THE CAPTAIN AND THE KING

Also by Myles Dungan

Speaking Ill of the Dead
How the Irish Won the West
The Stealing of the Irish Crown Jewels
They Shall Grow Not Old
Irish Voices from the Great War
Distant Drums

THE CAPTAIN AND THE KING

William O'Shea, Parnell and Late Victorian Ireland

MYLES DUNGAN

NEW
ISLAND

THE CAPTAIN AND THE KING
First published 2009
by New Island
2 Brookside
Dundrum Road
Dublin 14

www.newisland.ie

ISBN 978-1-84840-011-5

A CIP catalogue record for this book is available from the British Library.

Printed in the UK by CPI Mackays, Chatham ME5 8TD.

10 9 8 7 6 5 4 3 2 1

For Nerys
Diolch yn fawr fy nghariad

COPYRIGHT ACKNOWLEDGEMENTS

I gratefully acknowledge permission to quote from the following archive sources: the O'Shea Papers and other collections in the National Library of Ireland; the Joseph Chamberlain Manuscript Collection at the University of Birmingham; the O'Gorman Mahon Collection at the University of Chicago; the Davitt Collection at Trinity College, Dublin; the Parnell Collection at Kilmainham Gaol Museum; the Chief Secretary's Office Registered Papers at the National Archive; and the Gladstone, Campbell-Bannerman, Dilke and Escott Papers at the British Library.

CONTENTS

ACKNOWLEDGEMENTS

This exercise in disguised biography began life as the final paper delivered at a two-day RTÉ–National Museum seminar series in Collins Barracks in 2006, entitled *Speaking Ill of the Dead*, which was subsequently broadcast as a ten-part radio series. The piece itself (a 5,000-word distillation of a 15,000 word essay) was never broadcast and neither was it included in the RTÉ–New Island publication of the same name, which derived from the lecture series. I can justifiably claim that these were wise decisions on the part of the compiler of both the RTÉ radio series and the editor of the book. The fact that I myself fulfilled both roles is neither here nor there.

My thanks are due to:

Lorelei Harris, Managing Editor of Features, RTÉ Radio, who commissioned the original series; and to Adrian Moynes, Director of RTÉ Radio, who got behind the book project.

To Helen Beaumont of the National Museum for making *Speaking Ill of the Dead* come to pass in the first place. Let's do it again sometime.

Dr Martin Mansergh TD and Dr Patrick Wallace, Director of the National Museum (both contributors to *Speaking Ill of the Dead*), for persuading me, by example, to look at the totality of even the most obnoxious of historical personages.

Aonghus Ó hAonghusa and all the staff at the National Library in Dublin: especially Fran 'Man U' Carroll and Jerry O'Callaghan upstairs and Ciaran and John L. downstairs. The Library became both a second home and a haven. Though the microfilm machines did nothing for my fading eyesight.

Caitriona Crowe, of the National Archives, for all her assistance and advice, and especially for reintroducing me to the dark arts of extracting nuggets from the back-breaking volumes of the Chief Secretary's Office Registered Papers. There was gold in 'them thar' boxes – eventually.

Niall Bergin of the Kilmainham Gaol Museum for his help with the Parnell memorabilia, photographs and letters in the possession of the institution where he spent a productive incarceration.

Pat Power of the Parnell Society who brought to my attention and allowed me to reproduce certain documents donated to him by Mahon O'Brien before the latter's death and which include 'further and better particulars' of O'Shea's alleged affairs as itemised by his wife.

Roy Foster, who stimulated my curiosity in the Captain three years ago with the chance remark that O'Shea had been in Madrid when Pigott fled there in 1889.

Frank Callanan for patiently answering an email out of the blue when I was attempting to come to grips with the iron wills [*sic*] of Aunt Ben.

The Fulbright Commission for assisting me in not one, but two, projects. The first, for which a Fulbright Scholarship was forthcoming, is for another day. But in my spare time in Berkeley, when I detached myself from Thomas Fitzpatrick and the Treaty of Fort Laramie, I managed to fit in some work on O'Shea. Colleen Dube and Sonya McGuinness, you must have known I'd have some spare time!

David Kessler and all at the Bancroft Library at the University of California, Berkeley: a home for half of 2007. And also to whoever purchased, donated or stole the terrific collection of books on Irish history which Cal has in its undergraduate and research libraries.

Dr Patrick Geoghegan and Dr Ciaran Brady of Trinity College, Dublin, for reintroducing me to historical discourse with their *Contesting History* evening lecture series.

To Edwin Higel of New Island Books who said 'yes' to the whole idea two years ago and to Deirdre Nolan who did not immediately pitch me into the nearby Dodder when I told her the finished product might be a *wee* bit longer than we'd first envisaged.

*

But my undying gratitude goes to a former teacher who must have thought he had finished supervising my work three decades ago after I graduated with very little distinction from University College, Dublin. Especially since he had himself reached the security of retirement and must have imagined that he was safe from my clutches. But old historians never retire, they just emeritise, and a chance meeting in February 2007 resulted in a rash promise to read the work as it was produced. Despite the fact that it has almost doubled in length from what was originally envisaged, Professor Donal McCartney read, corrected and criticised every syllable. He has been a true guardian angel and I promise never to impose on his good nature again. Needless to say, any errors, major or minor, are entirely my fault and my responsibility.

*

On a purely personal level, my thanks to Cal (the cat, not the University) for being my familiar. To Amber, Rory, Lara and Ross for tolerating the many occasions of 'Yes, let's do that after I finish ...'

And, above all, to the patient Welsh poet and scholar who has seen our shelves groan with volumes of Irish 19th-century memoirs and histories, who lost me for weeks to the demands of the ex-Hussar, his wife and her lover, and who never complained once. Nerys, all I can say is a heartfelt *go raibh mile maith agat mo bhean cheile dhilis* and I am eternally grateful for your love. *Rwyn dy garu di.*

INTRODUCTION

'... a spruce, dandified man, filled with belief in himself and disbelief in others. He was the kind of gentlemanlike adventurer, cynically contemptuous under the guise of bonhomie ... who makes the world his oyster, and is disappointed with the size of the pearls.

Alfred Robbins on William O'Shea,
Parnell – The Last Five Years

Back in the 1970s, any student of history at University College, Dublin, who posed the question 'what if' risked being dismissed out of hand for attempting to hypothesise. The status of the hypothetical may not have changed in the academic world,[1] but the terminology has. The 21st century 'what if' is no longer a 'hypothetical' – it is a 'counter-factual'.

The complex web of relationships between Charles Stewart Parnell, Katharine O'Shea and William Henry O'Shea, one time Member of Parliament for Clare, gave rise to one of the most famous counter-factuals of Irish history. 'What if the split in the Irish Parliamentary Party had been avoided in 1890 and Charles Stewart Parnell had continued to lead the Irish nationalists in the British Parliament?'

As well as gliding over a few other salient facts, the question, of course, conveniently ignores an inconvenient morbidity. Parnell was dead by October 1891 and so, logically, beyond what he had already achieved, he would have played a very minor role indeed in Irish history. He had been almost two years in his grave when Gladstone introduced his second Home Rule Bill in 1893, a measure that was itself laid to rest by the House of Lords.

But that is the beguiling (and ultimately fatal) attraction of the counter-factual. Nestling within the basic 'what if' is the assumption that his health would not have failed had it not been for the intense, mean-spirited and gruelling series of by-elections fought by Parnell in 1891 against his former colleagues. He would have been able to remove the qualifier from the title 'Uncrowned King of Ireland' and achieve some form of reification.

Within that primary Parnellite counter-factual lies the assumption that the sexual affair between Parnell and Katharine O'Shea never happened. But there also lurk many secondary 'what ifs', some of which would allow for the existence of the liaison. For example, 'what if' 28 electors[2] in the Exchange Division of Liverpool had switched their allegiance from the Conservative to the Liberal candidate in the November 1885 General Election and given that candidate, Captain William Henry O'Shea, a bare majority and a seat in the House of Commons? Would this have been sufficient to buy his silence, in spite of the insuperable evidence that his wife was having an affair with his former party leader?

Or, failing the balm of a parliamentary seat, 'what if' the will of the principal O'Shea benefactress, Mrs Benjamin Wood, had been kinder to her niece's husband? Would the salve of a guaranteed income have allowed the increasingly diaphanous veil of secrecy over his wife's affair to remain in place?

To the notion of the 'counter-factual' allow me to add the idea of 'counter-hagiography'. Many biographers, besotted with their subjects even before they begin their research, have been sucked into the quicksand of hagiography. Although this is rare amongst modern writers, who tend to a more detached or revelatory style. In the case of 'the Captain' of the title, whilst hoping to come to terms with many of his previously unacknowledged complexities, this biographer has 'come to bury [O'Shea] not to praise him'. And, as Charles Stewart Parnell was far from being a saint himself, 'the King' will be subjected to a measured counter-hagiographical treatment as well.

The third point of this triangle, Katharine O'Shea, has been a reviled figure in Irish history. Her nickname 'Kitty' (an epithet applied to Victorian prostitutes), coined by a malevolent Tim Healy, encapsulates the narrative forced upon her by contemporary myth-makers. As Parnell was a legitimate Irish warrior-hero, without feet of clay, he was, *ipso facto*, suborned, charmed and seduced from his duty of care to the Irish nation by a self-seeking, amoral and destructive Englishwoman. It is a myth that has been laid to rest by a series of excellent biographies, which, perhaps, tip the balance a little too much in the direction of aggrandising her real significance.

In order to avoid any confusion engendered by the title of this volume, let me be clear from the start. You have just entered a biography of William Henry O'Shea, Victorian dandy, dilettante, go-between and cuckold. When it comes to the life and career of Parnell, I am more than content to stand on the shoulders of giants such as F.S.L. Lyons, Roy Foster and Paul Bew. The character and personality of Katharine O'Shea has been expertly reassessed, revised and rehabilitated by Joyce Marlow, Mary Rose Callaghan, Jane Jordan and, latterly, Elisabeth Kehoe. The extent to which the real nature of her character has also been re-invented will be dealt with in due course.

Which leaves the Captain! The remote and uninteresting third point of an isosceles triangle? Far from it. I admit to having been tempted, on the basis of a relatively small amount of research, to subtitle this volume 'The Cuckold, the Chief, his Wife and her Lover', thus further denigrating the man. To say that O'Shea has his detractors would be a polite understatement. In the course of his career he managed to antagonise some of the most celebrated names in British and Irish politics. He attracted or issued at least three duelling challenges in his lifetime, though none of them came to anything.[3] His contemporaries (and subsequent historians) have judged him harshly. He has been described as (and this is a mere cross section of contemporary ill wishers): 'a real dandy'[4]; 'that obnoxious individual'[5]; 'a vile hound'[6]; 'a blackguard ... the traitor we expected him to be'[7]; 'that slippery and piebald politician'[8]; and finally, one who has 'insight into so many details of Irish affairs, political and personal'.[9] It is difficult to disagree with any of those descriptions, even the concluding paean of praise, though that comes from the pen of the Captain himself.

But something much more interesting than a self-deluded *mari complaisant*, a broker, a carrier of messages devoid of ideas, emerges from O'Shea's correspondence. Granted, he managed to become both matchmaker and cuckold but when one can get beyond the blatant vanity, the overweening pomposity and the frequent risibility of the man, he becomes something more than just an irritating and hazardous political and matrimonial appendage. O'Shea the archetype is deserving of more study than O'Shea the husband, who failed even to become a focal *bête noire* of the Irish nationalist tradition. He lost out in that invidious contest to his (unjustifiably) loathed wife. In James Joyce's *Portrait of the Artist as a Young Man,* for example, 'Kitty' O'Shea, as well as the 'priests and the priest's pawns', comes in for dishonourable mention in the context of the downfall of the 'dead King' – there is not a single reference to the regicide himself.

O'Shea's narrative often resembles a harlequinade and his values feed into a number of neglected or notorious Irish Victorian tropes. But he is far more than the mere catalyst in a national tragedy. He is not simply some vagrant ray of light refracted through a prismatic Parnell – his spectrum may not begin at red and may stop well short of violet but the colours that do emerge merit close study.

He represents a strand in Irish nationalist politics that was partially eclipsed in 1880 and ruthlessly annihilated in 1885. But for his later notoriety he might be a relatively undistinguished member of an unenviable club whose president is Isaac Butt, whose secretary is William Shaw and whose ordinary members include long-forgotten names such as Richard O'Shaughnessy, Mitchell Henry, the O'Donoghue and the O'Conor Don. Chastised in the 1880s as 'Whigs' they were cold-bloodedly brushed aside by the 'advanced' nationalists led by Parnell, with the energetic support of Dillon, O'Brien and Redmond. Ironically the latter, in their turn, would be made redundant in 1918 by the more extreme nationalistic forces at play in the aftermath of the 1916 Easter Rising.

O'Shea, despite the jibe being tossed at him from the floor and platform of many a political rally, was never an unreconstructed Whig. But neither was he ever a convinced nationalist. He managed to straddle the two camps with a certain degree of success between 1880 and 1885, while blinding himself to the fact that, if he wanted a political career based in an Irish constituency, he needed to climb aboard the Parnell Express before it left the station in November 1885. Ultimately it was not a case of his missing the train. In fairness to him he simply declined to get on board. Consequently, although his name need not be inscribed on the tomb of the Unknown Whig, he is interred, politically, in the Mausoleum of the Unsung Maverick, along with the likes of Frank Hugh O'Donnell, John O'Connor Power and Philip Callan.

Another despised renegade of Irish political life was the inveterate 'place-seeker'. Patronage and preferment had long been an instrument of British policy in Ireland. On the basis that 'if you can't beat them, buy them', a succession of British ministries had managed to achieve their ends in Ireland (from unification in the late 18th century to pacification in the mid 19th) by opting for the politics of ennoblement and sinecure. The 'purchase' of two leading members of the Independent Irish Party of the 1850s, John Sadleir and William Keogh, was the most egregious recent example of this policy. Both men, MPs for Carlow and Athlone respectively, had been pledged to oppose any British government ill-disposed towards agrarian and ecclesiastical reform in Ireland. Both men had deserted the fledgling cause by accepting the positions of junior Treasury Minister and Solicitor General for Ireland in the Aberdeen Ministry.

The essential difference between the reviled Sadleir and Keogh and the equally corruptible O'Shea was that the Captain had little to offer that any British government appeared to be willing to buy. Hints as broad as the Shannon estuary, emblem of his constituency, gave way to the *rapprochement direct* when it came to attempting to satisfy his desire for a government position. But O'Shea had proved far too willing to supply his services voluntarily for any Liberal administration to feel the need to bribe him with the offer of a job.

Despite his desire for preferment by a Liberal government (a function of his perennial financial woes) O'Shea occasionally displayed a degree of feisty independence untypical of the average place-seeker. His steadfast refusal to take the Irish Parliamentary Party 'pledge' complicated his political career and brought him the sort of attention that a bona fide backroom huckster would wish to avoid. As he pointed out in a letter to the Roman Catholic Primate of Ireland in 1891, 'I need only have given a silent vote for Mr Gladstone's Home Rule Bill and my seat was as safe as any in Ireland.'[10] By then, of course, he was the servant of a different master and may have calculated that, by walking out of the House of Commons on 8 June 1886, he was making a gesture of loyalty to Joseph Chamberlain that would be amply rewarded. If this was what he believed, it was a grave miscalculation.

Arguably, O'Shea may also be numbered among the members of that sinister and darkly iconic substratum of Irish history, the informer. He remains innocent of all charges (and there have been many) of being in the pay of Dublin Castle, in the absence of any incriminating documentary evidence. But he is most assuredly guilty of constructive treachery in his various conspiracies to bring about the downfall of the man he came to loathe with all the passion of the vanquished. He did far more damage to a thriving nationalist cause in 1890 than the likes of Leonard McNally[11] had done to the United Irishmen almost a century earlier. He was also far more effective in thwarting the constitutional nationalist movement than even Britain's most celebrated and successful spy amongst the American Fenians, Thomas Billis Beach (Henri le Caron),[12] had been in stymieing the militant cause over a 20-year period. The fact that this was not his primary intention is of secondary importance.

On a slightly more positive note (but only slightly, given our latter-day experience of this particular political animal), O'Shea was a prototypical clientelist politician. Separated as he was from his constituents by a journey of two days' duration, he was not in the mould of the American ward heeling precinct captain. But in advance of the franchise extension of 1884, after which attention to one's constituents became a *sine qua non* for all but the most fortunate and favoured public representatives, he sought to exploit a culture of dependency in the western part of his Clare constituency and was modestly successful in gathering around him the makings of a political machine. He was hardly unique in this respect but he was, unlike many of his contemporaries, aware that he had a duty to his electors and that, in fulfilling this duty, he might be enabled to sustain his career, against all the odds, in the face of ideological opposition.

Ironically, in the context of Irish politics in the 21st century, the attention paid by O'Shea to the county and people of Clare went, essentially, unrewarded. Moreover, not only was his work unappreciated in many nationalist circles, it was also viewed with a certain suspicion in an Ireland where clientelism was often associated with collaboration (in the pejorative sense of the word). In the charged atmosphere of the 1880s the successful acquisition of political patronage for a borough or a county could backfire and be interpreted as uncomfortable proximity to the governing British élite.

In the context of the Victorian era in which he lived O'Shea probably has more in common with a celebrated fictional character than with any of the Irish politicians with whom he shared the green sward of the House of Commons. In many respects O'Shea *is* Phineas Finn, that charming and opportunistic mid-Victorian invention of the novelist Anthony Trollope[13] and the motive force of two books in the Palliser series, set in the world of mid-19th century British politics. There is something vaguely fictional and elegantly melodramatic about the career of O'Shea. He is, of course, his own invention, though his faction[14] is that of the classic 'unreliable narrator'. His is an auto-hagiography laced with special pleading, evasion and outright untruth and the reader of his biography is unlikely to share O'Shea's estimation of his own character. When it comes to his personal narrative O'Shea has none of the pragmatic self-awareness of Thackeray's Becky Sharp, the mercenary heroine of *Vanity Fair*.

Like Phineas Finn, O'Shea was fortunate in having a blinkered and generous father. He was, similarly, an above-average student of distinctly below-average commitment. He was ebullient, engaging and fortunate in his physical appearance. So, like Trollope's hero, he was the perfect template for a public man on the make. While his personal history deviates from that of Phineas Finn it rarely strays from the inherently fictional. He had an older mentor (the O'Gorman Mahon) with a quixotic career in politics and the military, whose duelling activities had left him with the smell of cordite and the aura of romance clinging to him. He sought long and hard for a more exemplary political chieftain before finding one in the quintessentially ambitious, infinitely resource-ful and fatally egotistical, Joseph Chamberlain. He married well and repented at leisure as his marriage sank into the welcoming embrace of a brand of journalism only a few degrees separated from the tabloid frenzies of our own times.

But just how different was he from the man whose career he contrived and conspired to end?

There are some interesting but less than significant similarities between the two men. Both have fallen victim, for example, to a latter day predilec-tion for mispronouncing their names. In the case of O'Shea this is perfectly understandable. The pronunciation he preferred was an anglicised affec-tation. He was, in fact, phonetically at least, William Henry O'Shee. This unorthodox rendering of a relatively common Irish name allowed one of the Captain's many detractors to satirise his wife as 'O'Shea who must be obeyed', *d'après* the heroine of H. Rider Haggard's popular novels of the late Victorian period. Parnell has, for decades, suffered a not dissimilar fate, based on the emphasis of the syllables of his name. He insisted that the stress be placed on the first syllable (as in *Par*-nell). Nowadays, all but a faithful few place the stress on the second.

A scan of the final lines of the Yeats' poem 'Come Gather Round Me Parnellites' illustrates the point:

> But stories that live longest
> Are sung above the glass,
> And Parnell loved his country
> And Parnell loved his lass.[15]

The two men came from a similar social background, at least in the sense that they were both landowners. Parnell had inherited the Avondale estate in County Wicklow from his father; O'Shea owned and rented out land in County Clare. But there the similarity ends. Parnell was as *ancien* as O'Shea was *nouveau*. In addition, Parnell was as Protestant as O'Shea was Catholic, with all that such a difference implied when it came to social status. The Parnell line stretched back beyond Sir John Parnell, Chancellor of the Exchequer in Grattan's parliament. The O'Shea line was attenu-ated, and considerably less exalted.

Neither man showed exceptional enthusiasm for learning in the English schools that they attended. It was there they acquired their other, most obvious, common characteristic: an upper-class English accent.[16] Both, however, displayed considerable aptitude and enthusiasm for horse-riding. Parnell employed his equestrian skills in the hunt, O'Shea in the Hussars.

Parnell was very much the rural establishment figure in his member-ship of the Wicklow Militia and his tenure as High Sheriff of the county. O'Shea sought entry to the establishment via the back door through the purchase of a military commission. Both appeared to enter politics almost as an afterthought and on the coat-tails of others.[17] Neither, in their initial period in the House of Commons, exhibited much talent for their chosen pursuit. But here again the similarity ends. After an apprenticeship in which he, wisely, kept his own counsel and absorbed the lessons to be learned from studious observation, Parnell went on to a stellar career in the British Parliament. The more nakedly ambitious O'Shea was alto-gether too eager to share his counsel but never threatened to distinguish himself as a parliamentarian.

However, it would be a mistake to see O'Shea as the mere lackadaisi-cal and glad-handing buffoon of popular myth and Parnell as the strategically adept and conscientious ideologue of Irish historical legend. Although Parnell could, when he chose, be resolute, hard-working and consistent in his political philosophy, he could also be irritatingly fickle, unnervingly whimsical and display an arrogance[18] and lassitude charac-teristic of his social rank and of the very class he, avowedly at any rate, sought to drive out of Irish political life. While O'Shea could be equally patronising and unctuous as well (this was not something of which Parnell could ever be accused), he was occasionally capable of displaying a shrewd political intelligence and had a surprising capacity for hard work.

Parnell managed to parlay the *ancien* aloofness and haughtiness of his social class into a successful, if dictatorial and absolutist, style of leader-ship. As one of his loyalists, Andrew Kettle (father of the noble and tragic Great War fatality, Tom Kettle) once perceptively observed, without seeming to be overly concerned at the fact, 'Parnell was not a democrat.'[19] O'Shea only succeeded in parlaying the *arriviste* superciliousness and con-descension of his 'Castle' Catholicism into provoking and alienating a disproportionate number of his fellow countrymen – and often seemed to relish this ability, since he rejoiced *d'épater les bourgeois*. Parnell turned his instincts and intelligence into a peerless political acumen that was placed at the service of a great cause. O'Shea, ultimately, placed his talents at the disposal of reactionary forces and the cause he served most enthu-siastically was his own.

But, in many respects, O'Shea was actually more radical than the man seen by most of his British contemporaries as a dangerous extremist until quite late in his political career. Despite being labelled a 'Whig', O'Shea associated himself in the English Parliament with the radical wing of the Liberal party. And his alignment was not entirely opportunistic (although largely so). He was an acolyte of Joseph Chamberlain, close to Sir Charles Dilke and friendly with Henry Labouchere, three men who, until the arrival of John Morley on the political scene, were the best known figures on the 'left' of the ruling Liberal party. It was his misfortune that the radical element of that party split over the issue of Home Rule in 1886 and that debilitating tensions preceded that split.

Neither did O'Shea's alleged Whiggery and Liberal-Unionist tendencies prevent him from forming a bizarre alliance with some of the most extreme nationalists in his constituency. While supporters of Parnell were intent on deselecting him as Irish Parliamentary Party candidate for the 1885 election (from very early into his tenure), his clientelism extended as far as cultivating members of the Fenian movement in Clare and in London. Doubtless this particular *démarche* was founded on the premise that 'the enemy of my enemy is my friend'. Both O'Shea and *his* Fenians were *ad idem* in their antipathy towards Parnellism. It would be hard to see O'Shea making any interjection on behalf of the Manchester Martyrs in the hallowed halls of parliament[20] and this misalliance can be viewed as a disregard for political principle and consistency. But it certainly adds an exotic layer of paint to the political portrait of the Captain.

Famously, Parnell also returned to the embrace of the 'hillside men', as he struggled for political survival after the 1890 split. In fact, both men had a Fenian in common. Patrick Neville Fitzgerald, Munster IRB leader, shared a platform with Parnell in December 1890 and was in a carriage behind his coffin at the lost leader's emblematic funeral in October 1891. In their own distinct ways both men can be said to have turned to the Fenians *in extremis* – in both instances such desperate measures were rewarded with the sort of result to be expected from desperate measures. Margaret O'Callaghan rejects the idea that Parnell's recourse to the hillside men arose out of any mental confusion, believing that 'Parnell's version of constitutional nationalism was effectively dead before Parnell's fall.'[21] O'Shea's version of clientelist nationalism was stillborn. His recourse to the Fenians had little to do with the breakdown of an ideology but emanated from a highly developed survival instinct – another quality he may have shared with Parnell – as well as a fascination with intrigue and a shared penchant for dressing up as soldiers.

O'Shea's egocentric, *mé féin* philosophy renders him a largely predictable figure. But occasionally he can surprise, as in the discovery in his correspondence of some well-thought-out and radical legislative ideas. In March 1887, though he was no longer a serving MP, he sent a detailed set of proposals[22] to Chamberlain embodying legislation for palliative measures in aid of impoverished parts of the west of Ireland (including his former constituency). This, transmitted through Chamberlain during his political 'Moses wandering in the wilderness' phase, became the basis of the Salisbury government's Congested Districts legislation.

In similar correspondence the following year, his assessment of the agrarian philosophy of the Parnellite movement, while self-serving, was also hard-headed and hard-hitting. He brusquely dismissed the proto-socialism of the Davitt wing of the agrarian movement. In probing and questioning some of its supposedly moderating influences, he drew attention to the *petit bourgeois* thinking which, he claimed, underpinned the land agitation. This, he contends, contributed to the dystopian nature of rural Irish society by satisfying the interests of only one faction. The natural constituency of this tendency was, '... the publicans and the avaricious shopkeepers ... to which classes the members of the faction themselves largely belong, or with which their pecuniary interests are inextricably bound up.'[23] Had he added graziers to the publicans and shopkeepers, the only class missing from the litany would have been priests, and O'Shea was not about to excoriate that particular faction.

O'Shea's distaste for publicans and avaricious shopkeepers emanated, not from any radical political idealism, but from a very Yeatsian, class-based contempt for those who 'fumbled in a greasy till' and, in that respect also, he was little different from Parnell. Most of his biographers and many commentators on the period have alluded to Parnell's innate conservatism, even to his latent Toryism. Two examples will suffice for the moment. The first is a line in his speech on the Land Bill in which he hinted at his vision of a post-Home Rule Ireland. 'We do not want the Irish landlords', he told the House of Commons, 'and the Irish tenants continually to live in opposing camps. As individuals, the landlords are well fitted to pick their place as the leaders of the Irish nation.'[24]

The second instance is his 1885 template for local government reform, as outlined to O'Shea and passed on to Chamberlain. It was the issue that was to cause a serious and, ultimately, irreparable rupture between the two political heavyweights. Parnell's version of local government reform was far more limited in scope than that of the Radical leader, albeit Chamberlain's more ambitious project was designed to vitiate the growing impetus towards Home Rule. One of the Parnellite measures that surprised Chamberlain was, in effect, a guaranteed local and national administrative role for Irish landlords. Having studied the document that O'Shea brought him, Chamberlain wrote to Morley, 'In one respect it goes much farther than I should have thought possible in the direction of a conservative policy since it proposes a separate representation of landowners both on county boards and on the central board in proportion to their rateable contributions.'[25]

As Paul Bew has pointed out in his excellent short biography of Parnell, he sought to bring about a form of 'pan-class nationalism'. His objective in championing the cause of land reform was very different from that of the 'neo-Fenians', men like Davitt, Patrick Egan and Thomas Brennan. Their attachment to the notion of peasant proprietary was posited on, especially in the case of Davitt, an expropriative social model. On a political level they sought to erase the last vestiges of the 'garrison' that had propped up British rule in Ireland. The landlords were the 'eyes and ears' of Dublin Castle. Once they were removed, a purblind Irish executive would struggle to maintain British hegemony. Parnell, however, had very different intentions to those of his temporary and expedient associates in the agrarian movement. He sought to establish 'a socially stable partnership between "reformed" landlords and a "satiated" class of peasants.'[26] Together this nationalistic alliance of the aristocracy and the peasantry would sound 'the last knell of English power.' It was a naive and anomalous, if somewhat audacious, dialectic. Clearly one of the many books left unread by Parnell was *The Communist Manifesto*.

If O'Shea was a 'Whig', then Parnell was a 'Volunteer'.[27] He made a habit, both literally and metaphorically, of genuflection towards the old Irish Parliament building on Dame Street and his frequently expressed aim was the restoration of Grattan's Parliament. Some have assumed that his surprisingly uncertain grasp of Irish history (inferior in many respects, for example, to that of Gladstone) led to his belief that Grattan's elitist brand of Ascendancy Home Rule was far more egalitarian than was actually the case. Such an assumption would be unsafe. It is just as likely that Parnell knew precisely the true nature of the Patriot Parliament and had no difficulty with its composition and its ethos. Since the closest Ireland got to Home Rule in his lifetime was a compromise bill designed by a British Liberal administration, Parnell could easily fudge his particular take on Irish self-government. O'Shea was not the only one who had little time for the febrile political dreams of shopkeepers and publicans.

Their relative stances can be seen as an issue of location. Both men, up to a point, defied the logic of their religion and social class. They located themselves in unexpected areas of the Irish body politic. Parnell – Protestant, Wicklow landowner, a prospective high Tory – chose to position himself (however briefly and opportunistically) on the radical extreme. O'Shea – Dublin-born, mid-west connected, son of a country solicitor, a putative Home Ruler – opted to oppose the Zeitgeist of advanced nationalism. Parnell could, so easily, have been the kind of figure to whom the likes of Isaac Butt would have been happy to concede power when the time came. O'Shea might well have been a Joseph Neale McKenna, who voted against Parnell's leadership in 1880, but by 1890 was siding with him in the internecine warfare following the divorce.[28] Both men, however, chose to locate themselves outside their stereotypical constituencies.

It is natural for a biographer to promise the revelation of unexpected complexities in their subject. It is natural for a biographer to promise revision of the status of their subject in the light of a close study of their lives. This biographer is no exception. While he enjoyed the drama of victimisation in the way that a hypochondriac (someone like Charles Stewart Parnell, for example) often 'enjoys' ill health, William Henry O'Shea is a far less deserving victim than Irish history has recorded. He should be removed, at least temporarily, from the repertory company of stock Irish villains and examined a little more closely. While his life's melody is never high opera, it is not entirely *opera buffa* either. And, although at times one needs to remind oneself of this fact, neither is it merely a constant and irritating whine.

In the case of the Captain, even if fresh analysis and reassessment proves too much of a stretch, there is always the personal narrative. The accompanying song may be muted but the story remains the same.

CHAPTER 1

A Dandy in the Making

Phineas himself did not boast much of his own hard work
when at home during the long vacation. No rumours of
expected successes – of expected professional successes –
reached the ears of any of the Finn family at Killaloe. But,
nevertheless, there came tidings which maintained those high
ideas in the maternal bosom of which mention has been
made, and which were of sufficient strength to induce the
doctor, in opposition to his own judgment, to consent to the
continued residence of his son in London. Phineas belonged
to an excellent club – the Reform Club – and went into very
good society.

Anthony Trollope, Phineas Finn

NEMESIS

It should never have been permitted to deflect the triumphal upward
progress of the junior member for the constituency of Clare. It should
have been a sublime moment in which he would emerge from the unruly
pack and take his place at the head of the hounds. The Master of the Hunt
was making a significant statement to the House of Commons. It was 15
May 1882. Less than two weeks had gone by since the Byzantine manoeu-

vrings of the Honourable Member for Clare had helped secure the release from Kilmainham jail of the person he described as 'the most influential Irishman of the day',[1] Charles Stewart Parnell. Barely a week had passed since the newly appointed Chief Secretary, Lord Frederick Cavendish, had been brutally murdered along with his Under Secretary, T.H. Burke, in Phoenix Park.

That tragic event had changed the political atmosphere. For a period of about four days Captain O'Shea had been allowed to profit from the perception that he had employed his negotiating skills adeptly in order to broker a rapprochement between the incarcerated leader of the Irish party at Westminster and the Liberal government. The police state, which had been created by two years of agrarian unrest, would begin to wither away. Hard-pressed tenants in danger of eviction because of hefty unpaid arrears of rent would be offered relief. In return, moderate Irish politicians (most British parliamentarians would have considered the phrase to be an oxymoron) would do their utmost to check the mounting violence in rural Ireland.

But the Phoenix Park murders had provoked an inevitable and, to some at least, regrettable change in direction for the Gladstone government. Conciliation was temporarily shunted into a siding. Coercion was back on the main line. Four days previously the British Home Secretary, Sir William Harcourt, had introduced a Crimes Bill, alongside which objet d'art previous Liberal coercive legislation looked like the daubings of a childish amateur. In addition a hostile England was asking questions about the release of the Irish nationalist rabble-rousers from Kilmainham jail. Had the government done the unthinkable and negotiated a deal with Irish political leaders who, no one had any doubt, fomented sedition and outrage?

Gladstone denied the very possibility. Just as future British administrations would never speak to terrorists, he rejected the notion of Her Majesty's Government negotiating questionable deals with the vaguely constitutional Irish party whose members sat across from the Treasury Bench. The compact, rumours of whose existence he sought to refute, was already being dubbed the 'Kilmainham Treaty'. To his dying day the Grand Old Man would deny that such an accord had ever existed.

Which was why Parnell was on his feet in the Commons chamber. He had some explaining of his own to do. While his parliamentary colleagues were glad to have him restored to the Mother of Parliaments, there was a wider constituency to which he urgently needed to cater. It was back home in Ireland, it was in the United States of America, and it was suspicious. Had the party leader bought his freedom by making guarantees, not only of his own good behaviour, but also that of his supporters? A lot hinged on his response. Should he fail to satisfy some of the more extreme elements on the far side of the Atlantic, sources of vital Land League funds might begin to dry up.

The Irish party leader was reading a letter to the House that he had, he claimed, written to Captain O'Shea on 28 April 1882 before his brief return to jail in Kilmainham, following a ten-day parole. That was the first white lie. The letter had actually been written on 29 April in Kilmainham itself. The document sets out terms which, the writer suggested, might lead to a reduction in outrage and agrarian tension in Ireland. His release had formed no part of any suggested understanding.

As Parnell lowered the letter from which he had just read and began to continue his observations, a voice rang out from the government back-benches opposite. It was that of the former Chief Secretary for Ireland, William E. Forster. He had resigned on 2 May in protest at the Cabinet decision to release Parnell and two other Irish MPs, John Dillon and James O'Kelly.

'Might I be allowed to ask the Honourable Member for the City of Cork,' Forster inquired, 'did he read the whole letter?'[2]

Members whose attention might have begun to wander were brought sharply back to the present. What was Forster getting at? The Irish party leader explained that what he had read had been supplied to him as a fair copy by his Honourable Friend, the Member for Clare. But if the Honourable Member for Bradford (Forster) had doubts on the matter he had no objection to any alternative version being read to the House. At this point O'Shea rose to his feet to intervene. As he attempted to explain he was shouted down by Tories smelling blood. The hecklers were demanding that he read the full text of the letter, assuming they had heard an edited version. O'Shea played for time. There was, indeed, a somewhat longer document but, regrettably, he did not have it immediately to hand.

Unfortunately for him, Forster did. It had been supplied to him by ... Captain O'Shea! There was no escape. He would now be obliged to read the document that he had truncated before handing his copy to Parnell. He must have watched with a sinking heart as it was passed from hand to hand and drew ever closer to him.

FROM O'SHEA TO O'SHEE

For a man who had a remarkable habit of snatching defeat from the jaws of victory, William Henry O'Shea was fortunate enough to be blessed with an excellent start in life.

Admittedly he was a Roman Catholic and, even in the Ireland of 1840 into which he was born, that could be a distinct disadvantage. O'Shea was the son of a Limerick solicitor with a prosperous Dublin practice. He was not, as his arch-enemy Tim Healy later wrote, the son of 'a Limerick pawnbroker designated by an unsavoury Gaelic nickname'.[3] Henry O'Shea was, by all accounts, a decent, hard-working man who had been called upon to sort out the financial mess left by his own father, also called William, before he could make his way in the world. The family estate in Limerick, Rich Hill, had been heavily mortgaged by William O'Shea Senior. Henry O'Shea, eldest of three brothers, managed to rescue the property from bankruptcy. He obviously put the experience thus acquired to good use and made considerable sums of money in the aftermath of the Famine by buying and selling encumbered estates, the property of bankrupt landlords.

His younger brother, John, was equally successful. He settled in Spain where a branch of the O'Shea family had lived for two centuries. There he founded a bank and married Señora Dona Ysabel Hurtado de Corcuera. The couple had five children. This was a family connection that William Henry O'Shea would frequently exploit.

Little is known about the third brother, Thaddeus, a mediocre trainer of bad racehorses, other than the metaphorically mixed information supplied on a family tree that 'he was ruined by horse-racing and went to the dogs'.[4] It was a fate his nephew later came close to emulating.

Henry O'Shea married Catherine Quinlan, daughter of a Tipperary man, Edward Quinlan. Accentuating the fervent Catholic strain in the family, she was a Countess of Rome and is described by Katharine O'Shea in her 1914 memoirs as 'a bundle of negations wrapped in a shawl – always in a very beautiful shawl ... assiduous in her practice of religion ...'[5] William Henry O'Shea had one sibling, Mary, who shared much of the sobriety and pietism of her mother and who, in later life, enjoyed the title of Lady of the Royal Order of Theresa of Bavaria. Her sister-in-law observed that Mary O'Shea's 'education had left her French in all her modes of thought and speech.'[6] Catherine O'Shea disapproved of her son's marriage to her virtual namesake. As one of Katharine's biographers, Joyce Marlow, has observed, 'Had she shown greater determination to prevent the marriage, Anglo-Irish history might have had a different shape.'[7] Yet another counter-factual!

The young William Henry O'Shea was sent to England to be educated at St Mary's College, Oscott, near Sutton Coldfield in Warwickshire. Founded in 1794, as well as serving as a secular establishment, it was also a seminary for the training of priests in the Roman Catholic archdiocese of Birmingham.[8] There O'Shea acquired a liberal education and an English accent that would stand him in good stead in certain quarters. Contrary to received wisdom and to the impression later conveyed by his former wife, O'Shea was an intelligent and capable student.[9]

The writer and diplomat, Wilfrid Scawen Blunt, was a contemporary of O'Shea's at Oscott and remembered him with something less than fondness. In his memoir of the Land War he observed that he 'hated him as cordially as the Irish do to-day. He was older than me,[10] a bit of a dandy, and a bit of a bully; and I can recollect well being chivvied all over the college by him with a fives bat he wished to chastise me with ...' Given that Blunt's father had 'fagged' for Byron at Harrow, he should probably have been better prepared for such juvenile rites of passage.[11]

O'Shea's father indulged him mercilessly. He was allowed to travel extensively, spending much time in France (where his mother eventually settled) and with his relatives in Spain. He became proficient in both languages. After Oscott he spent a short time in Trinity but he and Dublin's oldest institution of higher learning did not manage to agree with each other and he took refuge in the Army. Less well-known is a brief period spent in the capital city's other major seat of higher learning, University College, Dublin.[12] There he was fortunate enough to reside in the house of the distinguished Rector, John Henry Newman. Within three months he had tried the future Cardinal's patience to such an extent that Newman recorded, 'My youths, all through that O'Shea, or rather in the person of O'Shea, are giving me trouble – and I don't know how I can possibly stand another year. I think he must go at the end of the year.'[13] The comment vaults Newman to the front of a long line of patient souls who dearly wished to see the back of William Henry O'Shea.

On the basis that to lose one Dublin university might be regarded as a misfortune but to lose both looked like carelessness, O'Shea's father purchased him a commission in the 18th Hussars in 1858. He was a decent horseman and, at 5 feet 10 inches, looked good in a colourful cavalry officer's uniform on the back of a stallion. His father, seeing the commission as an entrée into more exalted social circles, reportedly advised the son to refer all his expenses and mess bills to Dublin. The obedient Willie duly obliged. Living up to an Army commission was an expensive process. His future brother-in-law, Midshipman Evelyn Wood, who didn't smoke, drink or gamble, reckoned he needed an income of £400 a year to cover his Navy expenses. O'Shea enjoyed all three vices and in less than ten years as a Hussar he racked up debts of £15,000. These were settled by his father. Incurring large debts and getting others to pay them were two of O'Shea's principal accomplishments.

Henry O'Shea did make some attempts to rein in his son's profligacy. He warned him at one point that if his expenditure continued at the outrageous level to which he had become accustomed his mother and sister would suffer reduced circumstances. The young Hussar may well have tried to curtail his extravagance for their sakes, but it continued to get the better of him. Eventually, under threat from his father's dwindling bank account, he was forced to resign his commission.

During his tenure as a dashing equestrian he had had frequent occasion to visit the estate of Sir Thomas Barrett-Lennard at Belhus, in Essex. It was a haven for those with a passion for horses. It was there that he renewed an acquaintance with a young woman whom he had first met in 1860 in her brother's house in Aldershot. He was a twenty-year-old cornet in the Hussars at the time, she was a fifteen-year-old coquette, more interested in the 'elderly and hawk-eyed Colonel of the regiment' than she was in the 'younger men'.[14]

FROM WOOD TO O'SHEE

Katharine O'Shea[15] (who was, at no point, ever known to her intimates as 'Kitty') was born on 30 January 1845, the thirteenth child of a lofty Church of England cleric, Sir John Page Wood, and his wife, Emma Caroline Michell. Her father was Vicar of Cressing in Essex and Rector of St Peter's, Cornhill. Her mother was a woman of considerable artistic talent. Katharine herself describes how Emma Wood had kept the young, impecunious couple afloat financially by painting and selling miniatures while her husband was a student at Cambridge. Later, having further developed her talent, she would exhibit larger and more mature works in London. Constable was a personal friend and Edwin Landseer was 'mothered' by her. She would also turn her hand to writing and became a successful novelist. She attracted the attention of no less a peer than Anthony Trollope who was a regular visitor to the Wood household at Rivenhall, in Essex.[16] In addition, according to her daughter, she was a 'fine musician'.

Katharine was the last of eight surviving children: two brothers had died in early childhood and three other siblings had not managed to escape infancy. She arrived on the scene a quarter of a century into her parents' marriage, by which time they were comfortably settled at the spacious and well-appointed Rivenhall Place whose grounds had been designed by Capability Brown. By the mid-1840s, the Woods were enjoying some of the fruits of the labour of Katharine's remarkable grandfather, Matthew Wood, a self-made 'Dick Whittington' who had come from a background in child labour to occupy the Mansion House in

London for two consecutive terms. He had also been a Liberal MP of radical bent from 1817 to 1843.[17]

With this in mind, at least one of his sons must have been an acute political disappointment to him. Katharine has described her father as 'a thoroughgoing Whig', though she may not have intended the phrase to have the sort of pejorative connotations it acquired in Ireland. Her father was wholehearted in his commitment to the hustings: he 'became a great influence in the county during election times',[18] she noted. He would bedeck his youngest daughter in orange ribbons[19] and have her drive him to election rallies. Her uncle, William Page Wood, later Baron Hatherley, was even more of a political *engagé*. He was a long-standing Liberal MP who served as Gladstone's Lord Chancellor in the administration of the late 1860s, the avowed mission of which, at least according to its leader, had been 'to pacify Ireland'.

Katharine, who appears to have been her father's favourite, was not just blessed with well-connected older relatives. Her siblings, too, either married well or attained a celebrity as noteworthy as her own subsequent notoriety. One exception was her sister Clarissa, who died when Katharine was just two years old. Two older siblings had already married and departed Rivenhall by the time Katharine, known in family circles as Katie, was a small child. In effect, she had two brothers and two sisters with whom she grew up.

Her sister, Emma, married Sir Thomas Barrett-Lennard when Katharine was eight years old. Sharing some of her mother's talents and interests, Emma dabbled in song-writing and poetry. She divided her time between Brighton and the Barrett-Lennard estate at Belhus. Katharine enjoyed spending vacations with her older sister on the south coast but was less enamoured of Belhus.

Katie's brother Charles, nine years her senior, would eventually become a local gentleman farmer. He would play a small but significant role in precipitating his sister's divorce by his own unremitting pursuit of what he saw as his entitlement to a share in a significant family legacy.

Evelyn, two years younger than Charles, was the most illustrious of the brood. His mother's 'idol', he was destined for a distinguished military career. Entering Marlborough College at the age of nine he became a teenage naval cadet and, as a sixteen-year-old midshipman, was wounded in the Crimean War in 1854. He narrowly avoided having an arm amputated after it was shattered by a cannon-ball. Like many of his peers in the Crimea (he returned there in 1856), he succumbed to typhoid fever and probably cheated death because his determined mother (defying the great Florence Nightingale herself) insisted on travelling to the region and bringing him back to England. He was one of the first men to be recommended for the newly created Victoria Cross (he was not finally awarded one until 1859). He served in the Zulu War, the First Boer War, the Indian Mutiny and the Egyptian conflict against Arabi Pasha, finally reaching the rank of Field Marshal, having transferred from the naval service to the Army.[20]

Katharine was closest, in age and disposition, to her sister, Anna. Five years Katie's senior, Anna 'had soft brown hair and a lovely skin, blue eyes that were mocking ... and a very pretty figure.'[21] Like her mother, Anna Wood would become a successful popular novelist who wrote under her married name of Steele. The name was almost the only thing she took from her marriage to Lieutenant Colonel Thomas Steele in 1858. It was a short-lived, and probably unconsummated, relationship lasting no more than a week. Apparently the eighteen-year-old Anna had been unaware that she would be required to have sexual relations with her new husband. Unprepared for that side of marriage she returned to the family home and steadfastly resisted all efforts to persuade her to renew the relationship.[22] Her sexual history would come into question again in 1890 in the case of *O'Shea* v *O'Shea and Parnell* (Steele intervening).

The Wood family always maintained that Anna remained a lifelong virgin. Katharine would famously, and fatally, dispute this in Divorce Court No 1, when she accused her sister of having had an affair with William O'Shea. One quote attributed to Anna Steele – 'Man is a very limited creature, very limited; I find infinitely more variety in woman'[23] – suggests that any sexual inclinations she might have had actually lay within the confines of her own gender.[24] Thomas Steele, not to be denied his conjugal rights, made numerous attempts to reclaim his bride but all were unsuccessful and, on at least one occasion, he came to blows with the future Field Marshal, her brother Evelyn. The Steeles never divorced.

The young Katharine Wood was an attractive girl – dark, both in hair colouring and complexion. As a teenager she was full-faced but later in life her puppy fat would obligingly disappear, revealing a formidable jaw. Her eyes were lively and would have been the most prominent feature of her face, but for a nose that always seemed to be slightly out of proportion with the rest.

Katharine's lack of formal schooling was more than compensated for by an enquiring mind and a thoroughly educative environment. She had merely to attend to the conversation at family dinners to acquire a grounding in the arts and politics. Alternatively she could, and did, absorb knowledge from guests at Rivenhall. One visitor was the young John Morley, then a journalist, later to be a Liberal Cabinet minister, Chief

Secretary for Ireland and 'one of my bitterest foes', as she puts it herself. She remembers Morley as 'a very slight young man with a hard, keen face, the features strongly marked, and fair hair.'[25] If he remembered her from that encounter it would have been as an intense and attentive young lady, eager to listen and to learn, who devoured his conversation. She had been delegated to entertain him because the rest of the family found him altogether too dryly intellectual. She marks the meeting as a sort of rite of passage, saying that as a result of holding her own with Morley she 'lost all awe of cleverness as such.'

So it was a bright, motivated and well-read young woman who, at the age of seventeen, met her future husband and nemesis, William Henry O'Shea, for the second time.

COURTSHIP AND MARRIAGE

The young Dublin-born Hussar cut a fine figure as a 22-year-old. Not being exceptionally tall, he carried himself well, though with a somewhat supercilious air. A rather bland face was given the illusion of greater character by an impressive moustache. His hair was thick and wavy. He was more Flashman than Phineas at this point in his life. Already he exhibited much of the arrogance and vanity, as well as some of the unctuousness, that would characterise his future personal and political relationships.

The reason for the renewal of an acquaintance that, according to Katharine's own account, had left little impact on her two years before, was the Brentwood Steeplechase. O'Shea, at the suggestion of Katharine's brother, Frank, had been chosen to ride a horse with the improbably ironic name of Honesty. Katharine hints that although Willie's prowess as a rider had earned him his place in Belhus, his hosts were not above patronising their Irish Catholic guest who affected the air of a sophisticated cosmopolitan. Katharine might have been expected to identify with the victim of such behaviour. As the youngest daughter, she was accustomed to being treated in an offhand manner and dismissed by her elder siblings. This was despite, or perhaps it was because of, her cultivated erudition and youthful intensity.

When it came to dinner, and the pairing-off of guests, Emma Barrett-Lennard, née Wood, was asked who would accompany her sister Katie to the dining room. Her facile and condescending response (and here it is necessary to bear in mind Willie's favoured pronunciation of his surname) was 'Oh she shall go in with O'Shea'. O'Shea was also the butt of a similar joke from some of his fellow Hussars at about the same time. In an effort to ingratiate himself with the Barrett-Lennards he had volunteered to take part in one of those dramatic divertissements, which, the novels of Jane Austen would have us believe, were a mandatory form of amusement in English stately homes.

Cast, incongruously and embarrassingly, as Queen Elizabeth in a Belhus frolic, he was further humiliated when his brother officers, in a droll *double entendre* took up the cry of 'Oh she is a jolly good fellow'. It quickly spread about the room. According to Katie, O'Shea 'glowered at them' and then 'with a look of withering scorn, picked up his skirts and stalked off "left" 'with as much dignity as he could muster.'[26] Which, by that point, would have been very little indeed.

However, the fact that young William Henry O'Shea was even circulating in such a drawing room, despite his Irishness (however muted) and his Catholicism, meant that he was punching above his weight. He himself, of course, would not have seen it that way. O'Shea, thanks to his cosmopolitan upbringing and élitist education, always carried with him a confident air of entitlement. The youngest, by five years, of a large family, Katharine, while bright and sure of herself, would have lacked much of O'Shea's brio. She was never allowed by her siblings to forget that she was the youngest of the family and was expected to be seen, admired even, but not heard.

On the occasion of their second meeting, O'Shea made the mistake of taking his cue from her brothers and sisters and patronising the seventeen-year-old Katie. She later recalled that, while he cut a dash in his outfit ('a brown velvet coat, cut rather fully, sealskin waistcoat, black and white check trousers, and an enormous carbuncle and diamond pin in his curiously folded scarf' – one can see where his father's money was being spent), he needled her to such an extent with his condescension that she 'promptly plunged into such a discussion of literary complexities, absorbed from my elders and utterly undigested [that] he soon subsided into a bewildered and shocked silence.'[27]

O'Shea evidently recovered from his perplexity very quickly, because before leaving Belhus on that occasion he wrote, and left her, a poem. When she showed it to her father he was less than pleased. Although he had a personal liking for the handsome Irish Hussar he may have had other ideas for his daughter than marriage to an Irish Catholic. His most immediate expressed intention was to keep her at Rivenhall for some years to come. Ironically, although the family lived on a large country estate, the Woods had few economic reasons to adopt airs and graces towards the likes of O'Shea. Their pedigree was not matched by their financial resources.

Later that summer, however, Katie and O'Shea met again. Gradually their meetings became more frequent – the poetry from the pen of the young O'Shea more prolix and more regular. He was far from being her sole admirer and it was only a serious accident that finally clarified her feelings about him.

The 18th Hussars were stationed in Brighton, a town that would acquire even greater significance for both of them in later life. O'Shea had taken his horse, Early Bird, for a gallop on the Downs. The riderless and bleeding horse returned to barracks at about the time O'Shea's absence was first noted and the alarm was raised. O'Shea was found on the Downs unconscious and remained so for six weeks. The Barrett-Lennards helped nurse him in barracks before removing him to Belhus when he emerged from his coma. Katie's concern for his health brought it home to her that her attachment was something other than mere friendship. O'Shea made his interest clear when, as she and Anna accompanied him to Belhus, he slipped a ring from his finger onto hers. It would not be long before he would repeat the process in more formal surroundings.

Henry O'Shea, concerned and indulgent parent, journeyed from Ireland to be with his son. He must have been sorely tempted, when Willie recovered his health, to offer a variation of the paternal speech of Polonius to Laertes, but probably realised it was already far too late. His gloom at his son's profligacy did not have long to run, however, as he died in 1865. His passing came during a difficult phase in the relationship between his son and Katharine Wood. Katie, still only twenty, had already begun to tire of her dalliance with the Captain, or at least that is what she claims in her appealing but often unreliable memoir. Whatever the truth, the two were separated for some time as O'Shea returned to Dublin after his father's death and then travelled to Spain to begin working in his uncle's banking business.

Towards the end of 1865 Sir John Page Wood fell ill. He died in February 1866 leaving his family in a parlous financial state. His lifestyle may not have been that of a typical English Anglican clergyman but his legacy certainly was. Lady Wood was left with virtually nothing. At this point a deus ex machina enters the narrative, signs the cheque and saves the day. And not for the last time either. Lady Emma Wood was rescued from financial embarrassment by her sister, Anna Maria. The two sisters had married two generations of the Wood family. Anna Maria was the widow of Sir John Page Wood's uncle Benjamin. As Mrs Benjamin Wood, she was, affectionately, known to the members of her extended family as 'Aunt Ben'.

With apparently limitless resources from the estate of her late husband, she settled an annual income on her sister that enabled Lady Emma Wood to avoid penury. It was the first act of generosity in a pattern that would, in the future, see her as a hugely influential paymaster, calling for tunes from the often frantically piping O'Sheas.

As Sir John's health deteriorated Lady Wood appears to have been as concerned for the welfare of his favourite daughter as she was for her husband. To arrest a decline in a distraught Katie's mental state her mother, overcoming an often vacillatory ambiguity towards O'Shea, sent for him to come and offer some comfort to her daughter. He returned, post-haste, from Spain and, after a brief stay, left behind the gift of a King Charles spaniel.

Touched by his attentiveness, and both emotionally and financially vulnerable after the death of her father, Katharine now overcame any misgivings she may have developed about matrimony and accepted William O'Shea as a life partner. But (with the significant caveat that she was writing in 1914 about a man she had come to loathe) her almost casual reference to their marriage suggests a distinct lack of enthusiasm on her part. 'I now yielded to Willie's protest at being kept waiting longer, and we were married very quietly at Brighton on January 25, 1867,'[28] is her only grudging reference to the happy event. The ceremony, which actually took place on 24 January, 1867, only went ahead after at least three postponements (it was first scheduled for 26 November, 1866) on account of a series of inter-family disputes over the marriage settlement. One of the delays was over the Woods' doubts about the ownership of land being settled on O'Shea by his mother. The legal firm representing Katharine's family noted that 'Mrs O'Shea objected to comply with our suggestion that the Title to the Irish property to be settled on Capt. O'Shea should be investigated'.[29] The settlement was not formally executed and attested by the trustees until four days after the wedding.

According to her brief account, because the best man and groom contrived to position themselves incorrectly, Katharine came close to marrying O'Shea's friend, Cunninghame Graham, until he, rather forcefully, pointed out the error to the celebrant. How different Irish history might have been had the vicar pressed on regardless.

In his account of the marriage from nationalist hell, Tim Healy has Evelyn Wood virtually force his sister on a reluctant O'Shea who is only persuaded to marry her by the lure of a settlement of £30,000. Like much of Healy's spicy memoir what the allegation lacks in accuracy it makes up for in entertainment value.[30]

After the ceremony O'Shea began the marriage as he would proceed, gracelessly. Singling out the wedding gift of a bracelet sent to Katie by an aunt, he appraised it sceptically and allocated it to the dog. Their honeymoon was spent in splendid boredom in a borrowed estate house and then it was time for O'Shea to begin some form of gainful employment. He had sold his commission in the Hussars and invested the proceeds (about £4,000) in a partnership in his uncle's bank in Spain. It was there the newly-weds spent the first full year of their married life. But not before a visit from Katie's new mother- and sister-in-law.

Neither of these pious Roman Catholic ladies had attended the wedding, disapproving as they did of 'mixed' marriages. Once the die was cast, however, they were prepared to accept that their son/brother had married a Protestant. Much like the formidable Lady Catherine de Bourgh in Jane Austen's *Pride and Prejudice* they were all 'condescension and affability' when they dined with the young couple in London. As Katie puts it herself, 'they were very nice and kind, and so gently superior that at once I became politely antagonistic ... they admired me, and very plainly disapproved of me ... they wearied me to death.'[31]

There was no meeting of minds when O'Shea and Katie called in on his mother and sister in Paris, on the long journey to Madrid. The self-righteous O'Shea females were scandalised when Katie insisted on bringing her lapdog, Prince, into Notre Dame Cathedral. She, bridling at their admonishments, scooped up the over-indulged canine and stalked off in high dudgeon. Her act of rebellion lacked only one essential to make it emphatic and complete: a sufficient grasp of the French language to enable her make her way home independently. The penalty for this linguistic deficiency was a rather strained journey in the O'Shea carriage back to her hotel.

Katharine O'Shea thrived in Madrid; she was charmed by the city, by the Spanish and even by her husband's relatives. One of these, Willie's uncle, John O'Shea, had some of the inclinations of his brother Thaddeus for gambling large sums of money. Fortunately he did not have his brother's aptitude for losing it.

While in Spain Wilfrid Scawen Blunt drifted back into O'Shea's life. Blunt, while working as a diplomat in Madrid, had become friendly with Willie's cousin, also called William O'Shea, the Duke of San Lucar. The Spanish relative had, according to Blunt, fallen on hard times after a cashier had embezzled money from his bank and his aristocratic wife had left him. He had been rendered penniless 'but being a careless pleasant fellow he had retained his gaiety and was still popular in Madrid society.'[32] Blunt failed to overcome his aversion to the Irish O'Shea whom he described as possessing 'pretentious, affecting English ways, and altogether inferior to my friend.' Vis-à-vis Katie, he adds, '... of his English wife, a pretty woman, I have but an indistinct recollection.'

Katie is vague about the specific reason for the end of their Spanish idyll but it appears that within a year John O'Shea had ceased to view his nephew with much avuncular affection, the partnership was ended and the young couple returned to England.

O'Shea then tried his hand at stud management, only to discover that having a good seat didn't necessarily translate into an ability to prosper in the bloodstock business. He rented an establishment at Bennington Park in Hertfordshire. With hindsight, Katie observed in 1914, 'we knew, of course, nothing of the enormous expense and many losses such an undertaking was certain to entail.'[33] She writes as if business failure was inevitable. Perhaps where her husband was concerned, this was indeed the case. He had a penchant for expenditure, both personal and business, not matched by any similar degree of application when it came to charging his customers (almost all personal friends) for stabling expenses. He might have been prepared to wait for his fees but his suppliers were not so patient. Before the enterprise collapsed, O'Shea attempted to improve his cash flow by gambling, with predictable results.

In 1869 he was declared bankrupt. Representations were made to Katharine's uncle, Baron Hatherley, for a position in the Treasury. The Lord Chancellor sent a cheque (made out to Katharine) but, wisely, was unable to offer Captain O'Shea a job. Somehow O'Shea managed to get his family (their son Gerard had been born in 1870) out of hock for a while, although he contrived to spend very little time in the home that had been provided for them in Brighton by the ever-generous Aunt Ben. Hints of O'Shea's neglect of his wife and children (three altogether – Gerard, Norah (1873) and Carmen (1874)) enter the narrative early on. He absented himself from the family home frequently and for lengthy periods. Lady Wood wrote of her son-in-law, 'Kate did not pay me the compliment of leaving O'Shea. He only gets there once a week.'[34] O'Shea was a fitful provider for his family and an even more unreliable companion to his wife. He delighted in the notion of being an indulgent Victorian paterfamilias but was not prepared to adjust his lifestyle accordingly. He preferred London society to quasi-rural domesticity and his business interests provided a convenient pretext for long absences. In later years, Katharine assumed that, while resident in London, he was also conducting a series of sexual affairs. She was certainly convinced that her husband was resorting to prostitutes. In an affidavit submitted to the Divorce Court in 1890 she even accused him of conducting an affair with a parlourmaid, Sarah Winsor, under their own roof in 1875.[35]

For a brief period Katharine, despite being the daughter of a Church of England cleric, toyed with the idea of adopting her husband's religion.

She went so far as to take instruction in the Roman Catholic faith. But, as she explains herself, 'I had before me two types of Catholics in Willie and his mother and sister, and both were to me stumbling blocks.'[36] Willie she described as a 'careless Catholic', though later, when they were informally separated, he would arrive at his wife's home on Sundays to take his children to Mass. These were the 'once a week' visits referred to by Lady Wood. His mother and sister were, in effect, religious zealots – 'such an immense piety and so small a charity'[37] – is how Katharine characterised their particular brand of bigotry. Later, on the birth of her third child (the last one by O'Shea), she was so far from any Pauline conversion to Roman Catholicism that she refused to attend the christening, preferring to stand in the porch of the Church where the event took place.

On occasions when it suited him, especially post-1880 and the launch of his political career, O'Shea liked to take advantage of his wife's personable qualities and skills as a hostess. Katie could be charming and vivacious when required and her husband often required it of her. One of his most promising business ventures was a sulphur extraction project in Spain. O'Shea worked his contacts in London to put together a consortium. When he based himself in Spain Katie was used to perform some extraction of her own, whenever extra investment was needed. She would be assigned the task of charming the company directors into coming up with supplementary finance. Suspicion surrounds her relationship with one of the directors, an associate of O'Shea's named Christopher Weguelin, one time Liberal MP for Youghal.

The journalist and Irish Parliamentary Party member T.P. O'Connor put it tactfully when he wrote that Weguelin 'was said at one time to have been very keenly interested in her'.[38] His parliamentary colleague, the waspish Tim Healy, was far less diplomatic. He accused Katharine (by then deceased) of having had an affair with Weguelin. According to the often notoriously unreliable Healy, Weguelin's name came up in documentation during the divorce case. 'You did not object to Christopher,'[39] she is supposed to have written to her estranged husband. This, and other rumours, added to the prevailing notion that O'Shea was not above 'pimping' his wife for their mutual benefit. The plausibility of the contention relies too much on Healy's allegation[40] for its own safety. However, O'Shea would not have been unique had he employed his wife's charms to advance his business interests.

Towards the end of the 1870s, leaving Katharine to take care of their three children, O'Shea departed once again for Spain and worked there for 18 months on the sulphur-mining enterprise. It was to be another of his many business ventures not crowned with success.[41] Fortunately for his wife she no longer had to rely on O'Shea's unpredictable income for the support of herself and her children. She, like her mother before her, had re-discovered Aunt Ben.

At one time Mrs Benjamin Wood's niece had reflected that her aunt was a slightly terrifying lady who 'always wore the fashions of her early Victorian youth'. Clearly Aunt Ben had mellowed towards Katharine by the 1870s, but a woman who was born in the 1790s can hardly be described as having had a 'Victorian youth'. A symbiotic relationship developed between the Georgian and the truly Victorian lady. A large house, Wonersh Lodge, was purchased for Katharine and her three children, across the park from Aunt Ben's impressive pile in Eltham.[42] All Mrs O'Shea's needs were taken care of and, in return, she became the daily companion of her octogenarian aunt.

Anna Maria Wood, a highly educated and cultured woman,[43] lived in Eltham Lodge, whose grounds had once encompassed a hundred acres of Crown land. By the time Katharine became part of her entourage the elderly lady had been a widow for almost half her life, her husband having died in 1845. Katharine O'Shea was not her only paid or kept companion. The novelist and poet George Meredith, also a friend of Katie's mother, received an annual stipend of £150 for reading to the old lady. Rather surprisingly he was not allowed to read to her from his own writings. He attempted to do so on more than one occasion but was, politely, asked to deny himself the pleasure.

Meredith's visits had begun in 1868 and didn't end until the mid-1880s when Aunt Ben was already in her nineties. The novelist was forced to accept some of the strange eccentricities of his hostess. These included a passionate pride in her parquet floors. In order to avoid excessive noise and dirt a series of rugs had been placed at strategic intervals. Staff and guests (including Meredith) were required to hop from one to another to progress through the house. A determined lady, Aunt Ben had ensured that the local railway line skirted, rather than bisected, her property. This made it impossible for the village of Eltham to have a station of its own. Her Francophone tendencies meant that she was especially fond of William O'Shea, with whom she could converse in fluent French.[44]

The arrangement between Katharine and her aunt greatly suited the Captain. He had returned from his Spanish sojourn poorer and none the wiser. After a short time connubial proximity began to pall with Katharine. Much to her relief, Mrs Wood's money secured a London base for O'Shea and provided him with a generous annual stipend. His visits to his wife and children became infrequent in the months after the conclusion of what we might describe as the Eltham Treaty. It was, perhaps, the most significant political victory ever achieved by O'Shea, apart from the destruction wreaked by his divorce in 1890.

So, by 1880, the O'Shea family consisted of two independent entities: one based at Eltham and one situated in London; both happily leading separate lives, but united in an official O'Shea Federation. The Federation, like many such institutions, operated more efficiently the less frequently its laws and precedents were invoked. The O'Shea marriage, although it was less than orthodox, sailed along with moderate contentment, based on the principle of 'the square of the distance'. By and large the farther William O'Shea was from his wife, the happier she was. At least that is how she represented the status quo in her memoir. But that was before her husband decided to fill his days by gaining a seat in Parliament and introduced a rogue element to a perfectly satisfactory arrangement.

UNCROWNED PRINCE

The 'rogue element' was a man of extraordinary political courage, skill and dedication. The latter quality may, at times, have been less than obvious to certain of his colleagues; the former may have been doubted by extremists who shared some of his aims; but no one could deny the strategic and tactical political genius of Charles Stewart Parnell. No man, other than Daniel O'Connell, inspired quite the same level of veneration and hope as he did amongst the people of 19th-century Ireland. However, in contrast to the gradual decline of the ageing Liberator, the fall of Parnell was precipitate and shocking. Things could have been utterly different had Captain William Henry O'Shea not been indulged in his whim of embarking on a political career by his wife's elderly aunt.

Parnell's life and career has been well documented. He could trace his ancestry back to the 1600s and the town of Congleton in Cheshire. The Parnells of the 17th century supported the Parliamentarian cause in the English Civil war and, after the Restoration, bought an estate in Queen's County (Laois). The Irish Parnells, prior to the arrival of their most illustrious scion, boasted a poet (Thomas, 1679–1718) and a Chancellor of the Exchequer in Grattan's Parliament (Sir John, 1744–1801). Sir John was known as the 'Incorruptible' because of his opposition to the Act of Union. However, according to Paul Bew, 'The less agreeable aspects of Sir John's politics were simply glossed over.'[45] One of those was his refusal to accept Catholic Emancipation, a fact which gives a more complete picture of the man whose reputation was exploited to some advantage by his great-grandson.

Sir John's son, William, inheritor of the Avondale estate in Wicklow, was a more appropriate, though less celebrated, role model for Charles.

William Parnell was a novelist and a Liberal MP for Wicklow. He was also far more willing than the former Chancellor to make political concessions to his Catholic neighbours.

Of even more profound influence were Parnell's own parents. His father, John Henry Parnell, was 'a man of generous liberal political temperament'[46] but no political pretensions or ambitions. His mother came from a family whose anti-English credentials would have been envied in the most Fenian of households. Delia Tudor Stewart was the daughter of an American admiral who had fought the British in the War of 1812, captured two Royal Navy ships and earned the sobriquet 'Old Ironsides'. Her removal to rural Ireland from the Boston and New York salons of her youth had done nothing to quell her innate anti-Englishness. This aversion, however, did not extend to the niceties. Her daughters, when they came of age, were duly presented at the court of Queen Victoria.

Parnell's father died in 1859, when Charles had barely reached his teens. His parents had lived separate lives for a number of years. Although the portion of his father's estate that fell to him was Avondale, the legacy was circumscribed by the purchase of land in Carlow that benefited his younger brother, Henry Tudor Parnell.[47] The consequent mortgage on Avondale and the family circumstances after John Henry Parnell's death resulted in the Parnells being forced to leave the County Wicklow estate pro tem, for a variety of different homes in Dublin and Paris.

At the age of six, the 'unmanageable ... Master Charley'[48] had been sent away to a girls' school in Yeovil, Somerset, '... to which I will always look back with the greatest reverence, affection and respect ...'[49] he told a political rally in nearby Portsmouth in 1886. He was, perhaps, gilding the lily for a local audience, as he only spent two terms there before being repatriated with typhoid fever. He was, by and large, tutored at home, until the age of fifteen when he returned to England with his older brother, John Howard, to be prepared for Cambridge in a 'crammer' school in Chipping Norton in Oxfordshire. Although not a keen or adept student, 'his days at Chipping Norton', according to his brother, 'were happy ones, and he thoroughly enjoyed riding, hunting, and playing cricket.'[50]

His four-year career (1865–9) at Magdalene College, Cambridge, was less than illustrious. His brother, who did not accompany him there, records Parnell's expressions of regret that he did not receive a better education or, more particularly, 'that he had not devoted himself with more application to such opportunities as he had for study.'[51] It was a disadvantage under which he would labour during his political career. Parnell's penchant for the scientific (he was a committed technophile) was apparent in his often forensic approach to political debate. It was not, however, matched by any great literary or allusive facility. Even elements like basic spelling and grammar, taken for granted by most Victorian public figures, did not come naturally to him.

There is a difference of opinion amongst members of his immediate family as to his Cambridge experience. His sister Emily insists that 'his Cambridge days were boyishly happy with all the "long, long, thoughts" of youth that distinguish an undergraduate's life.'[52] His brother, John, however, paints a picture of frequent quarrels with fellow students 'which often resulted in blows'. Whatever the truth, Parnell never completed his studies in Cambridge. A fortnight before the end of term, he was involved in a brawl in which he assaulted a Cambridge merchant named Hamilton. Twenty guineas in damages were awarded against him and he was sent down by the University authorities for the remainder of the term. He could easily have resumed his studies later that year but chose not to do so.

On a trip to Paris, where his mother and other members of his family were living, he met a young American woman, Miss Woods, from Rhode Island, with whom he fell in love. There was talk of an engagement. There was certainly an understanding of some sort. When her family journeyed to Rome he followed. However, her desire to keep him there was overcome by his native hypochondria. His fear of fever prompted him to return to Ireland. They met again in Paris some weeks later, at which point everything seemed set fair for a Newport wedding. Then, inexplicably, Miss Woods and family returned to the USA, without reference to the future or to any engagement. Parnell followed her to Rhode Island. There she informed him that she did not wish to marry him, as 'he was only an Irish gentleman without any particular name in public.'[53]

Parnell, crushed and disillusioned, returned to Avondale to lick his wounds. He threw himself, in particular, into the development of a sawmill on the estate. It was one of the few industrial outlets in the area and supplemented the income he received from rent. This, in itself, would have been more than adequate to afford him a prosperous lifestyle except that he was expected to provide, not just for himself, but also for his female relatives from the proceeds of Avondale.

So, in 1873, Charles Stewart Parnell was a fairly typical member of a privileged class enjoying his privileges. He was a resident, benevolent landlord with an estate of just under 4,000 acres. In short, he was a country squire. He rode with the local hunt, he was an officer in the Wicklow militia, he was High Sheriff of the county, he played cricket in summer (he was a competent batsman and wicket-keeper), and he made good use of his large shooting lodge at Aughavanagh during the hunting season. His only deviation from this proto-feudal template was his interest in engineering and science. Why, therefore, in 1874 did Parnell begin to reinvent himself and, according to many of his peers, betray his own birthright in a fifteen-year 'scorched earth' campaign for land reform and self-government?

The traditional explanation for Parnell's abandonment of the politics of his landowning class is that his rabidly Anglophobic mother, his unpleasant experiences in English boarding schools, his expulsion from Cambridge, and the arousal of his nationalistic impulses by the Fenian Rising of 1867, all conspired to fashion a true Irishman from unpromising Ascendancy marble. Leaving aside the debate over what exactly constitutes a 'true Irishman', this stereotype has long since been discredited by a succession of biographers. Parnell's initial response to the Fenian movement was as an enraged young militia officer expelling extreme nationalists from his Dublin home. They had been cultivated by his mother and his rebellious sister Fanny. His boarding school experience was far more positive than the literature of the period suggests was the norm for his English-born contemporaries. His decision not to return to Cambridge probably had as much to do with his growing responsibilities towards Avondale as it did with any disinclination to return to a putative hotbed of anti-Irish bigotry.

The execution of the Manchester Martyrs, Allen, Larkin and O'Brien, hanged in 1867 for their part in the accidental killing of a policeman after a botched rescue attempt, may have had some impact on his political formation or transformation. Certainly his celebrated intervention in parliament in 1876 would suggest as much. The Chief Secretary for Ireland, Sir Michael Hicks Beach, was hitting the disorganised and heterogeneous tribe that was the Irish Home Rule party for six in the House of Commons when he referred to the 'Manchester Murderers'. Parnell intervened, responding acidly that he did not believe 'that any murder was committed at Manchester.'[54] Parnell's brother and R. Barry O'Brien, his first biographer, are quite emphatic in their belief in a Fenian influence. Latter-day historians, such as Roy Foster, are less convinced.[55] When it came to his own evidence before the *Times* Special Commission in 1889, he himself downplayed it. But then, in a phrase from another era, 'he would, wouldn't he?'

The impetus may even have come from a sense of shame and humiliation at the nature of his rejection by Miss Woods. To be told, in effect, that he didn't – and would never – amount to anything, might have been the spur he needed to abandon his squirearchical comfort zone. If that was the case, this would be a richly ironic narrative circle. The career that was scuttled by a very public, albeit highly rewarding, love affair, may have been launched by a more private, but unsatisfactory, romantic experience.

That Parnell went into politics is hardly surprising. Despite his often-expressed abhorrence of public speaking and his initially faltering oratorical skills, this tyro-politician came from a long line of MPs. His father's lack of interest in political office had ended a sequence of Parnells in parliament (Irish or English) going back four generations. But this does not explain how he defied logic so emphatically and located himself far from his natural political home.

Roy Foster points to the Ballot Act of 1872 and the renewal of Tenant Right activity as motivating forces in this regard. Parnell cited both to the Special Commission as factors in his decision to enter politics. The former offered the hope and possibility of a changed political landscape. The latter was a natural concern for an 'improving' landlord, eager to avoid the sort of reactive agrarian turmoil and outrage inspired in aggrieved and impoverished tenants by the more regressive members of his class. An additional incentive, according to David Thornley, biographer of Isaac Butt, was the fact that the Ballot Act made entry into parliament a little easier for the impecunious. As the casting of votes could no longer be monitored the necessity of buying them was somewhat reduced.[56]

John Howard Parnell may offer us another clue in his biography of his brother. As a teenager Parnell took a keen interest in the American Civil War. It was a constant topic of conversation in the Parnell household. Delia Stewart Parnell was an apologist for the Northern cause. John Howard Parnell, as befitted a man who would eventually settle there, was a supporter of the South. Charles sided with his mother and, in a metaphor for the war itself, physical altercations between the two brothers were common when verbal argument on the subject proved inadequate. Did Parnell apply some of the logic of emancipation and liberation to his own country? It is tempting to see in Parnell the outline of an Irish Lincoln. The innate conservatism and reluctant radicalism of the American President would also be of a piece with the future Irish leader. Both men, out of principle, located themselves in a political territory where they were not necessarily comfortable.

But it may all come back to a different form of 'location' in the end. In this instance, 'location' in its geographical sense. Roy Foster has made a detailed study of County Wicklow in the later Victorian period and, in part at least, attributes Parnell's metamorphosis to 'the liberal attitudes of local gentry'.[57] The badger was not actually straying that far from his set. Also, his profound emotional ties to the county and its people gave him a solid base of personal acceptance, no matter how extreme his political beliefs might have seemed to some of his friends and neighbours. This acceptance allowed him the space to make an unexpected political journey. (At the end of his career it also ensured that many members of the local Roman Catholic clergy remained faithful to him.)

Whatever the cause, the first essay of this political chrysalis into local politics was on behalf of his brother, John Howard Parnell, who was defeated in the general election in Wicklow in 1874. Parnell had intended to go forward himself, but was disqualified because of his position as High Sheriff of the county. He would have been in the invidious position of being given responsibility for the count at the end of an election in which he had stood as a candidate. He was, however, perfectly entitled to stand in any constituency other than his native county. To the surprise of many, he declared himself to be a Home Ruler and, because of his political and social pedigree, was run by the Home Rule League as a candidate at the earliest possible opportunity.

A by-election in County Dublin in March 1874 was the first occasion on which he put himself in front of the electorate. It was a chastening experience for both. Parnell was virtually inarticulate. His tentative efforts at public speaking were capable of embarrassing not just the novice politician himself, but also his cringing audience. He went down to a thoroughly convincing defeat but, in the course of the campaign, enunciated a notion that would become largely relegated to a Parnell subtext in the years ahead. In a speech at Kingstown (Dun Laoghaire) he made the expected gesture in the direction of Home Rule, extolling the right to develop Irish industry and fisheries as one of its benefits. He then added that the people of Ireland 'should have their gentry living at home and spending their money amongst them, and coming forward on the public platform to represent the liberties of the country.'[58] It was a theme to which he would regularly return.

His second attempt, in a by-election in Meath in April 1875 (brought on by the death of the former Young Ireland veteran, John Martin), was more successful. In a strange portent of events in the Galway by-election of 1886, pressure was put on a local candidate to withdraw in order to allow Parnell to run and he did so with the support of the Roman Catholic Bishop of Meath. Acting as intermediary in the process of candidate selection was one Patrick Egan, a former Fenian, with whom Parnell would be even more closely linked in the years ahead.[59]

In the House of Commons Parnell would prove to be a far more apt student of politics than he had been of literature and history in Chipping Norton or Cambridge. He entered a parliament in which the Home Rule League, led by the distinguished barrister Isaac Butt, was a barely tolerated irrelevance. Because of the apologetic and supplicant approach of most of its leadership the issue of self-government for Ireland rarely caused more than the slightest tremor in the English body politic. An ostensible cohort of almost 60 MPs was far too few in number to have any significant impact in a parliament dominated by a huge Tory majority.

The Disraeli government felt no great need to 'pacify' Ireland as the previous administration of Gladstone had done. This neglect was accentuated by an indolent or demoralised Irish representation. In an era of unpaid MPs, many Irish members were absentees, forced by financial exigency to make a living outside of parliament.

Initially Parnell did not show any signs of rewriting the rules of this exclusive Gentleman's Club. For two years, while he made regular contributions and voted consistently, he kept his own counsel, by and large. His challenge to Hicks Beach in 1876 indicated that something was beginning to stir.

Prompted by a sense of deep frustration at an inability to get Irish measures (well short of Home Rule) discussed and the prospect of functioning as part of a small but committed alliance, the policy of obstructing the work of parliament was launched on a slumbering House of Commons in 1877. Parnell and the Belfast-born ex-Fenian, Joseph Biggar, began to filibuster and delay the work of parliament. No one expected much more from the acerbic, hunchbacked, one-time pork butcher Biggar, the member for Cavan. But the behaviour of the aristocratic young grandee, representative for the neighbouring county, was truly shocking. British MPs were appalled. Butt was horrified. Parnell and Biggar were unconcerned. Despite rebukes from all quarters, including public disparagement from their own party leader, the two Irish MPs largely succeeded in their campaign of consternation. They gathered allies as they went. Soon they were joined by fellow Home Rule MPs, such as Frank Hugh O'Donnell and another former Fenian, John O'Connor Power.

Parnell's claims that he was not exhibiting a merely destructive and blatant disrespect for the traditions of the House but was, in fact, upholding those traditions by defending minority rights, cut no ice with most of the chamber's 665 or so hostile members. But the tactics of the obstructionists played well at home in Ireland and amongst the Irish in Britain. Within months of unleashing the new strategy, Parnell had replaced Butt as President of the largely Fenian Home Rule Confederation of Great Britain. A thoroughly demoralised Butt died in May 1879. Parnell was forced to endure taunts that his actions had precipitated the death of his party leader.

By then Parnell may have been dimly aware of movement somewhere behind his left shoulder, as growing concerns about a possible repetition of the Great Famine began to seep out of the west of Ireland. At much the same time he would have been utterly unaware of another movement over his right shoulder. It was the fluttering into life of the political ambitions of William Henry O'Shea.

CHAPTER 2

The Representation of County Clare

This proposition had taken Phineas Finn so much by surprise ... What! he stand for Parliament, twenty-four years old, with no vestige of property belonging to him, without a penny in his purse, as completely dependent on his father as he was when he first went to school at eleven years of age!
Anthony Trollope, *Phineas Finn*

DEPARTURES

By 1879 the small cohort of Irish obstructionists in the House of Commons had managed to provoke and antagonise the British establishment and make considerable nuisances of themselves. But they were also gradually filibustering their way into a political cul-de-sac. On one level their campaign was an indictment of the inadequacy of Irish remedial legislation. However, their policy was unlikely to invite positive responses from the Tory government of Lord Beaconsfield (Disraeli).

As Parnell's most respected biographer, F.S.L. Lyons, has put it, he needed 'to broaden his base'[1] and the only viable movement he could make was toward the left, in the direction of the secretive cabals and enigmatic anterooms of Fenianism. His friendship with the journalist and adventurer James J. O'Kelly prised open the door. O'Kelly, a member of the Supreme Council of the revolutionary Irish Republican Brotherhood and an associate of Michael Davitt, met Parnell for the first time in Paris in the summer of 1877 and was favourably impressed. He wrote about the meeting to a fellow Irish–American journalist and employee of the *New York Herald*, the veteran Fenian John Devoy. Devoy had spent five years in jail for his part in the build-up to the rising of 1867 before emigrating to America and joining the revolutionary nationalist organisation, Clan na Gael. O'Kelly's endorsement of Parnell was part of a chain of events which would lead to a brief alliance of convenience between revolutionary and constitutional nationalism.

Parnell also needed to broaden his base of support in parliament and was not likely to be able to do so in any meaningful way until the government chose to go to the country. At that point he could, and did, canvass vigorously for Home Rule candidates of 'advanced' stripe. Until then he was obliged to live off the scraps coming from by-elections. In 1879 two of these took place in adjacent constituencies in the county of Clare.

Politically, Clare has always been something of a bellwether county. In 1828 it elected the first Catholic MP to the House of Commons in the form of the 'Liberator' himself, Daniel O'Connell. In the 20th century it would, famously, choose Eamon de Valera as its Member of Parliament. In the case of the former, the electors chose O'Connell in the knowledge that he might never be able to take his seat. In the case of the latter, it was with the knowledge that the prospective member had no intention of taking his seat. In 1879 the county was given two opportunities to select supporters of Parnell, and came through for him on both occasions.

Chosen to contest the vacant county seat (Sir Bryan O'Loghlen, one of the two sitting MPs, had been appointed a Commissioner of Appeal in Melbourne) was a remarkable individual, at that time in his eightieth year. Colonel James Patrick O'Gorman Mahon, who styled himself the O'Gorman Mahon, was a buccaneering figure who made even the soldier of fortune and frequent duellist James O'Kelly look staid by comparison. He was a Roman Catholic landlord from Clare who had nominated O'Connell for the Clare seat in 1828 and had fought to get the Emancipator elected. He had then represented the constituency himself, had fallen out with the O'Connell family, and had lost his seat. He took up soldiering and fought for 'half the armies of Europe'.[2] He married well but rapidly and efficiently went through his wife's wealth. He had the good fortune to be immortalised by William Makepiece Thackeray when the writer, as a young journalist, encountered him in London. Thackeray 'delighted in his exuberant manners and his irresponsible behaviour.' As a result the O'Gorman Mahon became 'the

O'Mulligan of Ballymulligan' in a series of sketches by Thackeray called 'Mrs. Perkins's Ball'.[3]

Mahon had ended his mercenary wanderings in the 1840s, and in 1847 was re-elected to the House of Commons from Clare as a dyed-in-the-wool Whig. Five years later, after losing the seat for a second time, he was back in military uniform again as a Lieutenant in the bodyguard to the Tsar of Russia. From there he ventured to South America and soldiered for a while on that continent. Along the way the highly argumentative Irishman defended his honour on countless occasions and, given the fact that he died in his bed in his nineties, was clearly one of the most successful duellists of the 19th century.

In 1879 Mahon, who sported a shock of white hair, an unkempt beard and was partial to wearing suits of Highland plaid, was reinventing himself as a Parnellite. As a confirmed contrarian the very unpopularity of the cause may have appealed to him. His biographer, Denis Gwynn, certainly thought so. 'The violent tirades against the Home Rule League which began in the English Press were quite enough to satisfy him that he was still playing a rebel's part in his old age as in his youth. And his still stronger passion for social distinction was fully gratified by the company in which he found himself, as one of the most picturesque landlord champions of Home Rule.'[4]

Playing on his association with O'Connell in the monumental 1828 by-elections, and glossing over any subsequent differences, the O'Gorman Mahon, half a century after his first electoral success, won the seat. He defeated a 'liberal' Tory candidate, local landlord Hector Vandeleur, by 1663 votes to 1530. The result might have gone to Vandeleur but for the presence in the race of a Liberal, anti-Home Rule candidate, the barrister Peter O'Brien[5] who drew away 807 votes. Some years later Parnell may have come to regret his decision to support the O'Gorman Mahon when the latter introduced a fellow Clare landlord to Irish political life, the ambitious William Henry O'Shea.

The other morale-boosting electoral success for Parnell came in the tiny constituency of Ennis, with an electoral roll of only 247 voters. Here Parnell's candidate was a journalist, Lysaght Finigan.[6] His principal opponent was the successful barrister William O'Brien, a nominal Home Ruler but, in reality, a Liberal. Parnell was energetic and highly visible in his support of Finigan, knowing, as he did, that one or two votes either way could decide the election and dictate the momentum going into the general election expected the following year. He spoke at a rally for Finigan in Ennis on 20 July 1879 and remained on for some time to canvass the constituency. His presence was probably crucial in swinging the election for Finigan who won by a mere five votes.

Despite these noteworthy victories it was extra-parliamentary activity that had much greater significance for Parnell in 1879, as he marked time hoping to sweep away the 'moderate' Home Rulers when Disraeli went to the country. In two significant instances events outside Parnell's control would conspire to move him in new directions. Growing in confidence and political nous, he managed to turn both to his advantage. A conversation that took place on a train in May 1878 brings these two strands together.

Parnell's travelling companion on that long journey to an Irish political rally in St. Helen's in Lancashire was the former Fenian prisoner Michael Davitt. As recounted in his personal history of the period, *The Fall of Feudalism in Ireland*, Davitt was politely turned down when he sought to recruit Parnell into the IRB.[7] A recently released Fenian prisoner, Davitt had been born into poverty in Mayo in the same year as Parnell's more salubrious birth in County Wicklow. His family had emigrated to Lancashire when he was a boy and it was there that he lost an arm in a mill accident as a child. Later, in the aftermath of the Fenian rising, he was jailed for gun-running and spent seven years of his life in British prisons.

On his release in 1877 Davitt more or less took up where he had left off. He had been curious to appraise Parnell for himself. When they eventually met, Davitt, like O'Kelly before him, was taken with Parnell. In a memorable and often-quoted phrase he described the obstructionist leader as an 'Englishman of the strongest type, moulded for an Irish purpose.'[8] In contrast to a number of other contemporary observers Davitt noted his travelling companion's sound grasp of Irish history.[9] But he was under no illusions about the extent of Parnell's radicalism. Davitt himself viewed the ill-fated Grattan Parliament of the late 18th century as having 'secured what appeared to be a further lease of legislative power for the landlords of the country ... ' Davitt's assessment was that 'Mr Parnell never went in thought or in act a revolutionary inch, as an Irish nationalist, further than Henry Grattan.'[10] However, long before his memoir of the period was written, Davitt had fallen out with Parnell on a wide range of issues.

Despite his sense of Parnell's innate conservatism, Davitt would become the principal instrument in catapulting Parnell into a brief marriage of convenience with revolutionary nationalism and a longer lasting, though equally utilitarian, relationship with agrarian reform.

His dismal lodgings in Dartmoor had not dulled Davitt's intellect. Abandoning the doctrinaire nationalism of diehard Fenians like the American-based O'Donovan Rossa and the novelist Charles Kickham, Davitt saw that antagonism between militant and constitutional nationalism was inhibiting Irish political development. From the time of his release he began to seek some form of accommodation between these disparate strands of the nationalist movement. In the so-called New

Departure,[11] the shift away from the sterile pursuit of a vague and neutered form of Home Rule and towards agrarian activism, he achieved his initial purpose.

Prompted by soundings and urgings from O'Kelly and Davitt (the latter on a visit to the USA in 1878) John Devoy urged a policy of collaboration between the Parnellites and the revolutionary movement. After a far from exhaustive series of consultations within the Clan he came up with a template for co-operation. This he cabled on 25 October 1878, as a courtesy, to Charles Kickham, the ageing, infirm, irascible and, as it transpired, irreconcilable President of the Supreme Council of the Irish Republican Brotherhood. Devoy must have had a shrewd idea of the response his initiative would elicit because he simultaneously published his proposals in the *New York Herald*.

Kickham was, in theory, intended to transmit the document to Parnell should he approve of its contents. He thoroughly disapproved, but the ideas contained in the 'New Departure' telegram were widely disseminated anyway. The conditions sought by Devoy in return for the support of American militant nationalism were:

> FIRST. Abandonment of the Federal demand and substitution of a general declaration in favour of self-government.
> SECOND. Vigorous agitation of the land question on the basis of a peasant proprietary, while accepting concessions tending to abolition of arbitrary eviction.
> THIRD. Exclusion of all sectarian issues from the platform.
> FOURTH. Irish members to vote together on all Imperial and Home Rule questions, adopt an aggressive policy, and energetically resist coercive legislation.
> FIFTH. Advocacy of all struggling nationalities in the British Empire and elsewhere.[12]

This seminal document of Irish nationalist history was reprinted in both the mildly nationalistic *Freeman's Journal* and the more militant *Nation* in November 1878 but did not elicit a response from Parnell. In essence, none was required. The message had been conveyed and received. It would be reinforced in a series of meetings the following year between Devoy and Parnell, brokered by Michael Davitt.

It was an agricultural crisis that ultimately precipitated the change in direction sought by Davitt. Atrocious weather and bad harvests, allied to the marginality of much of the land being tilled in the west of Ireland, led to fears of a renewed famine in 1878–9. The wider context was a fall in agricultural prices internationally. Once again, after a period of relative prosperity since the Great Hunger of the 1840s, smallholders found them-selves unable to meet their twice-yearly payments of rent. Many landlords were patient and sympathetic. Some were not, and the incidence of evictions began to escalate. Historians have argued about the gravity of the problem, some pointing out that many of those evicted were re-admitted to their farms as caretakers. But, whatever the truth, the fact of the matter is that the reverse side of the coin of eviction quickly re-asserted itself. The incidence of agrarian violence, or 'outrage' as it was officially characterised, began to soar. This described an arc from low-level threats and anonymous letters to assault and murder. J.L. Garvin, Joseph Chamberlain's biographer, has described the unrest, with only a certain degree of hyperbole, as 'agrarian insurrection ... the strongest native revolt for over two hundred years, it sought to disrupt the bases of the Cromwellian settlement and of British rule.'[13]

Davitt, who was above all a superb organiser, responded to the situation by collaborating with journalist James Daly in arranging for the staging of a rally in the most troubled region of the west, his native county of Mayo. It took place in Irishtown on 20 April 1879. It was prompted by the threat of evictions on the estate of the late Walter Burke. His executor, Canon Geoffrey Burke, a Roman Catholic priest, was seeking arrears from his brother's 22 tenants. Partly because of his 'ticket of leave' (parole) conditions, and in order to avoid any over-reaction on the part of the authorities, Davitt did not attend the meeting himself. Parnell's obstructionist ally John O'Connor Power, an egotist with whom he would soon fall out, was the only MP in attendance.

The resolutions passed by the meeting (drawn up by Davitt) were modest and aspirational. A 'reduction in unjust rents by local and Mayo landlords' was sought. However, the speeches from the platform by Thomas Brennan[14] and O'Connor Power went far beyond that. They called for the abolition of landlordism and for peasant proprietorship of their own holdings.[15] Whatever the wider ramifications, the Irishtown meeting had the desired effect on Canon Burke, who granted an abatement to his late brother's tenants.

Parnell might well have come to see the wisdom of placing himself at the head of a movement for agrarian reform without the prompting of Davitt. He might have won the support of individual Fenians in Ireland and the USA without the intervention of Devoy. But what is clear is that, with his agreement to speak at another Davitt-organised rally in Westport, County Mayo in June, despite the very vocal opposition of the powerful Roman Catholic Archbishop of Tuam, Dr MacHale, Parnell had crossed a Rubicon. He needed to place himself at the head of an extra-parlia-mentary movement to be assured of the votes required to shift the balance in the Irish Parliamentary Party towards active and interventionist nation-alism. His cause had not been assisted by the selection of Butt's replacement after his death in 1879. William Shaw, a sober Cork banker and acquiescent parliamentarian, had been chosen to lead the Home Rulers in the House of Commons. His elevation promised a continuation of the anaemic policies of his predecessor.

Parnell's Westport speech of 8 June 1879 begat one of the momentous phrases of the Land War. 'You must show the landlords that you intend to keep a firm grip of your homesteads and lands,' he urged the 8,000 strong crowd. 'You must not allow yourselves to be dispossessed as you were dispossessed in 1847.'[16] The election of Finigan in Ennis in July, the formation of the Land League of Mayo in August and the growing agri-cultural crisis propelled Parnell into the Presidency of the Irish National Land League in Dublin on 21 October 1879. Whatever understanding had been arrived at during a series of three 'summits' between Parnell and Devoy during the months of March, April and June (and there were sharply divergent interpretations) the committee of seven included four Fenians: Biggar, Davitt, Thomas Brennan and Patrick Egan. For a consti-tutionalist Parnell had chosen unconventional collaborators with whom to launch the next phase of his political strategy.

As a landlord himself, Parnell had chosen a paradoxical issue on which to make a stand. He was no Wat Tyler[17], but then neither did the Land League constitute a genuine Peasants' Rebellion. The organisation at whose head he placed himself was just as much under the influence of wealthy urban shopkeepers as it was under the guidance of impover-ished tenant farmers. Although unaware that they were, in large measure, conforming to a template identified by Marx and Engels, the good burghers of Ennis, Wexford, Galway, et al. were simply ensuring that in the context of an agricultural depression it was not the bour-geoisie who would suffer from bad debts. That would be the fate of the landlords. In a skilful exhibition of misdirection and sleight of hand the mercantile conjurors of the county towns of Ireland channelled fear, frustration and anger in the direction of the demesne. The landlords were, after all, not hard to demonise. In the words of R.V. Comerford, 'farmers and shopkeepers responded readily to the idea that agricultural rents lacked the moral legitimacy of other debts ... it was the landlords' bad luck that this viewpoint commanded widespread sympathy in and out of Ireland, even among people who proclaimed the sanctity of all other forms of property.'[18]

In the months ahead Parnell was required to perform a delicate balancing act, an 'inside–outside' strategy. He was hardly the first Irish parliamentarian to walk this particular tightrope. Even the avowed pacifist himself, Daniel O'Connell, had not been above pointing to the 'hillside men', shrugging his shoulders and muttering an '*après moi* ...' But it was a task almost designed for Parnell who was beginning to develop a line in politic vagueness that would stand him in good stead throughout his career. As one of his biographers, Robert Kee, has pithily observed 'imprecision was to be his fundamental strength.'[19]

It was, however, the 'outside' Parnell who arrived in the USA in January 1880, accompanied by John Dillon. At the time Dillon, son of the Young Ireland leader, John Blake Dillon, and former pupil of the Fenian leader James Stephens, was a strident Land League activist. Later that year he would become MP for Tipperary. Officially, the two men were there to raise funds for the Land League and for the relief of distress in the western counties of Ireland. In both of those aims they were highly successful. Parnell, however, was equally intent on winning over Irish–American activists. He sought to convince Irish America to put aside doubts about the efficacy of parliamentary action. He also hoped that some of the money raised by his endless speaking engagements (He and Dillon covered 11,000 miles and 62 cities) would be used to elect Home Rule candidates sympathetic to his activist and muscular approach.[20]

Parnell was preaching to the converted in their millions. The 1881 US census would reveal an Irish-born population of 1.85 million: 3.7 per cent of the total American population and almost 28 per cent of foreign-born inhabitants. Those born of Irish parents numbered 2.8 million.[21] In the course of traversing the United States, Parnell carefully tailored his fund-raising activities. In the more sedate districts he collected for the relief of distress in Ireland. Where he encountered a more radical audience, the Land League would be the stated beneficiary. The money thus collected would fund the organisational activities of full-time professional League activists and organisers, most of them neo-Fenians.

Parnell was careful in his speeches to yoke together the intertwined aims of land reform and self-government. His speech to an audience in Brooklyn on 24 January is typical. 'I feel very confident', he told New Yorkers, 'that the day is very near at hand when we shall have struck the first blow, the first vital blow, at the land system as it now exists in Ireland, and then we shall have taken the first step to obtain for Ireland that right to nationhood for which she has struggled so long and so well.'[22]

Such was the level of publicity attracted by this very American Irishman that the members of the US House of Representatives passed a resolution allowing Parnell to address them. It was not his finest hour as a public speaker. 'A painstaking performance' is Robert Kee's verdict.[23]

As the tour progressed he seems to have honed his rhetoric, doubtless becoming more attuned to the demands of his audiences. By the time he reached Cincinnati, Ohio, in the last week in February 1880, the call for self-government had become a far more aggressive demand for total separation. 'None of us, whether we be in America or in Ireland, or wherever we may be, will be satisfied until we have destroyed the link which keeps Ireland bound to England.' However, even that message, though overtly hard line, is capable of being parsed in a number of ways.

As the pilgrimage through Irish America progressed, it began to descend into organisational chaos. To save the tour boat from sinking altogether the young journalist and political activist Timothy Healy was brought out from Ireland to accompany Parnell. He was not there for long but he was responsible for at least one enduring epiphany. On 7 March 1880, in a speech of his own in Montreal, Healy coined the phrase 'the Uncrowned King of Ireland' in describing Parnell to his audience.[24]

The trip was curtailed by a curt telegram from Ireland summoning Parnell home. On 8 March Disraeli had called an early election, confident that he would defeat an unprepared Liberal party. For Parnell the game was on in earnest. The value of his covert courtship of the Fenians and his overt involvement in the campaign for agrarian relief and reform was about to be tested. He would spend the next month energetically supporting Home Rule candidates, though his efforts fell well short of a crusade. The extent to which he ran neophyte Parnellites against nominal Home Rulers has been exaggerated. The frequent opposition of Roman Catholic clergy (not to mention irreconcilable Fenians) and the need for candidates who could fund their own campaigns and incumbencies militated against a comprehensive attempt to oust the majority of the Shaw faction. By and large Home Rule MPs who exhibited even the vaguest support for the young Pretender were left to their own devices.

The Parnellite campaign was given some context, and something of a boost, by one of the last acts of Lord Beaconsfield as Prime Minister. His was an administration that had been preoccupied with foreign policy adventures and was largely oblivious to anything other than turbulence across the Irish Sea. Disraeli chose, before leaving office, to make Ireland an issue at the hustings. In a calculatedly intemperate letter to the Lord Lieutenant, the Duke of Marlborough, he noted that, 'A danger in its ultimate results scarcely less disastrous than pestilence and famine, and which now engages your Excellency's anxious attention, distracts Ireland. A portion of its population is attempting to sever the constitutional tie which unites it to Great Britain in that bond which has favoured the power and prosperity of both.'[25] For Parnell and his supporters it represented a welcome gauntlet.

THE CLARE ELECTION

In 1841 the population of County Clare was 286,000. One famine and forty years of emigration later it had more than halved. Of the 141, 457 souls who made the county their home just over half (76,073) could read and write. More than 50,000 inhabitants of Clare were wholly illiterate almost fifty years after the establishment of a partially state-funded primary education system in 1831.[26] The main economic activity was agriculture, the county being almost totally lacking in industry or indeed worthwhile infrastructure. The prospect of a railway line for the western part of the county had been dangled before the population for some time. Snail-like progress had been made on the building of piers and jetties on the Atlantic coast to facilitate fishing, but most Clare fishermen were still forced to land themselves and their catches in often perilous coves and inlets.

That the county was far from prosperous is also clear from the size of an electorate based on male suffrage and the ownership of property. Out of a population of around 70,000 males, fewer than 8,000 were entitled to vote in the two constituencies (Ennis and Clare) which made up the county. The population was largely scattered across rural Clare, the main centres of population being the centrally located county town of Ennis, Killaloe in the east and Kilrush and Kilkee to the west. Ennis, the county town, was, according to one 19th-century travel writer, intensely proud of '... its handsome drapery stores, of its brand-new waterworks, of its hundred and odd whisky-shops, and of its patriots.'[27]

Because of the two 1879 by-elections and the determined efforts of Parnell, the representation of the county was no longer entirely vested in the aristocratic families who had, by and large, held sway since the Act of Union. Names like Vandeleur, Conyngham, Fitzgerald and O'Brien (Roman Catholic and Protestant landowners) recur in the lists of MPs consistently returned for the two constituencies. In March 1879, if one counts the O'Gorman Mahon as a committed Parnellite, only Lord Francis Conyngham remained in place of the long line of Tories, Whigs and Liberal Home Rulers who had dominated the politics of the county.

And the political future of Lord Francis Conyngham was in considerable doubt. The Clare Farmers' Club, which took upon itself the endorsement of Home Rule candidates for the constituency, was being alternately drip-fed and force-fed information on his plans by the O'Gorman Mahon. Rumours abounded that Conyngham, whose health was known to be delicate, was not going to stand. In anticipation of that eventuality the jostling to replace him as a Home Rule candidate was intense.

What was clear was that from early March 1880 the O'Gorman Mahon fully intended, despite his advanced years, to put himself before the electorate again for one of the two seats in the County constituency. Assuming, of course, someone could be found to pay his election costs. These would probably be of the order of £300–400. The average amount spent by Home Rule candidates in the 1874 General Election had been £250.[28] Mahon was perennially hard up and specialised in testing the limits of credit and the patience of his creditors. Touting for business, a fellow debtor, Richard Pigott (of whom much more later), the editor of the quasi-Fenian *Irishman* and *Flag of Ireland* newspapers, had already written to Mahon inviting him to insert his election address in their advertising columns. He pointed out that 'both papers circulate largely amongst a class of electors who seldom see any other paper – a class which exercises no inconsiderable influence at elections ...'[29]

On 11 March Mahon appeared confident that both he and Lord Francis would stand together for the county. His Lordship was back from the Continent where he had gone to recover his health 'sacrificed by faithful devotion to Parliamentary duties.' Mahon wrote to a constituent that ' ... our gallant County shall never be reduced to the political degradation of being *misrepresented* by Whig or Tory. The matter is now in the hands of the people themselves!'[30] The rhetoric conveniently ignored his own Whig past.

William Shaw, anxious that a Parnellite should not replace the malleable Conyngham, was disappointed by consistent rumours that his man was about to stand down. In that event he had a candidate in mind, and he knew how to appeal to the improvident Mahon. 'There is a Mr McFarlane who may have ... cultivated the county.' The aforementioned McFarlane, whose name had suddenly emerged in local newspapers as a prospective candidate, had at least one thing, Shaw reasoned, to recommend him to the old Chieftain: 'he may coalesce with you and pay all the expenses, he is a dependable man.'[31] The Clare Whig newspaper, the *Freeman,* in introducing McFarlane to its readers, described him as 'a Roman Catholic gentleman residing in London, under the wing of the Roman Catholic bishop and clergy.'[32] He would quickly disappear without trace.

Another aspirant was anxious to secure His Lordship's endorsement, should the latter decide to opt out of politics. Five days after the calling of the general election Lord Francis received the following letter from a man who introduced himself as a former Captain in the 18th Hussars:

My Lord,

I have seen to my great regret that you do not intend to represent Clare any longer. This is to all who have the national cause at heart very bad news indeed. If the report be true and there be no one in whose candidature you feel an interest, I am ready to come forward, having been frequently urged to stand for an Irish constituency by my friend, the late John Martin.[33] I have some property in Clare and could therefore not be looked upon as a stranger. When the last election for Limerick city occurred I was asked to contest it but was at the time abroad, and although I have no doubt I should meet with good support there, I would on no account disturb the sitting members. The warm interest evinced by your Lordship in the Irish cause leads me to hope that you will in any case pardon this intrusion.

I am, my Lord, Your Faithful Servant, W.H. O'Shea[34]

But Mahon was not quite ready to abandon the notion of a joint campaign with Conyngham. Reassurances were being ferried from London to Clare to the effect that Lord Francis was about to declare his candidacy, despite abundant rumours to the contrary. Just over a fortnight before polling day Mahon's nephew, Captain Mahon, and one of his principal supporters, M.J. Kenny (a future MP for Ennis), experienced some turbulence while holding the line at a meeting of the Clare Farmers' Club. Some of the substantial yeomen of the county suspected that sand was being sprinkled in their eyes by their elderly member. Kenny wrote to Mahon saying that he had been forced to intervene at the meeting to defend his Chief when he had been attacked. 'I told the meeting that you laboured indefatigably and that Mr Parnell was enchanted with you. Your name was then received with enthusiasm.'[35]

Captain Mahon warned his uncle that, although a resolution had been passed endorsing the sitting MPs, 'if you both do not appear before or on Easter Monday ... they do not hold themselves pledged to the above. I need scarcely add that all your best friends have urged me to implore of you both to be in time if possible.'[36] His uncle duly turned up on the appointed day but without Lord Francis in tow – though his imminent declaration was promised yet again.

The concern and confusion in the Farmers' Club, not helped by Mahon's self-serving missives from London, was reflected in local newspaper coverage. On 11 March the conservative *Clare Journal* wrote Conyngham's political obituary, describing him as an MP 'who discharged the duties of his position with zeal and self sacrifice',[37] and noted that he would not be running. Elsewhere in the same issue it corrected itself. The following week the *Journal* sounded a warning. 'Doubtless the O'Gorman Mahon considers his seat so secure that it is absolutely unassailable, but ... it is not at all so improbable that another may be selected to fill the seat he now occupies, and that the O'Gorman Mahon may find out to his cost that in practically ignoring the county he has made a mistake.'[38] Further attacks followed from the *Journal* in the following days as it expressed scepticism about his claims that Conyngham was well enough to run.

The *Clare Freeman* was suggesting that neither of the two sitting MPs would go forward and that the also-rans in the 1879 by-election, Vandeleur and O'Brien, would triumph. Vandeleur would top the poll because of his support for the West Clare Railway and O'Brien would be returned 'owing to the prestige of his father's name and his family connections.'[39] The newspaper's own political tendencies can be gauged by its subsequent endorsement of Vandeleur: 'This gallant gentleman's avowed politics are [the *Freeman* was "pleased to learn"] Conservative, though of a moderate type.'[40] The newspaper later continued its assault on the alleged machinations of the O'Gorman Mahon by hinting that if Lord Francis Conyngham's election address to the voters of Clare was issued,'... it will more probably be without Lord Francis [*sic*] consent or knowledge.'[41] A younger O'Gorman Mahon would have called the editor out.

Soon a plethora of potential candidates were circling Conyngham's seat like vultures. One of the biggest employers in the county, H.C. Drinkwater, who was involved in reclaiming sloblands (marshland) along the Fergus River, was being touted in some circles as the possible choice of Parnell. On 30 March Drinkwater telegraphed Mahon seeking the sitting MP's support, but the man Parnell had chosen for Clare was his new-found friend James O'Kelly. He had, however, not yet shown his hand.

By the end of March there were only two declared candidates for the Borough of Ennis seat (Finigan and William O'Brien, QC – a Shawite Home Ruler) and two for the County of Clare (Mahon and Vandeleur).

Parnell once again materialised in Ennis on 30 March, a day later than scheduled, to offer his support to Lysaght Finigan. His tardiness was related to a fracas in Wexford when he had been assaulted while campaigning against a conservative Home Ruler, the Chevalier O'Clery.

O'Clery had the support of both the local clergy and, somewhat bizarrely, the Wexford Fenians. This tendency for Irish election rallies occasionally to degenerate into faction fights was underscored by the arrival at the Ennis meeting of a large group of 'slob' workers, employees of H.C. Drinkwater. Whether or not their employer had been jilted by Parnell and had instructed his charges to seek exemplary revenge, Drinkwater's men threatened to disrupt the Parnell–Finigan rally.[42] Parnell must have wondered if he was about to suffer bodily harm yet again.

From the platform Finigan warned the slobmen that 'if they committed any breach of the peace they would be well punished for it.'[43] The labourers had allegedly been promised a shilling each for drink if they successfully disrupted the meeting. Finigan warned that, 'If Mr Drinkwater was really the originator and prompter of this abominable plot he (Mr Finigan) would show him that an English capitalist could be sent to spend two years in an Irish gaol.'[44]

Drinkwater's faction certainly did their level best to breach the peace but were outnumbered by the Parnellite supporters and, but for the intervention of Finigan himself, their leader, a foreman named Kerin, would have been badly beaten by the crowd. Few of those attending the rally would have had a vote in the forthcoming election, but that didn't dampen the fervour of their support.

It was not until the beginning of April that the final list of candidates for the two Clare seats emerged. Long before that the O'Gorman Mahon had realised that Conyngham would not be running and began casting about for a replacement purse. He found a willing financier in Captain William Henry O'Shea, who was, of course, venturing someone else's money. O'Shea had received the imprimatur of Aunt Ben, not to mention her resources, to make a run for the County of Clare as a Home Ruler. What he did not tell his wife until after the election was that her aunt would be funding the entire Home Rule campaign for the county.[45]

Aside from the issue of finance it is not hard to see how the two men, despite the enormous difference in age and experience, would have been eminently simpatico. O'Shea had a refined ability to charm, flatter and amuse. He clearly used all his well-honed social skills on the octogenarian adventurer. O'Shea's letters to Mahon are waggish and affable but just sufficiently deferential to appeal to the older man's vanity. In addition both were cosmopolitan Europeans, linguists and hapless entrepreneurs. Denis Gwynn called them 'kindred spirits'.[46] He noted in his biography of Mahon that, 'Sharing the representation of the county with so active a young politician, who took care to treat his senior partner with every deference, the old man felt himself more than ever the chief potentate of his county.'[47]

Mahon advised his putative running mate not to await a definitive decision from Conyngham but to begin canvassing the constituency on a provisional basis. Thus, late March found O'Shea travelling the byways (highways were few and far between) of Clare. On 27 March alone he covered 42 miles, travelling through the villages of Broadford, O'Callaghan's Mills and Kilgorey before settling for the night in Scariff. Writing to his patron he flagged a strategy that would become one of the cornerstones of his brief political career, the cultivation of the Roman Catholic clergy. In the absence of an organised and disciplined Home Rule party they had become accustomed, in some constituencies, to selecting the candidates themselves.[48] 'I have been ordered by authority which cannot be disobeyed,' he wrote to Mahon, 'to send my address to the Priests but of course I shall not publish it until, and if, it becomes evident that Lord Francis cannot stand. The time is so short, however, that the delay that has occurred looks like throwing a chance away.'[49]

The priests did not let him down. Then, or a decade later.

TO THE HUSTINGS

Once the O'Gorman Mahon finally accepted that when Lord Francis said 'No' he actually meant it, O'Shea's address to the electors of County Clare was published in the *Journal*. It appeared in the newspaper (and some may consider the date appropriate) on 1 April 1880. As his avowed political manifesto it is worth reproducing in full:

> To the free and independent electors of the County of Clare,
>
> Gentlemen, I beg to offer myself as a candidate for the honour of representing your County in Parliament.
>
> Having been proposed as a member of the Home Rule League soon after its formation by my lamented friend, political guide and teacher, Honest John Martin, I do not make a mere time-serving profession in declaring for –
> HOME RULE.
> As an Irishman I hold that our country can never rest until its nationality is recognised in our own Parliament.
>
> If elected I shall work with the Active Home Rule Party, under its recognised leader.
>
> The Land Question is urgently pressing for settlement. That settlement should be thorough and final.
>
> Facilities should be given to tenants to become propri-etors of their holdings, and they should be protected from

the power which landlords now possess of arbitrarily raising their rents or capriciously evicting them.

I am, then, for Peasant Proprietors, and for Fixity of Tenure at Fair Rents as embodied in Mr Butt's Land Bill.

On the Education Question I shall be guided by the Bishops of our Church in seeking such further measures as are necessary to give Fair Play and full Equality in Endowments and otherwise to the Catholic Youth of Ireland.

The state of the Irish Franchise is a wrong. I shall cordially support the measures introduced by the Home Rule Party for its reforms. [*sic*]

The Grand Jury Laws, which are an anomaly, should be thoroughly reformed, so as to give those who pay taxes an effectual control over their expenditure.

These, gentlemen, are my political opinions on the leading subjects which now agitate the public mind. I believe they are in accord with those of the vast majority of the Electors of the County.

Should you do me the honour of electing me as your Representative, my Parliamentary Policy shall be shaped entirely by the course pursued by the Irish Home Rule Party, with whom I shall loyally act.

Holding property in the county my interests and yours are identical. I shall always be at your service and shall regard it as a duty to take counsel with you on all occasions in which Local or National matters are concerned, so as to be sustained in Parliamentary action by your approval and support.

I have the honour to be, Gentlemen, Your Faithful Servant,
W.H. O'Shea

It was a manifesto that was clearly designed to attract the endorsement of the Clare Farmers' Club. All the requisite buttons were pushed, from land reform (incorporating peasant proprietorship) to the extension of the franchise. The key reference, given his later history, was in his declared support for the '*Active* Home Rule Party under its recognised leader'. The crucial word 'active' had not appeared in the original draft of the address. This had been forcefully brought to O'Shea's attention at the convention of the Clare Farmers' Club when that organisation met to endorse its candidates in late March.

The meeting was chaired by Tulla-based priest Father Patrick White. He amply demonstrated the efficacy of O'Shea's policy of winning clerical hearts and minds by enthusiastically recommending O'Shea to the assembled members. He had made personal inquiries about the candidate and had been told, 'that he had on his side some of the respectability and influence of the county that had been opposed to them at the previous elections, and it required a man of his popularity and his associations with the county to oppose the Tory organisation.'[50]

Notwithstanding the suspicion that his labourers had been paid to disrupt a public meeting in the Ennis constituency, H.C. Drinkwater (who had disowned the activities of his employees) offered himself to the members as a Home Rule candidate. Watching proceedings quietly was James O'Kelly who had been sent to Ennis[51] at the bidding of Parnell. He brought with him a letter from Morrison's Hotel, Dublin, haunt of his leader. It read, 'I have succeeded in persuading my friend, Mr James O'Kelly, to place his services at the disposal of the farmers of Clare ...' Both men addressed the meeting. Drinkwater, despite being English, would have had some familiarity with the constituency. O'Kelly must have been somewhat bemused by what was going on; newspaper reports describe him as having 'had very little to say.'

In his speech O'Shea played the local card straightaway. He claimed to have been born 'on the brow of the Shannon and the first sight he had ever seen were the hills of his native county ...'[52] According to the Clare *Independent*, after recapitulating the essential elements of his address, he concluded by insisting that, 'He was not in favour of Whigs or Tories but was a true Irishman, and hoped they would select him.' He sat down to applause.

Some of the members, however, were unimpressed. Among the audience was the formidable Thomas Stanislaus Cleary, proprietor of the main nationalist newspaper of the county, the *Clare Independent*. Something of a newsmaker himself, Cleary was an editor/proprietor who both provided and supplied his newspaper with copy. He was a staunch Roman Catholic and a writer of sentimental and execrable religious and nationalist verse who wrote under a number of pseudonyms. The column inches devoted to his activities in the *Independent* would have been the envy of many 21st-century publishing magnates. At least some of those activities had come to the attention of the authorities in Dublin Castle where he was viewed with considerable suspicion. 'By the general tone of his paper and his speeches he excites the people to acts of violence ...'[53] was the view of the Executive. Although his paper had supported Vandeleur against the O'Gorman Mahon in the 1879 by-election, by March 1880 Cleary was a convinced Parnellite. He was known in some circles, at least according to his own newspaper, as 'The Parnell of Clare.'[54]

As O'Shea resumed his seat Cleary rose and began to quiz the would-be Member of Parliament. Why was there not a single mention of Parnell in his address? O'Shea avoided the question. He insisted that he had spoken very fully on the matter, his address was very explicit. Fr White then intervened on the side of the presumptive candidate, attempting to head Cleary off. The newspaper editor would not be deflected. 'Captain O'Shea must be prepared to work with the Active Policy of Mr Parnell or he will not be adopted by this Club ...', he insisted. The chants of 'Parnell, Parnell' coming from the floor left the President in no doubt as to the feelings of the meeting. O'Shea continued to maintain that 'my address is sufficient.' To renewed chants of 'Parnell', Cleary retorted that, 'The leader of the Home Rule party may not mean Mr Parnell at all in Captain O'Shea's opinion ...' At this point Lysaght Finigan intervened and insisted that O'Shea remove any ambiguity from the wording of his address. Finigan, a noted opponent of clerical domination of nationalist politics, would have relished crossing swords with the chairman as much as the overdressed prospective candidate. After a debate on the issue O'Shea conceded defeat and the word 'active' was duly added. At which point Drinkwater and O'Kelly bowed to the inevitable and withdrew. All was sweetness and light for O'Shea, but he had clearly planted doubts in the minds of some; doubts that would grow exponentially in the months ahead.

The O'Gorman Mahon faced no similar inquisition and sat contentedly wearing his favourite green scarf, the one he had refused to doff at the bidding of the High Sheriff of Clare while campaigning for O'Connell in 1828.

T.S. Cleary appears to have anointed himself campaign mascot for the two county Home Rule candidates. His many stump speeches in the days ahead contained few enough references to O'Shea or Mahon, dealt a lot with Cleary himself and involved lengthy diatribes against Tories and Whigs. In one instance, by way of introduction to O'Shea, he hinted at concerns that were already being expressed in nationalist circles about the prospective junior member for the county. 'Whatever may be said, you will find that Captain O'Shea will keep true to his pledges; he promised us in the Farmers' Club ... that he would support the Active Party, and if he ever fails to do so, I will be one of the first to denounce him.'[55] The praise was faint indeed, with more than a suggestion of damnation to follow.

The county campaign had barely begun in earnest when the borough election was decided. Finigan, once again, despatched William O'Brien, but this time by more than five votes. He was the relatively comfortable winner by 124 to 95. The electors for the county were afforded ample opportunity of running their eye over the three candidates. Two were very familiar; the third was an object of curiosity, unknown in the county, except by his own tenants. O'Shea was very much the 'coat-tail' candidate. He may have been providing the cloth, but the O'Gorman Mahon owned the coat. On 3 April the *Clare Freeman* reported from Tulla that 'the O'Gorman Mahon accompanied by Captain O'Shea ... made a long and characteristic speech, to a rather limited audience, as his arrival had not been announced'. The *Freeman* correspondent noted that 'Mr O'Shea also attempted to address the crowd but he utterly failed.'[56]

In the course of the campaign the first recorded meeting of the Captain and the King took place at a political rally attended by both men in Ennis. There is no record of O'Shea's impressions of Parnell at that time but, retrospectively, we have Parnell's comments on what he made of O'Shea. In the midst of their mutual antipathy in the late 1880s the Irish party leader observed to Katharine O'Shea, 'I was right when I said in '80, as Willie got up on that platform in Ennis, dressed to kill, that he was just the man we did not want in the Party.'[57]

The return of one Home Rule candidate in Clare was inevitable but the *Clare Freeman* made no secret of its hopes for the second seat. Writing about Hector Vandeleur campaigning in the coastal town of Kilrush it enthused about 'Mr Vandeleur's pleasing manner and natural courteousness ...' adding that 'When the learned gentleman removed his hat and rose in his carriage to address the assembled multitude, he was met by a ringing cheer ...' Accompanying the hybrid Liberal Conservative candidate was his brother-in-law, R.W.C. Reeves, who sported the campaign trophy of a black eye, the result of a stone thrown by a political opponent.

The Home Rulers experienced their own difficulties in the seaside town. According to a letter to the *Freeman* from 'An Elector' the two candidates had addressed voters from the windows of Williams' Hotel: 'The O'Gorman Mahon got a fair hearing, but some of the remarks of Captain O'Shea were objected to and several free fights took place.' The exact nature of the objectionable comments is left to our imaginations. Both men had then visited the church in nearby Knock on the following Sunday morning: 'They received, however, such a "warm" reception that they were obliged to beat a hasty retreat. They returned to town at about half past 11 o'clock with the windows of their carriage smashed.'[58]

Such a show of hostility was not reflected in the eventual result. When the votes of the county were tallied, Mahon and O'Shea had won comfortably. The senior member topped the poll with 3,383 votes; the new junior member was 250 votes behind, with Vandeleur a distant third, having polled only 912 votes. On the face of it at least Parnell had swept the county of Clare.

In a breezy letter to his new colleague O'Shea later reminded the O'Gorman Mahon of some of the other more colourful moments of the campaign. 'My Dear Chief ... I left you cursing and swearing for the carriage on the road to New Park,' he wrote, 'and I have often wondered which had the best of it when you at length, as I suppose you must have done, measured swords with the beggar women of Ennis after the election. The strength begotten of whisky could alone have saved me from the strangling embrace of the ragged Amazon who intercepted my passage over the bridge. I foiled her somehow, but her disappointed screech of "huzzay for Vandeloore!" rings in my ears.'[59] The 'whisky' in question was, of course, whiskey. It was a drink that O'Shea detested but had been obliged to consume in copious quantities in order to appear sociable to his more bibulous constituents.

O'Shea's ability to project the accommodating and positive side of his personality had been enough to counteract the evidence of his almost foppish appearance and his clipped Anglicised vowels. According to Katharine O'Shea, her husband's victory had come about in spite of his 'innate fastidiousness in dress [which] brought gloom into the eyes of the peasantry till his unfeigned admiration of their babies and live-stock, scrambling together about the cabins, "lifted a smile to the lip".'[60]

The announcement of the result was the signal for prolonged and excessive rejoicing in certain parts of the county. The same Kilrush where the Home Rule candidates had experienced such animosity, celebrated with a will. A correspondent who called himself 'An Elector' kept the *Freeman* readers informed. Between eight and ten o'clock on the night of the dec-laration 'the town was practically in the hands of the great unwashed. They carried burning tar barrels through the street hurraying for the O'Gorman Mahon and Mr O'Shea. Not satisfied with this method of testifying their great joy they smashed the windows of the houses of several respectable people who were supposed to be the admirers of Mr Vandeleur. ... The police are either guilty of culpable negligence or base cowardice ...'[61] Thirty extra Royal Irish Constabulary constables were called in from Tipperary to deal with the aberrant Home Rulers and at least one serious sabre wound was inflicted in the confrontation that followed.

According to O'Shea's own account something similar was going on in Tulla. 'I have a good many letters from Clare, of all sorts and sizes,' he wrote to the O'Gorman Mahon. 'I'm sorry to hear that our friend "Cock" Neill, chief of the Tulla Mob, after having failed in a well meant attempt to burn down the town in order to illuminate our victory, got fined at the next petty sessions. He is a great organiser of men and boys, and a born commander.'[62]

O'Shea may have been touched by the displays of delinquent loyalty, but such egregious and destructive enthusiasm prompts an obvious question. Either it was the case that the charismatic qualities of the two Home Rule candidates were so motivational that the fervour of their supporters knew no boundaries, or we must look elsewhere for the cause of such passionate merrymaking. Before a riot can be fuelled by alcohol the drink must be paid for. Is it conceivable that the Kilrush and Tulla carousers had been the recipients of inducements to cast their votes in a particular direction?

The defeated candidate certainly suggested as much in a statement issued after the election.

> To the Electors of the County of Clare
>
> Gentlemen – By a combination of influences, both misguided and illegitimate, I have been prevented from representing you in the Parliament about to be assembled. A knowledge of the peculiar tactics adopted against me increases my respect for those Electors who adhered to their principles, and, in spite of persistent pressure and solicitation, acted in accordance with the dictates of truth and honour.
>
> Hector S. Vandeleur, Kilrush House, Kilrush, Co Clare
> 8th April, 1880'[63]

Vandeleur had been promised enough votes to win both Clare seats for himself but in the end only 912 electors had delivered on their promises. The Clare *Journal* observed that guarantees of support were 'at least quadruple that of his actual supporters ... that he was grossly deceived the result has shown.' The *Journal* made the assumption that 'even the major portion of his father's tenantry did not support him'.[64]

It is hard to feel much sympathy for the Tory candidate after years of elections in which votes had been gained by members of the ruling oligarchy as a result of unashamed intimidation and corruption. This in a system of rotten and pocket boroughs fought on a restricted franchise which had still not been entirely swept away even by 1880.[65] If some form of bribery – petty, egregious, subtle or explicit – had been used to swing an election in Victorian Ireland it should not be the cause of much astonishment. Indeed had the Home Rulers 'sweetened' the electorate with money or alcohol they might well seek to justify their actions by insisting that they were merely neutralising similar activities on the part of their opponents. The sum alleged by O'Shea to have been spent during the campaign to elect two candidates, £2000, was considerably in excess of the average (£414)[66] expended by other successful Parnellites. It is tempting to assume that it was employed to enhance the lives of the people of County Clare.

There was at least one more hint that some of Aunt Ben's money had been used to purchase hearts and minds that could not be won over by rational argument. A month after the election, T.S. Cleary used the pages of his own newspaper to scotch a rumour that had gained currency in the county. In an article entitled 'Another Slander', there was an emphatic denial that Cleary had ever had any conversation with O'Shea 'with reference to money matters ... or that the question of money or value or reward or compensation was touched upon by Mr Cleary to Captain O'Shea before or after the election. Or that any threat or inducement was held out or implied by Mr Cleary to Captain O'Shea before or after the election.' Cleary's vigorous denial may be taken at face value but the rumour obviously flourished in a climate where such petty corruption was endemic.

Nationally the balance in the Irish Parliamentary Party had shifted towards Parnell, though not in any overwhelming fashion. Nominal Home Rulers (essentially Whigs who paid lip-service to the concept) had been returned in a number of constituencies. MPs like the O'Donoghue had been re-elected in Tralee (based on a franchise of 355 voters). His particular brand of insipid nationalism was typical of many Borough constituencies that proved not to have been a fruitful source of support for Parnell. Of the 21 *soi-disant* Home Rulers returned from Borough constituencies, only 5 voted to place him in the leadership.

Parnell had worked industriously for 'his' candidates and he himself stood for and won the constituencies of Meath, Mayo and Cork. He opted to sit for the latter, and his supporters won the resultant by-elections in the other two counties. Unionist opponents were often the least of Parnell's concerns. He had first to face down the 'enemy within' – Whig Home Rulers, the Fenians[67] and powerful elements within the Roman Catholic hierarchy, led by Archbishop McCabe of Dublin. Altogether sixty-three notional Home Rulers were returned in Irish constituencies. Two of those rapidly fell by the Liberal 'Ministerialist' wayside. Time would tell how many would throw in their lot with Parnell and whether he could wrest the leadership of the Irish party from William Shaw. Whoever was selected to lead the party in the new parliamentary session would be facing a Liberal administration. The British electorate had rejected 'Beaconsfieldism' and Gladstone had been returned to power with a comfortable overall majority of forty-six, the largest since 1832.

Meanwhile the newly elected junior member for Clare was luxuriating in his success and in the *faux* disapproval of his more conservative friends. After his electoral exertions he had stopped off for some rest and recuperation on an estate in north Wales. Writing to the O'Gorman Mahon he joked that 'Some of my friends profess great fear of the Communistic tendencies of "Citizen O'Shea", and ask me if I put petroleum on my handkerchief for scent. I see that our own People are having a bit of a skirmish in Dublin. I can only advise peace and concord to both sides.'[68]

The skirmish in question was a row between the two Irish party factions about the timing and location of the vote on the chairmanship of the party. Shaw wanted it in April, in Dublin. Parnell, many of whose elected supporters were based in England, preferred the decision to be made in London just before the parliamentary session began in May. 'Citizen O'Shea' gave a possible early indication of the direction in which his support might go when he indicated that he would be happy to attend the proposed Dublin meeting. The *Clare Independent* was not pleased with his decision.

'We regret that Captain O'Shea', Cleary wrote, '... should, in this that may be considered his first public act, not be found in accord with Mr Parnell. Of course it may be regarded as a small matter, yet it is a matter in which sides were taken and we know the electors of Clare would have been better pleased to find Captain O'Shea on the side of Parnell. We hope to see him there faithfully in future.'[69]

Even before that preliminary sortie from O'Shea some constituents had been hinting that they had some doubts about the man just chosen to represent them. At a post-election rally in Ennis the local Secretary of Trades (the closest thing in Victorian Ireland to a Union official) Michael G. Considine heaped plaudits on Parnell, Finigan and the O'Gorman Mahon. His praise for O'Shea was less fulsome. 'We all feel confident', he told the crowd, 'that Captain O'Shea will ... support that self-sacrificing patriot, Mr Parnell, but should he not, the men of Ennis and Clare know what to do when provoked to anger.'[70] The *Independent* reported that there were 'cheers for Captain O'Shea'; they might just as easily have been cheers for the threat implied by Considine.

A letter from a constituent to the O'Gorman Mahon highlights the fact that Aunt Ben's entire fortune would not have been enough to have ensured O'Shea's election without the support of his senior partner and his somewhat tepid endorsement of the policies of Parnell. 'Your colleague Capt O'Shea', wrote Thomas Studdert, 'was a singular success for a Stranger, but his canvass, in conjunction with the OGM [*sic*] Insured his return for Clare, you asked me to support him and I did so, and would act likewise by Tom the Devil, if you wished me to do so ...'[71]

The Unionist Clare *Journal*, in licking its wounds, was scathing in its assessment of the outcome of the election. '... it seems to us that the County of Clare has gained least of any other in Ireland in her representatives.' The O'Gorman Mahon, the paper claimed, was 'the embodiment of a chequered career' and had reached the end of his rope when it came to exploiting his part in the election of O'Connell in 1828.

For his part the *Journal* thought O'Shea to be too young and inexperienced and his electoral success:

> ... was due in the first instance, to the fortuitous circumstance that he was the proverbial man in the gap; and in the next to his acceptance of the active policy dictum, for had he not ascribed his adherence to that policy he would never have been accepted by the Farmers' Club. However he is now MP for Clare, and if the people have discharged a duty by him, it is now for him to discharge a duty by them. Honours that are lightly won are apt to be regarded lightly, yet we trust the converse will be the case in this instance.[72]

O'Shea could hardly expect much acclaim from a Tory newspaper but the fact remained that he had a lot to do to build up a support base of his own in Clare. In the months ahead he would set about doing just that with his characteristic élan and enthusiasm. Ultimately it was a course of action that would end in failure. When it came to consolidating his bailiwick, his instincts were flawless and his methodology sound – it was the times that were out of kilter. The *Journal* may have been correct about his fortunate position in 'the gap' in March 1880. But between that time and the General Election of 1885 the 'gap' closed, excluding the Captain in the process.

CHAPTER 3

Courting the King

The country can do nothing to put a stop to this black-guardism. When they've passed this Coercion Bill they're going to have some sort of Land Bill – just a law to give away the land to somebody. What's to become of the poor country with such men as Mr Gladstone and Mr Bright to govern it? They're the two very worst men in the whole Empire for governing a country. Martial law with a regiment in each county, and a strong colonel to carry it out – that is the only way left of governing us.

Anthony Trollope, The Land Leaguers

PARNELL V SHAW

Before the 1880 General Election 'it was still possible to see Parnell and the other obstructionists as no more than an irritant.'[1] The result had, at the very least, served to increase his nuisance value, but it remained to be seen whether he had managed to effect the return of enough like-minded MPs to seize control of the Irish party at Westminster. Some of the young men[2] who would become his most able lieutenants had been elected but he was by no means assured of a majority of votes when it came to the election of a chairman of the party for the forthcoming parliamentary session. His acolytes had done well, especially in the Land League stronghold of Connaught, but he had not secured anything even vaguely resembling a swingeing mandate from the people.

Parnell could count on the support of additional bodies. John Dillon, his companion on the American excursion, had been returned for Tipperary, and James O'Kelly, who had not been unduly chastened by his Clare experience, had been elected ahead of the Liberal grandee, the O'Conor Don, in Roscommon.[3] Thomas Sexton, a young journalist, had defeated the incumbent Captain E.R. King Harman in Sligo. His fellow officer, Captain William O'Shea, had met the Protestant landlord in Dublin and the latter had claimed to be 'glad of his beating' though he spoke 'in doubtful tones.'[4]

Another journalist, the London-based T.P. O'Connor, had taken Galway, while in Westmeath the publisher H.J. Gill and T.D. Sullivan, editor of the *Nation*, had taken the two seats. But the victory of William Shaw over Parnell's favoured candidate in County Cork, Andrew Kettle, had been a setback and the success of the proprietor of the *Freeman's Journal*, Edmund Dwyer Gray, against a Tory incumbent in Carlow did not necessarily augur well for the activists. Nor was there any certainty that the distinguished journalist and novelist Justin McCarthy would side with Parnell. In addition the return of the veteran Young Irelander, A.M. Sullivan, in Louth had been cancelled out by the triumph of the obnoxious Philip Callan. The mutual antipathy between Callan and Parnell (based largely on Parnell's loathing of Callan's excessive drinking) would continue for another session at least.

Furthermore the 'active' leader had been forced, in too many instances, to accept the credentials of some rather dubious 'Parnellites' on the basis that they could fund their own campaigns. O'Shea was a case in point, as was J.C. McCoan in his native Wicklow. Arch-opportunists like the O'Donoghue in Tralee, although they were dyed-in-the-wool Whigs, had even expressed a measure of support for Parnell in order to garner the 'gullible' vote.

There was not even a remote possibility that whoever was chosen to lead the Irish party would be able to unite its rapidly diverging wings. When the Home Rule MPs assembled in City Hall in Dublin on 17 May 1880, only 44 of the 61 members bothered to attend.[5] Edmund Dwyer Gray, MP for Carlow and Lord Mayor of Dublin, presided but was unable, according to the Dublin Correspondent of the *Times*, to 'obtain even a flimsy semblance of union.'[6] Listed among the attendees are some of the forgotten yeomen of the rearguard, ostensible Home Rulers, most of whom were eager to offer support to the Gladstone administration. There were names like Synan, Smithwick, O'Shaughnessy, Errington, Colthurst, Gabbett and their leader, Shaw. The new Irish politics, as exemplified by Parnell, Dillon and O'Kelly, had no further need of them and, with an impressive majority in the new parliament, neither did the incoming Liberal administration. Significant absentees included Parnell's nominal political allies Frank Hugh O'Donnell and John O'Connor Power. Both had valid reasons for absenting themselves, but the unstated reason was a growing personal animus. Neither could stomach the likely apotheosis of Parnell. O'Donnell, in his own version of the obstructionist narrative, saw himself at its head. O'Connor Power's simmering resentment was related to the almost casual manner of Parnell's angelic ascent into leadership of the agrarian movement.

Parnell was proposed by the oldest member of the party, the O'Gorman Mahon, resplendent in his green scarf. He urged the members 'not to be led to the right or to the left by Whig or Tory', thereby implying that the party was more conservative than the Hartington wing of the Liberals. Biggar seconded, pointing out that while a number of candidates had been elected on the basis of their support for Parnell, 'he was not aware that any member of the party had told his constituents he came forward as a supporter of Mr Shaw.' According to the *Times* 'a warm debate, enlivened by some personal sallies ensued' and continued for three hours. Among the thrusts was the reference by Sir Joseph McKenna to Parnellism as 'a braggart policy' and a row between Lysaght Finigan and Philip Callan. When the issue was put to a vote, Parnell's victory was narrow (23 to 18)[7] and an indication of the extent of the support he could expect in the new parliament. After the elevation of Parnell a lunch hamper arrived and 'a cloth was spread across the end of the table, and the observations of the disputants were heard amid occasional explosions caused by the opening of bottles.'

Most of the newly elected MPs voted with the majority. One of them, something of an unknown quantity, came to the attention of T.P. O'Connor, newly elected MP for Galway and at that time a successful 32-year-old, London-based journalist. The stranger sat with the O'Gorman Mahon who wore a 'suit of shabby tweed with the rather glaring colours of a Scotch plaid'. His companion, on the other hand, according to O'Connor:

> ...stood out from all his colleagues as the one well-dressed man in the place. He was a real dandy, though a tasteful one. His face and expression were in harmony with his clothes; he

had a round placid countenance, with the mutton chop
whiskers then almost universal; he wore what used to be
called a Prince Albert coat; his face was a little puffy and a
little pale, and his expression was somewhat impassive. He
gave me at once the impression of a man who had 'lived',
and had just come direct from the enjoyments of a club in St.
James's.[8]

O'Connor also noted that this handsomely accoutred newcomer,
Captain William O'Shea, cast his vote for Parnell.

Was O'Shea merely honouring an undertaking made, albeit under
pressure from T.S. Cleary, to the Clare Farmers' Club? Was he, as
Katharine O'Shea's biographer, Joyce Marlow, suggests, indulging 'his
gambler's instinct to back a winner'?[9] Was he simply following the lead of
his superannuated political patron, the O'Gorman Mahon? Or did he
expect some sort of advantage to derive from his support of Parnell, a
party leader with little or no preferment to offer at that time? Whatever
his motive he was less than convinced, in the aftermath of his decision,
that he had made the right choice. He telegraphed his wife that night
telling her what he had done but expressing the fear 'that Mr Parnell
might be too "advanced".'[10] Despite his misgivings he also requested her
to create a political salon by cultivating leading Irish and British political
figures. Parnell was on top of the list of desirable invitees.

TESTING THE LIBERALS

The Irish party had expected nothing much from the Beaconsfield administration and had not been disappointed in their low expectations, but
there was a natural sense of anticipation surrounding the Gladstone
Ministry. The great Liberal Prime Minister had, after all, been responsible for two major initiatives in Irish law, the Disestablishment of the
Church of Ireland in 1869 and the Land Act of 1870. Though the latter
in particular was a deeply flawed piece of legislation, they had established
the Grand Old Man's credentials on John Bull's other island as a
reforming Prime Minister. The members of the Shaw oppositional faction
of the Irish party were well disposed, by inclination and temperament,
towards supporting the Liberal government. Many signalled their disposition by taking up seats on the government benches.

The Parnellites too were prepared to adopt a watching brief in the new
parliament. However, they maintained their quasi 'observer status' on the
opposition benches. First indications from the new administration were
positive. The Queen's Speech on 10 May 1880 contained a promise not

to renew the coercion legislation introduced by the Tory government and acknowledged the need for land reform in Ireland, but, proceeding in Augustinian mode, the Liberals were taking a 'not just yet' approach.

An early testing of Liberal bona fides was on the cards and it came with the introduction, by O'Connor Power, of a bill to compensate tenants evicted for non-payment of rent for improvements made to their holdings during their tenure. The bill was, ostensibly, intended to plug one of the major loopholes of the 1870 Act. In fact it was also designed to precipitate positive action or sustained stasis on the part of the administration. The latter course would have been a signal for a return by the 'active' Home Rulers to some form of parliamentary obstruction. Instead the move had the desired effect and the Gladstone administration adopted the fundamental elements of O'Connor Power's measure. The Chief Secretary for Ireland, William E. Forster, a Quaker who had established a humanitarian reputation during the Famine, wrapped up many of O'Connor's proposals in the Compensation for Disturbance Bill. Forster, who began his Chief Secretaryship intent on conciliation, told the House 'if you pass the Bill it will put out the fire.'[11] The government also appointed a commission, under Lord Bessborough, to examine the working of the 1870 Act. The implication was that, on the back of its report, there would be further remedial legislation the following year.

The debate in the House of Commons on the Compensation Bill afforded the new member for Clare an opportunity to catch the eye of the Speaker (Mr Brand) for the first time. In the course of the second reading of the Bill, on 29 June, O'Shea rose to make his maiden speech. It was a brief (about six minutes) interjection into the debate. It was also unusual in that it was made by an Irish party member who had voted for Parnell but who was speaking from the government benches. He began by chiding the honourable gentlemen 'on the Opposition side of the House' (in other words, on the Tory benches) 'that the Bill was not likely to cause social revolution in Ireland, and that it was not expedient to oppose the measure even on behalf of the landlords themselves.' O'Shea placed his faith in the good sense of County Court judges who, under the auspices of the Bill, could be made responsible for distinguishing between 'fault and misfortune' when it came to adjudicating on evictions, 'to reduce exaggerated claims and reject fictitious ones.' While decrying the frequency of agrarian crime, he pointed out to the House that if the returns from constabulary districts were carefully examined 'they were largely made up of letters and notices' – threats rather than actual bodily harm. He advised the Tories, many of whom would have been landlords (as he was himself) anxious not to establish precedents that might migrate across the Irish Sea, that some concession was necessary to dilute the current agitation. 'As the proverbial tree escaped injury by bending to the storm, so landlords would do well to make some sacrifice now.'[12]

It was a sober and balanced contribution from a member who, while admitting to a vested interest, demonstrated a capacity to rise above special pleading. The *Irish Times* correspondent was suitably enthused by the speech: 'He made the ablest and most effective defence I have heard for the Bill. Mr Gladstone, as well as Mr Forster, was profuse in his approving plaudits and repeated "hear, hear"s.'[13] Closer to home, at least as far as the neophyte MP was concerned, were the plaudits of the *Clare Freeman*. 'Captain O'Shea has made his mark and if he continues as he has commenced Clare County will have no reason to regret conferring on him representative honours.'[14] The *Clare Independent*, while covering the speech, made no editorial comment whatever and did not even acknowledge that it was O'Shea's parliamentary debut. Cleary had placed the Captain on probation within a month of the commencement of the session. When it came to divisions O'Shea was already displaying the streak of disagreeable independence that would, ultimately, prove to be his undoing. In an interim report on the performance of the three Clare MPs the paper had judged them to be 'going on excellently and unitedly – if Captain O'Shea would be just a *little* more steady and stick better to the side of the old Chieftain in the divisions.'[15]

One issue on which the intensely Roman Catholic editor of the *Independent* was certainly not going to upbraid O'Shea was his stance on the admission to the House of the MP for Northampton, Charles Bradlaugh. An atheist (and Radical supporter of birth control), Bradlaugh refused to take an oath of allegiance to the Monarch insisting instead on his right to 'affirm' his allegiance. He cited the Parliamentary Oaths Act of 1866 as his authority,[16] but the Speaker allowed the House to adjudicate on the issue. Parnell, along with some of his more anti-clerical supporters like Lysaght Finigan, supported Bradlaugh in the teeth of opposition from, among others, the Irish Roman Catholic hierarchy. O'Shea voted with the Tories to exclude Bradlaugh. He was repaying the faith placed in him by the clergy of County Clare. Parnell, though he probably voted with his conscience on the matter, may also have had an eye on his extra-parliamentary (and excommunicated) Fenian support. Three years later on the same issue, when his focus was elsewhere, in a somewhat cynical volte-face he too voted to exclude Bradlaugh.

By the middle of July O'Shea was already making a habit of entering the division lobby with the government (and the followers of William Shaw) and voting against the Parnellites. So much so that the baiting epithet 'West Briton' was tossed across the floor of the House in his direction. He duly swallowed the bait. The occasion was the committee stage of the Relief of Distress (Ireland) Act (1880) Amendment Bill. Discussion centred around the building of railways as affording employment opportunities for impoverished labourers or tenant farmers. Shaw and his supporters viewed the provisions as straightforward 'relief clauses'. Parnell thought otherwise, seeing the programme as opening the door 'to very great jobbery and abuse'. Jobs, he suggested, would not go to 'starving peasants' but to 'well-fed railway navvies'. In the cut and thrust, the 'West Briton' jibe had been thrown at the Shaw faction. O'Shea, who had already antagonised his erstwhile allies in the Parnellite group by voting against Parnell's wishes and whose constituency was anxiously awaiting word on the development of just such a project, rose to defend himself against the allegation. He responded to the effect that:

> ... the taunt of being a West Briton fell harmlessly on him, one of the most Celtic of the Irish Members and he felt very strongly that those clauses ought to be carried; therefore whilst he regretted having voted several times that night against the hon. Member for Cork, he hoped the hon. Member would not consider that he had done so from any but his real motive ... it was the first step the Government had taken to develop public works, which were absolutely necessary for the West of Ireland, and especially for the very important county which he represented.[17]

The junior Member for the County of Clare was already proving to be something of a nuisance.

A fortnight later, on 26 July, the House of Commons passed the Compensation for Disturbance Bill by a majority of 67. The Parnellites, in a seemingly quixotic move, abstained. The move was actually to become a trademark of Parnellite tactics. Knowing that the passage of the Bill was assured, the Irish leader was able to make a criticism of its inadequacies by walking out of the House with his supporters.

A week later, on 3 August, the Tory- and landlord-dominated House of Lords threw out the Bill by a majority of 282–51 after a cursory two-day debate. John Dillon, newly returned from America to take up his seat, warned the House of Commons that there might be 'bloodshed and massacre to come' and returned to Ireland to advise farmers to begin military-style preparation for a strike against rent.[18] For Parnell, champion of parliamentary action, it was a serious blow. Masquerade he might as an extremist, but he was actually a committed, albeit unconventional, constitutionalist.

To anxious onlookers in Ireland the reactionary response of the Lords indicated the limits of what could be achieved through constitutional action. Parnell's 'inside' strategy would have to change, reverting from a watching brief to a more interventionist and obstructive line. On the basis that nothing could be expected from a pig except a grunt, the Lords was given a fool's pardon. Not so the government. Gladstone's administration had not prepared public opinion to accept Irish land reform and thus make it impossible for the Lords to oppose its will. Over the months that followed the Liberals would reap the consequences. The first of these was the renewal of the obstruction policy in the Commons. This was agreed upon at a meeting of Parnellite MPs three days after the curt message from their Lordships and carried through less than three weeks later when the Irish members forced an all-night sitting on the Irish Constabulary estimates.

Parnell's 'outside' strategy would also be ratcheted upwards, though much of what followed was not of his choosing and was beyond his control and direction. According to the authoritative *Annual Register* for 1880, 'Soon after the rejection of the Bill there were disquieting reports from Ireland. There were riots at evictions; tenants who ventured to take the place of evicted occupiers were assaulted, their property damaged, their ricks burnt, their cattle maimed; there was a mysterious robbery of arms from a ship lying in Queenstown harbour,[19] and it was said that a plot had been discovered for the blowing up of Cork barracks.'[20] The incidence of agrarian outrages had been climbing in the late seventies, from 236 in 1877 to 863 in 1879. In 1880 they soared to 2,590. There is a significant correlation with evictions, which were just over 2,000 in number in 1877 and 10,457 in 1880.[21] Within six weeks one of the highest profile murders of the Land War would lead to the death of Lord Mountmorres, a relatively impecunious landlord who was something of an easy target for the ad hoc brand of Fenian/Ribbon violence that pervaded. [22]The day before the murder, eviction notices had been served on a number of tenants on the estates of Lord Erne in Mayo by an obscure land agent, Captain Charles Boycott.

Captain William O'Shea, absentee Clare landlord, had been safely ensconced at a horse sale on his in-laws' estate of Belhus on the day Lord Mountmorres was murdered. Two days previously his wife's faithful family retainer, Lucy Goldsmith, had died but the former dealer in horse-flesh was, presumably, no longer mourning her passing. According to the *Times*, O'Shea '... secured the lady's bay, Banker, for 200 guineas.' He also bought 'the pretty grey mare, Poplin, which has been hunted by ladies in Leicestershire and which sold for 160 guineas.'[23] He may have been making the purchase on behalf of his two young daughters, Norah and Carmen, but if his wife's version of the state of their marriage is correct, he was most certainly not buying them for her. However, if her narrative is to be believed he might just as easily have been purchasing the ladies' mounts for one of his mistresses.

Earlier that month O'Shea had been busy in his constituency. Well before the end of the parliamentary session on 7 September, he had travelled to Clare, making Father Patrick White of Milltown Malbay his first port of call on Monday, 16 August. The two men discussed a forthcoming rally in support of land reform. It had all the trappings of a Land League meeting but was not described as such. Instead it can be seen as a Clerical–Liberal alliance, aimed at restraining agrarian criminality and moulding a local movement more susceptible to the moderating influence and control of the Roman Catholic clergy in Clare.

The meeting took place in the west Clare coastal town of Milltown Malbay on 5 September and it would be O'Shea's first platform speech in the constituency since his election the previous April. He had chosen the venue wisely. A couple of days before his arrival in Clare the bill for the provision of the Ennis and West Clare Railway[24] had been given its third reading and was awaiting the Royal assent. O'Shea had worked hard to smooth its passage. The line, when built, would begin in Ennis and terminate in Milltown Malbay. O'Shea might already have been an object of suspicion, and even hostility, in other parts of the county, but not on that particular part of the west coast.

The meeting, held under the shadow of a green silk banner installed by a group from Kilnamona, was attended by about 5,000 people.[25] O'Shea would later claim an attendance of 8,000. Among those present were 13 priests and a government reporter sent to record potentially seditious speeches. He could afford to relax during O'Shea's contribution. The meeting began with apologies from Lysaght Finigan (it was far from his Ennis bailiwick) and Parnell – both men were to address a more fateful rally in the county a fortnight later. The O'Gorman Mahon's fulsome and magnanimous letter of apology heaped praise on his younger colleague. Regarding the progress of the Ennis and West Clare Railway project the old Chieftain informed the people of Milltown Malbay, 'There is no portion of the county likely to derive more benefit, immediate and permanent than yours from the passing of this measure, and as an act of common justice I desire it to be recognised by all that to the zeal, energy and perseverance of your young member, Captain O'Shea, is the county indebted for the advantages which must inevitably accrue. Of course he always knew that I was ready to second him if circumstances arose to require aid, but he achieved the affair himself, and therefore to him alone should be accorded the well-earned merit of this favourable issue.'[26]

O'Shea was introduced by Father P.M. O'Kelly, who said that O'Shea 'had honourably reclaimed the pledge he had given on the hustings.' This led to cheers from the audience and cries of 'He brought us the railway'. O'Shea was in front of a home crowd and in his element. Taking a leaf out of the O'Gorman Mahon's book, especially in his absence, the Captain began where the Colonel usually left off, invoking the spirit of '28 and insisting, with considerable hyperbole, that the meeting was 'worthy of the palmiest days of O'Connell', before adding, a mite ungraciously, that the current audience was 'vastly improved in appearance and respectability and education' to those who would have attended the Liberator's rallies.[27]

O'Shea's agenda was not outlined in full. That would become clear in an obsequious letter to the Prime Minister the following week. He did, however, seek to undermine the collective and even quasi-syndicalist approach of the Land League when he suggested that he 'would have all these matters between landlord and tenant settled between man and man. In the case of his own tenants he had offered them arbitration.' This reference was rewarded by a member of the crowd whom one is tempted to suspect had been rewarded himself. 'There is no need of arbitration on your property,' a voice interjected. Taking this encomium in his stride, O'Shea reminisced about his first term at Westminster. He claimed that during the recent parliamentary session he had had an opportunity 'in the House of Commons of making the acquaintance of a number of very good Englishmen.' O'Shea was not being insincere, but he was risking obloquy in thus addressing people who had seen little evidence of the goodness of English legislators.

The nature of the meeting and the absolute control of the large cohort of clergy present can be gauged from the fact that there was no adverse reaction from the crowd. Had a similar sentiment been uttered from most other platforms up and down the country at that time the speaker would have been roundly abused. O'Shea went on to insist that, 'There never was a House of Commons more willing and more ready to settle this question equitably than the present House of Commons.' While O'Shea was not, according to his own lights, being deliberately disingenuous, he was teetering on the brink of selling political snake-oil to the susceptible.

The government reporter would have been called back into action towards the end of the meeting when a speaker from Kilrush related his experience of being rack-rented by a landlord. A distinctly immoderate and clearly audible voice inquired from the crowd, 'Why did you not shoot him?'[28] One wonders what O'Shea made of such a nakedly subversive comment.

Any reference to such an inflammatory remark was excluded from the extraordinary letter he wrote to the Prime Minister on 13 September.[29] The excuse offered to Gladstone for his temerity in proffering an account of an obscure public meeting on the west coast of Ireland was that the Grand Old Man had just recovered from illness and O'Shea wished to congratulate him and convey the good wishes of his constituents.

He also clearly wished to establish his credentials as a potential creature of the Liberal Party. Conscious of the Liberator's long political alliance with the Whigs after his accession to parliament, O'Shea was keen to point out that the meeting, organised by himself and 'one of the most influential priests in the West of Ireland' was conducted '... on the old lines of O'Connell's constitutional agitation, in favour of honest tenant rights with facilities for the gradual establishment of a peasant proprietary, where and when feasible. Every effort was made by the Land League to organise opposition and disturbance, but without avail.'

Referring to the Bessborough Commission, at the time having some difficulty in getting tenants to offer evidence, O'Shea attested that, ' ... my great object in organising the meeting and in going through the county, was to break down the conspiracy to prevent the tenant farmers giving evidence before the Commission. I have the Irish priests of the county, with one exception[30], with me in this important matter.' The use of the word 'conspiracy' puts him firmly in the ranks of hysterical English critics of the Land League agitation. He would employ the word again in 1882 in a crucial context and equally to the detriment of the agrarian movement.

He then proceeded to place the state of unrest in Galway and Mayo in an unfavourable light, especially in comparison with the '... purer Irish population of Clare, although, I confess, slightly contaminated here and there by the Returned Irish–Yankee plague, [but which] is radically sound so far. It reveres the tradition of O'Connell and respects the clergy, which is the only restraining force in Ireland.' He concluded by promising 'to keep the constituency in the ways of those who have gone before', before adding a postscript to the effect that '... my wife is neice [sic] of a member of your former Cabinet, Lord Hatherly [sic].[31] Shortly thereafter O'Shea, doubtless well pleased with his efforts, travelled to Paris.

Eagerness to flatter his 'betters' (and he had a very clear notion of hierarchy) was always a dominating trait in O'Shea's makeup. This introduction to Gladstone must have enabled that canny politician to build up a very clear picture of the nature of his correspondent (assuming the letter ever got past his diligent secretaries). Gladstone would have been well used to sycophancy. In that avocation O'Shea was *primus inter pares.*

A public meeting of a very different and far more auspicious nature took place in Ennis on 19 September 1880. There, Parnell advocated for the first time the policy that would almost come to define the Land League. Referring to recalcitrant landlords, agents, and especially 'land grabbers' who moved onto farms from which tenants had been evicted, he advised his listeners to send such an offender to a 'moral Coventry, by isolating him from his kind as if he was a leper of old'. In *The Fall of Feudalism in Ireland,* Davitt, correctly but gracelessly, refuses to give Parnell credit for originating the policy of ostracism. But within days Parnell's words would lead to such action being taken against Captain Charles Boycott in Mayo. As his employees melted away a force of Orange volunteers from Northern Ireland had to be brought in under armed guard to harvest his crops. Within two months his name had entered the lexicon as both a verb and a noun and was in common usage.[32] It remains there as a powerful reminder of the potential efficacy of collective action. In the knowledge that legislation was due in 1881 from the Liberal government, Parnell cautioned the Ennis meeting against apathy, 'Depend upon it that the measure of the Land Bill next session will be the measure of your activity and energy this winter. It will be a measure of your determination not to pay unjust rents; it will be a measure of your determination to keep a firm grip on your homesteads. It will be a measure of your determination not to bid for farms from which others have been evicted, and to use the strong arm of public opinion to deter any unjust men amongst yourselves – and there are many such – from bidding for such farms.'

The rhetoric was utterly different from the bland nostrums of Milltown Malbay a fortnight before. The meeting was chaired by a leading member of the Clare clergy who had not been charmed by O'Shea, Rev Matthew Kenny of Scariff. Perhaps with the Milltown Malbay gathering in mind, or simply as a reaction to O'Shea's sporadic voting record[33], Lysaght Finigan in his address to the crowd played on their growing doubts about the newly elected Clare MP. According to the account of the meeting in the *Freeman's Journal*[34], Finigan was fulminating against British agrarian policy when he digressed:

> *Mr Finigan:* ... there was one 'ism' which he must cherish and love and that was nationalism. [Cheers] He would say nothing of the men who had broken the promises made on the hustings.

A Voice: O'Shea
Mr Finigan: He knew there was a day of reckoning coming
and he would leave it to the people to judge.

Given the state of his, as yet unconsummated, relationship with Katharine O'Shea (see below), Parnell may have had mixed feelings about Finigan's implied censure. Indeed the lady herself had earlier been introduced to the people of Clare for the first time in a rather curious fashion.

After the Milltown Malbay meeting O'Shea had left for France. Attempts by T.S. Cleary to send him an invitation to the pivotal Ennis rally had been unsuccessful until Parnell advised Cleary to write to Eltham. His invitation elicited a response from Katharine O'Shea that was read out at the meeting. 'I received your telegram to Captain O'Shea last night and sent it on to Paris.'[35] It was a peculiarly bland debut for a woman whose future appearances on Irish political platforms would be more fraught and controversial.

That little episode, utterly insignificant at the time, was followed by the reading of a letter of apology from O'Shea, addressed, not to Cleary, but (typically) to the presiding cleric, Fr Kenny. Its air of injured innocence was characteristic of the man. 'You may be able to find an opportunity of telling the Ennis meeting (to which I have not been honoured with an invitation) that there will be no one at it who has a more intense anxiety than myself for a fair, full and final settlement of the land question.' Interestingly another absentee (we can safely ignore the absence of the octogenarian O'Gorman Mahon) was Fr Patrick White, who had found himself unable to make the journey from Milltown Malbay. It may be seen as indicative of the fact that some members of the clergy, while anxious not to be found too far behind public militancy on the land issue, still had still not fully made up their minds about Parnell.

STALKING THE CHIEF

By the time of the Ennis meeting Charles Stewart Parnell had become well acquainted with Captain William Henry O'Shea and his family. O'Shea had made sure of that. According to Katharine's own account in the revealing but unreliable *Charles Stewart Parnell: His Love Story and Political Life* (which is just as much her autobiography as it is her hagiography of the 'lost leader'), by 1880 the O'Shea marriage had been reduced to her husband taking his Roman Catholic children to Mass on a Sunday in Eltham and Katharine herself hosting occasional salons or soirées on O'Shea's behalf in London. Since his election to parliament the emphasis of those social gatherings had shifted from the maintenance of business contacts to the establishment of a new circle of political intimates.

If Oscar Wilde was the Irishman *du jour* for London hostesses with a cultural bent in the 1880s, in a more political ambience Parnell was the Irish prize. All the more so because of his famed reluctance to participate in the game. Katharine O'Shea used her favourite London hotel, Thomas's on Berkeley Square, for entertainment purposes. Her soirées evinced an eclectic neutrality when it came to the guest list, mixing prominent Parnellites, such as Justin McCarthy, with supporters of Shaw, such as Colonel Colthurst and Richard Power. Parnell had, according to Katie, been invited to more than one dinner, had accepted at least one invitation and then failed to show up. The empty chair had sparked off a discussion about his inaccessibility and 'his dislike of all social intercourse'. Her interest was piqued by the man and the challenge and, as she puts it herself, 'I then became determined that I would get Parnell to come, and said, amid laughter and applause: "The uncrowned King of Ireland shall sit in that chair at the next dinner I give."'[36]

Snaring her quarry would have been more difficult for a less resilient hostess. Parnell was notorious for ignoring his voluminous mail. Most days he failed even to open it. In future years he would have the loyal Henry Campbell organise his correspondence, but in 1880 only the young Tim Healy was permitted, or prepared, to sort through the backlog from time to time. Katie opted for the direct approach. In July 1880 she travelled to the House of Commons with her sister Anna Steele and sent in her card requesting Parnell to come and meet her in the Palace Yard. Somewhat surprisingly he did so.

Her account of the meeting, written almost 35 years later, is thoroughly romanticised but oddly affecting. Given what eventuated she can be forgiven an element of poetic exaggeration. 'He came out, a tall, gaunt figure, thin and deadly pale. He looked straight at me smiling, and his curiously burning eyes looked into mine with a wondering intentness that threw into my brain the sudden thought: "This man is wonderful – and different."' She chided him for not answering her invitations and he responded candidly that he had not opened his letters for some time. However, he promised to accept her hospitality at the earliest opportunity. What she claims happened next would become a central iconic image in their narrative:

> In leaning forward in the cab to say good-bye a rose I was
> wearing in my bodice fell out on to my skirt. He picked it up
> and, touching it lightly with his lips, placed it in his button

hole. This rose I found long years afterwards done up in an envelope, with my name and the date, among his most private papers, and when he died I laid it upon his heart.'[37]

A close reading of the iconography of the gesture by an Irish nationalist would have Parnell surrendering to the rose, symbol of English nationalism, with all the enthusiasm of a Sadlier or a Keogh. But, as with many close readings, we can assume that this was not the intention of the writer, not even subliminally. Who knows? The anecdote, which has all the hallmarks of Victorian romantic fiction, may even be true. Though Parnell would not have been renowned for either gallantry or flirtatiousness.

Within a short period Parnell acted on his promise and turned up at one of Katharine O'Shea's dinner parties. The other guests included Anna Steele, Justin McCarthy MP and her nephew, Sir Matthew Wood. After dining they went on to the Gaiety Theatre. Katie's version of events has Parnell paying scant attention to what was going on onstage. Instead he regaled her with his luckless romantic past and the ill-fated engagement to Katharine's near namesake. Following that revealing conversation, Katie began to make frequent visits to the Ladies Gallery of the House of Commons and the two commenced the intimate correspondence that continued until Parnell's death 11 years later and which is included in her biography of the man who signed himself 'your King'.

Wednesday afternoon drives in the country followed, during which 'we chiefly discussed Willie's chances of being returned again for Clare, in case another election was sprung on us. Both Willie and I were very anxious to secure Mr Parnell's promise about this, as the O'Gorman Mahon was old, and we were desirous of making Willie's seat in Parliament secure.' Parnell promised that 'he would do his best to keep Willie in Parliament, and to secure County Clare for him should the occasion arise.'[38] At this point in the relationship she was clearly following an agenda laid down by her husband. It was one that coincided with her own desires, as a distracted and busy O'Shea was an absent O'Shea. It was the very reason she had encouraged him to enter politics in the first place 'for I knew it would give him occupation he liked and keep us apart – and therefore good friends.'[39]

After the close of the first parliamentary session of 1880 she was certainly on his mind. Ten days before the Ennis meeting he wrote to her from Dublin. It reads like the letter of a man confident that the emotions he was revealing were reciprocated. '... I don't feel quite so content at the prospect of ten days absence from London amongst the hills and valleys of Wicklow as I should have done some three months since. The cause is mysterious but perhaps you will help me to find it, or her, on my return.'[40]

The great shame of Katharine O'Shea's book is that, when it comes to documentary material, we only hear one voice (and that is often an unfortunate simper). She does not include any of her own letters to her future husband. Some drafts, at least, of her correspondence with Parnell must have survived in 1914, but if allegations that her son Gerard was heavily involved in the editing of the book[41] are to be believed, it may well be that he wished to convey an impression of a predatory Parnell. The inclusion of encouraging letters from an acquiescent Katharine O'Shea would not have suited that narrative or indeed the thesis of the book, that William O'Shea was, largely, an unwitting and unwilling cuckold.

Why did Parnell allow himself to become infatuated with the wife of one of his parliamentary colleagues and occasional supporters? It is a question that has fascinated biographers of both the Irish leader and Katharine O'Shea, and is equally germane to a biography of the cuckolded husband. (The more important issue of the extent of his knowledge of the relationship is dealt with elsewhere.) Attempts to answer the question have ranged from the Freudian (she was an older woman[42] who gave him the love he never received from his mother) to the fanciful (the O'Sheas were British spies and the relationship was a highly successful seduction plot).

Parnell was certainly made aware by Katharine of the nature of her relationship with her husband. In 21st-century parlance, at least as far as she was concerned, they were a separated couple free to pursue other relationships. Accordingly Parnell has been exonerated by history of the charge of wilful adultery. How honest Katharine was with him in her representation of that relationship is another matter entirely. In her book she glosses over sexual matters but there is enough internal evidence in her narrative and in letters between the three principals to suggest that she was, for some time at least, engaging in a simultaneous sexual relationship with both men.

After an initial period of undeniably covert dealings with each other,[43] the relationship between Parnell and Katharine O'Shea cannot be characterised as a stereotypical or prosaic 'affair'. It became a thoroughly domesticated relationship. To all intents and purposes they lived as a couple in Eltham or Brighton for most of the decade in which they were together. In his letters Parnell would refer to Katharine with the slightly cringe-inducing diminutive 'wifie' and refer to himself as 'your husband'. It was probably this very domesticity and a clear sense of emotional security that attracted him to the arrangement. Allied to that was his own disregard for petit-bourgeois convention, especially when the ethical standards being set were those of the English bourgeoisie. Parnell's relative disregard for the feelings of the English nation, though its origins are much debated, was legendary.

One of Katharine's biographers suggests a plausible reason for Parnell's susceptibility to a ménage whose hazards he must have appreciated, notwithstanding his disregard for orthodoxy. Joyce Marlow declares ' ... the shy, reserved side of his nature meant that he suffered doubly from the occupational disease of the Irish parliamentarian – loneliness – cut off from their homes and roots as they were for at least half the year. ... That she was a married lady, that her husband was one of his Home Rule colleagues, did not enter into Parnell's calculations.'[44] Parnell was not the only member of the Irish party who became embroiled in an extra-marital relationship. Joseph Biggar, for example, was rumoured to have had numerous affairs.

Whatever Parnell's motives for putting his political career into obvious jeopardy, the fact remains that the affair progressed rapidly. The flirtatious correspondence of August and September 1880 had given way to a combination of intimacy and misdirection from October. In the wake of the Ennis speech Parnell, although committed to further engagements in Ireland, darted back across the Irish Sea in the hope of meeting Katharine. He must have been encouraged to do so by her response to his advances. He failed on that occasion because of the death of her maid, Lucy Goldsmith. His disappointment, as expressed in an almost frenzied series of communications, was palpable.

On or about 28 September, O'Shea, who had returned to London from France, travelled to Spain on business.[45] Parnell continued his Land League activities in Ireland until 7 October. It is probable that he spent much of the next ten days in Eltham, and that it was during this period the sexual relationship was consummated. On 17 October he wrote Katharine a letter which began, unambiguously, with the words 'My own love ...' From that point on their correspondence varied from the profoundly intimate to the studiously formal. Correspondence of the latter sort was designed to be produced to her husband or Aunt Ben when required. They would frequently refer to O'Shea in amicable terms as if the two men were close friends or associates.[46] However, the formal letters would also often include enclosures that Mrs O'Shea was asked to post or pass on for Parnell. The enclosures were confidential missives for Katharine and were intended for her eyes only.

In his habitually unapologetic fashion, Parnell often preferred to remain in England, presumably with Katharine, rather than fulfil obligations in Ireland. He failed to turn up for public meetings in his own constituency of Cork and in Roscommon. John Dillon was forced to cover for his absence in the southern capital; James O'Kelly and fellow local MP Andrew Commins dutifully picked up the slack in Roscommon.

When he did reappear he was almost unrecognisable, having shaved off his beard in the interim. It is not unreasonable to assume that this radical change of appearance was to abet his comings and goings in the vicinity of Eltham. Parnell was well aware that he was of considerable interest to the London press as well as to the London Metropolitan Police. While he may, at this point at least, have escaped the attentions of the former, in the medium term he did not succeed in evading the latter.

Katharine and Parnell were, occasionally, to be seen in public together in the initial period of the relationship, though this would have been in the context of O'Shea's lengthy absences from the London social scene, which would necessitate her escort to social engagements by another man. The journalist and controversialist Frank Harris, one-time editor of the *Fortnightly Review* and, much later, the author of the notorious memoir *My Life and Loves*, writes of seeing the two together at a dinner party given by Justin McCarthy. 'It must have been pretty early in Parnell's acquaintance with Mrs O'Shea, for she was seated opposite to him, and Parnell scarcely ever took his eyes from her face. At this time she seemed to me a sonsy, nice looking woman of thirty-three or thirty-five with pretty face and fine eyes, very vivacious, very talkative, full of good-humoured laughter.

So far, so good. But Harris then goes on to damage the credibility of his anecdote by referring to Katharine's 'exaggerated ... Irish brogue'. At no point in her life did Katharine O'Shea ever set foot in Ireland and she would certainly not have developed a natural Irish accent from O'Shea or Parnell, both of whom had the same aristocratic English inflection which she herself possessed. 'All the while she talked', Harris continues, 'the dour, silent, handsome man opposite devoured her with his flaming eyes. I remember saying in fun to Justin afterwards, 'If she were as much in love with him, as he is with her, it would indeed be a perfect union.' But kindly Justin would not admit the liaison. 'He's attracted,' he said. 'I think we all are. She's an interesting woman.' Soon, however, everybody knew that they were lovers and lost in a mutual passion.[47]

Ironically Parnell was openly resident at Eltham for the second fortnight in October. He was unwell (though he was quite a hypochondriac his health was often genuinely fragile) and O'Shea had insisted that he recuperate at Eltham. Robert Kee, who has a particular genius for tracking the movements of the principals in the Parnell history, has him in Eltham from 13-30 November.[48] During some of that time at least, O'Shea too was in residence. It must, at times, have been an uncomfortable *ménage à trois* for Parnell and Katharine, though there is little doubt that at this stage O'Shea was utterly unaware of what was going on behind his back. His own instincts in issuing the invitation to the Irish party leader would have been less than altruistic. His Machiavellian purpose was political self-preservation. Unaware of the true nature of the forces at work in Ireland, O'Shea would have assumed that a very public friendship with Parnell would guarantee his return for Clare at the next election, however he might vote in the division lobbies.

In this, as in other campaigns, he was happy to enlist the services of his gregarious and attractive wife. Whatever his attitude to their marriage he certainly still saw her as a partner. His letters to Katharine, right up to the mid-1880s, are, by and large, affectionately chatty. He generally made use of their pet names for each other, 'Dick' and 'Boysie' in the salutation and signature. Those nicknames were, however, being trumped by Parnell's 'Queenie' and 'King'. But when it came to O'Shea's political career, there was a happy coincidence of interests. Katharine and Parnell wanted to keep O'Shea in the House of Commons in order to keep his time occupied constructively and exclusively. It was just that Parnell was not keen for him to remain there as an Irish Home Rule MP.

In late November O'Shea returned to Spain on business and remained there for the entire month of December. Parnell was campaigning on behalf of the Land League in Ireland in the first week of December. His health must have recovered during his Eltham convalescence, because on 7 December he borrowed a horse and took part in the Curraghmore Hunt. It was a characteristic display of *insouciance* from a man who might well have had cause for anxiety. On 2 November he, along with a number of members of the Land League executive[49], had been indicted for seditious conspiracy to prevent the payment of rent, as well as a number of other charges. Parnell, typically, rarely exhibited the slightest concern about the machinations of Dublin Castle against him. In this instance he was justified in his blasé attitude. The trial was due to take place in Dublin in January. He suspected that no Irish jury, unless expertly 'packed' by the authorities, would ever convict him.

In early December he wrote Katharine an optimistic formal letter. It made reference to a postponed meeting with O'Shea, '... the special jury panel, of which we obtained a copy last night, is of such a character as in the opinion of competent judges to give us every chance of a disagreement by the jury in their verdict ...'[50] Just over a week later, however, in another formal letter he showed that he was not complacent to the point of carelessness. He wrote to her from Avondale, '... I have come here to arrange my papers and find a number which I should not like to destroy, and which I should not like the government to get hold of in the event of their searching my house in the troublous [sic] times which appear before us. May I leave them at Eltham?'[51]

Assuming the response was in the affirmative, he could have brought the hazardous papers over in person, because he spent Christmas in Eltham. Robert Kee speculates, on the basis of hints contained in his published correspondence with Katharine, that she may have been almost three months pregnant at the time and was about to miscarry. Parnell was obliged to return to Dublin on Boxing Day.

O'Shea, meanwhile, was still in Spain. The January pre-sessional meeting of the Irish Party in Dublin had been brought forward to 27 December to facilitate the accused in the State trial of the Land Leaguers. Katharine had been asked to inform O'Shea of the change of date but his business commitments kept him in Spain until January. He wrote from Madrid on 23 December, apologising for his enforced absence but adding that '... I hope and believe however, that the absence of a unit will be of no importance owing to the unanimity with which I am sure that the whole party must be inspired at the present crisis.'[52] In that absence his 'colleagues', many of whom would have, by then, become highly sceptical of the extent and nature of his support for Parnellite policy, decided to insist that all Irish Party members take their seats on the opposition benches. For most of the Whiggish rump of the party this was a bridge too far, and in January Shaw and 11 of his supporters disassociated themselves from the party. O'Shea was not amongst them. It would take more than a pious resolution to discourage him.

CHAPTER 4

Carrot and Stick

The House is sitting. The Irish members are talking of some
Bill of vital importance. One after another they get up, mad-
deningly irrelevant are their remarks, hideous is their English.
George Moore, *Parnell and his Island*

It is no use trying to soothe these tigers by stroking their
backs. They are avowed rebels and they are covertly assassins.
And that, I believe, is the state of mind of the leaders as well
as of the disciples.
Sir William Harcourt to William Ewart Gladstone, 9 July 1882

COERCION

To a 20th- and 21st-century Irish nationalist sensibility the Irish Parliamentary Party exemplifies compromise and, ultimately, political
irrelevance. The overwhelming Sinn Féin electoral victory in 1918 brutally
wiped the party off the political map in unprecedented fashion. Hence a
view prevails of the Irish party members as temporising moderates
incapable of leading Ireland into a new century. They had grown too close
to the English political beast and become establishment figures themselves.

The party was found guilty of treason by the electorate, by reason of absorption.

Such a notion of temperate inefficacy would have been risible in the late Victorian period. It was an era of alienation. In the early 1880s in particular, even to Liberals, the Parnellite wing of the Irish party would have been just as suspect as Sinn Féin in 1917. While not an absolute political pariah, Parnell was not someone to be negotiated with[1] and certainly not someone to be appeased.

His outsider status did not concern the man himself. The hostility of English politicians was something he quite relished (though some early alliances were forged with English Radicals), and not simply because of how it played to the Irish electorate. Sir Charles Dilke[2] told Parnell's first biographer, R. Barry O'Brien, that he attributed the Irish leader's success to his comfortable familiarity with, and contempt for, English institutions. 'He hated England, English ways, English modes of thought. He would have nothing to do with us. He acted like a foreigner. We could not get at him as at any other man in English public life ... This gave him immense advantage, and, coupled with his iron will, explains his ascendancy and success.'[3]

In the view of the British establishment, Parnell was preaching anarchy to the peasants and separation to the rest of the island.[4] He was regularly shadowed by Scotland Yard detectives and, in 1881, the Home Office hired detectives to follow him when he visited Paris early in the year. And not without some reason. While in the French capital in February 1881, Parnell met with William Lomasney who, some years later, would blow himself up in a failed attempt to dynamite London Bridge. Outside of parliament his popularity was even lower. He often moved about London armed with a pistol for his own protection.[5]

The assumption was that, not unlike the Sinn Fein of the 1970s and 1980s, the Irish party leadership was in a position to turn on and off the tap of violence at will. Though she is hardly a disinterested source, the judgment of Florence Arnold-Forster, daughter of the Chief Secretary, would be typical: '... it is impossible for those who were in Ireland during the Land League agitation of 1880', she wrote in her diary, ' to forget with what complete indifference (if not encouragement) these same men looked on the daily commission of private crime and outrage in the interests of a political cause which they thought at that period would be advanced and not hindered by such means.'[6]

Not that Parnell's standing with the orthodox Fenian movement was much higher. At about the time of his return to Ireland to contest the 1880 election, the IRB Supreme Council, under the aegis of Charles Kickham,

had withdrawn even the limited concession to constitutionalism of per-
mitting individual oath-bound members to participate in political activity.
The Fenians, however, did little more than make nuisances of themselves
as, for example, when a number of activists sawed through the supporting struts of a political platform in Athlone, County Westmeath, on 7
November, before Parnell was due to speak. The platform duly collapsed,
throwing the unfortunate James O'Kelly into the crowd. The *Freeman's
Journal* reported that Parnell managed to step backwards out of trouble
just before the crash. There is an interesting symbolism in the occasion on
any number of different levels.

As long as individual Fenians defied the Supreme Council, others
abandoned the organisation to work with the constitutional movement
and Clan na Gael money continued to flow from America, Parnell could
afford to do without the support of the doctrinaire nationalists. In fact the
overt hostility of the likes of the New York-based *Irish World* editor,
Patrick Ford (after initial wholehearted support), did him no harm in
rehabilitating himself with English opinion at an appropriate time.

By the middle of the decade Parnell's status had changed in the English
parliament. By then he had shed much of his 'slightly constitutional' image
and holding the balance of power was no hindrance to his rehabilitation
either. But in 1880 his disdain for custom and practice in the House of
Commons, his decision to place himself at the head of a popular agitation,
and the suspicion that he was directing agrarian outrage placed him
outside of the Pale of inclusion. He had been invited to the feast and had
smashed the best crockery. As a consequence, in January 1881 he faced,
for the first time, the full apparatus of the state in a Dublin court.

Months of rising levels of violence had forced the Liberal administration to take action. Murders would more than double in 1881.[7] Agrarian
'outrages' had been 25 per cent of total crime in 1879 – by 1881 that
figure had soared to 58 per cent.[8] The *Daily News* journalist Bernard
Becker was sent to Ireland at the end of 1880 to write a series of articles
on the state of the country. He spent most of his time in the counties where
civil unrest was greatest: Mayo, Galway, Clare, Limerick, Cork and Kerry.
Visiting the estate of Clare landlord Richard Stacpoole, he described a
state of virtual siege. 'To the question whether he goes in fear of his life,
he replies, "Not at all; I take care of that," and out of the pocket of his
lounging jacket he takes a revolver of very large bore ... he never leaves
his revolver; and he is in the right, for not two hours ago a local leader
declared to me with pale face and flaming eyes that he would "gladly go
to the gallows for 'um."'[9] Not all the inhabitants of rural Ireland were
extremist Ribbonmen but, at the very least, the era of servility had ended.

The attempt to hold the leadership of the Land League to account for widespread boycotting, non-payment of rent and intimidation (with maiming and murder as subtext) was something of a last throw by the Liberals. Gladstone's government had resisted the temptation to reintroduce Conservative coercion measures but now someone had to take the consequences for the state of unrest in Ireland. If the convictions of Parnell and his associates could not be secured *pour encourager les autres*, the alternative was the suspension of Habeas Corpus that had been sought of Gladstone by the Lord Lieutenant Lord Cowper in a letter to the Prime Minister on 23 November.[10]

Parnell's optimism about the result of the Land League trial, as expressed to Katharine in early December 1880, was such that he felt able to abandon proceedings and return to London for the opening of the parliamentary session. He would not have been pleased by the Queen's speech. Ireland was below Montenegro and Basutoland in terms of governmental priorities and the only solid promise was that coercion legislation was in preparation. Agrarian reform and some measure of land purchase were on the cards, but the quelling of unrest was the Liberal priority. The Irish leader warned that 'the peace and tranquillity of Ireland cannot be promoted by suspending any of the constitutional rights of the Irish people',[11] and later in the debate on the Queen's speech he threatened that the first arrest under new coercive legislation would be the signal for an immediate rent strike. Irish obstructive measures helped ensure that the debate on the speech continued for almost a fortnight.

The threat of coercion meant that O'Shea was able to paint himself in slightly greener colours. Already he was one of four 'Whiggish' MPs who had obeyed the Irish party injunction to take his seat on the opposition benches. Over the course of the next two parliamentary sessions O'Shea consistently and vocally resisted the introduction of police rule in Ireland. He began that opposition in the House of Commons on 10 January 1881 with an address in answer to the Queen's speech.

While recognising that Ireland was 'in a most dangerous state of revolution', he insisted that, 'Coercion was a folly of 1881, with a vile pedigree of 700 years ...' He warned the Government that '... Before they enforced coercion in Ireland they ought to exhaust every form of justice and generosity.' He also defended Parnell against allegations of collusion with the organisation of agrarian crime. Hansard recorded his remarks: 'He had heard, with great regret, the Chief Secretary for Ireland state that his honourable friend, the Member for the City of Cork (Mr Parnell), had by speeches knowingly inclined people to commit outrages. Now he would not call, even in the conventional language of the House, the honourable Member for the City of Cork his honourable friend if he did not know that he was utterly incapable of conduct of that kind.'

He concluded by pointing out that, 'Although he [Captain O'Shea] was not a Land Leaguer, and was suffering inconvenience, as a landlord, owing to its action, and although he regretted that those who had the ear of the Irish tenant should be given the advice that a fair rent was a rent fixed by himself, he must confess, as an unprejudiced person, it was the Land League which had brought the Land Question, one of the most dangerous to the Empire, nearer settlement ... A great measure, a worthy rival of the mightiest feats of statesmanship, would, without coercion, restore law and order in Ireland; law founded upon justice, order upon the contentment of a hopeful people.'[12]

Privately O'Shea was not quite so well disposed towards Parnell. His expressed opinions tended to depend on his audience. Statements in the House of Commons were for constituency consumption. A week after his endorsement of Parnell in parliament he had a different story for Herbert Gladstone, son of the Prime Minister and MP for Leeds. On 17 January Gladstone recorded in his diary that he had been told by O'Shea that '... time was all important to the League as the organisation was not perfected to defy coercion. Davitt, he told me, was the ruling spirit and the whole strength of the Fenians was enlisted in the Land movement. Parnell he declared to be a puppet in their hands but thoroughly honest and not touching a penny of the L.L. [sic] money.'[13]

Whatever his private views, O'Shea might have hoped that his publicly expressed opinions would go down well in nationalist circles in Clare. But the *Independent* was mute on the subject. Not so silent was a cabal within the constituency that was proselytising against their junior Member. Two months after his 'coercion' speech he was writing to the O'Gorman Mahon to tell him that 'I have had several letters from friends, lay and clerical, in Clare telling me that no stone is being left unturned by the clique against me.'[14]

Towards the end of January Parnell had returned to Dublin for the conclusion of the state trial. As he sat in court, the *Freeman's Journal* (which had not always been well disposed towards him) expressed surprise at his apparent buoyancy. 'There sat the Irish leader all day', wrote the *Freeman* court reporter with poetic hyperbole, 'waiting to meet his fate, with the same grave, sweet, tranquil earnestness as if the fate of a nation as well as his own were not in the balance.'[15] The following day the paper was able to report that Parnell's sanguine attitude had been entirely justified. The jury, as predicted by the Irish leader himself, had become totally bogged down and had been unable to reach a verdict. In a classic Irish bull the foreman had informed the judge that he and his colleagues were 'unanimous about disagreeing'. Parnell and his co-defendants were free to go, and it was brought home forcefully to the Gladstone government that Irish juries could not be relied upon to play their part in quelling unrest.

Partly in anticipation of just such an eventuality, and to demonstrate an intolerance of further civil turpitude, Forster had, the previous day, introduced the Protection of Persons and Property (Ireland) Bill, which would give the government power to suspend ordinary law in proclaimed districts (mostly in the west of Ireland).

That was the signal for a campaign of parliamentary disruption by a Parnellite faction much enlarged since the early days of obstruction. On 25 January the House was forced to sit for 22 hours by Irish members after Gladstone proposed that the Bill take precedence over all other Commons business. Six days later a 41-hour sitting began, and was only brought to a conclusion as a result of a coup by the Speaker. Acting on no rule of the House that he was able to quote, he simply closed the debate. Faced with an Irish party clearly prepared to abuse, ad nauseam, the traditional facility to filibuster the assembly, Gladstone introduced a resolution which, effectively, curtailed the right to obstruct and removed it from the Parnellite arsenal.

The suspension of Davitt's 'ticket of leave' (probation) on 3 February, for making inflammatory speeches,[16] led to Irish party protests in the House and suspension of 36 Irish MPs. Soon after that Patrick Egan, sensing that it would not be long before arbitrary arrest and the seizure of assets became government policy, betook himself to Paris with the Land League funds. The League's Treasurer and Treasury were now beyond the reach of the British authorities.

By arrangement with Egan the other leading members of the organisation, many of them Members of Parliament, were to gather in Paris for an executive meeting in the first week in February. The absence of such a large and influential cohort of Parnellite MPs was probably one of the reasons why it was left to O'Shea (who had been proving eminently loyal and supportive of the Parnellite line) to ask a question on 7 February about Davitt's treatment in prison.

According to contemporary memoirs, the Land League leaders waited in Paris for up to a week for the arrival of Parnell. He failed to appear and failed also to get a message to his colleagues explaining his absence. Concerned at his non-appearance after almost a week, they had sought the approval of Healy, then effectively acting as Parnell's secretary, to open some letters that had arrived at their hotel for Parnell. At the time Parnell was, according to Katharine O'Shea, seeking to avoid arrest by hiding out in her house, unbeknownst even to the staff. She claims that he remained with her for up to two weeks before leaving for Paris; she also fixes the date as having been in 1880. However, Robert Kee has tested this entire episode against Parnell's known appearances at the time and has concluded that the amount of time Parnell was missing was limited to a few days at most.[17]

Tim Healy's version of what followed diverges significantly from that of some of his colleagues. According to his strange account, one of the letters was opened and was found to be from a Manchester barmaid (he calls her Lizzie) with whom, Healy alleges, Parnell had an affair at around the time of the anti-Shaw putsch. The letter informed Parnell that she now had a small child of which he was the father. On their return from Paris, Joseph Biggar, according to Healy, sought out Lizzie. She was found:

> in a barely furnished garret, in bed with a baby. A likeness of Parnell (cut from the Dublin *Weekly News*) was pinned to her counterpane. Though in want, she was staunch to the father of her child, and never let fall a complaint. Her needs were provided for, and she was told where to apply should she require further help. This she never did, so Parnell must have made amends for his temporary neglect. ... The mystery of Parnell's absence from Paris had no relation to Lizzie, for he had then taken up with Mrs O'Shea, whose name was unknown to us at that time ...'[18]

Michael Davitt's explanation is far more plausible. He refers to the opening of the letters and claims that 'the first letter revealed the secret that afterwards worked his ruin. None of his most intimate associates had hitherto suspected the liaison in which he was found entangled ...'[19] T.P. O'Connor wrote about the incident that 'One of the letters was from a lady, it was scarcely glanced at; but it told enough ...'[20] The main problem with both accounts is that neither man was present in Paris at that time. According to F.S.L. Lyons, the family of John Dillon (who opened the letters along with Egan) was told by him that the letter had come, not from Eltham but from Birmingham.[21] However, Davitt and O'Connor's version of events is supported by Katharine O'Shea herself in her memoir.[22] According to Lyons it is from around this time that relations between Parnell and his two loyal lieutenants, Dillon and Healy, began to deteriorate. The latter refused to continue as the leader's secretary. It is reasonable to assume, therefore, that knowledge of Parnell's affair among the higher echelons of the party and Land League dates from this time.

The Protection of Persons and Property (Ireland) Bill became law on 2 March 1881. It was followed a couple of days later by a further measure called the Peace Preservation (Ireland) Bill, which, among other things, sought to prohibit the carrying of arms in proscribed areas. On 7 March O'Shea rose to speak against this second dose of coercion. His intervention was neither useful nor particularly constructive. He had been preceded by Healy who had been critical of the prospective powers of police search under the bill. Healy had made a passing reference to the searching of women. O'Shea, not to be outdone when it came to prurient Catholic self-righteousness, took up Healy's random notes and turned them into a sonata. He appealed to the government to accept compromise on the issue.

'They should give a woman the option of saying whether she would submit to immediate search', he seethed on behalf of the good women of Ireland, 'or whether she would be taken to the police station, where she would have protection against any abuse of power. The roads in the West of Ireland were very lonely.'[23] Harcourt, the Home Secretary, pointed out that the issue was going to be discussed under a later amendment and the debate moved on.

THE 1881 LAND ACT

The Bessborough Commision had reported in January 1881 and had expressed itself in favour of a more effective implementation of the Three 'Fs' (fair rent, free sale, fixity of tenure) than had been achieved in the 1870 Land Act. With one measure of coercion already through the House and a second wending its way, it was time for the Liberal administration to show that it had a benign side as far as Ireland was concerned. On 7 April, Gladstone introduced his second Land Bill with a characteristic two-and-a-half-hour speech. The measure was designed to appease Irish tenant farmers and, in so doing, undermine the Land League. The logical extension of the collapse of the League, as far as the government was concerned, would be an end to the ravenous beast that was rural unrest, in the absence of the organisation that was feeding it.

The Bill, as advised, placed Parnell in an invidious position. It was, he recognised, an 'imperfect measure'. It proposed the establishment of Land Courts to adjudicate on differences between landlord and tenant over rent. It was 'an act to control rent'.[24] It also held out insubstantial promises of tenant purchase, but fell a long way short of a peasant proprietary. Initially, rather than be out-manoeuvred by the man he dubbed the Grand Old Spider, Parnell temporised. The day after its introduction he described the measure in a speech in Birmingham as 'an honest and sincere attempt to deal with the land question'[25] A few days later, at a Land League meeting in Dublin, he pointed out that the Bill admitted 'the existence of rack-renting, eviction and landlord oppression, and acknowledges the necessity of such a radical change in the law as will put it in the powers of the farmers to become owners of their land ...'[26]

He announced, however, that the Irish party would be proposing amendments when the Bill went into committee. His apparent desire for accommodation did not go down well on the left. Egan fulminated in Paris, Patrick Ford ranted in New York. As far as the forces of militant nationalism and agrarianism were concerned, it was an inadequate response to a festering ill, an exercise in crisis management which had only emerged in the wake of intense political and extra legal activity.

The left felt that more of the same at home in Ireland would wrest even more concessions from a routed Liberal government. Parnell was able to toss them a bone when Dillon made a scathing speech in opposition to the Bill and was duly arrested under the coercion legislation. This should have been the signal for a rent strike. Instead Parnell persuaded his party colleagues to make their protest by walking out of the House and not voting on the second reading of the Bill. As was so often the case with Parnell, he was having his cake and eating it simultaneously. The Liberal majority would be more than sufficient to ensure the safety of the Bill without Irish support and this act of defiance would go some way towards appeasing the left.

His Janus-like approach, however, almost left his party behind. Only by threatening to resign did he persuade a majority of his supporters[27] to adopt his strategy. Even then 14 of them refused to follow his lead when the vote on the second reading took place on 19 May. Among the rebels was O'Shea.

Anyone who has ever paddled a canoe along the often stormy waters of the Avonmore river, which flows through Parnell's old home at Avondale, will know the challenge the Irish leader was presented with. At one moment a wave could hit him from the right. While he was responding and adjusting to that threat he would be washed from the left. Somehow he managed to keep afloat but it required all his deftness and authority.

The Bill spent two months in committee with Irish members proposing hundreds of amendments. Irish dissatisfaction centred on the inadequate provision for leaseholders. They were excluded from the terms of the Bill. A Liberal government might be prepared to mediate between landlord and tenant-at-will when it came to rent adjudication, but it was certainly not going to come between contracting parties. To do so would involve a minor cultural revolution. The issue of arrears also threatened to hole the Bill below the waterline. Only tenants in good standing were allowed to take their cases to the Land Court for rent adjudication. Thus thousands of the worst examples of hardship were effectively excluded from the operation of the legislation.

About halfway through the committee stage a Mercury was born. It is not entirely clear whether he had been despatched by the Gods, but on 10 June O'Shea wrote to Gladstone enclosing a proposal for compromise, devised by his own hand but carrying, he said, the imprimatur of Parnell. 'I am therefore in a position to promise,' he ventured, 'if the Cabinet will accept the proposal, that the opposition of Mr Parnell's party in the House of Commons will immediately cease, and that he will give the Bill an effectual support in Ireland, such support to be loyally afforded even if outwardly and for the moment prudently veiled.' In other words Parnell wanted to continue with his three-card trick.

It is hard to see how the memo enclosed would have had much appeal for Parnell at that time (except as a landowner himself). It was a proposal that had far more to do with the relief of property than of poverty and was not founded in realpolitik. It posited a situation in which excessive reductions by the Land Courts would 'reduce to beggary' many marginal landlords. O'Shea proposed that, in order to persuade the landowning class to come to voluntary agreements with their tenants, a state subvention should be introduced which would be a multiple (between 10 and 12 times) of the rent reduction offered. 'The inducement of receiving a sum of ready money with which to pay off liabilities', O'Shea enthused, 'would thus be given the landlord to meet the tenant half way, and avoid the risk, expense and uncertainty of the Court.' The central issues, for tenants at least, of leaseholders and arrears were despatched in a sentence at the end of the letter. The sum required to effect this glorious compromise would amount to around £15,000,000. 'But supposing that it were to rise to £20,000,000', O'Shea asked, 'would it not be a cheap process for the re-establishment of law and order?'[28]

The government evidently thought not. For that kind of money it could probably have bribed the tenantry into quiescence for a generation. Mercury returned three days later bearing news of a further consultation with Jupiter and promised, if his measure was accepted '... that the effect of this would be the *immediate* cessation of agitation in Ireland.'[29] His method of advancing the scheme is interesting. He could simply have introduced amendments in committee. Instead he chose to approach the Prime Minister directly. This reflects his desire for attention and to present himself as a confidant and close adviser to Parnell, a potentially moderating influence indeed. Like a good entrepreneur (which he wasn't) he had seen a gap in the market. The Liberals needed to deal with Parnell on Irish business but could not do so openly. He could remedy that deficiency.

Gladstone responded to O'Shea on 14 June with some warmth but was the bearer of bad news. He had brought the idea to Cabinet and regretted to report that 'we do not see our way to any form of action on the basis you propose.' Lord Spencer, a once and future Lord Lieutenant of Ireland, summed up the response when he told Gladstone, 'I do not like the idea of purchasing at the public expence [sic] low rents for Irish Tenants and Ready Money for Irish Landlords.'[30] O'Shea's handwritten note over the letter, the first he received from the GOM, is revealing. 'Important – Gladstone's answer to *the proposal made by Mr Parnell through me to break up the Land League* [my italics] on condition that a clause should be inserted in the Land Bill that any landlord granting a long lease at a reduction of rent, should receive from the Imperial Exchequer a capital sum equal to ten times the annual reduction.'[31]

Whether it was Parnell's intention to 'break up the Land League' or O'Shea's understanding that a compromise allowing the passage of the Land Bill would bring that about, is unclear. The government had enough votes to push the Land Bill through without doing any deals with the Irish members. Their assent would make the resolution of the land crisis much easier to achieve, but Gladstone had calculated that the carrot of the Land Court would be irresistible for the tenant farmer and would deprive the League of its shock troops. Parnell had done likewise. He had sufficient vision, and knowledge of the nature of agrarian unrest, to know that if the courts worked, the basis of Land League agitation would disappear (without necessarily dealing with many of the problems of Irish agriculture, which were not going to be solved by a mere resolution of the issue of rack-renting). Like Gladstone, but with entirely different motivation, Parnell only had to bide his time and the agrarian popular movement, over which his authority was never assured, would give way to the primacy of parliamentary activity, over which his control would be absolute.

The issue of whether the proposal emanated from Parnell or from O'Shea is also unclear. O'Shea's notation is not to be trusted entirely. In his mercurial role he often exceeded his brief. He may have wanted to believe, or have sought to persuade others, that the proposition came from Parnell. But it is difficult to see who Parnell might have been trying to propitiate by adopting such a programme. Had he presented it as his own, the extra-parliamentary left in Paris, Dublin, Mayo and New York would have vilified him. There was little in the plan to recommend it to his par-liamentary supporters. Only the Shaw faction of the party, many of whom were landlords themselves, might have approved, and he had no need or reason to pacify that faction. It is, however, just conceivable that Parnell was pursuing an agenda of his own. He had no wish, unlike many of his associates, to annihilate the Irish aristocracy. Rather, as we have already seen, he hoped that in a post-Home Rule Ireland, its members would adopt leadership roles. O'Shea's proposal would have guaranteed the futures of the sort of enlightened landlords to whom Parnell looked for that leadership. But he could not be seen to attempt to shore up their positions. O'Shea, on the other hand, could. However, on the balance of probability, it is safer to assume that O'Shea was flying solo, perhaps after some cursory consultation with a party leader anxious, for personal reasons, to satiate O'Shea's growing sense of his own importance and not displeased with the implications of the Clare MP's proposals.

O'Shea made one constructive contribution to the Commons debate during the committee stage of the Bill. His concern on this occasion was more apropos. He rose on 19 July to press the case for leaseholders excluded from the working of the Bill. He pointed out that many lease-holders had not benefitted from the 1870 Act, having been forced by landlords, anticipating the provisions of the legislation, into entering lengthy and disadvantageous contracts in 1869. He also pointed out that some tenants had had bad leases forced on them by Conservative landlords because they had voted for Liberal candidates at elections (the secret ballot had only been introduced in 1872) 'and he thought it was very hard that, seeing that the tenants had stood by the Liberal party in those days, the Liberal Party should not stand by them now ... and he was certain that great agitation would take place and great jealousy would spring up if Parliament left them out in the cold.'[32]

The Land Bill came before the House for a vote on the third reading on 29 July. It was essentially a free vote, a gift from Parnell, for the Irish party members. Twenty-seven supported the legislation. These included, rather unexpectedly, James O'Kelly. Parnell himself, and most of his dedicated followers, did not vote. This was purely for demonstration purposes. He wished to show the left that he would not countenance watered-down land reform. However, most of the Land League and Irish party irreconcilables were either in jail or in exile. Despite appearances to the contrary Parnell was listening to a different drumbeat. It was being sounded by the Roman Catholic hierarchy, the *Freeman's Journal* and substantial farmers. Its insistent rhythm was urging settlement. Just as surprising as O'Kelly's decision to support the Land Bill was O'Shea's choice. Like Parnell, he abstained. He may have calculated that he had more to gain by siding with Parnell over an issue that did not threaten the stability of his beloved Liberal government. The Bill was carried by a majority of 92 and became law on 22 August. It was severely mutilated by the House of Lords, but didn't suffer the same fate as the Compensation for Disturbance Bill.

O'Shea's spirited defence of leaseholders was something of a drop in the ocean when set against the 15,000 contributions made by various members on the Land Bill (6,000 from Irish MPs) over a period of 58 days.[33] Parnell alone proposed 150 amendments in committee. O'Shea intervened on four occasions. But his speech on 19 July was given added significance by the fact that when he made it he was in the midst of a private altercation with Parnell that had resulted in a challenge being issued and accepted. At any moment the Captain might have had to leave London for Paris to fight a duel with the Uncrowned King.

AN AFFAIR OF HONOUR

The episode of the threatened duel between Parnell and O'Shea in 1881 involves two contradictory accounts. The challenge was issued in July of that year by O'Shea. There is some documentary evidence to that effect. The question surrounds the date of the *casus belli*.

Katharine O'Shea claims in her Parnell biography that her husband arrived unexpectedly in Eltham in January 1881. He was 'very angry indeed with me because he had seen some men watching his lodgings and imagined that I had engaged a detective to do so.' Why O'Shea had made such an imaginative leap she doesn't say, but we are left to make our own assumptions when she tells us that the detectives had, in fact, been keeping another residence under surveillance, that of a friend of O'Shea's, adding that 'this friend's wife afterwards divorced him.'[34]

Parnell, who lived habitually at Eltham by that stage, was not home. But a portmanteau of his was in residence. This was found by O'Shea and occasioned a fierce argument between husband and wife. The quarrel culminated in O'Shea despatching Parnell's luggage to London and leaving Wonersh Lodge 'declaring he would challenge Parnell to fight a duel and would shoot him.' She supports this version of events by including a plaintive note from Parnell, dated 7 January, in which he requests her to 'kindly ask Captain O'Shea where he left my luggage.'

Appropriately that veteran duellist, the O'Gorman Mahon, was used as O'Shea's 'friend' or second[35] in the case, but his real friend appears to have been his sister-in-law, Anna Steele, who indulged in shuttle diplomacy between the parties and patched matters up. Although O'Shea had a habit of issuing or attracting challenges it is highly unlikely that any duel would ever have been fought. In the latter half of the 19th century, 'duelling was simply no longer socially or legally acceptable.'[36]

In one of a number of contradictions and blatant errors Katharine makes the distinctly odd claim that Parnell, in accepting the challenge, requested that he be allowed to continue his association with her after the duel, explaining that 'he [Parnell] must have a medium of communication between the government and himself and that Mrs O'Shea had kindly undertaken the office for him ...' If Parnell was so confident that he would still be alive after the duel had been fought he must also have been aware that there was a good chance his adversary would not, and therefore would be in no position to deny him anything. In addition, though Katharine did serve as an intermediary between Parnell and Gladstone, that was not to happen for another 18 months.

She also includes the text of an undated note from Parnell that was, presumably, composed in response to O'Shea's written challenge. The implication is that this was written in January. 'I replied to Captain O'Shea's note yesterday,' Parnell had written, 'and sent my reply by a careful messenger to the Salisbury Club; and it must be waiting him there. He has just written me a very insulting letter, and I shall be obliged to send a friend to him if I do not have a satisfactory reply to a second note I have just sent him.'[37]

However, she then goes on to publish four more brief letters (she calls them 'cypher' letters) 'bearing upon the matter of the threatened duel.' All were written in July 1881 and one, from 25 July, which asks for his 'travelling cap', makes reference to the possibility that he 'may have to go over to Paris or Boulogne some day this week.' The latter had long been a favoured destination for English duellists. The subtext of the final letter, written the following day, is that the matter has been satisfactorily resolved and no one is going to get hurt, 'so you need not send my cap.'[38]

Except for agreement on the basic issue – that a duel was to be fought – none of this squares with O'Shea's version of events. This was outlined to the divorce court in November 1890. There, O'Shea dated his discovery of the portmanteau as the middle of July 1881. He explained how, after a blazing row with his wife, he had walked all the way back to London and had gone immediately to Anna Steele, arriving there at 4.00 am. He had despatched the challenge that day. Meanwhile Anna Steele had spoken to Parnell who had denied the affair. O'Shea had then accompanied his sister-in-law to meet with his wife. He had accepted her assurances that nothing untoward was going on. The letter he wrote to Parnell issuing the challenge was entered into evidence. It had been sent from the Salisbury Club in London, on 13 July.

Sir,
Will you be so kind as to be in Lille, or in any other town in the north of France which may suit your convenience, on Saturday next, the 16th inst.? Please to let me know by 1 p.m. today where to expect you on that date, so that I may be able to inform you of the sign of the inn at which I shall be staying. I await your answer in order to lose no time in arranging with a friend to accompany me.[39]

In this instance all the evidence seems to point towards the accuracy of O'Shea's memory rather than his wife's assertions. Her own book supports his contention that he had descended on Wonersh Lodge in July and set off the chain of events discussed above. All the dated letters (other than Parnell's request for his luggage) were written in July. The undated note in which Parnell refers to O'Shea's 'insulting' letter contains a reference to his having sent a reply round to the Salisbury Club. It was from that address that he had received the challenge, a challenge dated 13 *July*.

If we look at their known movements in January 1881, it is clear that both Parnell and O'Shea were in England. Parnell had abandoned the Land League trial in Dublin on 5 January and, according to Katharine, had stayed with her in Eltham for 'some days' during which time he met Aunt Ben for the first time.[40] In recounting this period she makes no reference whatever to the dispute with her husband.

On 7 January 1881, Parnell might have had something more on his mind than his baggage. Parliament had just opened for its new session and on that day he was moving an amendment to the Queen's Speech with a lengthy address to the House. Three days later O'Shea made his contribution to the debate, the one in which he denied the possibility that Parnell was the evil genius behind 'outrage' (see above). Is it likely that the entire affair could have been resolved so quickly and that O'Shea could have been so buoyed by assurances of fidelity from his wife that he was prepared to make such a public and ringing endorsement of a man whom he had, a few days before, accused of committing adultery with her?

It is just possible that the discovery of the portmanteau was made in January and the threat of a duel was not pursued until July, but it must be deemed unlikely that there would have been such a long gap between anger and the desire for satisfaction.

Katharine got an opportunity to trump her husband's account of events in the divorce court with the publication of the Parnell biography in 1914. Controversy surrounds the real authorship of that work because she appears to have passed up a number of opportunities to 'set the record straight'. However, her voice is heard again, and it is a quite different voice, in Henry Harrison's 1931 work, *Parnell Vindicated: The Lifting of the Veil*. Harrison was a young MP who remained loyal to his chief in the aftermath of the disastrous Irish Party split in 1890. In the wake of the death of Parnell in October 1891, he had offered his assistance to his leader's widow. The offer had been gratefully accepted and the assistance proved to be invaluable. But Katharine Parnell (as she was then) told Harrison a very different story to the one that emerges from her 1914 book. In the latter (almost certainly 'influenced' by her bullying son) she and Parnell are portrayed as having consistently duped an O'Shea who was ignorant of the truth of their relationship. It is, in most of its essentials, his divorce court narrative, that of *un mari ignorant*. The tale she told Harrison was of *un mari complaisant*, of a man who had known of the affair from early on, had encouraged it but whose vanity had been affronted when a relationship, in which he had connived for his own advantage, turned into a genuine love affair.

According to Harrison's account, Katharine had confessed to him that O'Shea had, in effect, pimped her to the Irish party leader, 'He had been willing enough that I should attract Mr Parnell, that I should have an 'affair' with him of conventional impropriety, transient, involving no ties, no upset, a mere *atnourette* [fleeting love]. He was more than willing that I should go to humiliating lengths occasionally to win him for O'Shea interests, but the idea of my giving him all my love, of my being engrossed, appropriated by him, was quite another matter. That infuriated him.'[41]

All talk of a duel had subsided when O'Shea became aware that Parnell was perfectly willing to meet him in France. Katharine told Harrison that, 'he worked upon my fears for Mr Parnell to get him out of it.' He had written to Parnell suggesting that the Irish leader was not prepared to offer 'satisfaction'. 'Sir, I have called frequently at the Salisbury Club today and find that you are not going abroad. Your luggage is at Charing Cross Station.' This serves to reinforce the July over the January scenario. The reply from Parnell would have disabused him of the notion that the Irish leader was avoiding the confrontation: 'your surmise that I refuse to go abroad is not a correct one.'[42] Bizarrely that evening both men trooped through the divisional lobby together to vote, in a very small minority, against the government.

While Katharine reiterated to Harrison the arrangement whereby she would continue to see Parnell because of her employment as emissary, her account varies when she deals with the cause of the fracas:

All that fuss about the duel I think arose from some talk which came to Captain O'Shea's ears in such a way that he had to take some steps. Our affair had not been in existence for so many months, but I suppose that it had got to be known to some extent – for instance, the detectives probably knew. Somebody, a Minister, a colleague, an enemy may have brought it under his notice, or challenged him with it, in such a way that he could not ignore it altogether. When he had written his challenge to a duel and had received 'assurances' he could always say, as he did ultimately say, that he had taken appropriate steps ... [43]

The private detectives monitoring her husband's apartment building do not appear to have entered the picture at that stage.[44]

Why did Katharine insist that the quarrel had taken place in January and imply (despite herself supplying evidence to the contrary) that everything had been patched up early in 1881? It may simply have been an error on her part. It may also be something more noteworthy. A possible explanation suggests itself in the phrase she uses to conclude her description of the episode: 'From the date of this bitter quarrel Parnell and I were one, without further scruple, without fear, and without remorse.'

The insinuation made in the divorce court was that, in the wake of the resolution of the row, physical relations between Katharine and her husband proceeded as normal. That is certainly what O'Shea wanted the court to believe. 'The affectionate relations which had always existed between Captain O'Shea and his wife were resumed' was the appropriately delicate Victorian phraseology. It is probable that the reconciliation effected at the time did, indeed, involve a temporary resumption of sexual relations between the couple. That is an inference that we can draw from a phrase in a letter sent by Parnell to Katharine on 22 July 1881, from the House of Commons. '... I am very much troubled', he wrote, 'at everything you have to undergo, and trust that it will not last long.' However, Katharine had more than one reason for allowing O'Shea his conjugal rights. She did not simply need to persuade him that she was an obeisant wife, she needed to convince him that he was the father of the child she was carrying.

He was, of course, no such thing. Katharine had become pregnant with Parnell's first child around mid-May 1881. By July she would have been well aware of the fact and the window of opportunity during which she could convince O'Shea that he was the father was closing rapidly. It seems likely that she took the opportunity of the 'reconciliation' in July to bring this about. It worked admirably. When Claude Sophie was born the following February, O'Shea could reasonably have believed that he was the father of a premature child.

The notion of Katharine maintaining a simultaneous sexual relationship with the two men has made some observers uncomfortable. To Henry Harrison it was a truly unbelievable and appalling vista, one he described as a 'vile picture ... a lying picture'.[45] Even F.S.L. Lyons, writing in the more permissive late fifties, describes the possibility as 'only a theory'. [46] A theory it may well be, but there is ample evidence to suggest that, for her own reasons, Katharine maintained some sort of sexual relationship, albeit as a highly reluctant partner, until at least the first quarter of 1882. She was a canny pragmatist, among whose priorities was self-preservation and the protection of her family. Although we never see her letters to Parnell, it is clear that he was the romantic in the relationship.

However, there is more than a hint that 'the lady doth protest too much' in her assertion that she belonged, exclusively, to Parnell in the aftermath of the duel debacle. By fixing the date of that episode in January 1881 she may have been responsible for conscious or subconscious misdirection, guiding the reader away from any supposition that she maintained sexual relations with her husband. If she and Parnell 'were one' from mid January 1881, then there could be no doubt about the identity of the father of her fourth child. But if she accepted that the duel episode had actually taken place in July, the child's parentage was no longer a given.

At another point in her disjointed and occasionally implausible narrative she writes about the existence of Claude Sophie as if the child had never actually been conceived. O'Shea, she says, 'had no suspicion of the truth.' She avoids the obvious question of how O'Shea could have thought Claude Sophie was his child if he was not having sexual relations with her by simply ignoring that question. There is no evidence that her husband, notwithstanding his Catholicism, ever claimed that his child was the consequence of an immaculate conception. Logically, therefore, his equanimity at the fact of her birth (on 15 February 1882), derived from the reassurance that it was mathematically possible for him to have been the father. Ergo a compelling rather than a 'vile' picture of service to expediency emerges.

To Kilmainham

In the aftermath of the passage of the Land Bill, Parnell's priority was to restore the faith of the American militants and maintain the flow of funds from the USA. Picking a fight with the Speaker and having himself suspended from the House was one device he used. Another was to entertain the militant Fenian Henri le Caron in the Mother of Parliaments itself. The links of that particular irreconcilable to the Brotherhood went back to the abortive invasions of Canada in the late 1860s. Parnell sought to convince le Caron that he had not softened his line on peasant proprietary, the elimination of the Anglo-Irish 'garrison' and the ultimate separation of Ireland from the Empire. What he was unaware of until Le Caron materialised eight years later at the *Times* Commission to testify against him was that the 'American' was actually one of the most successful and resourceful spies within the Brotherhood and Clan na Gael and had relayed the gist of that conversation to Sir Robert Anderson, his spymaster in Scotland Yard, within hours of its having taken place.

Not all of Parnell's negativity about the Land Act was attitudinising. He would, over a period of five years, see the thrust of his critique endorsed by both Liberal and Tory governments, with legislation on arrears and leaseholders and a definite move in the direction of a peasant proprietary. Where he was wrong was in his scepticism about the efficacy of the Land Courts. He suspected (correctly) that tenants would turn to them en masse, and at a National Convention of the Land League in mid September he persuaded the organisation to sponsor a number of cases in order to test their credibility. But he was not optimistic that a government-appointed court would place the interests of the tenant on an equal footing with, let alone above those of, the landlord class.

Parnell didn't necessarily set out to provoke Gladstone (who had been incensed by his approach to the Land Act) or Forster but he was especially successful in antagonising the latter. A major rally in Dublin on 25 September 1881 had heard trenchant criticism by Parnell of the Land Act. It was followed by a torchlight procession through the capital and a theatrical gesture from Parnell as he passed the old parliament building in Dame Street.[47] There he stopped and pointed silently but eloquently at the site of Grattan's Parliament. Forster described Parnell to Gladstone on that occasion as being 'moved by his tail' and responding to pressure from his followers.[48]

In July Parnell had taken the step of reinforcing his propaganda machine. He lacked a newspaper that totally and accurately reflected his viewpoint and priorities. The *Freeman's Journal* and the *Nation* were supportive but often cleaved to an independent line. With funds from the Land League and the help of Patrick Egan he acquired three papers run by the virtually bankrupt Richard Pigott (*Shamrock*, *Flag of Ireland* and the *Irishman*) for £3,000. This had the dual effect of ridding Parnell of an often-trenchant critic (the papers tended towards a doctrinaire Fenian line, though this was a wilful act of cynicism on Pigott's part) and giving him another platform from which to berate the government and 'Buckshot' Forster.[49] A young *Freeman's Journal* writer, William O'Brien[50], became editor of the weekly periodical, *United Ireland*, fashioned from the merged Pigott titles.

The tempo of recrimination quickened in October. Forster had already written to Gladstone suggesting that the time had come to arrest Parnell. 'I think you will do great good by denouncing Parnell's action and policy at Leeds.'[51] Gladstone was due to make a major speech in the constituency he had bequeathed to his son. On 2 October the Irish leader made it far more likely that the Prime Minister would succumb to pressure from the Chief Secretary when Parnell made a provocative speech in his constituency insisting that soon the Crown would be the only link connecting Britain and Ireland. He also called for a massive reduction in Irish rents, from £17,000,000 to £3,000,000.

On 7 October in his Leeds speech the Grand Old Spider went in pursuit of the irritating gadfly. He denounced Parnell's policies and told his audience that where the Irish leader and his movement was concerned the 'resources of civilisation were not exhausted'. The threat to arrest Parnell could not have been made clearer. Two days later Forster wrote to the Prime Minister that 'Parnell's reply to you may be a treasonable outburst. If the lawyers clearly advise me to that effect, I do not think I can postpone immediate arrest on suspicion of treasonable practices.'[52]

The last salvo, and the final straw in this tit-for-tat sequence, came in Wexford on 9 October, when Parnell almost seemed to court incarceration. Invoking the spirit of the 'men of '98' he, famously, referred to Gladstone as a 'masquerading knight-errant' and a 'pretending champion of the rights of every nation except those of the Irish nation', adding that he was supporting the landowning class by 'bayonets and buckshot'.[53]

It was a night for phrasemaking. Later, when asked in a Wexford hotel who would take his place were he to be arrested, he responded even more famously, 'Ah, if I am arrested Captain Moonlight[54] will take my place.' Whether or not he was inviting the martyrdom of imprisonment (and the resounding approval of the militant element in Ireland and America), he was certain that the outcome of his arrest would be civil chaos. And so it proved.

On 11 October Forster crossed to England for a Cabinet meeting. He left instructions behind for the Commander of Forces in Ireland, Sir Thomas Steele, to prepare for the arrest of Parnell. The signal to activate the plan, dependent on Cabinet approval, would be the single word 'Proceed'. That approval was forthcoming at the ministerial meeting of 12 October and the state apparatus closed in on Parnell the following day.

Curiously it was a Cabinet decision of which Katharine O'Shea claims she was forewarned. The chapter of her book dealing with his arrest opens with the claim that 'On October 12th, 1881, I was in London on Mr Parnell's business – to ascertain the movements of the government.' She describes her health as 'delicate', an obvious euphemism for the fact that she was five months pregnant at the time. She waited, she says, in a house in Piccadilly until she was told that a Cabinet Council had been convened. Then, she claims, 'I wired in code to Parnell, to inform him that Forster had left for Ireland with the warrant for his arrest.'[55]

Unless she is a complete fantasist (a possibility which can never be ruled out in her case), this means that either she herself had rapid access to Cabinet-level discussions, or Parnell had put her in touch with someone who was privy to Cabinet secrets. If her contention is true, then Parnell does not appear to have been forewarned by the alleged telegram. On the night of 12 October he stayed in Morrison's Hotel on the corner of Dawson Street and Nassau Street, as he usually did whenever he was in Dublin. He was due to speak at a meeting in Kildare the following day.

At 8.30 on the morning of 13 October (Parnell was intensely superstitious, feared the number 13 and disliked the month of October) the porter told him that two policemen were downstairs waiting for him. One of them was the celebrated Superintendent John Mallon who would later crack the Invincible conspiracy (see p. 120). After Mallon and his constable had been shown up to Parnell's room and had read the charges to him, Parnell was given time to write a letter to Katharine. He was being arrested for inciting others to acts of intimidation and 'tending to interfere with the maintenance of Law and Order'. Mallon, having expressed the concern that the arrest might spark a riot, was glad to hear Parnell agree to be removed with a minimum of fuss. Within an hour he had been deposited in Kilmainham Jail. That night a violent storm hit the British Isles. It was a prelude to storms of a different kind that would wreak havoc on the island of Ireland for the next six months.

According to Katharine O'Shea her husband sent her a note inviting himself to dinner that night. However there is more than a suggestion in Parnell's correspondence that he had actually re-established residence in Eltham. On the day that Gladstone was ratcheting up tension in Leeds, Parnell had written a detailed note to Katharine about O'Shea's future movements. Both men were in Dublin at the time, but O'Shea was leaving for Wales the following day and thence, through London, to see the Papal Nuncio in Paris. 'This then', he had written, 'is the last letter I can send to you for the present through Eltham ...' Four days later he wrote, 'Your telegram this morning took a great weight off my mind, as your silence made me almost panic-stricken lest you had been hurt by that ____ [sic] and had not been able to get to town.'[56] The implication was that O'Shea had left for Paris, vacating Eltham in the process. Another obvious implication is that he had reasserted his conjugal rights and Parnell was aware of this fact.

On the night of 13 October O'Shea was, according to his wife:

> ... extremely pleased to be able to announce to me that Parnell had been arrested that morning. I knew his news directly I saw his face, and as I was really prepared for it I did not flinch, but replied languidly that I had thought Parnell 'couldn't keep out of jail much longer, didn't you?' But Willie was so fiercely and openly joyful that my maids, who were ardent Parnellites, were much shocked ... we got through dinner amicably enough, while he descanted upon the wickedness and folly of Parnell's policy and the way the Irish question should really be settled, and would be if it could be left to him and those who thought with him. He observed me closely, as he criticised Parnell and his policy, and reiterated his pleasure in knowing he was 'laid by the heels'.[57]

If this is true, it suggests that O'Shea had not been entirely convinced by the assurances of fidelity offered by his wife back in July. His obvious pleasure in the arrest of Parnell sounds largely personal. It belied his consistent opposition to Liberal government coercion policies and his own efforts on behalf of Irish political prisoners, many with views far more extreme than those of Parnell.

Before entering Kilmainham, Parnell had managed to post the hastily scribbled letter he had written to Katharine. It arrived the following day, and does not read like the missive of a man who had been given advance warning of his arrest. After the personal, he concludes with a significant political aside: 'Politically it is a fortunate thing for me that I have been arrested, as the movement is breaking fast, and all will be quiet in a few months, when I shall be released.'

He was correct in his assessment of the future of the Land League: in his absence the Land Courts would begin to do their work and do it so well as to inspire a rush of tenant farmers to rent arbitration. But as to peace in rural Ireland, that would be more elusive. As the months went on he would come to regret his handover of power to the mysterious and uncompromising Captain Moonlight.

CHAPTER 5

The Kilmainham Treaty

It was the tyrant Gladstone
And he said unto himself,
I never will be aisy
Till Parnell is on the shelf.
So make the warrant out in haste
And send it by the mail
And we'll clap the pride of Erin's isle
Into cold Kilmainham jail.

Dublin Street Ballad

NO RENT MANIFESTO

Within 48 hours of Parnell's incarceration he was joined in Kilmainham by Dillon (whose freedom had been short-lived), O'Brien and O'Kelly. He would have been immensely cheered by the arrival of the jovial O'Kelly, but less so by the company of the dour John Dillon. Also present to help him pass the time were Thomas Sexton, Andrew Kettle and the influential Land League Secretary, Thomas Brennan.

A response of some kind was required to the Castle coup. The Damoclean threat of a rent strike had been hovering over the government since the introduction of the coercion regime. A significant faction among the Kilmainham internees felt it was now time to lower the boom on the administration. O'Brien set to work and within three days of his arrest had compiled a 'No Rent Manifesto', calling on farmers to cease the payment of rent. It was issued on 18 October and was a document 'inspired by Ford and Egan,'[1] In its essentials it was the logical outcome of the New Departure, a call to radical action in the wake of the failure of appeasement. But it was not the kind of document to which Parnell would, ordinarily, have been expected to append his signature. Nevertheless he did so, along with Dillon, Sexton, Kettle, O'Kelly and Brennan. The names of Egan (in Paris) and Davitt (whose ticket of leave had been suspended and who was now in Portland prison) were added later.

Ironically it was Dillon and Davitt who were the most opposed to the document. Davitt was never consulted and later claimed that he would have opposed the policy on the grounds that the combination of the Protection of Persons and Property Act (coercion) with the Land Act (conciliation) made a rent strike unworkable and undesirable. Dillon was prevailed upon by O'Kelly to sign – though his misgivings were similar and based on the reality of a leaderless Land League.

What prompted Parnell to sign? He must have known that the promise of the Land Act was too tempting for many tenants to resist and that recourse to the Land Courts by even a significant minority would leave those who obeyed the Manifesto more exposed to retaliatory action by the forces of law and property. Katharine O'Shea claimed, in effect, that he succumbed to the wishes of the majority in Kilmainham. Frank Hugh O'Donnell held that Parnell was consciously seeking the suppression of the Land League. Conor Cruise O'Brien's analysis suggests slightly less Machiavellian motives. Parnell, he believes, was happy to give the extremists their heads while he was *hors de combat*.[2] He could not be held responsible for what he was convinced would be the utter failure of militancy.

Whether or not, by signing the Manifesto, Parnell actually sought the banning of the Land League, the organisation was duly proscribed on 20 October 1881. Its place was taken by the Ladies Land League, originally founded in the USA by Parnell's sisters, Fanny and Anna. This organisation was located to the left of the League itself and its operations were ruthlessly shut down by Parnell upon his release from Kilmainham in May 1882. This led to a sundering of relations with Anna Parnell, who was its motivating force. The Ladies Land League's endorsement of the Manifesto must be weighed in the balance against the vehement opposition of the Roman Catholic hierarchy, including even the normally supportive

Archbishop Croke of Cashel. The *Freeman's Journal*, too, came out in opposition to the strike, and even the *Nation* repudiated the document. Only *United Ireland* beat the drum in its favour.

There were potential dangers to Parnell's health in darkest, dampest Kilmainham, especially as the period of his incarceration neatly coincided with the Irish winter. Some of his colleagues fared badly. It was feared that Dillon would become a victim of tuberculosis and Sexton had to be released on health grounds. Parnell was fortunate, as were the other prisoners, in that Dr. J.E. Kenny, a Parnellite loyalist, was also detained at 'Her Majesty's pleasure'. Kenny regularly insisted on his 'patients' being removed to the hospital wing of the gaol where the regime was less spartan and forbidding.

Parnell was treated so leniently that he had the advantage of one of the biggest and most comfortable cells in the prison, gained five pounds in weight, played handball in the exercise yard and (consider the security implications and, indeed, the symbolism of this privilege), was permitted to practise with his airgun. Another compelling image, from R. Barry O'Brien, is of Parnell playing chess regularly and taking a lot of time over his moves.[3] Add to that the fact that Parnell was able to defy all reading curfews and smuggle out correspondence and it is questionable whether or not his imprisonment was worse than the alternative: presiding over the demise of a movement which had become something of an obstacle to his plans.

The prolonged stay was, however, psychologically onerous, especially for an expectant father who was forced to conceal his impending paternity. It also brought out some of Parnell's latent hypochondria and almost paranoid superstition. He once forced William O'Brien to burn a letter he had received from a fellow journalist whose children were suffering from scarlet fever. He also became somewhat demented by the profusion of gifts sent to make his stay in Kilmainham more comfortable; gifts which, because of their political tinge, were often green in colour. Green was his *bête verte*, and a wardrobe of green clothing designed to keep him warm went unworn and untouched.[4]

Visited by Maurice Healy, brother of Tim, with a draft Arrears Bill to amend the 1881 Land Act, he studied the document and quickly deleted one of the clauses. But as soon as he realised that, in so doing, he had reduced the number of articles in the Bill to 13 he immediately reinstated the offending clause.

In later years Parnell spoke to T.P. O'Connor about his sojourn in Kilmainham and was curiously positive about it: '... he himself told me that the time passed very pleasantly, that he had not been so happy for years. He was relieved, he said, from all sense of responsibility, and that to him was inexpressibly consoling. His health, however, I believe suffered from that period ...'[5]

Despite the less than draconian conditions it must have been difficult for Parnell to endure separation from Katharine. He knew that O'Shea was a frequent 'visitor' to Eltham and received occasional resentful letters upbraiding him for the contribution his absence was making to her unhappiness. Katharine could be less than stoical at times, and references in her correspondence to the effect that he was 'surely killing'[6] her would not have helped his frame of mind. On more than one occasion he refers to the fact that her most recent letter has left him full of anxiety. She appears to have been quite frank in her depiction of her situation and to have spared him few details. As early as 21 November he is writing to her in response to her declaration that she is 'a little less miserable'. O'Shea had been staying at Eltham for 'some days' and Parnell inquired anxiously, 'Has he left yet? It is frightful that you should be exposed to such daily torture. My own Wifie must try and strengthen herself, and get some sleep for her husband's sake and for our child's sake, who must be suffering also.'[7] The probable implications of that statement will be explored elsewhere.

Communication between the two was enabled by a combination of visitors, acquiescent warders, the ingenious use of accommodation addresses and invisible ink. Parnell proved himself to be as resourceful in jail as outside. Often, however, he failed to display the same grasp of the possible in Kilmainham as he did in Westminster. More than once he suggested that Katharine might be able to visit him. In November he proposed that she would be insinuated into Kilmainham as his cousin 'Mrs Bligh' (a nicely ironic touch). In early 1882 she was to be introduced as his sister. Presumably the more practical Katharine demurred; being heavily pregnant may have figured in her counter-arguments.

When her memoir of Parnell was published in 1914, it was one of the Kilmainham letters that caused most controversy among his erstwhile supporters and residual enemies. Written on 14 December 1881 he declares plaintively, '... my darling you frighten me dreadfully when you tell me that I am "surely killing" you and our child ... Rather than that my beautiful Wifie should run any risk I will resign my seat, leave politics, and go away somewhere with my own Queenie, as soon as she wishes; will she come? Let me know, darling, in your next about this, whether it is safe for you that I should be kept here any longer.'[8]

He may well have been calling the bluff of an understandably depressed woman or hinting that he was receiving too much information from Eltham, but some 20th-century critics and former associates of Parnell refused to believe that he could have countenanced abandoning the nationalist cause at the behest of Katharine O'Shea. Tim Healy, whose loathing for Parnell may have moderated over the years, but whose antipathy towards the woman he had dubbed 'Kitty' never abated, was scathing in his assessment of this revelation. 'Thus the leader of a movement mightier than O'Connell's', he wrote, 'proposed to forsake his comrades in the most critical hour, and abandon at a woman's whim Ireland's "magnificent and awful cause".'[9]

THE STATE OF THE NATION

The two pieces of legislation that most directly impacted on the country in late 1881 and through 1882 were William E. Forster's coercive vehicle, the Protection of Persons and Property Act, and Gladstone's remedial instrument, the Land Act. They were part of a pattern of schizophrenic 'good cop – bad cop' British administration in Ireland that would continue for a generation. Despite the rhetoric of activists like Davitt (who would travel an ideological road from peasant proprietary to land nationalisation), most Irish farmers were, in 1881, content to remain within the ambit of the landlord–tenant linkage. The Land League, to them, was a means towards shifting the economic balance within that relationship in their direction.

When the Land Commissioners began their work, there was an understandable scepticism. In advance of the Land Court convening in Clare, in early December, to arbitrate between the peasantry and the propertied class, the *Clare Independent* warned that patience was thin. 'There must be sweeping reductions, if there are any, for the case is not one to be pottered with; either a good job must be made of it or none.'[10] A fortnight later the newspaper was reporting, with not a little surprise, that reductions of between 20 and 40 per cent had been recommended by the Court on a number of Clare estates. Which begs the question: was O'Shea speaking as a landlord or as a spokesman for the tenant farmers of County Clare when he criticised the work of the Court in the House of Commons on 15 March 1882?

In response to a Private Member's motion to amend the Land Act he pointed out that '... the working of the Act so far had been a great disappointment to the tenant farmers in County Clare, who understood that official valuers would be appointed. He had spoken with many of them and they objected to a partly perambulating tribunal, some members of which went about valuing land on their own account. He thought the Commission ought to sit permanently in the towns, and take the advice of qualified professional men as to the value of the property with which they were dealing.'[11]

Despite O'Shea's caveats, the reality of Land Court assessments, which were bringing rents down towards Griffith's[12] valuation levels, was to lead to an eventual stampede of tenants (in good standing) to arbitration. The unsought corollary of this was the plight of those who, because of their circumstances, had no access. There was no solace for the leaseholder who, not being a 'tenant at will', had no recourse to the arbitrative process. Nor for the tenant in arrears, of whom there were over 100,000 (about 20 per cent of the total). So, in a sense, the Land Courts, while proving hugely beneficial to a highly influential segment of the agricultural population of Ireland, actually exacerbated the frustration of many poorer farmers.

Agrarian violence proceeded apace. It did so partly as a reaction to the arrest of the Land League leaders and, simultaneously, as a function of their inability to discourage civil strife. However, the raw figures for serious crime included instances of 'Ribbon' activity that had more to do with local feuds and jealousies than it did with any ideological imperative. A study of the, often tedious, proceedings of the Parnellism and Crime Commission in 1888–89 reveals ample evidence of this particular variety of social breakdown.

The inexorable rise of the 'outrage' figures was also stoked, in a minority of instances, by suicidally provocative landlords. These powerful relics of aristocratic authoritarianism were utterly unprepared to make concessions either to great need or political reality. Again, in O'Shea's constituency of Clare (where the MP himself gave his own tenants a reduction of 25 per cent) there were property owners such as the Morony family. As a consequence of disadvantageous leases entered into around the time of the 1870 Land Act, tenants on the Morony estate were, according to Fr Patrick White, paying two to three times the Griffith's valuation. The widow of the man who had forced those leases on Clare farmers, Mrs Morony, was in no doubt about where the blame lay for the recalcitrance of her tenants. 'They would pay their rents were it not for influence and bad advice ...' was her philosophy, as outlined to the *Clare Independent*. '... those who are poor owe it to their own idleness or imprudence, and the interference of the Land League.'[13]

But the statistics are also a simple index of anger, despair and anti-establishment resentment. The total number of 'outrages' for the ten months that preceded the passage of the Coercion Act was 2,379. For the subsequent ten months it was 3,821. If crimes like sending threatening letters and cattle-maiming are stripped out and the focus is entirely on crimes against the person, it can be seen that homicides almost trebled (from 7 to 20); instances of firing at the person increased threefold (from 21 to 63) and firing into dwellings virtually doubled (from 62 to122).[14] Much of this was connected to a provocative policing regime which, far from putting down dissent, merely encouraged it to prosper.

The coercion environment allowed the government to take action against activities like boycotting, which, in the absence of special powers, would not even constitute civil disobedience. In the case of Mrs Morony, three Milltown Malbay shopkeepers, Edmund Burke, William Hynes and Thomas McMahon (who were not Land League members), were threatened with arrest by the Special Resident Magistrate for the area, Clifford Lloyd. Their 'crime' was participating in a boycott against Morony. They were ordered to sell her goods under threat of imprisonment. On 21 March 1882, O'Shea raised the case in the Commons in a question to Forster. The Irish Secretary was unapologetic. There had been a conspiracy in Milltown Malbay 'to ruin a lady, and deprive her of the necessaries of life'. Clifford Lloyd had information that two of the shopkeepers, Hynes and McMahon, were ringleaders in the conspiracy. He also, gratuitously, pointed out that 'an unoffending old man in the service of the lady in question was shot in cold blood at his fireside'. It was left to O'Shea to ascertain that Hynes and McMahon were not under suspicion for that crime. The Commons was also favoured with an interesting snippet of information: out of a total population of just over 1,300 souls, 21 inhabitants of Milltown Malbay were in jail.[15]

The Resident Magistrate to whom Forster and O'Shea referred, Clifford Lloyd, was a new breed of law-enforcement mercenary. Six Special Resident Magistrates had been appointed to police the proscribed parts of the country, mostly west of the Shannon. Lloyd was probably the most reviled amongst nationalists. His approach to policing was paramilitary in nature and amounted to the imposition of martial law. The confrontational regime of Lloyd, who was a particular favourite of Forster, according to his daughter,[16] became something of a minor obsession with O'Shea. The Clare MP made frequent critical references to his activities in the House of Commons. In this he was *ad idem* with *United Ireland*, which referred to Lloyd (a convinced Unionist) in a January 1882 editorial as a 'Satrap', and observed that 'His gangs of ruffian soldiers may prowl about the roads at night; steal all they find; put all they meet into prison; get up outrages in order to put them down; handcuff every woman who thinks all the suspects ought to be provided with decent food; put their bayonets through every child who whistles *Harvey Duff*: How much nearer will they be to collecting the rents?'[17]

DICK AND BOYSIE

What was the true state of relations between O'Shea and his wife while Parnell resided in Kilmainham at the Chief Secretary's pleasure? There is much internal evidence to suggest that O'Shea was spending considerably more time at Eltham than had been the case before the aborted duel. Was he being more solicitous for his wife because she was carrying (as he believed) his child? Had he been brought to his senses as regards his neglect of his wife and family by the suspicion that she had had an affair with Parnell? He was certainly not monitoring his wife's activities as, unless he feared the onset of other suitors, the principal object of his suspicion was safely locked up in Kilmainham.

There is no doubt that during this period O'Shea still viewed Katharine as, at the very least, an acquiescent and nurturing partner. He regularly discussed business affairs with her and she was clearly kept informed of his setbacks as well as his (infrequent) successes. He also engaged with her in political debate, and on a level well above that of mere gossip. The O'Shea letters that make it into the Parnell biography are collected in a single chapter and are probably there at the instigation of her son. They are affectionate and chatty, right up to the end of 1885. His letters to her are those of a man still seeking to impress his wife with his little victories and consequential achievements. Much of this may be based on her proximity to the financial spigot that was Aunt Ben; some can be traced to the period of her involvement as a mediator between Parnell and Gladstone; and still more is connected to her 'friendship' with the Irish party leader. But, aside from the obviously self-serving elements, a genuine sense of fondness emerges from the correspondence.

It is hard to see how he could have maintained such a breezy and familiar tone had her side of the correspondence been curt and discouraging.[18] It may be that Katharine's responses were as warm and lively as his for diplomatic reasons only. She certainly had good cause for deceiving him into the belief that she was still 'Dick' and he remained her 'Boysie'. But her feelings towards her husband (albeit recorded more than 30 years after the events in question) at the time of Parnell's incarceration are far from positive and encouraging. 'I had to be careful now;' she wrote in 1914, 'Willie was solicitous for my health, and wished to come to Eltham more frequently than I would allow. He thought February would seal our reconciliation. Whereas I knew it would cement the cold hatred I felt towards him, and consummate the love I bore my child's father.'[19]

The use of the word 'reconciliation' is significant and suggests that O'Shea felt that their marriage had, in some sense, been renewed in the aftermath of the bitter row in July 1881. Towards the end of 1881 he was spending much time in Spain. Mid-December saw a share issue for the Union Bank of Spain and England, of which O'Shea was to be a director. It was 'established for the purpose of conducting general banking and commercial business between England and Spain'[20] and sought capital of £1,000,000 at £20 a share.

But, to Parnell's consternation, neither his Union Bank activities, nor indeed the new session of parliament in January, were enough to keep O'Shea away from Eltham entirely. On 7 January 1882 a concerned Parnell wrote, 'I do feel very anxious about you my darling and cannot help it. You must tell the doctor and never mind about ___. Could you not go to London or Brighton about the beginning of February? London would be best, if you could get him away on any pretext; but if you could not, Brighton would leave you most free from him. It is perfectly dreadful that Wifie should be so worried at night. I had hoped the doctor's orders would have prevented that.'[21]

The reasons for his concerns are apparent. O'Shea, assuming that 'his' child was not due until April or May, had been claiming his conjugal rights. The previous week Parnell had written, 'I am very nervous about the doctors, and you should at all events tell one of them the right time, so that he may be on hand, otherwise you may not have one at all. It will never do to run this risk.'[22] From this we can infer that Parnell was conscious of that fact that Katharine had been forced to lie to her husband about the date of her forthcoming confinement to throw him off the scent of adultery. A genuine premature birth (in early January, as opposed to the O'Shea 'premature' birth that would take place in February) would be potentially disastrous on two counts. In the absence of 'informed' medical help anything could go wrong and, in addition, not even O'Shea was likely to believe the child to be his if it was born in early January when he was not anticipating its arrival until the end of April.

F.S.L. Lyons in his majestic biography of Parnell is slightly reluctant to accept the 'unpleasant hypothesis'[23] that Katharine was having sexual relations with both men simultaneously. He also rejects the suggestion that Parnell was aware of O'Shea's assertion of his conjugal rights saying that Parnell's 'reaction would have been murderous if any whisper of it had reached him.'[24]

However, what other complexion can be put on Parnell's knowledge that Katharine was misdirecting her husband as to the birth date of her child? She can only have been doing this in an effort to convince O'Shea that the child was his. There had clearly been no admission of an affair and a pregnancy; *ipso facto* Parnell has to have known that she had had sexual relations with her husband in order to 'justify' her pregnancy. Far from feeling 'murderous' Parnell was more concerned with Katharine's feelings than he was with any (perfectly natural) personal jealousy. Even when he was told that O'Shea's visits were continuing in the wake of the birth of the child, Claude Sophie,[25] on 16 February, his reaction was relatively mild and designed to spare Katharine's feelings, 'If my own can make an arrangement now for him to keep away,' he wrote on 29 March, 'I think she ought to do so. It will be too intolerable having him about always. When I see Wifie again or am released, I can consider the situation, but until then, if you can you had best make some arrangement.'[26]

In this instance Katharine O'Shea's biographer, Jane Jordan, is probably closer to the truth than Lyons when she writes, 'One of the surprising things which the Kilmainham letters reveal about the relationship between Katharine and Parnell is the extraordinary frankness with which they appear to be able to discuss this continuing intimacy between the legal husband and wife. She seems to have made no attempt to hide unpalatable details from her lover, while on his part, Parnell expresses not his own jealousy, as one would expect, but only solicitude for Katharine.'[27] Indeed he makes a far better job of hiding any anger or bitterness from Katharine than she appears to have done where he was concerned.

In an obvious effort to dispel any doubts as to the parentage of the short-lived Claude Sophie, Katharine describes the child, at birth, as having 'the brown eyes of her father'.[28] Aside from the fact that babies are generally born with blue eyes that only come into their natural colour when they ingest sufficient melanin, she includes in her memoir a letter from Parnell on 29 March that contains the phrase 'I cannot consent to Wifie turning nurse even when brown eyes do come.'[29]

Her case that neither her husband nor any member of his family was aware of the child's parentage is far stronger. While in the throes of a correspondence with Joseph Chamberlain, which will be discussed below, O'Shea opens one letter, on 25 April, with the line, 'My Dear Sir, My child is to be buried at Chislehurst this afternoon and I do not intend to return to town unless you want to see me.'[30] A month or so after Claude Sophie's premature death, O'Shea's sister Mary wrote to Katharine in her most pietistic manner and sympathised with '… your grief at losing her, but, happy child, how glorious is her existence! What a contrast to ours, we who must struggle on, working out our salvation in fear and trembling!'[31]

THE GO-BETWEEN

As Parnell passed the time in Kilmainham ponderously considering his next chess move, large parts of rural Ireland passed into the hands of Captain Moonlight and his lawless cronies. Despite the protestations of the Land League to the contrary, one thing that does emerge from the Special Commission on Parnellism and Crime in 1888–89 is that there was at least a tenuous (and deniable) connection between elements of the League and agrarian violence. This might have taken the form of League members indulging in extra-curricular 'Ribbonism', or of Fenian members of the organisation taking advantage of civil ferment to forward their own aims. In certain instances League funds were used to pay for the legal defence of members indicted for crime. Forster openly admitted to the House of Commons that 'his policy had failed, that he had under-estimated the forces with which he had to contend'.[32] The only solution he had to offer was a further tightening of the coercion regime. Support for him and for his policies in the Cabinet was waning rapidly. As it became clear that the government and the Land League had reached stalemate, interest increased in the thoughts and the potential intrusion of the Kilmainham chess player into the anarchy that was rural Ireland. His incarceration had led to an increase in agrarian violence and to his lioni-sation by the irreconcilable wing of the national movement. Neither was a desirable or intended outcome for the Gladstone government. Whether or not he could turn off the tap of violence was immaterial. No one else could. So it was time Parnell was put back to work. The principal diffi-culty was that the government could hardly be seen to negotiate directly with, or even sound out, an inmate in one of Her Majesty's Prisons. All the more so when discussions with Parnell were unlikely to have the approval of the Chief Secretary or the Lord Lieutenant. Some form of discreet and reliable intermediary was required.

Over the period of Parnell's imprisonment a number of potential mediators came and went. The O'Gorman Mahon was the first. He visited Parnell in Kilmainham and was used by the prisoners to negotiate terms on a number of practical issues. These included Parnell's efforts to secure the releases of Dillon, Kettle and O'Kelly (Sexton was released on the grounds of ill health).[33] Mahon even went so far as to approach the Radical leader and Cabinet member, Joseph Chamberlain (President of the Board of Trade), and seek clemency for Parnell on the basis of a guarantee of good behaviour. When Chamberlain inquired as to what was the nature of the guarantee, the delightfully eccentric Clare MP responded, 'By God, if he doesn't behave, sir, I will shoot him.'[34]

Herbert Gladstone became peripherally involved in the process when he was approached by Frank Hugh O'Donnell, whom he described in his diary for 22 April 1882 as 'a Parnellite freelance, a man of conspicuous cleverness, with tongue and pen of vitriol.'[35] O'Donnell's message was that the Land Act was working and if an arrears measure were to be introduced by way of amendment the Act would be wholly successful. The word from Kilmainham was that Parnell had been shocked by the level of agrarian violence and that the Land League was looking for an excuse to withdraw the No Rent Manifesto. On the basis of the conversation Gladstone sent a memo to Forster. It was discussed at a Cabinet meeting the same day and afterwards the Prime Minister's son was approached by Joseph Chamberlain for more information. His interest in the matter, far removed from his own political bailiwick, was that he himself was in the midst of a backstairs negotiation with someone he told Gladstone was 'more to be trusted than O'Donnell.' That person was the indefatigable William Henry O'Shea.

O'Shea had been far from sated, or indeed discouraged, by his abortive attempt at mediation over the Land Bill the previous June. If anything, that failed compromise had given him a taste for the shadows where real political power is exercised. On 8 April, blissfully unaware of the coincidence of events that were about to propel him from relative obscurity, O'Shea chanced his luck with a letter to the Prime Minister. Admitting that the communication was entirely at his own initiative he, almost sentimentally, took the GOM back to the days of his own contribution to the white noise of the greater Land Bill debate. He inquired whether the Prime Minister had ever considered reverting 'to the compromise which I proposed to you last year. Judged by the only true light – the light of subsequent events – my estimate of the forces was correct, and the bargain offered wonderfully easy.' He suggested that 'terms might still be possible' before concluding with a challenge designed to pique Gladstone's vanity. 'Last year all that was needful could have been done as a mere matter of detail. To "save the situation" now, great audacity would be required but great audacity has often proved to be great statesmanship.'[36]

Were it not for an unexpected tragedy the letter and its implications might have become little more than an archival curiosity. Two days later Parnell was released on parole to travel to Paris where his sister Delia's son had died of typhus. The good ship Compromise was about to break free of the doldrums. O'Shea, like his celebrated brother-in-law, was its ambitious midshipman.

Gladstone's initial response to O'Shea's overture was similar to the conclusion of the démarche of the previous June. He reread the correspondence and indicated that he had no wish to reopen that particular Pandora's box.[37] There the matter might have rested had Parnell not arrived in London and felt the need to include O'Shea in the loop. In order to justify his first port of call, Eltham, he may have felt obliged to visit O'Shea in his London residence at Albert Mansions, near Victoria Station. This gave O'Shea the traction he needed to widen the scope of his initiative.

His reply to Gladstone on 13 April assured the Prime Minister that he had no wish to exhume the June 1881 proposals, although 'there was no detail of my proposal to which I had not previously obtained Mr Parnell's assent ...' He then chided Gladstone for having ignored his initiative the previous year before adding that '... At the eleventh hour, and even under the aggravated circumstances, I believe that the pacification of Ireland is by no means so difficult as it appears to be. But you must pay for it, and you must cease to ignore an important Irishman.'[38]

O'Shea then went into self-aggrandising overdrive. He made the utterly outlandish claim that 'The person to whom Mr Parnell addresses himself in many cases (much as I differ from him in serious matters of politics and policy) is myself. He considers, I believe, that I am not without insight into Irish affairs, necessities and possibilities, and he knows that no Member of Parliament has nearly so much influence with the clergy of the county that member represents, as I have attained.' Not content with an appetiser, which the Prime Minister must have found a little hard to swallow, he then offered an astonishing soufflé as dessert. 'Eighteen months ago', he claimed, 'Mr Parnell used every effort to induce me to take over the leadership of the Party. I mention these things (the last one is known only to two or three besides ourselves) as an explanation of what would otherwise appear to be fatuous officiousness.' His worst detractor could not have phrased it more aptly. It was one of the more fatuous claims made by O'Shea in a career peppered with examples of extreme fatuity.

However, despite past setbacks, O'Shea represented himself as a man of Job-like patience: '... I will try to mediate again. This time of course Mr Parnell has no part in the initiative.' After the lengthy self-regarding preamble O'Shea eventually got to the meat of his proposal. It was hardly new but it displayed a degree of common sense and practicality not in evidence elsewhere in the letter. Essentially O'Shea was suggesting – and the implication was that this emanated from his conversation with Parnell on 11 April – that a deal was possible. 'I believe that moral support of great power might be enlisted to aid you actively against agrarian outrage, and that effectual steps might be taken to hasten the acquiescence of the tenants in the spirit of the Land Act.' In return he urged the government to deal with rent arrears; in essence to fund the deficit between the 100,000 tenants in arrears and their landlords. 'Here you must give, not lend ... the proportion falling on the public[39] must be a grant, not a loan. The land must be left free from charge. Otherwise you will never hear the end of it, and far better leave the landlords and tenants to fight it out now, than to carry on a running fire for years.'[40]

Again it was a letter that could probably have been safely ignored by 10 Downing Street given that it emanated from a source that was hardly in good standing with the bulk of the Irish Party. However, the invocation of the name of Parnell, and the assumption that, despite O'Shea's disclaimer, the Irish party leader endorsed the sentiments expressed, elevated the initiative to a different plane entirely.

Within two days O'Shea had his prize: a response from Gladstone indicating that he should proceed with his efforts. 'I am very sensible', the Prime Minister wrote, 'of the spirit in which you write and I think you assume the existence of a spirit on my part with which you can sympathize ... the end in view is of vast moment and your letter is not the first favourable sign I have observed. Assuredly no resentment or personal prejudice, or false shame, or other impediment extraneous to the matter itself will prevent the government from treading whatever path may most safely and shortly lead to the pacification of Ireland ...'[41] The Prime Minister expressed misgivings as to whether a compact could be achieved but his instructions to O'Shea were clear – proceed with caution.

Gladstone's flexibility and sense of the possible is clear from his assurance that no predisposition to mistrust would be allowed to jeopardise any accommodation. A less forbearing but more typical approach was adopted by his secretary, Edward Hamilton, in his diary of 16 April. He writes with barely concealed contempt about the approach from O'Shea, and his tone suggests that he considers the mediator to be displaying a personal effrontery and the Irish party to be guilty of political impudence. 'His principal terms', he describes O'Shea's proposal irritably, 'are (1) a settlement of arrears by a *grant* and (2) an extension of the purchase clauses. In return for this, the Parnellites to exercise all their moral power to stop outrages (as if they were not bound to do so now in any case) and to cease all parliamentary opposition. It may be as well to know what the views of the Irish party are; but it seems impossible to have any direct dealings with them. They are probably not the least to be trusted. I expect O'Shea himself is, though a gentleman by birth and a brother-in-law of Sir E Wood, not of the "straightest".'[42] Fortunately Hamilton was not Prime Minister.

Gladstone forwarded O'Shea's letter to Forster, who was equally dismissive. On 18 April he replied to the Prime Minister, 'I return O'Shea's letter, he is a clever fellow but vain and untrustworthy. ... I do not believe he has the influence either with Parnell or the priests which he claims.'[43] He could be forgiven for making such an assumption but, as it transpired, he was as mistaken in his evaluation of O'Shea's influence as he was in his one-trick policy of continued intensification of the coercion regime.

As if on cue, although completely unaware of the Chief Secretary's resistance, O'Shea had begun the process of negating Forster's influence by making an approach to one of his most poisonous adversaries in the Cabinet, Joseph Chamberlain. The self-made businessman from Birmingham was, along with Sir Charles Dilke, the recognised leader within the radical, left-wing faction of the Liberal party. He was intensely ambitious, an inspired political organiser and had created an alternative power base for himself within the party through the National Liberal Federation in 1877. He was also part of a growing cabal against Forster in the Cabinet. One of his biographers, Peter T. Marsh, is sceptical about his sudden interest in Ireland. 'Chamberlain's intrusion into the domain of the man he so obviously despised deepened the suspicion that personal motives were at work.'[44] Dilke too was in no doubt about Chamberlain's motivation for getting involved in an issue far from his area of competence: 'Chamberlain will of course have but one object – i.e. to damn Forster. He always cared more about damning Forster than about anything else at all.'[45]

He had certainly exhibited, privately at least, little enough radical sympathy for the arrested Irish party leaders. Less than a week after the imprisonment of Parnell he was writing to fellow Radical John Morley, then editor of the *Pall Mall Gazette*, that 'It is ... war to the knife between a despotism created to re-establish constitutional law, and a despotism not less complete, elaborated to subvert law and produce anarchy as a precedent to revolutionary changes. If this be so what is the use of criticising in detail the means adopted? Coercion in any form is hateful to us, but coercion with a silk glove would be ridiculous. Why are we to be shocked at each new exercise of authority...'[46] Coincidentally, in the same letter he announced his total opposition to 'national independence' for Ireland.

So there was a happy coincidence of ulterior motives and ambitions involved in the collaboration of O'Shea and Chamberlain, which began when O'Shea forwarded to the President of the Board of Trade a copy of his letter to Gladstone accompanied by another 'I told you so' for the temerity of the administration in ignoring his June 1881 proposals. In seeking Chamberlain's support he concluded by pointing out that:

> I have myself good reason to dislike the Land League because it has touched me in the vital part, the pocket. But in my little way I have had sufficient nous to compromise with the inevitable. I lose, but not so much as I might. There is no use in bewailings, scoldings and perorations. You have to deal with men and things as they are and although time

and many hateful incidents have aggravated the difficulties, still I believe that it might be to the advantage of the Liberal party if its leaders were to try to compromise honourably and that such an effort might be met [by the most influential Irishman of the day][47] in a candid and moderate spirit.[48]

Chamberlain's response, though not entirely fulsome, was sufficiently positive to have encouraged O'Shea. Like the 'poor cat in the adage' Chamberlain's 'I Will' ('I think I may say that there appears to me nothing in your proposals which does not deserve consideration and which might not be the basis of subsequent agreement') was tempered by his 'I Dare Not' ('I am not in a position, as you will readily understand, to write you fully on the subject'). His reservations when it came to demarcation did not extend to diplomacy, at least where the Irish party and its powers of alienation were concerned: '... the Irish members have acted as if their object were to disgust, embitter, and prejudice all English opinion against the cause to which they have pledged themselves.'[49]

O'Shea was up and running. Incalculable rewards beckoned for this place seeker *par excellence*. Within 24 hours he had informed Gladstone and Chamberlain that he had spoken to Parnell whom he quoted as hoping that '... something may come out of the correspondence and certainly the prospect looks favourable.'[50] He sought, and obtained, their permission to forward their letters to Parnell. Gladstone – who was already looking forward to the impending, but as yet unannounced, 'retirement' of the Lord Lieutenant, Lord Cowper – was, in conjunction with Chamberlain, now set to undermine the position of a tired, disillusioned but principled and determined Forster. The Chief Secretary was intent on retaining the Land League leaders as virtual hostages. Their release would only come about in the event of a diminution in the levels of outrage or Cabinet agreement to the granting of additional police powers. Either development would render their continued detention unnecessary. 'Without the fulfilment of one or other of these conditions,' he told Gladstone, 'I believe their release would make matters worse than they are.'[51]

In point of fact Forster was only prepared to countenance the release of Parnell, in particular, if the latter went abroad and remained there for an indeterminate period of time.[52] The day after writing the letter Forster left Dublin for an important Cabinet meeting in London on 22 April. He was unaware of it at the time but a last-minute change of plan, which saw him leaving early to catch the boat-train from Westland Row station, may well have saved his life. Waiting to murder the Chief Secretary were members of a new and ruthless secret society, known to themselves as The

Invincibles. That Cabinet meeting was to betoken the endgame in the chess match for the Chief Secretary. It was agreed by ministers that Chamberlain was to pursue the back-channel negotiations with O'Shea. Herbert Gladstone's news of the approach from O'Donnell had helped the right Honourable gentlemen make up their minds that the time for compromise might be approaching. But Chamberlain was on his own. Sir Charles Dilke recorded in his diary that he was 'to be disavowed if he failed.'[53]

Parnell had returned from Paris on 19 April and gone straight to Eltham. Perhaps it was depression brought on by the imminent death of his first child or, more likely, the sombre air of his sister's household, but his letters to Katharine from the French capital are hypochondriacal and self-obsessed. On his return to Eltham he telegraphed O'Shea, who arrived at Wonersh Lodge on 21 April. According to Katharine, 'he wished to conciliate Willie as much as possible, and believed that his politics might now prove useful.'[54] In a desperately poignant image she describes the two men, her estranged husband and her lover, sitting downstairs in her dining-room working through the details of the arrangement that would become the Kilmainham Treaty, while she remained upstairs nursing the dying child both men thought to be theirs.[55] While the deal that would secure Parnell's release (though he insisted that was not a precondition) was being formulated, his first child died of obstructive jaundice.

Despite his belief that the deceased child was his, O'Shea did not let grief or mourning get in the way of ambition. On 22 April he met with Chamberlain and outlined what had been discussed with Parnell the previous night. The result was the compilation of a memorandum by Chamberlain, based on O'Shea's report, which, with some alterations, additions and refinements, would become the template for the settlement of long-outstanding grievances between the Irish party and the Liberal government. The memo read:

> If the Government announce a satisfactory plan of dealing with arrears, Mr Parnell will advise all tenants to pay rents and will denounce outrages, resistance to law and all processes of intimidation whether by Boycotting or in any other way.
>
> No plan of dealing with arrears will be satisfactory which does not wipe them off compulsorily by a composition – one third payable by tenant, one third by the State – from the Church Fund or some other source – and one third remitted by the landlord, but so that the contribution by the tenant and the State shall not exceed one year's rent each – the

balance, if any, to be remitted by the landlord. Arrears to be defined as arrears accruing up to May 1 1881.[56]

The intention of Parnell was that the government would move quickly on the arrears issue along the lines of a bill, sponsored by the Irish party, then going through the House.[57] His intention also was to remove O'Shea from the equation. Whether he had thought better of the Captain's role in the negotiations, based on their conversation of 21 April, or whether he had only involved him in the first place to gain unproblematic access to Eltham at an extraordinarily difficult time, is uncertain. But on 22 April he had sought a meeting with Justin McCarthy. The two men had met the following day, and Parnell had apprised his lieutenant of his thinking and authorised McCarthy to make contact with Chamberlain. He had then returned to Kilmainham on 24 April to await developments.

On 25 April he sent McCarthy a memo that he was allowed to show to Chamberlain, but which the latter would not be permitted to retain. It required a resolution of the arrears question in return for a rescission of the No Rent Manifesto. In addition, relief for leaseholders was sought, as well as an extension of the underdeveloped purchase clauses of the 1881 Act. 'If the result of the arrears settlement and the further ameliorative measures suggested above were the material diminution of outrage before the end of the session ... we should hope that the government would allow the Coercion Act to lapse and govern the country by the same laws as in England.'[58] The final sentence is significant as an indicator that O'Shea might already have exceeded his brief. In his enthusiasm to broker an agreement he had given Chamberlain and Dilke the impression that Parnell would either favour or not oppose a modified Coercion Bill.[59]

It is clear from a letter sent by O'Shea to Parnell on 24 April that the go-between had outlived his usefulness and was beginning to suspect that to be the case. He had hoped to see Parnell at Albert Mansions the previous day and had waited for the Irish leader to arrive. Giving up the ghost at 8.00 pm he had returned to Eltham, by which time the Irish leader was safely on his way back to Dublin having passed the chalice to Justin McCarthy. In the O'Shea papers in the National Library of Ireland this particular letter is prefaced with an explanatory note from O'Shea to the effect that it was '... written because certain ministers objected that there was no proof to bind Parnell to my statements and with the intention of ... getting an expression of confidence from Kilmainham'. In fact it sought some form of repudiation of McCarthy by Parnell and an assertion from the party leader that he still had faith in O'Shea. 'Mr

Chamberlain asked me', the Captain chided, 'if I was aware that another Irish member had made advances to the Government, I replied that if so, it was without your knowledge or authority ...' He concluded by pointing out that certain colleagues of Chamberlain's, sceptical in the extreme, wanted proof that O'Shea was, in reality, Parnell's plenipotentiary. Accordingly Chamberlain had 'suggested that you [Parnell] should write me a note to the effect that you are glad to have had the opportunity lately of conversing fully and freely with me, and that I have your confidence.'[60] Meanwhile, O'Shea continued his correspondence with Chamberlain as if nothing was amiss. The memo of 22 April was elaborated upon and refined. He was not going to be removed from the loop without a fight.

Parnell, perplexed by O'Shea's unexpected persistence, turned to Katharine. Sending a copy of O'Shea's letter he asked plaintively, 'What do you think I had best say to it? ... I told my friend in Jermyn Street[61] what steps to take, so that the matter referred to in enclosed will probably go on all right without, or with, the further participation of the writer.'[62] But Parnell underestimated the Captain's ability to make himself appear indispensable. Even on the day of the burial of Claude Sophie, O'Shea was in communication with his invaluable ally, Chamberlain, over an obscure argument related to the assessment of arrears.

On the day after the funeral (26 April), the Private Member's Bill being piloted through the House by the Irish party members came up for discussion. Gladstone took the opportunity to make a commitment to deal with the arrears issue while rejecting the Bill itself. O'Shea rose to applaud the Prime Minister and, simultaneously, reproach his *bête noir* Clifford Lloyd, saying that the arrears announcement 'would do more for the pacification of the country than any number of superior Resident Magistrates or police.' He then made a further plea for leaseholders. He noted that 'Nothing had tended more to unfortunate dissension and to greater crime in certain localities with which he was acquainted than the omission of leaseholders from the operation of the Bill.' Leaseholders had seen others benefit from the terms of the Land Act and 'It was extremely mortifying to them and it had created a sense of injustice in their minds that had led to horrible crimes.'[63]

Later that day he wrote, once again, to Parnell in Kilmainham. His sales pitch was simple. Gladstone had been reeled in. 'In my judgement,' he wrote, 'Mr Gladstone's statement contained what was tantamount to a promise to deal immediately with the burning question of arrears.'[64] Three days later he followed up the letter by arriving, uninvited and unwanted, at Kilmainham in person.

In the absence of any letter of comfort from Parnell, conscious that Chamberlain was still dallying with McCarthy and anxious to avoid being left at the altar, O'Shea had sought permission from Forster to meet Parnell. The caustic Chief Secretary had actually been agreeably surprised by some of the communications (from O'Shea) that Chamberlain had shown him. But now he wanted something directly from the horse's mouth. He willingly granted leave to O'Shea to visit Parnell. Though in writing to Gladstone on the day of the Kilmainham meeting he did not express much hope for a positive outcome: 'It is possible', he wrote, 'that O'Shea may bring back from Dublin a declaration by Parnell which may be published that he will not in future aid or abet intimidation ... I do not myself expect this.' Even if O'Shea was successful, Forster was still opposed to the release of his Honourable Friend, the Member for Cork. 'We cannot release these men without wakening forces in Ireland to an extent which I do not believe to be safe.'[65]

According to Katharine O'Shea, her husband was making the journey 'as he said Parnell was "so shifty" he could not be trusted to carry out any agreement that was not in writing.' In fact agreement was virtually inevitable. Parnell at large was now of far greater use to the administration than Parnell in jail. McCarthy and Chamberlain, left to their own devices, would have nailed down an agreement within days. But O'Shea was not going to see the prize snatched from his grasp, hence his display of bloody-minded determination. No one other than he was going to broker the deal that would end the Land War.[66] Despite a letter from Parnell designed to put him off ('If you come to Ireland, I think you had best not see me ...'[67]) he was going to finish what he had started.

He spent a good part of the day (six hours in total) in discussion with Parnell and, eventually, came away with his trophy. No one other than the two men knew what transpired. There have been varying accounts, for example, as to whether or not Parnell consulted in any way with his lieutenants in Kilmainham. But O'Shea emerged from the prison with a detailed letter from Parnell outlining definitively what he sought and what he had to offer in return. It is one of the seminal documents of the Land War and is worth reproducing in full. Although composed (in blue pencil on black lined paper)[68] on the 29 April it is dated the previous day. This was, presumably, with some thought of being able to claim, should the need arise, that it had actually been written before the meeting in Parnell's cell. O'Shea, the conspirator, would have been focused on just such minutiae.

Kilmainham's most celebrated prisoner wrote:

> I was very sorry that you had left Albert Mansions before I reached London from Eltham as I had wished to tell you that after our conversation I had made up my mind that it would

be proper for me to put Mr McCarthy in possession of the views which I had previously communicated to you.

I desire to impress upon you the absolute necessity of a settlement of the arrears question which will leave no recurring sore connected with them behind and which will enable us to show the smaller tenantry that they have been treated with justice and some generosity.

The proposal you have described to me as suggested in some quarters, of making a loan, over however many years the repayment might be spread, should be absolutely rejected, for reasons which I have already fully explained to you. If the arrears question be settled upon the lines indicated by us, I have every confidence – a confidence shared by my colleagues – that the exertions that we should be able to make strenuously and unremittingly would be effective in stopping outrages & intimidation of all kinds.

As regards permanent legislation of an ameliorative character, I may say that the views which you always shared with me as to the admission of leaseholders to the Fair Rent clauses of the Act, are more confirmed than ever. So long as the flower of the Irish peasantry are kept outside the Act there cannot be the permanent settlement of the Land question which we all so much desire. I should also strongly hope that some compromise might be arrived at this session with regard to the amendment of the tenure clauses. It is unnecessary for me to dwell upon the enormous advantage to be derived from the full extension of the purchase clauses which now seem practically to have been adopted by all parties.

The accomplishment of the programme I have sketched out to you wd [sic] in my judgement be regarded by the country as a practical settlement of the Land question and would enable us to co-operate cordially for the future with the Liberal party in forwarding Liberal principles and measures of general reform. And I believe that the Government at the end of the Session would, from the state of the country, feel themselves thoroughly justified in dispensing with future coercive measures.

Yours very truly,

C.S. Parnell[69]

The following day Parnell explained to Katharine that 'He came over to see me, so I thought it best to give him a letter, as he would have been dreadfully mortified if he had nothing to show.'[70] What he had to show was little different from what McCarthy had already shown Chamberlain, with one obvious exception. In his memo to McCarthy, enclosed in the 25 April letter, there had been no reference to détente with the Liberals. The stated desire to 'co-operate cordially' would be regretted cordially by Parnell in the weeks to come, but what had prompted its inclusion? Obviously the Captain had played some part in this extraordinary démarche. Paul Bew has no doubt that it was diabolical in nature. His contention is that O'Shea bludgeoned Parnell into adding the reference to a Liberal alliance because he required a titbit that McCarthy could not offer. 'It seems likely that O'Shea was only able to get such a result by means of compulsion. O'Shea had only one method of getting Parnell to do anything – blackmail. O'Shea may well have given Parnell the alternative of the exposure of his relationship with Mrs O'Shea.'[71]

The controversial British Conservative politician Enoch Powell concurs. In an article in the *Historical Journal* of 1978, Powell insists that Parnell was compelled to insert the phrase and did so only on the basis that the letter would be seen by Chamberlain alone and never published.[72] As we will see, O'Shea reneged on this guarantee, to the subsequent embarrassment of Parnell and, justly, of himself. The letter was taken to Forster as soon as he returned from Ireland. Powell goes on to claim, however, that O'Shea was even more devious than he is given credit for. He was also in the process of double-crossing Chamberlain in that the copy of the Parnell 28 April letter sent to the President of the Board of Trade did not include the 'offending paragraph'. This, the gold medal version, was for the eyes of the Chief Secretary and Prime Minister only.[73] Although he does not make such a citation himself, there is some support for his contention in the O'Shea manuscripts in the National Library of Ireland. There are two copies of Parnell's original, in O'Shea's handwriting, from one of which the relevant paragraph has been excised. So the Captain was toying with different versions. However, this theory is not supported by Chamberlain's own political memoir. Here, an O'Shea letter is reproduced from 1 May 1882 and is accompanied by an enclosure of a copy of Parnell's 28 April letter. It includes the reference to the Liberal alliance.[74] So whatever else O'Shea was trying to do, and whatever he might have said to Parnell in order to achieve his end, he was not trying to betray Chamberlain.

Had Chamberlain chosen to 'betray' O'Shea, however, a lot of mischief might have been avoided, as we shall see. According to the influential historian J.L. Hammond, in his *Gladstone and the Irish Nation*, it was

Chamberlain who had suggested to O'Shea that he extract a formula from Parnell in writing. Just as the Captain wanted something concrete to show for his efforts, so did the Radical leader. Chamberlain had also developed a personal affinity with the plausible former Hussar. As Hammond puts it, 'He had taken his pretensions and assurances at their face value, and, like many Englishmen, he found O'Shea an agreeable person, with the kind of Irish temperament that impresses Englishmen more than Irishmen.'[75]

Ironically, had he waited for 24 hours, he would have had his documentary evidence of Parnell's intentions. It was only when O'Shea was already on his way to Dublin that McCarthy showed the manuscript in his possession to Chamberlain. This version could just as easily have been presented to the grateful Cabinet by a triumphant Chamberlain as the later O'Shea version. And its source was a far more reliable plenipotentiary. But once O'Shea hit pay dirt, the whooping and hollering began in earnest. Rather like a child showing off his certificate of cycling proficiency, O'Shea was anxious that the command structure of the Liberal party should be forced to admire his handiwork. His first port of call was, surprisingly, not Chamberlain but the Chief Secretary himself. Perhaps he feared that were he to simply hand over the Parnell letter to Chamberlain it would be somehow merged with the McCarthy initiative and the credit for breaking the impasse would be shared. He wanted sole possession of the Kilmainham trophy.[76]

He called at Forster's residence bright and early on the morning of Sunday 30 April. Florence Arnold-Forster's diary records the domestic aspect of the visit. 'As usual on a Sunday, Father was not left long undisturbed. Before we had finished breakfast, Mr O'Shea arrived, and Father was called off to interview him in the library. 'An ambassador from Mr Parnell?' I ask when Father had left the room. 'Yes,' says Mother, 'I can't say how much I hate him having any negotiations with them.'[77] Forster's wife would be pressed urgently into service by her husband after O'Shea's departure as he hurriedly dictated a memo of the extraordinary interview.

After reading the letter the Chief Secretary had, whether by predisposition or genuine disappointment, professed his surprise that O'Shea had not extracted a better bargain from Parnell. He later described the olive branch to Gladstone as being 'less even than I expected.' He made the same point to O'Shea.

'Is that all, do you think, that Mr Parnell would be inclined to say?' Forster had asked disparagingly.

'What more do you want?' was O'Shea's initial, and quite reasonable, response. He made the fatal error, however, of then blurting out, 'Doubtless I could supplement it.'

Forster analysed the gist of the document wearily. 'It comes to this: that upon our doing certain things, he will help us to prevent outrages.'

O'Shea, now completely taken aback by the unenthusiastic response to his treasured prize, repeated, 'How can I supplement it?' Forster left him none the wiser, merely observing coolly that he would pass the letter on to Gladstone.

While O'Shea would have been delighted to hear that his letter was to be presented to the Prime Minister uncontaminated with any supplementary missives sourced through McCarthy, he was clearly concerned that Gladstone might share Forster's indifference. He began to trip over himself in justifying and enhancing the significance of the letter.

'Well there may be fault in expression,' he added unnecessarily, 'but the thing is done. If these words will not do, I must get others, but what is obtained is that the conspiracy which has been used to get up boycotting and outrages will now be used to put them down, and that there will be reunion with the Liberal party.'

Forster described them as 'remarkable words', and indeed they were. O'Shea had, in a single sentence, justified, not the Parnell letter, but the thrust of Forster's aggressive policy which identified the Land League as the source of agrarian crime and responded accordingly.[78] The Clare MP had linked the Irish nationalist political establishment to an organised conspiracy to provoke mayhem and violence. Subsequently O'Shea would deny the use of the word 'conspiracy', claiming that he had employed the phrase 'organisation', but the damage had been done. Rather than correct what could still be dismissed as a mere solecism, he went on to aggravate the damage.

According to Forster, as an earnest of his good intentions O'Shea then added that '... Parnell hoped to make use of Sheridan, and get him back from abroad as he would be able to put down the conspiracy (or "agitation" – I am not sure which word was used) as he knew all its details in the west.' The 'Sheridan' in question was P.J. Sheridan, a Fenian, a Land League organiser and a committed agitator for whom the RIC had been searching for some time. Forster was familiar with his record of legally dubious activity and the very mention of his name sealed the case as far as the Chief Secretary was concerned. In his memo to Gladstone he explained that, from his point of view, '... Sheridan is a released suspect, against whom for some time we have had a fresh warrant; and who, under disguises, has hitherto eluded the Police, coming backwards and forwards from Egan to the outrage-mongers in the west ...'[79]

By 11.00 am Forster had dispatched his memo to Gladstone and had begun to contemplate retirement. He was realistic enough to know that he was in a minority of one in the Cabinet in his opposition to the release of Parnell. He told his daughter that day '... that he should in all probability be out of Office on Tuesday night. Mr Parnell's offers – as made through Mr O'Shea – he thinks are worth nothing, but of course the document has been sent down to Mr Gladstone. "I wonder what he will think of what I have sent him?"'[80]

Gladstone thought very highly of it indeed. In his recounting of the meeting and his report to the Prime Minister, Forster, whose focus was elsewhere, ignored the offer of an Anglo-Irish Liberal alliance. But when Gladstone got hold of the actual letter that was the element upon which he immediately pounced. He took a much more sanguine view of the document and its implications. He recognised that, although Parnell had stressed the need for the resolution of issues other than arrears, they were not inserted as preconditions to an agreement. The 'deal' was straightforward enough. Tackle the arrears question and the No Rent Manifesto would be withdrawn; peace would be restored as a direct consequence of the palliative efforts of the Irish leadership.

Gladstone expressed surprise at Forster's pessimism. 'I own myself at a loss', he wrote, 'to gather your meaning when you say, "the result of his visit to Parnell is less even than I expected."' The Prime Minister then got to the nub of the matter as far as he was concerned. 'He then proceeds to throw in his indication or promise of future co-operation with the Liberal Party. This is an hors d'oeuvre which we had no right to expect, and, I rather think have no right at present to accept.' He then added an hors d'œuvre of his own for O'Shea and a putrid appetiser for Parnell when he concluded, '... On the whole Parnell's letter is, I think, the most extraordinary I ever read. I cannot help feeling indebted to O'Shea.'[81]

Late that night, having read Gladstone's eager response, Forster was drily downbeat with his daughter.

'Mr Parnell agrees ... that if we pass an Arrears bill he will undertake to do all he can to stop outrages. O'Shea considers the affair as good as settled.'

'But is Mr Gladstone impressed with this?' she had asked.

'Oh, Gladstone is delighted – he only thinks it's too good to be true.'

'He had better get Mr Parnell to take your place ...'

'Well that is rather the line of his ideas at present,' was the Chief Secretary's mordant response.[82]

Two days later, the instruction was issued to a reluctant Lord Lieutenant, Lord Cowper (who had himself resigned on 28 April and was awaiting the arrival of his replacement), to proceed with the release of Parnell, Dillon and O'Kelly from Kilmainham. O'Shea, ever the constituency politician, telegraphed his Clare base with the good news.[83] With the release of the MPs and a public hint from Gladstone that the Coercion Bill would be allowed to lapse, Forster bowed to the inevitable and quit his post. It was a huge relief while also being something of a personal tragedy for Forster. Years later Justin McCarthy would describe him as 'a good man gone wrong'. Charitably, the Irish MP acknowledged that the Quaker politician had 'meant well for Ireland ... and yet his administration seemed only to make things worse and not better day after day. The best conclusion at which I could or can arrive was that Mr Forster must have become disappointed with Ireland even before Ireland had become disappointed with him.'[84]

Edward Hamilton confided to his diary that Forster had timed his departure well. 'Instead of being considered a failure, he retires now in a halo of conservative glory and carries with him a very general feeling of sympathy. It is perhaps unkind to say so, but his vanity, which I think is undoubted, may have had something to do with his availing himself of this favourable opportunity of relinquishing a thankless post.'[85]

The political hara-kiri of 'Buckshot' Forster was a consummation devoutly sought by Parnell, but to his chagrin it was the Captain who had prevailed in helping to bring it about. In the eyes of the Liberal elite, and of the man himself, the concordat was his creation. It was his ill luck that the garment he had doggedly woven was unpicked less than a week later with the emergence from obscurity of the Invincibles and their date with destiny in Phoenix Park.

CHAPTER 6
Mayhem

A FEMALE is at the bottom of every conspiracy. Look for
the woman in the Kilmainham Treaty Mystery, and you will
find her in O'SHEA!

Punch, 27 May 1882

THE PHOENIX PARK MURDERS

The first issue in the wake of Forster's resignation was the succession.
Earl Spencer was already bound for a return to the Viceregal Lodge.
In his case the job carried a Cabinet position. This made it moot whether
the Chief Secretaryship would be of similar status. Chamberlain was the
popular favourite for the poisoned chalice. He was seen as the right man
to carry out Gladstone's moderated policy. Certainly his new acolyte,
conscious of the possibility of a reward for his own good offices, was keen
that he move from the Board of Trade to Dublin Castle. Hearing rumours
that Chamberlain was having doubts about accepting the position (which,
at that point, had not even been offered), O'Shea wrote to him urging him
to take it. 'I hasten to assure you', he ventured, depicting himself as
Parnell's chosen representative on Earth, 'that if you accept it, it will be a
point of honour with Mr Parnell to work as if for himself to secure the
success of your administration.'[1]

Chamberlain's response to this maladroit and transparent approach was disappointing. 'Many thanks for all your kindness. At present no offer has been made to me *and I sincerely hope it never will be*. I should like to see an Irishman in the post and I intend to put this view to Mr Gladstone.'[2] O'Shea might have been thoroughly delighted at the notion had the 'Irishman' in question been himself. But the name being touted was that of the former Irish party leader and Liberal ally, William Shaw. He moved to crush the Cork banker's phantom candidacy before it gained traction.

'Your note has greatly disappointed me.' he responded. 'Circumstances are not ripe for an Irishman. Shaw is at present a political cripple. Possibly, in good time he may be reset. But he has unfortunately spoken at various times of Parnell in such terms that the latter will not forgive the appointment at present.'[3] The implication was that Parnell had some sort of unstated veto over the appointing of an Irish candidate to the post. The idea may have been unpalatable to Chamberlain but, in reality, it was probably close to the truth. As regards Shaw the other insuperable reality was neatly expressed by Dilke in his diary when he observed that Shaw was practical enough to realise that, in the by-election that would follow his appointment,[4] he would be unlikely to get sufficient voters in Cork to return him to Westminster.[5]

Not content with taking the chance that such a disqualifying mark would influence Gladstone's final decision, O'Shea took it upon himself to write to the Prime Minister and canvass for Chamberlain. He began in his most servile yet simultaneously conceited manner, 'My Dear Sir, I am astonished at my audacity in writing to you', he opened, 'but having insight into so many details of Irish affairs, political and personal, at the present moment, I must risk being misunderstood.' He repeated his evisceration of Shaw, added a few thrusts against another rumoured candidate, the Radical Shaw Lefevre, before concluding, with breathtaking pomposity and impudence, 'If Mr Chamberlain goes to Ireland I can undertake that Mr Parnell will work for his success as heartily as if he were working for himself.'[6]

A head of steam was building up behind Chamberlain, but Gladstone had, it would appear, no inclination to promote the Radical leader. Hamilton professed to be mystified at the notion, '... unless as seems probable Chamberlain gave out himself that he would be ready to accept the offer, were it made to him. Mr G., I believe, hardly for a moment ever contemplated the idea.'[7] Had he done so he might, according to Florence Arnold-Forster, have had the blessing of the previous incumbent whose supporters were 'anxious to see him [Chamberlain] accept the post much in the same spirit ... in which they would like to watch him handle a red-hot poker.'[8]

Whether or not Chamberlain had actively sought the position, he seems to have been seduced by the public clamour that the job should be his. Dilke wrote in his diary on 3 May that 'Chamberlain, who had decided to take the Irish secretaryship if offered to him, was astonished at having received no offer.' After dithering for two days and being turned down by potential candidates, Gladstone looked to the young, largely untested, Lord Frederick Cavendish. In making the appointment he laid himself open to a charge of double partiality.[9] Cavendish was married to his niece and was the brother of the powerful Whig leader, Lord Hartington, in many ways Chamberlain's Liberal party alter ego. The passing over of Chamberlain was, according to Tim Healy, a mistake on Gladstone's part. Ireland became part of the collateral damage of Chamberlain's pique. 'A permanent estrangement now began with Gladstone', Healy wrote, 'who wanted to rivet to his side the Marquis of Hartington ... Perhaps, too, Lord Spencer preferred an aristocrat to a commoner in the post, but the letting down of Chamberlain meant misfortune to Ireland.'[10]

In his resignation speech to the House of Commons on 4 May 1882 Forster was as dignified as it was possible to be in the face of a number of, probably contrived and certainly theatrical, entrances of former detainees, made while he spoke. On a potentially difficult day for her own father, Mary Gladstone watched from the gallery as Forster addressed the chamber, 'He was nervous and not wise and suspects came in at various times, Dillon looking deathly, O'Kelly fat and jolly ...'[11] Gladstone must have had some concern that, should Forster choose to be vindictive, he might well reveal something at least of the machinations of the previous week. As far as Forster's own daughter was concerned there was never any danger of that. She had written in her diary for 3 May, the eve of Forster's statement, that 'as long as the matter is in Father's keeping the Government is safe.'[12]

Parnell, consciously and deliberately, or with the Napoleonic luck that finally abandoned him in late 1890, contrived to enter just as the former Chief Secretary intoned the words 'the honourable Member for Cork'. Forster's subsequent remarks were drowned out in a cacophony of welcome from his Irish party colleagues.

The set pieces in the House that day were an exercise in damage limitation. Both the government and the Parnellites had a vested interest in denying that any deal had been done to secure the release of the 'suspects'. The government risked being castigated for caving in to a policy of agrarian terror, while the Irish leader had no desire to leave himself open to the charge from the left of having sold out the Land League, lease-holders, labourers and tenants in arrears in order to exit Kilmainham and cosy up to the Liberals.

Watching her adoptive father in action, the intensely loyal Florence Arnold-Forster was conscious that 'The idea of an "arrangement" in which Mr Gladstone, Mr Parnell and Mr O'Shea were all mixed up, had got possession of the Conservatives, and once or twice in the course of the evening they came dangerously near the truth.'[13] The Tories' mood had not been improved with the news that Michael Davitt was to be released from Portland Prison. The 'Treaty that never was' was already beginning to pay dividends, for one side at least.

To his dying day Gladstone steadfastly denied that any agreement even vaguely constituting a 'treaty' had been reached between the government and Parnell. In an interview with R. Barry O'Brien not long before his death he told the London-Irish writer, 'How ridiculous! There was no treaty. There could not be a treaty.'[14] He was technically correct in that the government had been careful to leave no documentary evidence of a bargain; the only significant literature on the subject came, in the main, from O'Shea and from Parnell himself. Chamberlain had been eager to cover his tracks with O'Shea. As long as the credit accrued to him, he had no need of documentary proof of his diplomatic skills, other than exploratory letters. He even moved to suppress any possible impression of a verbal agreement. In a boastful letter to his wife on 1 May 1882, O'Shea referred to a conversation in which the Secretary of the Board of Trade had sought 'to impress upon me that if a row ever occurred and an expla-nation was called for we were agreed that no negotiations had taken place between us, but only conversations.'[15]

When Parnell got to his feet to address the House after Forster had concluded, he was quick to disabuse the Tories of the notion that there had been any preconditions set for his release, on either side. After a fulsome Gladstonian 'hear, hear', he went on to deliver on the first instal-ment of their understanding, making the obvious and unexceptionable observation that a settlement of the arrears issue would lead to a diminu-tion of violence in Ireland and would enable him to use any influence at his disposal to further dampen down outrage. He then resumed his seat. Watching the speech, Mary Gladstone noted that Parnell 'substantially acknowledged the change in his tactics ...'[16] According to Hamilton, her father was not overly enraptured with the performance but adjudged that it would 'pass muster.'[17]

Like the Tories the *Irish Times* was suspicious, but, for the moment at least, could prove nothing. In an editorial it speculated that there was more to this episode than met the eye. The paper even questioned the very future of the Union itself:

> Assuming that we have all the stipulations disclosed – which is to assume a great deal (might not a question be asked whether any form of Home Rule is included?) – the payment to the Irish party for helping the Government to rule Ireland from the Castle, will be, as has been said, the loan of a sum of money to tenants to pay arrears. We are glad that the tenants are to get help. We urged that it should be given to them long before Captain O'Shea appeared in the character of a Minister-Plenipotentiary between England and Ireland. ... But now that the idea has been taken up, it will be necessary to moderate the transports of popular joy until we see what exactly Mr Parnell has agreed with the Government to do.'[18]

All sides now settled down to await developments. Parnell had to devise a formula to convince his supporters (Davitt and Dillon being principal amongst them) that he had not sold the pass. Gladstone could begin to speculate on what an alliance with a potentially powerful Irish faction at Westminster might bring. O'Shea could wallow in his new-found cachet and dream of portfolios to come. Unfortunately, however, none of the high contracting parties to the 'treaty that never was' were afforded any time to rest on their laurels. They were wrenched from their reveries by a set of highly efficient and devastating surgical knives.

The shadowy Society of the Invincibles was, itself, unfamiliar to the likes even of Superintendent John Mallon before 6 May 1882, although individual members would have been well known to Dublin Castle detectives. There is more than a suspicion that this small, clandestine band of assassins was, in part, funded by Land League money disbursed by Patrick Egan, and it was certainly abetted by prominent Land League members like Frank Byrne, Secretary of the Land League of Great Britain. Byrne's wife was alleged to have brought over from London, concealed in her clothing, the expensive surgical knives used by the Phoenix Park murderers.[19]

On a mild spring evening, Saturday, 6 May, the new Chief Secretary, Lord Frederick Cavendish, somewhat capriciously decided to accompany his Under Secretary, T.H. Burke, on foot from Dublin Castle to the Chief Secretary's Lodge (now the US Ambassador's residence) in Phoenix Park. Along the route the two officials were overtaken by a number of men who attacked them with murderous intent. The received wisdom is that their target was the unpopular Burke, an Irishman associated with the coercive administration of Forster and Cowper. Cavendish was either killed defending his colleague or to avoid the survival of any witnesses to the atrocity.

On the day the murders took place Parnell, Dillon and O'Kelly were on a train from Weymouth to London, the former seeking to convince a recently released and highly dubious Michael Davitt (not to mention a sceptical Dillon) that the new understanding with the Liberal government was an opportunity rather than a capitulation.[20] Eventually the four men (essentially agreeing to disagree) settled into a parlour game in which an uncharacteristically jovial Parnell apportioned offices in an Irish Home Rule administration. O'Kelly would be Chief of Police, Dillon was an obvious Home Secretary, the absent Sexton would be Chancellor of the Exchequer and, no doubt with some relish, the putative Prime Minister appointed Davitt to the post of Director of Prisons.[21]

The men went their separate ways, Parnell continuing his journey to Eltham. The following morning, a Sunday, Katharine O'Shea deposited Parnell at Blackheath Station so that he could catch a train to London in order to renew his discussions with Davitt. She waited in her carriage while he went to get a newspaper for her. Reading the paper – the Sunday *Observer* – as he returned, he stopped in his tracks a few yards from her and went rigid. He stood frozen to the spot until she called out in anxiety. Approaching her he held open the paper and pointed to the headline, 'Murder of Lord Frederick Cavendish and Mr Burke.'[22]

A short time later Parnell was in Davitt's room in the unofficial Irish party HQ, the Westminster Palace Hotel. 'His face was deadly pale', Davitt wrote, 'with a look of alarm in the eyes which I had never seen in any expression of his before and after.' According to Katharine O'Shea, before he had even started out on the journey from Blackheath to London Parnell decided he had only one option. 'I am going to retire at once, and for good, out of Irish public life,' he told Davitt, 'I shall have no more to do with Irish movements.'[23] Soon a number of other Irish MPs arrived and, with considerable expedition, Davitt composed a manifesto 'to the Irish people' condemning the murders in outraged prose.[24] It was signed by Parnell, Davitt and Dillon.

Parnell then left with Justin McCarthy to seek more information on the murders and to mend fences with political allies. They called on Dilke first.[25] He advised keeping a cool head and, according to McCarthy, was taking his own advice, even going so far as to suggest that he might be offered the post of Chief Secretary. McCarthy continues, 'When we were leaving, Dilke drew me aside and spoke of the extreme unwisdom of allowing Parnell to walk about the streets that day in London. He said no one could tell when someone might recognise him and, thinking he was responsible for the murders, make an attack on him.'[26]

Next they visited Chamberlain. The Secretary of the Board of Trade wrote his account of the meeting in the early 1890s, after a series of spectacular altercations with Parnell. His account may well be accurate, but it is less than gracious.

'Parnell was white as a sheet,' he wrote in his *Political Memoir*, agitated and apparently altogether demoralised. At the time I thought he was abjectly afraid for his own life which he said was in danger. "They will strike at me next," were his words. He asked me, "What shall I do – what can I do?" I said, "Your first duty is to denounce the assassins and to endeavour to secure their apprehension.'[27]

Both Chamberlain and Dilke attempted to dissuade Parnell from resignation. But his first port of call that morning had been Albert Mansions where he had already written a letter to Gladstone offering to resign, leaving O'Shea to transmit it to the Prime Minister. This O'Shea did, wrapping his own mundanities around it. At a time of grave crisis he assured the Prime Minister that, 'I shall telegraph to the Bishop of Killaloe and all the Parish priests in Clare to convene meetings and denounce the murders and express sympathy with you. ... Do not consider my tender of sympathy a mere form. I feel the blow *as if it were a family misfortune*.'[28]

In his note of reply Gladstone ignored O'Shea's sympathetic blandishments and, politely but curtly, responded to the salient point of the letter. 'My duty does not permit me for a moment to entertain Mr Parnell's proposal, just conveyed to me by you, that he should, if I think it needful resign his seat; but I am deeply sensible of the honourable motives by which it has been prompted.'[29]

In observing Parnell on that ghastly Sunday, Dilke also described a man who had completely lost his famous sang-froid and had begun to internalise the tragedy of the deaths of Burke and Cavendish. 'Parnell came to see me with Justin McCarthy,' He wrote in his diary. 'He was white and apparently terror stricken. He thought the blow was aimed at him and that if people kept their heads, and the new policy prevailed, he himself would be the next victim of the secret societies.'[30] Dilke is probably exaggerating Parnell's fear for his own personal safety. Advised by Chamberlain against walking the streets of London for fear of retaliation from angry English mobs, Parnell ignored the advice and went about the city in plain view. According to McCarthy Parnell remonstrated with Chamberlain, saying that, '... he had done no wrong to anyone, and that he intended to walk in the open streets like anyone else. Some men from the top of an omnibus passing us called out – "There's Parnell!" whether in friendship or animosity I don't know – but otherwise we were unnoticed.'[31]

During the conversation with Chamberlain O'Shea had arrived. His capacity for independent and mischievous action had not been sated by his letter of sympathy to Gladstone. In 1888, in his evidence to the Special Commission, O'Shea insisted that after the meeting with Chamberlain he and Parnell had taken a cab together. In the course of the journey the Irish leader '... said that he was in personal danger, and he asked me to get police protection for him.' He had duly obliged, when, by coincidence, he was summoned to a meeting with the Home Secretary, Sir William Harcourt, to discuss the issue of the outstanding warrant for the arrest of P.J. Sheridan. While there he made a formal request for police protection for Parnell and for himself.[32] When it came to his own evidence at the Commission, Parnell would vigorously deny that he had ever made such a request. Justin McCarthy's account that the two men had left Chamberlain's house together supports Parnell's, rather than O'Shea's, version of the affair. It is idle but amusing to speculate what Harcourt might have made of the request, given that he already had detectives shadowing Parnell on a regular basis anyway. He certainly took delight in discovering that Parnell was now, as he saw it, hoist by his own petard and proceeded to leak the story to the Press.[33]

In reality Parnell was more concerned about the impact the murders would have on the thawing Anglo-Irish relationship. In 1883 the *Annual Register*, recording the political events of the previous year, could take a disinterested, unemotional and logical view of the Phoenix Park murders: 'A little reflection ... brought most men to see that the murders were in all probability designed rather to discredit the Land League party than that they were the outcome of even its most violent partisans.'[34]

Such understanding sentiments, however, were in short supply in London on 7 May 1882. Florence Arnold-Forster recounts an incident in the Westminster Palace Hotel when a man approached Dillon, Davitt and O'Kelly at breakfast and called them 'assassins'. He was about to attack them when a waiter intervened.[35] Davitt himself was full of praise for British restraint, particularly that of the normally excitable Press, which ' ... acted on the whole admirably, under the great provocation of a crime so calculated to appeal to English passion.'[36] In his biography of Gladstone, John Morley makes a similar point saying that, 'With one or two scandalous exceptions, the tone of the English press was sober, sensible and self-possessed.'[37]

Given the embarrassment O'Shea was to cause Parnell by seeking police protection, it is ironic that the two men and Katharine O'Shea dined *à trois* at Eltham that night. Katharine describes both men as 'gloomy and depressed'. Parnell must have been aware that it was only a matter of time before the government was obliged to respond to the

Phoenix Park atrocity with a renewal of coercion. As the three sat together, waited on by a parlour maid, a large engraving of the members elected to the House of Commons in 1880 spontaneously crashed to the ground. The ever-loyal Katharine has O'Shea display a far more nervous reaction than Parnell. Later, however, the latter indulged his superstitious nature by describing the incident as 'an omen, I think, darling, but for whom? Willie or me?'[38]

Parnell went out of his way to represent the horror of the Irish nation at the slaying of Burke and Cavendish. On 8 May he made a dignified speech in the House of Commons roundly condemning the atrocity. A few days later *United Ireland* (which would later gloat at the murder of James Carey, one of the informers whose information broke the Invincibles) replaced its usual front page political cartoon with a blank space that contained the legend: 'In token of abhorrence and shame for the stain cast upon the character of our nation for manliness and hospitality by the assassination of Lord Frederick Cavendish, Chief Secretary for Ireland, and of Mr Thomas Burke, Under Secretary, in the Phoenix Park, 6th May, 1882.'[39] But nothing he or anyone else could do was going to prevent the inevitable recrudescence of special powers and rule by diktat.

The irony of Sir William Harcourt's introduction of the Prevention of Crimes (Ireland) Bill on 11 May 1882 was that it was, to all intents and purposes, a template devised by Cowper and Forster before their resignations. The former Chief Secretary had actually offered to take up his old job again in the wake of the Phoenix Park assassinations. But it was to Dilke that Gladstone had turned first. He was offered the job but without an accompanying Cabinet portfolio. On the, not unreasonable, grounds that he would be simply an executor of the policies of his senior Cabinet colleague, Lord Spencer, he declined, though urged by Chamberlain himself to accept.[40] Gladstone opted instead for a lesser light in the Radical firmament, George Otto Trevelyan.[41]

As Trevelyan contested the by-election ordained by his appointment, the pugnacious Home Secretary was pushing through (with considerable enthusiasm) this new measure of coercion. Among the Bill's provisions was the replacement of trial by jury – in certain cases – by three-judge courts, increased jurisdiction for magistrates, and enhanced powers of search for the police. The Lord Lieutenant was also to be empowered to arbitrarily suppress public meetings and newspapers. An Arrears Bill had been introduced at around the same time but it was the mailed fist rather than the velvet glove that exercised the Irish members. In some respects vigorous opposition to the Bill allowed Parnell to enhance his tattered reputation with the nationalist left. But the Parnellites were fighting a losing battle. As *United Ireland* put it, forlornly '... the ingenuity and the argument all upon one side, the votes and the brute force mostly on the other side ...'[42]

THE IDES OF MAY

There was little enough ingenuity in evidence on the Irish side of the House on 15 May 1882. In the context of vehement Irish opposition to the Crimes Bill and vestigial Tory suspicions that the release of the prisoners and the Phoenix Park murders had not merely been an unhappy coincidence, the government bowed to demands that the Kilmainham Treaty (the name was already in common parlance) be debated. Ordinarily, provided all the principals stuck to their stories and, to use a latter-day expression, 'stayed on message' the government might have been expected to emerge relatively unscathed from the debate. The maverick and problematic element, however, was a quietly seething William E. Forster, the loose cannon on the deck.

Forster was suspected, by Edward Hamilton among others, of having encouraged a number of damaging press leaks, so he was seen by some Liberals to have a track record in petty betrayal. He had certainly told his daughter about the April 28 letter and she was aware that he would bide his time waiting to see if the full text would be revealed to the House. In her diary for 15 May she wrote, 'Father had told me a week ago that, if any part of the letter was referred to, he should insist on the whole being produced – so what he did, disagreeable as it was, was not on an impulse of the moment to be regretted afterwards.'[43] Forster may not have regretted what transpired, but O'Shea certainly would.

Government denials that any 'deal' had been done which secured the release of Parnell and the other political prisoners from Kilmainham were widely disbelieved. The pervasive conviction that the government was economising with the truth was exacerbated in the Commons when Gladstone refused to accede to demands for the publication of the correspondence that had led up to the Treaty. The Prime Minister claimed that the documents in question consisted of letters written between members of the House and that their production came under no rule of the House of which he was aware. 'In fact,' he added, 'I think it would be open to objection as tending to diminish the responsibility of Her Majesty's Government.'[44]

Parnell, despite being afforded this opportunity to keep his own counsel, rose with surprising alacrity and read what he claimed to be the letter of 28 April 1882 from himself to O'Shea. As he did so, Forster sat in the back benches opposite waiting to pounce '... his furrowed brow and gleaming eyes portending trouble',[45] according to Tim Healy. When Parnell omitted the sentence, holding out the possibility of future collaboration with the Liberals, Forster went straight into action. Barely able to contain himself he almost shrieked, 'That's not the letter.'[46] That intervention is not recorded in Hansard, a decorous publication that often tidied up awkward moments like this. It merely quotes his follow-up: 'Might I be allowed to ask the hon Member for the City of Cork did he read the whole of the letter?'

There is little doubt that both Parnell and O'Shea were taking a gamble. Had Forster made a copy of the Parnell letter before passing it on to Gladstone? Had he retained that copy after leaving office? It must have been clear to Parnell as he faced the former Chief Secretary across the floor of the House that the answer to both questions was a resounding 'Yes'. What the *Times* referred to in an editorial the following day as the 'amateur diplomacy of the Member for Clare'[47] was about to be exposed.

'The House of Commons has known many dramatic moments,' Tim Healy wrote almost half a century later, 'but in my 38 years there I never felt such emotion as at that interruption. Parnell paled. Gladstone's face mantled with pious resignation. Chamberlain sat erect like a soldier who knew that the password had not been rightly rendered and that the guardroom yawned for a culprit.'

Parnell, who needed to recover quickly from this setback, replied that 'I did not keep a copy of the letter in question. My hon Friend, the Member for Clare, has furnished me with a copy, and it may be possible that one paragraph has been omitted; but, speaking for myself, I have no objection to the hon Member, if he desires it, communicating the whole of the letter as I wrote it to the House.'

At this point O'Shea got to his feet. Beaten back by shouts from the House to 'read the letter', he resorted to prevarication. 'I have not the document with me,' he pointed out to the baying Tories. But Forster was ready to oblige. The former Chief Secretary passed a copy to O'Shea who must have watched it approach with all the enthusiasm of a French aristocrat beholding the guillotine during the Terror. He tried to pass it back to Forster who declined to accept it. Henry Labouchere, sitting beside the Captain, then tried to return the letter to the former Chief Secretary 'who smiled, shook his head again and referred with his forefinger the paper to the Member for Clare.'[48]

O'Shea managed to mumble an 'I do not think it is fair', before bowing to the frenzy of the parliamentary sans-culottes and reading the letter in its entirety. The *Irish Times* reported, '... The Captain has a musical voice and as he went on the House listened till the Member for

Clare came to the words "It would enable us to co-operate for the future cordially with the Liberal party". This was the magic spell. Here was the note that the cold chain of silence had hung o'er so long. In short the cat was out of the bag ..."[49]

The Conservatives were exultant. The Liberals silent. The Irish dismayed and embarrassed. Healy's declared reaction in his memoirs, although refracted through a prism of subsequent animosity, was one of acute dismay, '... No word-painting can bring to life the sensations of that hour. We felt that the Chief had lowered the flag, and had tried to deceive alike his countrymen and the British. His attempt to suppress what Gladstone styled the "hors d'œuvre" filled us with disgust.'[50] With hindsight, post-divorce, some of his erstwhile supporters were inclined to the simplistic notion (hinted at in satiric form in the *Punch* extract quoted at the top of this chapter) that Parnell had engineered his release from prison to enable him to spend time with his mistress.

T.P. O'Connor was the first Irish MP to recover his equilibrium. He was not about to allow Forster his vengeance without retribution. The former Chief Secretary remained silent when asked if the Kilmainham letter had come into his possession as a member of the Cabinet. The inference of the question was clear, Forster was honour-bound to maintain confidentiality whatever the circumstances of his departure from the top table. When O'Connor repeated the question Forster, no doubt stung by its implications, was starting to explain that it had been given to him by O'Shea himself when the Speaker interrupted and rescued him, by ruling that O'Connor had not been entitled to pose the question. Instead Gladstone was quizzed about his claim, in the light of the letter's contents, that no deal had been done with the Irish party. His response is the one to which he clung consistently. 'I did say,' he insisted, 'and I repeat now, that there never was the slightest understanding of any kind between the hon Member for the City of Cork and the Government. The hon Member for the City of Cork asked nothing from us, and he got nothing from us. On our side, we asked nothing, and got nothing from him.' The following day the *Times* objected to the disingenuous nature of the assertion, pointing out that 'It may be technically accurate to contend that there was no compact, but the undisputed facts show an understanding to have existed ...'[51]

Were it not for Gladstone's Episcopalianism, his rationalisation might be described as Jesuitical. Either he was lying barefacedly to the House or he had managed to convince himself that no agreement, still less a 'Treaty', had taken place, even in the face of overwhelming documentary evidence to the contrary. Those who lacked the Grand Old Man's belief in his own absolute integrity thought otherwise. In future years whenever any reference was made in Gladstone's presence to the concordat that had ended the prison stalemate, the Liberal leader would deny its very existence in emphatic and often surly terms.

Much later that night Gladstone rose again on a motion seeking leave to introduce the Arrears Bill. After the Prime Minister's contribution O'Shea attempted to redress some of the damage he had inflicted earlier in the day. His avowed intention was to prevent a 'grave injustice' being done to the government, to Parnell and, least important of all, to himself. Healy was sitting beside Parnell as O'Shea rose and records the Irish leader as muttering, 'This d____ fellow will make a mess of it as usual!'

His speech was a combination of the pretentious, the overly dramatic and the falsely humble. According to his own account, his highly attuned political antennae had picked up, in the midst of the aggravation over arrears, 'a general sense of weariness – a state most conducive to the proposal of a truce and to the ultimate hope of a permanent peace.' But how to bring this about?

Resorting to a heightened state of unctuousness, he informed the House that on 8 April he had taken it entirely upon himself to write to the Prime Minister, 'to take the liberty of submitting to him a statement on Irish affairs as they presented themselves to his poor judgement.'[52] In his account he then metamorphoses into a Mozartian figure, surprised by the arrival of the Mysterious Stranger who inspires his final great Requiem.

O'Shea recalled that three days after despatching his humble musings to the Grand Old Man, Parnell himself had 'quite unexpectedly' called upon him, following his temporary release for the purpose of attending his nephew's Paris funeral. Glossing over the fact that his honourable friend's first port of call had actually been the Eltham home of the Member for Clare's wife, O'Shea averred (as outlined in Hansard), 'Their conversation, indeed, was merely that of personal friends, and certainly not of political allies, which the House was aware they had never been held exactly to be.'

Parnell had urged O'Shea to campaign to secure a promise from the government 'of making the contribution from the state a gift, and not a loan ... [and] ... to stay eviction by the introduction of an Arrears Bill.' O'Shea claimed to have then asked a single question: 'Suppose that ... the Government should rise to the situation ... should you not consider it your duty to use your immense personal influence for the purpose of assisting in the preservation of law and order in Ireland?' When he received a reply in the affirmative, O'Shea claims to have quickly ended the conversation and shortly afterwards Parnell took his leave and 'left for Paris'. The winking and nodding was over and the Captain had his instructions.

He outlined his version of the sequence of events that had led to Forster coming into possession of the original draft of the Parnell Kilmainham letter of 28 April. He candidly admitted that he had not been able to charm Forster into a mood of compromise. He also conceded that Parnell had not been pleased that he had handed the letter directly to the Chief Secretary. When it came to the deleted sentence, O'Shea informed the House that he had exercised his own discretion, or 'indiscretion, as the case might be'. Believing that the promised co-operation might be seen as a 'bid for release', he had 'begged that the sentence in question should be expunged.' When Parnell had asked him for a copy of the letter, he had despatched the amended version and that was what the Irish Party leader had read to the House. O'Shea, gallantly, took all the blame for the misunderstanding on his own shoulders. He concluded with an appeal to Forster to 'be a little more tolerant' and recognise that politicians occasionally said or wrote things they subsequently regretted and wished to recant. O'Shea piously demanded of the former Chief Secretary that he 'turn his eyes from the exaggerations of the past to the possibilities of the future.'

That was altogether too much for Forster, who rose and proceeded to take a wrecking ball to O'Shea's case and to his pretensions. So far the former Chief Secretary had restricted himself to keeping Parnell honest. Now he began to read from the memo he had made of his conversation with O'Shea, in his house, on 30 April.[53] This, of course, included O'Shea's unfortunate use of the phrase 'what is obtained is that the conspiracy which has been used to get up boycotting and outrages will now be used to put them down.'

The word 'conspiracy' echoed around the chamber like a thunderclap. O'Shea stirred himself and insisted that he had not used the expression. He had referred to the 'organisation'. Forster stuck to his version of the nomenclature but claimed not to see much difference between the two anyway. He then went on to recount how O'Shea had told him that Parnell proposed to guarantee peace in the west of Ireland by using P.J. Sheridan as his enforcer. Sheridan, Forster reminded the House, was wanted by the police. He was astonished by the proposal but 'I did not feel myself sufficiently master of the situation to let him see what I thought of this confidence.' O'Shea sat in assenting silence.

Forster concluded by summarising what he was being asked to support. Sheridan, a man he believed to be 'engaged in these outrages' was clearly 'so far under the influence of the hon Member for the City of Cork that, upon his release, he would get the assistance of that man to put down the very state of things which he had been promoting.' This, in return for action on the question of arrears. The former Chief Secretary managed to make the arrangement sound rather like a latter-day protection racket.

It was Parnell who came to O'Shea's rescue, though he must have been seething at this further evidence of the latter's overweening capacity to improve on his instructions and exceed his mandate. He thanked his 'honourable friend' and only gently chided him for having delivered the Kilmainham letter into the hands of the one person most likely to use it to ill effect: 'I do not wish to find fault with him for having handed it to the right honourable Gentleman, the Chief Secretary to the Lord Lieutenant, although, certainly, I had no intention that it should have fallen into his hands.'

He then attempted to repair the damage done by Forster's injection of the word 'conspiracy'. Opting instead for O'Shea's more neutral 'organisation', he denied having expressed any sentiment of the kind Forster had attributed to O'Shea. What he had been trying to convey was his conviction that 'Moonlight' outrages were undertaken by the 'smaller tenantry on the estates who were unable to pay their rent, and who were attempting to intimidate or coerce the larger tenantry who were able to pay', on the basis that if the landlords were not receiving any rents they would be forced to come to terms. The introduction of an Arrears Act would obviate the necessity for the poorer tenants to continue any such campaign of intimidation. As regards Sheridan, he (Parnell) acknowledged that his name, along with that of Davitt and Egan, had been mentioned, as persons vital for the process of convincing small tenants to accept remedial legislation on arrears. He claimed to have no information of any kind that would lead him to accept Forster's evaluation of Sheridan.

The Members of House were left to decide for themselves whether to believe Forster's or O'Shea's account of the meeting. O'Shea would return to the fray in the correspondence columns of the *Times* four days later,[54] still ineffectually disputing Forster's representation of the facts. But even an observer as antipathetic to Forster as Michael Davitt contended that '… posterity, Irish as well as English, will be more inclined to believe Mr Forster's word than that of the other witness to what transpired.'[55]

The debate then rolled on into the following day's sitting. Gladstone was called upon to defend his position again when questioned by the Conservative MP for Devon North, Sir Stafford Northcote, Leader of the Opposition in the House of Commons, who wanted to know whether there had been any 'personal interviews' between Government Ministers and Parnell.' It was clear from Gladstone's response that the involvement of O'Shea as go-between effectively insulated him from even the most incisive questioning. The Member for Clare was a solid buffer between the

Grand Old Man and accusations of consorting with the enemy. Gladstone was able to assure the Leader of the Opposition that no such interviews had taken place.

When asked about his communications with O'Shea, the Prime Minister insisted that, in any letters that had passed between them, he believed himself to be dealing with the advice and opinions of the Member for Clare. He did not view him as a stalking horse or a mouthpiece for the views of the Irish leader. In support of this position he quoted a line from O'Shea's letter of 13 April in which the latter stated that 'This time, of course, Mr Parnell has no part in the initiative.'[56] As O'Shea had, in the past, acted as an emissary of Parnell he had clearly wished to demonstrate that on this occasion he was acting at his own instigation.

Some of the running was made for the Opposition by a future Chief Secretary for Ireland, Arthur Balfour, nephew of the Tory leader, Lord Salisbury. He, incisively and entertainingly, 'recollected that in a comedy of Molière's the hero declared that he had not sold his goods, but had only given them to a friend, who had, in exchange, given him some money. There was no sale. There had only been a free exchange of gifts.' Balfour was having none of it. His analysis was starkly simple:

> Each party, before the transaction took place, knew perfectly well what they were going to give, and what they expected to receive. The Government were going to give the honourable Gentlemen their liberty and a bill with regard to arrears. The honourable Gentlemen were going to give the Government peace in Ireland and support in Parliament. However that transaction might be disguised by words, there was no doubt whatever that it was a compact ... The Executive was degraded by negotiating with these men.

Sir Walter Bartellot, the MP for West Sussex, attempted to stoke the fire a little further when he inquired of O'Shea (who sat silently in his place) if there was any truth in the rumour '... that the President of the Board of Trade carefully read the letter through, and suggested that the last paragraph should be omitted from the letter?' It was Chamberlain rather than O'Shea who rose to deny that any such a conversation had ever taken place. He did, however, accept that O'Shea had expressed misgivings about the concluding paragraph and suggested that he wanted to withdraw it. Chamberlain claimed not to have paid much attention to O'Shea's professed wish 'because I could not see what authority he had to withdraw any part of the letter ...' He insisted that he had set so little store by the conversation that when Parnell had read the amended letter to the House the previous day he had not even noticed that the offending paragraph had been withdrawn.

Chamberlain then went on to offer little comfort to the squirming O'Shea. He addressed the issue of O'Shea's conversation with Forster. He dismissed as unimportant the question of whether O'Shea had used the word 'conspiracy' or 'organisation'. Describing Parnell as a 'cool, calculating person ... whom we all know to be a Gentleman of great ability', he contended that Parnell would not have 'committed the supreme folly of saying to anyone that the organisation he had always maintained to be a legal and praiseworthy organisation was at any time a conspiracy used for getting up outrages.' He then inserted the knife. The members of the House were offered the vision of a bumbling O'Shea speaking foot in mouth and they accepted it with some amusement. 'I confess that even when it came as a report of a conversation with the honourable Member for Clare, I arrived at the conclusion that these might have been the words of the honourable Member for Clare himself – in which case it would have been a matter of small importance.' Here he was interrupted by laughter. O'Shea, presumably, did not share in the general merriment.

After a vituperative intervention from Frank Hugh O'Donnell in which he heaped scorn on Forster, a chastened O'Shea rose once again for what should have been a stalwart and steadfast defence of his position. Questions had been raised about his dealings with Forster and Chamberlain that he needed to answer. His contribution, far from being assertive and convincing, was brief and defensive. He spoke for just over a minute. He described the actions of Forster in reading his memo of their conversation as contrary to the 'code of conduct common among gentlemen'. He reiterated that he had not used the word 'conspiracy' but 'had been assured the Land League "organisation" would be used for the maintenance of law and order'. He did not think, therefore, that he was 'quite as clumsy' as Chamberlain seemed to believe. Before resuming his seat he taunted Forster with the accusation that he was 'disloyal to his old friends and malignant to his old enemies'. Given the damage done to O'Shea's credibility in the course of the debate, his gibes must have felt to Forster like being set upon by an ageing, toothless terrier, though his daughter, observing from the Ladies' Gallery found them 'personally insulting to father'.[57] Forster rose to make only one riposte. 'I adhere', he insisted, 'to the statement that the word "conspiracy" was used.'

An unsought and unacknowledged complication for O'Shea, consequential on his embarrassment and on the very act of abandoning his relative obscurity in the House, was that he became the object of scatological gossip. Henry Lucy, parliamentary correspondent of the *Daily News* (part owned by Henry Labouchere), also wrote the 'Essence of Parliament' column in *Punch* under the pseudonym Toby MP. Lucy appears to have had something of a fondness for O'Shea but was privy to the rumours about the Katharine–Parnell relationship. Writing a satiric contribution to his Toby column about the Kilmainham Treaty debate, he observed (in the persona of the fictional MP): 'By the way, interesting discussion to-night among Members near me, as to the grammar of the thing. When we ask, "Who negotiated the Treaty of Kilmainham?" should we answer "O'SHEA" or "O'SHIM"?[58] Of course you would say "*he* did it" not "*Shea* did it". Therefore, O'SHIM, though unparliamentary, seems ... preferable to O'SHEA. Must consult the SPEAKER.'[59] The humour might be somewhat laboured for 21st-century tastes but the allusion is clear.

A New Mercury

Were his public humiliation not enough punishment for the Irish MP, there was a private sting in the tail at some point during the week of his Commons embarrassment. It was one that he was not aware of at the time. By dint of his noisy diplomacy, O'Shea had vaulted himself into the public consciousness for the first time. He quickly became an object of curiosity and, its handmaiden, gossip.

O'Shea had the misfortune, through no real fault of his own, to fall foul of the formidable William Harcourt, a Home Secretary with some of the less endearing qualities of a Doberman. According to the diary of Sir Charles Dilke, on 15 May, before his mortification in the Commons, O'Shea had been approached by Chamberlain, sent at Gladstone's behest '... to see if Parnell could be got to support the new coercion bill with some changes.' When he found this out, Harcourt was livid and at least some of his animus was channelled towards the entirely innocent O'Shea. His estimation of the Clare MP would not have been improved by that day's events in the chamber.

According to Dilke, one of the consequences of this attempt to soften Harcourt's bill was a stormy Cabinet meeting on 17 May at which the Home Secretary threatened to resign:

> He told the cabinet that the Kilmainham Treaty would not be popular when the public discovered that it had been nego-tiated 'by Captain O'Shea, the husband of Parnell's mistress'. He informed the Cabinet that he knew that in the previous year, 1881, O'Shea had threatened Parnell with divorce pro-

ceedings, and that it was only because of Mrs O'Shea's discovery of the adulterous relations of her husband, which put him in her power: that O'Shea had shut his eyes and made the best of it, but that after this it would hardly 'do for the public form' to use O'Shea as a negotiator.[60]

In his capacity as overlord of the British police force and given his antipathy at this point in his career to the Parnellites, Harcourt would have made himself aware of police reports on Parnell's movements and have known about his sojourns at Eltham in the absence of O'Shea.

There are, however, two problems with this particular piece of evidence that the existence of the O'Shea–Parnell triangle was common knowledge in certain circles by the middle of 1882. The first is that Dilke could not have directly witnessed the Harcourt diatribe, as he was not a member of the Cabinet. However, it is known that Chamberlain often spoke to him about Cabinet affairs and he was also a confidant of Harcourt. The second difficulty is that there was no Cabinet meeting on 17 May.[61] However, this is something of an incidental detail. Dilke could simply have got his dates wrong. The noteworthy thing is that, by mid 1882, awareness of Parnell's relationship with Katharine O'Shea, though still contained within a tiny elite, had spread beyond Wonersh Lodge. Furthermore, many of those who were privy to this information were in a position to make detrimental use of it, should they so choose.

Another consequence of O'Shea's disastrous performance in the House on 15 May was that his role as a mediator (always circumscribed by Parnell's reluctance to use his good offices) was assumed by his wife. During the Kilmainham transaction O'Shea had been more 'impotentiary' than plenipotentiary. His credibility was based entirely on the government perception that he was a trusted emissary of Parnell. In truth he was nothing of the kind. Now, in the wake of his leading role in the political embarrassment of the Irish leader on 15 May he was supernumerary as far as Parnell was concerned. While he did continue to play a part in various backstairs negotiations in the years ahead, and continued a surprisingly full political relationship with Parnell, it was as a perceived ambassador from Highbury.[62] Certainly no significant interaction would have taken place with Parnell were it not for the fact that the Irish leader found it convenient to placate the husband of his mistress. O'Shea would, very quickly, become Chamberlain's creature and do, largely, his new master's bidding. A great proportion of his surviving correspondence from this point onwards is with the Birmingham Radical.

Where his influence could be used by the Irish party (he became involved with efforts to allow Egan to return to Ireland, for example) he was still occasionally employed by Parnell. But in his dealings with Chamberlain he complained frequently of finding Parnell difficult to work with and cast doubt on his good faith and 'honour'. In one letter he refers to Parnell as being '... in a "moony", drifting state of mind, nowadays, with which it is difficult to keep one's temper.'[63]

O'Shea's sense that he was still very much at the centre of things meant that he continued to address himself directly to Gladstone. On 9 June he wrote to the Prime Minister asking for a meeting, decrying the 'course into which affairs have drifted' and offering 'to be of use in setting them right'.[64] The reply came, on this occasion, not from Gladstone but from Edward Hamilton informing him that the Prime Minister had '... yesterday placed Mr Chamberlain in full possession of his views on the situation with a view to communicating with Mr Parnell ... he thinks that on the whole it would be best if you would kindly see Mr Chamberlain and make known to him any suggestions you may have to make to meet the present difficulties'. It was a polite but emphatic dismissal coming just over a week after a new avenue of communication with Parnell had been opened. O'Shea's services were no longer required.[65] Perhaps by way of consolation he was invited to a dinner in 10 Downing Street four days later.[66]

Opposition to the Crimes Bill and the virtual restoration of the mutually hostile status quo in relations between the nationalists and the Liberals meant that Parnell still needed someone to mediate between himself and the government. It would have to be someone with sufficient gravitas and Liberal credentials to be acceptable to Gladstone and, more importantly for Parnell, someone utterly trustworthy, without an agenda and who would not improve on their instructions. Thus did the niece of Gladstone's former colleague, the late Lord Hatherley, enter the frame.

In an effort to reach some accommodation with the Irish over the Crimes Bill, Gladstone agreed to a meeting with Katharine O'Shea on 2 June in Thomas's Hotel in London. She had written to him as a friend of Parnell's, an honest broker hoping to effect some sort of compromise that would allow the promise of the Kilmainham accord to be fulfilled. He had accepted her invitation, suspecting her to be something much more than a mere friend of the Irish party leader and assuming that she would be a more reliable mouthpiece for Parnell than her husband had been.

That censorious guard dog, Edward Hamilton, was appalled at what he saw as the Grand Old Man's misguided chivalry. In a diary entry for 20 June 1882 he notes that:

She seems to be on very intimate terms with Parnell; some say his mistress. It would have been far better for Mr G. to decline point blank to see her or communicate with her; but he does not take the view of the 'man of the world' in such matters. He never attributes false motives to other people, and so never makes allowance for the effect which the attributing of false motives to himself has. Were the fact of his having seen this woman known, it would give encouragement to the supposition that the Government pay too much attention and heed to the Parnellite party.[67]

The assignation in Thomas's Hotel was one of three[68] that took place between the Prime Minister and Katharine O'Shea over a relatively short period of time. There was also a lengthy correspondence that waxed and waned at times of political crisis. When pressed into service she performed her new role admirably. Her main shortcoming was an unfortunate tendency to importune on behalf of her husband who, as he began to wear out his welcome in Clare (see the following chapter), became desperate to secure a salaried government position of almost any kind.

O'Shea's business interests were also a cause of concern for him and for his wife. In early May, almost as an afterthought, he mentions in a letter to her that 'I am getting quite hopeless, and the dates of payments are staring me in the face.'[69] In an undated letter, possibly in response, she wrote to him that '... I wanted to tell you that I am so worried about your business for you and I fear you must be [also].' He may have been facing the seizure of his assets, since she inquired '... would it be wise to make over your interest in the Irish land and anything that could be touched to your mother or to some man you can trust until March or until the time you will be free from risk?' There is even a hint that he may have been involved in some form of illegality: 'It seems too great an issue to leave anything to the chance of its being found out – and I do hope you will take immediate steps to protect yourself in every possible way.'[70] At the time O'Shea was still involved in the Union Bank of Spain and England. It may be that his problems were related to the need to capitalise that fledgling institution. Equally, as he claimed many years later to Chamberlain, they could have been related to his own profligacy and 'non payment of rent' on his Clare estates.[71]

These, and other letters, call into question yet again the exact nature of the relationship between husband and wife. Granted, Katharine's concerns could be those of a wife worried about the continued ability of her husband to support her. Except that O'Shea had never been able to

Katharine O'Shea, née Wood, in 1873

Captain O'Shea as a cornet in the 18th Hussars, *c.* 1860

Anti-clockwise from left: Parn[ell],
1880. A portrait given by him [to]
Mrs O'Shea soon after their fi[rst]
meeting. Photograph by Mr P[arnell's]
nephew, Henry Thomson

Wonerish Lodge, North Park,
Eltham

Parnell on horseback, 1880

Katharine O'Shea in 1880.
This portrait was carried by
Parnell until his death.

Parnell in 1881

Dec: 15th

My own darling Queenie

Nothing in the world is worth the risk of any harm or injury to you. How could I ever live without my own Katie, and if you are in danger my darling I will go to you at once. Dearest Wifie your letter has frightened me more than I can tell you. Do write my darling and tell me

Facsimile of letter from Parnell to Katharine, 14 December 1881

that you are better —
I have had nothing from
you for several days.
I am quite well and
strong again. We
have made arrangements
so that everybody will
be allowed to feed
himself for the future
the poorer men getting
so much a week —
Your own husband

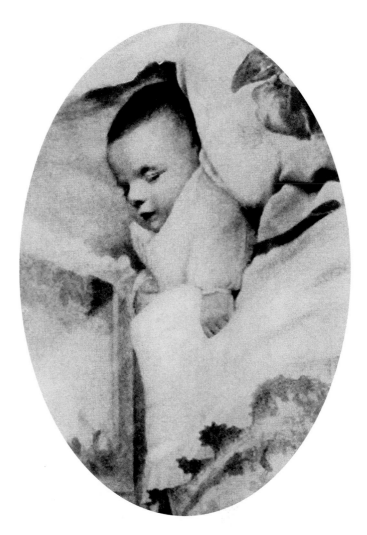

Claude Sophie, born 15 February 1882, died 21 April 1882

Cartoon from *Punch*, 20 May 1882, in the wake of the Phoenix Park murders

THE IRISH FRANKENSTEIN.

"The baneful and blood-stained Monster * * * yet was it not my Master to the very extent that it was my Creature ? * * * Had I not b[r]
into it my own spirit ?" * * * (*Extract from the Works of* C. S. P-RN-LL, M.P.

support his family properly for any length of time and both his wife and, to a considerable extent, the man himself depended on Aunt Ben for sustenance. It is apparent from much of the correspondence between husband and wife, published in her memoir, that there was a great deal of affection between O'Shea and Katharine. His letters to her are intimate on a domestic rather than a romantic level. They lack the mawkishness and sentimentality of Parnell's correspondence but indicate, at the very least, the existence of a continuing respect and friendship between the O'Sheas. It would not be for some time that Katharine O'Shea would come to see her husband as a vicious adversary. In 1882 he was more of an annoying but tolerable complication.

Either from her concern for his financial state or, just as likely, her determination to get him as far away as possible for as long as was feasible, Katharine used her assignations with the Prime Minister to plead for the late T.H. Burke's old job for her husband. Cerberus himself, the ever-diligent Edward Hamilton, decided that this (or the acquisition of some other place) had been the O'Sheas' plan all along. (Certainly O'Shea was eager to capitalise on his wife's entry into the corridors of power.) On 29 August, after a second meeting between Katharine and Gladstone, Hamilton wrote, 'Mr G. thinks the Government is under *some* obligation to O'Shea. I can't admit this at all. There never befell a greater misfortune than to have to take heed of that man's information.'[72]

Gladstone (whom J.L. Hammond believes may have doubted the rumours of an affair, because of Katharine's determined efforts to get her husband a job) took that obligation seriously enough to go as far as to circulate a memo around his Cabinet, seeking their opinions on the possibility of some form of government employment for O'Shea. 'I wish to represent to those of my colleagues who have any considerable amount of civil patronage at their disposal, that Mr O'Shea has rendered spontaneously considerable service to the Government ... the debt is made; and so is the desire to have it acknowledged.'[73] His secretary was livid: Hamilton wrote in his diary, 'There never was a man who played a difficult part more awkwardly, and who unconsciously so discredited those he intended (as I believe) to assist, but to assist with motives of self advancement. Mr G. will not get much sympathy on this account from his colleagues.'[74] In case the likes of Earl Spencer was inclined to be sympathetic (an unlikely eventuality) Hamilton was proactive in his unstinting denunciation of the O'Shea family. Writing to the Lord Lieutenant in September 1882 he expressed his annoyance at the volume of the correspondence emanating from Eltham. 'I can't say how greatly open to objection [are] these continued communications from Mrs O'Shea (whom rumour reports to be no better than she ought to be) ...'[75] The scathing reference to Katharine was an unsubtle reminder to the Red Earl of the *ménage* at the heart of Mrs O'Shea's appeals on behalf of her husband.

Of course Hamilton was perfectly right in his diary entry, the Cabinet response was underwhelming.

Gladstone had already tried to fob Katharine off in September by invoking the dreaded Earl Spencer and suggesting that any such appointment would be in his gift. That elicited a disappointed response from O'Shea: 'Yes, I'm afraid that the Grand Old Humbug is gammoning us. It is very handy of him to be able to put the claims on Lord Spencer's shoulders. Of course, Lord Spencer would not stand out one moment against the GOM's real wish.'[76]

Spencer was aware of Katharine's campaign on behalf of O'Shea. Though he felt it 'quite right that Mrs O'Shea should have unbounded faith in her husband', it was a faith he did not share. In response to a question from Gladstone about O'Shea's suitability for the position, Spencer was scathing: 'The post is one which requires the highest administrative qualities of an experienced Official, and if I were to judge of Captain O'Shea from the volumes of letters which he pours in to the Chief Secretary and to myself on every conceivable subject, I can hardly think of a man more unfitted for the Place.'[77] O'Shea himself suspected that Spencer's favoured candidate for the job was Edward Jenkinson, his former Private Secretary, once a civil servant in India. Jenkinson was Assistant Under Secretary for police and crime at Dublin Castle. O'Shea was not to know that such an appointment was highly unlikely. Jenkinson was probably far too valuable to Spencer at that time, in his capacity as his Dublin-based spymaster.

O'Shea's financial problems were of such a magnitude that he had written to Katharine in late September signalling difficulties with his involvement in the Union Bank of Spain and England: 'I am sorry we cannot manage the bank any longer ...' He was borrowing from friends and concluded with a *cri de cœur*: 'I don't see any way out of it at all, and believe the end is at hand.'[78] Years later, after his divorce, he would candidly admit to Chamberlain that during this period he had been in great financial difficulty because of his 'extravagant personal outlay'.[79] He estimated his annual income (mostly from the rent roll of his holdings in Clare) at £2,500 per annum and his wife's allowance from Aunt Ben as £4,000 per annum.

Katharine, having failed in her efforts to provide O'Shea with a remunerative income, now appears to have taken advantage of his insolvency to secure her freedom from any further conjugal visits. In the aftermath of the death of Parnell, and while his widow was involved in a damaging lawsuit with her siblings over her Aunt's will, Henry Harrison, in the role of self-appointed amanuensis-cum-protector, had access to Katharine's legal papers. In *Parnell Vindicated*, he claimed to have come across a document written by O'Shea from the 1882 period. This suggested to him that Katharine had agreed to transfer £600 a year from her allowance to her husband 'on condition that he continued to leave her quite free and did not attempt to interfere with her life'[80] (Harrison's terminology). This was referred to explicitly by the, often coy, Harrison as her 'agreed conjugal freedom'.

This could have been presented to O'Shea by his wife as a simple codification and/or continuation of their de facto separation. Equally she might have justified it by insisting that, after the death of Claude Sophie, she did not want to risk any further pregnancies. Alternatively, knowing that his back was to the wall and he needed funding at any cost, she may have taken the opportunity of telling him the absolute truth about her relationship with Parnell, assuming he was not already aware of it. In Harrison's view, 'Money had been the magnet to which the needle of Captain O'Shea's compass had always been true.' It may be of some significance that the O'Shea letters cease to feature in her memoir after October 1882 and don't recur until October 1884. Ironically, when they resume, they do so on pretty much the same basis as before. If O'Shea had indeed given Katharine her conjugal freedom, at a price, in October 1882, 'Boysie' did not seem too perturbed that his 'Dick' had given birth to a baby girl in March 1883.

CHAPTER 7

The Member for Clare

'All politics is local.' (Thomas P. 'Tip' O'Neill)

THE FIXER

The Victorian era was a period of great institutional political change in British history. The Reform Acts of 1832 and 1867 had hugely increased the franchise and virtually abolished the notorious 'pocket' and 'rotten' boroughs. The Ballot Act of 1872, which introduced the secret ballot, had made it even more difficult for vested interests to intimidate voters. The 1884 Franchise Act would, it was anticipated, complete the process by adding hundreds of thousands of new names to the voter roll. In the final quarter of the century there was far greater pressure on an MP to actually represent the interests of his constituents. The import of these changed circumstances was slow to dawn on the junior member for County Clare.

When O'Shea put himself forward for the constituency, he was intent on the consequent benefit he could derive from his new associations in the House of Commons. He had an early Victorian inverted view of politics as an extension of the gentleman's club. It was possible to doze in the library and eat the occasional lunch there or take a more active role in club activities. Admittedly there was the added irritant of needing to return to one's electors every five to seven years, but in the interim one was not required to be too concerned about them.

The taunts aimed at his lethargy and his diluted nationalism in the course of the crucial Ennis mass meeting in September 1880, gibes which would have been relayed to Katharine by Parnell, alerted him to his predicament. Barely six months into his tenure as an MP he was already facing sullen rebellion among his constituents. They were unhappy with his decision, despite his declared support of Parnell, not to sit on the opposition benches. They were displeased with his patchy voting record. They were unimpressed by the infrequency of his interventions in Commons debates. Granted O'Shea's Hansard entries were a virtual torrent in comparison with the unsteady trickle of those of the O'Gorman Mahon[1], but the Old Chieftain served an entirely different, and largely psychological and ceremonial, role in the nationalist cause.

O'Shea was a quick learner. His politics were not going to change; he continued to pursue an independent line during his period in the Commons. If he were to be returned to parliament in an election that could come at any time, he needed an alternative strategy. His unique relationship with Parnell was one element of that strategy. His cultivation of his constituency, particularly the western part, was the other.

Over a five-year period his fruitless search for a political coup that would make his position invulnerable (his work on the Kilmainham Treaty and the later Central Board project are cases in point) was matched by an energetic advocacy of the economic, and even narrowly financial, interests of his constituents. He visited Clare on a regular basis (averaging at least two lengthy trips a year), though his property holdings in the county required his presence there as well as his political interests.[2] On every visit he would cleave ever more closely to the bosom of Mother Church. His most frequent house calls were to the priests of Clare. In London he used a network of contacts, and his political clout with the Liberal establishment, to extract financial concessions from an often tight-fisted government. He formed the sort of paradoxical alliances often required of pragmatic politicians. He nurtured a group of loyalists who worked and propagandised on his behalf. And he was always on hand to trumpet his own achievements to acquiescent journalists or to defend his political reputation in the correspondence columns of daily newspapers.

In many respects he was the very model of a 21st-century political operator. While paying a respectable amount of attention to his legislative duties[3] and operating at the highest echelons of power with some of the great beasts of British Victorian politics, he was also a clientelist politician *par excellence.* A study of the Chief Secretary's files for the six-year period of his tenure in the House of Commons reveals a public representative who was prepared to pepper the Dublin Castle administration with correspondence on behalf of his constituents. The same cannot be said of his more nationalistic or even his Whiggish colleagues. In the case of the former there was an inbred suspicion of making representations to that particular bastion of British administration and a conviction that they would, in any event, probably be ignored.[4] The inactivity of the latter was a function of the sort of indolence of which O'Shea was guilty in the early part of his tenure and a growing conflict with their own increasingly disillusioned constituents.

O'Shea also grasped the importance of public relations in dealing with the electors of Clare. When he was not supplying local and national newspapers with details of his activities, he was writing letters to the editors for publication in the correspondence columns. Few good deeds went unnoticed, few slights went unanswered. He was as apt to write to the *Clare Advertiser,* as he was to adorn the letter columns of the *Times* itself. Stories in the Thunderer tended to end up being reprinted in one of the many local papers in County Clare[5] anyway. He was merciless when he felt he had been misrepresented in any way, even if this only amounted to a sin of omission. In August 1882, for example, he must have bent the ear of the *Freeman* London Correspondent, J.M. Tuohy, who was, consequently, forced to acknowledge that 'Captain O'Shea's name was omitted from your Parliamentary report on yesterday as having both spoken and voted against Mr. Clifford Lloyd's salary.'[6]

O'Shea's final gesture towards modernity actually derived from an old-fashioned stress on the importance of patronage. He used his, often scarce, financial resources (or more correctly those of Aunt Ben) to attempt to build up something resembling a political machine in Clare. In anticipation of a redrawing of boundaries after the 1884 Franchise Act, he seems to have made a conscious attempt to ingratiate himself, in particular, in the western part of the county. On more than one occasion his supporters were called upon to deny rumours and outright accusations that they had accepted money from him.

One of his more successful parliamentary projects was the Ennis and West Clare railway. Aside from any long-term infrastructural benefit, the people of the county saw the railway as '... a much better panacea for the existing distress than wholesale emigration.'[7] A parliamentary question from O'Shea on 23 November 1882 had pointed out that employment on the building of the line would greatly relieve the distress then being experienced by labourers in the county.[8] He returned to the theme in

February of the following year during the debate on the Queen's speech, suggesting that the Treasury had an obligation to support the project given the difficulty of getting money from 'the market'.[9]

The railway, which was supposed to have already been given the green light, was the subject of negative rumour by early May 1883. The *Independent* and the *Freeman* both carried editorials casting doubt on the future of the project. Ennis Board of Guardians shared some of that pessimism during their May meeting. The following year O'Shea dangled the subject before the Prime Minister, handing him a letter in the House.[10] This achieved little other than drawing a rebuke from the Downing Street Cerberus himself, Edward Hamilton, who requested that in future the Captain should direct all such communications to the Cabinet office as '... If given to Mr Gladstone at the House they run the risk of being mislaid.'[11]

Final parliamentary approval and government funding for the Ennis and West Clare Railway came in August 1884 and the Clare Grand Jury[12] guaranteed capital investment of £163,000 to enable building to commence. Work began on the railway on 3 November 1884 but, in a very Irish inversion, the first sod was turned in Milltown Malbay on 26 January 1885. Despite the good work done by O'Shea, the man chosen to wield the shovel on that occasion was Charles Stewart Parnell. In attendance was a 40-year-old Cork-born tramway entrepreneur, William Martin Murphy. He would rise from obscurity to become a Parnellite MP in 1885 and achieve notoriety in his more accustomed tramway role in the Dublin Lockout of 1913.

One of O'Shea's earliest and most sustained campaigns was on behalf of the fishermen of the Atlantic coast of Clare. Just a month before the adverse reaction to his name at the Ennis mass meeting in September 1880 he had forwarded a petition (which he had duly signed himself) to the Office of Irish Fisheries, seeking funds to develop a harbour at Goleen Tullig near Loop Head, one of many small Clare inlets '... which remain in the same rude wild shape in which the sea formed them.'[13] O'Shea's constant argument was that, for minimal investment, dangerous harbours could be made safe for the currachs[14] and small boats of Clare fishermen allowing them '... to fish three or four times the length of time they were able to do so at present'.[15] Just before Christmas he was able to tell the fifty or so fishermen who had petitioned that the development money would be made available. In July 1882 the *Clare Advertiser*, which circulated mainly in the western part of the county, drew O'Shea's attention to the need for a new pier at Cappa, near Kilrush. Thus began a letter-writing and lobbying campaign which would culminate in success, but which would come to be used against him by political opponents in the constituency.

In the manner of an American big city 'ward heeler' he and the O'Gorman Mahon had their 'precinct captains', local factotums who looked after their interests on the ground. Two of the loyalists he shared with Mahon were Ennis-based businessman Edward Finucane and Michael G. Considine, local trades secretary and popularly known as 'Dirty Mick'. Considine[16] deferred only to Mahon in his devotion to Daniel O'Connell. According to one tongue-in-cheek account '... the grime on Mr Considine has a romantic origin. It is the fakir's robe of filth. When he was only a budding patriot, the great Liberator once kissed him. Mr Considine determined that the cheek sanctified by the embrace of O'Connell should never again be profaned by water, that the kiss should never be washed off.'[17] If Finucane was Mahon's eyes in the constituency, Considine was his ears. And most of what was passed on to the veteran nationalist was drawn to the attention of his junior colleague. What he didn't pick up from the likes of Finucane and Considine, O'Shea could glean from his regular conversations with the clergy of the county, principally his main ally, Rev Patrick White of Milltown Malbay.

The highly personalised politics of Clare, as practised by O'Shea, involved many representations on behalf of individual constituents. One of his particular obsessions was Post Office positions. The Liberal government Chief Whip, Lord Richard Grosvenor (later Baron Stalbridge) was subjected to a barrage of requests for postmasterships for nominees of O'Shea. One such request, towards the end of 1884, drew an exasperated response from Grosvenor: '... while willing to meet your wishes for post offices for which you have a particular candidate, and about which you write to me, I should not be acting in accordance with the rules and customs of the office which I hold were I, on every occasion, to place the entire P.O. patronage at your command ...'[18]

O'Shea had sought to influence two appointments: one was for the Post Office of Dunsallagh. He was aggrieved to discover that his favourite, Clancy, had been passed over in favour of a man called Campbell, 'a Scotch Tory'. Although on a later occasion O'Shea admitted to loathing the process of this particular form of advocacy, he could not afford too many reverses. An aura of efficacy clung to his representations and added to his reputation as a political resource. Conversely, the failure to secure an appointment '... did some injury to my influence in the neighbourhood.'[19] So was he being mischievous when, in April 1885, he spoke in opposition to a suggestion from Thomas Sexton that MPs should have the appointments of postmasters and assistant postmasters in their gift. 'No,' said one of the foremost practitioners of that particular dark art, '... They were pestered with applications from persons seeking to obtain appointments ... In his opinion it would be better that all Departments should make their own appointments. ...'[20]

On other occasions personal approaches on behalf of constituents would backfire spectacularly. As an neophyte MP before he became a seasoned veteran of the 'quiet word', O'Shea had interceded in what appeared to be a hardship case. He sought a pension for the dismissed former Master of Kilrush Workhouse, '... now living with some poor relations, who are not in a position to support him. ... he is altogether without resources.'[21] Other letters in the file told an entirely different story. The Master, a man called O'Brien, had been dismissed for a series of infractions and complaints against him. One of those involved '... a female officer named Nash [who] being with child had at the Master's instigation abstracted certain medicines from the Surgery with the view of securing abortion ...' O'Shea's approach, made jointly with Mahon, was, unsurprisingly, rejected out of hand.

Arguably, in the context of the early years of his tenure at least, many of O'Shea's efforts on behalf of disadvantaged constituents were of no value when it came to raising his profile or increasing his popularity among the actual voters of County Clare. It depends on how you defined a constituent. If, as a public representative, you equated the term with 'elector' then you did not concern yourself with those whose property holdings did not entitle them to a vote. The actual voters were not people who, relatively speaking, needed that much assistance from an interventionist public representative. With the limited franchise they tended to be shopkeepers, men of property, businessmen – in a word ratepayers. Also, in the context of the Land War the electorate was, almost uniquely, driven as much by ideological considerations as the merely pecuniary. This was accentuated in proscribed counties like Clare that were being subjected to quasi-military rule. But at some point in his tenure, clearly disillusioned with his prospects of acquiring a 'place' in government, O'Shea became very earnest in his desire to continue his career as MP for Clare. At around that time (1884) the focus of government was on the extension of the franchise. The electorate of county Clare was about to be doubled, the borough of Ennis would disappear and the county itself would split into two constituencies. The new voters would not all be men of substance (and I use the word 'men' advisedly – female suffrage was more than three decades off). They would include the fishermen who needed piers and harbours on the west coast and labourers who would be grateful to the man who provided work on a rail project. These were the men, O'Shea decided, who were going to make up the bulk of *his* constituency.

O'Shea's need to appear so well-connected that his services to Clare were well nigh indispensable coincided with a subtle change in thinking at Irish executive level. In the wake of the Kilmainham Treaty and the departure of Forster an era of tentative collaboration between the Irish civil service and the previously untouchable Parnellites was ushered in.[22] By 1884, Lord Grosvenor, in his response to being pestered by O'Shea over postmasterships, declared '... more than once I have been told that "the Parnellites get all they want".'[23] Research by Parnell scholar Alan O'Day suggests that it was the less militant Home Rulers, rather than the out-and-out Parnellites, whose constituents benefited more from official patronage.[24] As a moderate Home Ruler with a perceived influence over Parnell, O'Shea was in a position to exploit this development. O'Day describes him as 'the most persistent applicant for favours'.[25]

In a society where politicians are eager to share their clientelist successes with their clients it is almost inconceivable that any members of that breed would seek to conceal concessions extracted from an administration. But such was the case in late Victorian Ireland. 'Irish Party MP's found it expedient to disclaim the deals which they were negotiating with the government ... The new militant Ireland was not prepared to stand by and watch the Parnellite party's strength sapped by ministerial favours.'[26] O'Shea, however, could allow himself free rein. As a lukewarm adherent of the prevailing Irish Zeitgeist, O'Shea needed other ways of justifying his existence. Ironically, in some quarters, his very success in wringing concessions from Dublin Castle and London made him even more objectionable. It merely confirmed suspicions that he was far closer to Gladstone than Parnell. To the purists, Irish public representatives should not have to adopt the begging bowl approach or accept crumbs from an anathematised Imperial administration. In the context of a Home Rule parliament concessions would become entitlements and representations on behalf of individual constituents would be unnecessary and even unpatriotic.[27] The notion of a tempered or qualified opposition pending achievement of one's ultimate aims didn't gain that much currency. The memory of Sadlier and Keogh was still fresh.

THE EXECUTION OF FRANCY HYNES[28]

The most notorious miscarriage of justice in late Victorian Ireland was probably the execution of a 60-year-old Galwayman, Myles Joyce, for his alleged involvement in the horrific Maamtrasna murders. These took place on a remote shore of Lough Mask in County Galway[29] on 17 August 1882. John Joyce (unrelated to Myles) and his family were brutally murdered. Myles Joyce was one of three men hanged for the murder in

Galway Jail on 15 December. His execution went ahead despite the fact that the two men who were hanged with him admitted their part in the massacre and exonerated Joyce. Although he spoke only Irish, his trial had been conducted in the English language. His only translator was an unsympathetic policeman.

The Maamtrasna killings distracted attention from, and had a major impact on, a lesser-known miscarriage of justice involving a constituent of O'Shea's, Francis Hynes. Hynes was convicted of and hanged for the murder of John Doloughty, a 60-year-old agricultural labourer with seven children, in Limerick Jail on 11 September 1882. The murder of Doloughty had taken place on Sunday 9 July as he was returning to his home near Knockaneane after Mass in Ennis. He had been shot in the face, lingered for a number of hours, and died the following day. While still lying at the scene of the crime, in answer to a question from Resident Magistrate Captain Hugh McTiernan, he had identified Francis Hynes of Toureen as his killer. It was a case that, for a variety of reasons, would exercise the county, the country at large, the Irish party and the members of parliament for Clare.

The two men had a previous history of antagonism and intimidation. Hynes was the son of a once-prosperous Clare solicitor and farmer (his mother had died when he was a child) whose family was involved in a dispute over land with another local farmer, James Lynch. It was a feud typical of the period and of a kind that added an element of personal malice and political confusion to the Land League campaign. Lynch had been accused by the Hynes family of being a 'land grabber'. It was an accusation frequently levelled in disputes involving bad blood between neighbours. James Hynes, father of Francis, had been subletting his farm to Lynch when he was evicted. He had fallen on hard times, a victim of mental illness. The farm had then been taken directly from the landlord by Lynch himself. Doloughty, a herder once employed by the Hynes family, was now working for Lynch. He had, willy-nilly, become embroiled in the row. He had remained loyal to Lynch despite threats of boycotting and a nocturnal visit the previous October by three masked men during which his life had been threatened and shots fired at him. After that incident he had been permitted to carry a revolver. He had been armed at the time of his murder but his gun had not been loaded. On the basis of alleged threats made against Doloughty by members of the Hynes family, Francis Hynes had been bound over to keep the peace the previous year. Captain McTiernan had also revoked the gun licence of Charles Hynes, a brother of Francis, after the shooting incident at Doloughty's house.

On the day of the murder a local physician, Dr Dixon, had been one of the first on the scene. He had found Doloughty mortally wounded and unconscious. It was Dixon who had informed the police and fetched a local priest, Father Loughnane. At both the inquest and the subsequent trial of Francis Hynes, Captain McTiernan testified that when he had arrived on the scene the victim had been conscious. When asked who had killed him, he had said 'Francy'. When questioned further he had identified Francis Hynes as his assailant. McTiernan (who appears to have had his own antagonism towards the Hynes family[30]) had then broken into the local schoolhouse, returned with pen, ink and paper and had written a statement on behalf of Doloughty. It read simply, 'I am now dying. I declare that Francis Hynes killed me by firing a shot at me.'

An order was issued for the arrest of Hynes and, at around 5.00 p.m., Constable Richard Doyle had come across him in Hackett's public house in Barefield, a couple of miles from the scene of the crime. Doyle had taken a short cut across the fields to the pub, crossing a stream in the process. When he challenged Hynes, who threatened to resist arrest at first, he noted that the legs of his trousers were wet and his boots looked grey, as if the polish had been washed off. It was a detail which was not overlooked by the jury and seemed to discredit his alibi, corroborated by a number of fellow drinkers, that he had been in the bar since at least 2.00 p.m. Hynes was unarmed but two packets of shot were found in one of his pockets.

An inquest into Doloughty's death, before coroner John Frost,[31] took place two days after his death. The doctor who had carried out the post-mortem examination, Dr William Cullinane, had also attended Doloughty by the roadside at around 5.00 p.m., a few hours after he had been found. He testified that the victim had a number of shot marks on the face and the upper part of the head. He had extracted a number of grains of shot, some of which had passed through both eyeballs and were found near the bone next to the brain. The doctor had attempted to speak to Doloughty but 'From the time I first saw him he never spoke, except once, when he made an attempt but said nothing intelligible.'

The victim's identification of Hynes was mentioned by a number of witnesses but the verdict was that Doloughty had 'died from gunshot wounds inflicted by some person or persons unknown to the jury'. Frost had sought to add the word 'maliciously inflicted', but curiously 'several of the jurors said there was no evidence of malice produced'. It was all too much for the Coroner who commented 'Surely, gentlemen, you don't think it was through love any person committed the deed. I will take the verdict, but I do not agree with you ...' The jury members had asked a lot of questions, their thrust had been to discredit Doloughty's identification of Hynes. Frost's irritation is a microcosm of the frustration of the authorities in their attempts to enforce law and order on factionalised communities, divided by the Land War, that were offered few reasons to respect civil authority.

Those same civil authorities were not going to risk grappling with Clare jurors when it came to the trial of Francis Hynes. That opened in the Commission Court in Dublin on Friday, 11 August 1882, under the magisterial Mr Justice Lawson, an unpopular judicial ogre who had been slated for assassination by the Invincibles. It was one of the first capital cases taken under the aegis of the Crimes Act and the jury would only have been peers of Francis Hynes had he been a well-to-do, middle class, Dublin Protestant gentleman. Three members had addresses in Grafton Street, the others came from the leafy suburbs of Rathgar, Ballsbridge, Churchtown and Kingstown. In such an environment it was entirely appropriate that the prosecuting counsel was Peter 'The Packer' O'Brien, QC, MP. The accused, described as '... a fine looking young man, only twenty years of age, and six feet four inches in height', pleaded not guilty when the charges were read out.

Background evidence was offered of the feud between Lynch and the Hynes family. This amounted to Francis Hynes and his brothers making major nuisances of themselves. On one occasion Lynch had had his grass stolen and a similar amount of grass had miraculously appeared on Hynes land. The jury was told that John Doloughty had developed something of an obsession about 'Francy' Hynes in particular. The dead man was, apparently, terrified of his young neighbour. His fear was exacerbated by the fact that the two men lived only 600 yards apart.

Evidence from Fr James Loughane tended to cast doubt on the statement of Captain Hugh McTiernan. The priest had been able to overhear the conversation between the Resident Magistrate and the dying man and the implication of his evidence was that Doloughty had been barely conscious, far from lucid, and that McTiernan may have put words into the victim's mouth. Loughnane stated that he had heard the Magistrate ask Doloughty, 'Which of them? Is it Francy?' There was also evidence from Doloughty's widow who (assuming she had not been intimidated) cast doubt on the nature of the relationship between the accused and the victim. She claimed that there had been no animosity between the two and that Hynes had given Doloughty a number of 'presents' over the previous two years.

Originally the jury was to have been sent to the Gresham Hotel for the night. Instead its members were given a choice between two alternatives: the European and the Imperial. They opted for the latter. More evidence was heard on Saturday 12 August and at 4.10 the jury retired to consider its verdict. It returned one hour and fifteen minutes later with a guilty verdict, and Francis Hynes was sentenced to be hanged in Limerick prison on 11 September. On the basis of the evidence offered the *Freeman's Journal* commented editorially, with considerable restraint, 'The circumstances of the case were in every sense most lamentable. We cannot think that the evidence will so far satisfy the public conscience as to induce it to regard the capital sentence on Hynes with equanimity.'[32]

And there the matter might have rested, had it not been for the extraordinary coincidence that *United Ireland* editor William O'Brien had shared a hotel corridor with members of the Hynes jury on the night of Friday 11 August. The letter he wrote about their activities that night to the editor of the *Freeman's Journal* would open a can of worms, and close the cell door on the *Freeman* proprietor and Irish party MP, Edmund Dwyer Gray.

The tale told by O'Brien, and its aftermath, brings to mind the most famous satiric couplet from Alexander Pope's mock-epic poem, *The Rape of the Lock*:

> The hungry judges soon the sentence sign,
> And wretches hang that jurymen may dine. (Canto iii)

In theory these twelve good men and true were supposed to have been locked up for the night, have been kept apart from members of the public, and to have had a decent night's sleep, given that the life of a young man might depend on their attention to detail the following day. Instead O'Brien recounted how three, or possibly four, of them got drunk and cavorted in their cups around the hotel. One even invaded O'Brien's room and shouted, 'Hallo, old fellow, all alone?' before beating a hasty retreat when met with a venomous response. O'Brien concluded his letter by saying, 'I leave the public to judge the loathsomeness of such a scene upon the night when these men held the issues of life and death for a young man in the flower of youth.'[33]

When hotel employees were subsequently questioned by reporters, it emerged that an even more serious infraction of the rules of procedure had occurred. The jurors had not only drunk a spectacular amount of alcohol,[34] but half of them had spent part of the evening in the hotel's billiards room fraternising with members of the general public.

None of which cut any ice with Justice Lawson. When the matter of the adverse coverage was raised in his court on Monday 14 August by an aggrieved jury foreman, one William George Barrett of Kingstown, the judge was suitably incensed. Not at the behaviour of the jurors or the dereliction of duty by their attendants but by the publication of 'outrageous' articles by the *Freeman's Journal*. The proprietor of that newspaper, Edmund Dwyer Gray MP, who also happened to be High Sheriff of the City of Dublin and the man ultimately responsible for the conduct of the jury, was ordered to appear before the court. When he did so, despite attempts by O'Brien to offer testimony justifying the publication of the letter and subsequent editorial comment, Lawson dismissed all exculpatory detail, silenced O'Brien by having him removed from the court and threatening him with jail, and sentenced Gray to three months in Richmond Prison and a fine of £500 for contempt of court.

As High Sheriff Gray was now, technically, obliged to take himself into custody. To overcome this farcical situation, Lawson added to the black humour by ordering the Coroner to commit Gray to jail. The *Freeman* owner was put into a hired cab and accompanied by a guard of mounted police on his journey to Richmond. The comedy of errors continued when the Superintendent of the Guard fell off his horse and his sword dropped into Gray's carriage. Eschewing heroics, the MP did not use the weapon in a desperate attempt to escape.

The controversy now separated into two, not quite equal, parts. The *Freeman's Journal*, the main nationalist daily newspaper, which might have been expected to campaign vigorously for clemency for Hynes, was preoccupied with a campaign to force the release of its own proprietor. At no point was Gray's incarceration treated as being of more significance than the probable execution of Hynes but, nonetheless, the Gray issue did become a distraction.

Both matters were raised in parliament. Oddly, though he did work behind the scenes to secure clemency for Hynes, O'Shea chose not to take this route. MPs like Philip Callan, Frank Hugh O'Donnell and, principally, Thomas Sexton, spoke on the Hynes case in the House of Commons. O'Shea did not. In addition to the doubts over the safety of the verdict prompted by the behaviour of up to half of the jurors, there was a challenge to the verdict based on the actual composition of the jury. On 15 August most of the Irish party members were in Dublin for the dedication of the O'Connell Monument, so it was left to the mavericks to take on the government regarding this issue. Philip Callan raised the matter of jury packing with the Attorney General for Ireland, W.M. Johnson. Describing Lawson as 'the pet of the Prime Minister', the colourful Louth MP pointed out that a number of perfectly good men had been excused from the jury purely because they were Roman Catholics. Forty-nine jurors had been empanelled, the Hynes defence team had challenged eleven and the State had stood down twenty-six before the final twelve men were chosen.[35]

O'Donnell put it more bluntly: '... if it was a fact that the Government were about to try men for their lives by juries from which all men professing the same religion, and the religion of the Irish people, were excluded, then the universal opinion must be that they were being put to death, not by any system of justice, but by a system of judicial assassination.'[36]

O'Shea's first involvement in the case was a telegram to the Hynes family telling them that the 'Attorney General acknowledges the necessity of inquiring into charges against members of the jury in the case of Francis Hynes with a view, if true, of commuting capital sentence.'[37] O'Shea's optimism might have been better placed had it not been for the carnage in the family home of John Joyce on 17 August. The sense of revulsion generated by the Maamtrasna murders in Ireland, the UK and the USA was almost akin to that which had greeted the Phoenix Park murders three months earlier. Each of the five deaths in the Joyce cottage was a nail in the coffin of Francis Hynes. Close to 60 murders had been committed in Ireland during the Land War, for which no one had been punished.[38] That list included the murder of a Chief Secretary. In that sort of atmosphere it was always going to be well nigh impossible to override a verdict of guilty, no matter how dubiously it had been arrived at. This was especially so in the case of the first such outcome secured under the newly minted Crimes Act.

Within County Clare, and nationally, an ultimately futile campaign was waged on behalf of Francis Hynes. Precedents were cited in which dying victims had wrongly identified their killers. Precedents were cited in which convictions had been quashed when it emerged that the jury had been 'contaminated' by public contact. The contempt laws and issues of freedom of the press in a police state were parsed and scrutinised. At a political level more attacks were aimed at the jurors in the case and demands were made for a sworn public inquiry into the events of the night of 11 August in the Imperial Hotel.[39] In the absence of an Irish Court of Appeal, the only recourse for the supporters of Hynes was a commutation of the sentence by Earl Spencer, the Lord Lieutenant. He first set his face against an inquiry into the frolic of the jury, indicating that he would make up his mind purely on the merits of the evidence in the case.

O'Shea, still working behind the scenes, was chosen to present a memorial to the Lord Lieutenant signed by the most influential personalities in County Clare: these included Justices of the Peace and landlords who had a vested interest in discouraging agrarian crime. While staying in the Shelbourne Hotel in Dublin he wrote, once again, to the Hynes family promising that 'I am leaving, and shall leave no stone unturned for that poor boy.'[40] The following day O'Shea was involved in an accident on the way from Westland Row station to the Shelbourne. The cab in which he was travelling turned a corner in Lincoln Place awkwardly, the horse fell, and O'Shea was thrown from the car breaking his left forearm. He was in considerable pain when he presented the Memorial to the Lord Lieutenant pleading for clemency for Hynes on 29 August.

The request for a pardon was based, in part, on the need '... to restore tranquillity to our county.' It argued that '... the execution of the said Francis Hynes would give a rude shock to a community settling down after a period of much excitement. We may add that this execution would inflict deep pain upon an unusually large circle of respectable relatives in the county of Clare and elsewhere.'[41] Within three days the grandees of County Clare got their answer from the Queen's representative in Ireland. He saw no reason 'why in the case of Francis Hynes the law should not take its course.'[42] The *Freeman* noted, again with some moderation, that if Hynes was hanged 'we believe that when the present excitement dies out it will be recognised that a grave mistake has been committed.'[43] *United Ireland*, somewhat preoccupied with the funeral of the Fenian leader, Charles Kickham, was more caustic: '... if it is ruled that the irregularity does not vitiate the verdict, it is hard to see why juries might not repair to Orange lodges to drink the pious and immortal memory while considering their verdict ...'[44]

The campaign for a pardon continued unabated. O'Shea, spurned by the Lord Lieutenant, tried the Chief Secretary,[45] before attempting to cash in some of his credit with the Prime Minister himself. At a time when he was using his wife's correspondence, on Parnell's behalf, with Gladstone in order to advance his own claims for a government position, he also prevailed on her to use her influence on behalf of Hynes.

On 26 August, the day before his accident, he had written to her from Dublin about the presentation of the Memorial to Spencer. 'Lord Spencer said that in so grave a matter, and one in which such a momentous responsibility lies on him, it would not do to discuss the matter, but that the matter would be fully weighed etc., etc., etc.'[46] After failing to convince the Lord Lieutenant, O'Shea had obviously asked his wife to go directly to the Prime Minister. She refers in her memoir to Hynes[47] being a 'distant connection'[48] of O'Shea's, but without any elaboration. Either the matter was not such a high priority with her, or she may not have appreciated the urgency of the situation, because she did not write to Gladstone until 12 September. She coupled her request on behalf of Hynes with one of Parnell's on behalf of a convicted man called Walsh.[49] Gladstone replied on 14 September 'that he would certainly bring the appeal under the notice of Lord Spencer.'[50] At that point, unfortunately, it was all too late for Francis Hynes. He had already had his appointment with Marwood, the hangman, in Limerick prison the previous day.

Special Resident Magistrate, Clifford Lloyd, had taken the precaution of reinforcing the prison on the day of the execution. The extra troops were not required. Limerick remained quiet as Hynes went to his death at the end of a rope. In an editorial the following day the *Freeman* took the opportunity to call for the creation of a Court of Criminal Appeal and said of the executed man that 'To the last Francis Hynes maintained his innocence ... We wonder if those who might yesterday have arrested his doom have any misgiving today as to the wisdom of their ultimate decision.'[51] *United Ireland* carried a drawing of Hynes taken from his only extant photograph and reported that 'The poor youth, who ... was called out to die for Judge Lawson's dyspepsia and his juror's headaches, died firmly and tranquilly.'[52] The Unionist *Evening Mail* congratulated Earl Spencer on his 'firmness ... [and] vigour' and continued to solicit donations to its Doloughty Fund, one of the contributors to which was Justice Lawson.

Shortly after the verdict the Lord Lieutenant toured the west of Ireland. His police and military escort numbered in the dozens. Up to ten RIC men had to escort Captain McTiernan to divine services every Sunday. The Ennis parish chapel was now devoid of choristers, other than those of the professional classes, because of McTiernan's membership of the choir.[53] Shortly thereafter he was transferred to Enniskillen. Edmund Dwyer Gray was released from Richmond prison after six weeks. Justice Lawson, though critical of his paper's condemnation of a jury under Gray's control, agreed to remit half of his sentence. On 11 November would-be assassins failed in an attempt to murder Lawson. In late October the Prime Minister announced that in the wake of the Gray case the government proposed to alter the law on contempt of court. In December special directions were given to the Dublin Metropolitan Police for the protection of the jurors in the case.

In the week of the failed assassination attempt on Lawson, in a courtroom in Bootle, Liverpool, James Hynes, father of the executed man, was committed to a lunatic asylum for care and treatment. In court he had shouted out, 'A man who has received a collegiate education – who took honours at the University forty years ago, is he to be treated as a lunatic?' He only agreed to remain silent when asked to do so by an Irish-born policeman. Before being committed he threatened to 'bring actions against Judge Lawson'.[54]

O'Shea, it must be said, could have done a lot more for Francis Hynes. He was walking a personal tightrope at the time of the reprieve campaign.

Looking to a government job to solve his perennial financial difficulties, he opted not to take up the issue in parliament and publicly embarrass the Liberal government.[55] He worked, almost exclusively, behind the scenes, failing even to appear at a mass meeting in the Mansion House in Dublin on 6 September. The meeting was addressed by an emotional O'Gorman Mahon. His efforts were typical of his customary working methods. He had already begun to perfect his clientelist approach. Unfortunately for Francis Hynes he had also discovered its outer limits.

THE END OF THE BEGINNING

The honeymoon period enjoyed by O'Shea as MP for Clare, as already illustrated, was painfully short. Within a few months of his election he had been identified by zealous nationalists as a Whig in neat clothing. But he was never an unreconstructed Whig. He was capable of toeing the militant Home Rule line in spasms and was still attending Irish party meetings like a conforming Parnellite in early 1884.[56] After mutterings in his own constituency he saw the wisdom (albeit temporarily) of sitting on the opposition benches. By the end of 1882 he was slightly unconstitutional but not dangerously so, quasi-nationalist and semi-Whiggish, but not egregiously so. He had vigorously supported the Liberal government's Arrears Bill (collateral benefit from the Kilmainham Treaty), which had eventually been rammed through the House of Lords with the assistance of Irish Tory peers intent on getting back some of the money they were owed by their tenants. This was despite the fact that their English brethren saw the Bill as an attack on property rights and feared its implications for England.

The *Irish Times*, observing the new Clare MP's progress, probably put it best:. 'Half a Land Leaguer and half a Whig, Mr O'Shea was like the harlequin in comedy with one side green and the other buff.'[57] But in his play for redemption among 'advanced' nationalists he was not helped by the hostility of many within the Irish party. He was hugely unpopular with swathes of his Irish colleagues from an early stage in his parliamentary career. Although not without charm and joviality towards his fellow man, where many of the Irish MPs were concerned (mainly the lesser lights) he adopted a supercilious air, mimicked their accents and described them in correspondence and conversation as 'the Boys'[58]

William O'Brien, far from the unsophisticated 'yokel', despised the condescending O'Shea from his introduction into parliament as Mallow MP in 1883 . 'My only public exchange with him in the House of Commons', he wrote in his memoirs, 'was once when he demonstratively cheered some suggestion of mine in debate. My comment was this: 'I am sorry, Mr Speaker, to have incurred the applause of the honourable and gallant member for Clare. I want no further proof that I must have been in the wrong. I beg to withdraw and apologise for my suggestion.'[59]

In a letter to Lord Richard Grosvenor, Liberal Chief Whip, in December 1884 O'Shea acknowledged the antipathy of his fellow Irishmen. 'I am detested by several of my countrymen in the House of Commons as the 'restraining influence' and because they have a shrewd suspicion that they have often voted for the government because of my management.' We can assume that the 'restraint' in question is restraint of Parnell. He goes on to boast, 'That I have not attended a meeting of Irish members of any political organisation in London since the week before the second reading of the Irish Land Act, and that I never receive intimation of such meetings or whips.'[60] The claim, designed to polish his Liberal credentials with Grosvenor, was palpably untrue. He had regularly attended Irish party meetings since 1882, though by December 1884 he had ceased to do so.

Apart from the occasional spasmodic heckle or remark at a public meeting there was no coordinated move against O'Shea in his constituency until September 1883. But in early 1881 he had become concerned by what his supporters in the constituency were telling him. He wrote to the O'Gorman Mahon that 'I have had several letters from friends, lay and clerical, in Clare telling me that no stone is being left unturned by the clique against me.' He appealed to his senior colleague to come to his defence and suggested that Mahon should write to the local Clare papers on his behalf. He even enclosed a letter with suggested wording for this encomium:

> I consider it my duty to the dear old county to point out that Captain O'Shea is constantly working to advance every interest of Ireland and that he stood shoulder to shoulder with me day and night in opposing the Coercion Acts, against which we voted 108 times. I know the men of Clare, their generosity and justice, and I am confident that they will listen to me when I tell them that Captain O'Shea is a representative of whom they have every reason to be proud.
>
> Yours Faithfully,
> The O'G Mahon.[61]

It was a public relations ploy that O'Shea would seek to use consistently when he perceived himself to be in political difficulty. But in this, as in other cases, he was not necessarily appealing for intervention in the right quarters. The O'Gorman Mahon was under almost as much pressure as O'Shea.

Despite O'Brien's personal dislike of O'Shea he rarely used the pages of *United Ireland* to vent his animus against the Clare MP. Most of the other Irish Members who crossed Parnell consistently voted against his wishes or were unreliable in their support (into which latter category O'Shea certainly fell), regularly felt the lash of Parnell's newspaper. Frank Hugh O'Donnell was depicted in its pages as a lightweight court jester, while John O'Connor Power was a 'vulgar apostate'.[62] O'Shea did not suffer a similar fate. He was dealt with more harshly in the other major nationalist weekly, the *Nation*, but O'Brien tended to leave him alone. This was in spite of evidence advanced by his own publication.

On a weekly basis, while the House of Commons was in session, *United Ireland* alerted its readers to the voting patterns of Irish MPs. They were judged to have voted 'For Ireland', 'For England' or been 'Absent'. At the end of each parliamentary session these figures were aggregated and published. So that, for example, in September 1884 a table appeared in the paper indicating the loyalties of every Irish MP on 15 separate measures of Irish concern. The Limerick MP Richard O'Shaughnessy (who was duly rewarded with a government position some weeks later[63]) was the most pernicious offender, having voted on nine occasions 'For England' and been absent for five more 'Irish' divisions. The next most serious offenders were the two Kerry Whigs, the O'Donoghue and Sir Rowland Blennerhasset, who had voted 'For England' on three occasions and been absent for most of the other votes. However, alongside these dyed-in-the-wool 'nominals'[64] was O'Shea. He too had voted 'For England' on three occasions and had missed eight other votes of importance to Ireland.[65]

The newspaper, commenting on the figures, declared that 'The Irish public have a keen eye for the systematic laggard, shirker and sneak.' Despite this *United Ireland* continued to ignore O'Shea's sins against nationalist orthodoxy. We must assume that O'Brien was either under specific instructions on the matter from Parnell, was anticipating his leader's wishes or, aware of parliamentary and Fleet Street gossip, pursued the line of least resistance by drawing as little attention as possible to O'Shea. A barb aimed at the Captain for attending a ministerial dinner to celebrate the Queen's birthday and a letter on the front page entitled 'The Representation of County Clare', represented the extent of the damage O'Shea suffered via *United Ireland* in 1883. The letter, published in early March, read:

Sir,

I have waited in vain for a length of time to see would any man have even the courage to ask, through your paper, how long are we to be misrepresented in Parliament by Captain O'Shea, ex-Hussar? Now that the Government are putting all their forces forth, with the avowed intention of stifling the national cause, it should be the duty of patriotic men to band themselves together as one, and at any cost secure to Mr. Parnell more than the necessary forty members to defeat Mr. Gladstone's gang.

Yours, One of the Misrepresented,
Milltown Malbay, January 23 1883

Unlike the correspondence of a similar nature running in the *United Ireland* letters column at the same time, which regularly excoriated the unfortunate Richard O'Shaughnessy as a 'nominal' Home Ruler, 'One of the Misrepresented' failed to draw a crowd. There were no supporting or contradictory letters in the weeks that followed.

The rebellion can properly be said to have begun in September 1883. The first significant straw that took to the wind did so at a public meeting in Kilrush; a town to which, ironically, O'Shea had been paying particular attention. In the aftermath of the proscription of the Land League Parnell had moved to create a new popular political organisation, the Irish National League, over which he exercised more complete control. The National League was established in October 1882 and in the year that followed branches began to pop up, like resilient daisies, all over the country. By the end of 1884 Clare had a complement of more than 50 branches whose activities, personalities, prognostications and occasional acrimonious disputes were exhaustively reported in the Clare newspapers (other than the conservative *Clare Journal*) and even *United Ireland*. More often than not meetings were for the committed, engaged and ambitious members of a self-selected local oligarchy. There was also a quasi-judicial element to many of the branches, as the National League monitored the activities of local farmers and ensured that they conformed to the template established under the Land League. Alleged 'land grabbers' would, for example, be summoned before branch meetings to show cause why they should not be boycotted.

On the fringes of this structure was a younger, freewheeling element, which could be called upon as unofficial 'enforcers' or, if its members chose to do so, might operate independently in displays of what Frank Hugh O'Donnell had dubbed 'Ribbon–Fenianism'. The composition of the executive and the nature of the (legitimate) activist element of most branches varied considerably, but tended to comprise a literate, educated, relatively wealthy and often urban cohort. Insofar as there was an Irish provincial middle class in the late 19th century, its members tended to dominate the discourse of the Irish National League at branch level. Even in small rural towns it was the local parish priest who was likely to be chairman or president of the National League branch, while the shop-keepers or tradesmen were more likely to be secretary or treasurer than was a cottier or labourer. Thus, when peasant farmers were being instructed to abandon farms they had 'taken' after the eviction of a sitting tenant, it often had the appearance of 'town' lecturing 'country', or the burgeoning middle class dictating to the peasantry. It was a pattern that would persist into post-Independence Ireland.

Supplementing what was, in many respects, an alternative local government /policing structure, was the occasional mass meeting at which localised policy issues and decisions, already thrashed out at branch level, were tested before a wider constituency, and validation was sought for campaigns being conducted at a national level. Where a significant national figure was available to address those meetings (Davitt, Healy, Biggar, or even Parnell himself) their nature changed entirely and local issues were largely shelved in favour of an enthusiastic expression of support for policy at national level. Whatever the nature of the meeting in almost all cases local RIC men would attend and make notes on the content of platform speeches.

The public meeting on 26 August in Kilrush was, primarily, local in nature. It had been called at short notice but still attracted a crowd estimated by the often over-enthusiastic *Independent and Munster Advertiser* at 10,000. The platform was dominated by the relatively well-to-do. There were a number of elected Poor Law guardians, a Limerick solicitor, an academic and the editor of the *Kilrush Herald*. Unusually the chair was not taken by a local priest, none of whom appear to have been in attendance. O'Shea still had the clergy of Clare in thrall.

The principal resolution passed at the gathering was to the effect that '... considering [the] zeal and activity essential to success in Parliamentary representation in Ireland, we express a decided want of confidence in some of the representatives of Clare.' The other purpose for which the meeting had been called was to introduce to the assembly 'the future Member for Clare'. He was a man called Moran,[66] a Limerick solicitor who told the people of Kilrush that '... he was glad to be amongst them that day to rouse them into action, for during some time past he noticed that the West was asleep. They were not supporting the National cause in the way they should ...' Of course, it was a futile gesture. Replacing O'Shea as nation-alist candidate in any forthcoming election was one thing, substituting an aspiring politician from the neighbouring county of Limerick who had not been endorsed by Parnell was entirely different. The *Independent and Munster Advertiser* was distinctly unenthusiastic. As far as Clare was concerned, '... there is no neighbouring county going to dictate it a lesson ...' The meeting was described as a 'farce'. There was only one caveat: 'if Mr Parnell recommends him, we will fight his battle against all comers.'[67] The implication was that such a possibility was remote.

At the time of that meeting Kilrush did not have a National League branch. Three weeks later one was formed and it appears as if O'Shea had moved in the meantime to shore up his position in the town. One of the motive forces behind the move to establish a local branch was one John M. Nagle. He would become to O'Shea what Edward Finucane, from his Ennis base, was to the O'Gorman Mahon. Nagle was a hardworking 'ward heeler' and consistent champion of O'Shea in the fledgling machine politics of County Clare. At the inaugural meeting of the Kilrush branch, however, he was not prepared to show his hand. Harking back to the public meeting at which a motion of no confidence in O'Shea had been passed, he spoke ambiguously in declaring, 'There is nothing unreasonable in selecting good men to represent the aspirations of the overtaxed ratepayers ... and oust in perfectly constitutional manner those chickenhearted dolts who are alike indifferent to the wants of rate payers and sorrow-stricken paupers ...' To his listeners he could well have been advocating a change in representation. But he could also have been hinting at the emergence of 'Boss' O'Shea, the man who would deliver for the people of Clare.

O'Shea's brand of watered-down nationalism was proving increasingly unpopular in an environment where militancy was becoming de rigueur, especially in the more impoverished west of Ireland. Murder and outrage continued apace. The ready availability of dynamite had allowed the old extremist O'Donovan Rossa, from his American base, to supervise a bombing campaign in the UK. British public opinion required some sort of security response in Ireland. Naturally the continuation of military-style rule in proscribed parts of the country encouraged further Ribbon—Fenian activity. The most spectacular Irish crime of 1883 had actually taken place in August, outside the country, when the former Invincible turned informer, James Carey, was assassinated while making his way to a new life in South Africa. Superintendent James Mallon had broken the Invincibles by breaking Carey, but the extremists had apparently demonstrated their ability to pursue and dispatch traitors even though their movements had been shrouded in the very darkest veil of secrecy.[68]

In that sort of atmosphere the martial law regime of Clifford Lloyd in Clare had not been allowed to relax. The man himself was needed elsewhere but the policies he had put in place continued. Reports of his imminent departure had been published before and proved false, but on 8 September 1883 the *Independent* triumphantly announced, 'Mr. Clifford Lloyd has been appointed Inspector General of Reforms in India, and we are assured by the London papers he will leave by the end of the week for that unfortunate country. He was to have gone to Egypt as Inspector General of something else, but the cholera was there before him and, consequently, Egypt was saved.'[69] In the end the *Independent* was both right and wrong. Lloyd was leaving the country but his destination was Egypt. Cholera was not going to check the hand of the Empire. Despite Lloyd's departure the thrust of his policies remained firmly in place. On Sunday 23 September another public meeting was due to take place in Milltown Malbay. It was to be addressed by Biggar and M.J. Kenny, the new MP for Ennis who had replaced Lysaght Finigan (see below). On the eve of the rally, apparently on the basis that posters advertising it bore the slogan 'God Save Ireland', it was banned on the order of Earl Spencer. The search for a scapegoat, other than the rather obvious figure of the Lord Lieutenant himself, then began. The searchlight lingered on O'Shea. A rumour began that he had been seen leaving Dublin Castle and that it was he who had requested the authorities to suppress the gathering on the basis that his own position would be challenged from the platform. It was arrant nonsense but indicative of the state of mind of many of his constituents vis-à-vis their MP.

O'Shea dealt with the situation in similar fashion to the whispering campaign against him in 1881, by applying to a colleague for public support. In this instance the colleague was Parnell himself. A letter had been despatched from Palace Chambers, Westminster, for publication in Clare newspapers.

My Dear O'Shea,

I am very much surprised to hear from you that a calumny has been circulated about you with reference to the proclamation of the Milltown Malbay meeting. I can vouch that the statement that you were seen leaving Dublin Castle, either on Friday, the 21st September, or on Saturday, the 22nd, is absolutely false, as on both those days I had the pleasure of seeing you at a distance of several hundred miles from that place, and I was the first, on the following day, the 23rd,

to bring you the news of the proclamation, which you attributed solely to Mr Jenkinson's hostility to yourself.

Yours very truly,
Chas S. Parnell[70]

The letter had undoubtedly been written by O'Shea; it had his fingerprints
all over it. It spoke of an intimacy between Parnell and O'Shea and cleverly
turned the incident to his advantage by implying that, far from being in a
position to extract such favours from the Castle's security chief, the devilish
Jenkinson was ill-disposed towards the champion of the oppressed people
of Clare. The public backing of the Irish party leader had the desired effect
on T.S. Cleary, who wrote in the *Independent* about the mill wheel that had
created the rumour and 'the danger of disruption through the action of
party cliques'. It was precisely what O'Shea wanted to hear. One might
even speculate that he had started the rumours himself except that there is
no evidence whatever for this. The only downside for the Captain was a
bilious attack by Biggar, reported in the same issue of the *Independent*, at
a National League meeting in Dublin where he noted on his trip to the
county that 'Captain O'Shea, every one assured him, had not the shadow
of a chance of ever sitting in Parliament again for Clare.'

This positive public relations exercise was reinforced a fortnight later
by another O'Shea press release. In late October he visited the constituency
himself. He had a double purpose, but both were related to his political
career. He spent time working his support base amongst the clergy and in
the western part of the constituency. His efforts were now concentrated
on Kilrush, Milltown Malbay and the west coast of the county (it was there
that he bestowed most of his political favours) and on assembling a nascent
political machine that would allow him to prevail against the 'advanced'
nationalists of Clare in any electoral contest.

His second object involved the use of his tenants in what, in modern
terms, would be described as a 'PR stunt'. His property was divided
between lands in Derrynaveigh, near Sixmilebridge in the south-western
part of Clare and Cappnahanna near Murroe across the Shannon in
nearby north-east Limerick. In late October O'Shea visited both areas
and, on the strength of a rent abatement of 25–40 per cent, extracted from
the tenants a glowing memorial which was then carried by local and
national newspapers, even appearing in the *Times* under its Dublin correspondent's byline. The tenants (17 in all) denied rumours circulating
through parts of Clare 'to the effect that Captain O'Shea had been treating
his tenants harshly and was unkind to them. Now we hereby declare that
the same is false and that there is not a shadow of a shade of truth in such

a report ... We are happy to acknowledge that Captain O'Shea has been always uniformly kind, considerate and indulgent to us.' By way of illustration they pointed out that before he had even stood for the county when the potato crop was threatened (in 1878) he had told his agent to issue seed potatoes 'gratis'. The conclusion was vintage O'Shea: 'Mr Parnell himself, our great leader, could not do more for his tenants ... We are truly grateful to Captain O'Shea, and are sorry that any one could be found to malign so good and great a man.'[71]

When *United Ireland* referred in their coverage of the story to the fact that the abatement had come about as a result of rent arbitration, O'Shea's response was rapid and effective. He pointed out that the reduction had been voluntary and requested that the newspaper print his statement as fact. *United Ireland* meekly complied.[72] He may well have been gilding the lily in the complexion he put on the arrangement to *United Ireland*. On 18 August 1883 he had written to the publisher T.H.S. Escott: 'I am going to Ireland next week. There I have law and arbitration with some of my tenants (unable as yet to distinguish between gold and rubbish in Landlords, especially if the Landlord be a member of Parliament) ...'[73] This suggests that the abatement may not have been entirely voluntary but O'Shea was not going to have his generosity called into question. Neither was he going to be put in a position where he could not exploit his move for its inherent political capital. It was a substantial risk on his part, given that he depended on his rents for a sizeable part of his income.

In between the original abatement and the *United Ireland* retraction O'Shea ventured even further out of character. On 30 October, at a meeting of the Land Reform Union in London, Michael Davitt spoke on the theme of 'Land for the People'. It was a phrase that Davitt had been subtly remoulding to encompass the nationalisation of land rather than mere tenant ownership. The resolution moved at the meeting read, '... each nation should hold the entire soil in its territory as national inalienable property, to be administered for the benefit of the whole of the people of England, Ireland and Scotland respectively.'[74] Among the attendees listed in the *Times* report was Storey, the Radical MP, Phillip Callan and ... William Henry O'Shea. Given their mutual antipathy it is hard to fathom what O'Shea was doing there, other than to establish his radical credentials and associate himself with the iconic figure of Davitt. He was as much out of place as a fox at a hunt ball. The *Times* reported that when Davitt came forward to speak 'the entire audience rose to their feet and cheered him most enthusiastically'. It is difficult to see O'Shea abandoning his seat to acclaim one of his leading *bêtes noires*. But then it is equally difficult to see how he became involved with a group of even less obvious bedfellows – the Irish Republican Brotherhood.

CHAPTER 8
Alliances and Dalliances

Captain O'Shea is a good specimen of an Irish gentleman fortune hunter. Handsome, educated equally in the drawing-room, on the turf and in the Stock Exchange; at least he *was* ... The turf and the Stock Exchange having failed him, Capt O'Shea decided to take up the trade of politics, and at the last General Election astounded his Conservative friends by enlisting in Mr Parnell's ragged regiment, and being returned for an Irish county as a Home Ruler – as mild a Home Ruler as his secret masters would permit.

Anonymous English columnist, reprinted in
Clare Advertiser, 27 May 1882

COURTING THE BROTHERHOOD

It is said that desperate times call for desperate measures, but was O'Shea so concerned about the safety of his seat that he felt the need to seek support from members of an organisation whose objects he did not share and whose methods he deprecated? The answer appears to be that yes, he was.

O'Shea brokered a safe passage for ex-Fenian, Patrick Egan, to allow him to return to Ireland from his Gallic exile. Not that Egan would have been gratified by the Captain's intercession on his behalf. O'Shea corresponded with Spencer on the subject in June 1882. This was presumably at the request of Parnell who, at the time, was anxious to exert more control over the Land League funds in Paris. These had become depleted under Egan's stewardship and the suspicion was that some of the League's finances had been used for dubious activities supported only by the ex-Fenian and the truculent wing of the organisation. Parnell was determined to curb the Treasurer's powers. After Parnell re-asserted his authority over the purse-strings of the movement Egan resigned and migrated to the USA. He finally settled in Nebraska but remained a significant factor in Irish nationalism.

It is evident from his own notation above the Spencer letter that O'Shea was more concerned about obtaining the release of a Clare prisoner named Patrick Frost than he was about securing the return to dear old Erin of the conspiratorial Egan. Spencer had been unable to locate an inmate who fitted O'Shea's description precisely but was able to tell him that two prisoners of that name had been released in June 1882.[1] The prisoners in question were both named Patrick Frost. Both had been arrested at the same time and were links in a chain that tied O'Shea, by association, into relationships with a number of men considered by the authorities to be members of the IRB.

The Frosts had been arrested along with 16 others on 17 February 1882 on treason felony charges. The arrests were based on information received from an unidentified informer. The Frosts were among nine men who had been picked up and brought to the police barracks in Tulla. An immediate boycott had been put in place and no carts were made available for hire by locals to allow the men to be taken to Ennis. Arrangements were made by the RIC to move them the following day. Simultaneously, another group of nine men had been rounded up in Scariff. Among them was a 21-year-old farmer's son, Martin Crotty, and an 18-year-old, John Clune. As far as the RIC and Special Resident Magistrate, Clifford Lloyd, were concerned, the men arrested were at the centre of agrarian disturbances and many, if not all, were also members of the IRB. They were held on remand for two weeks as Lloyd put pressure on the Under Secretary, T.H. Burke, to allow them to be released and rearrested under the Protection of Persons and Property Act. Lloyd told Burke that 'The 18 arrests are absolutely necessary to prevent further bloodshed in the Barony of Upper Tulla. We cannot remand further. All 18 are notorious rebels in the locality and our information is I believe sound and reliable.'[2] On 27 February Forster rubber-stamped the request of his protégé.[3] The men were released from Ennis prison on 4 March and as they walked outside the gates they were immediately rearrested and brought to a number of different prisons for indefinite periods of time.

Over the weeks and months that followed, O'Shea peppered the Chief Secretary's office with correspondence, and Forster himself with parliamentary questions, about a number of Clare men in custody under the Coercion Acts (men who were without recourse to Habeas Corpus) and treason felony legislation (which required charges to be brought). Among his 'clients' were the 18 Tulla and Scariff 'suspects'. On 22 March 1882 he wrote to Forster about the treatment that had been meted out to the men who had been arrested in Tulla. He railed that they ' ... were placed in a cell about 7 feet by 8 feet. In this cell they were all confined until 3 p.m. when they left for Ennis.'[4] They had spent more than 24 hours in a lock-up known locally as the 'black hole'.

O'Shea then had the galling experience of watching Thomas Sexton steal his thunder a week later by asking Forster a parliamentary question about the treatment of the Tulla prisoners. O'Shea did not attempt to hide his annoyance at being upstaged. He dashed off a complaint to Forster pointing out that 'I was yesterday put by you in the position of an Irish member against whom the charge would undoubtedly and plausibly be made of having neglected a complaint from the county which he represents, and allowed it to be taken up by a really patriotic and unsparing opponent of the Ministry. I very much regret my foolishness...'[5]

A contrite official in the Chief Secretary's office explained that 'The report on the subject was only received on the same day that Mr Sexton's question was asked or a communication would have been made to you before, and when answering Mr Sexton's question Mr Forster did not at the moment remember that you had written to him on the subject or in his answer he would have stated that his reply was intended also as an answer to your communication.'[6]

One by one the prisoners were released. The Frosts were already back in Clare when O'Shea inquired after them on 22 June. Two other members of the group, Martin Scanlan and Martin Crotty had been deemed suitable for release by 27 April. The case of Crotty is particularly interesting. March 1882 was not the first occasion on which O'Shea had made representations on his behalf. Neither was this the first time on which he had been 'lifted'. In July 1881 O'Shea had questioned the Chief Secretary about the arrest of Crotty for an attack on a house in Tomgraney, near Scariff. O'Shea claimed that Crotty had a cast-iron alibi. He had been on the way to Nenagh Fair to sell cattle when the attack had taken place. Forster's reply was curt and uninformative; he held that there were reasonable grounds for suspicion in the case and left it at that.[7] A month later O'Shea visited Limerick Gaol and spoke to a number of prisoners, Crotty amongst them. The *Freeman's Journal* reported that the Clare MP '... has been for some time exercising his influence for their release and came specially here from London to ascertain more particulars concerning their cases. The interview with each of the "suspects" was of very long duration.'[8] Another of the men to whom O'Shea spoke on that visit was Patrick Slattery. Slattery was associated with the Clune brothers, Matthew and Bryan, of Carrahan, Tulla, and John O'Connor of Feakle (see p. 237). Six months earlier the County Inspector of the RIC had written of them 'I know of no worse men in the county of Clare.'[9]

But neither was the interview in Limerick prison the first occasion on which O'Shea had made some intercession on behalf of Crotty. An entry in the index in one of the huge ledgers of the Chief Secretary's Office Registered Papers in the National Archives indicates that O'Shea wrote to Forster about Crotty on 9 August, a fortnight before the Limerick prison meeting and some time after his parliamentary question. Unfortunately the relevant file[10] has gone missing but the ledger entry does show that O'Shea was actively pursuing Crotty's case. The young man had, despite Forster's brusque comment, been released without charge for the Tomgraney attack in 1881 (possibly as a result of representations from O'Shea) but had then been arrested again in February along with 17 others, as outlined above.

But who was Martin Crotty? What do we know about the young man whose path crossed that of his MP on at least three documented occasions? Was he a young innocent caught up in a military-style sweep by an over-enthusiastic and ambitious Resident Magistrate on the basis of dubious informer evidence? Or did he have a more sinister side?

Crotty was from Poulagower, Scariff. His arrest file, which includes an official 'Recommendation for Arrest' form under the Protection of Person and Property Act, gives a clear indication of what the local civil authorities felt about him. His character was described as 'bad', his economic circumstances 'fair', and he was being recommended for arrest for 'Treasonable practices – being a member of the IRB – also intimidation against the payment of all rent in the district.'[11] A handwritten note appended over the name (but not the signature) of Clifford Lloyd added, 'There is good private information that the above named is an important member of the above society and his character as known to the police fully supports this information. I have personally inquired into the recommendation and consider the arrest absolutely necessary to prevent further bloodshed in this district.'[12]

O'Shea was to become something of a conduit for testimonials and character references written on behalf of prisoners to assist in obtaining their release. When visiting Clare he would regularly attend court cases involving charges of involvement in agrarian crime. His enthusiasm for the cause drew praise from the *Clare Advertiser*, which noted that 'Captain O'Shea is rendering good services to the "suspects" of the county by his interrogatories to the Irish Chief Secretary in Parliament.'[13]

Whether his activities were entirely based on political self-interest and expediency, or were mixed with an element of altruism is not revealed in his correspondence. Certainly his prison work was done with an eye to the ballot box, but an unintended effect was that he earned the gratitude of elements of the Fenian organisation in County Clare. There were a number of Fenian sympathisers and activists among the prison population throughout the 1880s. O'Shea may not have been aware *ab initio* that he was making representations on behalf of extreme republicans, but when he did become conscious of the fact he was quick to turn it to his advantage.

Of crucial importance in this regard was his involvement in the aftermath of the so-called 'Crusheen conspiracy'. On 20 May 1882 near the village of Crusheen in the northern part of Clare, not far from the Galway border, an attempt had been made on the life of a man named Ford by a group of 'moonlighters'.[14] Ford had fought back and the would-be assailants had run off abandoning one of their number, John Tubridy, who had been wounded in the fracas. Tubridy, a father of five, was a 30-year-old shoemaker. At the subsequent winter assizes he had been sentenced to penal servitude for life. In order to gain restitution of that sentence he had agreed to identify the other members of the group that had attempted to murder Ford. He did a lot more besides.

Tubridy's story – which he told, among others, to Clifford Lloyd – was that he had joined the Irish Republican Brotherhood on 31 October 1879. The men he had identified as his co-conspirators in the attempted murder of Ford had done likewise. In January 1882, at a meeting in Ennis, this faction had become a Ribbon–Fenian group when ' ... the society was transformed into an organisation to do away with landlords, agents, bailiffs, and spies.' One of its earliest victims had been a man called Ned Kennedy, shot for taking a farm from which the sitting tenant had been evicted. By the time Tubridy had finished with his statement, he had implicated 13 men he alleged to be Fenians involved in agrarian outrage. Collectively, according to his story, they had been responsible for two murders, seven attempted murders, and twenty-four firings into dwellings. *United Ireland*, in a mocking editorial commentary, congratulated Tubridy on his apostasy: ' ... what joy must have been yours, when, ushered into the presence of Mr Clifford Lloyd, your soul was thrilled with the proud consciousness that now you had become like him, a labourer in the glorious Castle vineyard.'[15]

In prosecuting his regime in Clare, Clifford Lloyd was learning from the example of Mallon in his Phoenix Park murder investigation. He was engaging in what O'Shea described as 'fishing prosecutions'. He rounded up large numbers of suspects in the hope that one or more of them would crack, just as James Carey had done when interrogated by Mallon. In the Crusheen case they had been handed to him on a plate by Tubridy. In another separate round-up in Milltown Malbay he had seized a number of men who were about to emigrate and was holding them without charge. 'Every effort was made to induce one or another to give evidence, whether true or false, against the rest, in order to save his own skin,' O'Shea told the House. 'He could not conceive anything more likely to drive men to the commission of crime than such a state of affairs.'[16] Lloyd was also accused by the *Independent and Munster Advertiser* of having overstepped the line in his interrogation of one suspect, P.K. Sullivan who, it claimed, was '... cajoled into speaking on matters he had no knowledge of ... ' Adding that Lloyd had 'no right to play upon the sensibility of any timorous witness'.[17] O'Shea appealed to the Attorney General for Ireland to examine both cases, reject the uncorroborated evidence of convicted prisoners, and withdraw the charges.

Such public displays of support for men suspected, by the authorities at least, of being guilty of conspiracy to murder, allied to his constant carping at the 'Satrapy' of Clifford Lloyd, went down well in some Clare-based Fenian circles. He would make use of this extremist support in a number of future political escapades.

PARLIAMENTARIAN

Perhaps the best word to describe William Henry O'Shea's parliamentary career would be 'chequered'. It was a patchwork quilt with fine intricate stitching in some places, over-elaborate suturing in others and some shoddy, haphazard workmanship throughout.

During the sessions of 1883 and 1884, when he was well established as an MP, he managed to be available for a vote on the removal of additional railway ventilators from the Thames Embankment and to offer an opinion to the House on the subject of the Swansea, Oystermouth and Mumbles Railway Bill, while missing 22 out of a total of 35 divisions of Irish concern. He also voted against the Irish party in four of the divisions for which he was present.[18] He was prepared to return to Westminster from his sister's deathbed in Paris[19] to vote with the government at the behest of Chamberlain,[20] while being absent for crucial votes on Harcourt's Crimes Bill.[21] To his credit, when he was actually present he voted consistently against Liberal coercion measures. All, of course, to no avail.

He contributed to government defeats,[22] allowed the Liberal administration off the hook by dint of abstention or absence,[23] and came dramatically to its rescue on at least one occasion.[24] It is possible to deduce when he was under most financial pressure by dint of observing his occasional long absences from the House. During those periods he spent time in Spain, France or Portugal. He was sporadically absent on constituency business in Clare when the House was in session, but on those occasions he would be gone for less than a fortnight. When trying to sort out his business affairs on the Continent he could be missing for weeks. As his tenure as Clare MP began to wind down, so did the frequency of his parliamentary questions and interventions into debate. During his brief sojourn as MP for Galway he didn't ask a single question or participate in even one parliamentary discussion.

In the late Victorian era, when outstanding parliamentary rhetoric, exceptional debating ability and a masterful capacity for procedural manipulation were skills prized far above low profile service to a constituency, O'Shea was never going to figure among the parliamentary giants. On the rare occasions when he injected himself into heated debates on controversial issues, he was too easily disconcerted and flustered and unable to think on his feet. The Kilmainham Treaty 'Massacre' of 15 May 1882, is a case in point. Twenty-four hours *after* the most serious attack on the credibility of his parliamentary career he was back in the House with his pointed retorts. But the moment had already passed, and even then he was reduced to merely suggesting that his principal antagonist (Forster) was failing to behave like a gentleman in what was, in essence, a bear pit with a civilised veneer.

If the negotiable currency of the Victorian parliamentarian was interventions in debate and parliamentary questions (in itself a highly debatable premise), then O'Shea was under-resourced. Over a career that began in April 1880 and ended in June 1886, he caught the Speaker's eye on fewer than 200 occasions. This compares wonderfully well with the contribution of his constituency colleague, the O'Gorman Mahon, who challenged the House on a grand total of 16 instances over a similar period (albeit he lost his seat in the General Election of November 1885). But compare his performance to that of Parnell, a leader whose lieutenants often accused him of having a lackadaisical attendance record and who spent six months in jail. The Irish leader managed to make 1,600 interventions during those two parliaments. The political gadfly Frank Hugh O'Donnell, who admittedly did enjoy the sound of his own voice, spoke 1,262 times over a six year period – his seat disappeared after the constituencies were redistributed in 1885 and he didn't stand in the

November election of that year.[25] On that basis O'Shea was hardly overextended.

Fewer than half of his questions or interventions related to Ireland, almost one fifth referred to military or constabulary matters, a dozen questions concerned the House of Commons smoking room or facilities for reporters in the Palace of Westminster, and he managed to look after his own business interests as well by asking ten questions about Anglo-Spanish matters.[26]

In his first year in the House he did not make a single reference to Clare. He expressed concern about the '... defective ventilation and noxious exhalations in and about the House ...', but not about his constituency. As his difficulties in Clare became apparent that pattern changed, slowly at first and then more radically. From 1880–85 more than 60 per cent of his 'Irish' interventions related to his constituency (57 out of 93). Almost half of those came in his most active year, 1882 (26 of 34 'Irish' interventions), at a time when he was preoccupied behind the scenes with matters of high politics. He may have spent a considerable portion of his time that year dealing with the Kilmainham Treaty but he didn't neglect the Kildysart Poor Law Union.[27]

Untrammelled by allegiance to a wider national cause, O'Shea could concentrate his energies on personal and local issues. Some of the former concerns were predictable, others quite unexpected. His questions, for example, over treaty negotiations between Britain and Spain were those of an entrepreneur with important Iberian business interests. But there is no such obvious reason for the three questions (all posed in 1882) about the first tentative plans for the Channel Tunnel, other than the fact that the responsible minister was Chamberlain who could have invited the queries.

He also became embroiled in the controversy over the alleged assault on the redoubtable Lady Florence Dixie. Lady Florence was the sister of the ninth Marquess of Queensbury (father of Lord Alfred Douglas and scourge of Oscar Wilde). She was a friend of the Queen, a novelist, travel writer and became the first female war correspondent when she was sent by the *Morning Post* to cover the Anglo-Zulu War.[28] A strong advocate of Home Rule for Ireland and her native Scotland she was, nonetheless, opposed to the activities of the Land League. Her questioning of the use to which League funds were being put during the 1883 dynamite campaign threw her together with the renegade nationalist journalist Richard Pigott, from whom she commissioned research into the agrarian movement. The fruits were published in a pamphlet called *Ireland and her Shadow*, which concluded that the League championed 'the doctrines of the communist and the infidel'.[29] Her vociferous condemnation of the agrarian campaign (partly inspired by a lengthy stay in Mayo) had made her a number of enemies and attracted death threats.

On 17 March 1883 Lady Florence had presented herself at Windsor Police Station, near London, in a state of extreme agitation and dishevelment. She told the police an utterly bizarre story. She insisted that while walking in a nearby park with her St Bernard dog, Hubert, a gift from her husband in the wake of the threats against her life, she had followed the dog into a shrubbery and had there been accosted and assaulted by two men with strong Irish accents. Both men were dressed in women's clothing. One had slashed at her twice with a sharp knife. The story caused an immediate sensation. Queen Victoria despatched her faithful aide/bodyguard/companion, John Brown, to examine the shrubbery for himself. The London Metropolitan Police investigated, identified a number of suspects, but got no further. Her story was accepted as gospel by many, but dismissed as a self-publicising hoax or fantasy by others.

O'Shea entered the fray with a series of parliamentary questions in late March 1883. This was probably at the behest of Parnell[30] who did not wish the issue to be taken up by any of his lieutenants. The Captain's first bite at the controversy came three days after the alleged fracas in Windsor when he asked Sir William Harcourt, the Home Secretary, 'whether the police had come to any definite conclusion as to the alleged murderous attack on a lady near Windsor, on Saturday the 17th instant; and, whether considering the gravity of the comments on the subject by the Press, Her Majesty's Government intend to institute a public inquiry into the circumstances of the case?'[31] The subtext of O'Shea's inquiry was the effect the hysterical tabloid babble surrounding the case was having on feelings towards the Irish community in Britain, already being exacerbated by the dynamite campaign.

Within days he put another question down on the order paper that was highly incendiary. O'Shea's PQ alleged that, on a previous occasion, Lady Florence had forged a letter and hoaxed the public, claiming that it had been written by the Zulu chieftain Cetewayo. *Ipso facto*, he inquired, was the alleged assault another hoax and '... whether as a result of the inquiry into the affair near Windsor and the professional examination of the cuts in Lady Florence Dixie's clothing, the police have not come to the conclusion that the lady is an impostor?' The *Irish Times*, informed of the tabling of such a question, waxed apoplectic. It was in no doubt that O'Shea had cast aspersions on the honour of an aristocratic lady of impeccable family who was being threatened by the proscribed and sinister Land League: '... the onus of the proof lies upon Mr O'Shea alone; and we have never before had an Irish member making such an allegation against a lady. The Cabinet messenger to Kilmainham is bound to make good his imputation, and the public will listen to what he has got to say for himself ... The League at all events has its chance now ... But if it fails to make good the charge of imposture, that charge will have a recoil and imposture is a very ugly word.'[32]

In the end the storm blew itself out without spilling over onto the saucer. O'Shea thought better of the wording of the question and when he rose to put it to Harcourt on 29 March the phraseology was much more anodyne, merely inquiring of the Home Secretary whether the police had come to any conclusion on the matter. Harcourt responded in like manner. 'The accounts in this case rest mainly on the statements of Lady Florence Dixie,' he declared, skirting, while simultaneously hinting at, the issue of her credibility. 'The investigations of the police into this matter have not resulted in discovering any further circumstances in confirmation of it.'[33] As 'Toby MP' (Henry Lucy) put it in the pages of *Punch*, '... exit Lady FLORENCE. Pretty good joke in its way. But some jokes, like every dog, have their day, and this has had a week.'[34]

The episode, relatively unimportant in itself, illustrates the fact that, as far as Parnell was concerned, O'Shea still had his uses. While Katharine O'Shea was now accepted as the extra-parliamentary emissary between Parnell and Gladstone, she could not function on the floor of the House of Commons. O'Shea continued, though not exclusively, to fill that niche. He operated in the no man's land between the Irish and Liberal trenches as a phantom Whip, bringing Parnell's offers of procedural cooperation to Chamberlain and Dilke, and returning with the government response. Like a bottom-feeding fish he was essential to the continuity of the food chain, but shared the fate of the bottom-feeder in being under-appreciated by those further up the chain. As a conduit between two groups who, at that point in Anglo-Irish history, did not wish to appear to be too close to each other, he served a practical and constructive function. He did much of the work that, in a different environment, would have been undertaken by Lord Richard Grosvenor and his Irish party counterpart Richard Power. Provided, that is, his role was that of a mere cipher. As we shall see, it was when O'Shea exceeded his brief that things were apt to go awry.

One episode that almost went askew through no fault of his, illustrates the nature of his political 'consultancy' role. In August 1883 he had been involved in a procedural tryst between Parnell and the Liberals, in which the Irish leader, for his own reasons, had agreed not to delay the Bankruptcy Bill and the Corrupt Practices Bill. O'Shea was obviously very pleased with his handiwork. The *Irish Times* parliamentary correspondent described how he appeared in the chamber as the debate on the Bankruptcy

Bill began: 'We discerned an omen in the apparition. The gallant Captain was radiant, not to say resplendent. Got up in gorgeous array, with the rose of victory in his buttonhole, and a suggestion of successful diplomacy beaming from every lineament of his expressive countenance ...'[35] O'Shea, according to the newspaper, had come to an arrangement, on Parnell's behalf, with Chamberlain. Unfortunately a few practical details had been overlooked. O'Shea was in the chamber to witness the results of his exertions but neither Parnell nor Chamberlain were present. No one had told the Irish party member Arthur O'Connor that a deal had been done and, assuming the nationalist imperative was to continue making a nuisance, he was moving an adjournment. O'Shea was forced to exit the chamber hurriedly and go in search of Parnell. When the Irish leader rushed onto the floor of the House he managed to rescue the transaction by instructing a baffled O'Connor to withdraw his motion.

In addition to O'Shea's continuing utility for Parnell both men were joined at the hip when it came to the ramifications of the Kilmainham Treaty. The work of John Mallon and the Dublin Metropolitan Police had borne fruit in the first quarter of 1883 with the trials in Dublin of the accused in the Phoenix Park murders. The evidence of the informer James Carey at the end of February 1883 allowed Forster to raise his *idée fixe* once again in the House of Commons. He drew Parnell and O'Shea into a renewed debate on the consequences of the still-disputed concordat. Carey had told the court about the activities of Land League organiser P.J. Sheridan who, he alleged, had moved around the west of Ireland disguised as a priest. Wherever the shadowy 'Fr Murphy' went, it was suggested, murder and mayhem soon followed. Carey also claimed in court that the money which had funded the Invincibles' activities had come from the Land League (a very good reason for Parnell to want to scotch the activities of Lady Florence Dixie a month later) and that the surgical knives used to kill Cavendish and Burke had been provided by Frank Byrne, Secretary of the Land League of Great Britain. Forster used Carey's testimony to renew his offensive. He tested the rules of the House to their limits and was given the sort of leeway an Irish member would not have been granted. While allowing that Parnell himself had not 'planned or perpetrated outrages or murders ...', he alleged that the Irish leader had '... either connived at them or, when warned, did not use his influence to prevent them.' This drew a rebuke from the Irish leader who shouted 'It is a lie' across the floor of the House at the former Chief Secretary. Forster continued his attack and then resumed his seat.

Parnell, at first, displayed both the utter contempt he felt for Forster and his disdain for English opinion by remaining silent in the face of the

Bradford MP's onslaught. To the chagrin of his party colleagues he remained in his seat. His only reaction was 'a scornful smile'.[36] The following day (23 February) he went on the offensive at the insistence of his party. Prowling at his heels, ready to snipe at Forster, was a vengeful O'Shea. Parnell, with a considerable degree of disingenuousness, dismissed Carey's testimony as the fantasies of an informer conjured up for the benefit of his interrogators. His sharpest cut was a recommendation, since the government was intent on pursuing the policy of coercion, that Forster return to his desk in Dublin 'to help Lord Spencer in the congenial work of the gallows in Ireland'. An element of Parnell's defence, which he emphasised was being made for the benefit of the Irish electorate and not the House, was Forster's exclusion of any reference made by O'Shea in April 1882 to the need for the assistance of Davitt, Egan and Boyton, as well as the menacing Sheridan. After he had finished, O'Shea rose but introduced an element of farce by simply walking out of the chamber to the raucous delight of the assembly. He was, however, back very shortly with a copy of Hansard from 16 May 1882. He quoted from the debate that day in support of his contention that Forster, in compiling the memo of their meeting of 30 April 1882, had deliberately omitted mention of any Land League organiser other than Sheridan. O'Shea reiterated his claim that he had stressed the equally important role that would be played by the others in quelling what Forster had misquoted him as describing as a 'conspiracy'. 'I would ask,' he concluded, 'why did he not keep a note of the whole con-versation? Did he wish to hoodwink his colleagues?'[37]

A fortnight later O'Shea followed up his defence of Parnell (and of his own credibility) with a letter to the *Times* in further refutation of Forster's attack in the Commons. Like so much of O'Shea's writings, speeches and activities it combined intelligent discourse and subtle argument with a thudding pomposity. He opened with the startling statement that 'Whatever may have been the differences between Mr Parnell's views and mine on matters of politics and policy, he is my friend and I hope you will allow me to defend him.' He then rehearsed the arguments he had made in the Commons, elaborated on them by the inclusion of some well-researched references to Hansard, and accused Forster of '... trying to drive out of bounds a considerable man, with the aid of whose talents and influence exercised, as I believe they would be, for moderation and within legality, a gradual and peaceful solution of the Irish problem might have been found.'

But, characteristically, he couldn't resist injecting himself into the argument. On a personal note he hypothesised, 'Supposing, for the sake of argument, that Sheridan be the dangerous character which Mr Forster and Carey describe him to be, and even that in a confidential conversation with Mr Forster I had mentioned, as the latter erroneously imagines, that Sheridan had been engaged in a conspiracy to get up outrages; might not Mr Forster by the public statement that I had informed on Sheridan have cost my life to the gang?' As if that wasn't enough he concluded with a typically self-aggrandising anecdote:

> The House of Commons and the public know Mr Parnell only as the man of hard, cold, undemonstrative bearing. I have seen him with the mask off. When the news of the murders in the Phoenix Park reached London he came to me, and if ever a public man was overcome by horror and grief for public crime, it was he. He then and there drew up an address announcing in a few words his retirement in despair from political life. I myself approved of this course under the circumstances, but I insisted on an hour's delay in order that I might consult with other heads than mine. In deference to their counsels I eventually prevailed upon him with great difficulty to alter his determination.[38]

It was an O'Shea formulation with just enough truth to pass muster in his own imagination, but it was still breathtakingly arrogant and utterly nonsensical.

HUSBAND, COLLEAGUE, FRIEND

Whatever mutual ulterior motives brought the O'Gorman Mahon and William Henry O'Shea together in the first place, their relationship developed over time into one of considerable warmth and genuine friendship. O'Shea's letters to Mahon are chatty and irreverent, while still maintaining an element of deference. The younger man was careful to stroke Mahon's sizeable ego, seeing his own vanity mirrored in that of his potentially prickly, but ultimately avuncular, colleague. In 1885 Mahon might well have saved his Clare seat by disavowing O'Shea. He chose not to do so. When the divorce controversy convulsed the party (Mahon had returned to parliament after a by-election in Carlow in 1887) he chose to believe O'Shea's version of events and repudiated Parnell.

But the two Clare MPs do appear to have had at least one major difference of opinion which threatened to lead to yet another resort to 'powder and steel'. The dispute originated from a piece written in, of all places, the Preston *Guardian*, hardly a source much consulted by the Irish electorate, still less by the voters of Clare. But the *Clare Journal*, in a piece of opportunistic mischief-making, picked up the story and reproduced it verbatim in its issue of 17 July 1882, while describing the *Guardian* as 'an ultra Liberal journal'. According the Lancashire paper's London correspondent, Mahon had, shortly before, been invited to dinner by Forster: 'He accepted the invitation and even boasted of it afterwards. This step was regarded as high treason, and The O'Gorman Mahon is now formally Boycotted. His colleague in the representation of Clare is one of the bitterest denunciators of his treasonable act, and has formally acquainted The O'Gorman Mahon that he cannot hold any further communication with him.'

The *Journal* then added its own pithy commentary, opining that 'We really cannot see what social amenities have to do with a man's politics, though it is said the most trenchant weapon yet discovered for knocking patriotism out of an Irish Member is a good ministerial dinner. Still we cannot believe that any number of dinners in this particular department of mastication and mutability would make the old veteran of '28 swerve from his allegiances.'[39]

A letter in Mahon's papers indicates how personally offensive he found the article. It is from a supporter named Bernard J. Molloy. O'Shea had already telegraphed the *Journal* denying the report and demanding that the paper print a retraction. Mahon had apparently asked Molloy to speak to O'Shea and refer him to a 'friend' – the old duellist intending to settle the matter in traditional fashion. Molloy informed the Colonel that 'I took the responsibility upon myself not to do so ... As you desire so much to maintain your friendly relations with him I ... sincerely hope this incident may not impair it.'[40] On 22 July the *Clare Advertiser* had reported that O'Shea had written to Kilrush denying the story. Had he not done so he might have found himself staring at a doughty 82-year-old antagonist down the barrel of a duelling pistol.

His relationship with that other aristocratic figure with whom he had avoided such an encounter, Charles Stewart Parnell, is hard to fathom at this juncture in both their lives. The extent of O'Shea's awareness in 1883–84 of his wife's relationship with the Irish party leader will be discussed elsewhere, but Parnell's knowledge of his own sexual affair with Katharine O'Shea did not prevent him from having a thoroughgoing professional relationship with her husband. The staggering nature of the assertion of O'Shea in his 8 March 1883 letter to the *Times* that Parnell '... is my friend and I hope you will allow me to defend him ...' is only astonishing with hindsight. Whether through ignorance, acquiescence or blatant ambition, in the mid-1880s O'Shea was eager to engage in a professional collaboration with Parnell. Whether through vulnerability, guilt or expediency, Parnell was content to encourage that collaboration.

This is not just evident in the swathe of letters from this period between O'Shea and Chamberlain, in which the former purports to represent or reflect the thinking of Parnell on a range of issues. In March 1884 the two men also became involved in a project that brought them together in a highly visible fashion. This was the Irish Purchase and Settlement Company, established in 1883 to take advantage of a provision in the Tramways and Public Companies (Ireland) Act, 1883, of a government grant of £50,000 'for the purpose of removal and settlement'.[41] The principle behind the enterprise was to seek share capital of £250,000, add it to the government finance, purchase estates around the country, and establish a form of internal migration by settling impoverished farmers from the west of Ireland on the purchased land. 'The farms of those who go will be consolidated with the farms of those who remain' was the optimistic claim of the published prospectus. Parnell was the company chairman and among the directors were Radical MP Jacob Bright (son of John), *Freeman* proprietor and former Richmond prison inmate, Edmund Dwyer Gray, Galway MP Colonel John Philip Nolan, and Queens's Counsel and Liberal MP, Charles Russell, who four years later would searchingly cross-examine O'Shea at the *Times* Special Commission hearings, and the Captain himself.

United Ireland hailed the experiment in its 29 March 1884 issue, declaring, 'It contains the germs of two critical experiments – the creation of an occupying proprietary, and the establishment of home settlement in substitution for emigration ... we trust Irish people far and wide will be found eager to bear a hand in the work.' Unfortunately few such eager participants ever emerged. The project, while excellent in theory, never worked in practice. The preposterous failure to fill out the relevant administrative application form in time meant the company was not eligible for government funding. Few subscribers could be found to purchase shares, despite Parnell's efforts to get, for example, Boards of Poor Law Guardians to contribute.[42]

The success of the Irish Land Purchase and Settlement Company also depended on a major change of culture in parts of the country. The logic of the experiment lay in the purchase of a number of sparsely populated livestock 'grazing' estates and the substitution of more population-intensive tillage farming. Only one property was ever purchased: the 2,700-acre Bodkin estate in Kilcloony, County Galway, bought for £43,000.[43] In a speech in Tuam around the time the sale was being negotiated Parnell made the point that 'vast areas of cultivatable land, which are now left without anything save bullocks and sheep, shall once more afford a home and sustenance to mankind.'[44] Unfortunately this particular swallow did not make a summer and the company was wound up with embarrassing rapidity. Accompanying Parnell and Colonel Nolan (towards the end of May) on the inspection tour of the Kilcloony estate (though this fact was not acknowledged in the *Nation* coverage of the story) was Captain O'Shea. In his biography of Parnell, F.S.L. Lyons suggests that travelling with O'Shea and Parnell 'must have taxed Colonel Nolan's diplomatic and conversational powers to the utmost.'[45] In fact Parnell and O'Shea were on excellent terms at this point. After the Galway excursion they abandoned their chaperone and spent some time together in Avondale.[46] This amicable relationship is all the more extraordinary when it is borne in mind that Katharine O'Shea was three months pregnant at the time with her sixth and last child, Frances Katie Flavia (Katie), who was born on 27 November 1884.

Katharine's fifth child, Clare Gabrielle Antoinette Marcia Esperance O'Shea, known as Clare, had been born on 4 March 1883. Katharine makes no reference whatever to either child in her memoir and their existences were downplayed to such an extent that when Henry Harrison became part of Katharine's domestic circle in 1891 he was surprised and delighted to discover that Parnell had two children. In the divorce proceedings in 1890 both were named as O'Shea's children but it was later tacitly acknowledged by all concerned that Parnell had been the father.

But did O'Shea still have reason to believe that he might, conceivably, have been father to one or both of Parnell's girls? Here T.P. O'Connor's recollections are useful if somewhat contradictory. In his *Memoirs of an Old Parliamentarian*, Tay Pay (as he was affectionately known) has an extraordinary account of a visit paid by O'Shea and Parnell to the London offices of the *Freeman's Journal* near the Victoria Embankment. His information came from the newspaper's London correspondent, J.M. Tuohy, a man, according to his fellow journalist, 'incapable of inventing any event'.

Tuohy's account of the interview has O'Shea proffering a letter for inclusion in the correspondence columns of the *Freeman*. It was the letter of 8 March 1883, (see above) also published in the *Times*, in which O'Shea defends 'my friend' (Parnell) against the allegations of Forster in the House of Commons on 22 February. Parnell then reached into his pocket and pulled out a piece of paper that he showed to O'Shea. He then 'asked him whether he should also supply this information to the *Freeman's Journal*. O'Shea nodded an assent, and Parnell handed the document to Mr. Tuohy.' It was the announcement of the birth of a daughter to Mrs O'Shea, wife of Captain O'Shea; the kind of notice that might have been expected to emanate from her husband rather than Parnell.

O'Connor then guardedly speculates on the ongoing relationship between husband and wife by introducing hearsay evidence based on what Henry Labouchere had told him about a conversation he had once had with O'Shea. 'The story of O'Shea to Labby was that Mrs O'Shea used to pay him occasional visits at Albert Mansions and – I need not be more precise, but suggest the humiliating and shameful compromises which married women who have a lover sometimes have to submit to. At that I have to leave it.' If O'Shea's story was true, and a sexual relationship of sorts persisted between husband and wife in 1883–4, then he could have had reason to believe that he was the father of Clare and Katie.

He probably would not have been interested in more than the occasional conjugal visit from his wife. O'Connor also refers to the widespread belief that O'Shea was a serial womaniser.[47] In his memoir he recounts a story of passing by O'Shea near Vauxhall Bridge Road; the Captain was in the company of a lady. The Liverpool MP always made it a rule to be discreet in such cases. He passed by the pair in such a way that O'Shea could imagine he had not been spotted. However, later that day in the House of Commons the Captain approached him. 'He began eagerly to enter into an explanation as to the identity of the lady with whom he had been walking. He told me, but whether true or false I do not know, that the woman I had seen him with was a maid to a very important lady of the social world with whom it was his duty to conciliate or to consult. I could not help thinking even at that time his manner suggested that of a man – as the Americans say – covering his tracks.'[48]

Apart from the name assigned to Katharine's fifth child,[49] her baptism in a Roman Catholic Church in a ceremony organised by O'Shea himself suggests either ignorance of the true situation, a high degree of complicity, or an assertion by O'Shea of his parental and conjugal authority. The baptism took place in Brighton on 2 May 1883. Given Katharine's reaction to the baptism of Carmen (see p. 15) she can hardly have been happy at the child of two Protestant parents receiving the initiation rites of the Roman Catholic Church.

A few weeks after the baptism of Clare the slowly disintegrating wall of silence which surrounded the Parnell–Katharine O'Shea affair was significantly breached, at least according to the highly dubious source, Tim Healy. In June 1883 he ran as a candidate for a vacant seat in Monaghan, which he duly won. In the course of the campaign, however, a telegram arrived for an absent Parnell at the hotel in Monaghan town where the candidate and his entourage were staying. It was opened by Newry solicitor and Wexford MP, J.F. Small. It read, according to Healy, 'The Captain is away. Please come. Don't fail – Kate.' Healy upbraided Small for opening the telegram but the situation could not be rectified as the solicitor had disposed of the accompanying envelope. Small, wisely, decided against showing the contents to Parnell. He did, however, at a later date show the telegram to one of Parnell's inveterate opponents in the Irish party, the bibulous Philip Callan, who made good use of the threat of revealing the information. When Parnell eventually became aware of what had happened, Small's political career went into a rapid decline and he did not figure in the General Election of 1886.[50]

Just as with 'Lizzie of Blankshire' this story has a ring of fantasy, invention or exaggeration about it. Parnell and Katharine were seasoned in the dark arts of postal duplicity by 1883. It is hard to imagine that she would have sent him an open communication unless it contained some element of personal encryption. Furthermore, the Captain was not 'away'. While the campaign was going on in Monaghan O'Shea was in London. He is recorded by Hansard as having spoken six times in the House in the month of June 1883.[51] Given his propensity for descending on his wife's abode without warning, he was never safely 'away' unless he was out of the country. At the end of the month of June and into July he did visit his constituency of Clare but Parnell was well aware of that and sought to meet him there after his own Cork electors held a banquet in his honour on 4 July. Parnell was in the process of assessing for himself the viability of a future O'Shea candidature in Clare. He had already spoken to one of the Captain's principal sponsors in his run for the seat in 1880. He wrote to Katharine (openly) on 4 July, 'I have had several conversations with Fr White, who is a very superior man, and has impressed me very much. I intend to make it my first business to look up west Clare and trust that Captain O'Shea may be able to meet me there.'[52]

There is no evidence from local Clare newspapers that Parnell ever made it to west Clare on that occasion, unless he travelled incognito. But he does appear to have gathered further intelligence on O'Shea's political predicament. A couple of days later he wrote to Katharine from Dublin letting her know that he was to meet her husband in the capital city rather than in Clare, '... shall see him Wednesday evening or Thursday morning and do what I can. I fear his position in Clare is irretrievable.'[53] Both their efforts were focused on keeping O'Shea content and occupied. In this regard the retention of a seat in parliament was a *sine qua non*.

So whether peaceful relations were based on a clear mutual understanding or continued deception, the fact was that throughout 1883 and well into 1884 Parnell and O'Shea behaved publicly as two men with friendly personal and professional relations, albeit not attempting to hide their political differences. T.P. O'Connor described their public dealings as 'ostentatiously fraternal'. O'Shea, when sitting on the government benches, would constantly cross to the other side of the House to speak with the Irish leader: 'Whenever O'Shea came across the House to Parnell, the attitude of Parnell to him was always that of an elder brother – indeed, the attitude of a brother advising or even reproving a younger brother. I remember one day hearing Parnell say to O'Shea, "I think it would be very foolish" – evidently discussing some action which O'Shea contemplated, and O'Shea seemed to submit to the advice.'[54]

The atmosphere changed, however, in the late summer of 1884.

REDISCOVERY

The previous winter Katharine had rented a house in Brighton in her own name (as she had been entitled to do since the passage of the Married Women's Property Act of 1882). It was chosen because it had taken Parnell's fancy. But, indicating that he was still head of one of her households, O'Shea had countermanded her choice and forced/persuaded her to opt instead for the seaside house of 8 Medina Terrace in nearby Hove. He was a frequent visitor himself, as was Parnell, at O'Shea's invitation. In her memoir Katharine writes about the two men discussing the Local Government Bill 'at all hours, as Parnell wished to find out what the views of Mr Chamberlain and the Tories were – better ascertainable by Willie than others.'[55] She recounts how O'Shea spent Christmas in Hove with his children while she returned to Eltham to be with her aunt. There is no mention of whether her youngest child accompanied her or remained on the south coast. At Eltham she was joined by Parnell.

According to her account, O'Shea travelled to Ireland in January,[56] just when he was beginning to come under renewed local and national pressure over the retention of his seat. She then claims that he returned to the UK in February, said goodbye to his children in Brighton and left the country for Lisbon. At the end of that month the lease on 8 Medina Terrace ran out and the family returned to Eltham. Although she makes no reference to it, within a matter of weeks she was pregnant with Katie. At this point in her narrative she blithely skips from February to May 1884 (and the O'Shea visit to Avondale, see above), and thence to late October when she describes herself as being 'ill'. In fact she was a month away from giving birth. She also records that 'Captain O'Shea was coming to Eltham a good deal.' She writes as if nothing much had happened in the interim, but O'Shea's account to the Divorce Court of events in late 1884 tells an utterly different story. However, when compared with the known facts, neither account is entirely credible.

Katharine is clearly incorrect in suggesting that O'Shea had departed for the continent in February. He questioned the Chief Secretary on the Crimes Act on 29 February 1884. He voted with the Irish party against the government on Parnellite amendments to the Land Law (Ireland) Act on 5 March, and pops up at regular intervals with questions or speeches throughout the month and into early April. He does not disappear from view until after 7 April. Why she insisted that he was not in England in March will soon become clear.

O'Shea, on the other hand, wanted to stitch into the record that he had left England for Portugal and Spain in *March* and had returned in July or August 1884. He was certainly in Lisbon in early May as the *Independent and Munster Advertiser* reported that he had fallen ill there.[57] But he had returned by the end of the month as he was touring the Kilcloony estate with Parnell and Colonel Nolan.

Both O'Shea and his wife had diametrically opposed agendas. Katharine, albeit without any reference to her pregnancy or the birth of her daughter, wanted O'Shea out of England in March so that he could not be advanced as the father of Katie. Conversely O'Shea had to convince the divorce court that he was her father. He claimed as much in direct evidence. It was an integral piece of the mosaic he constructed for the divorce court which, when seen in its totality, created a poignant picture of a wronged and deceived husband. As it happens his account of his departure date appears to be more accurate than hers. What followed was mostly pure invention. 'In July or August I heard vague rumours that Mr Parnell had been seen at Eltham,' he told the court.[58] This prompted him to write an aggrieved letter to Parnell on 4 August 1884.

'You have behaved very badly to me,' he complained trenchantly. 'While I have often told you that you were welcome to stay at Eltham whenever I was there I begged of you not to do so during my absence, since it would be sure at the least sooner or later to cause scandal.'[59] In the same letter he also indicated his intention to resign his seat and take his family abroad. Three days later Parnell responded coolly that 'I do not know of any scandal, or any ground for one, and can only suppose that you have misunderstood the drift of some statements that may have been made about me.'[60] Far from trying to dissuade O'Shea from resigning, he requested him to do so towards the end of the parliamentary session so that the by-election could take place during the recess.

What 'vague rumours' had O'Shea heard that had prompted such an extreme response? In all probability it was nothing that he had heard, but rather the evidence of his own eyes. A letter sent by Katharine the same day, 7 August, conveys the salient information that they had had a heated discussion a couple of days before. In early August, when that argument took place, she would have been roughly 23 weeks pregnant, something she could hardly have hidden from her husband. It was this discovery, and presumably the certain knowledge that the child was not his, that had sparked off his renewed anger. Later, when their relationship reached a new low in 1887, he would claim that she had hidden her pregnancy from him. At that time she responded to the allegation by declaring that 'Your assertion that I at any time "concealed the fact of my being in the family way" is simply a foul lie ...'[61] If, as we have speculated, Katharine had obtained her 'conjugal freedom' from O'Shea in October 1882 he might have been able to convince himself (as he had successfully done in the case of Claude Sophie) that he was the father of Clare, born six months later. But he knew with absolute certainty that he was not the father of Katie (to whom he referred in the divorce Court as 'Frances').

A hint of this is contained in O'Shea's own notation on some of his correspondence. Atop a brief letter from Chamberlain, of December 1884, is his observation that it was 'Mr Chamberlain's letter regretting I cd [sic] not come to dinner because of my sister's desperate state. I think she died on 8th December '84 *a few days after the birth of the last child*'[62] [my italics]. When writing to Chamberlain in April 1882, after the death of Claude Sophie, he had referred to the funeral of '*my* daughter'. In the case of the birth of Katie the terminology is much more impersonal, the definite article is chosen over the personal pronoun. This suggests what was subsequently (though only privately) acknowledged to be the case, that Katie was Parnell's child. This was despite the fact that on 4 December 1884 the *Times* announced the birth of another daughter to 'Captain O'Shea and his wife Katharine'.

For a second time O'Shea had accused Parnell of having an affair with his wife. Interestingly on both occasions he had chosen to complain to him in writing rather than confront him directly. That would have been enough to have ended most friendships, professional or personal. It might also have been expected to prompt a verifiable estrangement between husband and wife. But the triangular relationship simply continued just as before. O'Shea and Parnell remained as collaborators on a political level. O'Shea's letters to his wife (which reappear in her memoir from late October 1884 onwards) resume, in tone, where they left off – the chatty and intimate correspondence of married partners. Why did O'Shea light the fuse, then stamp it out and retire? Presumably because he had two excellent reasons for doing so: the potential professional rewards of a political understanding with Parnell and the personal financial gain to be made from continuing to deceive the censorious Aunt Ben.

We can be morally certain that, by the autumn of 1884, O'Shea had no further reason to doubt the rumours that surrounded his wife and Parnell. The only thing that could be presented as an argument against this thesis is that his sexual relationship with his wife had continued into early 1884 at least. Otherwise he would have been aware that he had been cuckolded when his wife's pregnancy became apparent. The 4 August letter suggests that he had no grounds whatever for believing himself responsible for Katharine being 'with child'. But it seems to have taken some little time for the logic of his situation to dawn on him. There is evidence that as late as October 1884 Parnell and Katharine were still involved in misdirecting or deceiving him as to Parnell's movements and, as we have already noted, in that month Katharine acknowledged that O'Shea was coming to Eltham 'a good deal'. But at some point, possibly after the birth of Katie, an understanding or accommodation, clear or tacit, was reached between the three.

It was around this time that Katharine began the building of an extension to Wonersh Lodge, a workshop and study for Parnell in which he could work on his beloved scientific experiments and investigate the heavens through his favourite telescope, brought over from Ireland. In early January 1885 Parnell, the thoroughgoing equestrian, had two horses, 'President' and 'Home Rule', shipped over from Ireland to be stabled at Eltham. For Parnell there could be no clearer gesture of relaxed domesticity. This was not a couple that expected to be surprised by any further unforeseen visits from a suspicious husband. O'Shea, for the time being, could see very plainly where his interests lay. He might not have been happy with the arrangement but, as long as some element of discretion was maintained, he did not concern himself unduly.

From this point a significant proportion of the formal correspondence between the three has the air of contrivance about it. This is reflected, for example, in letters such as the one in which O'Shea invited Parnell to spend part of Christmas at Wonersh Lodge[63] and Parnell's formal request of Katharine for permission to lodge his horses at Eltham 'for a few days'.[64] They read as if they are for the benefit of the credulous Aunt Ben. Astonishingly this sort of pretence was still maintained by O'Shea in 1887, long after relations between the three had soured beyond the point of redemption. On 27 December the *Times* Dublin Correspondent reprinted a story from the *Cork Examiner* to the effect that 'Mr. Parnell is spending the Christmas holidays with Captain O'Shea at North Park, Eltham ...' Had such an arrangement, in fact, taken place it would by then have taken more than their Galway tour guide, Colonel Nolan, to have broken the ice between Parnell and O'Shea.

CHAPTER 9

Unseated

I dreamt that I dwelt in Westminster Halls
And that I was the Member for Clare.
And of all who assembled within these walls
I had the best right to be there.
I thought that at twenty-five pennies a head
The electors I bought in a lot;
And the very first night that I went into bed
My pledges at once were forgot.

Clare Independent, 5 April 1879

THE MAN ON THE TRICYCLE

It is striking when consulting Hansard for the decade of the 1880s how much of the time of the House of Commons was taken up with Irish affairs. In addition to the marquee issues of land legislation and coercion there was a multiplicity of local matters raised by Irish MPs, as well as discussion of the application of legislation of a general nature to a specifically Irish context. With 103 Irish MPs, most of whom were not aligned to any governing party and many of whom were independently minded and dismissive of the niceties of Commons traditions, the House was never far from the next Irish question, intervention or filibuster. One exception was the year 1884. With the Liberal government preoccupied with electoral reform and its imperial adventures in the Sudan, Ireland slipped far down the administrative agenda. The Coercion regime was firmly in place until the end of the 1884–85 session so there was little onus on the Liberals to enact any further palliative measures.

Instead Gladstone's government concentrated on rectifying the deficiencies of Disraeli's 1867 electoral reforms. The introduction of the Ballot Act in 1872 had been Gladstone's previous boon to British participatory democracy. But being able to vote in secret was of little use if one possessed insufficient property to be allowed vote in the first place. The 1884 Representation of the People Bill (along with the Redistribution Bill which would alter the shape of constituencies in Britain and Ireland) was designed to greatly lower property qualifications and hugely increase the franchise. Of course if it had that effect in Britain, the results in Ireland would be similar. It did not take a political genius to realise that more Irish voters meant more Home Rule seats and more influence for Parnell.

Attempts to exclude Ireland from the terms of the Bill and to reduce the number of Irish seats were both successfully resisted with the result that the Irish electorate more than trebled, rising from 226,000 to 738,000 voters.[1] The disappearance of the borough constituencies (such as Ennis) with the electorate numbering in the hundreds (rather than the thousands of the county electoral areas) also played into the hands of the Parnellites. A Whig or a Tory candidate might have some chance of winning a seat in the context of a restricted franchise,[2] but not when the average electorate was around 7,000. The Reform Bill was passed in December 1884. It was supported by the bulk of the Irish members, including the likes of Sir Rowland Blennerhasset and the O'Donoghue. The familiar turkey/Christmas metaphor is inescapable. *United Ireland* predicted that 'The Nominals, of course, will be entirely swept away or replaced by Nationalists.'[3] And so it proved.

At least one leading Liberal was conscious of the implications of this sweeping change. Radical leader, Joseph Chamberlain, looked forward to a fundamental realignment in British politics. A doubling of the British electorate and the inclusion in electoral politics for the first time of a significant working-class element held out the prospect of, at the very least, the Radical faction dominating the Liberal party after the next election. This was due in 1886 at the latest. A likely consequence of that would be the flight of the Whigs to their natural home in the Conservative party and the destruction of one of the pillars of Gladstone's leadership, his presence as peacemaker and mediator between the Liberal left and right wings. When the possibility was added of the Randolph Churchill-led faction within the Tories (often referred to as the Fourth Party) breaking away from its moorings, then the prospect beheld by Chamberlain was rosy indeed.

Chamberlain's interest in Ireland and the Irish party (already considerable) increased exponentially. There was talk of Parnell returning to parliament after the next election with 83–85 pledged candidates ready to do his bidding. There was also the newly enfranchised Irish vote in British urban constituencies to be taken into consideration. If directed to support Radical candidates, it would further increase Chamberlain's leverage within the Liberal party. The Birmingham businessman, whose talents were underused at the Board of Trade, would have seen the Irish party as natural, if potentially quixotic, allies of the Radicals. In the context of class politics most Irish voters were members of an underclass that should have been a naturally radical constituency. Their representatives often came across as fire-breathing populists. One of the leaders of the Irish agrarian movement, Michael Davitt, was a socialistic supporter of land nationalisation. The likes of William O'Shea, accused in Ireland of being a Whig, were comfortable with the company and, by extension therefore, the policies, of Chamberlain and Dilke. If Chamberlain was to realise his ambitions of shifting British politics to the left and wresting the leadership of the Liberals from the aged Grand Old Man, he needed a Liberal–Irish alliance that owed allegiance to him rather than Gladstone.

Of course he miscalculated on a number of fronts simultaneously. O'Shea's allegiance to Chamberlain and Dilke was not ideological, therefore he was not a political marker by which one could assess the politics of those who viewed him as a Whig. Even the term 'Whig' itself, as applied in an Irish context, had a rather different connotation. In British politics a Whig represented the landed interest and was, essentially, a conservative politician with liberal pretensions or inclinations. In Ireland, while the term did have 'class' applications, it was a rolled-up term of abuse that encompassed sins of collaboration and political avidity. Gradually it would be replaced by the much more descriptive 'West Briton'.

Where Michael Davitt was concerned, while his iconic status in the agrarian and nationalist movements was guaranteed, his socialist interpretation of that wonderfully ambiguous phrase 'the land for the people'[4] had been undermined and marginalised by Parnell. Neither were the Irish parliamentary firebrands as radical as the Liberal establishment took them to be. It is intriguing that even by 1884 – two years after the Kilmainham Treaty – the association of the Irish party with the continuation of 'outrage' in Ireland conferred on its members an ongoing pariah status.

While there were some direct contacts between the government and the Parnellites, when the likes of Chamberlain wanted to find out the thoughts of Parnell they, by and large, didn't consult the man directly but went through intermediaries like O'Shea and Labouchere. Chamberlain overestimated the potential radical sympathies of Irish members whose occasional obstructionism and bloody-mindedness disguised their innate conservatism. It was a conservatism shared by their leader.

Chamberlain also underestimated the power of the political philosophy that motivated the Irish MPs who sat on the opposition benches. Irish nationalism of a Parnellite hue would, in 1885, sweep away Whiggery and Toryism. That much was predictable in 1884. But it would also resist the blandishments of O'Shea's brand of clientelism and trump Chamberlain's radicalism into the bargain. Such eventualities did not preclude an alliance of convenience between 85 Irish nationalists and a potentially larger cohort of Radicals led by the Birmingham MP. But when the priority of the nationalists was to take a major step in the direction of the legislative independence of Ireland and a priority of the Radical leader was the preservation of the Union, a political marriage was not in the tea-leaves.

The impression conveyed when one reads the correspondence surrounding an attempted démarche by Chamberlain in 1885, which has to become known as the 'Central Board' scheme (sometimes referred to as 'National Councils'), is of a man peering 'through a glass darkly'. Here was someone conscious that his own English working- and lower middle-class constituency was dubious about political fraternisation with the Irish. He was also dealing with an alien political culture, while being himself guided by instincts more attuned to the British midlands or the Houses of Parliament than the Bog of Allen. His lighthouse was a place-seeking Irish politician uncertain of his own bearings and intent on enhancing his own reputation. And the object of his courtship was a notoriously opaque figure who saw little to gain by encouraging Chamberlain's political ambitions.

Chamberlain did not want the Liberals to go into an 1885–86 election with nothing in the Irish cupboard other than a further (inevitable) dose of arbitrary search, arrest and detention. He sought a way to retain elements of coercion, while softening the blow with an earnest of positive Liberal intentions. In concert with O'Shea, he began exploring models for future Irish local government. Towards the end of November 1884 O'Shea forwarded a document to Chamberlain, which he claimed reflected Parnell's views on 'a considerable measure of County Government' as well as the suggestion that the revivifying of coercion be limited to one year.[5] He also, apparently, enclosed a copy of the Prevention of Crime Act with excisions from Parnell that constituted his view of what form renewed coercion legislation might take.

On 17 December Chamberlain responded to a letter from a Walsall solicitor, W.H. Duignan, which sought his views on the future governance of Ireland. Duignan had just returned from a cycling tour of the country and had been struck by the inadequacies of British administration there. With a clear view to the circulation of the letter Chamberlain allowed Duignan to show it to interested parties. It encapsulated his viewpoint on matters of Irish concern, principally with regard to what he characterised as local government. He expressed support for a large measure of Irish self-administration, including responsibility for education, transport and agriculture. He acknowledged that the local legislators '... would, of course, be invested with powers of taxation in Ireland for these strictly Irish purposes.' As a former Mayor of Birmingham, Chamberlain knew 'how much good could be done through popularly elected local government.'[6]

The letter was, presumably, intended as a bridge-building exercise. It served as an illustration of the possibilities inherent in an Irish–Radical alliance (with Chamberlain as Prime Minister in a more left-leaning Liberal administration as subtext). If so it displayed a lack of sensitivity and political nous not untypical of paternalistic British would-be champions of the Irish cause. In the course of offering blithely to come to Ireland and 'make a speech or two' in favour of such proposals and suggesting that 'If they were carried out the Irish people would have entire independence as regards all local work and local expenditure ...', he managed to add the astonishing comment that, in such an event, 'Irish newspapers and politicians would find occupation, I hope, more congenial than that of bullying English officials and the English house of commons ...' Obviously the *Skibbereen Eagle* and its like were taking their toll on the Tsar of Birmingham.

But the first shoots of defeat for his proposals were not in the disparaging subtext but in the opening paragraphs. There Chamberlain emerged as an unrepentant Empire Loyalist who could '... never consent to regard Ireland as a separate people with the inherent rights of an absolutely independent community ... if nationalism means separation, I for one am prepared to resist it. Sooner than yield on this point I would govern Ireland by force to the end of the chapter.'[7] The latter point was hardly calculated to be of any assistance to someone who was looking for a deal on coercion. But it was the categorical opposition to anything even vaguely resembling Home Rule that must have struck those favoured with copies of the document (Parnell and Healy amongst them). It afforded a simple explanation as to why Chamberlain was prepared to advance what

were, by the standards of day, meaningful concessions to Irish nationalist opinion. His proposals were designed as an alternative to total
separation or legislative independence. They were designed to pull the
teeth of any concerted drive towards Home Rule.

Parnell was prepared to study what Chamberlain had to offer, but only
qua local government. When he examined detailed proposals emanating
from the Radical leader, which were passed to him by O'Shea, he warned
the intermediary 'In talking to our friend you must give him clearly to
understand that we do *not* propose this local self government plank as a
substitute for the restitution of our Irish parliament but solely as an
improvement of the present system of local government in Ireland.'[8]
Parnell's own ideas on the issue reflected his wider political agenda.
Chamberlain's proposals were more far-reaching, enabling and comprehensive than Parnell's. They envisaged not just increased powers for local
councils, but also the creation of a Central Board in Dublin, which would
exercise some of the powers that might have been expected to be within
the purview of an Irish legislative assembly. Parnell's alternative proposal
downplayed this element, while acknowledging the need for a Central
Board of some kind. Interestingly Parnell, in outlining his more modest
template, added the rider that 'For the purpose of these elections the representatives of the landowners would have a separate elective power
proportionate to that of their constituents in the elections to the County
Boards.'[9] The Wicklow squire was not about to allow the peasants the
run of the estate on their own. Unsurprisingly, the central body designed
by the Birmingham Radical contained no such provision.[10] Equally significant, for entirely different reasons, was the fact that Parnell's proposals
were contained in a document signed, not by him, but by O'Shea. In all
the correspondence in the course of the controversy the only important
documents signed by Parnell were two letters to O'Shea that would come
back to haunt the Clare MP.

Parnell's injunction to O'Shea to be emphatic with Chamberlain about
the exact scope of the negotiations proved to be an inconvenience for the
emissary. Back in December 1884 O'Shea had represented the embryonic
proposals of Parnell as sufficient 'to satisfy the Irish people'. Now, in
January 1885, the Irish leader was making it clear to the go-between that,
while the proposals he was formulating would 'satisfy the Irish people',
when it came to local government they were not be taken as any sort of
final solution to the issue of legislative independence. Parnell's Councils
and Central Board were administrative bodies only. This put O'Shea in a
bind. He could not see Home Rule as a realistic concession that would
ever be forthcoming from any British government and he wanted to be

one of the architects of a lesser 'peace deal' that would catapult Chamberlain into Downing Street (and himself into the Chief Secretary's Lodge in Phoenix Park). He replied on 6 January 1885 to Parnell's warning: ' I have kept our friend fairly informed, and I now scarcely know how to act, inasmuch as your letter would appear to convey, on the eve of coming to close quarters in the negotiations, that I am still to demand one of the widest extensions of political and popular administration imaginable, at the same time withdrawing any offer of party advantage or parliamentary peace.'[11]

O'Shea sought a meeting with Parnell on 7 January but, according to Katharine O'Shea, 'Parnell did not think it well to keep this appointment, as he distrusted proposals coming from this quarter as to Irish affairs.'[12] Instead he reiterated his position in writing on 13 January. In his letter to O'Shea he quoted from Chamberlain's correspondence with Duignan insisting that Chamberlain's template 'would cross the border-line between legislative and administrative functions ...' He spelt out clearly for O'Shea the limitations of his negotiating mandate: 'The two questions of the reform of local government and the restitution of an Irish parliament must, as I explained to you from the first, be left absolutely separate.'[13]

On 18 January, restrained by Parnell's double lock, O'Shea met with Chamberlain. In his political memoir Chamberlain would later claim that O'Shea had not informed him of the narrow parameters laid down by Parnell for the negotiations. This assertion was later underscored by his biographer J.L. Garvin who, recognising the crucial long-term implications of the misunderstanding, declared that: 'What led him [Chamberlain], however, to take action in a way that altered everything in politics was the assurance to him that the scheme was Parnell's 'own proposal' for a 'final settlement'. O'Shea suppressed the letters proving, with other evidence, that finality on this basis never for a single moment was contemplated or suggested in public or private by the Irish leader.'[14]

This has led to the assumption by many writers that O'Shea, a dog with a bad name, made no reference to Parnell's letters of 5 and 13 January in his discussions with Chamberlain. If this is the case then a question remains. What did the President of the Board of Trade mean when he said in a letter to John Morley three days later, when referring to the objectives of the Irish party, that '[They] profess to desire independent government and possibly separation.'?[15] If that information had not come from O'Shea, where had it come from? Henry Harrison, no advocate for the Captain, has asserted that 'there is no evidence that any such assurance that Parnell's scheme related to "a final settlement" was given or accepted by Chamberlain through Captain O'Shea ... such evidence as is available points to the opposite conclusion.'[16]

Aside from what he did or did not learn from O'Shea on 18 January, Chamberlain can have been under no illusions whatever about Parnell's stance on administrative versus legislative independence after the reports of the speech Parnell chose to make in his constituency on 21 January 1885, in which he famously observed that 'no man has the right to fix a boundary to the march of a nation'. He could have been talking about the restrictions laid down by Chamberlain himself. He certainly believed that he stood a far better chance of achieving his ultimate aim by convincing Gladstone of the wisdom of introducing Home Rule. If the Central Board controversy proved anything to Parnell, it was that Chamberlain's opposition would be a major obstacle to negotiate on the road to Home Rule.

On the strength of a lengthy conversation with Chamberlain, O'Shea chose, as was the norm in these circumstances, to convey the Radical leader's thoughts to Parnell in the form of an aide-memoire. Sent on 19 January to Morrison's Hotel in Dublin, it was probably meant to be informal and disarming. It was akin to a written expression of O'Shea's considerable verbal powers of charm and persuasion. If that is indeed the purpose, and it is probably an overly charitable suggestion, it was lost in the translation. Later described by Chamberlain as 'an odious letter, cynical, personal, mean ...'[17] and by O'Shea himself as 'the inconvenient letter', it is O'Shea at his worst, indiscreet, undiplomatic, dismissive, sneering and smug. It presumed greatly upon his 'friendship' with Parnell and, according to the Radical leader himself, it misrepresented Chamberlain's position in a highly embarrassing fashion.

The letter begins by disparaging W.H. Duignan as 'the man on the Tricycle', a person by the name of 'Dignum'. He continues to call him Dignum throughout the letter. The reason becomes clear later. To have done otherwise would have been to have missed the opportunity for a clever pun at Duignan's expense, since he observes of the Walsall solicitor's sense of his own importance that 'Dignum saw a chance of making himself *dignior* ...'; not, of course, something of which O'Shea could ever be accused. He went on to depict Chamberlain as someone who was having second thoughts about his widely circulated communication with Duignan, though 'in no way ashamed' about the opinions expressed therein.

Getting to the crux of the issue, he observed: 'I explained the position in which you are placed, and as long as you are practical for the time being, Chamberlain does not appear to mind the determination which you are expressing in your speeches of recovering Grattan's Parliament.' This can be seen to lend succour to the argument advanced above that O'Shea had informed Chamberlain of Parnell's warning to him. But one cannot help getting a nagging feeling that Chamberlain's insouciance may be because O'Shea had managed to convince him that such aspirations were pious platitudes on Parnell's part designed to appease 'The Boys'.

O'Shea succeeds in tarring Chamberlain's proposals with the brush of political expediency. He manages to represent them as a mere sop to obtain the support of the Irish, rather than as a desirable end in themselves. He quotes Chamberlain as warning '... that all this might be premature, that I was proceeding somewhat as if he were already Prime Minister and I Chief Secretary.' In summing up he represents his mentor as being prepared to go along with Parnell's proposals and to seek to restrict the extension of coercion to one year. In return Parnell will '... establish a distinction between your friends and foes in the government ...' This is a blatant indication that Parnell is expected to offer more overt support to the Radical cause. O'Shea also suggests that he adopt a cynical pose of opposition to a renewal of the Crimes Act, while actually allowing it to proceed. Chamberlain had told him, he avers, that his own supporters would be better pleased if he ignored Ireland, 'But he is anxious to settle Ireland, and he will work steadily and fairly with us if you will put him in a position to overcome objections by the argument of 80 votes.' He concludes with the assumption that Parnell will be able to enforce the acquiescence of the party to such a policy: 'When the centurions give the word "right about turn" the rank and file will, like true men and devoted soldiers, show their excellent discipline by immediate obedience.'[18]

Not only did this communication prove to be a significant hostage to fortune, it was also a breathtaking exercise in misplaced *realpolitik*. In its essence it may not have been too far from the truth, but it made absolutely no provision for a motivation on either side that deviated from absolute political cynicism. It was the philosophy of the huckster and neither of its intended readers saw themselves in that light. So confident was O'Shea that he was on the same political wavelength as Parnell and Chamberlain that, after despatching the letter to the former he sent a copy to Katharine. We do not know precisely why he did this other than, perhaps, to impress her that he was still very much at the centre of events. He asked her to forward it to Chamberlain. This she did, with very little attention to security or confidentiality (see below). Parnell did not reply to the letter. Chamberlain did so almost immediately and his response was the most stinging rebuke O'Shea ever suffered from his mentor's pen:

> Speaking frankly as a friend should do, I must say that you have a most damnable habit of letter writing. Take the present case; you came to me for a chat, and I talk to you, according to my wont, fully and openly – perhaps even indis-

creetly – about Irish affairs *et omnibus aliis*. If you thought the conversation of sufficient interest to justify you in transmitting your general impressions of it to any third person, I have no right to complain, though even here I think it would be better in such delicate matters to reserve the communication for oral intercourse, and not to trust it to the post. But you go much further! You send me a detailed précis of the interview according to your recollection of it, winding up with the heads of a cut and dried treaty of alliance, as to which I will only say that it resembles the late Lord Brougham's nose in its most important characteristic, namely that it is all on the one side. You ask me to approve of this document, which you send to me in an envelope which arrives open on two sides, whether by design or accident, I know not.

I can only reply that your report of the conversation seems to me to omit much that I considered of importance, and to include some things that I cannot accept as accurate, at all events without much qualification. Beyond this I cannot go in correspondence. I will talk with you as often as you like, and I cannot, of course, control your private correspondence, only you must please not make me responsible for it.

One thing, however, I must make clear, the time has not arrived for any negociation [*sic*] or agreement. I am very glad to know Mr Parnell's views on local government, which in principle seem to be the same as my own. If this turns out to be the case I shall be glad to find that we are working on the same lines. As to any support he may be able to give English Radicals in matters in which they are interested I will neither ask nor receive a pledge. Experience alone can show if there is any possibility of co-operation between the Irish party and the English democracy.[19]

As well as being a rebuke of O'Shea's indiscretions, the letter was intended to convey the impression of Chamberlain as an idealistic political purist, as a man of substance who was above grimy and hard-nosed political deals. He had been far less fastidious when he had told William O'Brien in the smoking room of the House of Commons on one occasion, 'You can have an Irish Republic, so far as I am concerned, if you will only first help me to dish the Whigs.'[20]

On the same day as the forthright rebuke of his messenger Chamberlain wrote to John Morley that 'I am beginning to be a little uneasy on the subject of Captain O'Shea's volunteered communications. I believe him to be perfectly honourable and sincere but he has a perfect mania for diplomacy and seems inclined to press matters forward as if he were actually negotiating a treaty between two high contracting parties.' He described O'Shea's letter to Parnell as '... a somewhat cynical account of our conversation, distorted to suit his own views. If such a work were published, it would be fatal to the work of reconciliation, for it would degrade the whole matter into a mere partisan bargaining, in which a bribe for Mr Parnell's support was to be offered by the radical party ... my impression is that a solution of Irish difficulties will be rather delayed than hastened by his officious but well-meant interference.'[21]

Despite his irritation with O'Shea, Chamberlain persevered with his efforts. In March he wrote to Spencer inquiring what elements of the Crimes Act he wished to retain and what could be jettisoned. Spencer, smelling a rapprochement with Parnell, was unable to enlighten him. As time went on O'Shea became more pessimistic about the fate of the scheme he had nurtured and for which he had such high hopes. Parnell was apathetic and O'Shea saw his prospects of the Chief Secretaryship[22] beginning to evaporate. He had written to his wife in early 1885 holding out the prospect of the position in a government with Chamberlain as Home Secretary. 'This is an enormous thing', he wrote, 'giving you and the Chicks a very great position.'[23] Given that two of the 'chicks' were Parnell's, it was either a letter written to be shown to Aunt Ben or an attempt to open up a line of negotiation which would result in his wife agreeing to spend at least some of her time in Phoenix Park, for the sake of appearances.

Towards the end of March Chamberlain got his answer on coercion. With some amendments Spencer sought the reintroduction of the Crimes Act. Alongside it he was wise enough to recommend some palliative legislation to take the sting out of Irish opposition to coercion. Chamberlain was not sanguine: '... it will lead to a bitter and prolonged parliamentary conflict and will prejudice the Liberal party at the general election,' he suggested. Instead of the minimalist proposals of Spencer on land purchase and local government he proposed his own Central Board scheme as it '... affords, in my opinion, the only hope of ultimately securing better relations between the two countries.'[24] A fortnight later he circulated a document to Cabinet that incorporated elements of his own and Parnell's proposals. In the interim the Roman Catholic primate Cardinal Manning, Archbishop of Westminster, had been added to the mix. He had spoken to Irish Catholic bishops and had discovered them to be suspicious of Home Rule (including, apparently, Archbishop Croke) and better disposed towards an enhanced scheme of local government. He offered his good offices to determine if such a proposal could be agreed upon by the Gladstone Cabinet. He pronounced himself satisfied with Chamberlain's 25 April template when it was shown to him, as were the Irish bishops.

The same, however, could not be said of the Lord Lieutenant. On viewing the proposals (which he described as 'Mr Parnell's'), while accepting those elements that applied to local councils, he rejected the Central Board notion as it removed most of the responsibility for the governance of Ireland from Dublin Castle: 'It takes from government all patronage ... I see a further grave danger in constituting a representative body which may assume to itself the right of speaking for the Irish nation ... It is very probable that we should find the present Irish Parliamentary Party, the Healys, and O'Briens and T.P. O'Connors, managing and leading this assembly.' Presaging the 1886 campaign to plough Home Rule under he concluded, 'The idea of this will create well nigh a panic among the well affected people of Ireland, and I doubt whether Ulster will agree to it ... [and] we shall hand over control of local affairs to men who have shown themselves unfit for government.'[25] Spencer was also unbending on the Crimes Act, insisting that it be renewed for three years. The Chief Secretary, Trevelyan, on the other hand, was '... in favour of the scheme as affording the *only* chance for solving, or seriously investigating, the Irish difficulty.'[26]

O'Shea kept a diary of the 'Crimes Act Crisis' as he dubbed it and noted on 28 April that if Spencer's arguments were enough to sway the Cabinet away from the Central Board scheme and towards a three-year sanctioning of coercion, Chamberlain and Dilke proposed to resign. O'Shea felt that if they did so their Radical allies, Trevelyan and Shaw Lefevre, would follow suit and precipitate a Cabinet crisis. Over the next few days he shuttled between Parnell, Chamberlain and Manning. First he secured the agreement of Parnell to the scheme. The Irish leader endorsed the plan without much enthusiasm – Manning described Parnell's acceptance as 'guarded, and I do not take it as more than not opposing it.'[27] On 30 April O'Shea, Chamberlain and Dilke were assuring each other that a Cabinet rupture was about to take place. If the Central Board plan was rejected, the Radicals would withdraw. If it was accepted they assumed Spencer and Hartington would go. Gladstone was 'strongly in favour'.[28] O'Shea confessed to his wife that the principal reason why he 'was anxious about the Local Self-Government Scheme[29] is that if Chamberlain has power, which I think he will in the next Parliament, he will offer me the Chief Secretaryship, or the equivalent position if the name is abolished, if the boys will let me have it. Gladstone ought not to know this.'[30]

As was his wont, O'Shea was also working the press assiduously. On 8 May he dined with Edmund Dwyer Gray and '... inspired a leader for the *Freeman* in favour of the local self-government scheme.'[31] The issue was debated in Cabinet on 9 May and narrowly rejected. Contrary to what they had told O'Shea, neither Chamberlain nor Dilke resigned at that point. Their decision might have been dictated by the refusal of Trevelyan to countenance resignation over the issue. He had written to Chamberlain: '... I do not think that difference of opinion on this matter is a sufficient reason for bringing it about.'[32] It might also have been influenced by Parnell's blasé attitude towards the offer to resign. O'Shea wrote to his wife the day before the crucial Cabinet meeting that ... 'Mr Parnell is very unsatisfactory. He told me last night, with a sort of wave of chivalry, that I might convey to Chamberlain that he didn't hold them to the bargain; that they were free to compromise with their comrades if they chose. He does not much care for anything except the vague and wild politics which have brought him so much money.'[33] The reference was to the Parnell Tribute and the letter, which he must have expected to be shown to Parnell, was a calculated insult to the Irish leader and an indication that O'Shea needed to be propitiated.

The next step taken by the government precipitated the withdrawal from Cabinet of Chamberlain, Dilke and Shaw Lefevre. The decision to renew the Crimes Act led to the three men tendering their resignations.[34] Whether it actually prompted them to resign is a moot point. It has been suggested that their decisions had less to do with a principled opposition to coercion than with an impatience to hasten an election to be fought on radical terms and on the basis of an enlarged franchise. The resignations hung fire for a time until they became irrelevant when the Tories and the Irish party combined on a trivial budgetary issue (whisky duty) to defeat the government. Gladstone, much to his relief, was not obliged to reintroduce a Crimes Act. Instead he dutifully resigned and left it to the incoming Conservative caretaker government, under Lord Salisbury, to decide what to do.

There was a coda to the Central Board affair, though it was not directly related to that six-month tussle over local government. In his original letter to W.H. Duignan, Chamberlain had offered to travel to Ireland and take the proposal directly to the Irish people. In the wake of the government defeat he and Dilke revived the idea of an Irish speaking tour. The difference now was that the Central Board proposals had been rejected, the Radicals were seen to be simply making a play for Irish support, the Liberal government had shown itself to be married to coercion, and Parnell was opening channels to the Conservative caretaker administration to see if he could extract more from them than had been on offer from the Liberals. The travel arrangements of Chamberlain and Dilke became the subject of controversy. Cardinal Manning had offered assistance, which was then withdrawn when the government fell. According to Dilke's biographer, Roy Jenkins, the Cardinal '... preferred his political friends to be ministers'. In a letter to Dilke he declined, in a memorable phrase, to be 'godfather to Hengist and Horsa'.[35] His opposition may have had as much to do with the prospect of a Tory government more sympathetic to denominational education than the Radicals. The June 27 issue of *United Ireland* fulminated against the proposed trip, pouring vitriol over the two Radical politicians in the process. They were accused of 'cynical hypocrisy' and the whole project was condemned as a 'mere electoral manoeuvre ... to curry favour once more with the Irish people'.[36]

The thin-skinned Chamberlain considered the article to be a breach of faith on the part of Parnell. Though the campaign against the trip had been concocted by O'Brien and Healy, there is little doubt that Parnell had a hand in stirring the brew. As always he was ruthlessly unsentimental about disparaging two figures who had been relatively sympathetic to the Irish cause when it served his greater ends. He refused to ally himself with Chamberlain in what he saw as the beginnings of a campaign to oust Gladstone. The Central Board negotiations had taught him what to expect from Chamberlain on Home Rule. He hoped for much more from the Liberal leader.

For his part Chamberlain was aghast at being so ill-used after taking the risk of moving far ahead of his Cabinet colleagues in proposing major institutional reform for Ireland. He wrote to O'Shea, requesting that the letter be passed to the Irish leader, 'I think that Mr Parnell is bound as a gentleman and a man of honour', he declared, 'to take steps to correct the impression, which appears to prevail among some of his supporters, that he is hostile either to our visit or to the scheme for local government which has been prepared on lines laid down by himself.'[37] It was a theme to which he would revert some years later. Parnell had not heard the end of the Central Board scheme. What he had heard, however, was the first shot in a war with the Radical leader that would become increasingly bitter and destructive in the years ahead.

This dying phase of the Central Board controversy also had a hugely deleterious effect on his professional relationship with O'Shea. The Captain was growing tired of being treated like a political postman. The *United Ireland* diatribe reflected on him and he took up the matter with Parnell. To Chamberlain he communicated the Irish leader's implausible explanation that O'Brien had been out of the country when the article was written and that the Tipperary MP was his sole conduit when it came to the editorial policy of the newspaper. 'Mr. Parnell assured me', he added, 'that he took the earliest opportunity on Mr O'Brien's return to explain his favourable views and wishes with regard to your visit with Dilke to Ireland.'[38] However, given that *United Ireland* had expressed a view, it would be difficult to reverse what had been said. Tellingly, however, Parnell made no attempt to prevent a recurrence of the attacks in the newspaper.

As regards the Central Board scheme, now that Parnell was cosying up to the Tories, it was defunct: '... although I laid particular stress on the many assurances of (in my opinion) a binding nature, which I had taken you from him, regarding the present business, he did not appear to be disposed to go any further.'[39] O'Shea assured the Radical leader that he was, nonetheless, '... endeavouring to impress on him the quackery of the Tories and the folly of losing the substance in grasping at the shadow.'[40] As regards how to save face over the proposed Irish journey in the wake of the *United Ireland* savaging, he advised Chamberlain '... if eventually we should think it advisable to drop the idea of the journey, it can be done quietly and without announcement. On the other hand, if you should go, you do not require any introductions from an "English Bishop".'[41]

In his correspondence with his wife he was far less diplomatic. He cut loose at the Irish leader in a manner that marks a departure from previous manifestations of mere annoyance and frustration. His anger that rigor mortis had set in to the Central Board negotiations was accentuated by the signals he was getting from Parnell that another run at the Clare constituency was not a viable option.

In an undated letter to Katharine from around this time he expressed the embittered belief that, 'No rational beings who have had dealings with Mr Parnell would believe him on oath.' He told her that '... he has recently said that he is under no obligation or promise to me! ! ! ! ! ... the man who, after promising to assist in every way Mr Chamberlain's journey to Ireland, can let his paper the same week abuse him like a pickpocket, is not to be respected by Mr C, and I have already told the scoundrel what I think of him. The worst of it is that one looks such a fool ...'[42]

Regarding what must have been the same conversation with Parnell, he had told Chamberlain, 'although my temper is that, not of an angel but of an archangel, I made believe to lose it yesterday afternoon.'[43]

His anger with Parnell was exacerbated by stresses of a different kind related to his perennial financial woes. He kept Katharine closely informed of all his business dealings, presumably so that she would be aware of the basis for the next bail-out request to Aunt Ben. In the same letter where he disparages Parnell's trustworthiness he told his wife, 'I am worried, if not out of my wits, out of my hair. The little left came out this morning after a sleepless night, and I am balder than a coot is. Such fun. I wonder whether I shall die soon, or if the day will come. Would I had understood it had come when I was asked to go to Kilmainham.'[44] Leaving aside the evidence that the Captain was a man with a morbid nature, the final comment is typical of O'Shea's ability to reinvent his own history. It is absolutely possible that he actually believed he had been asked to 'go to Kilmainham' rather than having been earnestly advised to stay away.

The political and the financial umbrage coalesced in another letter to his wife a couple of days later. O'Shea had obviously been making no secret of his anti-Parnell pique around the Palace of Westminster. He had shared his chagrin over the Central Board debacle and his problems in Clare with a number of MPs mainly, as it happens, Tories. All had made appropriate noises of sympathy which had duly validated his resentment. 'None of them, of course, knew the absolute baseness of it. But to all I replied: "Poor devil, he is obliged to allow himself to be kicked to the right or the left and look pleasant. But he has the consolation of having been well paid for the pain –£40,000 – the tribute of the priests and people of Ireland!"' O'Shea could not reconcile himself to the fact that such an undeserving general as Parnell had been offered tribute by the people, while so worthy a centurion as himself was being dragged behind the chariot in financial chains.[45]

THE BEGINNING OF THE END

Almost from the outset of his tenure as Clare MP O'Shea had encountered hostility on account of his perceived indifference to the Parnellite cause. This began to intensify as the prospect of a general election loomed. It had started to crank up in earnest on 6 January 1884 when, at a public meeting in Scariff chaired by his clerical nemesis Rev Matthew Kenny, a no-confidence motion in O'Shea was passed 'as he has violated his pledges, and ceased long since to act with Mr Parnell and the Irish Party.'[46] Kenny had, unfairly and inaccurately, characterised O'Shea as having consistently '… sanctioned the brutal and reckless policy of coercion'. Nearly two years later, in a speech in Liverpool, Parnell would exonerate O'Shea of any such sins.[47]

In their first issue after the Scariff meeting the *Nation*, in reporting the event, took O'Shea to task itself:

> It is clear that if Captain O'Shea desires to retain the representation of Clare he will have to proceed on different lines

to those he is at present following. The constituency which returned O'Connell has too much public spirit to remain satisfied at seeing itself represented by a mere Whig, and there is a strong opinion in the county that Captain O'Shea is inclined to cast in his lot with this particular section of politicians. He received fair warning on Sunday of the fate in store for him if he does not give more loyal support to Mr Parnell than he has been giving for some time past.[48]

Edited by T.D. Sullivan, who was married to Tim Healy's aunt, the newspaper's stance on O'Shea reflected the growing undercurrent of defiance and independent action surrounding some of Healy's activities. The growing rift between Healy and Parnell would become a chasm after the former's attempted putsch during the Galway by-election of February 1886. *United Ireland* ran a short report of the meeting without comment.

One of the principal nationalist dilemmas regarding the Clare MP was encapsulated at a second meeting a fortnight later in Tulla. In an era where public representatives were not remunerated, O'Shea, despite his many failings, was at least able to fund his sojourn in the House of Commons at a time when it was difficult to get viable candidates to stand for election because of the expense involved. For example the Ennis MP, Lysaght Finigan, had failed to sustain himself as a full time representative. He had retired from the House of Commons in August 1882 on health grounds,[49] though it was suspected that the real reason was the loss of an income of £400 per annum as a journalist. Within six months he was restored to 'full health' and working as a barrister.[50]

The Tulla branch of the Irish National League turned its attention to practicalities. To unseat O'Shea it would be necessary to fund a local candidate. The branch offered to come up with the sum of £30 per annum towards a nationalist MP's salary and encouraged other branches to do likewise.[51] It was alleged at the meeting that any stirrings against O'Shea were futile as rumours were '... industriously circulating that his candidature for the county, whenever the next election comes off, will have the approval of Mr Parnell.' A second speaker probably hit the nail on the head when he observed that, 'I believe the author is Captain O'Shea himself; that he has been telling his few friends throughout the county that from the great personal friendship, outside of politics, which exists between himself and Mr Parnell, that Mr Parnell will endorse his candidature.'[52] O'Shea, had he not had good intelligence on the ground anyway, would have become aware of the purpose of the meeting as it was reported on by the *Times* Irish correspondent who suggested, with masterful understatement, that 'The junior member for Clare does not appear to have succeeded in securing the complete confidence of his constituency ...'[53]

There was worse to come for O'Shea at a meeting in Milltown Malbay in late February. By then it would have become known to his constituents that, despite having attended the pre-session Irish party meeting in Dublin on 4 February, O'Shea had opted to return to the government benches. The meeting was chaired by one of O'Shea's earliest and most enthusiastic supporters, Rev Patrick White. He reminded his listeners that, before his election, their MP had promised to support the policies of Parnell '... which promise he has betrayed'.[54] O'Shea had always boasted about the backing he had among the clergy of County Clare. That highly influential support was beginning to erode. His voting record was too 'ministerialist' even for their moderate tastes.

But elsewhere in the county, especially in the south-west and in the coastal areas to the west, O'Shea had his staunch defenders. His solid graft on behalf of certain interest groups in the constituency was beginning to pay dividends. An editorial in the *Kilrush Herald* made it known to '... such selfish fault-finders beyond Ennis that Mr Parnell will recommend Captain O'Shea for Clare at the next election.' And the writer made it plain why this was a thoroughly desirable outcome. 'Since his return for this county the Captain has been unceasing in his exertions to procure grants from the Government to promote public works and extend our piers and harbours, and has been successful to a very great extent. This is more than can be said of his notoriously untruthful maligners ... it matters very little to the people where the honourable member sits as long as he does his duty to Clare, to Ireland and the Irish leader ... [Clare] will take no notice of the drivelling of those few and insignificant weather cocks ...' The abused meteorological fowl were, the writer made it plain, from Tulla and Scariff.[55] It might have been written (or commissioned) by the Captain himself. Indeed it would not have been beyond him to have done either.

It also heralded, no pun intended, a local letter-writing campaign on O'Shea's behalf. This was undoubtedly inspired by the Captain and his supporters and highlighted his efforts for the county. It ignored or played down his support of the government.[56] In fact, the implication of the message being purveyed by the Captain's cheerleaders was that the benefits he had been able to wrest from the administration had been forthcoming precisely because he sat on the government benches. It was a straightforward clash of pragmatism versus idealism – one that would continue as a subtext in Irish nationalism into the 1920s.

It was a debate and dilemma neatly summarised, from the Clare perspective, in a considered letter to the *Independent and Munster Advertiser* in late March 1884, written under the nom de plume, 'Tattler'. The writer acknowledged the existence of that body of opinion that wished to retain O'Shea because of his clientelist skills and influence. They wanted him to continue in office 'to further works of public utility in the county'. Whereas, 'Tattler' observed, others held that 'influence with the government is about one of the worst qualifications an Irish national representative could have ...'[57] The letter then concluded, sagely, with a question about the extent of O'Shea's usefulness should the Tories be returned to power at the next election.

By this time resolutions of no-confidence had been coming so thick and so fast from Irish National League branches all around the county that the *Independent and Munster Advertiser*, the main Parnellite newspaper in Clare, came off the fence and pronounced sentence. 'Captain O'Shea has not the confidence of the democrats of this locality,' stated the leader writer, 'neither will he have their support if he should come forward at the approaching general election.'[58] In the same issue was a damning assessment by Davitt of O'Shea's status as '... the unofficial ambassador of the Gladstone administration ... when any governmental policy requires either the neutrality or co-operation of the Irish representatives the member for Clare is the Government medium for diplomatic intrigue.'

But, quite apart from O'Shea's usefulness, there was one other factor which worked in his favour: the silence of Parnell. If his print outlet, *United Ireland*, had been charitable to O'Shea by dint of the consistent omission of the sort of scathing criticism visited on other 'nominal' Home Rulers, the absence of any comment from Parnell represented munificence itself. A consistent thread through speeches made on behalf of O'Shea was the lack of any instruction or lead from Parnell on the subject of his future candidacy. One of his staunchest supporters in Kilrush, John M. Nagle, put it succinctly at a meeting seeking to censure their MP, when he said, '... until our leader sounds the trumpet of his condemnation, your obedient servant will never fling a stone at a gentleman who, though he does not talk much, is always endeavouring to alleviate the sufferings of the Irish people.'[59] A way around this particular crux was sought by the highly antagonistic Irish National League apparatchiks in Kilrush when they wrote to Parnell '... requesting of him to give an expression of opinion on the conduct of the county members as there was a resolution of want of confidence proposed which would be considered at a further date.'[60] The response was akin to that of the oysters to the Carpenter in Lewis Carroll's 'The Walrus and the Carpenter', 'answer came there none'.

There was another issue at play as well, and that was a parochialism within Clare itself. As regards the future career of William Henry O'Shea the county was already beginning to divide into the two sections that would, ironically, be formalised in the Redistribution Act the following year. East of Ennis and in the county town itself, O'Shea had few supporters. West of that line it was a different matter. It is apparent that, from the moment he became aware of how the old county constituency was going to be divided, he put most of his efforts into the assiduous courtship of west Clare.[61] He had already been seen to bestow infrastructural largesse – in the form of the railway, pier development, and an orphanage in Kilrush – on that portion of the county. His profile in Kilrush in particular allowed him to build up, in the two years before the 1885 election, if not a political machine there, at least a body of worthy and vociferous apologists.

In yet another public meeting in Ennis, which sought to condemn the Captain, one of the speakers, a John McInerney from Cratloe, articulated this position, 'The people of the eastern part of the county were not at all satisfied with conduct of Captain O'Shea as one of their representatives [groans]. They did not want any backstairs politician, but a man who would stand by the side of Mr Biggar and Mr O'Brien.' As he made this point, standing by *his* side was the selfsame Mr Biggar. The old Belfast Fenian took the opportunity for a free shot at the Captain. 'That, honourable gentleman', he commented waspishly, 'would make a very good advertisement for a tailoring establishment, but if he had any other good qualities they were not visible to the naked eye.'[62]

The negative east Clare rhetoric was reinforced a couple of weeks later by a newspaper report that exhibits all the classic evidence of an O'Shea self-promotional exercise. The pattern he had adopted was to assist the advancement of a project and then secure printed eulogies from grateful (and prominent) beneficiaries. In this instance the lucky west Clare village was the coastal Carrigaholt on the Shannon estuary. He had been pressing the government to proceed with the building of a harbour there. This had enabled him to approach the local parish priest who duly wrote to the *Independent and Munster Advertiser* that '… the efforts of the gallant member for Clare deserve the grateful recognition of our poor people.' As if that wasn't enough, there was confirmation from the Board of Works that O'Shea, although consigned to his sickbed in Lisbon, had been prepared to dip into his own pocket to ensure that work on the harbour proceeded. This, according to the Board, would not now be necessary as his representations had secured £16,000 in government finance. 'Nevertheless,' wrote Commissioner John Blake, an Irish Liberal MP, 'the people of Clare, especially the seaboard population, ought to feel much indebted to you for the willingness you evinced to offer your personal security in order that there should be no delay in proceeding with the construction of the much needed piers ...'[63] In any political environment other than one where, atypically, ideology trumped expediency, it would have been a master-stroke. Of course neither Blake nor the parish priest were to know that O'Shea did not have the financial resources to kick-start the project (without application to an increasingly reluctant Aunt Ben) and was therefore bluffing.

In August 1884 Tim Healy drew up a parliamentary pledge binding Irish MPs to an unbending Parnellite whip. Even had O'Shea been prepared to take that pledge, it is unlikely he could have run again for Clare, such was the activists' antipathy towards him. But he had no intention of taking the pledge. That was one of the few places to which O'Shea was not prepared to go in his tenacious fight to hold on to his Clare seat. Yet he had no desire to simply go 'gentle into that good night' as men like Richard O'Shaughnessy had already done, and as other 'nominals' would do,[64] quite meekly, in 1885. He had another ace up his sleeve when it came to the defence of his realm: the Irish Republican Brotherhood.

THE FENIAN RISING

O'Shea had worked hard for the release of the suspects held in the Crusheen 'conspiracy' case in 1883. In October 1884 he sought to reap the rewards of his efforts with a visit to the village. He wanted to stage a rally that would send a message to the rest of the constituency. But, by then, the only group that could guarantee him a decent reception was the local Fenian organisation.

The IRB had two reasons to offer support to a man who was to nationalism what they were to pacifism. Some Fenians had a decidedly ambiguous attitude towards Parnell. While many, but by no means all, had been prepared to involve themselves in agrarian agitation (not all of it legal) for the greater good, when the Land War began to fizzle out as the Land Commission did its work the situation changed. The very idea of constitutional politics was anathema to many of them and Parnell was anxious to move away from populist activism towards a more 'parliamentary' model. The leading Munster representative on the Supreme Council, Patrick Neville Fitzgerald, epitomised the contradictions of many individual members of the movement.

He had taken over P.J. Sheridan's duties when that Land League activist had handed out one IRB weapon too many to non-Fenians.[65] As an experienced gunrunner in the Munster region, Fitzgerald would have been unhappy at the extent to which agrarian outrage attracted the wrong sort of attention from the foot-soldiers of Clifford Lloyd and jeopardised IRB arms caches. He was also dismayed at the extent to which American resources, large but not unlimited, were being channelled into organisations other than his own. His idea of a rapprochement with Parnell was to stand as an Irish party candidate but to adopt the abstentionist approach of a Rossa or a John Mitchel. His determining philosophy when it came to Home Rule was 'there is no such thing as a halfway house to liberty.' To his way of thinking, and it was a mode shared by many Fenians, it was verging on the criminal that Irish politicians were prepared to 'tune their fiddles to catch Paddy's ear with a new tune of a cheap form – a Home Rule Bill.'[66]

It was just that sort of unreconstructed Fenianism that could actually accommodate itself to a slightly reconstructed Whig on the basis that 'the enemy of my enemy is my friend.' O'Shea, although his political credo could hardly have been more different, was perceived as harbouring a similar level of ambivalence towards Parnellism as the Fenians themselves. In addition he championed the cause of Clare 'suspects' and prisoners, many of whom, if not actual members of the IRB, certainly swam in the same gene pool. Add to that his single-minded campaign against the activities of their mutual *bête noire*, Special Resident Magistrate Clifford Lloyd, and it was a marriage made somewhere between heaven and purgatory designed to keep O'Shea from a political limbo.

One of the newspapers that consistently voiced support for O'Shea, the *Clare Advertiser* based in Kilrush,[67] carried an editorial in March 1885 that suggests a further reason why the Fenians might have been indebted to the Captain. The *Advertiser* noted that 'His constituents have reason to be much pleased with the exertions of Capt O'Shea MP who has effected a reduction in the Police Force of this county, and consequently a great saving of taxation to the community – Bully for the junior member from Clare, who is proving himself to be the right man in the right place.'[68] A reduction in policing activity (which had assumed a highly militaristic tinge during Lloyd's hegemony, especially in arbitrary search and arrests), afforded more protection to the hard-earned arms dumps of Patrick Neville Fitzgerald.

And so the Crusheen Fenians got the faithful, and the village band, to come out for O'Shea on Sunday 19 October 1884. At least three members of the platform party can be identified, on the basis of prison lists, Dublin Castle files and internal evidence, as probable Fenians[69]. Two more had served time in prison under the Coercion Acts. It was a platform peculiarly uncontaminated by the presence of the clergy who could not afford to be openly associated with known members of an oath-bound secret organisation. O'Shea made it up to them by paying a visit to two local priests after the rally.

In a speech that pushed no republican buttons (and would not have raised the heartbeat of the RIC sergeant taking notes) O'Shea claimed some of the credit for 'moulding' the Arrears Act and pointed out that '... it has kept many a poor hearth warm and saved some of the most hopeless and helpless of our people in their little homes.'[70] While he was cordially welcomed, he only raised a cheer whenever he invoked the name of Parnell, something that would not have gone down too well with the doctrinaire Fenians in attendance. He told his wife in a letter sent from Limerick the following day, 'It took me all my time with some of them to allow a vote of confidence in Parnell to be put to the meeting yesterday.' But he seems to have been buoyed up by the gathering, claiming that '... the Fenians have now shown such an extraordinary support that, as they themselves say, there will be murder in the Co Clare if I am opposed.'[71] One presumes he is not to be taken literally. He certainly overestimated the influence of the Fenians on the votes of Clare nationalists.

In a subsequent letter to Dilke he continued to enthuse about the experience: '... the Fenians (who however deluded in their aspirations are grateful) consider themselves under obligations ... for timely warnings and some assistance to honest and repentant brethren when "in trouble".' The reference to 'timely warnings' is intriguing but unexplained. He had so much confidence in his new allies that if the National League continued to pass motions of censure in him he believed they 'had better look out for squalls.'[72] So pleased was O'Shea with his display of Victorian 'radical chic' that he actually drew more attention to it by complaining to Spencer about the size of the police presence at the demonstration. A reply (it appears to have been initialled by the shadowy Jenkinson) enclosed a number of police reports and expressed the '... hope that you will be able to assure Capt O'Shea MP that the Police had not the slightest intention to do anything but show respect to Capt O'Shea.'[73]

As we will see later, O'Shea's association with the IRB, while it was an affair of convenience, went some way below a surface of mere mutual expediency and was of extended duration. On the basis of a document sent to his wife in December 1885, it appears that O'Shea was beholden to P.N. Fitzgerald himself, through his association with a Clare republican, John Malone.[74] He was also to become involved with an entirely untrustworthy London Fenian, George Mulqueeny. This association would continue for some time and involve both men in highly questionable activities, much of which it is impossible either to fathom or to ascertain fully.

O'Shea probably came across Mulqueeny when he campaigned for the election of a Liberal candidate, Samuel Montagu, an Orthodox Jewish merchant banker, in the Tower Hamlets division of Whitechapel in the East End of London. His association with Montagu was more than simply political. It is evident from letters to his wife that Montagu was advising him in a number of financial and legal transactions involving investments in Cuba and an action being taken against O'Shea and other directors by the Union Bank of Spain.[75] O'Shea was concerned throughout 1885 about his business dealings and had to make a number of journeys to Spain to try and sort things out. As usual his wife's aunt bankrolled him, and continued to complain about having to do so. In early April he sent Katharine a self-pitying letter from Madrid where he was engaged in his regular struggle against insolvency: 'If Aunt accuses me of extravagance you can truthfully tell her that my sister's illness was an immense expense to me. This hotel is simply ruinous, and I never have anything but 1s 6d wine.'[76]

The quid pro quo for Montagu's financial assistance (which may well have been of a practical as well as an advisory nature) was O'Shea's involvement in the Whitechapel election. In this he participated with gusto and used some of the techniques he had already employed in Clare. His first move was to enlist the support of Chamberlain for Montagu's candidacy. He asked the Radical leader to send the banker a letter of congratulations on being selected to run telling him that 'I have taken a good deal of trouble in the organization of the borough and have secured the Irish vote.'[77] Having obtained his letter he later asked Chamberlain to come down to the East End and speak on behalf of Montagu. Chamberlain demurred, suggesting that if O'Shea wanted 'a special "shine" in the East ...'[78] he should recruit Morley instead.

O'Shea's efforts to garner the Irish vote in the East End for a Liberal candidate came at a time when Parnell was making overtures to the Tories, who were in power under Salisbury in a caretaker capacity, and prior to his recommendation to Irish voters to choose Conservative candidates over Liberals in the November 1885 election. T.P. O'Connor and William O'Brien were intent on neutralising O'Shea's efforts and a mass meeting of Irish voters in the East End was addressed by O'Connor and told in graphic terms that though the Tories' '... hearts were black ... if they voted for the Conservatives it was not because they loved them, but because it was expedient and because they hated the Liberals more.'[79] In an account of the meeting O'Shea (diplomatically referring to the Fenians as 'my friends') told Chamberlain it had been arranged '...that "One of Them" should be chairman.'[80] In the *Times* of 17 August the Chairman is reported as being one P.J. Mulqueeny, President of the Tower Hamlets Branch of the National League.

George Mulqueeny was a clerk in Victoria Docks in London and he seems to have taken a peculiar pleasure in intrigue of all kinds. Involved with the National League he was also a close associate of fugitive Frank Byrne and, according to Michael Davitt, an informer in the pay of Scotland Yard[81] as well as O'Shea's 'bag carrier'.[82] T.P. O'Connor, who was familiar with the man before he achieved a brief notoriety during the *Times* Commission proceedings in 1888, wrote that he '... resembled Carey in assembling in his bosom professions of religion, violent revolutionary sentiments, and the seeds of ultimate treachery to the things which he vehemently expounded ... He was vain of the sound of his own voice, and used to speak at small branch meetings of the National League around London.'[83]

O'Shea hinted at his association with Mulqueeny and other London-based Fenians to Chamberlain when he referred to them in a letter as 'leaders of opinion in the Tower Hamlets'. He had spoken at a meeting there on Monday 24 August at which he had favoured his audience with 'words of wisdom'. It is O'Shea at his cynical best: 'By "words of wisdom" I mean the grossest adulation of Dilke and yourself and the Fenians, "advanced nationalists". An extract from the speech is being printed for distribution among my deluded countrymen.'[84] Ultimately Montagu won Tower Hamlets in spite of, rather than because of, the Irish vote. O'Shea, through his wife, sought from Parnell an exemption for Montagu from the injunction to the Irish community to vote Tory, but this was not forthcoming. Less important than the Irish vote may have been the fact that, according to Katharine O'Shea, '... his opponent was obnoxious to all parties.'[85]

THE END

In his efforts to retain his Clare seat O'Shea waged a battle partly by land, but mainly by sea. His efforts to secure funding for a pier at Cappa, near Kilrush, involved a bureaucratic battle to wrest control of the pier from the Shannon Commissioner and the Board of Works. That campaign and his continued support for the Goleen fishermen drew a rueful (and highly exploitable) response from the Galway MP, Colonel Nolan, Chair of the Fishery Piers and Harbours Commission. 'Owing, no doubt, to your exertions,' Nolan wrote, 'Clare has already got exactly five times the average per fisherman of the maritime counties.' The admission drew paeans of praise from the already well-disposed *Advertiser*: '... could stronger testimony be adduced', the newspaper inquired rhetorically, 'to show that Captain O'Shea is fully alive to the wants of a much neglected class in society? There is no bunkum or braggadocio about Captain O'Shea, he is the steady silent working man; and his exertions for the release of political prisoners, are items to his credit, which should not be forgotten.'[86] A latter-day spin doctor would not dare to have written such sycophantic copy for even the most valuable client.

Not that it was all plain sailing for the redoubtable Captain. Where Cappa pier was concerned, a mischievous rumour was circulated in May 1885 that O'Shea had insisted on the aristocratic Clare landlord, Colonel Vandeleur, being appointed as one of its trustees. A public meeting was called in Kilrush to condemn the 'course of action ascribed to Captain O'Shea'. The chairman, a local priest, refused to allow any condemnation to take place until O'Shea had had a chance to answer the charge. His supporters, including *Clare Advertiser* editor, John A. Carroll, suspected that he had been traduced by 'a snake in the grass'.[87]

O'Shea rose to the challenge so magnificently as to almost prompt, once again, suspicions that he had begun the rumour himself. A letter was despatched to the editor of the *Kilrush Herald* on 5 May 1885 in the aftermath of successful representations made by the Captain himself and a local justice of the peace (Michael Glynn) to a House select committee. Referring to the meeting held '... to protest against some imaginary intentions of mine with regard to Cappa Pier. Such proceedings must tend to reflection on the part of the very few who are unfriendly to me. If the perpetrator cannot play a more plausible trick he may as well give up the cap and bells. I am glad to say that my unremitting efforts for several years will soon be crowned with success, and the people of Kilrush will have Cappa Pier ... In the meanwhile we can afford to watch with indifference the wriggling of the small fry about it.'[88] A second meeting, to which Glynn reported that there was no foundation for the rumour, was characterised by a refusal on the part of his emboldened supporters to be silenced by O'Shea antagonists. Carroll reported that, 'Several of Captain O'Shea's friends rallied to defend the gallant gentleman from unkind aspersions flung at him without rhyme or reason ... A very lively scene followed, on which a warm vote of thanks was ultimately passed to Captain O'Shea – the prisoner's friend and friend of all in favour of Cappa Pier – and of the county at large.'[89]

As the campaign against O'Shea intensified there were more aspersions from the Kilrush National League, whose members were anxious to discredit him in any way possible. In January, in a gesture unconnected with a love of music, O'Shea had contributed five pounds to the funds of the Kilrush Brass Band. The donation had been prominently featured in the *Advertiser* and no other donor (not even the local JP, solicitor or hotel owner) had contributed more than ten shillings. Within six months the donation was being represented by the local rumour mill as a bribe to individual members of the Band from the MP. The Band was ordered by the National League branch to be subjected to a boycott, in an example of the sort of abuse of process that often characterised the deployment of that particular weapon. Band leader, Michael O'Meara, had resigned from the League, partly at least because of the venom directed at O'Shea during the Cappa pier controversy. As a consequence he was singled out for particular contumely. He had turned, perhaps ill advisedly, to O'Shea for a public assurance that the donation had not been an attempt at political seduction by the MP. O'Shea was happy to give this and his refutation of the charges against the unfortunate O'Meara was printed in the *Advertiser*. 'I have paid no money to the Band,' he wrote, 'or to any member of the Band except my subscriptions, which have been duly acknowledged in the newspapers. The accusation, therefore, is a calumny on the Band and an insult to myself.'[90]

O'Meara was not the only person to have been subjected to such allegations. A week later John M. Nagle, long time champion of the Captain, was forced to refute allegations that he, too, had been suborned by O'Shea's largesse. In an impassioned letter to the *Independent and Munster Advertiser* he insisted that 'never did I accept the smallest British coin'[91] While there must remain a suspicion that O'Shea might well have used Aunt Ben's money to purchase support in West Clare,[92] there is no documentary evidence to justify such a contention. And the allegations of his increasingly virulent political opponents may be given relatively little weight in such an argument.

With an election looming O'Shea's optimism was beginning to fade. A long letter to Chamberlain sent in early September captures his increasing uneasiness, his bitterness and his fundamental lack of awareness of the political forces that were shaping the Ireland of the 1880s. It was written in transit while he was taking his mother, now 'feeble in health' from Ireland to Paris. He described his relations with Parnell as '... very strained. He asked me last month to shoot at Avondale but I thought it well to refuse.' His advice from his Clare supporters was to avoid the constituency for the time being, '... the people are "wild" and will not listen to moderate counsel for the moment.' He then exhibits utter naivety in asking Chamberlain if '... in one of your forthcoming speeches you could possibly manage to give me a lift.' That O'Shea would imagine any speech of Chamberlain's would give him a lift in Clare indicates how utterly out of touch he was with the political exigencies of his own constituency.

He continues this chronicle of a political death foretold with a *cri de cœur* that such a speech might underscore the fact that he is a hardworking politician, '... not inferior in ability to other Irish members, I have been content constantly to efface myself in debate in order otherwise to gain substantial advantages for the Irish people; and that my influence, apart from the Kilmainham Treaty, was a more potent factor throughout the Parliament than the speeches and antics of those who now take to themselves the credit of everything that has been attained.'[93] That this Lament of the Mistreated Ward Heeler may have had some inherent element of truth is irrelevant. The fact is that O'Shea was not the man for those particular times.

Chamberlain suggested in his reply that his sometime political protégé persuade a Clare priest to write in praise of the Captain and that he would respond with the sort of statement O'Shea sought. In this instance O'Shea was well informed about the realities of Clare politics. There was no succour to be had from that source, '... although almost all the Parish priests and most of the Curates are really anxious that I continue in the representation of Clare, I greatly doubt, such is the reign of terror, that I shall be able to find anyone to write to you. Each one will think that the duty ought to be performed by his next neighbour ...'[94]

In desperation O'Shea, rather surprisingly, turned to Mulqueeny. The 'bag man' wrote to Chamberlain, allowing the former President of the Board of Trade to respond positively and warmly. He concentrated on the defunct local government proposals,[95] highlighting O'Shea's valuable role as a catalyst in that failed effort at reform and describing the Captain as '... a most earnest Nationalist Irishman [who] has yet shown himself able to appreciate the difficulties surrounding the question and from whom, accordingly, I have often derived valuable suggestions. If all his colleagues had been as fair-minded, I believe that we should long ago have been able to settle all those burning questions which now keep Ireland in a state of agitation which is as hurtful to her prosperity as it is unsatisfactory to England.'[96] It is hard to envisage copies of the encomium being passed around Clare hearths for constituent perusal in the long evenings approaching *Samhain*.

Meanwhile, what of O'Shea's superannuated 'partner in crime', the O'Gorman Mahon? His soundings were similar to those being conveyed to the junior member. Edward Finucane, Mahon's self-appointed lieutenant in Ennis since the death of Michael Considine, wrote to the Chieftain in late October that there were local manoeuvres afoot (disapproved of by Parnell) to displace him as MP. Finucane was emphatic that '... this ingratitude towards you – is to be perpetrated so as no excuse need be given for getting rid of Capt O'Shea!!'[97] The O'Gorman Mahon, even though there was ample opposition to his own continuation, would be collateral damage in the fight against O'Shea. In the same letter Finucane also refers to 'a clan of fellows posing as extreme nationalists ...'

who wanted to run P.N. Fitzgerald as a Home Rule candidate. There was indeed a rumour in late 1885 (see above) that Parnell had approached Fitzgerald and asked him to run[98] as a Home Ruler. But there is another intriguing possibility.

As we shall see, where the Galway by-election of February 1886 was concerned, O'Shea and his Clare Fenian allies hatched a plan (which came to nothing) of running a candidate who would, at the last minute, withdraw in favour of O'Shea.[99] It is conceivable on the basis of Finucane's information and of the prevailing rumour surrounding Fitzgerald, that this was actually the repetition of a scheme that had been contemplated for Clare in November, 1885, but had been abandoned in the light of the local antipathy towards O'Shea. Not that Clare opposition was the deciding factor in Parnell's decision not to risk O'Shea in the constituency. That was founded on the veto of the likes of O'Kelly and O'Connor.[100] And that, in an emphatic example of 19th-century democratic centralism, carried more weight with Parnell than the resolutions of National League branches in Clare.

Ironically the growing clamour for a county-wide public selection convention to choose two local candidates to run for Clare was just as much anathema to the highly centralised Irish party as it was to the highly vulnerable O'Shea. Such a suggestion was deprecated in a statement from National League secretary and Westmeath MP, Timothy Harrington. He intimated that such a development would not meet with Parnell's approval. Fr Patrick White was to draft a programme for such a convention. This was sent to the League central office in Dublin and drew no response whatever. Parnell had a template of his own. Candidates would be chosen at private meetings attended by delegates representing local branches and local clergy. These meetings would be chaired by a sitting MP from outside the constituency. Once a candidate had been chosen, the waiting public would be presented with the fait accompli at an open mass meeting. In the case of Clare, local branches were allowed to nominate their favourite sons, but this was a mere exercise in phantom democracy. The convention, held on 2 November and chaired by Tim Healy, was intended simply to ratify Parnell's choices for the two constituencies. The party travelling from Dublin for the event included both men.[101]

The tempo of the campaign against O'Shea had increased to such a degree that the impetus for his deselection was already irreversible by the time Michael Davitt spoke in Kilkee in mid-October and hammered the stake through his heart. To the cheers of his listeners he expressed the hope that '... in the future historic Clare will not allow itself to be misrepresented by sham Nationalists or by Whigs in disguise.'[102]

Four days after he was refused the imprimatur of the National League to contest the Clare seat, O'Shea issued a Shakespearean farewell address to the electors of Clare. It was a dignified valedictory, more resigned Othello than ranting Lear. He had done the county some service, he believed. 'I have served you faithfully, and in some measure perhaps not altogether fruitlessly. Amongst you I leave many dear friends and, I believe, few personal enemies.'[103] Whatever about the former contention the latter was impossible to justify, but it is conceivable that the revisionist in O'Shea actually believed it.

The *Freeman's Journal* wrote a charitable and wholly premature political obituary.[104] It ticked off his achievements, the Kilmainham treaty, the Arrears Act, the Archbishop Walsh controversy and the extension of the full terms of the Franchise Act to Ireland. It claimed that he had broken faith with no one (a point that might have been disputed by Fr. Patrick White) as '... he never formally identified himself with the Party led by Mr. Parnell, though he often, on critical occasions, voted with it, and frequently exerted himself to promote the same objects ...' The editorial comment concluded with a *caveat* and a clear reference to Chamberlain, '... the influence which he undoubtedly possessed with certain English statesmen was, we believe, steadily used to induce them to regard Irish affairs from an Irish standpoint. Possibly Captain O'Shea thought that in keeping himself in touch with English rather than Irish parties he was able to do better service to Ireland. Be that as it may, now that he is about to retire, it is only bare justice to call to mind the part he took in the stirring politics of the last five years.'[105]

In a letter to the *Freeman* proprietor, Edmund Dwyer Gray, O'Shea appeared philosophical about his fate while still hitting out at Parnell, insisting that 'I need not expect a kind word from the man who is under obligations to me as weighty as was ever one politician to another.' Perhaps his relative optimism in his correspondence with Gray was prompted by his penultimate sentence. 'I have no doubt Chamberlain will get me back into politics before very long.'[106] Chamberlain would certainly make one further effort to get his henchman back into the House of Commons, but it would be for his own devious strategic purpose.

Thus ended William Henry O'Shea's brief but rousing tenure as the representative of County Clare. Phineas Finn had suffered a similar setback and he had recovered. The question was, would it be a case of 'O'Shea Redux'?

CHAPTER 10

The Member for Galway

'The party' ... required that the candidate should be a safe man, one who would support 'the party' – not a cantankerous, red-hot semi-Fenian, running about to meetings at the Rotunda, and such-like, with views of his own about tenant-right and the Irish Church. 'But I have views of my own,' said Phineas, blushing again. 'Of course you have, my dear boy,' said Barrington, clapping him on the back. 'I shouldn't come to you unless you had views. But your views and ours are the same, and you're just the lad for Galway. You mightn't have such an opening again in your life'

Anthony Trollope, *Phineas Finn,*

MERCURY AGONISTES

The defeat of the Liberal administration in June 1885 had brought a caretaker Conservative ministry to power. It was led by Lord Salisbury and was to remain in office until a general election. This was delayed by franchise changes under the electoral Reform Act of 1884 and could not take place until November. A period of calm in Ireland was heralded by an indication from the Tories that coercion would not be renewed and that a new land purchase measure would be introduced. The replacement of the unpopular Earl Spencer with the more sympathetic figure of Lord Carnarvon added to the impression that a pragmatic, businesslike Tory government was prepared, at the very least, to de-intensify sullen Irish agrarian resentments and to gently prise rather than dash the cudgel from the hand of the 'Irish Frankenstein'[1]. Later, when measures were introduced benefiting Roman Catholic schools, the 'Tory nationalists' (Davitt's phrase) within the Irish party were suitably mollified.

Where some of his followers saw little hope of extracting concessions from the party of property, Parnell saw opportunity. He 'sought to exorcise the debilitating dependence on the Liberal party which had been the endemic weakness of parliamentary nationalism'.[2] In so doing he had no intention of engaging in a retributive campaign destructive of any prospects of a future alliance, but he wished to test the limits of Tory indulgence. In fact between the time of the fall of the Gladstone Ministry and the general election, Parnell was involved in a tortuous series of simultaneous explorations with the Tories, the Liberals and the 'Fourth Party'. The only parliamentary faction with which he was not in meaningful contact during that period was the Radicals.

Through the auspices of Justin McCarthy and Sir Howard Vincent,[3] Parnell, somewhat against his better judgment, properly began his flirtation with the Tories when he met the newly appointed Lord Lieutenant in a vacant house in London on 1 August. The two men would later offer different versions of the substance of that meeting. As Parnell was seeking to gain political advantage with his account, which came twelve months later during the Home Rule debate, we should probably rely more heavily on that of Carnarvon. Typically, Parnell had preceded the meeting with a stout public denial that there had been any dialogue with the Tory government. He remained within the boundary of literal truth by a mere 24 hours.

Carnarvon was acting with the guarded acquiescence of the Prime Minister. Salisbury, however, had made it clear in advance to his Lord Lieutenant that he thoroughly disapproved of the notion of Home Rule for Ireland and that he would not serve in a government that thought otherwise. So, in spite of his own personal predilection in favour of some form of legislative independence for Ireland, there was little Carnarvon could do other than to indicate his sympathy for Parnell's arguments, sound him out on a number of Irish issues, and report back to Cabinet.

Parnell may or may not have left the empty house on Hill Street having achieved a compact of some kind, but what ensued, put at its starkest, was a series of overtures which saw both parties manifestly bidding for Irish support while resolutely denying that an auction of any kind was taking place.

Casting around for an Irish policy of some kind Gladstone recalled a document sent to him by Katharine O'Shea in January 1885 which purported to represent Parnell's views on the subject of local government in Ireland.[4] Liberal Whip, Lord Richard Grosvenor, was delegated to use the O'Shea (*femme*) channel to ascertain if this still accurately represented the Irish leader's thinking on the subject of Irish institutional reform. Either Grosvenor simply took his time in making the inquiry (Gladstone had asked him to do so on 6 July, he waited for more than a week before complying), or the conspiracy theorists who discerned a grandiose Machiavellian Liberal plot to buy Irish support were absolutely correct in their paranoid assumptions. On the very day he wrote to Katharine inquiring if the document (a copy of which O'Shea had given to Chamberlain in mid January) still reflected Parnell's thinking, Herbert Gladstone had made a speech in his Leeds constituency declaring his personal support for a measure of Irish Home Rule. Whether or not this was the first forward press in an intricately choreographed series of dance moves that would lead to the Damascene conversion of Gladstone *père* to Home Rule must remain a 'not proven'. But if it was, the bait was taken. Katharine responded to Grosvenor's heavy hint with a declaration that 'nothing less than a scheme on the lines of Herbert Gladstone's speech at Leeds would now be considered.'[5] Two further letters from Grosvenor on 23 and 28 July extracted no elaboration. None was required. Later Gladstone himself, indicating the significance of the issue, wrote to Katharine and was dealt with much less curtly than his Chief Whip. In reply Parnell (by the hand of Katharine) upped the ante considerably. He now sought the '... granting to Ireland [of] a constitution of a similar nature to that of one of the larger colonies ...'[6] In his reaction, on 8 August, Gladstone thanked Mrs O'Shea for 'a very interesting letter', but made it clear that he was not prepared to venture 'into any counter-bidding of any sort' against the Tories. With that the Grand Old Man took off for boating trip to Norway and waited for events to navigate their own course.

For his part Parnell was in no position to indulge in such passivity. In a speech made in Dublin on 24 August, which was badly received in the British press and most political circles, Parnell threw down the gauntlet. The policy he enunciated was simplicity itself: 'I hope that it may not be necessary for us in the new Parliament to devote our attention to subsidiary measures, and that it may be possible for us to have a programme and a platform with only one plank, and that one plank National Independence.'[7]

The wood from which the 'one plank' would be fashioned was, meanwhile, being seasoned in the headquarters of the National League in

Sackville Place in Dublin. There 35 Irish MPs signed up to a pledge that offered no room for ambiguity or lack of commitment: 'I pledge myself that, in the event of my election to Parliament, I will sit, act and vote with the Irish Parliamentary Party; and if at a meeting of the party, convened upon due notice specially to consider the question, it be determined by a resolution, supported by a majority of the entire Parliamentary Party, that I have not fulfilled the above pledge, I hereby undertake forthwith to resign my seat.'[8] It was recommended to the constituency conventions that would choose Irish party candidates to decline to consider any person who was unwilling to sign the pledge. Captain William Henry O'Shea was just such a person.

Reaction to Parnell's declaration for Independence came swiftly. In a speech at Warrington on 8 September, Chamberlain denied the very idea of Irish 'nationhood' and declined to bargain for Parnell's support on the basis of Home Rule. But then, perhaps unwisely, no effort had been made to keep the Radical leader in the tight loop of those parleying tentatively and feeling their way gingerly towards some form of accommodation. More significantly, in his mid-September address to his Midlothian constituency, Gladstone had spoken positively about some nebulous form of self-government for Ireland but only in the context of maintaining the unity of the Empire. When it came to Salisbury's turn to handle the grenade three weeks later, his cautious expression of neutrality was sufficiently anodyne not to discourage Parnell.

The territory had now been demarcated, in the case of the Tories, by remaining undefined. Parnell had a dilemma on his hands. He suspected that the hysterical *Times* reaction to his 24 August 'one plank' speech, that an Irish parliament was 'impossible'[9], was closer to the heart of Tory thinking than the sympathetic noises from Carnarvon's corner. A further inquiry from Grosvenor about his own current state of mind came the day after Chamberlain had slammed shut the radical door on Home Rule. Despite this, Gladstone's Midlothian address encouraged Parnell to believe that a better bargain might be struck with the Liberals. But a Home Rule bill of any kind from that quarter would be doused in kerosene by the House of Lords and returned to the Commons in a haze of smoke and flame.

Parnell also feared that a sizeable Liberal majority in the 1886 session would nip any Home Rule ardour in the bud. The rationale was compelling. Only if the parliamentary arithmetic was tight could the Irish nationalists expect to influence the policy of either party in any meaningful way. Parnell was unaware that the Grand Old Man, in a culmination of the process he had himself initiated in 1869 with the Disestablishment of the Church of Ireland, was on his own personal road to a Home Rule Damascus. And even had he known what was going through Gladstone's mind he would probably have mistrusted such an epiphany.

Nationalist logic dictated support, in the short term at least, for a party that was pledged not to renew coercion and which, through the Ashbourne Act, had advanced the cause of peasant proprietary. By supporting the Tories the intriguing possibility was that a vastly augmented Parnellite grouping might hope to hold the balance of power between Conservative and Liberal. Thus it was that T.P. O'Connor composed a stirring manifesto calling on Irish voters in Britain to support the Tories. He found his party leader reluctant to sign. On 30 October Parnell, through Katharine O'Shea, had sent a document to Gladstone with the provocative but unambiguous title 'A Proposed Constitution for Ireland'. He had surmised that it might get a more sympathetic reception in Hawarden than Hatfield.[10] It called for a unicameral Irish parliament of three hundred members, special arrangements for the representation of the Protestant minority, with '... power to enact laws and make regulations regarding all the domestic and internal affairs of Ireland ...'[11]

A very public dialogue based on this highly confidential document ensued. Both men, in effect, negotiated remotely from election platforms until Gladstone made it clear that he did not intend to commit himself publicly to a set of proposals which he had admitted privately (via Grosvenor) were 'of great interest to him'.[12] The Liberal leader's consistent line was that Parnell should have recourse first to the government of the day to see what, if any, concessions on Home Rule he could extract from the Tories. He undertook to adopt a bipartisan approach to any Conservative legislation on the matter. He even approached Tory MP Arthur Balfour, Salisbury's nephew, and intimated that the Liberals would not oppose the government if agreement could be reached between the Tories and the Irish. Suspecting deviously partisan machinations on the part of the Liberal leader designed to immerse them in an Irish legislative bog, Salisbury, privately accusing Gladstone of hypocrisy, let the chalice pass.

If we are to go by the word of Henry Labouchere (which should always carry a clear warning as to absolute veracity) in a letter to Chamberlain, then Gladstone was, at the time of his son's pronouncement, already trying 'to unite the Party on Irish legislation and to make that his *cheval de bataille*'. But, sensibly, he sought some earnest of Irish support. Labouchere, who didn't specify what sort of Irish legislation Gladstone might have in mind, was probably trying to gratify his Radical master when he added that the Liberal leader should be wary because

Parnell '... never makes a bargain without intending to get out of it, and that he has either a natural love of treachery, or considers that promises are not binding when made to a Saxon ...'[13]

Parnell's reluctance to sign the manifesto and tie a blue ribbon around the parcel containing the Irish vote in Britain had much to do with his instinct that a better deal could be done with Gladstone than Salisbury.[14] It may also have been related to the language of the document. 'Tay Pay' had wandered over to the dark side when compiling the manifesto, which urged Irish voters to oppose 'the men who coerced Ireland, deluged Egypt with blood, menace religious liberty in the school, the freedom of speech in parliament and promise to the country generally a repetition of the crimes and follies of the last Liberal Administration.' It was incendiary prose that left hardly a single bridge unburnt.

Parnell had a further, compelling but purely personal, reason for his reservations about O'Connor's manifesto. It related to the political future of William O'Shea.

TIOCFAIDH ARMAGH

The opposition of the mass of his constituents, his inconsistent voting record, his tendency to lose his way in the House of Commons and sit on the government benches, and his refusal to take the party pledge, all guaranteed that O'Shea was not going to be allowed to contest the Clare constituency as a member of the Irish party. But, even more than those disqualifying factors, it was his unpopularity with the members of the Irish party that copper-fastened the case against him. O'Shea could be, and frequently was, a man of great charm and considerable charisma. Even his wife admitted that 'He was witty, and his wit was a little cruel; a raconteur, his stories lost nothing in the telling, and as a diner out he was much sought after. But his set did not include the then Irish party.' When it was pointed out to him that most of his Irish colleagues were his equal in ability, intelligence and, in some cases at least, education, his response demonstrated his gift for the putdown. He could 'rejoice in, but could not sit with, unvarnished genius'.[15]

His connection with Chamberlain also made him an object of suspicion in a party largely populated by Davitt's 'Tory nationalists'. Chamberlain's political philosophy, as outlined in the quasi-socialistic 'Radical programme'[16] of 1885 and anticipated in advance in countless speeches and pamphlets, was too expropriative, anti-clerical and free-thinking for their tastes. Even though O'Shea's alignment with Chamberlain was blatantly careerist, rather than indicative of any radical beliefs of his own, he was found guilty by association.

It was probably the fact that O'Shea made little effort to disguise his contempt for the bulk of the Irish members that most antagonised them. Katharine O'Shea recounts one incident where she was told by Parnell that an irate and inebriated Irish MP had lain in wait in the lobby of the House intent on actually killing O'Shea. Fortunately he had been too drunk to carry out his mission. 'But I wish Willie would not annoy them all so much,' Parnell had observed. 'From what I could make out, Willie smiled at his pronunciation of "Misther Spaker, Sorr". Willie's smile is a bit of a twister sometimes.'[17]

Despite overwhelming evidence to the contrary O'Shea clung to the daisy of conviction that he could stand once more for Clare until the roots of that tenacious plant finally gave way. This appears to have taken place in a conversation with James O'Kelly. In a letter dated 23 October 1885, written from Avondale, Parnell told Katharine that he had sought the advice of T.P. O'Connor as to whether O'Shea had a chance of passing muster with the party for another run in Clare and 'he was positive he had none, pledge or not'. The following day O'Shea had interrupted a conversation between Parnell and O'Kelly. Probably on foot of an unfavourable reaction from Parnell to his demand for a nomination he had sought O'Kelly's opinion. When he told O'Kelly that he did not intend to take the pledge, the latter '... told him at once that it was not in the power of mortal man to get him in for any National constituency without it ...' Even Parnell himself, O'Kelly insisted, could not do it. According to Parnell, ' He then decided to give it up, and it was arranged that he should stand for a constituency in the North which we do not intend to contest and where he will have a chance.'[18]

That day O'Shea sent a white flag letter to Gladstone.'Owing to intrigues I am unable successfully to contest either Division of Clare without taking a "pledge", which I cannot subscribe for many good reasons, including the impossibility which it would involve of giving your policy the humble support which I am always anxious to offer it.'[19]

He indicated to Gladstone the bones of a deal which, he hoped, would assure him of a return to parliament, but as a Liberal rather than an Irish nationalist. '... if I stand for Mid Armagh as a follower of yours, he [Parnell] promises the votes and active assistance of his supporters there who number within 600 of the Orangemen and Presbyterians combined. If adopted by the Liberal Party for Mid Armagh therefore, my election would be secured.' He moreover offers, 'I am thus accepted, to give the Liberal candidates his best assistance in four other Ulster constituencies, in two of which, at least, he holds the balance.' The four constituencies where a gift of the nationalist vote would enhance the prospects of a

Liberal victory were East Down, North Antrim, North Armagh and North Derry. In the second prong of a pincer movement on the same day, Katharine O'Shea began a rolling correspondence with the unfortunate Grosvenor, asking him to intervene with the Ulster Liberals and observing with some pathos, 'I shall feel so much obliged if you will write and tell me if you think there is any chance of Mr O'Shea's getting a seat. I am sure he will be a very good supporter of the Liberal party.'[20]

At this point O'Shea was still waving. The drowning would follow as he got into greater difficulties.

There were a number of problems with this particular Operation Rescue. First was the spirited independence of the Northern Liberal franchise from its theoretical London masters. Led by T.A. Dickson MP they had their own ideas about who they should run as their Mid Armagh representative. Secondly, as O'Shea to his chagrin quickly discovered, was the difficulty of the ethno-religious arithmetic. The Protestant plurality was far in excess of the 600[21] or so souls referred to in O'Shea's letter. It was almost double that figure, a margin that even a made-over O'Shea at his most plausible could not hope to breach. In a conversation with Archbishop Daniel McGettigan, the northern prelate had impressed on O'Shea, '... the danger arising out of the bigotry of the Presbyterians and he believes that, however Liberal they may be and however strongly they may promise to support the Party, all would be merged into religious animosity at the last moment and they would universally vote against the Papist.'[22]

Thirdly, the Northern Liberals wanted another sweetener before they would even contemplate such a deal. Parnell would have to add South Tyrone to the pot. As South Tyrone was a potential nationalist seat, for which no less a personage than William O'Brien had been nominated, that was distinctly unpalatable to the Irish party leader. Nonetheless he was on the verge of having O'Brien's candidacy withdrawn when the necessity evaporated. It was O'Shea himself who pulled the plug on the manoeuvre, writing to Grosvenor and, with regret, withdrawing his candidacy.[23]

The final difficulty was of O'Shea's own making. He had been instructed to stay well away from the constituency while the triangular negotiations between Parnell, the Ulster Liberals and Grosvenor were taking place. But he had already been seen visiting the county. A Tory MP and former member for Derry, Lord Claud Hamilton, now a member for Liverpool, had spotted O'Shea on a train travelling through Portadown on 24 October and pointed him out to a group of Orangemen.[24] Grosvenor told Katharine in early November that O'Shea had discussed his plans to run for the constituency,[25] presumably with Hamilton,[26] and with the cat out of the bag, in order to avoid accusations of collusion, the conspiracy to foist O'Shea on Mid Armagh had to be aborted.

O'Shea kept Chamberlain and Katharine informed of what was happening. His letters to both reveal a self-deluded, self-pitying and politically dangerous loose cannon. In the expectation of the collapse of the house of cards then being constructed on his behalf in Ulster, O'Shea expressed particular bitterness to both about what he claimed to be Parnell's obligations towards him, 'P[arnell] if he had acted fairly would have placed the acceptance of my candidature, irrespective of everything else as a *sine qua non* before his party, the alternative being retirement from the leadership.'[27]

It is, on the face of it, an astounding contention. On what basis, other than the preservation of his silence about the sexual relationship between Parnell and his wife, could O'Shea claim any such 'promise' or 'obligation'. Why should Parnell run O'Shea for anything other than the mythical Chiltern Hundreds?[28] Conscious that some explanation of his extraordinary hold over the Irish party leader was required, O'Shea set about designing an edifice that would withstand the curious prodding of inquisitive onlookers. Initially the structure in question took on the outline of a pyramid. O'Shea might have demanded Clare or Mid-Armagh on the (specious) basis that he had secured Parnell's release from Kilmainham. Just that pretext would actually be advanced later. But his first construction was Egyptian in nature and probably without foundation.

Among the O'Shea papers in the National Library of Ireland is a draft of a sullen letter to Parnell in which O'Shea seeks to *remind* him '... of your promises to secure my re-election to Clare. As it may possibly be that you will deny them. I think it right to leave you no excuse in the way of forgetfulness ...' The narrative then reverts to the day of an important parliamentary vote on government policy in Egypt. No details are given, but it is more likely to have been around the time of the General Gordon mission to Khartoum in 1884 than to the 1882 Arabi Pasha conflict. Parnell, O'Shea alleged, had been anxious to secure his support in opposing the Gladstone administration's Middle Eastern policy. According to O'Shea:

> You begged of me to vote with you and your words, which
> I took down within five minutes after they were spoken,
> were "in any case I will, of course, do my very best for your
> re-election, but if you vote with us tonight I promise to
> secure it for you without any trouble." On several other
> occasions you entered into a similar engagement, and on one
> of them at Eltham long afterwards, you asked me to think

over the matter well and let you know which division of the [county] I wished to represent and you wd. [sic] arrange the matter. It is not very long since I wrote from London choosing the Western division. There is much more to be said but this is enough.[29]

The champion of the Clare fisherman had landed a red herring. Parnell's only obligation to O'Shea was based on blatant, though possibly unspoken, blackmail. There had been a censure vote in the House on government policy in Egypt and Sudan on 19 February 1884,[30] but on that occasion O'Shea was marked absent.[31] T.P. O'Connor writes in his memoirs about a subsequent vote on 15 March, in which the support of a 'member whose vote was considered doubtful' because it meant 'going against the government' had been harvested at the last minute by Parnell.[32] Whether or not Parnell did request O'Shea to shelve his regular support of the government on that occasion, it is highly unlikely that he would, in the wake of the much-publicised animosity towards O'Shea in Clare and the obvious antipathy of his own lieutenants, have made such a guarantee. The draft smacks of a familiar exercise by O'Shea in *ex post facto* justification. It appears to be a unilateral attempt to intimidate Parnell into adopting an agreed fiction to rationalise his otherwise inexplicable efforts on behalf of someone who had only offered lukewarm support to the Irish party in the outgoing parliament. As a man of honour Parnell, in the narrative concocted by O'Shea, was obliged to keep his word. Hence his exertions on behalf of a nationalist apostate.

As it happens, if this is indeed the division to which O'Shea was referring, then the thesis that he was searching for even a semi-convincing rationale is thoroughly reinforced. The vote was described by the Home Secretary, Harcourt, as a 'trap'. It took place on a Saturday when Labouchere surprised a sparsely attended House, brought in to pass supplementary estimates delayed by the chamber's preoccupation with the Middle Eastern crisis, by introducing a motion critical of the government's incursion into the Sudan. It was a ploy that had clearly been pre-arranged with the Parnellites, other radicals and the Churchill wing of the Conservatives to catch the administration unawares. The government just managed to scrape together a majority of 111 to 94 and fend off an embarrassing defeat at the hands of one of its own backbenchers. So the support of O'Shea would have been very useful. The problem is that O'Shea was absent from the division. So even if Parnell had guaranteed his return for Clare in exchange for his support that day, the 'agreement' would have been voided by O'Shea's failure to vote.[33]

By early November O'Shea was holed up in the Shelbourne Hotel feeling distinctly unwell (he suffered from gout) and utterly sorry for himself. He told Chamberlain that he had 'quite given up all hope of re-election' and that, in his view, where Parnell was concerned he was 'dealing with a dishonourable man'.[34] His ailment did not inhibit his ability to write letters and only served to accentuate his sense of personal grievance. In a letter to Parnell he remonstrated with the Irish leader over the Mid Armagh debacle and declared that:

> ... you are bound to act with regard to myself in a way very different to the one which you have hitherto followed. You were all along aware that I would take no such pledge as you have formulated, consequently the adoption of it by yourself and your friends has nothing to do with me ... you are under the clearest obligation to declare to your friends that you insist on my being returned to Parliament *quand même*, and that if the necessary steps are not taken for this purpose you will resign the leadership of your Party.[35]

In his communications with his wife his rage against the inevitable dying of the light of his political career alternated with bouts of extreme self-pity. He dismisses her efforts on his behalf (which would intensify in the weeks ahead), complains that his daughters have not written to him, and pouts that 'no one cares for me except my poor old mother'. But he also berates Parnell in the sort of language that is far from the mere vernacular of a disappointed place-seeker: 'I have been treated in blackguard fashion,' he moans, 'and I mean to hit back a stunner. I have everything ready; no drugs could make me sleep last night, and I packed my shell with dynamite. It cannot hurt my friend [Chamberlain] and it will send a blackguard's reputation with his deluded countrymen into smithereens.'[36]

Energetically stirring the pot and nurturing O'Shea's *idée fixe* that he had been defrauded and deluded by Parnell was the Birmingham Svengali himself. He advised the Captain solemnly that '... you have been shamefully used and have much greater reason for complaint than myself, although I am not by any means satisfied with the way a pledged word has been kept.'[37] Chamberlain's expressions of sympathy, or sublime mischief-making depending on your point of view, undoubtedly had an edge to them. His tone was based on his knowledge of the real hold O'Shea had over Parnell and the implied threat that existed to the Irish leader's political future. Chamberlain was at that time occupying a ringside seat at the continuing humiliation of his radical ally, Sir Charles Dilke. Dilke had been accused of conducting a two and a half year affair with the young wife of a Scottish lawyer and Liberal MP, Donald Crawford. In the face of a threatened divorce action (which came in February 1886) Dilke was attempting to salvage his political career.

The Birmingham MP was well aware of Parnell's predicament. He would have been privy to the information about the O'Shea–Parnell affair that had seeped into Cabinet circles in 1882, courtesy of Sir William Harcourt. Had he remained unaware, he would have been informed by a letter from Labouchere in October/November 1885.[38] The 'Christian Member for Northampton' (this was a Labouchere joke – covertly agnostic, he contrasted himself with his friend and openly atheist Northampton colleague, Charles Bradlaugh) was at his gossipy best. He wrote:

My Dear Chamberlain,

I have received a long letter from O'Shea asking me to denounce Parnell for not supporting him, and he says that he is going to see you. Here are the real facts. Parnell is – or is supposed to be – the lover of his wife. He told me several times that he would do all he could for him, but that it was very difficult. I found out from the 'boys' that the difficulty was in their knowledge of the love affair, and in their not seeing why on account of it he was to be treated better than others who had given a half support to Parnell. Of course it is impossible to explain this to him, as we must assume that he knew nothing of the domestic detail. I write you this, to put you up to the facts, but don't say that I wrote at all to you about it to him.[39]

Just over a week after his Ulster humiliation O'Shea had the opportunity to extract some measure of revenge on his nemesis. Parnell paid an apologetic courtesy call on the Captain in the Shelbourne Hotel to sympathise over their joint failure to have him contest the Armagh seat. We only have O'Shea's version of what happened, conveyed in a letter to Chamberlain. The high notes must surely be removed from O'Shea's livid falsetto, but even if a portion of his account is accurate it was an astonishingly uncomfortable interview for the Irish leader. It is also highly revealing as to the new state of relations between the two men. Their interactions may have been, at an official level, about politics, but there is little doubt that both men were well aware of the subtext. O'Shea writes:

> Parnell called on me yesterday afternoon and began to
> mumble something about sorrow that I had not seen my way
> to contest Mid Armagh and hope that an English seat might
> yet be found for me. I soon cut matters short by telling him
> that I did not want any more beating about the bush, that no
> man had ever behaved more shamefully to another than he
> had behaved to me, and that I wished to hold no further
> communication with him. He enquired whether I wished
> him to leave and I replied, most certainly. He then crossed
> the room and held out his hand. I informed him that I would
> not touch it on any account. I do not suppose that he has
> feeling enough to have felt the blow long but I never saw a
> man slink out of a room more like a cur kicked out of a
> butcher's shop.[40]

From what we know of Parnell's character, more particularly his iras-
cibility and a pride that often leaned over into arrogance, it was not the
kind of lecture he would have tolerated from anyone else in his personal
or political retinue. O'Shea was '… using the kind of language to Parnell
which that proud man would have suffered from no one else'[41] It may
well be that O'Shea's account is as grossly exaggerated as it is self-serving.
It certainly reeks of bravado, self-aggrandisement and a transparent effort
to reassure Chamberlain that, despite all his reverses, he was still his old
cocksure self. But if it even vaguely resembles the truth of what occurred,
there can be very little doubt that either: a) Parnell bit his tongue for the
sake of Katharine; or b) Parnell bit his tongue rather than provoke a confrontation which might lead to an accusation of adultery from an irate
and vindictive O'Shea.

THE CARPET-BAGGER

Having declined to undermine the constituency selection structures by
running an unpledged candidate for a safe nationalist seat, having failed
to capture a Liberal nomination in Ulster for O'Shea, and responding to
the appeals of Katharine to find her husband a constituency, Parnell did
all that remained within his power to do and shifted his focus to the most
'Irish' city in Britain, Liverpool. In so doing, according to one of his many
biographers, he was demonstrating his abject subjection to Katharine's
'whim of iron'.[42] In up to half a dozen Merseyside constituencies the Irish
vote was bound to be an important or decisive factor.

Parnell's efforts on behalf of the Captain were not entirely based on the
implied threat of the exposure of his affair with Katharine. He was also

under pressure from a determined Mrs O'Shea. 'I was very anxious', she wrote in her memoir, 'that Willie should remain in Parliament. Politics were a great interest to him and gave him little time to come down to Eltham. When he did so the perpetual watchfulness and diplomacy I had to observe were extremely irksome to me. Years of neglect, varied by quarrels, had killed my love for him long before I met Parnell ...'From this it is clear that Katharine's motives for keeping her husband in politics were not simply to facilitate him in ignoring her relationship with Parnell. It was far more basic and self-centred than that: it was because '... I could not bear to be near him.'[43] She admits that it was her will that drove the endeavour to find O'Shea a constituency. She claims that the true reason for Parnell's Trojan efforts on behalf of a man he would come to loathe, if he did not do so already, were on account of 'my desire'. However, she is not so inane as to ignore the elephant in the room: '... ugly rumour had already begun the campaign of brutality that, not daring to meet its foe in the open, wars with the dirty word.'[44]

In this regard she might have been referring to the antics of Philip Callan in Louth. Throughout the final days of the election campaign Parnell devoted himself almost exclusively to the task of getting O'Shea elected in Liverpool. He even told his own election agent that he would be unable to campaign in his Cork constituency. An exception was a side trip to Louth to speak out against the candidacy of Callan, whom he despised as a drunk and a veritable faucet of political leaks. Parnell campaigned in Louth in favour of his preferred candidate, Joseph Nolan. He would also have been aware, assuming the Monaghan election telegram story is true, that Callan knew about his affair with Katharine O'Shea and was bruiting the rumour about the constituency as he clung on for his political life. On 3 December Parnell was in Louth to speak on behalf of Nolan. While there he witnessed Callan, incandescent with rage, come as close as anyone had ever done on a public platform to revealing his secret. Contrasting the Irish leader's efforts on behalf of O'Shea with his decisive opposition to his [Callan's] candidacy, the former Louth MP wondered aloud what it was that O'Shea possessed to recommend him in such a way. 'What was there in his political character or private history superior to that of Phil Callan and his wife that Mr Parnell should malign and traduce him [Mr Callan] and support with his best exertions Captain O'Shea?'[45] Callan's apparently gratuitous reference to his own wife would have gone over the heads of all but the initiated. But to Parnell the message could not have been spelt out more clearly.

Callan refused to take his defeat and retire. Within a month Parnell was writing to Katharine warning her that the deposed Louth MP was

'... plotting to do all the mischief he could to members of the Party ...', principally to the party leader himself. He was threatening to challenge the result of the election and, in the process, would accuse Parnell of succumbing to the desire of a 'lady in London ... Of course the point he will make is that I did not oppose him on account of his bad character and conduct, but because she wished me to, and upon this peg will be sought to be hung other statements and questions. Is it not ingenious?'[46]

When it came to securing O'Shea a nomination in Liverpool, Parnell was leaving it late to locate a constituency with a sizeable Irish population that did not already have a Liberal candidate. Arguably he actually played a mere supporting role up until the days immediately before nominations closed. Before that a single-minded campaign of letters, telegrams and personal encounters by Katharine eclipsed anything Parnell was able to accomplish. Within hours of reluctantly accepting that a run for Mid-Armagh was out of the question, Katharine opened up a diplomatic barrage against an extremely patient Liberal Chief Whip, Lord Richard Grosvenor. The Grand Old Man himself was a secondary target. There is no cause whatever to doubt her when she says, 'I grimly determined that I would make Lord Richard Grosvenor's life a burden to him until I had landed Willie safely on the Liberal benches.'[47]

The Exchange Division of Liverpool was identified as the most fertile territory for an O'Shea candidacy as a Liberal. T.P. O'Connor was already slated to run in the Scotland Division with promising prospects of becoming an Irish MP with an English base. Parnell was prepared to canvass the Irish votes for Liberal candidates in four other sections if the Liberal party would run O'Shea in Exchange. The difficulty for the Liverpudlian Liberals was that, tempting though the offer was, a candidate called T.E. Stephens had already been nominated for Liverpool Exchange. In addition assurances were required by a wary O'Shea that Grosvenor and Gladstone endorsed the plan to run him. To a woman of Katharine's determined, or simply desperate, qualities the obtaining of supportive telegrams from a prime minister and his chief whip for a candidate whom, up to that point, was known only as an Irish nationalist,[48] was a mere bagatelle. Not only did she secure a telegram of support from Grosvenor, she even secured the Chief Whip himself. Despite being in the middle of a hard-fought general election campaign he agreed to travel to Liverpool and assist in the process of convincing or brow-beating the local Liberal establishment to jettison Stephens and run O'Shea.

His visit was preceded from O'Shea's point of view by a very welcome message. 'I am very glad', wrote the Chief Whip, ' that you have decided to issue your address to the Exchange Division of Liverpool as a Liberal and thorough supporter of Mr Gladstone; you will, I hope and trust, gain the unanimous support of all Liberals as you deserve it, and I am sure that it will give Mr Gladstone great pleasure to hear that you are the selected Liberal candidate and both he and I will welcome your return to the House of Commons – he authorises me to say that he wishes you heartily success and so do I.'[49]

Lest there be any illusions about why Grosvenor was prepared to thus inconvenience himself at a time when his services were required elsewhere, it is important to bear in mind that all this was taking place prior to any official indication from Parnell as to the best use of the Irish vote in Britain. With Irish party support still to play for, Grosvenor was prepared to indulge the frenzy of the woman who had become Parnell's intermediary with the Prime Minister. Of course he was also aware of the reason for the urgent drive to return O'Shea to parliament. When he arrived in Liverpool in the early hours of 21 November, he was heard to tell one of those who greeted him that Parnell 'sleeps with O'Shea's wife'.[50] Gladstone, although he steadfastly denied actual knowledge of the affair itself[51] until after the divorce, was certainly privy to the rumours at this time. In the case of Dilke he is alleged to have dispatched Labouchere to buy off Crawford.[52] In this instance he must have suspected, at the very least, that he was dispatching Grosvenor to achieve a similar purpose.

All of which was contributing to Parnell's reluctance to sign O'Connor's blood-curdling anti-Liberal manifesto. If he signed he would be forced to explain his support for a Liberal candidate in the Liverpool Exchange Division.[53] In addition, even the ruthless and unsentimental Parnell must have felt some twinge of guilt at turning on the Liberals after Grosvenor and Gladstone had so willingly facilitated Katharine's Liverpool strategy. But then the Irish leader was usually someone who looked far beyond the personal to the wider picture before him. He signed the manifesto, to the subsequent discomfiture of the Liberal party in the general election. In the spirit of 'democratic centralism' that pervaded his reign, he did not inform all of his principal followers of his move. Healy later claimed that he read about the manifesto in the paper.

To take the bare look off O'Shea's candidacy Parnell filed his own nomination papers for the Exchange Division and those of John Redmond for nearby Kirkdale. Then, at the last minute, he announced that he intended to withdraw and advised Irish voters to support O'Shea. Stephens, the other Liberal candidate, also withdrew but his name remained on the ballot paper. A sequence of letters from Chamberlain indicates how close run a thing it was just to secure a slot for O'Shea. On 17 November he was congratulating the Captain ('I am sure that the party could not make a better choice')[54] on the good news that he was to run. He followed the good wishes with an obviously solicited endorsement similar to the one sent earlier to Mulqueeny. Three days later, after the issue had been thrown into doubt by local opposition, the former Mayor of Birmingham was excoriating Merseyside Liberals, 'I am surprised at nothing from Liverpool politicians but they seem on this occasion to have exceeded their venal imbecility ...'[55] The issue had been in doubt right up to the day before nominations closed. Grosvenor, having 'interviewed Stephens', reported to O'Shea (who passed on the bad news immediately to Birmingham) that '... it was useless; that Stephens would not retire; that if I persevered Stephens would, he feared, "round on us"; and that my duty to the party was to give up.'[56] Chamberlain was sympathetic and critical of the Chief Whip's powers of persuasion or intimidation. 'What is the point of a Whig if he can't get rid of a fellow like Stephens?'[57] he responded dismissively, while acidly observing of the 'vote Tory' manifesto: ' So P has declared war after all. I suspected that he would and I think his conduct makes any *rapprochement* with the Radicals impossible.'

After the withdrawal of Parnell and (albeit reluctantly) Stephens, O'Shea was opposed only by a local Tory named Baily. Parnell had got the horse, in the form of the Exchange Division electorate, to the water, but he still had to persuade the voters to swallow O'Shea. This he did, with energy, false enthusiasm and counterfeit sincerity. At a major rally on 23 November in support of Redmond and O'Connor, he also asked for votes for the other Irish candidate. His advocacy of the candidature of O'Shea (who was hissed when first referred to by name) was based on the fact that 'Captain O'Shea is an Irishman, and also belongs to the religion of the majority of Irishmen, and that he has performed an important service in reference to the passage of the Arrears Act, under which, I suppose, fully 100,000 poor tenant farmers in Ireland were saved from the immediate risk of eviction and extermination.' Thus far his speech, as reported in *United Ireland*, only merited 'slight applause'. He then explained to his listeners that O'Shea was '... entitled to an exception being made in his favour from the terms of the manifesto ...' because he had been closely observed by Parnell himself and '... in no case was he found in the lobby in favour of coercion.' The 'slight applause' now became 'applause'. He then had the audacity to blame the Tory candidate for having '... driven me away from the contest in the Exchange Division by persisting in his candidature.' And, having identified the reason why the Irish voters in the constituency would not have the pleasure of casting their ballots in his favour, he concluded with a less than ringing endorsement: 'I should say to the Irishmen of the Exchange Division, if you desire to vote for Captain

O'Shea as an Irishman and as a Catholic, I see no reason why you should not ...' It was hardly calculated to send the troops into action with a song in their hearts, but then Parnell must have been straining every sinew to make his sham rhetoric sound convincing. More because their leader had concluded his address than out of any great enthusiasm for their Liberal candidate, the crowd managed to raise the decibels to the level of 'cheers'.[58]

Parnell, in backing O'Shea, had pushed some of the right buttons. He had reminded the Irish voters of the Exchange Division that, despite his other, less endearing qualities, O'Shea was their co-religionist and he had a principled opposition to martial law. It wasn't much, but arguably it was better than the pompous address O'Shea himself issued to the voters. As reported in the local press it informed the electorate that 'Captain O'Shea tells the electors of Exchange that he is an advocate of the widest possible measure of local government. As an Irishman, he appeals to his fellow countrymen as one who, 'while maintaining the integrity of the Empire, and increasing its solidity' is anxious to 'heal the injuries and remove the rancour of centuries".'[59]

But nothing, it seemed, was good enough for O'Shea. He continued to denounce Parnell's behaviour towards him to anyone who would listen. It is not hard to read into his constant carping a vicarious and apolitical denunciation of Parnell's sexual relationship with his wife. His grumbling must have appeared graceless and ungrateful (which it was) to the Merseyside Liberal onlookers. Parnell was forced to telegraph Katharine to get her to 'send W a tip to be civil'. The *Irish Times* became aware that 'The wing of friendship has moulted a most notable feather in the case of Mr Parnell and Captain O'Shea. It is news indeed to hear that the gallant go-between of the Kilmainham Treaty has turned his sword upon the chief who treated him worse than Othello treated Cassio. There is something poetical in the vengeance Captain O'Shea proposes to take ...'[60] Rarely can a newspaper have been so correct, so far in advance of the denouement of their story.

Despite O'Shea's palpable sulkiness (he had been reluctant to contest an English constituency in the first place) Parnell was unstinting in his exertions on behalf of the petulant candidate. According to T.P. O'Connor, the Irish leader '... was ubiquitous, persuasive, pathetically appealing to everybody to help in the return of Captain O'Shea.' O'Connor noted that in his platform speeches Parnell excoriated the Liberals in the spirit of the manifesto while '... supporting a candidate who was a Whig of the Whigs, without the excuse of the English Whig in his nationality and his party ties.'[61]

All Parnell's dogged efforts were in vain. Despite his urging the Irish voters that 'We must return the three Irishmen',[62] Baily, the Tory, eventually prevailed by 55 votes (2,964 to 2,909, with 36 votes going to the redundant Stephens). The result opens up another counter-factual vista. What if a mere 28 Bailly supporters had voted instead for O'Shea? Would the Captain have been a loyal and contented Liberal member for parliament with no axe to grind? The possibility is remote. Wherever there was an axe available, O'Shea always seemed to manage to locate a convenient grindstone.

In the weeks and months ahead the Captain would himself become a millstone, threatening to retard Parnell's progress and, on at least one infamous occasion, almost dragging him under the millrace. That was when O'Shea decided he wanted one of T.P. O'Connor's parliamentary seats. As he couldn't have the Scotland Division of Liverpool, a suggestion he had actually made to a horrified Parnell some weeks before, he would have Galway instead.

THE DRESS REHEARSAL

Gladstone, in one of his more fanciful moments, had once opined that the extension of the franchise in Ireland would ensure the return of a much larger cohort of Liberal MPs. It proved not to be one of his most inspired analyses or premonitions. The 1885 General Election resulted in the obliteration of Liberalism in Ireland. Eighty-five Home Rulers were returned (Parnellite at that – the 'nominals' went the way of their Liberal allies) and eighteen Tories.[63] When the success of T.P. O'Connor was added to the Irish total, it made the parliamentary arithmetic very interesting indeed from Parnell's point of view. The Liberals had been returned with 335 seats, while the Tories had won 249. The Irish, for the first time in British parliamentary history, held the balance of power. The Conservatives would find it impossible, and the Liberals extraordinarily difficult, to govern without the Irish Parliamentary Party. The impact of the Irish vote is difficult to assess. Chamberlain reckoned that Irish electors had swung 25 contests in the direction of the Tories. T.P. O'Connor, who was rather less objective, put the number at 65, 19 of which had been in London.

The Tories, awaiting whatever the logical outcome of the new arithmetic might prove to be, remained in office. The virulent Manifesto notwithstanding, Parnell began immediately to make overtures to the Liberals. They might be more amenable after being savaged by Irish voters. Gladstone, Parnell calculated, was far more likely to link arms with him and walk down the thorny path of Home Rule than Salisbury. It would also be easier to sustain the Liberals in power than a Tory minority administration. Letters to Gladstone flowed from the pen of Katharine like Vesuvian lava. Enclosures reflecting proposals with which her very good friend Mr. Parnell had favoured her, were included. One of these referred his friend Mrs O'Shea to his Proposed Constitution of October that he vouchsafed as a 'final settlement' (the words for which Chamberlain had waited in vain) of outstanding issues between Britain and Ireland. The covering letter was a conjurer's deployment of flattery, cajolery, misdirection and bluff.

'I have always felt', declared Mr. Parnell (from his Eltham redoubt), 'that Mr Gladstone is the only living statesman who has both the power and the will to carry a settlement it would be possible for me to accept and work with. I doubt Lord C[arnarvon]'s power to do so, though I know him to be very well disposed. However, if neither party can offer a solution to the question, I should prefer the Conservatives to remain in office, as under them we could at least work out gradually a solution of the Land question.'[64] The Grand Old Man ignored these blandishments and waved Parnell in the direction of the Tories to whom, as we have already noted, he promised a bipartisan approach to Irish legislation and was firmly rebuffed by Salisbury. Enter Gladstone *fils*.

In an interview that appeared first in the *Leeds Mercury* on 17 December 1885, Herbert Gladstone, in an unguarded or carefully engineered moment, made a purely personal or deeply political comment that did or did not reflect the thinking of his father on the subject of Home Rule. It was as precise as that. He told three companions that it was his belief that his father was on the verge of committing to legislative independence for Ireland. The three, being journalists, printed his remarks. They were hummingbird comments, but they still had wings. Gladstone repudiated his son but no one quite seemed to believe that Herbert's remarks had not been inspired by the ambition of the Grand Old Man to return to Downing Street, and there to continue his self-appointed mission to pacify Ireland. This time, so the speculation went, he was proposing to achieve his end by cutting some of the chains that bound her to Britain. The conversation, Herbert Gladstone's own personal and scaled-down 'unauthorised programme' was immortalised as the 'Hawarden Kite'.

It was going to be difficult for the Tories to trump the mouth-watering prospect of Home Rule and they made no effort to do so. There was a reluctance on the part of the Conservatives to continue to govern with the support of the Irish anyway, and when (against the wishes of Carnarvon) the government adjudged that the renewed growth of outrage in Ireland warranted the re-imposition of coercion, that reluctance had metamorphosed into a death wish. At the behest of Chamberlain the Liberal–Irish

Parliamentary Party *coup de grâce* was not administered on foot of an Irish issue, but as a consequence of a banal amendment to the Queen's Speech by one of his henchmen, Jesse Collings, on agricultural policy.

This resulted in yet another reiteration of those words Queen Victoria least liked to hear – 'Prime Minister Gladstone'– and the prioritisation by the new administration of a policy with which she was distinctly uncomfortable: Home Rule. It had taken a little over ten years, but in that decade Parnell had, more than anyone else, advanced the cause of Irish self-government from the anonymity of the opposition benches and the sloughs of obstruction to the very centre of the Cabinet table. He did not have much time to enjoy his success before the Captain came calling again.

O'Shea had had it in mind to trade in the fisherman of Carrigaholt and Cappa for those of the Claddagh for quite some time. He had already discussed the impending parliamentary vacancy in Galway with Chamberlain shortly after his Merseyside setback. On 9 December Chamberlain had advised him that 'I hope the Galway proposal may bear fruit. I need not say how glad I should be to see you in again.'[65] On this occasion O'Shea was not letting his imagination entirely run away with him. He had at least some support, having renewed his acquaintance with 'the real boys' as he called his Fenian friends in Clare. A few days before Christmas he wrote to Katharine from Albert Mansions where he had had an interesting visitor: '... a Fenian chief called.[66] His friends wanted to see me, so I went with him, and was introduced to some of the principal "men". They thoroughly understood that my political views and theirs are "as the poles apart", but they say they will stick to me through thick and thin.'[67]

Among the topics discussed was the forthcoming by-election in Galway, for which the writ had not yet been moved. According to O'Shea, the Fenians wanted a contest for the seat rather than see it go, by default, to a Parnellite. The enclosure he included from 'the Fenian Chief' (dated 23 December) has already been discussed in part. It connected O'Shea to P.N. Fitzgerald, the Munster representative on the IRB Supreme Council. But it also contained an intriguing proposition. The 'Fenian Chief' advised:

> Come to Limerick, giving timely notice, so that all may be prepared. Bryan Clune will meet you in Limerick, where everything can be arranged. All I can say is that if Bryan Clune stands for Galway it will be pretty hard to beat him, and if at the last moment he yields to the request of his Clare friends and retires in favour of any person, that person will be rather safe. When the friends were in trouble you gave

them a helping hand, and they don't forget it. We stand to the man that stood to a friend and a friend's friend. God save Ireland![68]

The Bryan Clune in question was a Clare Fenian who had been a scourge of the authorities in the area around Carrahan, near Tulla. He was described in 1881 by the local police Inspector as being '... dreaded by all the well disposed persons in the neighbourhood'.[69] In an earlier report Clune and his brother Matthew had been called '... men of very indifferent character and who are suspected of being connected to the Fenian Brotherhood.'[70] In addition to firing into homes, shooting and intimidating local farmers and instituting boycotts,[71] they were also believed to have stolen dynamite and detonators from a local mine. The 32-year-old Clune had been recommended for arrest under the Protection of Persons and Property Act almost as soon as it had been passed, but managed to avoid incarceration without trial until the end of October 1881. As a 'suspect', his case was regularly reviewed to see whether it was safe to allow him to be released. Clifford Lloyd had consistently declined to recommend his release, on one occasion endorsing a note from an RIC officer who insisted that '... as far as I am concerned I would rather that *any* suspect were released except Bryan Clune and Patrick Slattery.[72] I look upon Clune as the most dangerous suspect at present in gaol. It was he who organized this county in the matter of secret societies and I am sure that his release would do a great deal of harm.'[73] Clune was not released from Naas prison until 29 July 1882.[74]

There is more than a hint, where O'Shea's Fenian conspiracies are concerned, of boys playing at revolution (in the case of the Fenians) and a love of intrigue (in the case of O'Shea). Both parties had an exaggerated sense of their own significance. Other than the reference to Fitzgerald, we have no idea if the Fenians in question were of any real organisational consequence. That they would be prepared to engage, even in a coalition of expediency, with a Whiggish politician lacking any meaningful power base, suggests not.

In a letter to the *Times* on 25 December 1885, Labouchere would articulate the threat posed to Ireland by British statesmen refusing to negotiate with constitutional nationalists. 'The Nationalists are the Girondists, the Fenians are the Jacobins ... Mr Parnell and his political friends have substituted constitutional agitation for lawless and revolutionary agitation. He has only succeeded in this by persuading his countrymen that his action will result in success. If he be doomed to failure, the Fenians will once more gain the upper hand in Ireland.'[75] 'So be it', was the tacit response from

O'Shea, the arch-constitutionalist. As the immediate environment was unable sustain his political life, he was journeying into a dark hinterland. Blinkered by his newly acquired loathing for Parnell, and desperate for Irish allies, he was happy to make common cause with the Fenian/Jacobins who, for their part, should have been leading the aristocratic Captain to the guillotine in a tumbril. But such was the overarching power of the Parnellite faction at that time that neither of these odd bedfellows had that much to lose from a loose association.

But O'Shea was not naive enough to believe that the IRB was going to get him elected to the Galway city seat, soon to be vacated by O'Connor. Only one man had that sort of power and influence and he was someone to whom O'Shea had privileged access. 'And now came the demand we expected from Willie ...' is how Katharine phrases it in her memoir. The justification for the demand had shifted somewhat. Egypt was no longer the issue. Kilmainham had reasserted itself, pushing back to the top of O'Shea's Pandora's box of duties, obligations and favours performed. That and the more intangible suggestion that 'Parnell had long before solemnly promised him his support should the occasion arise, soon after their first meeting indeed.'[76]

O'Shea's case was enhanced by a letter from Chamberlain (once again it was probably solicited), which neatly coincided with his own thinking and seemed more like peremptory command than observation:

> In the present condition of Irish affairs, it is more than ever unfortunate that you have not found a seat. Is there any chance of your standing for one of those now vacant by double election in Ireland? Surely it must be to the interest of the Irish Party to keep open channels of communication with the Liberal leaders. If any possible co-operation is expected, it is clear that a great deal of preliminary talk must be held, and at present I doubt if any Liberal leader is in direct or indirect communication with the Irish representatives. Certainly I find myself very much in the dark as to their intentions and wishes.[77]

Self-servingly interpreted as a request from the Radical leader for a seat to be found for O'Shea this letter was to become the basis (in the upper echelons of the Irish party only) for what was to follow. Home Rule was shimmering on the horizon but, so the argument went, it would prove to be a mere heat-haze or mirage unless Chamberlain could be persuaded not to actively obstruct Gladstone's new departure. The Radical leader was known, in the past, to have opposed legislative independence for Ireland. Barely a week after the Hawarden Kite had flown past Chester, he had told Labouchere, 'I am not going to swallow Separation with my eyes shut.'[78] His friend had warned him against the logical consequence of his opposition, the necessity to forge a pact with the card-carrying Unionists of the Liberal Party, the Whigs. 'They may ally themselves with you, re Ireland,' Labouchere had warned, 'but this will be for their benefit, not yours. Nothing would give them greater pleasure than to betray you with a kiss, for you are their permanent bogey.'[79]

We can reject any notion of altruism on Chamberlain's part in his advocacy of O'Shea's return for an Irish constituency. He was well aware of the hold his protégé had over Parnell. It was, after all, one of the reasons why he was so useful. He was also crystal clear in his analysis of the effect that Parnell running O'Shea would have on the Irish party. At best, from his point of view, it would split the party and end the growing impetus towards Home Rule legislation. At worst it would expose fault lines and reveal just how cohesive the enlarged Irish party was as a unit. In the admirable study, *Parnell and his Party*,[80] Conor Cruise O'Brien makes the point that 'even supposing that he acted from admiration of the Captain's diplomatic gifts and pity for his unrepresentative condition – the effect of his action was not altered; it was a severe and early laboratory test of the solidity and loyalty of the new Irish party.'[81]

In late December, two days after the Hawarden Kite had begun to change the political landscape, Chamberlain had written to Edmund Dwyer Gray in much the same vein as revealed in his correspondence with Labouchere. Gray warned Parnell that the Radical leader was 'unfriendly and sulky'. Parnell, who would have been well aware of Chamberlain's attitude to legislative independence for Ireland, implied in a letter to Gray on Christmas Eve 1885, that this was new information. 'You seem to intimate that O'Shea's influence upon Chamberlain, if it were exercised, might be of service,' he continued. He was, of course, clutching at straws. He then tried to put the onus on Gray to approach leading members of the Irish party to have O'Shea nominated for Galway.[82] Gray, sensibly, did not bite. He expressed extreme scepticism about the actual influence O'Shea wielded over Chamberlain. He also queried the Captain's suggestion that Chamberlain's sulkiness was because the Irish party had failed to find him an Irish seat. 'You are much better able than I am to judge how much salt may be required to digest his arguments,' declared Gray before closing the door on pleading the case for O'Shea to an Irish party Star Chamber. He advised Parnell '... openly to take the responsibility. No one else can do it – the intervention of no one else could do any good – least of all mine.'[83]

But all of this was mere prologue and pretext. O'Shea's supposed influence over a figure who would be a crucial factor in the forthcoming political battle for Home Rule offered the Emperor some clothes. It provided Parnell with the flimsy excuse that would allow him to bludgeon through O'Shea's unpledged candidacy for the nationalist seat of Galway.

At first the notion was rejected by Parnell as impossible when the two men discussed it, because O'Shea steadfastly refused to take the Irish party pledge. 'He would sit where he liked, and vote as he pleased,' the Captain had grumbled. Then, as was his wont, he went *pour chercher la femme*. 'Willie would give me no peace,' Katharine wrote. 'I must see Mr Gladstone, Lord Richard Grosvenor, Mr Parnell. It was nonsense to suppose that with all the "wire-pulling" I had had to do, I now had not the small amount of influence he required to secure him a seat in parliament.'[84] O'Shea threatened, to his wife, to stand for the constituency anyway, with or without the support of Parnell. The Irish leader could foresee such an eventuality exposing fissures that he knew to exist within the supposedly monolithic Parliamentary Party. He warned Katharine that 'I can force Willie upon Galway, but it will be such a shock to my own men that they'll not be the same again ... I'll propose him if only he will consent to take the party pledge. Tell him I cannot insult the others by proposing him without that.'[85]

Katharine's diplomatic efforts were of no use. O'Shea was obdurate and abusive: of her, of Parnell, of Grosvenor and of Gladstone. Parnell was given no choice. Better a controlled and carefully orchestrated campaign designed to keep O'Shea a safe distance from his constituents, than the free-for-all of an insurgent candidacy. 'I'll get him returned,' Parnell promised, 'I'll force him down their throats, and he can never again claim that I have promised and not performed. It will cost me the confidence of the party, but that much he shall have ...' With that, the stage was being prepared for the dress rehearsal of the disastrous party split in 1890. Parnell had already told T.P. O'Connor who the candidate was going to be. According to Katharine's account, '... he laughed with the rare flash of humour that sometimes beset him in unlikely moments. "You should have seen his face, my Queen; he looked as if I had dropped him into an ice-pit." Captain O'Shea was returned for Galway.'[86] Of course, not being a first-hand witness, she left out the rather interesting bit in the middle.

Meanwhile, back at the ice pit, T.P. O'Connor's '... blood ran cold. I saw the disastrous consequences which must follow ... and I thought it was my duty there and then to adopt all means to save Parnell from this tragic and disastrous mistake.'[87] He had his own candidate in mind, as had the local organisation in Galway.[88] Now they were being trumped by

'... a hated candidate, Captain O'Shea, in order to close his mouth as to the relations between Parnell and his wife.'[89]

O'Connor, appalled at the implications of what was being done in the name of the Irish Parliamentary Party, moved quickly to thwart his leader. He first sought out one of O'Shea's principal adversaries within the party, Joseph Biggar, at the Metropole Hotel. The meeting offers a comic vision not easily forgotten, '... when he jumped out of bed', O'Connor recalled, 'clad in a strange garment like a bearskin, he looked so grotesque that his image at that moment remains with me still as the ridiculous part of a great tragedy.'[90] Biggar's reaction on hearing that Parnell was going to nominate O'Shea was characteristically blunt and brusque. 'He won't sit for Galway ... I'll stop it. Damned Whig.'[91] Both men set out straightaway for Dublin, telegraphing Tim Healy in advance with the news.

As Healy relates it, he received a telegram from O'Connor on 5 February 1886, informing him that Parnell had chosen to nominate O'Shea for the seat. O'Connor was offering to resign rather than accept O'Shea if Healy would join him. The Liverpool MP urged Healy to write a letter at once to the *Freeman's Journal* condemning Parnell's action. Healy's (unpublished) letter to the *Freeman* was vitriolic in its demolition of the Captain: 'For six years he sat in Parliament on the Government side of the House, and on nearly every critical occasion he either voted against the Irish Party, or else kept prudently away from embarrassing divisions. If, now that he has failed to secure a seat on any other conditions, Captain O'Shea announces himself as a Nationalist, prepared to take the pledge of the Irish Party, the deathbed character of his repentance would be so apparent that his sincerity would at once be questioned ...'[92]

But if O'Connor, Biggar and Healy were gaining some impetus in their frontal assault on Parnell's position, he was outflanking them with great rapidity. The rebels needed to generate enough opposition from within the party to forestall Parnell in advocating O'Shea's candidacy. Once his support found its way into the public domain, there would be no option but to confront their party leader openly and risk one of the cleavages that was already opening up becoming an un-navigable chasm. But it was already too late for that. Not long after Healy's letter arrived at the offices of the *Freeman*, it was followed by an election address from O'Shea announcing Parnell's support for his candidature. Edmund Dwyer Gray immediately spiked Healy's letter. When Healy tried to persuade Gray to publish, Parnell's erstwhile political opponent observed tartly, 'My dear Healy I once tried a fall with Parnell and got the worst of it. I'm not going to try it any more.'[93] William O'Brien, describing the intervention as 'midsummer madness',[94] warned Healy against opposing Parnell publicly and advised that he overcome his ' ... instinctive repulsion for O'Shea ...'[95] and accept the inevitable.[96]

The publication of the address was enough to dissuade T.P. O'Connor from taking the escapade any further. He would not involve himself in a public act of disloyalty to Parnell, whatever he thought of O'Shea. Biggar and Healy, however, were both determined to end O'Shea's political ambitions and continued on to Galway to rally opposition to the Captain and the King. O'Shea had beaten them to the battleground, but when they got to the city they found that support had formed behind a local candidate, Michael Lynch. Biggar and Healy quickly addressed a meeting in favour of Lynch during the course of which Biggar made a number of scathing allusions to O'Shea. According to R. Barry O'Brien he even informed the electors of Galway that O'Shea had been chosen as their candidate because he was the husband of Parnell's mistress.[97] Unfortunately these colourful phillipics, if they ever saw the light of day, do not survive, as Healy claims he managed to persuade the local *Freeman* correspondent, W.H. Brayden, to omit them from his reports. Given that newspaper's support for Parnell it is unlikely that any public utterances of this nature would ever have got into print.

Healy and Biggar had solid political grounds for an appeal to the Galway electorate against the wisdom of choosing O'Shea as their MP. But the clinching argument they had in their armoury, that Parnell was blatantly buying off the husband of his mistress with a nationalist seat in parliament, was one even the often intemperate Biggar would likely have expressed more circumspectly. There is a divergence of opinion over how far Biggar actually went, in public, on that occasion. Two young Galway journalists were present at the rally: Thomas Marlowe, a future editor of the *Daily Mail* and John Muldoon, later an Irish party MP. In his version of events, told to T.P. O'Connor, Marlowe is emphatic that Biggar stated, '... that Parnell was giving the seat to O'Shea because Mrs O'Shea was his mistress ... Biggar made the allegation in question in the plainest language, and declared that nothing would induce him to be a party to such a transaction. Healy also spoke, in entire agreement with Biggar, but I cannot recollect that he repeated the statement as to Parnell's reason for putting O'Shea in.'[98]

Muldoon, who set down his account in 1930, has a very different recollection. His impression was that, while Biggar was explicit in his *private* statements to local apparatchiki, including Lynch, that 'The candidate's wife is Parnell's mistress and there is nothing more to be said ...',[99] he resisted what must have been an overwhelming temptation to share this intelligence with the good people of Galway. It is not possible to reconcile the two accounts, but it is reasonable to suggest that the repercussions of any such public exposure of the Parnell–O'Shea affair would have been instant, irreversible and utterly appalling. All the more so as the cuckold himself was observing proceedings.

While Healy and Biggar denounced his candidacy in Eyre Square, O'Shea looked on forlornly from the window of his room in Mack's Hotel and heard himself being colourfully described as 'a Whig grub'. Spotted by Healy as he spoke, the future Governor General of Ireland dropped the broadest possible hint that if O'Shea didn't withdraw from the race he risked exposure. 'We may yet have to raise other issues in this election and we shall not fear to do so before we allow the honour of Galway to be besmirched.'[100] Healy was rampant for the moment, but the Head Prefect was on his way. His arrival had been preceded by a telegram from the Irish party whip, Deasy, warning Biggar and Healy that Parnell would resign if O'Shea was not returned.

For the next two days Healy and Biggar were subjected to a flurry of telegrams from various prominent members of the party condemning their divisive actions. Parnell himself wired Lynch advising him that 'the responsibility resting upon you or anybody else who attempts to weaken my power and influence at [the] present juncture will be grave.'[101] He also appealed to Biggar's sense of loyalty with a confidential telegram. According to Healy's account in *Letters and Leaders*, 'It recalled their long comradeship, the combats they had endured together, the fidelity which each had shown the other, and implored him that now when the Irish Cause approached the winning-post he would not thwart the purposes of his old and faithful friend.'[102] Biggar was not going to be swayed by Parnell's sentimental appeal. So incensed was he that he proposed to respond with a single line: 'Mrs O'Shea will be your ruin.' Healy claims he persuaded him to write instead the scarcely less provocative: 'The O'Sheas will be your ruin.'[103] So thick was the traffic of telegrams and so vital the correspondence that the Galway telegraph office was kept open for business on a Sunday to accommodate it.

Meanwhile, the Captain, increasingly enervated by the hornet's nest he was stirring up, was making copious use of the unexpected Sunday opening of the Galway telegraph office himself. He loosed off five telegrams to Parnell that day (Healy and he, at one point, were sharing the office facilities to dispatch urgent messages). One of O'Shea's telegrams was typical: 'All hope gone unless you can come at once. Things have gone so far that the presence of anyone except yourself would not save the situation. O'Shea.'[104]

Not even the Bishop of Galway himself could 'save the situation' for the Captain. As was his wont, O'Shea had sought to enlist clerical assistance from the outset. He had spoken to Dr Carr, Bishop of Galway, and asked for his support. Thus far the Roman Catholic clergy of Galway had remained neutral in the row, but had been notably absent from the meeting that had nominated Lynch. This may have been because of his former connections to the IRB. It could equally be ascribed to an unwillingness to oppose Parnell. Of course it was attributed by O'Shea himself to the fact that his opponent was unable to attract 'the slightest sympathy on the part of respectable members of society, clerical or lay.'[105] While he claimed that the Archbishop of the adjoining diocese of Tuam 'was in the fullest sympathy with my candidature', he conceded that Carr and his clergy, 'with reluctance', were forced to adopt 'an attitude of expectation and reserve'. Healy, hardly an unimpeachable source, especially on this issue, later claimed that 'The Bishop, the Most Rev Dr Carr (soon to be translated to Melbourne as Archbishop) told us that O'Shea had gone down on his knees before him and vowed there was no truth in any allegation which connected his wife's name with Parnell.'[106] The Bishop had also asked O'Shea to withdraw from the election.[107] According to Muldoon it was O'Shea's proposer and namesake, Fr Joseph O'Shea (a distant relation), who actually raised the issue of the affair on the basis of Biggar's statements. O'Shea vigorously denied the allegation and said that he would shoot Biggar if he heard him repeat it.[108]

Despite his obvious unpopularity the Captain still found it difficult to curtail his natural arrogance and bluster. Healy alleges that O'Shea was visited by Sir Thomas Brady, a Fisheries inspector, and asked to withdraw his candidacy. When O'Shea not only refused, but suggested that Parnell himself would shortly be in Galway to lend his support, Brady reacted with incredulity. Pointing across Eyre Square from the front door of the Great Southern Hotel, O'Shea asked Brady whether he saw an errand boy making his way across the road. When the Fisheries inspector replied that he did, O'Shea bragged, 'Well I'll make Parnell run faster on my errands to-morrow than that fellow is hopping now.'[109]

While Healy and Biggar were making mischief in Galway, Parnell had been quick to rally party support behind him. Few, if any, of the Irish party members had any regard for O'Shea, but they were conscious of the risk of a Parnell-supported candidate failing to carry Galway while Gladstone and Parnell were collaborating on the formulation of the Home Rule Bill. T.P. O'Connor, who had begun the campaign against O'Shea, had done a complete about-turn. William O'Brien tried to persuade Healy by telegram to do a similar volte-face. A petition signed by most of the prominent members of the Irish party (with the exception of Healy's so-called 'Bantry bunch', his brother Maurice, *Nation* editor T.D. Sullivan, and a number of others) was dispatched to the *Freeman's Journal* to put further pressure on the Galway rebels. At this point Healy and Biggar were far out on a limb. There was no escaping the political reality that, as a chastened T.P. O'Connor phrased it, 'If Mr Parnell pinned himself publicly to the support of Captain O'Shea, then it became a question of his leadership ... even the lesser evil of Captain O'Shea's election was to be accepted.'[110]

Parnell took personal charge on 9 February 1886. Along with a number of his key lieutenants, including O'Brien and a reluctant O'Connor, he took the train to Galway to bend the city to his will. Healy had warned O'Brien that there would be a monumental row if Parnell arrived and suggested, with ill-advised bravado, that this would be a good time for the Irish leader to indulge in his penchant for missing trains. On the journey to Galway O'Connor, concerned at what horrors might emerge if a confrontation was provoked, pleaded with his leader to take a lenient attitude with Healy. Parnell responded by drily echoing Gladstone's famous Leeds speech of 1881 and insisted that he would use all the 'resources of civilization' in his treatment of the Cork rebel. He then accused his former secretary of having been 'trying to stab him in the back for years, and that he was doing so now, thinking the opportune hour had come.'[111] It has been suggested that Healy was indeed seizing what he perceived to be an opportunity to oust Parnell from the leadership of the Irish party. In retrospect the mutiny in Galway would appear to have been a singularly inauspicious occasion on which to launch a *coup* unless the pretender proposed to slash and burn his way to the Chieftaincy. However, it may have looked very differently to Healy at the time.

An as yet subterranean crevice had opened up between the two men. Healy had been anxious to convey to the Liberal leadership that Parnell was not the only point of light in the Irish party. Through Labouchere, for example, the extraordinary message had been conveyed to Chamberlain in December 1885 that 'Parnell is half mad. We always act without him. He accepts this position; if he did not we should overlook him. Do not trouble yourself about him. Dillon, McCarthy, O'Brien, Harrington and I settle everything.'[112] Fuelled more by personal ambition and animus than by any profound ideological difference the fault line between the two would widen in Galway before cracking wide open in the most brutal manner possible in November, 1890.

Not since Enniscorthy more than five years before had Parnell been abused by an Irish crowd. But, as he alighted from the train in Galway station and faced shouts of 'To Hell with Parnell and Whiggery', he must have been given pause at least. Local feeling was running high against his candidate. 'The large railway platform was impassable,' O'Connor recalled, 'with a wild, excited, terrible crowd, shouting furiously, wildly hostile to Captain O'Shea; ready to drink the blood – figuratively – of anybody who came to support him.'[113] Somewhat awed by the actual presence of the King himself the Lynch mob vented their spleen on the more familiar figure of their local MP. Someone attempted to knock his hat off with a stick and Parnell intervened on his behalf, leading the portly TP away to safety. Rather courageously, given the mood of the chanting crowd, O'Shea had put in an appearance at the station to greet the relieving force, '... the whiteness of his face was as palpable as that of his elaborate collar,'[114] O'Connor recalled. Parnell brushed him aside brusquely, marched towards the nearby hotel and, almost immediately, went into conclave with an apprehensive Healy and a still recalcitrant Biggar. Neither of the rebels had believed Parnell would come to Galway in person, assuming that his threats to do so were simply designed to force them to withdraw their opposition, According to Healy's account Parnell's approach to the crisis which both men had contrived to engineer amounted to little more than a crude statement of *l'etat c'est moi* 'Suddenly;' Healy wrote in his memoir 'Parnell put forth his arm with an eloquent gesture, declaring, 'I hold an Irish Parliament in the hollow of this hand.[115] The man who strikes at my hand strikes at the hopes of the Irish Nation!'[116] O'Connor's account of the confrontation is markedly different.

'On occasions of great excitement like this, Healy has almost always given way to his somewhat excitable temperament, and he has the gift of tears. He sobbed, and the tears streamed down his cheeks as he made his explanation...' Healy rejected the claim that his actions were out of personal animosity towards his leader. 'Parnell and the men around the table – all of them hostile to Healy, personally and politically – remained silent; I broke the silence by saying, "I certainly do not believe that".[117] Whether or not the surrender was as abject as depicted by O'Connor, the essential fact was that Healy capitulated. Knowing (through Labouchere) of the extent of Chamberlain's antipathy towards Home Rule, he did not buy in to the 'party line' of O'Shea as persuader. But collegiality won out and he climbed back in from the buckling branch.

Not so the redoubtable Joseph Gillis Biggar. The steely Northerner was utterly unrepentant. At one point in an impassioned speech, he veered so close to making an allusion to 'the terms on which we all felt the seat had been sold to O'Shea'[118] that Healy leaped from his chair and made to silence him. But Biggar avoided any direct reference to Katharine O'Shea and restricted his arguments to the well-rehearsed political objections to O'Shea's candidacy.

Silencing Healy and agreeing to differ with Biggar was only half the battle, however. Parnell was now called upon to address a highly partisan crowd and convince them that they should abandon their chosen candidate and adopt a Whig instead. Wisely, in what was one of the most important speeches in his career, he chose not to mention O'Shea. Instead he played on the awareness of his listeners that the potential *rapprochement* with the Liberals, currently the subject of tentative negotiations, would be jeopardised if his authority was challenged in any way. He repeated the line about holding Home Rule 'in the hollow of this hand'. To O'Connor, who was often sceptical about Parnell's rhetorical abilities, it was a *tour de force* that swayed the crowd: '... You could almost feel the shudder of terror and of subjugation which swept through the audience, brought back from its howling fury to the sepulchral silence of a death chamber.'[119] O'Connor's florid phrasemaking disguises the fact that it was not until William O'Brien made essentially the same point a short time later that the sullen crowd was actually won over.

When the din of the whole affair had died down, O'Brien wrote to thank Dillon for not intervening. The letter gives some indication of the damage done to Parnell: 'Your feelings and ours about O'S[hea] are, of course, the same: loathing. So is our feeling about the infamous way in which P[arnell] has put him forward and slighted the party. The question was, in the special circumstances of the moment, whether we should swallow O'Shea or utterly destroy our movement and party at its brightest moment for a personal reason which we could not even explain.' The latter comment is indicative of the discreet manner in which the affair was discussed by Parnell's more loyal lieutenants. The only further hint at what the entire shambles had really been about comes later in the letter, when he says of his leader 'he is plainly bound by some influence he cannot resist'.[120]

But the object of Parnell's visit had been achieved. He had dealt with the situation 'with a characteristic mixture of recklessness and calculation, bluntness and plausibility, ferocious determination and diplomatic address.'[121] Lynch withdrew his candidacy and Parnell remained in Galway to campaign on behalf of O'Shea. A reference by him in a speech to an agreement from O'Shea to sit on the Irish benches in the future was misinterpreted as implying that O'Shea had agreed to take the party pledge. When he had won the seat O'Shea displayed unexpected ethical qualms that voters might have chosen him in this mistaken belief. (In truth they had little alternative, other than to stay at home). He expressed his concerns to Bishop Carr and wondered whether, in the circumstances, he should resign his seat. Having, in all probability, come by it as a result of tacit blackmail, he apparently had no wish to retain it as a result of false pretences. The Bishop advised him to consult his mentor and accept the adjudication of Chamberlain. The Birmingham Solomon found in his favour and O'Shea withdrew his threat to resign.

For Parnell there was some satisfaction in the outcome. The Healy insurgency had been smoked out into the open and subdued. He had wielded absolute power over a reluctant party. He had, for the moment, silenced the irritating O'Shea. He had also, unbeknownst to himself, passed Chamberlain's stress test with flying colours. But there was too much downside for Parnell to have been pleased with his handiwork. There were limits to the ability of a leader, even one as charismatic and commanding as Parnell, to assert himself as brutally and, apparently, idiosyncratically, as he had done in Galway. Though never the most consistent of leaders, Parnell[122] had insisted on the introduction of a pledge largely predicated on loyalty to himself. He had then abused that loyalty to ram through a candidate who refused to take that pledge. He had demanded that both his party and the people of Galway not jeopardise his political credibility at a crucial time. In so doing he had done severe damage to that very same credibility. Chamberlain, and others, might have been secretly impressed at this exhibition of raw political power but it had come at an undoubted cost. In addition his liaison with Katharine O'Shea, known only within a largely tolerant élite circle, was now in the public domain. It was no longer merely the subject of gossip in fashionable London clubs, it had permeated into the street corners of the city of Galway. No one was more aware of that than the city's new Member of Parliament.

The official line taken in *United Ireland* was to gloat at the disappointment of the British newspapers, which had predicted that the uprising would end Parnell's leadership. Although the speeches of Healy and Biggar were reproduced (they could not fail to be, as they had already been carried in the *Freeman*) it was suggested that both men had opposed O'Shea *before* they had become aware that he had the support of the party leader. As soon as they had discovered the truth, Healy and Biggar had 'waived their objections to his candidature in deference to the request of their leader ... And so ended the Last Prophecy of Irish Disaster.'[123] The following week the result of the poll, a facile victory for O'Shea, was announced at about the right length without editorial comment and without any outcry in the Letters column.

Understandably the stance taken by the other major nationalist weekly, T.D. Sullivan's *Nation*, was radically different. In a scathing editorial, Healy's uncle (by marriage) described the running of O'Shea as 'a deplorable mistake', insisting that:

> ... much of the reasoning which we have seen put forward
> for the purpose of reconciling the public mind to that pro-
> ceeding is hollow and unworthy of the principle of Irish
> nationality. We have never met an Irish member who had
> any trust or confidence in Captain O'Shea as a politician, or
> who desired to have any political association with him.
> Today, because of great and unparalleled pressure exercised
> in his favour by the leader of the Irish party, he is able to call
> himself member for the Nationalist borough of Galway ...
> That would not be because of Captain O'Shea's merits, but
> because of the status of his patron ...'[124]

Left behind on the battlefield was a wounded and, temporarily, stricken enemy. Unlike the acquiescent Edmund Dwyer Gray, Tim Healy was not so chastened that he would retire permanently into his shell. In addition, events subsequent to the Galway mutiny exacerbated the factionalism within the party. The absence of T.D. Sullivan's signature on the petition supporting Parnell had been noted in certain quarters, as had been the caustic editorial in the *Nation*. As Lord Mayor of Dublin he had conceived the novel idea of beginning his year in office with a banquet from which Castle dignitaries would be excluded and to which ordinary tradesmen would be invited. This egalitarian gesture was almost negated by a poster campaign in Dublin urging workingmen to boycott the event. The argument that such behaviour was a spontaneous outburst and not indicative of a new Parnellite authoritarianism or a pervasive ethos of guilt-by-association did not weigh heavily with the Bantry faction.

The Press, too, while offering only oblique hints of the true state of affairs, was emboldened by the audacity of Parnell's behaviour. The Unionist Dublin *Evening Mail* on the day the result was announced made mention of 'a toast of some elderly wags – the family friendships of the O'Sheas and Parnells – it seems simple enough, but there is more in it than politics apparently.'[125] The *Times*, in its commentary, also sailed close to the wind. 'There must be, it is hinted', whispered the normally raucous 'Thunderer', 'good grounds for Mr. Parnell's choice ...' It went on to quote, without attribution, one of the more facile justifications from a *Freeman's Journal* piece supportive of Parnell: 'a man in his position fre-quently cannot disclose his reasons; to divulge them would be to destroy them.'[126] The juxtaposition, while hardly devastating, did Parnell few favours. Neither did the newspaper's political verdict on the debacle. As far as the *Times* was concerned, Parnell had failed the Chamberlain exper-iment. The suppressed revolt in Galway 'shows how difficult it will be for the Liberals to carry on a long Parliamentary campaign with such restless and passionate allies.'

But what of the new Member for Galway? The *Irish Times* reported that, reverting to type, one of O'Shea's first self-appointed tasks was to visit the Claddagh fishermen 'to ascertain in what way he could promote their interests ...' However, the newspaper suggested that 'many of his future colleagues are rather bitterly inclined towards the Captain, who will probably find himself cold-shouldered to a considerable extent ...'[127]

And so it proved. O'Shea was to discover that the game had not been worth the candle. T.P. O'Connor observed that, in the wake of the Galway fiasco and the seepage of rumours of blackmail and adultery into a wider public domain:

> There was undoubtedly an entire change in the atmosphere of the House of Commons towards O'Shea. His wit, his good humour, his suave manners, had made him not a popular personality, but certainly not a repellent member of the House. There was a general uneasy impression that he had purchased his seat in Galway at a price which no man of honour would pay, and the more or less detached air which he wore, his silence, and his general absence from his seat in the House of Commons, increased the sense of his being an isolated and not respected figure.[128]

O'Connor's impression is supported by Hansard, which does not record a single intervention by the Galway MP into any debate or a solitary parliamentary question in the 1886 session that had already begun when he made his return to Westminster.

Never one to spurn an opportunity to abuse former associates,[129] Lord Randolph Churchill was one of the first parliamentarians to make O'Shea feel distinctly unwelcome. In a speech at Paddington shortly after his Pyrrhic victory in Galway Churchill was recorded as observing that O'Shea was 'a person who from every point of view is absolutely repugnant and loathsome politically'.[130] Understandably upset at reading such a devastating assessment from a man he considered to be a part of his social circle, O'Shea wrote to Churchill looking for '... an explanation satisfactory to both of us'. What he got was an assurance from the Tory MP that he had been misquoted and that O'Shea's loathsomeness was entirely political and referred solely to the antipathy of the Irish party.[131] The explanation seemed not only to satisfy O'Shea, but also to please him so much that he drew attention to the original remarks by writing to the

Times. In so doing he took the opportunity not just of setting the record straight on Churchill's gibe, but of entirely reinventing the Galway narrative.

In contradicting Churchill's 'mistaken' views on the by-election, he claimed that 'I did not seek the representation of Galway without the knowledge that the local candidate had declared that he would not proceed; that I was received with cordiality by the bishop and clergy; that every fisherman in the Claddagh would have voted for me on the Monday just as he did on the Thursday ...' From arrant nonsense and fantasy he moved on to conspiracy:

> The opposition was organised outside the borough. For strategic purposes, the local candidate was induced to reconsider his decision ... The moment it was rumoured that I was in need, volunteers poured in from Clare, and I was provided with a bodyguard of men as determined as any in Munster ... I have no hesitation in saying that if there were a vacancy to-morrow and I were to stand for either division of the county from which I was 'compulsorily retired' by astute manipulation in November, Lord Randolph Churchill's expression would receive a decided contradiction.[132]

Once again O'Shea's breathtaking capacity for self-deception was equalled only by his ability to inflict his delusions on others.

It has to be assumed that, stated or unstated, the price of Parnell risking his leadership and the very unity of his party for O'Shea was that he and Katharine would be left alone and be allowed to conduct their domestic life together unhindered by her husband – as, by and large, they had been up to that point. The achievement of his ambition of a return to Westminster, no matter how humiliating the circumstances, allowed the Captain, for the moment, to relapse into his 'subsidised somnolence'.[133] But, in the words of the temporarily vanquished Healy, 'No gain for Ireland came by propping up Parnell's worm-eaten pedestal, and within four years O'Shea remorselessly overthrew it.'[134] For the moment, however, in the words of F.S.L. Lyons, 'Parnell was safe. But what Galway showed beyond question was that his safety still depended upon the co-operation or connivance of Captain O'Shea. And this in turn depended upon the satisfaction of Captain O'Shea's ambitions.'[135]

In a postscript to the 'mutiny', one of Parnell's most faithful and steadfast followers, Edward Leamy MP, cited a story he had been told by William O'Brien. Biggar and Healy, after an uneasy dinner with Parnell, had left Galway. Parnell had drawn O'Brien into his hotel room. According to Leamy, O'Brien had said that something like a sob escaped Parnell. He then told the *United Ireland* editor, 'I know all that my friends' action today meant. It was the first favour I ever asked of my countrymen, and it will be the last. From this day forth, this fellow can do no further mischief.'

'Alas!' Leamy observed bitterly and entirely accurately, 'The "fellow" was only setting out on his cured path of still more mischief.'[136]

CHAPTER 11

Crown Steward and Bailiff of the Chiltern Hundreds

I asked him whether Home Rule had not come to mean to
the average Irishman the turning of sixpences into shillings,
and what he [Parnell] thought would happen if the people of
Ireland ever woke up to find that even under Home Rule the
sixpences were still only sixpences ...

Lord Ribblesdale, *Impressions and Memories*

The interregnum between the second and third ministries of William
Ewart Gladstone was considerably shorter than that between his first
and second. Disraeli had held sway for almost seven years in the 1870s.
Salisbury's reign was closer to seven months. He would more than atone
for the brevity of his first ministry in the years ahead. Gladstone, who
had shown a readiness to adopt a 'push and pull' approach to Ireland,
came back into power in early 1886 with a radically different approach.
Rather than tinker around the edges, he had resolved to go to the heart
of the conflict between Britain and Ireland and offer a permanent solution
by means of a measure of Irish legislative independence.

Parnell, who had fought a long agrarian battle under the banner of
'the land for the people' was about to do so again, but this time '... "the
land for the people" took on another meaning. It now meant the land in
a political sense: Home Rule, freedom, self-government, or whatever
shorthand slogan sufficed.'[1] To some Irish tenant farmers, an increasing

proportion of whom had begun the process of buying out their landlords (under the aegis of the Land Purchase Act introduced by the short-lived Tory Chief Secretary, Ashbourne), the metamorphosis may have come as a welcome change. The old slogan was open to unsafe interpretations, socialistic notions that were anathema to a rising peasant proprietary. They had struggled to achieve ownership of their land. In offering their acquiescence in a new struggle for the realisation of a universalist ideal, they were ensuring that the redistributive implications of Davitt's philosophy were neutered. In their adherence to the new brief they were joined by their pastors. The Roman Catholic Church shelved its suspicions and began to promote the cause of Home Rule enthusiastically.

Gladstone brought a draft version of his Home Rule Bill before Cabinet in March 1886. Chamberlain's reaction can be gauged from a brief note sent to O'Shea after he had got sight of the Prime Minister's proposals a fortnight before they were formally presented to Cabinet. 'I fear that our arrangement is past praying for now,' was his pessimistic appraisal. O'Shea, to give him his due, sought some form of accommodation. He included a number of amending suggestions in a letter to Chamberlain on 19 March, suggesting that 'If this in any way might meet your views I would send for Mr Parnell.'[2] At this point Chamberlain had already indicated to Gladstone that he would resign when the draft Bill came before Cabinet.

O'Shea made a second sortie on 25 March in a memo designed to, as he saw it, clarify Chamberlain's thoughts on Home Rule. Quite why Chamberlain would need the dark corners of his mind illuminated by O'Shea or why the Prime Minister might require further elucidation on a philosophical disagreement that had already emerged at Cabinet level is not clear. What is apparent is that O'Shea cannot have been acting with his mentor's approval and, when the Captain went on a solo run, the consequences could range from mild confusion to utter turmoil.

Taking a leaf out of Parnell's book, O'Shea wrote a letter in the third person to his wife outlining his view of Chamberlain's attitude to the Gladstonian template for Irish legislative independence. He then sent a copy by hand to 10 Downing Street.[3] While fully acknowledging the difficulties of the situation,' he wrote, 'Mr O'Shea refuses to believe that a compromise is still impossible. Too much faith need not be placed in the statements of the mischief makers who say that Mr Chamberlain is absolutely determined to accept none ... *Mr Chamberlain is known to be in favour of Home Rule* [my italics] and of a settlement of the Land question, so that these great affairs can be with him only a question of degree.'[4] In the light of Chamberlain's vehement opposition to Gladstone's proposals in Cabinet and later in parliamentary debate, to describe him as favouring Home Rule is a perplexing statement.[5] It is indicative of counter-intuitive thinking on O'Shea's part, which had more to do with his own ambitions than with any profound concern about the implications for the Home Rule legislation. Chamberlain's resignation would greatly reduce O'Shea's capacity to influence. With the prospect of an almost inevitable split in the Liberal party, and the possibility of the government being forced out of office, that capacity would disappear almost entirely.

Whatever his motives or authority for his actions the intervention achieved no purpose. On 26 March 1886 Gladstone brought historic proposals to Cabinet for a legislative assembly for Ireland with powers of taxation, government appointment and responsibility for most internal affairs. After some cursory questions about the extent of Irish sovereignty,[6] Chamberlain and Trevelyan resigned their posts and left the room. Between then and the introduction of the Bill on 8 April, Parnell began a series of private jousts with Gladstone and John Morley (the new Chief Secretary) to ensure that a Bill acceptable to the Irish party emerged. Meanwhile, dismayed Radicals attempted to prevent the sundering of their faction within the Liberal party. The day before Gladstone brought the Bill to parliament, Labouchere was still cajoling Chamberlain in an attempt to change his mind 'Any number of British Radicals expressed their hope this afternoon in the House that you would see your way to approve of Mr Gladstone's amended Bill. They are all most anxious that you should be the Elisha of the aged Elijah, and aid in getting this Irish question out of the way.'[7] His erstwhile leader responded with obvious regret 'Nothing would give me greater pleasure than to come back to the fold. Unfortunately I am told today on the highest authority that the scheme to be proposed tonight will not meet the main objections which led to my resignation, I am very sorry, as I was in the most conciliatory mood.'[8]

In her memoir Katharine O'Shea places herself very much at the centre of things on the momentous day, 8 April 1886, when Gladstone rose to introduce the first measure of self-government for Ireland in over a century. She claims that the Prime Minister was waiting for a telegram from her indicating Parnell's assent for him to proceed with the introduction of the Bill. Naturally, or the scene would not be sufficiently dramatic, everything was left until the last minute. She had been told by Parnell that the measures to be introduced 'will do as a beginning' and that she could give her written consent to the Grand Old Man. 'His messenger was so late that I simply snatched Gladstone's letter from him and, scribbling my "Yes" on the enclosed Government form, sent my waiting servant flying to the telegraph office with it.' One wonders what she did with the redundant messenger. Unfortunately, because of this governmental tardiness, she was unable to be in the House of Commons when the Bill was introduced, '... this Bill that I had taken so often in its swaddling clothes from parent to foster parent, and I was very much disappointed at not being present at its introduction to a larger life.'[9] Given the greatly expanded circle of those with knowledge of her relationship with Parnell, it was perhaps just as well that she did not take her seat in the gallery. Had she done so she would have had the added satisfaction of watching her husband leave the House of Commons as an MP for the last time.

According to Herbert Gladstone, Katharine's account, which does sound quite preposterous, was completely untrue. In a chapter of his autobiography, specifically set aside for the purpose of debunking a number of Katharine O'Shea's claims about her relationship with his father, he asserts that the story '... arises either from hallucination or sheer invention.'[10] He also rejects her estimate of the number of meetings that took place between them – his tally is three in all – and points out that the lengthy correspondence between the two was largely one-sided, except at moments of crisis in the Anglo-Irish relationship.

Notwithstanding the absence of Katharine O'Shea there was a palpable sense of tension and of occasion about Westminster on 8 April 1886. Mary Gladstone, who accompanied her father from Downing Street to the Commons for the first reading of the Bill on that day, has an excellent, if extremely partial, record of the event in her diary:

> Every spot was covered. The floor had seats up to the table like the free seats in a church – the air tingled with excitement and emotion, and when he began his speech we wondered to see that it was really the same face – familiar voice. For three hours and a half he spoke – the most quiet, earnest pleading, explaining, analysing, showing a mastery of detail and a grip and grasp such as has never been surpassed. Not a sound was heard, not a cough even, only cheers breaking out here and there – a tremendous feat at his age.[11] His voice never failed – we wd. [sic] not judge of the effect yet, only that deep and anxious attention and interest were shown throughout and the end was grandly cheered. I think really the scheme goes further than people thought. It is astonishing [in] its faith and courage ...[12]

Sitting in the gallery with Mary Gladstone was Lucy Cavendish, wife of one of the most tragic casualties of Anglo-Irish bitterness. As Gladstone drew breath after his marathon speech, the shape of the opposition quickly became apparent. Across the aisles the Tories were baying but on the Liberal side of the House, in addition to Chamberlain and a Radical Unionist cohort, there was also antipathy towards Gladstone's new measure from the Whigs, led by Hartington. Even with the solid support of 86 Parnellites, unless hearts and minds were changed, the sums did not add up for Home Rule.

One of the most serious defections from the Radical Unionist faction was that of Chamberlain's valued friend and ally, Sir Charles Dilke. He was having personal difficulties of his own at the time. Donald Crawford had sued for divorce, citing his wife's alleged adultery with Dilke. On the advice of his lawyers and of Chamberlain, the baronet did not give evidence in his defence and was fortunate when the presiding Judge, Sir Charles Butt,[13] ruled that he had no case to answer. Paradoxically he then granted Crawford his divorce. As Dilke's biographer put it 'Apparently Mrs Crawford had committed adultery with Dilke but not he with her!'[14] It was O'Shea who broke the news to Chamberlain that Dilke was going to support Home Rule. The news would have come as a huge personal blow to the Birmingham MP. In his response to O'Shea's letter the disbelief he expresses is apparent: 'If D[ilke] is really taking the line you suppose I can only say he has not given me the slightest indication of it. I am afraid he feels that his seat, already very unsafe,[15] is made hopeless by the division of opinion; but I have not had the least intimation of any change of purpose on his part in consequence. Please send me full particulars.'[16]

O'Shea proved to be far more loyal to Chamberlain than to his Galway electorate. Although he pointed out on a number of occasions that he would never vote against a Home Rule Bill,[17] the implications of what he left unsaid were apparent. The *Times* Irish correspondent reported that O'Shea, like Chamberlain, was opposed to the measure that would see Irish MPs no longer sitting in Westminster. He was also recorded as having said that he had 'no hope of the measure passing'. Adding two and two together, the *Times* hazarded that O'Shea's support was 'doubtful'.[18]

A week before the second reading of the Home Rule Bill, when certain realities were becoming apparent (namely the strength of opposition in the Commons and the virtual certainty of defeat in the Lords even if it did pass through the lower House), O'Shea sent an oddly buoyant letter to Chamberlain. It is one of those communications (rather like the 'inconvenient letter' to Parnell the previous year) which, one suspects, may have been written while under the influence of the alcoholic stimulants whose frequent consumption had led to O'Shea's severe gout. In any event it bore little relationship to reality and amply demonstrates, yet again, that when it came to spinning fantasies O'Shea was an even more accomplished weaver than his wife.

It opened with the extraordinary line, 'My Dear Chamberlain, I can say anything I like in Galway now. I am the most popular MP that has represented the Borough for a quarter of a century!!'[19] He enclosed an extract from a newspaper report of a speech he had made recently in his constituency and complained that although the local *Times* correspondent, Dr Patton, had telegraphed a full report to London, the editor had suppressed it.

The report, which was of a 'meeting' alleged to have taken place in a Galway hotel, was O'Shea 'rampant'. The MP had, supposedly, advised his audience that 'The Galway election had struck a heavy blow at political blackguardism.' A sympathetic voice had then shouted, 'It would be bad for Healy and Biggar to be in Galway today against your honour's orders.' O'Shea had then continued by declaring that '... he was proud that his constituents were well satisfied with the choice they had made, but he would take that opportunity of saying that no man could have behaved more nobly than his late opponent, Mr Lynch, who protested against the gross deception that had been practised upon him, and who was now as warm a supporter of his (Captain O'Shea's) as there was in the borough.'[20]

The report itself had prompted Healy, still licking his wounds from the by-election, to re-open the case. He had written to Lynch inquiring whether O'Shea had accurately represented him in the address. In his reply Lynch alleged that the 'meeting' in question had never actually taken place, 'but was manufactured by Captain O'Shea in the office of the paper which gave it local circulation'.[21] Given O'Shea's previous form there is little cause to doubt Lynch's information. He also denied that he had been put under pressure or subjected to 'gross deception' by Healy and Biggar to run for the seat.

Healy then wrote a derisive letter to the *Freeman's Journal* in which he utterly demolished O'Shea's pretensions. He pointed out that the Captain had, contrary to his assurances to the Galway electorate, not taken his seat with the Irish party. Still worse, 'He has repaid Mr Parnell's generous intervention on his behalf by counter-working his policy on Home Rule, a measure which he has tried to induce at least one Radical member to oppose unless the conditions of his friend Mr Chamberlain be accepted. In fact I do not hesitate to say that he has shown himself a defiant enemy of Mr Parnell ...' The personal sting, however, was in the tail, since he concluded:

> Until now ... no one has taken any notice of this political castaway, whom all parties alike despise, but, emboldened by impunity, he appears to suppose that all concerned in the

Galway election, except himself, are bound by 'the cold chain of silence', while he is free to offer his unbiased opinion on that event to a chance hotel audience ... He has now plucked up courage to attack us only because he is degraded enough to suppose that Mr Parnell would regard a retort upon his malignity and an exposure of his treachery as a reflection upon himself; but he misjudges as grossly the leader we are proud to follow as he does the men whose forbearance up to the present he has rewarded by an unprovoked and graceless onslaught, made, too, at a time when everyone had combined to forget him.[22]

O'Shea's response was one of shell-shocked scorn. 'To be abused by Mr Healy is as gratifying to my feelings as to be praised by those whom I respect,' he informed the Editor of the *Times*. Not content to leave well enough alone, he then painted an unlikely scenario of a penitent Healy having attempted a reconciliation with him, brokered 'through a gentleman in Dublin'.[23] He speculated that Healy's venom was a consequence of his own rejection of those overtures. This, of course, only prolonged the surreal correspondence and offers another example of O'Shea's ability to jump off the jetty in a suit of armour. Healy's splenetic response to the suggestion that he had attempted to appease O'Shea was carried in the *Times* the following day. In it he reached new heights of creative invective. 'His statement is simply a lie; and if the honourable and gallant member can produce any credible testimony to prove that I have ever spoken of him, in public or in private, except with loathing and contempt, I will canvass Galway for him in a white sheet in the coming election.'[24]

Not even such a disturbing image deterred O'Shea. He now tried to stand up his allegation that Healy had sought his friendship. Never one to avoid controversy when there was a convenient cesspit to be stirred, O'Shea relished this valedictory moment in the public spotlight. He was becoming convinced that the Liberal–Parnellite alliance was conspiring to bring about his undoing. On the day he despatched his letter to the *Times*, he told Chamberlain, 'I am assured it was the Liberal whips who asked him to attack me.' He also gleefully added that 'Mr Parnell asked Montagu and Nolan on Friday to warn me that he believed I should be murdered if I voted against the bill.'[25] To lend credence to his unlikely claim that Healy had sought a reconciliation, he went in search of the 'gentleman in Dublin'. This was none other than Peter 'The Packer' O'Brien, future Chief Justice of Ireland.[26] His response to O'Shea's approach seeking confirmation of his allegation ended the matter abruptly.

'Healy never expressed to me in any way whatever a desire to be reconciled with you', an irate O'Brien telegraphed O'Shea in London, 'nor did I ever tell you that he did. I write quite astounded at your telegram ... Healy always spoke of you in most contumelious manner ... do not introduce my name into this matter ... there is no shadow of foundation for so doing.'[27] The following day a deflated O'Shea was obliged to inform the readers of the *Times* that the mysterious 'Dublin Gentleman' had declined to confirm his assertion and, 'no doubt owing to my refusing to listen sufficiently when he spoke to me about Mr Healy, I was mistaken in supposing he was commissioned to speak to me.'[28]

THE DEMISE OF THE LAST IRISH WHIG

The sands were fast running out on O'Shea's parliamentary career. Given the intransigence of the Whigs, the fate of the Home Rule Bill was already in the balance. When a letter from John Bright, expressing his disapproval of the measure, was read out at Radical meeting[29] on 31 May, this sealed the opposition of more than fifty members of the Radical faction. John Morley described it as the 'death warrant of the Bill'.[30] Defeat would spell the end of Gladstone's third ministry and a general election, which would be fought on the issue of Home Rule.

O'Shea had, despite his claims to be venerated by the fishermen of the Claddagh, already worn out his welcome in Galway. His machinations on behalf of Chamberlain had guaranteed that there would be no help from Lord Richard Grosvenor or Gladstone in finding him an English constituency this time around. Nor would Chamberlain be in a position to shoehorn him into a radical seat in his Midlands bailiwick if one were to become available. O'Shea was associated with the man, not the philosophy. Not even a dyed-in-the-wool Tory would have mistaken him for a Radical.

O'Shea was under no illusions that the end was nigh. On 1 June, the morning of Chamberlain's scheduled contribution to the debate on the second reading of the Bill, O'Shea wrote to him that 'I look forward with equanimity to my approaching exclusion from political life.' In anticipation of his departure from the corridors of power, he was concerned about his legacy. In a recrudescence of the Central Board controversy there had been allegations (not just from Irish members) that O'Shea had misled his mentor about Parnell's intentions for the National Council/Central Board scheme. Edmund Dwyer Gray had attacked Chamberlain in the House the previous night and the Radical MP Shaw Lefevre had told O'Shea that 'he would have acted differently at the time, had he not been induced to believe that Messrs Parnell and co [*sic*] were in favour of the project.' 'I hope, therefore', O'Shea requested of Chamberlain, 'that you will think the matter of sufficient importance to mention it in your speech this afternoon, and that you will declare that you have unimpeachable evidence that neither in this matter, nor in the many others in which I was engaged, did I try to "make a fool of" you.'

He concluded his letter by gloating over the inevitability of the defeat of Gladstone's brave essay at a final settlement of ancient Anglo-Irish animosities by congratulating Chamberlain on having scattered his adversaries. 'You have made no mistake throughout the business, and your right honourable friend, your enemy, has been delivered into your hands.'[31]

The day after Chamberlain's speech, which, as one might expect, was not well-received on the Irish benches, O'Shea wrote one of his more obsequious letters of congratulation. 'I may be prejudiced but having heard public speakers in many countries and in perhaps greater variety than any member of the House, I hold that I never listened to a speech of such power as yours.'[32] The great Birmingham Radical had returned to a theme he had injected into the wider debate when the Bill had first been introduced. He had then advocated an as yet undefined form of federation rather than outright legislative independence. But he could not overcome the widespread feeling, especially on the Irish side of the House, that this démarche was 'smoke and mirrors' designed merely to obscure his steadfast opposition to any form of separation. Ignoring the flattery, Chamberlain responded with the hope that O'Shea would come to his own defence on the Central Board issue. He offered to approach the Speaker and get O'Shea a place in the debate, the better to advance the case that Parnell had been duplicitous during the Central Board negotiations. Wisely, envisaging the reaction on the Irish benches such a contribution would provoke, O'Shea opted to remain silent.

Parnell spoke on the Bill on the last full day of debate, 7 June. Like Moses he had led his people to the Promised Land. He must have felt that not only would he not bring them all the way himself, but that his entire nation would remain in the marches of legislative independence for some years to come. Despite his stirring Cork speech of 1885 he was prepared to accept boundaries being set to the march of his nation even were the Bill to pass. He insisted, however, that the assembly that would emerge from a Government of Ireland Act would have more power and responsibility than his beloved Grattan's Parliament. The Irish executive would not remain under the control of London, as it had in the 1780s, but would be answerable to an Irish parliament. He dealt, not always utterly convincingly, with Ulster, finance, religious differences and education. Morley described the performance as 'one of the most masterly speeches that ever fell from him.' He spoke with a passion that was 'not the mere dialectic of a party debater'.[33] It was what was expected of him, it was undoubtedly heartfelt but it was for the record and for home consumption. It did not change the parliamentary arithmetic in any way. The Government of Ireland Bill fell by 343 to 313[34] and the Liberal government resigned.

Reflecting the immensity of the issues involved it was the largest Commons vote ever recorded in British parliamentary history. Including the Speaker, 657 members were present out of a total House of Commons cohort of 670. Conspicuous by his absence in either lobby, but present in the House on the night, was William Henry O'Shea. Unlike Joseph Chamberlain (and 92 other Liberals) he did not vote against the Bill. But neither could he bring himself to put the interests of his Galway constituents over the disapprobation of his mentor and vote in favour. As with many other potentially embarrassing votes in the past he took the line of least resistance and walked out of the House. The reason offered for his abstention was that, like Chamberlain, he was opposed to the removal of Irish MPs from Westminster. In his case it was a more plausible pretext. O'Shea could not have envisaged a political career outside of the context of the House of Commons. But, as in the case of Chamberlain, it must be seen as a pretext. He also pre-empted the electors of Galway by jumping before he was pushed. He resigned his seat. It was the last time he would 'walk out' on an important Commons vote. 'As a sanguine agent his lights were extinguished. As a sinister principal his part was beginning.'[35]

The poet Wilfred Scawen Blunt who, it will be recalled, had attended the same secondary school as the Captain, had said of O'Shea, 'his name will be handed down in infamy through Irish history to the remotest generation'.[36] Blunt's attitude may have been coloured by being chased around their school by a youthful O'Shea wielding a fives bat, but bear in mind, this assessment was written more than three years before the divorce proceedings.

Why O'Shea resigned at that point has always been something of a puzzle – his abstention had ensured that he could not be returned to the next parliament in any case. F.S.L. Lyons speculates, albeit rather tentatively, that it might have been because he became aware of how widespread was the knowledge of his wife's affair[37] among a Liberal leadership, soon to be widely dispersed and in search of new alliances after the trauma of the Home Rule vote. This theory is reinforced by a sentence of O'Shea's in a recriminatory letter sent to his wife a few months after the defeat of the Bill: 'I make no attempt to put your name in the newspapers,' he wrote, 'Indeed, one of the effects of its having been there has been to end my public life.'[38] Thus any prospect of political advancement from the government of the day was unlikely. In addition, with former Liberal Cabinet members likely to be in coalition with the Tories, prospects were even worse from a government with a Conservative majority.

But there may have been a far simpler reason. O'Shea had the born narcissist's capacity for self-delusion. Even if we were to accept that he actually believed his own evaluation of his popularity in Galway (could anyone be that deluded?), he would have known that his brand of clientelist politics was facing a barren future with the Liberals out of office. Equally his own chances of political advancement and acquisition of a place, notwithstanding the possibility of a Chamberlain Cabinet post, would vanish once the British electorate handed Gladstone his hat. But none of this would have necessitated his resignation.

It is more likely that, like the practical and realistic politician he was often capable of being, he made a virtue of necessity. Rather than repeat the embarrassment of having his own constituents deny him a run at a parliamentary seat he anticipated the inevitable, while taking a leaf out of the book of former Waterford MP John Blake. In his second farewell address in just over six months he acknowledged that '... his views are not shared in by his constituents. Honourable feelings suggest that he should resign his seat, which he accordingly does.'[39] Rather than wait around for the decline of the light he was able to take the moral high ground. Once again, Othello over Lear. He had strangled the thing he loved rather than see it killed by others.

United Ireland was unimpressed by the sight of the former Hussar falling on his cavalry sword. Referring to him as a 'traitorous Irishman' it observed that 'The Irish party mustered to the division with splendid discipline. The one disgraceful exception was Captain O'Shea, who absented himself. Within twenty-four hours of the division he made the atonement of announcing his resignation. The reparation would have been touching if the dissolution of Parliament had not been announced by the same post.'[40] With the prorogation of parliament O'Shea lost the only government position he had ever managed to occupy: Steward and Bailiff of the Chiltern Hundreds.

So, by his own hand, ended the political career of the last Irish Whig. He succumbed to the fate of Shaw, O'Shaughnessy, the O'Donoghue, the Blennerhassets and the brontosaurus. He had artificially outlasted them by a few months, sustained by his undue influence on the leader of the Irish party. His had been a singularly undistinguished career, marked by notable lack of accomplishment. He left no footprints, originated no private members legislation, made no profound, dramatic, far-reaching or passionate speeches. He was not even particularly useful lobby-fodder. His absences outnumbered his votes and his behaviour pattern in divisions was unpredictable.

His decision to leave politics did nothing to propitiate an incensed James O'Kelly. The Irish–American MP challenged O'Shea within hours of the defeat of the Home Rule Bill. 'Sir, As one of the members of the Irish Party who helped to get you elected by the people of Galway, I regard your abstention from voting on the Home Rule Bill as a personal injury also of such a nature as to entitle me to demand from you a personal reparation.'[41] But this was to be yet another unfought O'Shea duel. He failed to respond to being 'called out' by the pugnacious O'Kelly until August, explaining that he had been out of the country and had not received his fellow MP's challenge. In that genteel and exquisitely insincere Victorian manner he apologised for the delay in replying to a man who had indicated a desire to kill him. He then went on, 'Notwithstanding every desire to be courteous I cannot seriously entertain the pretension that my action with regard to a division in the House of Commons is any concern of yours.' Next, he risked antagonising O'Kelly even further by claiming to have effected his release from Kilmainham. He reminded O'Kelly of their conversation in Dublin in October 1885 and insisted that it '... must have accentuated your knowledge that nothing would ever tempt me to surrender my political independence'.[42]

The 1886 election returned a Conservative government led by Salisbury, which would have a considerably longer life span than his first ministry. It was a government that, because of its alliance with the Liberal Unionist grouping led by Hartington, had no need to offer even the slightest pretence of sympathy with the objectives of the Irish party. Salisbury's nephew, Arthur Balfour, was ensconced in the Irish Office within the year. It heralded a renewal of the 'stick' approach, with occasional glimpses of that conciliatory accompanying vegetable, the carrot.[43] So unpopular would Balfour become that, when he once asked a Roman Catholic priest unsympathetic to nationalism whether he (Balfour) was as reviled as Parnell claimed, the priest is said to have replied, 'If our flocks hated sin half as cordially as they hate you, there would be no use for priests in Ireland.'[44]

Chamberlain was unrepentant. As the election outcome became clear, he had told O'Shea that 'The beaten party are very bitter but they will have to get over it or remain in the cold permanently. The only chance for a Liberal government is a reunion of the Liberal party and this can only be obtained by a frank recognition on the part of the Ministerialists that they have made a mistake and that they will never do it again.'[45] It was the tail wagging the dog, while managing simultaneously to make the clucking noise of an irritated headmaster. Attempts were made to at least bring the radical element of the Liberal Unionists back into the Gladstonian family,[46] but these foundered and Chamberlain was left to his new Tory allies.

His relationship with O'Shea continued unhindered. By early September the Captain was on the lookout once again for ministerial favours,[47] this time from Churchill. Chamberlain was offering to use his influence. In his biography of Churchill, Roy Foster points out that the Captain was employed by the new Chancellor of the Exchequer 'as a link to conservative Irish bishops'[48] But his uses as a conduit would have ended when Churchill peremptorily resigned in late December 1886, leaving Chamberlain even more isolated. O'Shea continued to operate as a confidant and intelligence gatherer[49] for the Radical Unionists. Though it is difficult to see what useful Irish intelligence someone as circumscribed as the Captain would have had to offer, he somehow managed to keep himself sufficiently well briefed to interest Chamberlain.

His reputation for 'springing' extreme republicans had spread and, though out of office, he continued to offer his services. In early 1887 he was making representations on behalf of one of the more celebrated Irish political prisoners of that period, P.W. Nally. Nally came from a highly respectable family in Mayo and in 1882 had been elected as a Poor Law Guardian. He was a consistent critic of agrarian outrage and had even been issued with a gun licence by a local RIC inspector who asserted that Nally would 'lead a useful and loyal life'.[50] What the Mayo RIC did not know had not escaped the attention of Edward Jenkinson in Dublin Castle. Nally was to the IRB in Connacht what Patrick Neville Fitzgerald was in Munster. He was also known by the top British-based secret policeman, Robert Anderson, to be importing arms. On the evidence of an informer (Andrew Coleman), Nally was arrested for conspiracy to murder and jailed for ten years. Nally had already served half his term (and had become something of a *cause célèbre*) when his father, W.R. Nally, wrote to O'Shea to see what miracle could be wrought by the Captain.

O'Shea was eager to involve himself in such a high-profile case. On 4 February 1887 he replied to a letter from Nally Sr: 'I need not tell you', he declared, 'that the times are greatly against us in our efforts, and now that Lord Randolph Churchill has left the Ministry it is much more difficult for me to get attended to. I have been thinking about speaking to another minister, but I am very much afraid it might be premature to go to him expressly on the subject and I have been seeking an opportunity of referring to the subject on meeting him in society.' O'Shea then illustrated one of the essential differences between his approach and that of conventional Irish nationalist politicians, while, at the same time, demonstrating his innate pettiness. 'It is a great shame that the paid Patriots didn't say a word for your son this time twelve months when they were in full Gladstonian sunshine ... Any chance I see I will grasp at; you may depend on it.'[51]

Whether it was on account of his greatly diminished influence or the determination of the British authorities to continue to make an example of Nally, O'Shea's efforts came to naught. Nally did not, in the end, actually serve his full term. But that was only because he died, aged 36, in Mountjoy Prison, days before he was due to be released in November 1891. Efforts had been made, with a promise of clemency and other rewards, to get him to testify on behalf of the *Times* at the Special Commission on Parnellism and Crime (see below). A Dublin coroner's jury held that his 'naturally strong constitution' had been broken by 'the harsh and cruel treatment to which he was subjected ... for refusing to give evidence on behalf of the *Times* at the Special Commission.' At his funeral the same green flag was draped over his coffin as had enveloped that of Parnell himself two months before.[52]

THE WILDERNESS YEARS

In Ireland the larger fight for Home Rule had obscured the fact that, economically, the country was on a road leading back to 1879. The increased importation of American agricultural products had forced prices down in the vital British market where cash crops (in Irish terms the rent-paying produce) were sold. Many tenants were no longer capable of paying even the judicial rents fixed by the Land Courts under the terms of the 1881 Act. During the Home Rule debate Parnell had been able to keep the lid on confrontational agitation, but with the hope of legislative independence vanquished and evictions on the rise again there was little incentive, whatever Parnell might say or do to the contrary, to continue to hide agrarian militancy under a bushel. In September 1886, in an atmosphere of rising tension and militancy, O'Shea had forwarded to Chamberlain a report sent to him from Clare about the arrival of General Sir Redvers Buller. The General had been sent with an armed force to quell unrest in the south-west. It was apparent from the information O'Shea was getting that Fenian–Ribbon groups were eager to exploit the situation: '... to send an Englishman and a "renowned General" was to put a lot of eggs in one basket.' O'Shea's correspondent had observed, '... the Boys are very "cock-a-hoop" about what is coming.'[53]

Opposition came to a head with a limited reintegration of agrarian populism and parliamentarianism in late 1886. This occurred when John Dillon took matters into his own hands and advocated a renewed policy of withholding rents. Appropriate action was to take the form of an offer by the tenant of a reasonable rent and the depositing of that sum in a central trust for each estate in the event of a rejection of the offer by a landlord. The notion was formalised by National League Secretary, Timothy Harrington, in an article in *United Ireland* entitled 'A Plan of Campaign'. The funds held in trust were to be used to assist evicted tenants and any farmer who attempted to move onto evicted farms would be subjected to an immediate boycott. The land issue was returning to the top of the political agenda. The 'Plan of Campaign' movement, led by Dillon, Harrington and William O'Brien, spread quickly. This was despite the opposition of Parnell.[54] By early 1887 the Plan was being treated by the civil authorities as an 'unlawful and criminal conspiracy'. Serious illness, described by Parnell himself as a kidney aliment and by other observers as the degenerative Bright's disease,[55] reduced his capacity to oppose a policy he saw as endangering the Liberal alliance. It also led to long absences from parliament in the first crucial months of the new Tory regime.

Meanwhile, although his precise future was uncertain, Chamberlain continued to exhibit some interest in Irish affairs. Of course, in the aftermath of his defection over Home Rule he became an object of loathing for the members of the Irish party and was treated accordingly in the House. When reconciliation with the Liberal party was on the cards via the Round Table Conference of early 1887, he had complained to Harcourt about the behaviour of the Liberal's new allies towards him. 'As to the Irish, please bear in mind that I am only human. The brutes have been abusing and insulting me up to the very last moment, and nothing will induce me to turn the other cheek to the smiter. If you want me to be civil to them, you must bring pressure to bear on them to treat me with ordinary courtesy.'[56] When it was clear that Chamberlain's rehabilitation was no longer on the cards, Harcourt, a convert to Home Rule, responded acidly, 'You complain of bitterness displayed against you, but I wish sometimes you would consider how much you do to provoke it ...'[57]

O'Shea counteracted his political withdrawal symptoms by assisting the cause of his mentor with '... shrewd suggestion ... [and] no contemptible intelligence or purpose.'[58] This was especially the case when it came to the first seeds of what would develop into the Tories' Congested Districts legislation in the latter part of Balfour's Dublin Castle regime. In some of his correspondence with Chamberlain in the 1887–88 period O'Shea went to great pains to, in effect, draft legislation for the relief of poverty and distress in the western counties of Ireland. When the bitterness is stripped out of his commentary, he also reveals himself as quite an astute, if caustic, observer of Irish late-Victorian political mores. In short, some of his correspondence with Chamberlain during this period is surprising to anyone who has grown accustomed to O'Shea the intriguer and the self-pitying ingrate. He displays considerable political maturity, an attention to detail, and even an empathy with the Irish agrarian under-class. Also evidenced is a lordly contempt for the rising Irish mercantile middle class and substantial farmers. All of which places him, politically, in that awkward ground between the aristocrat and the radical. Was he motivated by a *faux* aristocratic scorn for the *petite bourgeoisie*, or by a genuine sympathy for the labourer and small farmer? At times instinct actually seems to triumph over interest. But there is always the suspicion that O'Shea was tailoring his language and his sentiments to appeal to the radical within Chamberlain that had not been suppressed by his adherence to unionism. Still, this is an unexpected O'Shea. Of course he regularly reverts to type even during this backroom phase of his political life, and he emerged from it as insufferable a figure as he had ever been.

His counsel must be seen in the context of the failure by Parnell to push through a Land Bill to deal with the renewed economic difficulties that had prompted the Plan of Campaign. In parallel was the need of the Tories to produce a leavening policy for Ireland to sugar the pill of coercion and the desire of Chamberlain to influence that policy. This was exacerbated in the wake of the murderous attack in September 1887 by police on an angry crowd in Mitchelstown County Cork, which led to three deaths and the application of the sobriquet 'Bloody' to the name of Arthur Balfour. In framing a solution to the endemic problem of the over-population of the west of Ireland in relation to the resources of its much-depleted soil, O'Shea at first returned to the migration policies espoused by Parnell, with his support, in 1884. His approach to migration as a solution combined elements of common sense, awareness of some of the unpalatable realities of Irish rural life, and a withering assessment of Parnellite pretensions and policies – which, he felt, ought to be treated with extreme caution.

When he discusses a renewal of the idea of moving non-viable farmers from settlements in the west to potential tillage farms farther east, he enters a major caveat, warning against the breakup of 'the fat pastures of Meath and of the Golden Vale',[59] because of the contributions they were making to the wealth of the country. This can be seen as defining the limit of his sympathy for the agrarian underdog or as an unsentimental assess-ment of the realities of the Irish agricultural economy. However, he does not allow this exception to negate the value of the policy, nor does he diminish the difficulties of putting it into effect.

'We may as well make up our minds to face the inevitable; no consid-erable scheme of migration can be carried out without a considerable ejectment of graziers ... to be effective it must be compulsory and compulsion must result in the removal of a good many tenants holding grazing farms.' Part of the difficulty he envisages would come from within the ranks of the Irish party itself:

> I doubt whether the average Irish member of the period has any very deep sympathy with the 'small men'. It is true that the latter were easily levied *en masse* and, with the labourers, have served as private soldiers in the Land War. Like the labourers, too, they have generally fared but poorly in the distribution of the spoil. But the class feeling of several of the present representatives of Irish constituencies would probably dispose them rather to favour the interests of tenants of holdings larger than those from which families would be shifted, and in some cases of holdings to which families must actually be shifted.

This bears out Roy Foster's contention that while the Land War was couched in 'the language of social revolution and expropriation', the actual outcome, although redistributive, was far from socially expropriative.

Not unexpectedly, O'Shea found it impossible to resist an attack on the English-based Irish party members like O'Connor and McCarthy as 'Irish cockneys ... who learn and repeat the lessons of agrarian agitation by rote, and their teachers are not the men whom migration would benefit.' For Parnell he reserves his particular disdain: 'In his heart he detests, in conversation he has often denounced, the Irish tenant farmer of every class and condition, but he despises the "small man" with exceptional bitterness.' While such an observation can be dismissed as mere bile, his assessment of the nature of the local leadership of the agrarian movements and the National League deserves more attention:

> When not shopkeepers, the local leaders of the League are almost inevitably 'strong' or at least comparatively strong farmers ... Office in the League has been extremely useful in the effecting of arrangements of all kinds, and much of the land grabbing of the last few years has been the reward of those who have held it. The castes in Irish agrarian society are marked with vivid distinctiveness. The best farm labourer is held to be unworthy of the daughter of a hut and half a dozen acres of cutaway bog, while there is little or no sympathy between the damsel's father and the farmer with a plough.

His advocacy of the policy is, however, ultimately based on its political desirability: 'there can be no question as to the political expediency of the exercise ... the effect, on the whole, would be extremely advantageous, and the general emancipation from care – for it would be nothing less, at least for the time – would inevitably produce an immense change for the better and afford abundant satisfaction to the "patriotic" feelings of what is, after all, a very important percentage of the population.' He concludes by suggesting that were such a policy to be introduced the Irish party would have no option but to support it, whatever their genuine feelings might be. He assures Chamberlain that their real sympathies '... have never been with the tenants whom [they] used only as a counter in the game, but with the publicans and the avaricious shopkeepers, many of the latter being gombeen men, to which classes the members of the faction themselves largely belong, or with which their pecuniary interests are inextricably bound up.'[60]

One of the features of the recurrence of agricultural recession in the mid-1880s was a widespread restriction on credit. This was not just a function of anxiety on the part of bankers, but a refusal on the part of merchants and shopkeepers to extend credit to farmers fallen on hard times. In one memo to Chamberlain, O'Shea attempts to disabuse him of the notion of the solidarity of the generous and charitable Irish shopkeeper sustaining the impoverished farmer through hard times, '... Englishmen are easily gulled by such stuff. In Ireland, as elsewhere, dealers ensure [sic] themselves against such risks by the prices they charge. What difference is there between disguised usury and open usury; a man may have to pay 50 per cent just as surely on "goods supplied" as on money lent.'

In something of a return to the ill-fated Central Board concept O'Shea also pointed out to Chamberlain that the introduction of any such policy on a widespread scale presupposed the delivery of a measure of local democracy. The aristocratic Grand Jury system, already creaking, was unsuited to the execution of such major change. The implication here was that at the helm of that particular system was the very oligarchy whose property would need to be compulsorily acquired to facilitate migration. County boards or councils, elected by ratepayers, would have to be created to expedite such a policy. Also, in a pre-echo of the full-blown Congested Districts Act, a number of counties should be 'scheduled' for the sort advantageous treatment abhorred by the vestigial laissez-faire philosophy of British late-Victorian administrations.

Correspondence between the two men on the development of structures which would inhibit or reverse the rising tide of agrarian activism continued for 12 months and allowed Chamberlain to present O'Shea-inspired proposals which would be woven into the fabric of the Tory policy of 'killing Home Rule with kindness'. O'Shea boasts to Chamberlain in one letter that he has just received a telegram informing him that 'my proposals were approved without alteration of a word by a Cabinet committee.'[61]

By that stage the relationship of O'Shea and Chamberlain had evolved into one of connivance rather than collaboration. They were working together on a project far less benign than the resettling of peasant farmers. They were engaged instead on the settling of old scores.

DOMESTICITY AND DISSENT

The Galway by-election seems to have marked a Rubicon in the triangular relationship between O'Shea, Parnell and Katharine. It has been suggested by some, Frank Hugh O'Donnell amongst them, that it was in Galway that O'Shea first became aware of the truth of the affair between the Irish party leader and his wife. It is probably more accurate to suggest that it was in Galway that he became aware that: a) it was a relationship he was no longer going to be able to turn to his political advantage; and b) public knowledge of the affair was now widespread. Galway marks a nadir in his dealings with Parnell; in particular because it was during that fateful by-election that what he thought to be his secret (or at least something known only to a very narrow circle) had percolated down to the sans-culottes, largely via the uninhibited conversation of Joseph Biggar.

For the better part of two years Parnell and Katharine had been living as man and wife in Eltham. They were domestic and political partners. In the words of Donal McCartney, '... Katharine O'Shea provided him with all the comforts of a home life that he had not known, and a companionship that allowed him to open up his heart and his mind in a way that he never did with his political colleagues.'[62] Their domestic arrangement was about to be seriously disrupted as O'Shea moved to the brink of divorce and then, for his own reasons, pulled back from that particular abyss for the time being.

Having extracted all he could, for the moment, from an increasingly restive Parnell, he continued to take advantage of what he thought to be his wife's privileged access to the Prime Minister. Their correspondence, largely one-sided, had maintained a businesslike aspect since its inception in 1882. This was despite Katharine's occasional references to her husband's desire for a salaried place of some kind in government. But a note to Gladstone on 16 April 1886 amounts to little more than a begging letter. Once again the favour being sought is for her husband who has clearly seen the writing on the wall in the wake of the introduction of the

Government of Ireland Bill the previous week. The appointment being sought for him by an apparently desperate Katharine (she refers to his 'very great pecuniary difficulties') is one of a colonial nature. Was this an attempt to extract him from his financial difficulties while simultaneously removing him from England? She explains in the letter that her aunt will '... assist my husband out of his present difficulties, for my sake, if she can see any hope of his getting any lucrative occupation – *but* if not, she will not help him, so you will understand how important your answer is to us in every way.'[63] In a polite response Gladstone said that he did not want to interfere in the patronage of his ministers. As Katharine records, 'his manners were perfect'.[64]

One of the pillars upon which O'Shea founded his frequent allusions to Parnell's obligations towards him was the decidedly shaky structure of the Kilmainham Treaty. Obtaining the Irish leader's release from jail was constantly trotted out to justify, both publicly and privately, Parnell's continuing and otherwise incomprehensible generosity towards the Captain. Illustrating the pitch of animosity in their dealings with each other is O'Shea's letter to his wife just a week after her 16 April intervention on his behalf with Gladstone. At some point around that time she must have informed him that Justin McCarthy had been Parnell's chosen intermediary. She may even have taunted her husband, in the midst of recriminations over the precise nature of her relationship with Parnell, with the suggestion that if he had not secured the Kilmainham treaty the highly respected 'Irish Cockney' would have done so anyway. This drew down on her a fusillade from her husband whose principal political achievement was being impeached. He was not going to be politically cuckolded by McCarthy. He cited a conversation with Gladstone, post-Treaty, during the course of which the Prime Minister had said, '... he believed that no one but myself could have carried out the business, and in the course of conversation he had occasion to add a very decided expression of his very poor opinion of Mr McCarthy.'[65]

Having addressed her reinvention of his personalised version of history, he returned to the main issue between them, Parnell: '... I have scores of times pointed out to you, that however innocent in themselves, the frequent visits of a man to a woman, during the absence of her husband, they are an offence against propriety, and are certain, sooner or later, to be observed upon by society.'[66]

On May 24 1886 the *Pall Mall Gazette* published a snippet entitled 'Mr Parnell's Suburban Retreat'. Its exact purpose is uncertain, unless it is seen as simple reportage. It was an account of an accident at 11.45 p.m. on the night of 21 May, in which a coach (Katharine's), with Parnell as its passenger, had collided with a florist's van. Nobody was hurt and the incident would hardly have been deemed newsworthy had Parnell not been involved. No one questioned how the *Gazette* had come by news of the accident. It was either the only paper to have been informed of the event or the only one that considered it worth carrying. The sting was, as always, in the tail. The *Gazette*, after outlining the bare facts of the case allowed itself the supplementary comment that during the parliamentary session Parnell made his home in Eltham, 'From here he can often be seen taking riding exercise round by Chislehurst and Sidcup.'[67]

To the uninitiated, of course, the piece was utterly meaningless and banal. To those in the know it served to affirm the suspicion that the Irish leader was in permanent residence at Wonersh Lodge with Katharine O'Shea. The report was, in all likelihood, a dart aimed from the desk of the *Gazette* editor, the extraordinary Victorian journalist, W.T. Stead. Son of a Congregational minister and radical Nonconformist, he had succeeded to the editorship of the newspaper after the election of John Morley to a Liberal seat in parliament in 1883. His agenda was driven by his politics and his moral righteousness. His social conservatism, allied to his sensationalist journalistic instincts, was by then well on the way to destroying the political career of Sir Charles Dilke. Stead had begun by believing and supporting him in the Crawford divorce scandal, but had then turned on Dilke ruthlessly and helped ensure that his Chelsea constituency did likewise in the July 1886 general election.

Fellow journalist T.P. O' Connor knew Stead well. 'He was honest and histrionic, pugnacious and sensitive, narrow and intolerant in religion, what in America they would call a Fundamentalist; in temperament half crusader ... he was too good a fanatic to be a real journalist and too real a journalist to be a good fanatic. He belonged by training and by conviction to the straitest sect of the straitest Nonconformists; he had their passion for sexual morality.'[68]

Stead's alternately prurient and muckraking approach to journalism had earned him three months in jail in 1885 for a technical infraction of the law in compiling a series of reports ('Maiden Tribute of Modern Babylon') on juvenile prostitution and 'white slavery'. For many years afterwards he liked to flaunt his convict's uniform.[69] A convinced Home Ruler, Stead had, up to 1886 at least, managed to overcome his censorious nature and allow Parnell the benefit of the doubt when it came to his relationship with Katharine. He told T.P. O'Connor on one occasion that he had been aware of it for some time, ' ... he said to me broadly and in almost a casual way: "The question I am now considering is whether I should ruin the Irish Party by exposing the *liaison* between Parnell and

Mrs O'Shea". Speaking still in that same tone as of almost commonplace occurrence, he told me that he had actually sent for Captain O'Shea[70] and put the question to him whether it was true or not that his wife was the mistress of Parnell.'[71] O'Shea had denied the allegation but Stead was morally certain that Parnell and Katharine were cohabiting with the tacit approval of the husband. His disinclination to publish details of the affair was, in all likelihood, connected to his knowledge of the damage it would do to the Home Rule cause.

It would appear that the 24 May story may have been a warning shot across the bows, not of Parnell (although that might have been a secondary purpose for the moralistic Stead) but of O'Shea himself. The Captain was known to be in cahoots with Chamberlain during the debate on the second reading of the Home Rule Bill, which had begun on 10 May. Stead, despite his political radicalism, was noted for his antipathy towards Chamberlain and would have been eager to print anything to give pause to his attempts to build a radical consensus against self-government for Ireland.

O'Shea immediately put the matter on a legal footing by contacting the London law firm of Freshfield and Williams[72] and seeking an explanation from his wife for the article. Her response was verging on the blasé. 'I do not see that it has anything to do with us', she observed and dismissed the report as mischief-making on the part of Healy and his allies: '... I was sure there would be no end to their spite after your Galway success.'[73] She called on him the following day (26 May) and brought a letter from Parnell, written from the offices of the Irish Parliamentary Party, and which she claimed had arrived that day. It offered a plausible explanation for the incident. 'Dear Mr O'Shea – Your telegram in reference to the paragraph in the newspapers has duly reached me. I had two horses placed in the neighbourhood of Bexley Heath, and turned out to grass. I am very sorry that you should have any inconvenience about the matter.'[74]

O'Shea seems to have been willing to accept this explanation – at least that was what he told the divorce court three years later. He does not, however, explain why he did not object to a far less oblique item in the *Pall Mall Gazette* a week later, which specifically identified Wonersh Lodge as Parnell's residence. The anonymous reporter also wondered why 'Mr Parnell's personal appearance changes so often ...'[75]

From around this point in the broader O'Shea narrative it is clear that all correspondence between the three parties involved, and some letters from them to others, becomes more than just a simple means of communication. O'Shea had no need to write to Katharine on 24 May 1886 to inquire about the meaning of the *Pall Mall Gazette* story. He was already well aware of the fact that Parnell was frequently in residence there during his own lengthy absences. Aside from the multitude of opportunities he had at his disposal to deduce or come by this information, he also had an increasingly obstreperous son, fashioned in his own image and rapidly acquiring many paternal characteristics, who would have informed him of the fact. Gerard was later enlisted by his father as co-conspirator. So the correspondence can be seen as multi-purpose, with the language therein operating simultaneously on a number of different levels. The letters were designed, if necessary, for public consumption and were later used for just this purpose. The fact that O'Shea retained copies of his letters and of Katharine's replies is also an indication that an endgame was in sight, at least as far as the Captain was concerned. O'Shea was playing the part of the indignant husband and expecting Katharine to dissemble. This she duly did – for her to have done otherwise in writing would have forced his hand. He was thus enabled to accept her written reassurances for as long as it suited him.[76] As the correspondence grew so did his case that he was a deceived husband.

But the language could also be quite circumspect, allowing for the possibility of a future reconciliation or, at the very least, a return to the *status quo ante* Parnell. For example, O'Shea never accused his wife of adultery. He merely made repeated use of the term 'scandal', thus leaving open the interpretation that he was simply accusing his wife of indiscretion in her pursuit of a platonic relationship with Parnell.

On another level the correspondence must be looked upon as a communication between two people who are both well aware of what is going on but cannot acknowledge the fact. To do so would be to greatly weaken their respective positions. O'Shea's letters to his wife in 1886 and 1887 can be seen as tacit warnings to her that his patience is wearing thin and that he will seek to end the affair or the marriage unless hints and rumours are kept out of the newspapers. It was the plethora of suggestive articles that drove him almost to the steps of the divorce court in 1887, rather than the affair itself. This palimpsest of meaning and intent means that few unchallengeable assumptions can be made from this phase of the O'Shea–Katharine correspondence, though cogent theories can be advanced.

Despite the element of surreal shadow-boxing inherent in the correspondence, neither side could be entirely certain of the total connivance and complicity of the other. O'Shea was an infrequent visitor to Wonersh Lodge in 1886, although he told the divorce court that he journeyed there and back on a number of Sundays with Parnell. If this was the case he must have turned a blind eye to the extension built for Parnell's use and stayed well away from the stables where Parnell's horses were housed.

For their part, unsure that the Captain would keep his distance and concerned lest the *Pall Mall Gazette* report would excite the curiosity of others, Parnell and Katharine removed his horses from Wonersh Lodge to an adjacent rented facility known as 'the lower stables'. In addition, throughout 1886 and 1887, Parnell and Katharine took out short and medium term rentals, either in Katharine's name or under a Parnell alias,[77] in a bewildering variety of locations in London and along the south coast. This was done either to forestall an impromptu O'Shea visit or to avoid a repetition of the *Pall Mall Gazette* coverage.

What was being spoken rather than written between Katharine and her husband at around this time may well have involved less circumspection. In an interview given by Parnell just after O'Shea had filed for divorce, and reported in the *Freeman's Journal* of 30 December 1889, he said of his residence at Eltham that '... Captain O'Shea was always aware that he (Mr Parnell) was constantly there in his (Captain O'Shea's) absence during that period, and since 1886 he has known that Mr Parnell constantly resided there from 1880 to 1886.'[78] This suggests that, at around the time of his failure to vote for Home Rule, O'Shea was directly informed, verbally, by either Parnell, Katharine or both that they were common-law partners. In his evidence to the *Times* Special Commission, O'Shea told the Attorney General that 'certain things came to my knowledge at that time which absolutely destroyed the good opinion I had hitherto held of Mr Parnell.'[79] This would appear to reinforce that theory. However, in response to a question from the young Henry Harrison in 1891 about the state of the Captain's knowledge of the affair, Katharine responded, 'Did Captain O'Shea know? Of course he knew. I do not mean that I or anybody else told him in so many words, *except once* [my italics] and that was in the course of so angry a scene that it may have sounded rather as a defiance, a repudiation of himself and of his claims to control me. There was no bargain; there were no discussions; people do not talk of such things.'[80] It is likely that the heated argument referred to here happened in the middle of 1886. From this point onwards it became more and more difficult for the couple to preserve even the illusion of *politesse*.

After his resignation from parliament, O'Shea told the divorce court in 1890 that he had brought Katharine to Eastbourne, lodged her in the Queen's Hotel and betook himself to the spa resort of Carlsbad for medical reasons. While there his attention had been drawn to an article mentioning his name. An American friend had begun to read it out and had then seized up with embarrassment when she realised the implications of what she was reading. It referred to Parnell being in residence at Eltham. Once again he had written to Katharine for an explanation, to the

Queen's Hotel where he had left her, and had got a telegram in reply advising him that it would be much better for him to look after his health than to concern himself with such reports.

O'Shea then set about establishing a construct that would either force his wife to end the affair with Parnell or prove invaluable to his case in a divorce suit. On 20 August he wrote to her proposing to put new domestic arrangements in place from 1 October. These involved the setting up of a house to which he would take the children. He rejected her suggestion that they live in Brighton and that she visit Eltham regularly as 'it would allow the scandal to continue unabated ...'[81] He also issued a warning to her to discontinue all communication with Parnell. The letter had not been posted but had been given to his children to convey to his wife. It drew a stinging riposte from Katharine, which intermingled injured innocence, scorn and subtle threats of financial ruin.[82]

Dear Willie,

You have written me many mean and unpleasant letters, like the last, which even you were ashamed to give me yourself and obliged the children to convey to me; it is one of the most mean and insolent you have ever written. You have quite surpassed yourself ... You speak of provisional arrangements to commence from 1st October, under which you will provide a house for myself and the children. I shall be obliged by your letting me know by return of post where the house is to be, if away from Eltham, my aunt says, she will not give one penny to me either for the support of myself or of the children, or of course for yourself either. She also says that she understood she was asked to buy the lease and furniture and pay the rent of your rooms at Albert Mansions when you required them to live in. If you mean to take a house for us away from Eltham let me know as I would arrange with Anna and Charlie[83] for one of them to come and live here. They always said they would come if I ever left Eltham. Of course in that case you will provide all income for the children, and myself ...[84]

There she rested her case, safe in the knowledge that O'Shea was unable to function without being financed by Aunt Ben. The apparently gratuitous reference to Albert Mansions was a reminder to her husband that if her aunt was no longer the sole provider for the family he would be forced to give up his London bolt-hole. If he wanted domesticity and connubial bliss he would have it in abundance. It is unlikely that the Captain would either have desired the realisation of what he proposed, or expected Katharine to comply. So we may assume that this construct was purely for later public consumption.

In a further letter on 13 September O'Shea counter-bluffed. Instructing her to have no further communication with Parnell, he tacitly accepted the impossibility of moving beyond the domain of Aunt Ben. His suggested alternative was that she should have a room prepared for him in Eltham. This, he said, had been mooted by her own brother, Sir Evelyn Wood, 'as the only chance of mitigating the scandal on the children'.[85] This letter was later read out in court. Had the divorce been contested it might have proved a hostage to fortune, as O'Shea had, of course, contended all along that he was always very much a part of domestic arrangements at Eltham. Any competent barrister would have raised serious questions about this contention. It may well have been this glaring anomaly that prompted one of the jurors to ask some awkward questions about O'Shea's relationship with his family before he and his colleagues retired to consider their verdict.

Katharine's dismissive response to O'Shea's (hardly serious) suggestion has, as her biographer Jane Jordan puts it, 'a very modern ring to it'.[86] 'I have not the slightest intention of allowing you to make the rest of my life utterly miserable by nagging at me from morning until night at Eltham,' she scolded him, 'I only desire to be left in peace with my children.'[87] It was a brusque and fittingly cruel dismissal of his qualities as a husband.

There were similar 'eruptions' from Albert Mansions in response to a report in the *Sussex Daily News* of a Parnellite tryst with Katharine in Eastbourne in September 1886. The *Pall Mall Gazette* was back in the picture once again on 18 December 1886. O'Shea was taking his son, Gerard, to a boxing exhibition at the Cannon Street Hotel in honour of a prizefighter called Jem Mace. On his way there he saw a piece in the newspaper that announced 'Mr Parnell is at present paying a visit to Captain O'Shea at Eltham.'[88] O'Shea went straight to the top with a letter to Stead in which he pointed out that 'The fact is that I have had no communication whatsoever with Mr Parnell since May. You have been deceived, probably by some Parnellite, because there are dogs of his, I am told, who in return for the bones he throws them snap when they think it safe. I have considerable cause of complaint regarding notices equally unfounded which have previously appeared in the *Pall Mall Gazette*, and I should be glad to show you how you have been made the victim of your misplaced confidence.'[89] He asked to meet Stead the following morning.

The two men duly met on Monday 20 December. According to Stead, O'Shea emphatically denied the truth of the rumours surrounding his wife and Parnell when asked directly by the *Gazette* editor. 'He assured me in the most positive terms that there was absolutely no truth in the current reports as to any intimacy between Mrs O'Shea and Mr Parnell; that he was perfectly secure in the fidelity of his wife, and though he said many strong things to the detriment of Mr Parnell politically, he asseverated in the most emphatic terms possible that he had never had any reason whatever to suspect Mr. Parnell of improper intimacy with his wife.'[90] Stead pronounced himself highly sceptical of O'Shea's assurances and called the interview 'one of the most curious that I have ever had'. Either O'Shea was lying to Stead in December 1886, or to the divorce court four years later, because he submitted documentary evidence to prove to the court that his suspicions had been aroused more than six months previously.

The *Gazette*, while not exactly forcing open the floodgates, emboldened other newspapers and journals to enter the lists themselves, much to O'Shea's annoyance. In February 1887 *Saint Stephen's Review*, a Tory weekly, carried an item about a complaint by Parnell made against the owners of a cab company concerning a driver's behaviour. The article pointed out Parnell's strange habit of changing cabs when he visited 'his residence – or rather Captain O'Shea's residence – at Eltham ... his complications have told considerably on his nerves and he has a constant fear of being waylaid,' the *Review* clucked coyly. Once again Katie's response was cool. 'No one thinks anything of *St Stephen's Review*, and that is so evidently the old rumour again that I think you will be very unwise if you take any notice of it. I do not understand what it means in the least, but I am quite sure that if anyone finds they have been able to take a rise out of you by it, that they will go on for ever.'[91] The article, however, prompted Parnell to take up the rental of a house in London at 34 York Terrace. According to Katharine's account, he lasted on his own there for about three weeks before returning to Eltham.

Sir Charles Dilke recorded in his diary on 13 February 1887, based on information from nationalist MP P.A. Chance, that O'Shea 'was going forward with his divorce action against Parnell'[92] and that Parnell had no plausible defence. The evidence suggests that Dilke was correct, that the Captain was indeed building a case. The *quod erat demonstrandum* may have been commissioned from his own son in mid-April 1887. As a pretext for legal intervention it bears a striking resemblance to the incident manufactured in 1889 with this end in view. On 13 April O'Shea received a letter from Gerard, whom he represented as having previously been reluctant to discuss his mother's domestic arrangements. His son's transformation into a champion of his father's honour seems unconscionably sudden, but he had undoubtedly become disenchanted with the constant presence of Parnell at Eltham and was spending more time with the

Captain. In the letter Gerard began by telling his father that he had returned home that day and heard, '... that awful scoundrel Parnell talking to a dog ... Perhaps I ought to have gone in and kicked him, but I am anxious to avoid unpleasant scenes with my mother. And I also think that it is better for you to know about it before giving him a thrashing, as you, of course, understand more about these things than I do. However, if you wish me to kick him you have only to say so, and it shall be done on the first opportunity.'[93] The language (if indeed he wrote the letter) and the mindset suggest that Gerard was something of a chip off the old block. His subsequent history bears out that belief.

The letter, pretext or not, escalated the simmering tension between the O'Sheas into an immediate crisis and set in motion full-scale legal intervention. The couple met on 14 April and had what was later described as a 'very painful interview'.[94] That euphemism was divorce court language for a blazing row in which, if he had not done so verbally already, O'Shea seems to have abandoned his 'scandal' motif and opted to characterise his wife's relationship with Parnell as an extra-marital affair. That is the subtext (always of vital importance in the case of the O'Sheas) of the letter she sent him on 17 April. She sought from him a written expression of the demand he had made of her at that meeting, adding that 'At the same time I must tell you that if you put it in such an offensive manner as you did on Friday it will be impossible for me to accede to it, both for my children's sake and my own, for you have no right to give such a reason for my not meeting any one.'[95] Despite her obvious anger, Katharine still managed to suppress her indignation for long enough to dangle the ultimate prize before her husband. In the second part of this letter (not read out to the divorce court) she refers to an enclosure. This was Aunt Ben's new will, which she was taking to the family solicitor, Horatio Pym, for legal advice. 'I desire to have his opinion as to whether it is sufficiently formal, or whether it would be better to have a more formal one made by him carrying out her intention ...' It was like waving a canteen of water in front of a parched desert traveller. The will bequeathed Aunt Ben's considerable fortune to Katharine and Katharine alone. None of the other members of the Wood family were to benefit.

His response was the first explicit indication that the couple was destined for the divorce court in the short term; or, at the very least, that O'Shea wished his wife to believe that to be the case. He dismissed her blandishments and the unsubtle reminder of the financial power she held over him should the new will be formalised. He pointed out, with irrelevant exactitude that 'The effect of your Aunt's will, of which you send me a copy, is that if she survives you the children will not have a penny

Parnell, 1886, from a photograph by W. Lawrence, Dublin

Clockwise from top:
Punch cartoon, 1888, after O'Shea's
Times Commission evidence

8 Medina Terrace, Hove

Sketch of O'Shea at the Parnell
Commission, 10 November 1888,
The Illustrated London News

Sketch of Sir Charles Russell at the
Parnell Commission, from *The Illustrated
London News*, 13 April 1889

Clockwise from top: Sketch of Pigott under cross-examination at the Parnell Commission, 1889. From *Cassell's Illustrated History of England*, 1889

Walsingham Terrace, Brighton – the house where Parnell died.

Punch cartoon, 18 August 1888, anticipating damning Times Commission evidence.

DR. M'JEKYLL AND MR. O'HYDE.

"SEPARATISTS."

Douglas . . . . Mr. Gl-dst-ne.   *Marmion* . . . . Mr. P-rn-ll.

Douglas. "THE HAND OF DOUGLAS IS HIS OWN;
AND NEVER SHALL IN FRIENDLY GRASP
THE HAND OF SUCH AS MARMION CLASP!"—*Marmion*, Canto VI.

Cameo of Katharine, 1891

Cameo of Parnell's daughter Clare, with permission of Kilmainham Jail Museum

Cameo of Parnell's daughter Katie, with permission of Kilmainham Jail Museum

Parnell's grave in Glasnevin Cemetery. Photograph taken shortly after his interment.

of her money.'[96] The likelihood of Katharine pre-deceasing her nonagenarian aunt was actuarially negligible.

He also declined to put his demand of the previous Friday in writing and instead advised her to consult her aunt's solicitor.[97] The couple's relationship was being further complicated at this time by the fact that Gerard O'Shea had decided not only to make common cause with his father, but also to move in to Albert Mansions. Katharine was insisting on his return, if only to convince Aunt Ben at a particularly delicate time that nothing was awry. Pym's involvement on her behalf included the demand that Gerard return to Eltham.[98]

But the solicitor's main concern was in communicating his client's obdurate denial of anything improper in her relationship with Parnell and her refusal to sever communications with him. Not only that, but she suggested that it was O'Shea himself who had encouraged her friendship with Parnell in the first place. The implication was clear. For the moment there was a mere suggestion of encouragement, but if matters were to get out of hand that might easily be elevated to allegations of connivance. Pym informed O'Shea on 22 April:

> I have seen Mrs O'Shea and laid before her your wishes.
>
> She most indignantly and emphatically denies that you have ever had the least ground for the very unworthy suspicions you have chosen to affix to her credit.
>
> The particular friend you alluded to is and has been a rare visitor at her house and he only became a friend of the family upon your introduction and by your wish. Were she now to forbid him the house it would involve her either in an admission that there had been some ground for your complaint or that she was behaving with a discourtesy which the past friendship and kind favors [sic] shown to you by that friend do not deserve.
>
> She therefore, although anxious to do nothing to cause you annoyance, must decline to peremptorily close her doors on the few and far between visits this friend is ever likely to make.[99]

O'Shea's reply suggests that he was hoping for better from Pym. He had obviously anticipated that the solicitor would impress on Katharine the seriousness of the situation.

'What I ask[ed] you to advise Mrs O'Shea about was this, and only this,' he wrote, 'That reports being wide and strong as to her relations with Mr Parnell, it would for her children's sake be expedient that she should declare her renunciation of communication with him. You have either given her this advice or you have not. However this may be, I understand that she refuses to recognise what I hold to be her duty to her children.'[100] It is not clear whether O'Shea was seeking a private or a public declaration from his wife.

A week after the introduction of Pym as a new factor in the equation, O'Shea abandoned his attempts to influence Katharine and laid his complaints directly at the doorstep of Parnell himself. 'It has come to my knowledge', he informed the Irish party leader, 'that in the face of the scandal which has been largely disseminated by your own associates and which I have no reason to believe you have ever made any effort to curb, you continue to communicate with and to meet Mrs O'Shea. I now personally call on you to discontinue all communication direct or indirect with her.'[101]

If it was indeed the case that O'Shea was gathering material for a divorce suit something must have happened to dissuade him from taking this course of action in 1887. It would certainly have been inimical to his financial interests at that time. Faced with the publicity that would have surrounded such a move and the suspicion that she had been misled for years, Aunt Ben would, almost certainly, have altered her will once again. It may well be that O'Shea was simply gathering material with a view to a divorce court foray as soon as the old lady finally died. On the other hand he might have run out of patience and been intent on blackening Parnell's character irrespective of the financial cost. So what caused him to back off when he did? The open warfare between the O'Sheas subsided in May 1887 and was resolved to the Captain's satisfaction in June. Aunt Ben's money was undoubtedly a consideration, but something else had emerged which seemed bound to discredit Parnell even more effectively than divorce proceedings involving him as co-respondent.

On 7 March 1887 the *Times* had begun a series of articles called 'Parnellism and Crime' which sought to connect the Irish Parliamentary Party and the Irish National League directly with outrage and murder. The initial impact of the series had disappointed the chiefs in Printing House Square, but they knew that their issue of 18 April would stir readers out of their apathy and indifference. On that day, right in the middle of the O'Sheas' worsening marital row, the newspaper published its infamous facsimile letter which allegedly carried the signature of Parnell and which linked him to the Phoenix Park murders (see below). Familiar with Parnell's signature,[102] O'Shea 'exulted ... Parnell was doomed.'[103] O'Shea could now afford to allow the *Times* to destroy the career of the man he had come to loathe while he waited until after the death of Aunt Ben to exact his own personal revenge.

In the interim, however, he was able to claim a minor triumph, though the concession was owed more to his son than to himself. It was, officially at least, on Gerard's behalf that Katharine capitulated. Only a mother's love would have forced her to acknowledge the proxy complaints of a son who was fast developing into the loathsome bully that his father had been for decades. Her surrender was sufficiently abject for O'Shea to step aside and let the *Times* do its worst: 'My dearest Gerardie, I now write to confirm my telegram to you, in which I said that I was willing to meet the wishes you expressed regarding Mr Parnell. I am most anxious that everything should be made as pleasant as possible for you, and that nobody should come here who is in any way obnoxious to you, and therefore I readily agree that there shall be no further communication, direct or indirect, with him.'[104] The following day she gave notice to the landlord that she intended to give up the use of the lower stables and in another letter to her son inserted a defiant message for his father: 'I must tell you again, I am not afraid of any proceedings ...'. Her recalcitrance was little more than a pose. She had been forced to acknowledge in writing that there *were* valid grounds for her to discontinue her relationship with Parnell.

Like one of the boxers to whose exhibitions O'Shea was growing fond of taking his son, her husband had won the round on points. Katharine's letter had been prompted by a threat from her son that she would never see him again. It was supported by a legal threat from her husband.[105] He had neither the need, the incentive, nor the inclination at this stage, to confirm to his own satisfaction that Katharine was adhering to her guarantee. To have discovered that she was not would have forced his hand prematurely.

On 27 December 1887 the *Times* Dublin correspondent reported that Mr Charles Stewart Parnell was spending the Christmas period with the O'Sheas at Eltham!

CHAPTER 12

Star Chamber

The gauntlet's down! In tourney days
The Knight who failed the gage to raise
Had courted instant shame.

Punch, 30 April 1887

BELLING THE CAT

On 4 March 1887 Richard Pigott, renegade Fenian, journalist, black-mailer and pornographer, wrote a letter from Anderton's Hotel in Fleet Street, London, to Archbishop Walsh, Roman Catholic Archbishop of Dublin. It was enigmatic and conspiratorial, informing Walsh that his correspondent was 'aware of the details of certain proceedings that are in preparation with the object of destroying the influence of the Parnellite Party in Parliament.' He was not in a position to offer specific detail, except to say that what was involved was the 'publication of certain statements purporting to prove the complicity of Mr Parnell himself and some of his supporters with murders and outrages in Ireland, to be followed in all probability by the institution of criminal proceedings against these parties by the Government.'[1] Other communications in similar vein followed. Two years later Pigott would become an object of derision when he claimed that the letters, because they were sent to a prelate, were subject to the seal of the confessional.

The Archbishop was not to know at that time that Pigott, always a shady and unsavoury character at best, was particularly well-informed about this oligarchic conspiracy. That was because it was his activities that had given the principal antagonists of the Irish nationalist movement the ammunition they required to launch a determined effort to discredit Parnell and his followers. That the material with which he had supplied them was fabricated was, at this point, known definitively only to Pigott himself. That was because *he* had fabricated it.

Archbishop Walsh replied in politely dismissive fashion and retained some of the letters.

Three days later the *Times* published the first of a series of articles, 'upon "Parnellism and Crime", the object of which is to remind the public of certain facts connected with the Home Rule agitation which are too often permitted to drop out of sight.'[2] The newspaper's attitude to Irish self-government was well known. The opening article was long on unionist rhetoric, applied obscure phrases like 'moral hebetude' to Parnell, reheated some old chestnuts, seemed just as concerned at embarrassing the Liberals as the Irish party, and promised far more than it delivered. The publication coincided with the replacement of Sir Michael Hicks Beach as Chief Secretary for Ireland with Arthur J. Balfour, nephew of the Prime Minister, Lord Salisbury.

That was not the only coincidence. What the newspaper sought to do was to equate Irish constitutional nationalism with political violence and outrage. Their equation was founded on a syllogism based on logic that was not peculiar to the *Times*. More Imperial than empirical, the rationale was that Irish legislative independence would do violence to the Empire. Therefore the advocates of Home Rule were supporters of violence. It was a philosophy that was not far removed from that of the incoming Chief Secretary. Balfour was intent on introducing a form of coercion 'that refused to distinguish between different kinds of nationalists. The constitutional party, the cattle hougher, the back street assassin, the boycotter, they were all the same: criminal because they were nationalist.'[3] A cartoon in *Punch* at around the time of his appointment was explicitly critical of what was represented as a pusillanimous Tory policy towards Irish unrest and outrage. It contrasted the robust approach of the *Times* with the more considered measures of Hicks Beach. Lord Salisbury is portrayed as Macbeth. He is clutching two daggers: 'Coercion' and 'The Law'. Behind him the *Times*,[4] in the guise of Lady Macbeth, her arms outstretched, is demanding the daggers and upbraiding him, 'Infirm of purpose! Give me the daggers! I'll show you how to do it!'[5]

The *London Charivari* need not have concerned itself. Balfour, the coercion dagger, would remain unsheathed during Salisbury's eventful tenure. The ghost of Forster must have smiled beneficently from the shades on 7 March 1887.[6] But his successor's forceful policies would be tempered with more social and economic concessions than 'Buckshot' had felt able to proffer. Balfour's second *poignard*, according to the widely accepted thesis of historian L.P. Curtis, was not 'The Law' but 'Conciliation'.[7] While the *Times* tolerated the latter, its enthusiastic validation was reserved for legislation like the Chief Secretary's new Criminal Law (Amendment) Bill. By yet another coincidence (assuming one believes in such possibilities) a vote on that very Bill was due on the day the newspaper disinterred the buried lead of its 'Parnellism and Crime' series on 18 April, with the publication of the infamous 'facsimile' document.

This seismic reproduction purported to be a letter over Parnell's signature, though not in his hand. It was dated 15 May 1882 and the text read:

> Dear Sir,
> I am not surprised at your friend's anger, but he and you should know that to denounce the murders was the only course open to us. To do that promptly was plainly our best policy.
>
> But you can tell him and all others concerned that though I regret the accident of Lord F. Cavendish's death, I cannot refuse to admit that Burke got no more than his deserts.
>
> You are at liberty to show him this, and others whom you can trust also, but let not my address be known. He can write to House of Commons.
>
> Yours very truly,
> Chas S. Parnell

The genesis of the *Times* letters (a number of others were published incriminating the likes of Egan, Davitt and O'Kelly, and linking the League to the Invincibles) goes back to a pamphlet entitled 'Parnellism Unmasked'. Written by Pigott, whose erstwhile 'advanced' political affiliations had taken a backseat to the exigencies of feeding himself and a young family, the pamphlet brought him into contact with Edward Caulfield Houston, an impressionable Unionist journalist in his mid-twenties who had worked for the *Times* office in Dublin and had taken up a position as Secretary of the newly formed loyalist organisation, the Irish Loyal and Patriotic Union, established to defend Ireland against Home Rule.[8] Houston, seduced by Pigott's circle of seedy contacts and hopeful that one or more of them shared the penchant for betrayal of the former *Irishman* editor, retained his services in the higher cause of establishing links between Parnell, his principal supporters and violent political crime.

This had resulted in a new lease of life for the impecunious Pigott, a vapour trail of anonymous contacts, plausible associates, trips to Lausanne and New York, and a financial transaction with shadowy Fenians in Paris (never seen by Houston), which produced a bag said to have been abandoned by the fugitive Frank Byrne. It contained a number of incriminating letters. This was manna from heaven to the young Dublin unionist. Gradually, as Pigott realised that Houston had considerable financial backing from other fervent supporters of the union, the first batch of letters was augmented with more sensational documents. Long before then Houston had already become a purveyor himself. He had failed to interest Hartington and W.T. Stead, before a non-committal *Times* editor, George Buckle, passed him on to the newspaper's manager, J.C. MacDonald. *Times* proprietor, John Walter, and the newspaper's legal adviser, Joseph Soames, then became involved and, as 'the story told by Houston was entirely consistent with suspicions that had long been entertained in Printing House Square',[9] the decision was taken to purchase the letters. At no point did anyone ask Houston about the provenance of this unexploded literary bomb. Their collective minds may have been elsewhere. Houston had first approached the *Times* during the same week in which Gladstone had introduced the Government of Ireland Bill.

The *Times* then set about verifying the signature of Parnell.[10] This was not an easy task since the Irish leader was notorious for his reluctance to append his signature to anything. An advertisement offering ten pounds for the autographs of a number of notable politicians attracted three usable examples of Parnell's hand. On this basis a handwriting expert (G.S. Inglis) confirmed that the signature on Houston's document was that of Parnell. It was only when the newspaper approached the eminent barrister, Sir Henry James, to consult with him about the potential fallout of publication that vague misgivings emerged. This was not the first time James had seen the letters and on the previous occasion he had formed the impression that Pigott had been involved in their procurement. That had been enough to end his interest in the matter. The *Times* representatives, however, were unfamiliar with the name and, astonishingly, 'nor was it regarded of sufficient importance to require the consultation of those members of the staff of the paper who were specially conversant with Irish affairs.'[11] It was an omission the 'newspaper of record' would come to regret.

The 'Parnellism and Crime' series had begun in a low-key fashion. In the second article, published on 10 March 1887 (carrying no by-line – they were written by a Dublin Catholic journalist, J. Woulfe Flanagan, son of an Irish judge and a Balliol contemporary of H.H. Asquith[12]), O'Shea's role in the Kilmainham Treaty and the Sheridan controversy had been cited. But was the Captain aware of what was to come? It seems he may well have been. Certainly he was friendly with Houston. He told the Special Commission in October 1888 that they were acquainted and the Chamberlain papers contain a chatty letter sent by the young journalist to the Captain in March 1889, which presupposes a friendship of some duration. It has been speculated that O'Shea had been made aware by Houston of the existence of letters which incriminated Parnell and that he came by this information in June 1886. Houston was aware at that point of the contents of the letters, although he had not yet purchased the originals. This is offered by some as the explanation of an enigmatic comment he made to the divorce court in November 1890, which went unchallenged. While dealing with the *Pall Mall Gazette* article of 24 May 1886, O'Shea had digressed from his discussion of his marital difficulties. He had, he claimed, accepted his wife's assurances that the article was without substance, but added that he had then come by other information prejudicial to Parnell: 'I had found out something that had nothing to do with the matter, and I desired her again before I went abroad to have no communication whatever with Mr Parnell.'[13] When he finally saw the facsimile reproduced in the *Times* almost a year later, he 'exulted'[14]. He was more familiar than most with Parnell's handwriting. Michael Davitt was struck by 'the staggering similarity of the signature'.[15] O'Shea must have felt that his quarry had been cornered, albeit by another hunter.

There is no definitive account of Parnell's reaction to the appearance of the damaging facsimile. Katharine O'Shea's version is full and thoroughly entertaining but unreliable right from the outset.[16] She begins by mixing up the date of the first *Times* article (7 March) with that of the appearance of the facsimile letter (18 April). She then claims to have shown him the newspaper. Later that day when questioned by Timothy Harrington as to whether or not he had seen the article, Parnell claimed total ignorance of it and had to have it shown to him. His response to it was one of characteristic impassivity. 'He put his finger on the S of the signature', Harrington recalled, 'and said quite calmly, as if it were a matter of the utmost indifference: "I did not make an S like that since 1878."'[17] Harrington had been appalled by his leader's apparent lack of awareness of the gravity of the situation. His insouciance suggests that he had already seen the paper, though in his evidence to the Commission he claimed that he did not 'take' the *Times*. Katharine described him as having maintained a similar sang-froid, merely remarking to her imperturbably, 'Wouldn't you hide your head with shame if your King were so stupid as that, my Queen?'[18] She spoils her narrative, however, by having Parnell back in Eltham early that evening when he was, in fact, awaiting an opportunity in the House of Commons, partly at the keen insistence of his lieutenants, to refute the allegations of the *Times*. One episode that does ring true is her anecdote about a copy of the *Times* piece which was cut out and left on the gates of Wonersh Lodge.

The arcane rules of the House of Commons meant that, in 21st-century terms, an entire news cycle had passed before the Irish leader was able to get to his feet (at 1.00 a.m. on the morning of 19 April) and vigorously denounce the *Times* document as a 'villainous and barefaced forgery'. The delay and the manner of the denial (the Tories were, predictably, unconvinced but so were a number of Liberals) led Alfred Robbins, London Correspondent of the *Birmingham Post*, to comment that 'The whole affair was as miserably mismanaged on the Nationalist side as it was relentlessly pressed on the Conservative ...'[19] Parnell's refusal to sue the *Times*, though sensible (he was advised that he would never convince a London jury of his innocence and the support of a Dublin jury would be worthless), added to the conviction of those negatively predisposed towards the Irish leader: that the newspaper would not have published the letter unless it was genuine.

Almost from the moment he first set eyes on the *Times* facsimile, Parnell saw the hand of O'Shea hovering over the piece. He became obsessed with the, not unreasonable, assumption that the Captain had the motive and the opportunity for forging his signature. It was a view not shared by Tim Healy who, despite his low opinion of O'Shea, was, by his own account, one of the first to suspect the hand of Pigott. He persuaded Henry Labouchere to identify the Kingstown-based journalist as the forger in his newspaper *Truth* within three days of the appearance of the facsimile. The two men then awaited a response. A week later Pigott asked *Truth* to publish a letter of denial but no lawsuit followed.[20]

The controversy died away almost as quickly as it had arisen. That was partly because its object was in no position to stoke it. Parnell fell ill and, in the weeks that followed the *Times* 'scoop', made few appearances in the House. Alfred Robbins wrote of his physical appearance in late May 1887, '... those who have seen him within the past few days have been astonished at the alarming change in his appearance a few weeks have made.'[21] The Tory press put it down either to malingering or a guilty conscience.

The entire affair could have become an unresolved nine-day wonder, but for the irrational intervention of the 'irritable eccentric',[22] Frank Hugh O'Donnell. Speculation as to why the former nationalist MP (no lover of Parnell) decided that he had been libelled in the *Times* articles ranges from an egotistical desire for a return to the limelight, through being egged on by fellow 'Parnellophobe' Philip Callan, to collaborating with Joseph Chamberlain (and, by extension O'Shea) to destroy the Irish leader's career. O'Donnell's own explanation for why he broke ranks and sued, as outlined in his *A History of the Irish Parliamentary Party*, is singularly unconvincing. It began, he asserted, with an intervention designed to distance Parnell from Frank Byrne and escalated into a claim of defamation in November 1887.[23] His own special pleading merely exacerbates the suspicion that he was 'only an irascible Quixote, insulted by the windmill.'[24]

When the case (*O'Donnell* v *Walter*) was heard, O'Donnell's counsel did not even put him in the witness box.[25] The *Times* was represented by the Attorney General, Sir Richard Webster. He was operating in a private capacity, but in accepting the brief managed to reinforce the aura of an oligarchic conspiracy, encompassing the government and the *Times*, which permeates the entire affair. He spent three days, from 2 to 5 July 1888, justifying the allegations of the *Times* and introducing more of the fruits of Pigott's penmanship. It was these latter documents, containing as they did a crucial spelling error, which were to contribute to the forger's ultimate undoing.

The *History of The Times* suggests that O'Donnell might have been used as a 'stalking horse'[26] by Irish members eager to test the mettle of the newspaper in a court of law. If so, he was the most broken down nag imaginable. O'Donnell had not even been singled out by the *Times* until he drew attention to himself with a letter to the paper on 17 June 1887. The *Times* itself offered the derisory comment about its opponent that 'We have never written one word to suggest that Mr O'Donnell, distinguished while a member of the House of Commons for his vanity, his garrulity, his inconsequence, but certainly for nothing worse, was of the stuff of which conspirators of that sort are made.'[27] Tim Healy hinted darkly in his memoir that 'To bring a libel action against the *Times* required means, and O'Donnell had none. The reader must, therefore, make up his mind as to whether, in provoking this bogus trial under the pretence that he had been attacked, O'Donnell was merely spiteful, or was an agent for (or in collusion with) an undisclosed principal.'[28]

O'Donnell himself acknowledges that he was considered by at least one Irish MP to be 'a damned bonnet[29] for the *Times*'.[30] Clearly the *Times* could, had it chosen to do so, have published the new letters as it had done the old. But with Webster and his colleague Sir Henry James reading them aloud to the court, the newspaper was able to insinuate the material into the public domain with the protection of qualified privilege. O'Donnell himself claimed that 'Parnell presided over the whole direction of the case'.[31] He produced evidence, in the form of a memo from his legal representative, of a meeting with Parnell; added to which the Irish leader did, along with O'Donnell, get access to the *Times* 'discovered' documents, but it seems likely that Parnell's interest in the case was belated, reluctant and peripheral.

This recrudescence of the case (according to Davitt, Parnell had asked O'Donnell not to proceed[32]) served to reinforce the notion that the Irish leader and his associates had much to hide. Chamberlain, admittedly not the least partial source, encapsulated these suspicions in a letter to his young American fiancée, Mary Endicott,[33] in the wake of the *O'Donnell* v *Walter* case, when he observed that '... such a journal as the *Times* has a great reputation to keep up and would never bring accusations lightly ... it is almost certain Parnell would go to a court of law if he were not afraid of the cross examination.'[34]

The *O'Donnell* v *Walter* fiasco forced the hand of Parnell. Back in April 1887 he had asked for a Select Committee of the House of Commons to investigate such an egregious accusation against one of its members. Now he did so again. But the Conservative government was more inclined to 'try a revolution as well as a man'.[35] It did so with some prompting from a vengeful Joseph Chamberlain. Still angry with Parnell for what he saw as his breach of faith over the Central Board issue and irked by the 'Judas' taunts of the Irish members for his role in the unthreading of Home Rule, he persuaded the Leader of the House of Commons, W.H. Smith (a good friend of the *Times* proprietor through his bookselling business) to give Parnell more than he sought. Rather than a limited Select Committee, Chamberlain proposed a full-blown judicial Royal Commission of Inquiry ('to the great confusion of Mr Parnell and his friends') to investigate not just the facsimile letter but 'all the charges against the leaders of the Irish party. I am convinced that this Commission will elicit some astounding facts and if the result is to show that more than one member of the so-called Nationalist party has been dabbling in assassination, the effect would be prodigious.'[36] This contrasts with what he told the House of Commons in a debate on the Commission's findings in March 1890, when he declared, 'I never heard of the Commission until it was suggested by the Government'.[37]

Just as the 'Thunderer' had ignored the advice of its Irish staff when allowing Pigott into the wheelhouse, the Salisbury administration excluded the Irish law officers from its counsels. In fact even its own senior law officers were dubious about Smith's chosen course of action. Sir Edward Clarke, the Solicitor General, discussed the matter with the Attorney General. 'Webster was not in favour of it, and I was thoroughly against it.' The Attorney General advised Smith that he (Webster) should not become involved in the case. Later he wrote to Clarke that 'Every day I curse Chamberlain and the Unionists for their obstinacy ...'[38] The Special Commission was, in Randolph Churchill's words, a 'trial of political opponents'. It was a unique collaboration between the British conservative political and media establishments to put Irish nationalism in the dock. The *Times* letters, Parnell's main bone of contention, were relegated to the status of a significant minor issue, superseded by the indictment of all the leading members of the Irish Parliamentary Party on charges laid by the *Times*. The Members of Parliament (Charges and Allegations) Bill was railroaded through in a matter of weeks in July 1888, with the Leader of the House at one point in the debate on the second reading referring to 'this great trial', before correcting himself and talking instead about 'this great enquiry'.[39]

Three judges were appointed to preside over the 'great trial'. The Commission President, Sir James Hannen, was President of the Probate, Divorce and Admiralty Court. Mr Justice A.L. Smith was a High Court judge, as was the third jurist on the panel, Mr Justice Day. None had any obvious political sympathies, nor had they ever been Members of Parliament. Ironically there was more Irish objection to Day than to Hannen or Smith, despite the fact that he was an English Catholic. He was perceived as having little sympathy for Home Rule. Throughout proceedings Day maintained a granite-like mien on the bench. According to Parnellite journalist Edward Byrne of the *Freeman*, the Irish leader was always 'highly amused at the vacant expression on the face of Judge Day'.[40] Over the course of months of evidence he did not make a single intervention.

CENTRAL BOARD REVISITED

The debate on the Special Commission Bill saw the renewal of the hostilities between Parnell and Chamberlain that had lain, more or less, dormant since the defeat of the Home Rule Bill. In a weasel-worded contribution on 23 July Chamberlain began with some transparent flattery of Parnell before chiding him for not challenging the *Times* in a court of law. In an exhibition of rank hypocrisy, given his behind-the-scenes involvement in championing a Royal Commission, he expressed his personal preference for a parliamentary Select Committee as the proper forum for such an investigation. He then concluded by recommending the most expansive terms of reference possible in order, so he said, to afford the Irish party a golden opportunity to efface the charges laid against its members.[41] The supremely narcissistic Chamberlain was so well pleased with his rhetoric that he told his fiancée '... one man said that in all his experience he had never seen the House listen with such rapt attention.'[42]

Cognisant of the fact that revenge is a dish best served cold, Parnell bided his time before repaying Chamberlain in kind. Late on in the evening sitting of 30 July he clinically eviscerated the politically homeless Birmingham Radical. He accused Chamberlain of having hidden behind Irish members (O'Shea was not referred to by name), while engaged in internecine conspiracies, and of transgressing Cabinet confidentiality. 'I care very little for the opinion of the right honourable gentleman,' he declared icily, 'I have never put forward men to do dangerous things which I shrank from doing myself, nor have I betrayed the secrets of my colleagues in council ... If this inquiry be extended into these matters – and I see no reason why it should not – I shall be able to make good my words by documentary evidence which is not forged.'[43] His devastating phillipic was accompanied by a Greek chorus of Irish members chanting 'Judas, Judas'. The duel went into a second day when Parnell resumed his attack on 31 July after having been interrupted by the adjournment. Chamberlain defended himself by maintaining that the Kilmainham Treaty negotiations had been carried on with the full knowledge and approval of Gladstone (a contention which the Liberal leader showed a marked reluctance to support) and that the Central Board scheme had been devised by Parnell himself and then unceremoniously dropped as he sought a better offer from the Tories.

At that point the Captain was piped on board. Chamberlain's biographer J.L. Garvin disingenuously refers to O'Shea as having 'blundered into print'[44] with a letter to the Times on 2 August 1888, although a piece of correspondence quoted in his own book captures the essential truth of the matter. On 1 August Chamberlain told his fiancée that 'tomorrow there will be a letter from O'Shea in the *Times* which ought to complete Parnell's discomfiture.'[45] Miss Endicott had already been introduced to the Captain in April when Chamberlain, in writing to her, had described him as 'an amusing Irishman ... He is a great supporter of mine and has been very useful to me occasionally in all Irish matters, but like all Irish politicians he is, I am afraid, unscrupulous and cynical ...'[46] Not, of course, that anyone could have accused Joseph Chamberlain of such heinous sins.

Chamberlain, wholly altruistically and scrupulously, convened with O'Shea to settle old scores with Parnell. He would come to regret his coalition with the Captain, based as it was on a desire to believe O'Shea's bilious assertions about Parnell's moral depravity. Given his almost certain knowledge of the real reason for the Captain's loathing of Parnell, he displayed very poor judgement in his choice of ally. It is morally certain that O'Shea encouraged Chamberlain in his belief that Parnell had been the motive force behind the Central Board scheme. While the Captain may not have misled the Radical leader in 1885 (see above), he almost certainly did so during the resurgence of the controversy. O'Shea's letter, when it appeared, was a masterly concoction of special pleading and innuendo, peppered throughout with the very cynicism which Chamberlain had sought to deprecate. It is ironic that, in using O'Shea as an attack dog, he was guilty of one of the principal charges laid against him by Parnell.

O'Shea began, in the *Times* letter, published on 2 August 1888, by suggesting that the real differences between the two men were minor. He then, gratuitously, suggested that in the aftermath of the Phoenix Park murders Parnell's principal concern had been with the preservation of his own life rather than the atrocity visited on others. He referred to the Kilmainham letter of 28 April as Parnell's 'surrender'. Moving on to the Central Board controversy he declared that 'The scheme was altogether Mr Parnell's, and Mr Chamberlain adopted it with considerable hesitation because of its not being sufficiently consonant with Radical principles ... Why the latter should repudiate it is a mystery; the original claim to its creation and construction exists not only above his signature, but in his own handwriting.'[47] He concluded by claiming that Chamberlain also had in his possession a copy of the expiring Crimes Act, with amendments in Parnell's own hand. This portrayed the Irish leader as a political opportunist prepared to rail against coercion while, in reality and for his own ends, countenancing its reintroduction.

In his response on 6 August Parnell challenged Chamberlain to publish any Central Board plan which bore his signature (he was well aware that no such document existed). He issued a similar challenge *in re* the alleged copy of the Crimes Act. He then, once again, sketched out clearly the differences between his local government template and that of the former President of the Board of Trade. He concluded by reiterating his insistence that Chamberlain publish whatever documents he had and declared that 'It will be found from them that, although he now accuses us of double dealing, he must have been early in 1885 fully acquainted with the views which I now explain to you.'[48] A curt letter from Chamberlain the following day declared simply, 'I accept Mr Parnell's challenge, and will forward to you in the course of a few days a full statement of the communications initiated by him which passed between us in 1884 and

1885.'[49] In taking up Parnell's gauntlet, Chamberlain was exhibiting his customary degree of confidence in his own political instincts and rectitude. But he was also putting his faith in O'Shea's veracity and integrity.

The rekindling of the Central Board squabble must have seemed like old times for O'Shea. He was back centre stage once again, shielding his mentor from the poisoned arrows of his despised accuser. When the two men had met on 1 August to jointly concoct O'Shea's letter to the *Times* much more than 'who said what' back in early 1885 had been discussed. After O'Shea had left, Chamberlain immediately wrote a memo of their conversation. Its contents reveal the extent to which O'Shea was acutely aware and well informed of certain aspects of the *Times* campaign against Parnell, as well as the extent to which he had succumbed to some of the gossip and black propaganda surrounding the affair. The memo reads as follows:

> Mr. O'Shea called today. He states that he has heard from members of the Irish party in London that the first letter signed C.S. Parnell and printed in facsimile in the *Times* is undoubtedly genuine, and that the body of the letter is written by Mr McSweeney, who died two years ago and who was a clerk to Mr Byrne.
>
> He also says that the cheque which Parnell sent to Mr Byrne was a cheque from the Irish League forwarded for the purposes of the English League, and was passed over to Mr Byrne by Parnell. It is not therefore a cheque of Mr Parnell's own.
>
> It is reported in the Irish party that Mr Henry Campbell, Mr Parnell's secretary, has been poisoned, some persons believing that it was done by Mr John O'Conor, others asserting that it was a case of attempted suicide.
>
> Mr Henry Campbell, according to Mr O'Shea, was one of the Treasurers of the Invincibles.[50]

O'Shea's information is an amalgam of the intriguingly accurate, the vaguely plausible, and the outrageously erroneous. The cheque referred to in the second paragraph of the memo was one of the cornerstones of the *Times* case against Parnell. It was from the Irish leader and was alleged to have been paid by him to facilitate Byrne's escape from London to Paris after he was implicated in the Invincible conspiracy. The *Times* had in its possession an acknowledgement of the cheque written by Byrne after he had fled to Paris to avoid arrest. O'Shea's information was unerringly accurate and the possible source will be discussed later. The information about Parnell's dourly loyal secretary, the northern MP Henry Campbell, was purely speculative, while the allegation about McSweeney was, at that time, conceivable, given that his name had come up in the *Times* argument in *O'Donnell* v *Walter*.

But the main business between the two men during this period was their attempt to further undermine Parnell's already battered credibility. After accepting Parnell's challenge, Chamberlain had written to Miss Endicott, 'I shall be working as hard as I know how, looking over old documents and papers. I have just finished a draft reply which I must submit to O'Shea to see if his memory tallies with mine, and which I think will be a pretty hard nut to crack ...'[51] O'Shea announced that he had sent for a box of his papers and hoped 'to prove Parnell's mendacity as a *point de départ*.'[52]

Things began to go wrong very rapidly for the reunited conspirators. When he consulted his own archive for the period, one of the first things O'Shea discovered was a copy of the facetious letter which he had written to Parnell on 19 January 1885, the one to which Chamberlain had taken grave exception and which O'Shea himself had dubbed 'the inconvenient letter' (see p. 193). He realised, to his horror, that Parnell, or more to the point the putative Invincible Treasurer Henry Campbell, would have retained a copy of the letter. With considerable chagrin he alerted Chamberlain:[53]

> It has crossed my mind that Parnell may have founded on this letter his charges against you, although it would be the meanest thing in the world to use a letter written when I was on terms of the closest intimacy with him in order to injure a third person who was not only not cognisant of its contents, but actually repudiated it as soon as he became aware of their nature ... What, however, I want to say now is that I fully admit that the letter did not contain or pretend to contain a literal account of our interview, but was rather my own version of it interspersed with my own comments on the political situation suggested by the general personal observation. I cannot at this distance of time separate what was yours from what was mine in the picture I drew, but if Parnell should be capable of the indescribable meanness of using such a letter to damage you, you may rely on my being ready to state the true facts, even though they do not redound very much to my diplomatic reputation.[54]

Given the enterprise in which he was engaged with Chamberlain, his suggestion that any attempt at exposure by Parnell would be a breach of trust and honour is utterly risible. But the existence of this golden hostage to fortune put Chamberlain in a dilemma and, ultimately, stayed his hand. He had no recollection of the letter in question or of his remonstrating with O'Shea after he had seen it. In accepting Parnell's challenge to produce documentation to back up his claims, he had relied on O'Shea's verbal assurances that proofs existed which would demolish the Irish leader's case and that it was Parnell who had been the prime mover in the Central Board scheme. It was an exquisite conundrum that he outlined to his future wife. 'What will happen if this letter is produced? In my own defence I must throw over O'Shea, and say what is the truth, that he grossly misrepresented me; but then if he misrepresented *me*, may not he also have misrepresented Parnell? And he is my chief witness against Parnell. Altogether it is a nice dilemma ... By the indiscretion and unworthiness of the agent selected, I am quite likely to be represented as animated by ambitions of the meanest and most selfish kind ...'.[55]

Of course it was beyond his own comprehension that Chamberlain might, indeed, have operated in 1885 with anything less than the loftiest of motives. He was never one to doubt himself or his essential goodness, so it was far easier to shoot the messenger. As he told his fiancée the following day after a meeting with his debased Mercury, '... it is provoking to find that one has been compromised by somebody else in a matter which was really undertaken with the most disinterested motives ...'.[56] He displayed a marked disinclination to accept any responsibility for his own monumental misjudgement in affiliating himself with an ally whose motives were far from disinterested.

Chamberlain raised the white flag in a letter to the *Times* on 13 August. In it he professed to be puzzled over 'what is now the issue between us'. His understanding was that Parnell wished to repudiate any notion that he approved Chamberlain's 'plan'. This so-called plan, he contended, '... was never at any time worked out in detail, and it was not the subject of any discussion with Mr O'Shea. I am consequently quite ready to admit Mr Parnell's disclaimer of any assent to it.' He appended to the letter the scheme O'Shea had brought him from Parnell and declared, with transparent magnanimity, that having perused all the documentation related to the controversy 'there was nothing in any of these communications of which Mr Parnell had cause to be ashamed.'[57] It was an exhibition of dismal abseiling, disguised as a leisurely climb-down.

For J.L. Garvin, as for his biographical subject, there was only one villain in the piece. He attempts to gloss over this abject defeat for

Chamberlain by declaring that 'He had got to the truth. O'Shea, meaning to exercise ineffable finesse in his negotiations, had always in effect misrepresented the inner mind of each man to the other. Chamberlain remained on terms of distant civility with the ex-envoy, but never again gave an opening to his diplomatic talents.'[58] For his part, O'Shea wanted to claim victory in the controversy with a letter to the *Times* in mid-August. He suggested to Chamberlain that he (O'Shea) would stress that 'Mr Parnell has not replied to Mr Chamberlain's letter. I therefore beg of you to allow me to note for future reference that there is now no denial of Mr Parnell's authorisation of the Irish local government scheme presented by me to Mr Chamberlain in January 1885.'[59] But, failing to arouse Chamberlain's interest, he dropped the idea.

O'Shea's career as envoy and confidant of the Merchant Prince of Birmingham was indeed at an end. But he may well have had other uses. In the Shakespearean tragedy to follow, he was about to forsake his role as Cassio and take on the much meatier part of Iago. It has been argued (and steadfastly denied) that Chamberlain coached him in his portrayal of the treacherous traducer of Othello.

THE SPECIAL COMMISSION

Preliminary hearings of the Special Commission in Probate Court No 1 in September 1888 were a rude shock to the *Times*. The newspaper had been hoping that a libel template would be adopted to govern proceedings, and that Parnell and his 64 co-accused parliamentary colleagues[60] would have to do what O'Donnell had signally failed to do – prove that the newspaper had gravely misrepresented and defamed them. Instead Justice Hannen and his two associates ruled that the tribunal would proceed on the basis that the Irish members had been 'indicted'. The burden of proof lay with the *Times* and it would have to produce witnesses to support its charges. In addition the *Times* would have to bear the cost of the 'prosecution' of the case. Despite the fact that the newspaper was at all times aided and abetted by the government,[61] it was an unexpected and unwelcome turn of events.

Attorney General, Sir Richard Webster, and Sir Henry James reprised their roles in the Whitehall farce that had been *O'Donnell* v *Walter*. Webster had been singularly unsuccessful in persuading his political masters that he should resile from the case. Salisbury was having none of it, telling Leader of the House, W.H. Smith, that Webster's defection would suggest that the *Times* case was weak. His resolute insistence that the state's chief law officer lead for the newspaper served still more to 'demonstrate the extent to which the government were prepared to go to link their fortunes with those of the *Times* to achieve the grand objective of bringing down Parnell.'[62]

Former Irish MP and future Lord Chief Justice, Sir Charles Russell, by now having permanently forsaken his attractive retainer from the *Times*, led for Parnell and most of the 'accused' Irish party members. He was assisted by a future Liberal Prime Minister, Herbert H. Asquith. Other Irish MPs were represented by Frank Lockwood, later a Solicitor General. Davitt (prominently listed among the malfeasants) and Biggar did their own pleading, as did Tim Healy whose involvement as counsel for the Irish party members had been vetoed by Parnell. The Irish leader was not just at loggerheads with Healy. He and Russell, both accustomed to getting their own way, found it difficult to co-operate. Michael Davitt was often forced to intercede between the two men as peacemaker. Russell was convinced, with some justification, that Parnell had no interest in the wider case being prosecuted against the entire nationalist movement, and was only concerned with the issue of the *Times* letters and his own personal reputation.

It had been assumed that the Commission would be quick to address the issue of the ever-growing number of incriminating letters. Such was not the case. Instead the tribunal began with an often mind-numbing litany of petty grudges and avarice masquerading as agrarian activism. Within days it had become bogged down in an opening speech by the Attorney General attempting to establish links between stirring platform speeches made by the likes of Parnell, Healy, Sexton, Harrington *et al* and 'outrages', ranging from threatening letters to murder. If the *Times* was to prove its case it had to establish a connection between speeches it claimed to be seditious and acts of violence which followed. Webster began, on 22 October, to read them into the record. On the third day of his dreary monologue he aroused a degree of interest when, referring to the Phoenix Park murders, he asserted confidently that 'Captain O'Shea will testify that Mr Parnell unwillingly signed the manifesto in which the murders were denounced. Captain O'Shea's testimony will also show that Mr Parnell could have stopped outrage, treaty or no treaty.'[63]

Then, in the midst of utter tedium,[64] a ripple of excitement. On 31 October, on only the second day of direct testimony, the *Times* produced a surprise witness. At least Sir Charles Russell insisted that the insertion of Captain William Henry O'Shea at this stage in proceedings was a surprise, and he objected to having such a significant witness 'sprung' on him. Webster explained that O'Shea's presence was dictated by the fact that he was about to leave for the continent and was not expected back for some months.[65] However, Parnell does not seem to have been taken aback. Alfred Robbins noted that the normally tardy Irish leader was 'punctual in attendance at the opening of the Court'[66] on this particular day and wondered why.

Although O'Shea had been subpoenaed by the Parnellites, he was attending as a *Times* witness, having invited the newspaper to subpoena him as well. He had been courted assiduously by the editor, George Buckle, through Edward Caulfield Houston, who was by now working virtually full-time on the newspaper's case. According to Henry Harrison, who held the feet of the *Times* to the fire many years later when he successfully challenged the newspaper's version of events in its official history,[67] 'Captain O'Shea was provided as a witness for *The Times* by Mr Joseph Chamberlain, MP, at the *written request* of Mr George Earle Buckle, the Editor of *The Times*.'[68] The substance of Harrison's contention is confirmed by a letter from O'Shea to Chamberlain in August 1888. He had just been served with a subpoena by Lewis and Lewis, solicitors for the Parnellite side, and assumed that he was being called to provide '... evidence relating to 1884–1885. I met Buckle at dinner last night. I told him I would have nothing to do with "charges and allegations" but that I had no objection to talk about the Kilmainham Treaty, which I, as usual, minimized to the utmost. He is evidently most friendly to you.'[69]

O'Shea later tried second-guessing Parnell's tactics in issuing him with a summons to appear before the Commission. He assumed that Russell would question him about the events of April 1882. 'Parnell's Plan of Campaign is this: he puts me in the box; on the ground that he wishes to show that Ministers who had the fullest knowledge of the secret service of Dublin Castle, were so certain of his being clear of all connivance with crime that they were willing to take his support in Parliament ...'[70]

As his date with the Special Commission approached, O'Shea grew nervous and sought some evidence of support and solidarity from Highbury. He had been fobbed off by Chamberlain's secretary when he had asked for a meeting 'to exchange impressions as to old events before going into the witness box.'[71] Chamberlain was understandably reluctant to become nursemaid to the Captain's anxieties. He wrote to Mary Endicott that he considered O'Shea to be 'indiscreet and therefore a dangerous person'.[72] He clearly conveyed his lack of enthusiasm to O'Shea who, after a telegram requesting 'all letters, memoranda and telegrams of mine between 1882 and 1886'[73] did not elicit the response he had expected, telegraphed his former mentor in ill-tempered high dudgeon the following day. 'Much obliged but cannot give or take the trouble you indicate. I will fight my own battle and entertain my own opinion of Liberal Unionist chivalry. O'Shea'.[74] It was the only occasion in a correspondence that had begun in 1882 that the worm ever turned.

Chamberlain's response was one of injured innocence: 'The remark in your telegram is uncalled for and not justified by anything I have said or done.' He implicitly dismissed the significance to him of much of O'Shea's extensive correspondence by insisting that the only letters of importance he still had in his possession covered the Kilmainham Treaty and Central Board periods. He would forward whatever he could locate, but '... A great deal has, however, gone into the waste paper basket and it has always been a chance whether letters of this kind were preserved by me or not.'[75] He also expressed regret that '... you cannot spare time to run down here for a night when we might have talked over any matter that remains in doubt ...' Chamberlain's conciliatory tone had the effect of rapidly mollifying an anxious prospective witness and the old balance in their relationship, heavily weighted in favour of the Birmingham Radical, was quickly restored.

O'Shea had expected to be called within a couple of days of the commencement of proceedings at the Commission, but reckoned without Webster's desire to leave no questionable Land League speech uncited. He did react unfavourably, however, to the Attorney General's invocation of his likely testimony. Writing to Highbury he declared, 'I never said that Parnell refused to sign the Manifesto denouncing the Phoenix Park murders. On the contrary, I have always believed he was very glad to have the support of Davitt and Dillon for the purpose. I have always said, and I maintain, that he bewailed to me his lot of having to affix his signature to a document drafted in so turgid a style, in order to pander to the vanity[76] of a bombastic writer like Davitt. He objected not to the proclamation, but to the style of the Proclamation.'[77]

O'Shea looked furtive and anxious as he entered the witness box, though, as we shall see, this was not entirely related to the ordeal ahead. Alfred Robbins described his physical appearance as 'shabby genteel'.[78] He was not the spruce, dandified figure of old. *United Ireland* was, not unexpectedly, even less complimentary, describing O'Shea as a 'sleek, odoriferous, furtive professional pimp and go-between, an entirely contemptible and unclean thing as everyone now can see in this strong glare, one of the vermin species, a flabby musk-rat needing but a prod for such a smell to arise.'[79] Others were rewarded by the appearance of his trademark gold eye-glasses, of which one onlooker was said to observe, 'He uses them with an 18th-century grace'.[80] According to Robbins, O'Shea was palpably nervous and ill at ease. He suggested that both Webster and Russell tiptoed around him, 'for neither trusted him and each suspected he might say too much.'[81]

Punch, in one of the first examples of what became weekly reportage of the Commission, did a Toby MP-style take on proceedings. 'O'Shea in box all morning and far into afternoon. Doesn't seem to like it; shaved off whiskers in order the better to face ordeal. But no use. In unbroken line below him sit old familiar friends.' The writer went on to describe Parnell as 'pale-faced, haggard-looking, staring with reproachful eyes'; Davitt as 'taking notes'; Healy as 'speechless with anger'; and Biggar 'smiling a ghastly smile, and thinking of the days that are no more, when he went down to Galway, and, in defiance of Parnell, pulled O'Shea's hair and scratched his face. A trying ordeal for the once *debonnaire* [*sic*] but now decidedly damaged Captain. Some signs of quailing at first. Strong disinclination to meet the four pair of gleaming eyes ...'[82]

Webster first took his witness back to the Kilmainham 'negotiations' – the word brought Russell to his feet straightaway and was amended to 'communications'. The *Times* was anxious to establish that Parnell was in a position to turn the tap of violence on and off as it suited him. The names of Egan and Sheridan were frequently invoked in order to associate them indelibly with that of Parnell. Very quickly the examination, probably by accident but possibly by Machiavellian design, strayed into territory that was potentially embarrassing for both O'Shea and Parnell. Referring to the period of Parnell's parole from Kilmainham in April 1882, the Attorney General asked the Captain when he had first become aware of Parnell's temporary release from Kilmainham. This elicited the following dialogue:

> *O'Shea*: Mr Parnell called upon me, I saw him.
> *Attorney General*: Where were you?
> *O'Shea*: At number 1, Albert Mansions.
> *Attorney General*: Had you any other house?
> *O'Shea*: Yes, at Eltham ....
> *Attorney General*: Were you not well then, or why were you at 1, Albert Mansions?
> *O'Shea*: I had had an attack of gout from which I was recovering. Mr Parnell first went to Eltham. I was unable to go there, and he came up to me.[83]

For those in the know, or those privy to rumour and innuendo, it must have been a moment to savour. The initiated would have been aware that Eltham was, by now, the Uncrowned King's official English palace. It could have been a subtle warning to the watching Parnell on the part of a well-informed Attorney General, but it is more likely that the hapless Webster, still wishing he was anywhere else but bogged down in recent Irish history, had just blundered into an inessential line of questioning and had to be pulled out of the way of the oncoming train by O'Shea's hastily manufactured attack of gout. The impression of the watching Alfred Robbins was that 'All through this, O'Shea was manifestly trying to repress his excitement, but his hands trembled a great deal, while Parnell looked eagerly yet gravely towards him the whole time.'[84]

Next O'Shea was quizzed about the events of the day after the Phoenix Park murders and here he pressed home his first stiletto into Parnell's back. He repeated his mantra that, though Parnell had been greatly shaken by the murders of Burke and Cavendish, his main concern had been for his own safety and that he (O'Shea) had been asked by the Irish leader to secure police protection. He also disabused a no doubt disappointed Webster of the notion that Parnell had been unwilling to sign the manifesto drafted by Davitt. He told the Attorney General that 'He said he disliked signing so bombastic a document, but it was necessary to pander to Mr Davitt's vanity, and allow him to draft it ...'[85], conscious that both men were sitting only feet away from him, he must have enjoyed the mischief he had caused by thus quoting Parnell.

Later he generously compensated the *Times* for contradicting Webster by advancing its central case that Parnell was surrounded by men of violence and mayhem. Discussing Harcourt's unwillingness in April 1882 to grant amnesty or safe passage back to Ireland to Sheridan, he told the Attorney General that, in recounting this to Parnell, ' I told him that I had been informed that Sheridan, whose warrant was cancelled at my request on the previous Thursday, was a murderer and a concocter of murder ... Mr Parnell told me he did not know how to communicate with him directly, but knew a person who could do so, and he went for the purpose of seeing that person.'[86]

His next thrust was more in the nature of a sabre jab to the jugular. Seven of the *Times* letters were produced bearing Parnell's alleged signature. Although professing himself not to be a handwriting expert of any kind, O'Shea identified each in turn as genuine. 'If these letters came to me, I should say they were written by Mr Parnell.'[87] In cross-examination Sir Charles Russell later tried to undo the damage but was unable to browbeat O'Shea into retracting his identification of a signature with which, it had already been satisfactorily established, he would have been extremely familiar. Altogether Webster's examination of the witness took up just over a third of his day in court. As far as that wily and experienced observer Alfred Robbins was concerned, O'Shea's direct testimony, as it progressed, had a dual purpose: '... to do a good service to Chamberlain and an ill-turn to Parnell, which seemed the only points clearly to emerge from what he testified.'[88]

When it came to Parnell's suspicions of O'Shea's involvement in the Pigott forgeries, curiously, it was the Captain himself who raised the issue, not once but twice. Even more strangely he did so under cross-examination. He told Russell, unprompted, that he had come before the Commission 'in order to refute the slanders which had been circulated about me by Mr Parnell and his friends with regard to these letters.'[89] Russell ignored him and carried on with his questions. Later, when asked about his relationship with Houston, he volunteered details of a conversation in which, 'He [Houston] repeated what I had heard in other directions; namely, that Mr Parnell and his friends had stated that I was engaged in a conspiracy to get these letters; in fact that it was through my instrumentality altogether, or in part, that these letters were got, and as I never stab a man in the back I was very anxious to come here and declare on my oath that it was not.'[90] At the end of October 1888 there were still a good four months to go before the exposure of Pigott as the forger of the *Times* letters, so O'Shea was taking a chance in publicly identifying the rumours circulating around himself. After a few brief questions on the subject Russell passed on to other matters. Given his obvious anxiety to raise the issue it is curious that O'Shea did not arrange with the Attorney General to be questioned on the subject in direct evidence. Why did he leave the matter to the vagaries of cross-examination, in which he had no opportunity of setting the agenda?

And Russell's own agenda was intriguing in the extreme. He had insisted that he was unprepared to cross-examine O'Shea because the witness had been taken out of turn. Whether or not this was designed to lull the Captain into a false sense of security and play on his customary self-assurance is uncertain. According to Michael Davitt, Russell only rose to question O'Shea at the insistence of himself and Healy. He recorded in one of his notebooks used to store ammunition for his own interrogation of witnesses that 'P[arnell] & Sir C[harles] R[ussell] wanted to put off X examination.'[91]

But despite his reluctance Russell had been well briefed on some of the Captain's more questionable activities. Davitt, self-appointed intelligence officer of the Parnellite case, had done his work well. For the first time the names of Houston and Pigott were introduced into evidence at the Commission. O'Shea acknowledged that he had been approached by Buckle through Chamberlain to give evidence and then deposed by Houston. He volunteered no further information about the ILPU secretary and was vague about who exactly he was. From Pigott he ran the proverbial mile. He professed himself ignorant of the man's first name, though he was aware that Pigott was 'the former editor of a Dublin newspaper'.[92]

He recounted how, in conversation with Houston, the younger man had referred to the rumours surrounding O'Shea's involvement in obtaining the *Times* letters. He was uncertain as to whether 'the report spread about was that I was connected with some men of whom Pigott was one.' When Russell inquired, 'You personally do not know Mr. Pigott?', O'Shea responded, 'To the best of my belief I have never seen him. I certainly do not know him.' So fleeting was this entire exchange and so incomprehensible was it to all but a small few, that the *Daily News* reporter, John MacDonald, whose reports would be collected in a single, invaluable volume, either missed or entirely dismissed the debut of the forger himself at the Special Commission.

But he did not miss the introduction of the shadowy George Mulqueeny, which followed on immediately. His name was first mentioned by O'Shea himself in response to a question related to Frank Byrne, English Land League secretary. O'Shea testified that Mulqueeny, in early 1886, had told him of a letter which he (Mulqueeny) believed to have been taken from the Land League offices in London. The letter, written on 8 February 1883, was an acknowledgement of the receipt of £100 from Parnell. The *Times,* which had the original in its possession, was claiming this as proof that the Irish leader had facilitated the flight of an accessory to the Phoenix Park murders. Mulqueeny had maintained to O'Shea that the police had the letter. O'Shea had asked Chamberlain to make inquiries, had been told there was no such letter in the possession of the authorities and had let the matter drop. O'Shea claimed to have given no credence to the central allegation. He could hardly have said otherwise as he later stood, with Parnell's support, for the Galway seat.

Russell then began to evince a serious interest in Mulqueeny. O'Shea was unable to say where he lived, observing vaguely that 'he called upon me recently and he told me that he had left his house.'[93] He accepted that Mulqueeny had been useful to him in the London East End election campaign of Samuel Montagu. It was around that time that the two men had met. Out of the blue Russell then inquired, 'Is Mulqueeny a member of any secret society?' O'Shea claimed not to know, other than that Mulqueeny admitted to being 'an advanced nationalist' who had never told him that he was a member of any secret society. At this point Russell's questioning, informed by the meticulous research of Michael Davitt, became even more specific. O'Shea was asked did he know of a woman called Mrs Lynch, proprietor of a public house in Wardour Street in London called 'The Golden Lion'. The public house/hotel was actually owned by Mrs Lynch's father, a man from Mayo named Peter Cowell.[94] O'Shea admitted that 'I have been there once.'[95] His visit had been to receive a testimonial from a number of 'advanced nationalists'. Refusing to identify them as Fenians when pursued on the matter by Russell, he explained that they had got up a petition in support of his renewed candidacy in Clare in the 1885 election. Their support for O'Shea, according his own account, was based on their extreme nationalist views and their antipathy to the activities of the Land League: '... the men of their party in the County of Clare were always great supporters of mine, and were very much devoted to me, and I presume these men, some of them, were friends of theirs. These are the old Nationalists,[96] and I always told them how foolish I thought their adventures were, but who hate outrages as much as I did myself.'[97]

This Fenian gathering had been the work of Mulqueeny. At the time of O'Shea's evidence it is possible that Davitt was unaware that Mulqueeny, in addition to being a member of the IRB in London, was also an agent of Edward Jenkinson and had been in the pay of the secret service for at least 12 years. He was now being handsomely remunerated by the *Times* for his services.[98] In 1889 Davitt was informed of this fact by a renegade private detective formerly employed by Joseph Soames on behalf of the *Times*. He went by the *nom de guerre* of 'Thompson', but his name was W.J. Reynolds. His decision to assist Davitt in combating the ongoing activities of the *Times* and Houston (with assistance from a now unemployed Le Caron) was prompted by the fact that he claimed Soames owed him £138 and refused to pay. Reynolds was able to tell Davitt quite a lot about Mulqueeny, including the fact that he occasionally went under the alias 'Mr Barker' (it appears that he had a fondness for dogs), and had once been convicted for assaulting a police officer and for reckless driving.[99] So when Mulqueeny introduced O'Shea to his fellow Fenians in Cowell's in Wardour Street in 1885, he had been operating as a double agent. In which case he was in good company, because amongst the enthusiastic 'Fenians' in the pub that night was another employee of 'the Service', one W.J. Reynolds.[100]

The picture became still murkier when Russell began to question O'Shea about some other services he suggested had been rendered to the Captain by Mulqueeny. Had the Cork-born shipping clerk been sent to Paris by O'Shea in order to make contact with the 'professed dynamiter'[101] Patrick Casey? The insinuation was denied. O'Shea claimed to know very little about Casey. Had he paid Mulqueeny his expenses for the Paris trip? O'Shea denied the specific allegation, but admitted that he had 'frequently' given Mulqueeny money. He excused this generosity by claiming that 'I liked him, and I liked his father, and when they want money I have often given money to them – to Irishmen, very often.'[102] Throughout this lengthy passage with Russell, Robbins noted that O'Shea 'became more and more nervous. He unfolded his arms; leant an elbow on the ledge and his head on his hand; frequently wiped his face; hurriedly stroked his chin; and almost turned his back on his cross-examiner.'[103]

The, by now distinctly uncomfortable, witness was then prompted by Russell to discuss Mulqueeny's connection with an Irish–American nationalist whom O'Shea names as General Caroll Thavies. The man was, in fact, General Charles Carroll Tevis, an American Fenian who, as it happens, was also a British Foreign Office spy.[104] Carroll Tevis, it appeared, objected to Mulqueeny's involvement in the O'Shea 'testimonial'. It was after an altercation with Carroll Tevis that Mulqueeny went to Paris in search of Patrick Casey. Russell's questions hint that Mulqueeny's mission, inspired by O'Shea, was to seek Casey's signature on the Clare election 'testimonial', or to warn him about something. About what we are not informed. All such suggestions were irately denied by the witness.

Russell may simply have been on a fishing expedition or attempting to throw mud indiscriminately, but his questions suggest a wealth of research and investigation into some of O'Shea's more questionable associations. Davitt[105] had found himself a very important confidant, Edward Jenkinson, the former 'spymaster' (and, despite his work for the Spencer administration in Dublin Castle, a Parnellite sympathiser) who had fallen foul of the Tory administration of Lord Salisbury in 1886 and had been dismissed. He supplied Davitt with an invaluable store of highly confidential information, gleaned during his involvement in the world of intelligence gathering in Ireland, dating from 1882.

United Ireland poured scorn on the Captain's '... half confession that he was the associate of extreme Nationalists – hillside men as he called them – and that he spent money amongst them because he was fond of their fathers. For their own sake, we trust they have committed none of their secrets to the Captain.'[106] *Punch*, for its part, satirised O'Shea's cloak and dagger activities. 'Mulqueeny took me there', the magazine pilloried the conspiratorial Captain, 'in a four-wheeled cab, blindfolded ... took bandage off my eyes when we entered the room. Rum lot, seen through tobacco smoke. Smell of lemon in whiskey. Somebody hit me on small of back with flat side of sword. Then I signed my name in red ink (they said it was blood). They all swore at Parnell; said I ought to be Chief Secretary.'[107]

One other noteworthy exchange took place between Russell and O'Shea before he was allowed to begin his journey to Spain. Apropos a suggestion made by John Morley that Parnell had been in regular, personal contact with P.J. Sheridan, the Captain insisted that he had not believed the claim at the time it was made. He then began skating on very thin ice indeed with an immediate caveat. He volunteered the information that 'certain things came to my knowledge at that time, which absolutely destroyed the good opinion I had hitherto held of Mr Parnell.'[108] Sensibly Russell did not attempt to ascertain what it was that O'Shea had discovered that was so prejudicial to his client. This reference and Webster's Eltham faux pas were the only occasions on which O'Shea's matrimonial difficulties broke close to the surface.

Russell had undoubtedly put O'Shea under considerable pressure. A number of unexplained names had been placed in the public domain, which would have indicated to O'Shea that Parnell was aware of some of his covert activities. O'Shea's usefulness to the *Times* had been somewhat neutralised when Russell had managed to get the witness to accept that 'I believe Mr Parnell to be absolutely free from any connivance with outrages.'[109] He had also admitted that, while he thought the *Times* facsimile signature to be genuine, he did not believe the letter itself to be so. But the Captain had successfully weathered most of what the distinguished advocate had thrown at him without doing any serious injustice to his hatred of Parnell. O'Shea left the witness box well-satisfied with his performance. Hinting to Chamberlain that a matrimonial upset had preoccupied him before he began his evidence, he pronounced himself victor in the bout with Sir Charles Russell.

'I went into the witness box yesterday under a very heavy load of anxiety owing to matters in themselves apart from Charges and Allegations. Once it came to fighting Russell, however, all went well and I had him down round after round. People here seem to think that my manner of putting the case will not be disadvantageous to you.' He then, almost flippantly, made the astonishing allegation that 'Campbell, Parnell's sec[retar]y, offered Mulqueeny a short time ago money to leave England and on being refused threatened him with assassination.'[110] O'Shea seemed to reserve some of his most startling claims for the ever-loyal Henry Campbell. Chamberlain, no doubt pleased that O'Shea had not sold the pass on any one of a number of issues, was suitably complimentary to a man already well pleased with himself. 'I need not tell you with how much interest I followed your evidence,' he wrote. 'You will perhaps be glad to know that I have had an account from a thoroughly trustworthy source & am assured that both the manner and the matter were excellent. This confirms the impression I derived from reading the *Times* report.'[111] A lot had been at stake for O'Shea and he would not have relished the association of his name with the likes of the infamous Patrick Casey, but now that the ordeal of cross-examination was over he could bask in the good opinion of his mentor and in his own self-satisfaction.[112]

United Ireland suggested that Chamberlain and O'Shea deserved each other. The Parnellite mouthpiece had long since ceased soft-pedalling in its approach to the Captain, '... who changes his masters like a cur dog, and bites today the hand that fed him yesterday. To pleasure the patron of today he is ready to pimp and spy to ruin the patron of yesterday. More degraded still, if that may be, is the character of the treacherous coward who, willing to wound and yet afraid to strike, employed so base a tool for so base an object. Now, at least, Mr. Chamberlain has fairly earned his title of "Judas".'[113]

EXPOSURE

In the context of the Special Commission O'Shea is a mere footnote. His initial significance, that of being the first witness of any centrality, dissipated as, one by one, the real principals gave their evidence. In between these occasional oases of political excitement was a desert of cultural and economic tedium. The cavalcade of *Times* witnesses who testified as to the effects of agrarian crime on themselves and their families offers an invaluable snapshot of the frequent brutality of life in rural Victorian Ireland, but it did little or nothing to incriminate the Irish Parliamentary Party hierarchy.

By the end of 1888, other than their tantalisingly brief appearance before O'Shea, the *Times* letters had still not seen the light of day. The suspicion grew that the often tiresome process of hearing evidence from policemen, unreliable informers (some of whom denied their depositions when they got into the witness box) and the genuinely traumatised and bitter was not merely prologue. Houston denied to O'Shea in late December that 'the evidence about the letters has been reserved owing to any doubts of its sufficiency', but rumours were rife that the *Times* was no longer confident of proving their validity. Knowledge of the paper's reliance on the word of Richard Pigott was becoming more widespread and was inspiring little confidence in the supporters of the *Times* case. O'Shea wrote to a newly remarried Chamberlain[114] just after Christmas that '... if, as I suppose, Pigott is a principal witness, he is likely to be easily attacked for there is little doubt he has done many things for money in his career as a patriot, and besides his constitution is much weakened by drink.'[115]

The exposure of Richard Pigott as the man responsible for forging the *Times* letters is a familiar tale. In brief, as already indicated, he had been identified early on in the process by the Parnellites as a suspect. This was in spite of Parnell's unwavering conviction that O'Shea was responsible.

Patrick Egan, now based in the USA, had become intrigued by the similarity of some of the phrases in the letters (some of which had, allegedly, been written by or addressed to him) to elements of the correspondence he had entered into with Pigott at the time of the purchase of his newspaper titles by the League. He had passed his suspicions on to the Parnellites and to Henry Labouchere, with whom they worked very closely during this period. In early December Egan had written to Labouchere that 'I hope you will be able to squeeze the truth out of Pigott in the way you say, as I should dislike terribly to see him profit in any way by his villainy. I do not believe there is a single thing in the suspicion against O'Shea ... The fellow is incapable of playing the role of heavy villain. I am quite convinced that the forgery part of the scheme was the sole work of Pigott.'[116] Labouchere had already made one attempt, in October 1888, to persuade, bully or cajole Pigott into admitting that he had forged the letters.

The evidence of Edward Caulfield Houston provided an illuminating preamble to the demolition of Pigott. The young journalist did his side no favours with his tale of furtive Parisian meetings, in the course of which he had purchased a bag of letters without establishing their provenance or the source of supply. It became clear to the onlookers that he had relied entirely on the bona fides of Pigott; that he had desperately wanted to believe, for his own political reasons, that the cache was genuine, but that he had sought to distance himself from his source by destroying their correspondence. The evidence of J.C. MacDonald, the *Times* General Manager, had been little more impressive. He made it apparent that the newspaper had spurned the sort of checks and balances that might have been expected before publishing material that was calculated to destroy the reputations and careers of a number of prominent and distinguished individuals. Then it was the turn of Richard Pigott.

When Sir Charles Russell rose to cross-examine Pigott on 21 February 1889 the courtroom was crowded. Pigott was a squat, bald man with a large, bushy, white beard; Robbins described him as 'a coarsely composed and rather cheapened Father Christmas'.[117] Russell had a number of elements in his favour. The first was the witness's correspondence with Archbishop Walsh in March 1887. The Archbishop had returned a number of Pigott's many letters on that occasion but, unbeknownst to the forger, had retained some and had passed these on to the Parnellites. Russell was therefore quickly able to catch Pigott out in a direct lie by getting him to deny that he had had any foreknowledge of the *Times* allegations. As soon as he had done so, the first of the Walsh letters had been produced. It was all downhill for the counterfeiter from that point onwards.

Russell had begun his cross-examination in curious fashion. Handing the witness a pad, he had requested him to write out a number of words; these included his own name, the words 'livelihood', likelihood', 'Patrick Egan' and 'proselytism'. Finally Pigott was asked to write the word 'hesitancy'. This he did. When the sheet was handed back to the defence team, Frank Lockwood was heard to whisper, 'We've got him'; the word 'hesitancy' had been spelt 'hesitency'. Russell, however, ignored the item at the time and carried on with his cross-examination. It was a clinical and devastating filleting of an increasingly confused and distressed witness. At times Pigott was so implausible and so obviously lying that the court, including the judges themselves, was reduced to helpless laughter. Russell played the witness like a matador. Pigott squirmed and sweated in the box. The *coup de grâce* came, in the richest of ironies, courtesy of Egan and Frank Hugh O'Donnell. Pigott's letters to the former had been characterised by a number of misspellings. A study of the new cache of *Times* letters revealed during *O'Donnell* v *Walter* had highlighted similar spelling mistakes. One of these was an idiosyncratic spelling of the word 'hesitancy'. It was pointed out to Pigott that he had spelt the word, when asked to do so at the outset of his testimony, in exactly the same fashion as an alleged letter to Egan included in the *Times* cache. Davitt, looking on as Pigott dug his own grave, commented 'this was a process of slaying the slain'.[118] The Commission adjourned on Friday afternoon with the forger utterly discredited. All that remained was for Russell to extract a confession from him the following week. His hope was then to coerce Pigott into implicating other, more prominent, individuals in his activities. He never got the opportunity. Over the weekend (after confessing his misdeeds to Labouchere and then retracting) Pigott escaped to Paris. From there he travelled to Spain. Either an attempt to cash a bogus cheque in a Madrid bank or an unwise telegram to a solicitor representing the *Times* revealed his whereabouts to the authorities, but when police attempted to arrest him he put a gun into his mouth and blew his brains out.[119]

The Commission continued, despite the fact that the *Times* was forced to withdraw the letters as bogus. Later Parnell successfully sued the newspaper for £5000. The Irish leader himself gave evidence two months after his vindication. In the interim he had been lionised by the Liberal establishment. His first appearance in the House of Commons after Pigott's humiliation and flight had provoked a standing ovation from his own supporters and those of Gladstone. The Liberal leader's daughter wrote in her diary that 'Parnell will be for the time as light an angel as he has been dark as a devil.'[120] A series of orchestrated events, including an unlikely public handshake with Earl Spencer, had cemented the alliance between the Liberals and Irish nationalists. Chamberlain was suitably tart and resentful in his assessment, written for the benefit of the exiled O'Shea, seething in Madrid:

> The effect has been to render the Parnellites exultant; but I think they are a little premature ... My own private opinion is that six months hence it will all be forgotten, and that no permanent impression will have been made either way. For the time, however, it is giving the friends of Home Rule a distinct advantage. It is extraordinary that the 'Times', which must have been fully warned of Pigott's character, did not take more pains to verify his statements before putting him into the box. They have been badly advised and have to pay a heavy penalty.[121]

On the day Chamberlain wrote to O'Shea he may have read the *Times* account of the evidence of a mutual acquaintance. If so, he made no reference to the event in his letter. The highly blurred George Mulqueeny had suddenly come into focus at the Special Commission the previous day.

He had the distinction, coveted or unenviable, of being the final witness put forward by the *Times*. For the first time we get a description of the mysterious clerk. 'He was a shortish, thick-set young man, with a bull-doggish, self-complacent, conceited, but not unintelligent expression.'[122] He had left Cork nine years before to work in London. It transpired that he had been subpoenaed by Lewis and Lewis in September and, like his own mentor, Captain O'Shea, had, a month later (in October 1888) been enlisted by the *Times* via a subpoena. Mulqueeny acknowledged in his direct evidence to the Attorney General that he was a member of the Irish Republican Brotherhood. He had also, for a time, been on the executive of the Irish National League of Great Britain and this had brought him into frequent contact with the League's secretary, Frank Byrne. Through Byrne he had also become acquainted with a man called P.J. Tynan, identified in 1883 as the enigmatic 'No 1', who, like Byrne, was a leading member of the Invincibles. The witness, to the delight of the *Times* side, testified to having seen Tynan in the League offices in London on a number of occasions. Mulqueeny, by his own admission, had been paid £1 by the *Times* for every day the Special Commission had been sitting.[123] The newspaper must have felt it was getting value for its money.

From his employer's point of view the crux of Mulqueeny's testimony concerned the sight he had been afforded, in a drawer in the National League London office, of the parcel of knives allegedly carried to Dublin by Frank Byrne's wife and used in the Phoenix Park murders. But, from O'Shea's perspective, of much greater significance was Mulqueeny's knowledge of the letter from Byrne to the League Executive, written from his Paris bolt-hole on 8 February 1883, which acknowledged receipt of a cheque for £100 from Parnell. The cheque had been requested of the Irish leader as the funds of the League in Britain were barely in the black at the end of 1882. Mulqueeny testified that Byrne had appropriated a portion of the funds and the money had been used to get him to safety in the USA. Mulqueeny was vague and forgetful when it came to questions about what exactly he had told O'Shea and what he might have done on his behalf. All he would accept was that, if the Captain had said his informant on the subject of the Byrne letter was Mulqueeny, then that was good enough for the man himself as, 'To my mind he is a thoroughly honourable gentleman'.[124] Implied in Asquith's cross-examination was Davitt's assumption that O'Shea had persuaded the Corkman to steal the letter and had then passed it on to the *Times*, which had published it in facsimile form as further damning evidence of Parnell's depravity.

The truth is probably more banal. Mulqueeny had told O'Shea that the Byrne 'acknowledgement' letter had been seized by the police. O'Shea testified that he had informed Chamberlain who had then questioned Harcourt on the subject. A search had revealed no sign of any such letter. Yet, just over two years later, the *Times* had the original.[125] There is no reason to doubt O'Shea's testimony, more particularly as, in December 1888, he reminded Chamberlain of the quest for the elusive letter and declared that '... I am told that Harcourt may have told you the truth when he said he knew nothing about the letter in question; it was in another department, or was being held, as it were, "officiously", at the time; but I have not pierced the mystery.'[126] Given the level of government support of the *Times* case, once the letter had been found, it was only a matter of time before it would find its way into the newspaper's files.

The Attorney General also asked Mulqueeny a number of questions about Henry Campbell. He was unable to tell Webster, from his own knowledge, that Campbell was a member of the IRB,[127] but the *Times* barrister hinted darkly that this was indeed the case. As regards O'Shea's allegation that Campbell had threatened to have Mulqueeny assassinated, that accusation had come in a letter to Chamberlain on 1 November 1888. This was a week after the *Times* had issued the Cork-born Fenian with a subpoena (probably at O'Shea's suggestion). If Campbell did threaten Mulqueeny, it could have been connected to fact that he was about to become a *Times* witness. It must also be borne in mind that the defendants had been first to issue Mulqueeny with a subpoena. This suggests that they were not overly concerned at what he might have to say against Parnell and were eager to explore his relationship with O'Shea. At the very end of his testimony (it was actually the final piece of *Times* evidence) Mulqueeny was asked about his only interview with Parnell. In reply he produced a letter from Campbell that had sought a meeting. The letter was dated 3 December 1888, more than a month after O'Shea had told Chamberlain about the alleged threat issued by Parnell's faithful secretary. Either the allegation was untrue, and no threat had been issued by Campbell, or Mulqueeny was not sufficiently intimidated to want to avoid a further encounter with Parnell's dogged sentinel.

DANGEROUS LIAISONS

It is not possible to come to any definitive conclusion about the extent of O'Shea's contact with the labyrinthine world of Fenians, spies, double agents and informers in the mid- to late 1880s. His only admission was a single visit to the Golden Lion in Wardour Street for a meeting with a group of well-disposed London Fenians. However it is unlikely that this was as far as it went. There is an interesting parallel between the Captain's dealings with Mulqueeny and his relationship with Chamberlain. Just as O'Shea provided Chamberlain's cordon sanitaire against contamination by Irish nationalist politics, Mulqueeny was O'Shea's buffer in his dealings with British and Continental Fenians. Just as the great English Radical could (and did) occasionally disavow O'Shea's actions and statements, the Captain could (and did) claim ignorance of activities conducted by Mulqueeny that were likely to have been at his instigation and for his benefit.

Although O'Shea was a noted and talented intriguer, he was a mere innocent abroad when he launched into the fractured and internecine hell that was Parisian Fenianism. The city appeared to have become an important continental base in the 1880s for Irish–American, Fenian and Clan na Gael dynamite and terrorist plots against the British state. Add to that treacherous cocktail a bewildering multiplicity of British double agents, agents provocateurs, informers and undercover policemen and neither Dante nor Milton would have had the vocabulary to do poetic justice to such an inferno. But outward appearances can be deceptive and this particular conspiratorial ferment flattered only to deceive. It was all an illusion fostered by bar stool revolutionaries, egged on by British agents and reported hysterically by both gullible and complicit English and Irish newspapers. Owen McGee, historian of the IRB, puts this illusory landscape into perspective when he writes, 'This new style of "Fenian fever" Tory propaganda in the British and Irish press was so prevalent that many contemporaries, as have some historians, believed that an Irish revolutionary movement existed in Paris during the 1880s. This was not the case.'[128] Hair-raising plots were hatched, which were never given expression outside of the fertile imaginations of their creators. Grand schemes were devised by *soi-disant* agitators who were often working for different branches of the British secret services or even for different spymasters within the same service. In the USA the republican movement had splintered into a number of antagonistic units warily eyeing each other. In Paris, as befitted the home of the great farceur, Feydeau, it was all more fiction than faction.

The Byzantine Paris republican scene was so circumscribed as to make ordinary decent conspiracy virtually impossible.[129] An indicator of its debased and treacherous nature was the fact that some of Davitt's knowledge of O'Shea's activities was founded on information coming from the militant republican, General Charles Carroll Tevis, who was secretly working for the British Foreign Office, and from Patrick Casey, who was equally compromised. Even more profoundly indicative of the inconsistency and impermanence of alliances in this covert world was the fact that Davitt's other principal source had once been the leading British spymaster in Ireland, Edward Jenkinson. The latter was partly motivated by his antagonism towards the man who had supplanted him in Irish counter-espionage activities in London, Robert Anderson. Anderson, as beloved of the Tories as Jenkinson had been of the Liberals, was, meanwhile, energetically collaborating with the *Times* by secretly contributing articles to its 'Parnellism and Crime' series. It was a world in which nothing was quite as it seemed.

O'Shea's activities, mediated by his proxy Mulqueeny, involved some element of direct or indirect contact with the likes of the Philadelphia-born John P. Hayes[130] (a Jenkinson informer), General Charles Carroll Tevis, and 'dynamitard' Patrick Casey (described by Davitt as 'in service',[131] meaning the British secret service). Casey was a fantasist who endlessly hatched unrealised plots with his brother Joseph. Russell's cross-examination of O'Shea, in which he made good use of interviews conducted by Davitt in Paris with Carroll Tevis (a relatively amiable conversation) and Hayes (conducted virtually at gunpoint), was an early indication to the *Times*–government side that the defendants were privy to information that would be profoundly embarrassing if it ever got into the public domain. This included bogus schemes (such as the infamous Jubilee Plot, designed to disrupt Queen Victoria's 50th anniversary celebrations) devised by spymasters and spies to mimic genuine terrorism. These had had the double intent of discrediting Irish nationalists of all hues and heightening demands for even higher levels of security.

In a small black notebook that he entitled, somewhat self deprecatingly, 'Notes by an Amateur Detective', Davitt recorded some of the investigative work he undertook on behalf of the defendants in the Special Commission. This was mainly conducted in Paris. Most of his efforts were directed against Pigott but, like Parnell, he believed that O'Shea was integrally involved in the ILPU–*Times* campaign to discredit the Irish leadership. He set out three primary goals in his notes to himself. The first was to 'Connect Pigott and Callan[132] with the others as accomplices or as instruments or dupes'. The 'others' in question included the cast of outrageous characters referred to above, such as the Caseys, Hayes, and Carroll Tevis. His second objective was to 'Connect some of the crowd with O'Shea and the disposal of the letters to the *Times*'.[133] The 'crowd' to which he referred was the motley gathering that enjoyed the hospitality of Peter Cowell in Wardour Street. This included Pigott, Callan and yet another agent provocateur, Captain Darnley Stewart Stephens (see below).

Davitt questioned Cowell and his daughter (Mrs Lynch) on more than one occasion. Although he extracted valuable information from them on a number of issues, he was unhappy with the responses he got on others. For example, he was unable to confirm his suspicion that O'Shea was an associate of the unsavoury conspirator Captain Stephens. He wrote in his amateur sleuth's notebook that 'Cowell denies that he knew O'Shea visited Stephens in Wardour Street ... says people could go up to S's room without he [C] observing them, as he was constantly engaged at the bar.' He was also frustrated by Cowell's reluctance to connect two of Parnell's undying enemies. 'Cannot (will not?) remember O'Shea meeting Callan at W. St.'[134]

One of Davitt's more garrulous (but not utterly reliable) sources was Patrick Casey, to whom he spoke in Paris on a number of occasions. It was Casey who had told Davitt about the visit of Mulqueeny on O'Shea's behalf in 1885, which had also been put to him under cross-examination by Russell. The information was passed on during an interview that took place between the two men over a period of two days. This had happened a fortnight or so before O'Shea's Special Commission evidence. Mulqueeny had been sent to Paris to 'warn C[asey] against H'.[135] Although Davitt, in his notes, often abbreviates the name of Edward Caulfield Houston as 'H', in this instance the initial probably refers to the sham republican and Jenkinson double agent, John Patrick Hayes. Davitt is not specific as to why Casey would need to be warned about Hayes (the two had previously collaborated amicably) and whether the warning was coming from Mulqueeny himself, from O'Shea, or, just as likely, from a London-based spymaster. Davitt had also recorded Casey's version of Mulqueeny's other purpose. 'Mul[queeny] said O'S[hea] had sent him and that he (O'S) had suffered much at hands of P[arnell] partly for his devotion to cause of extremists. Praised O'Shea as one of the 'right sort' – family of patriots etc. ...'Mulqueeny had written to Casey in 1885 seeking his signature on the Wardour Street memorial. When the two men met, Casey had declined to sign. He told Davitt that he himself had never met O'Shea – Mulqueeny, the Sorcerer's apprentice, had acted as intermediary.[136]

Davitt also spoke to General Carroll Tevis in Paris. The Irish–American described a visit he had made to London at the instigation of Hayes. Mulqueeny had attended one meeting, which formed part of that visit. In the course of conversation an argument had broken out and Hayes had threatened to shoot Mulqueeny. The former American General offered in mitigation that at least the volatile Hayes had not produced a revolver in tandem with his threat. The encounter has an air of the surreal to it, given that all three men, albeit probably unbeknownst to each other, were in the employ of various counter-intelligence agencies of the British administration. Not surprisingly, according to Carroll Tevis the entire trip had been unproductive. Davitt noted that '... H[ayes] tried to get parties in London to come to see Gen, but few of any note came.'[137] By his own admission one of those who did was Captain O'Shea.

Davitt's suspicions do not constitute proof that O'Shea was deeply involved in the shadowy and unreal London–Paris axis of conspiracy, counter-intelligence and disinformation, whose members were often *soi-disant* Fenians actually working for the British security apparatus. But the 'Amateur Detective' certainly saw the imprint of the Captain in some of the black propaganda and illegality that emanated from this murky under-world.[138] In an entry in his highly informative notebook he locates O'Shea's activities in a chain of events which began with the exportation of the knives used in the Phoenix Park murders and culminated in the Pigott forgeries. He wrote that 'Mulq[ueeny]'s evidence would tend to estab[lish] the incident of the brown paper parcel – knives – and the account of same by M[ulqueeny] to O'Shea as one of the primary sources of Parnellism and Crime. O'Shea must have related this and possibly the £100 letter (which Mulq may have stolen from Palace Chambers) to Blennerhasset,[139] Chamberlain, Buckle and others. Houston would therefore be likely to know of these facts & Pigott probably got them from Houston & shaped some of his forgeries accordingly.'[140] On the basis of this theory it was O'Shea's connections with Fenianism, in this instance in the shape of Mulqueeny, which had helped launch the *Times* on the road to the Special Commission.

After the disintegration of Pigott, Russell proclaimed loudly in Probate Court No 1 that '... we deliberately say that behind Houston and Pigott there is a foul conspiracy'.[141] Parnell was still convinced, even after the admissions of a forger whose story kept changing depending on the audience and the incentive, that O'Shea was behind the forgeries. As Frank Callanan puts it in his biography of Tim Healy, Russell was 'somewhat constrained in his development of the charge of "foul conspiracy", by reason of the central role ascribed by his client to W.H. O'Shea in the conspiracy.'[142] Davitt maintained that an ad hoc committee of three government ministers was 'in active league with Houston and the Loyal and Patriotic Union'.[143] He only named one of its members, Home Secretary Henry Matthews, a former MP for the Dungarvan constituency. It was hoped by the defendants to go on the offensive after the collapse of the 'letters' module of the *Times* case and prove collusion between the newspaper, the government and the Irish Unionists by forcing discovery of documents belonging to the Irish Loyal and Patriotic Union. But the Commission justices ruled against them and, shortly thereafter, Russell and his co-counsel withdrew from the proceedings. It had been hoped to establish, for example, that government money had been made available to the ILPU to fund Houston in his efforts to discredit Parnell and the Irish party. It was not until 1910, after Sir Robert Anderson had revealed his role in writing some of the original *Times* articles, that the former government official whose job it was to collate the material being supplied by Dublin Castle to the newspaper, William Henry Joyce, revealed the precise level of collaboration that had taken place.

Meanwhile Edward Caulfield Houston appeared unabashed and unruffled by the perfect storm that had been unleashed around his young head in the wake of the Pigott debacle. A letter to O'Shea, describing his deceased partner in intrigue as a 'poor wretch', amply demonstrated his lack of penitence:

> We are in a perfect muddle over here, and I have the honor [*sic*] and glory of being one of the best abused men in town ... My idea is that the first batch were genuine, and that the facsimile letter wh[ich] was amongst them was a bona fide document.[144] But of course the truth will never be known & whatever chance existed of such a desirable condition of things was entirely removed by the panic stricken lawyers withdrawing the whole of the documents. There have been many lamentable features connected with the case but this has been worst of all.[145]

It was to become part of the mythology of the *Times* protagonists that Pigott had not forged all of the letters. Ironically their principal antagonist, by then totally exonerated, would have been happy to agree with them, but for his own highly personal reasons.

Could Parnell have been right? Did O'Shea have some involvement with the Piggott forgeries? According to one of his early biographers, Parnell '... prowled about London in search of evidence which could convict him.'[146] He is even said to have disguised himself and visited Wardour Street in an attempt to identify O'Shea as a party to the intrigues taking place there. Davitt includes Piggott in the Golden Lion clientele. That is not to suggest that the Captain and the counterfeiter actually met there, but O'Shea may well have been aware of the ILPU search for documentation to discredit Parnell. He was certainly eager to locate the Frank Byrne letter once Mulqueeny had told him of its existence. He was also interested in the suggestion that the likes of Carroll Tevis, John P. Hayes[147] or Patrick Casey might have had letters in their possession incriminating Parnell. One of the implications in Russell's questioning of O'Shea was that he had despatched Mulqueeny to Paris on more than one occasion to talk to Casey. Although the bibulous and imaginative Casey 'knew nothing about Irish revolutionary affairs except rumours',[148] his name had been mentioned publicly and privately as a 'notorious dynamitard'. Is it likely that O'Shea would have wanted the signature of a man with such a reputation on a testimonial, even a Fenian one? Is it not more plausible to suggest that O'Shea had got wind of the fact that Casey, an associate of Frank Byrne, might be in a position to discredit Parnell and that was a reason for Mulqueeny's diplomatic mission(s) to Paris?[149]

Bizarrely, the men coyly described by O'Shea in Probate Court No 1 as 'members of the old Nationalist party'[150] were not the only denizens of Peter Cowell's intriguing establishment in Wardour Street. Cowell appears to have also welcomed Unionists into his all-embracing establishment. The Golden Lion had also been frequented, for a time at least, by a man code-named by Michael Davitt 'Major Yellow'. The description offered, that 'Yellow had been a British officer [and] was a native of Ireland',[151] is close enough to O'Shea himself to make one wonder at first. But 'Major Yellow' was, in fact, Captain Darnley Stewart Stephens, as is clear from Davitt's invaluable notebooks. He was a former employee of Edward Jenkinson and was yet another agent provocateur. He had been employed to tempt Casey into revolutionary action but had failed and had later been dismissed by Jenkinson for drunkenness. He re-emerged at the centre of an anti-Parnellite propaganda group based in Wardour Street, which, in 1886, produced a pamphlet called 'The Repeal of the Union Conspiracy; or Mr Parnell, MP, and the IRB'. According to Davitt, 'It was compiled chiefly from the drunken ravings of Kasey [sic] and other Paris "dynamiters", the "revelations" of the spy Hayes, Pigott's pamphlet, "Parnellism

Exposed",[152][*sic*] and the statements of Captain O'Shea's friend, George Mulqueeny.'[153] Any suggestion that O'Shea was intimately involved in plots to discredit Parnell, either in collaboration with Fenians, or the *Times*, or both, is, of course, pure surmise. But there is little doubt that he was well connected and familiar with a number of people involved in the world of espionage or undercover police work. Another of those was a man named by Michael Davitt as 'Sinclair'. Davitt describes him as 'a handsome man in the prime of life with light hair, blue eyes, strong resolute face, lightish mustache, military bearing and no beard'.[154] His real name was Matthew O'Brien and he was a highly colourful, resourceful and ruthless character. O'Shea knew of him as the grandson of a well-known solicitor with land in Clare. O'Brien had 'bumped into' Chamberlain on board an Atlantic steamer around the time of the latter's wedding in the USA in late 1888. O'Brien was able to tell Chamberlain during that encounter that Richard Pigott had already confessed to Labouchere in mid October 1888 that it was he who had forged the *Times* letters. This impressive intelligence on the part of O'Brien was owing to the fact that, a month before, O'Brien/'Sinclair' himself, while working for the Parnellites, had managed to coax Pigott over to London. There he had been confronted by Labouchere and Parnell and had agreed to confess to the forgeries on receipt of £1000. But before he delivered on his promise he had recanted.

In response to a letter from Chamberlain recounting this extraordinary conversation, O'Shea's assessment of O'Brien was shrewd.[155] 'He has passed under many names', warned the Captain, 'and is as great a scoundrel as ever crossed the Atlantic.'[156] 'Sinclair' had been recommended by Patrick Egan to perform investigative work for the defence during the Special Commission. However, as it transpired, he was also being paid by the *Times* and his loyalty was to the newspaper. O'Brien was first on the scene at Pigott's house in Sandycove Avenue after the latter's disappearance in February 1889. When Davitt got there 24 hours later most of the potentially embarrassing documentation in the house had been removed.

It is impossible to tell exactly how far O'Shea actually penetrated the jungle of what was the neurotic and duplicitous wing of militant Fenianism. But, on the evidence of Davitt's detective work, he certainly knew more than he admitted to the Special Commission. Was he, for example, privy to the *Times* attempts to persuade the former Fenian, Land League organiser and self-confessed Invincible P.J. Sheridan, to leave his Colorado ranch and testify for the newspaper in exchange for the sum of £20,000? This was something that Parnell might have had far more reason to fear than the forgeries of Piggott or even the potential revelation by

O'Shea of his affair with Katharine. As Patrick Maume has shown, there is evidence that Parnell, in the aftermath of the Kilmainham Treaty, allowed himself to be sworn into the IRB by Sheridan.[157] His motive might have been to convince Sheridan that the Treaty was a mere change of tactics, but that the extremist strategy of the previous two years was still in place. Maume's theory is supported by a note in the Davitt papers from Matthew O'Brien, alias 'Sinclair'. When the defence became aware that the *Times* was negotiating with Sheridan, Parnell demanded that a message be passed on to Patrick Egan in Nebraska to the effect that Sheridan was to be prevented 'at all cost and risk' from testifying for the newspaper. O'Brien claims that Parnell intended for Sheridan to be killed if he attempted to travel to London.[158]

*

Conspiracy theorists tend not to believe in coincidence. In which case there is much for them to chew over in one of the most extraordinary coincidences in the life of William O'Shea. In his evidence to the Special Commission he had insisted that, although he was aware of the existence of Richard Pigott, 'To the best of my belief I have never seen him. I certainly do not know him.'[159] A few days later he departed for Madrid for a lengthy period.[160] In the wake of Pigott's flight from London in late February 1889 he had travelled first to Paris. From there he had made a two-day journey to Madrid, arriving on 28 February. O'Shea takes up the story in a letter to Chamberlain written in early March:

> About 7 p.m. on Thursday week I saw a man, accompanied by another with the superscription 'Intérprete, Fonda de Embajadores', enter the Café Ingles in the Calle de Seville. Having seen portraits of Pigott, and read descriptions of his appearance in newspapers, I observed the former, who called for a bottle of beer and an English newspaper. I suppose the interpreter took him to the café in question because it is the only one (I think) where an English paper is taken in. I was soon convinced that the stranger was Pigott: he quartered the paper ... his hand trembled; then he looked around the café through an eyeglass, rose suddenly, touched the interpreter on the shoulder, and left hurriedly. I mentioned the matter to the President of the Chamber and other friends whom I met in the course of the evening, and hearing of the suicide a few minutes after it occurred the next day, I had no doubt of the identity. I am sorry the Attorney General

had not the opportunity of examining Pigott, although judging by the wretched manner he has conducted the case I am not sure he would have made much out of him. Still, Labouchere's conduct has been very suspicious and something might have 'transpired' as reporters say.[161]

Although disposed to comment on the widespread suspicion prevailing at the time that Labouchere had, by dint of bribing Pigott, provided him with the money to facilitate his flight, O'Shea makes no comment whatever on the astonishing nature of the happenstance that placed him in the same location as the most sought after fugitive in Europe; a man who now stood accused of the crime of which O'Shea himself had been suspected. This chance meeting begs many questions, but one will suffice to cast some doubt over O'Shea's version of events. If he was so convinced he had just seen a notorious forger who was being pursued by the British authorities, why did he not immediately report the matter to the Spanish police? The letter has an air of *ex post facto* justification about it, as if it was written to cover the eventuality that a meeting between O'Shea and Pigott had been witnessed by a third party. However, it is unlikely that O'Shea would have agreed to such a rendezvous in a well-known Madrid watering hole frequented by British expatriates. Nonetheless we are still left with the most basic question of all. Why did Pigott choose Madrid as his destination in the first place?

By the time Pigott showed up in Madrid, one thing would have been abundantly clear to the Captain. Parnell had slipped his bonds. The *Times* had badly missed its intended target. Not only was Parnell free, but he was bathing in the purifying light of the vindicated. Under cross-examination the Captain had been asked by Russell, 'Have you said you would be revenged on Mr Parnell?' O'Shea refused to swear that he had never uttered such words and then added, gratuitously, 'I have never been revenged on him ...'[162] Now, it appeared, the *Times* was not going to be the channel of his vengeance. The 'outraged valet of politics'[163] would have to take on Parnell himself. The primary impediment to such an enterprise was that he was in not in a viable position to do so.

But his principal obstacle was removed when Mrs Benjamin Wood died in Eltham on 19 May 1889, aged 96.

CHAPTER 13

Divorce

There are times when the insignificance of the accuser is lost in the ingratitude of the accusation.

'Stonewall' Jackson

It was perfectly well known that the O'Sheas were practically separated before Parnell came on the scene, but any weapon is good enough to beat a dog with ...

Frank Harris, *My Life and Loves*

THE MADNESS OF AUNT BEN

The Victorian era saw an exponential expansion of the public arena, that area of collectivity where people share elements of their lives and leisure, where the private becomes public and the exclusive becomes communal. This was, in large part, due to the reduction in the cost of national and local newspapers in an era of greatly increased literacy. It was an age in which inexpensive public relations (otherwise known as cheap publicity) became possible; this was just as dangerous and double-edged a phenomenon to those who profited from it then as it is at the dawn of the 21ˢᵗ century. One of the first beneficiaries of these new and expansive opportunities for publicity was the extraordinary French acrobat Jean Francois Gravelet, better known as Blondin. His almost incredible performances on a high wire stretched across the iconic Niagara Falls became legendary, thanks to the proliferation of American newspapers eager to create 'celebrities' and glorify spectacle. Blondin's larger than life exploits, which included carrying his genuinely petrified manager on his shoulders across the Falls on a rope two inches wide, provided the popular press of the USA and Europe with an heroic figure who managed to surpass himself with each new daring feat.[1]

He also provides us with an interesting metaphor for the career of his fellow Victorian, Charles Stewart Parnell. Like Blondin, the Irish leader managed to keep his balance while performing previously unbelievable feats of derring-do on the political high wire. Like Blondin, he had managed the seemingly impossible task of carrying his party on his back as he stepped gingerly across a narrow rope suspended over a torrent which had the potential to sweep him, and them, to political oblivion were he to stumble.[2] Unlike Blondin, however, the Irish political *funambule* was not allowed to die in a peaceful retirement having achieved everything for which even the most exceptional of individuals could have devoutly wished. The Captain successfully saw to that.

The details of the O'Shea divorce proceedings have been explored in many narratives, but there are still a number of unanswered questions surrounding aspects of the case. One of the great mysteries is why the defence was so disastrously mismanaged. Comparisons between the two men are normally odious, but where their high-profile involvements with the courts are concerned there are many regrettable similarities in the histories of Frank Hugh O'Donnell as plaintiff and Charles Stewart Parnell as defendant. In light of contradictory versions of events leading up to the divorce, there will never be a definitive answer to the question. But there can be few arguments about the consequences for Parnell of the absence of any detailed inquisition of the half-truths and special pleading which characterised William O'Shea's unchallenged submissions to the divorce court.

Neither will we ever know the truth of Parnell's allegation that the action taken by O'Shea was simply a continuation of the ILPU/Times v *Parnell* war by other means. The court docket may have read *O'Shea* v *O'Shea and Parnell (Steele intervening)*, but most Irish nationalists (in advance of hearing the evidence) assumed that the real struggle was that of *Parnell* v *Walter and Salisbury (Chamberlain intervening)*. There are many hints that it was Chamberlain who screwed O'Shea's courage to the sticking place as he was pressurised to abandon his action.

*

The death of Aunt Ben liberated Parnell and Katharine from imprisonment without trial at Eltham. In the absence of the need to tend to her
dying aunt, Katharine was in a position to let out Wonersh Lodge (in
whose vicinity Parnell was far too familiar a figure) and move permanently
with her children to Brighton. There, in two rented houses in Walsingham
Terrace, Parnell would become an equally well-known figure. The couple
made little effort to disguise the fact that they were living together. Largely
missing from this domestic idyll was the increasingly recalcitrant Gerard
O'Shea. He had done his Army entrance exams in late 1888 (the reason for
O'Shea's return from Madrid a month after his Special Commission
evidence) and was no longer permanently resident with his mother.

But the death of Aunt Ben also liberated O'Shea. There could no longer
be any financial ramifications resulting from untoward publicity. Indeed
for O'Shea the passing of Mrs Benjamin Wood finally closed off the possibility of any benefit accruing from her will. Her fortune, left entirely to her
favourite niece, was carefully bequeathed (in a new will of March 1888)
outside of the terms of his marriage settlement. While his children stood to
gain, assuming any of the legacy remained intact upon the death of his wife,
he could not touch a single penny himself. There is little doubt that the
spectacular failure of the *Times* to engineer the political annihilation of
Parnell and the removal of Aunt Ben from the restraining equation emboldened the Captain to take the step he had seemed ready to take in 1887.

The prologue to the divorce petition of 24 December 1889 began while
Mrs Benjamin Wood was still alive and was founded in an attempt by
Katharine's siblings, Charles Page Wood, his brother Evelyn, and their
surviving sisters, to have Aunt Ben ruled *non compos mentis* in the wake
of her testamentary generosity to their sister. Around the time of the
writing of an 1887 will, there had been much jostling for position and a
sudden renewal of interest by the Woods in their aged aunt. It was not the
kind of concern that pleased Aunt Ben however. She accused Charles and
Evelyn Wood, in particular, of attempting 'to deprive her of her right to
manage her own affairs'.[3] Katharine could not prevent the unwelcome
visitations of her brothers, but spent the duration of their stay seething
downstairs with nothing but her own agenda for company, while they
pursued their own upstairs in their aunt's bedroom. After one visit,
Charles Page Wood had noted that 'Katie looked black as thunder,
evidently hated my coming. Aunt wished me to stay to lunch and cheered
up so much that she offered to drive me to the station altho' she had not
left the house for 10 days. She took me to Bl[ac]kheath and begged me to
come again to see her.'[4] As one can imagine, such an outcome would not
have been calculated to improve Katharine's temper.

These preliminary sorties, in response to the April 1887 will, meta-morphosed into a full-scale petition to the Courts of Lunacy after the confirmation of Aunt Ben's intention to leave everything to Katharine in March 1888. In her desperation to prove that her aunt was mentally competent, Katharine exhibited once again that profound sense of enti-tlement that characterised many of her actions. She sought the assistance of no less a personage than the Prime Minister himself. Katharine had engaged the services of Gladstone's personal physician, Sir Andrew Clark, to examine Mrs Wood. He pronounced her sane and competent after an examination in April 1888. He was, however, slower to commit his opinion to paper than the impatient Katharine desired, and she wrote to Gladstone asking the Prime Minister's assistance to expedite the produc-tion of the official report. She even prevailed on Parnell to write to Gladstone stressing the urgency of the matter. Her persistence (not to mention sheer effrontery) achieved results and she had her positive medical assessment of Aunt Ben by 20 April. The eminent physician found the nonagenarian to be 'attentive, capable of apprehension and reflection and in reply coherent and logical ...'[5]

In response the Wood family deposed another niece of Mrs. Wood, Anne Courage, wife of the brewer, Robert. As a disinterested yet concerned relative who did not stand to benefit from the will, there was some prospect that she would be viewed by the court as an honest broker. She visited her aunt on 25 April, accompanied by her husband, and testified that, 'I found it most difficult to speak to her as she understood nothing of the present day and as regards the past I could not get her to remember even her own family. She asked me who I was and I had to tell her over and over again ...' According to Anne Courage her Aunt claimed that her nephews Charles and Evelyn were dead. She concluded that, 'My said aunt did not refer in any way to the proceedings in this matter. I do not believe that she understands anything about them in fact her memory is most defective. She is quite childish and amuses herself with her own thoughts which ramble wonderfully and she is totally incapable of managing her own affairs or of understanding them.'[6]

But it was the evidence of the professional that proved crucial. Clark's report was preferred by the court to that of Anne Courage. The lunacy suit ended in triumph for Katharine, but only postponed, *post mortem*, the resolution of the Wood family testamentary dispute. The will[7] was disputed by Katharine's siblings on the basis that she had exercised undue influence on their aunt, thereby depriving them of their rightful shares of the Wood inheritance.

THE BRUISED REED

As we have seen, the day after he testified to the *Times* Commission O'Shea had written to Chamberlain hinting that something other than 'Charges and Allegations' had been on his mind as he had entered the witness box. Two days later (3 November) he confided in the Liberal Unionist the private matter, which had so troubled him that it had over-shadowed even that vital and controversial evidence. '... the anxiety I felt was occasioned by the fact that Mrs O'Shea was under a written engage-ment not to communicate directly or indirectly with Mr Parnell, and the latter under a written order not to do so with Mrs O'Shea. I daresay a great many people have some notion of the state of affairs, but I am most anxious for my children's sake that nothing about it should be actually published because a very large fortune for them may depend upon its not coming into print.'[8] Chamberlain's response to this neat encapsulation of O'Shea's dilemma, written while on honeymoon in Paris, was belated, neutral and non-committal. It also tacitly acknowledges that he had an awareness of O'Shea's marital problems in advance of being informed by the husband himself. 'I sympathise with you in your domestic anxieties which must have added very much to the wear and tear of the last few months,' he declared, 'I have felt that I could not say a word to you on the subject until you spoke to me, but I have appreciated the strain to which you have been subjected.'[9]

Twelve months later much had changed. The bomb primed by the *Times* had failed to detonate under Parnell, and Aunt Ben no longer wielded a censorious sword, thus enabling O'Shea to detach himself from the *ménage à trois*. When the Captain sought to attach himself and his children (as an intervener) to the Wood family probate case[10] he had something of interest to the Field Marshal and the other relatives of Katharine O'Shea. This was no less than the mouth-watering prospect of a divorce case that would establish that his wife had concealed the truth about her affair with Parnell from Mrs Benjamin Wood in order to safeguard her hold over her aunt's inheritance.

Before taking any steps on the divorce issue, however, he first consulted the oracle of Highbury. Enclosing a handwritten copy of the *Pall Mall Gazette* piece of 24 May 1886 on Parnell's 'suburban retreat', he outlined the details of the *Driekaiserbund* into which he had entered with the Wood brothers in order to deprive his wife of the totality of Aunt Ben's fortune. He claimed, in relation to the Wood siblings, male and female, '... that I possess their affection, esteem and sympathy in a very marked degree.' No doubt of greater interest to Chamberlain was the ominous reference to his marital, rather than his testamentary, difficulties. The

Captain's phrasing makes it clear that he and Chamberlain had already discussed the possibility of divorce.

'Now to revert to the other business,' he began. 'Owing to some recent circumstances it is under consideration whether some strong action should not be taken by me, and I am anxious that you (and a few others) should be rightly informed. One of the principal difficulties in my way lies in the necessity, in case of legal proceedings, of putting my son (who is devoted to me) in the witness box against his mother.'[11] In addition to the copy of the *Gazette* piece, he also enclosed Katharine and Parnell's responses to that article as well as his wife's letter to Gerard O'Shea agreeing to forego further contact with the Irish leader.

Whatever the truth about the previous state of his knowledge, Chamberlain was certainly fully informed now. His reply is interesting. 'I am sincerely sorry that you should have such just cause of anxiety and trouble,' Chamberlain sympathised. He then added, 'I have never listened to scandalous reports affecting my friends & in your case I have heard nothing & know nothing beyond what you have told me.'[12] This assertion is rather difficult to accept given his membership of the Cabinet in 1882[13] and the information he had received from Labouchere. It also directly contradicts the line in his letter of 5 December 1888, quoted above, where he makes it clear that he was aware of the rumours surrounding O'Shea's marriage ('I have felt that I could not say a word to you on the subject until you spoke to me ...'), but natural delicacy prevented him from broaching the subject.

An unanswerable question surrounds the extent to which Chamberlain was involved, along with Tories and other Unionists, in a 'conspiracy' to cajole and occasionally jostle O'Shea towards the divorce court in order to destroy the career of Parnell. Henry Harrison quotes the above letter in his *apologia* written in 1931, *Parnell Vindicated*, and insists that some of the correspondence at around this time between the two men was for 'show' purposes only, designed to vindicate the Captain's stance that he had only recently confirmed his wife's long-standing adultery. O'Shea told Chamberlain in the 13 October letter that he had found out on 13 June 1887 that the *Gazette* story was 'true', and that Parnell was living with Katharine at the time of the accident. Harrison suggested that the correspondence had also been manufactured to imply that Chamberlain had been blissfully ignorant of the entire affair until a matter of weeks before O'Shea filed for divorce. The discrepancy between Chamberlain's response to the December 1888 letter and that of October 1889 proves nothing, but suggests that Harrison might be correct. Of course a 'show' letter on its own does not a conspiracy make.

A claim by the normally reliable *Birmingham Post* correspondent Alfred Robbins, however, points towards some level of foreknowledge on the part of Chamberlain's allies that a move against Parnell was imminent. Robbins was approached in September 1889 by someone he describes as 'on the inside of the Liberal Unionist machine' and asked whether Parnell would be ruined by a divorce, O'Shea 'being believed to be willing to take proceedings'. Robbins advised against the use of 'so very bruised a reed as O'Shea' to highlight a relationship that was already common knowledge.[14]

The covert world was certainly taking an interest in the divorce. Sir Robert Anderson, Assistant Commissioner of the Metropolitan Police, compiler (though as yet unidentified) of some of the 'Parnellism and Crime' articles, and the man who had offered Beach/Le Caron to the *Times*, was getting reports from the CID of the surveillance of Parnell's Tresilian Road rental house where he was spending time with Katharine. Freelance spy Nicholas Gosselin, a former Jenkinson loyalist now working for Balfour, reported to his master that O'Shea, having filed for divorce, 'was in a great state of terror' and might not be prepared to proceed. He suggested that, even if the Captain were to prove unreliable, there was still ample evidence of Parnell's adulterous activities that could be used to discredit the Irish leader.[15] This suggests that the ruling Conservative Unionist political élite, in whose interest it was to see Parnell brought down, was aware that O'Shea might prove infirm of purpose. This possibility, in addition to the likelihood that he might be bought off, may have prompted members of that Tory establishment to counter-bribe or threaten him into following through on his divorce petition. In a self-pitying letter to Chamberlain in the wake of the trial, O'Shea had complained that 'Nobody except myself knows what a fight it was or the influences, religious, social and pecuniary, that were brought to bear in the hope of "squaring" me.'[16]

There are hints that O'Shea feared a nationalist 'conspiracy' *against* himself, which had less benign intentions than bribery. There is a possibility that a clear and direct challenge to the political career of Parnell may well have turned many an Irish nationalist 'fancy' to thoughts of violence. In August 1890 O'Shea was hearing footsteps. His paranoia was based on a suspicion that Parnell had elements at his disposal that could rid him of a turbulent husband. He told Chamberlain, 'Information has been obtained that a conspiracy is at work ... "for the purpose of effecting my ruin". It has not yet been ascertained whether the "ruin" is to be moral, material or physical. I am told that Messrs Pat Egan, Fitzgerald and Michael Davitt direct the matter.'[17] Assuming the 'Fitzgerald' in question was Patrick Neville Fitzgerald, the Fenian organiser must have been regretting profoundly the assistance offered to O'Shea at the time of the Galway by-election in 1886. O'Shea was convinced that a man called John Louden, an Irish barrister and former Land Leaguer, was one of the leaders of this cabal.

Louden had fallen out with the Land League in 1881 and, on the strength of that mutual animosity, had been recruited and paid handsomely by the *Times* to damage his erstwhile allies at the Special Commission.[18] Having benefited from the newspaper's largesse, he had then reneged on the deal, the *Times* discovering that he '... was on the most intimate terms with, and constantly in the society of, Mr Davitt.'[19] O'Shea was perhaps closer to the truth than even he imagined. An examination of the papers of the distinguished 'amateur detective' offers evidence that not only was the Captain correct, but that Davitt himself was involved in an effort to secure documentary evidence that would damage the case against Parnell and Katharine. A week before the divorce trial Louden wrote to Davitt from Mayo, declaring that 'I do not intend to visit London for a long time. I did all I could in the matter to which you refer as far as my funds would allow me. To obtain proofs – to make a complete crushing case – large sums were necessary which I could not obtain. In a case of the sort one cannot get proof – documents etc. – without money. Yet those concerned would not spend a shilling. Anyhow, enough has been done to spoil the game of the ex-Hussar.'[20] There is no indication of who exactly the thrifty 'those concerned' were. It could have been concerned supporters of Parnell and Katharine, their legal representatives, or the couple themselves.

While he was under observation, O'Shea's faithful and resourceful sentinel, James Thomson (see below p. 342), was taking his employer's personal security very seriously indeed. 'I am watched by gangs of most disreputable looking men and women on whom some person or persons must be spending a good deal of money. Thomson continues anxious as to my personal safety and has made me promise never to go anywhere on foot after dark.'[21]

Aside altogether from the potential for violent repercussions, the edgy Captain would also have had sound financial reasons for abandoning his suit. In pure investment terms the divorce petition was a serious financial risk. A positive result for O'Shea might be turned to his advantage in the probate action. Proof of connivance on his part and the crumbling of his case would result in major costs. He calculated himself, in February 1891, that his various lawsuits, including the divorce, a number of libel/contempt actions, and the ongoing probate case, had cost him £5,300 to that point. He told Chamberlain that he had 'adopted the system of paying my way pretty regularly as I went along'. He declared proudly, and with suspicious ostentation, that this had been achieved with considerable difficulty 'but without help from anybody'.[22] He then proceeded to seek a loan of between £400 and £800 from Chamberlain to tide him over a short-term crisis in order to avoid being 'at the mercy of a very dangerous enemy of mine'. Either in deference to Chamberlain's potential political reservations, or (as Henry Harrison might contend) in the expectation of some possible future examination of his correspondence, the Captain pointed out that 'As this matter has nothing whatever to do with costs or with lawsuits, no one could say that there was a political motive attached to the transaction.'[23]

O'Shea's tone suggests that he feels he has been left to bear an excessive financial burden by the Unionist establishment and deserves to have some of his costs defrayed. Chamberlain did advance a loan[24] of £400, but conspiracy theorists should bear in mind that this was done months *after* the divorce had been granted. He did so despite financial difficulties of his own at the time and on the basis of absolute confidentiality. He was aware of the complexion that could be put on such a transaction by his enemies. In expressing his profound gratitude, O'Shea added conspiratorially, 'It will give us an opportunity of observing whether our enemies have a supernatural detective force at their disposal because, as you say, they seem to find everything out. But no one less acute than the Devil himself ought to be able to unravel a *secret-a-deux*.'[25] The thrust of the correspondence suggests (Harrisonian allegations of double-talk notwithstanding) that if Chamberlain was involved in an anti-Parnellite plot with O'Shea as an agent provocateur he was not making any contribution to the finances of the putative cabal.

However, some of Chamberlain's biographers, while offering no positive proof, suggest that he was indeed complicit in some form of Unionist–Tory divorce conspiracy. Peter Marsh says the divorce was 'a bomb which he had encouraged Captain O'Shea to ignite under Parnell', adding that 'the prospect was sweet enough for Chamberlain to swallow his distaste at the renewal of an embarrassing relationship.'[26] Richard Jay expresses the belief that 'Most historians would now agree that O'Shea's change of heart towards an affair that he had not only condoned but also benefited from politically for years was rooted in political rather than private motives. As he noted to Chamberlain, "He who smashes Parnell smashes Parnellism."'[27] Jay suggests that O'Shea's hints that he was coming under financial pressure to settle (and as we shall see they were heavy and frequent) meant that 'Countering the Parnellite offers was perhaps practical help that Unionists might have offered ...' It is important to emphasise, however, that there is no documentary evidence of any 'conspiracy' to keep O'Shea's feet to the fire. Nor would any but the most optimistic expect there to be.

Had Chamberlain been involved in any such conspiracy his enthusiasm must have waned with the entry of counter-charges by the defendants to the effect that O'Shea had colluded in the adultery. The Liberal Unionist's own knowledge of the affair could have led him to the conclusion that such a charge might well be proven. In that eventuality collateral damage would certainly be inflicted on anyone in proximity to O'Shea. Chamberlain would also have realised that an allegation of connivance on the part of the defendants amounted to an admission of adultery on their part. In which case the objective of any putative conspiracy had been achieved and awaited only the confirmation of the divorce court.

A commentator as knowledgeable as T.W. Moody saw a pattern in the workings of Chamberlain. In his essay on the Galway election he speculates that the Radical leader's intervention to secure an Irish seat for O'Shea in 1886 was of a piece with this pattern. 'It may well be that for Chamberlain the Galway affair was the preliminary move in an offensive that was to culminate, after the fiasco of the Special Commission, in the fatal divorce court proceedings of November 1889.'[28] In his introduction to Harrison's *Parnell, Joseph Chamberlain and the* Times, Moody writes that 'Captain Harrison has established beyond question (1) that the story told by O'Shea in the divorce court was a tissue of lies, and (2) that O'Shea was one of the instruments employed by great political forces to ruin Parnell and involve in ruin both the Home Rule cause and its English champion, Gladstone ...'[29] But despite Harrison's earnest arguments and some interesting circumstantial evidence, the case remains unproven. In the absence of persuasive evidence, while we may suspect the hand of Chamberlain and others[30] in ensuring the appearance of O'Shea in the divorce court, we must act on the assumption that his motives for taking such a grave step were largely personal and financial.

Whether or not Chamberlain played a conspiratorial role in the upheaval, in his response to the lengthy October 1889 letter of O'Shea he was certainly not counselling caution. 'I am not sure that the boldest course is not always wisest,'[31] was his recommendation when it came to the Captain's suggestion that he might pursue his wife and Parnell through the divorce courts. Chamberlain had sound personal and political reasons to encourage O'Shea in his pursuit.

Cardinal Manning had no such incentives and O'Shea's ill-advised pursuit of the approval of Mother Church for the course on which he was about to embark was to prove frustrating and counter-productive. His diary entry for 19 October records a meeting with the Primate of the Roman Catholic Church in England in which the Captain advised Manning that '... while anxious to conform with the regulations of the Church, I saw no way outside applying for a divorce. He [the Cardinal] said he had been told of the scandal, but had dismissed it from his mind. He asked whether I had proof of actual infidelity. He read a paper on which I had transcribed copies of *Pall Mall* paragraph, May 14th, 1886;[32] he expressed great sympathy and much grief. Finally he asked whether a separation deed could not be arranged. I said it would be useless. He begged me to give him time. To this I agreed.'[33]

O'Shea would have cause to regret his prevarication and there is little doubt that he was ill-used by the artful Manning in the ensuing weeks. There followed an unconscionable delay on the part of the Cardinal. O'Shea wrote to remind him of his undertaking a week later. Exactly what sort of response to the notion of a divorce suit O'Shea could reasonably have expected from a Roman Catholic prelate, other than benign neglect, it is difficult to divine. But he was certainly entitled to expect that confidentiality would be maintained. Instead Manning appears to have consulted not only Sir Charles Russell, but Parnell's solicitor, George Lewis. Eventually access to a Roman Catholic Ecclesiastical Court was offered by the dilatory Cardinal. O'Shea baulked at the prospect of having to lay out all his evidence before a religious court (in which Parnell and Katharine would be expected to appear), which would then report to Rome. The best that could be hoped for from such a source was a Church annulment. In his final reply, in a series of letters between the two men which continued for a month, he reminded Manning of what he described as the 'personal and political treachery' of Parnell in the Central Board affair in 1885 and suggested, in declining the Cardinal's offer of an Ecclesiastical Court, that 'It cannot, therefore, astonish your Eminence that I should hesitate to approach a tribunal before which a person who is thus known to us both to be unworthy of credit, might make statements without the curb which, in an English court, having the right to administer an oath, the possibility of a prosecution for perjury would perhaps provide.'[34]

Despite his hand having been stayed by the Church Laggard until well into the festive season, O'Shea was utterly unsentimental in the timing of his approach to the divorce court. His petition was entered on Christmas Eve 1889. The ultimate pretext for the divorce proceedings was consistent with O'Shea's conduct throughout. Rather than risk a direct confrontation with his wife or Parnell, his son was delegated the task of entering the Walsingham Terrace house and playing the offended party. As he informed a vacationing Chamberlain, sweltering in the sand dunes of Egypt at the time, 'He called unexpectedly at one of his mother's houses there (she has two) and found a lot of Mr Parnell's things some of which he chucked out of the window. There was a dreadful scene and on our return to London we went to the lawyers and settled that an action should be immediately instituted.'[35] The 'unexpected' visit was probably as contrived as his son's sudden and appalled discovery of Parnell talking to the family dog two years before. Lyons has referred to it sagely as 'the fuse that detonated a mine already well prepared.'[36] The account offered to Chamberlain is slightly at variance with that of his own counsel in the case. Sir Edward Clarke in his memoirs (admittedly written 30 years after the event)[37] fixes O'Shea's personal 'discovery' of his wife's infidelity as October–November 1889 and insists that his client told him that he himself had 'found Mr Parnell's dressing utensils and some of his clothes'.[38]

According to Henry Harrison (quoting Katharine O'Shea's future solicitor Bourchier F. Hawksley as his source), when counsel was first consulted on O'Shea's behalf the papers were returned and new instructions called for on the basis that 'the facts relied upon as evidence showed knowledge of such long standing that they presented a clear case of condonation by the husband.'[39] Counsel in question was Lewis Coward QC who, according to Clarke, first approached him on 4 February 1890 'to tell me that he had an important divorce case in hand which gave him much anxiety'.[40] This would appear to tally with Hawksley's information. However, no date is given by Harrison for that initial briefing. It is likely that Coward was still concerned about many elements of the case in February 1890, even if the inherent weakness of the brief had already been rectified by some form of remedial action. Therefore it is conceivable that Gerard O'Shea's visit to Brighton had been arranged *after* the rejection of the original brief, when a new narrative became necessary because of the inadequacy of the evidence presented to Lewis Coward. O'Shea's discussions with Manning in November 1889, which suggest that he had not finally decided to sue for divorce at that time, would not have precluded him from having had counsel briefed provisionally.

The sensational news of the divorce petition took some time to percolate from the Inns of Court to Fleet Street, no doubt due to the intervention of Christmas. The *Evening News and Post* was one of the first to announce the fact that O'Shea had finally shattered the increasingly porous wall of silence surrounding his marriage. It wasn't until 30 December that an exultant *Times* carried the news that 'A petition for divorce has been filed by William Henry O'Shea of 124 Victoria St Westminster, and justice of the peace in Co Clare, against his wife, Mr

Charles Stewart Parnell being co-respondent. The grounds alleged are the adultery of Mrs O'Shea during the period from April 1886 up to the date of the petition ...'[41]

The *Evening News and Post* had preceded its bald announcement with an exclusive interview. Its correspondent had called on O'Shea at his rooms to confirm the story and 'was shown up into a cosy sitting room'. Gerard O'Shea was with his father and was permitted to remain despite the reporter's obvious embarrassment. The *News* reporter was offered a cigarette and a seat and the brief interview began. With calculated insouciance the Captain calmly confirmed the details of the report and concluded by politely thanking 'your editor for having the courtesy to ask me before publishing the fact'.[42]

The loyally Parnellite *Freeman's Journal* went on the offensive immediately. 'The man who has outlived and lived down the calumnies and forgeries and perjuries of the ill-omened gang of the Commission need be very little troubled over this Houston-O'Shea-cum-*Times* scandal. Its authors and agents only cover themselves more thickly with the mire of the most abandoned turpitude.'[43] It was a refrain culled from Parnell himself, who had responded to O'Shea's thrust with a couple of his own. In an interview with J.M. Tuohy, the *Freeman's* London correspondent, Parnell had invoked an O'Shea–Houston plot hatched in the interests of the *Times* in order to mitigate the sum in damages the newspaper would be required to pay on foot of the admission of the Pigott forgeries. He then made a frankly astonishing and unguarded claim. 'Mr. Parnell also said', according to the *Freeman*, 'that he had constantly resided at Mrs O'Shea's house at Eltham from the end of 1880 to 1886. Captain O'Shea was always aware that he (Mr Parnell) was constantly there in his (Captain O'Shea's) absence during that period, and since 1886 he has known that Mr Parnell constantly resided there from 1880 to 1886.'[44] In effect, while claiming connivance on the part of the Captain, Parnell was admitting the adultery and justifying the grounds of the divorce (assuming he was not claiming that relations between him and Katharine were purely platonic in nature). It is just as surprising that this interview does not seem to have been quoted back at him in the months that followed when he assured certain colleagues that he would emerge unscathed from the divorce action.

The following day the *Freeman* printed Houston's and O'Shea's denials of any plot to destroy Parnell, while itself commenting optimistically that '... Mr Parnell does not commit himself lightly to assertions of that kind, and in due time he will be ready with his proofs.'[45] On 4 January the *Freeman* went further in its analysis of the divorce petition. In an article written by Tuohy the newspaper charged O'Shea, 'with bringing this suit, not for the purpose of vindicating himself or of obtaining that redress to which he is entitled, if the allegations in his petition are true, but for the purpose of assisting the *Times* and others in their attack on Mr Parnell.'[46] Tuohy also described the petition as a 'vile accusation sprung upon him [Parnell] like the last attempt of a moral assassin.' O'Shea sued the paper and won an action against the *Freeman* for contempt of court, claiming that the article jeopardised his divorce case by questioning his bona fides.[47]

On New Year's Day 1890, Michael Davitt made an emphatic entry in his diary starkly assessing Parnell's prospects should O'Shea convince the divorce court of the justice of his case. 'The Parnell O'Shea business still the talk of the town,' he wrote, 'Most people spoken to seem think it won't do P much harm "anyway". This huge mistake. O'Shea being cuckolded does not lessen much (if any) the crime (if ever committed) of adultery with another man's wife. If O'Shea proves his case P must step down and out. Hope sincerely he will come out all right.' Davitt was already focused on a possible life after Parnell and he also noted, '... If P falls Heaven save us from a Dillon leadership.'[48]

After his initial outburst to the *Freeman*, Parnell was more disposed to keep his own counsel. He made no further public attempt to stand up his plausible and widely credited, but ultimately unsupportable, allegations of a Unionist conspiracy. In response to a sympathetic address from Ennis Board of Guardians[49] in January 1890 he wrote, 'I venture to suggest that this charge ... may be more advantageously met with the deadly weapon of silent contempt.'[50]

However, on at least three occasions in meetings or communications with political allies, Parnell was less than silent in his contempt. He told Davitt, for example, 'that he would emerge from the whole trouble without a stain on his name or reputation.'[51] At the time Davitt, rather naively, chose to take this as a denial that any adultery had taken place. When writing his memoir of the period, *The Fall of Feudalism in Ireland*, however, he was inclined to the rather more realistic view that 'what was possibly working in his mind at the moment was a firm belief that the person who instituted the suit would be induced to withdraw it from the courts ...' In January 1890 William O'Brien had written a supportive letter to Parnell and his leader had replied, 'I thank you very much for your kind letter which I shall always highly prize. If this case is ever fully gone into, a matter which is exceedingly doubtful, you may rest assured that it will be shown that the dishonour and the discredit has not been on my side ...'[52] The suggestion was that the case would not come before the courts, the emphatic implication being that if it did O'Shea's connivance would be trumpeted before the press and the nation.

The third reassuring statement was perhaps the most significant and the most misleading. Gladstone was, understandably, becoming more and more concerned as the divorce trial date approached. Less than a week before the divorce petition had been filed, Parnell had experienced an apotheosis of sorts when he had been invited to Hawarden to discuss the possible template for Home Rule in a future Liberal administration. When the news broke that O'Shea had made his much-contemplated move, the Grand Old Man might have regretted the invitation. Certainly his senior colleagues were concerned about Parnell's future. John Morley, in congratulating George Lewis on the *Times* concession of £5,000 to Parnell in his libel suit in early February 1890, had struck up a conversation with the solicitor. Writing to Harcourt a short time later he had squarely predicted, on the basis of what Lewis had told him, the end of the Irish leader's political career. 'He told me much else, which cannot well be written down. I can only say that when the time comes, Walter will have his five thousand pounds worth of revenge. It will be a horrid exposure, and must, I think, lead to the disappearance of our friend.'[53]

As time wore on and Parnell remained studiously silent, in public at any rate, about how he proposed to deal with the allegations of the cuckolded husband, Gladstone became more concerned for the future of the alliance on which he had pinned much of his political reputation. Just a few weeks in advance of what he later called the 'dire wreck' of the divorce, John Morley, at the behest of Gladstone, had a long conversation with Parnell in the Metropole Hotel in Brighton. Despite the fact that the meeting took place on Parnell's 'patch', he contrived to be more than two hours late. They discussed Land Purchase, the possibility of Lord Spencer returning to Ireland as Viceroy,[54] and the impossibility (according to the man himself) of Parnell becoming Chief Secretary. Finally Morley got around to asking the question that must have been on his mind since he left London. In the light of the forthcoming divorce proceedings, was there a possibility of the Irish leader's 'disappearance' from politics? Parnell expressed amused astonishment.

'My disappearance! Oh no. No chance of it. Nothing in the least leading to disappearance, so far as I am concerned will come out of legal proceedings. The other side don't know what a broken-kneed horse they are riding.'[55] Parnell was reverting to his mantra. He had couched the divorce in impersonal terms, as a Tory political conspiracy. Morley was 'delighted to hear that', but elaborated in his memoirs that 'I inferred from his talk of the broken-kneed horse that he meant there would be no adverse decree.' This was the information duly communicated to a relieved and delighted Gladstone, who was told 'there were grounds for an impression that Mr Parnell would emerge as triumphantly from the new charges, as he had emerged from the obloquy of the forged letters.'[56] On the basis of his own account of the Metropole meeting (which took place on 10 November, barely a week before the divorce trial) the Liberal lieutenant was responsible for some gilding of Parnell's lily.

Whatever he told Gladstone, he does not appear to have been completely convinced by Parnell's bravado himself. That day he wrote to Harcourt that 'Edward Clarke has some terribly odious material in his hands and if he uses it, our man will be destroyed, or at any rate made impossible for a long time to come. I regard it as certain that the Irish will not throw him over in any case, and if they don't, nobody else can.'[57]

*

For a man whose political instincts had proved so adept over the years, Parnell's handling of the divorce is suggestive of someone who had either lost his touch, delegated unwisely or, more likely, both. Much of the handling of the defence case devolved to Katharine, a woman described by George Lewis (after she had disagreed with him once too often and they had dispensed with each other's services) as 'a very charming lady but an impossible one'.[58] The balance of probability and the weight of available anecdotal evidence suggests that Parnell's central preoccupation was to terminate the marriage of O'Shea and Katharine and to make her his own wife.[59] As was so often the case her objectives were complex and less than romantic. Initially both Parnell and Katharine simply denied the adultery and seemed prepared to challenge in court any evidence O'Shea might present. As this was likely to be overwhelmingly to their detriment, it was never a viable course of action and must be assumed to have been a necessary holding position in terms of legal bargaining, not to mention pubic perception. Later Katharine would make two counter-charges; both were surprising for different reasons and one was utterly inimical to a viable defence.

Katharine's course seems to have been dictated by her previous experience with her husband. O'Shea had offered no prior indication that he was a man of principle. On the contrary, where his domestic arrangements were concerned, he was absolutely corruptible and had already been 'bought off' on a number of occasions for a variety of reasons. Her assumption was that the divorce would be no exception, but that his price would be higher than before. She was probably correct in her assessment but, unfortunately, she did not have the financial resources to test it adequately. Had she inherited Aunt Ben's money without experiencing the attendant problems, there would probably still have been a divorce, but the proceedings might have taken an entirely different course. O'Shea repeatedly indicated to Chamberlain that there were large sums of money being offered to him to withdraw his petition.[60] Sir Edward Clarke was 'quite uncertain as to what would happen' when he went into court on Saturday 15 November.[61] By which he meant that he was unsure whether his client would show up to pursue the case.

In the months following the death of Parnell his wife told Henry Harrison that they had assembled evidence of no fewer than 17 instances of adultery on the part of O'Shea.[62] In an affidavit sworn on 24 July, 1890 the actual number falls well short of that figure. The deposition alleges that O'Shea 'between the years 1868 and 1890 ... habitually committed adultery with divers prostitutes and other women whose names except as hereinafter stated are at present unknown to the Respondent ...' It goes on to name specifically the parlour-maid Sarah Winsor (see below – Chapter 1), a Spanish mistress Maria Dominguez (with whom O'Shea is alleged to have had an affair 'in the years 1877 and 1878') and his sister in law Anna Steele. The affidavit also claimed that at the time of the 'duel' incident[63] in July 1881 O'Shea had also physically assaulted his wife when she was pregnant.[64] As these allegations were never advanced and tested in a court of law (other than that against Anna Steele) they must be treated with caution.

Katharine's intention was to use her financial resources to persuade her husband to allow her to divorce him on the grounds of adultery and cruelty. It was this possibility that prompted Parnell to make optimistic comments about the case to Davitt and O'Brien. His assurance to Morley, even though it was made late in the day and smacks of the lie direct, may also have been prompted by optimism that money would be found from some source to deflect O'Shea. The Captain himself told Chamberlain that 'The last offer was made to me through my son the evening before the trial and was equivalent to over £60,000.'[65] However, in reality, the probate case had long since put an end to that strategy. Aunt Ben's inheritance was frozen pending the outcome of the case, and with the divorce proceedings to be played out first there were few who would have lent Katharine as much as £20,000 on the strength of her defeating her siblings in court and inheriting most or all of the legacy. When it came to bribing O'Shea, the money was simply not there for the purpose.

Hence, the alternative strategy. This involved the counter-argument on Katharine's part that her husband had actually encouraged the affair and had even egged her on to initiate it. Subsequently, she alleged, he had connived in maintaining the relationship for his own benefit; what Henry Harrison has pithily described as 'covenanted blindness'.[66] There is no doubt that her allegations were credible. Had he been challenged by competent counsel, O'Shea would have had a difficult time explaining many of his actions as well as his frequent inaction, already discussed in previous chapters. However, the collusion defence was totally self-defeating. *Ab initio* it contradicted the simple denial of the affair and effectively 'sold the pass' on that issue. If proven and accepted by a jury, it also meant that no divorce could take place. O'Shea's connivance would have invalidated his claim for a legal termination of his marriage. This, according to Katharine at least, was precisely what Parnell did not want.[67] In addition, the admission that adultery had indeed taken place would have done Parnell untold political damage.

What, for want of a better word, can be described as Katharine's 'strategy' in the divorce case, is further complicated by her own invidious position. Given Parnell's desire for a divorce we must assume that the connivance counter-charge, while eminently provable, was entered *pour encourager le Capitaine*. A withdrawal of the allegation could have been used as a bargaining counter in the attempt to buy off O'Shea. Certainly Katharine did not want her husband getting into the witness box to refute allegations that he had been a knowing accomplice by producing evidence (documentary and anecdotal) of his continued affectionate relationship with his wife. In the course of such testimony he might be expected to refer to the parentage of Claude Sophie 'of whom the Captain mistakenly supposed himself to be the father'[68] (the words of Sir Edward Clarke). There can be little doubt (as outlined elsewhere) that Parnell was aware of O'Shea's belief that he had fathered the dead infant and of the basis for such a conviction. Too detailed an examination of the Captain, however, on his claim to have been the father of Clare and Katie, might open an entirely different can of worms for Katharine. It has been suggested elsewhere in this work that she continued a (highly reluctant) sexual relationship with her husband beyond the birth of Claude Sophie. It has not been suggested that Parnell was aware of that relationship. If O'Shea was called upon to give evidence that he had no basis for the belief that he was being cuckolded until 1886, he might well testify that the continuation of his sexual relationship with Katharine up to the mid 1880s offered some grounds for that opinion. Katharine would hardly have wanted any doubt cast on her carefully constructed personal narrative that she had been a neglected and abandoned wife since the late 1870s, and involved in a 'monogamous' and exclusive affair with Parnell since 1880.

But the gravest blunder of all, and one which almost beggars belief, was the specific counter-allegation made by the defendants that O'Shea had had an affair with his sister-in-law Anna Steele. This was doubtless prompted (whatever the truth of the allegation) by the probate case and the deterioration in the relationship between the Wood sisters. Evidence could be produced of the early morning visit by O'Shea to Anna Steele in the course of the July 1881 'duel' episode, but, as she could claim to have been the honest broker in that dispute, either Katharine had additional evidence of an affair between the two, or this was an egregious example of petulance winning out over common sense.[69] The imprudent allegation allowed O'Shea, already in possession of the moral high ground, to scale the highest peaks of self-righteousness when he got into the witness box.

O'Shea made a vehement denial of the charge to his court of first resort, Chamberlain, 'You can imagine the indignation of her brothers and sisters. Low as she has sunk with him before, I confess I was astounded when I heard of the depths to which Parnell has now dragged her.'[70] Parnell's inability in this and other instances to control Katharine's infamous 'whim of iron' would contribute to the approaching humiliation in the divorce court. He may have relied on assurances from her that her husband would, as O'Shea put it himself, be 'squared'. In the end, either O'Shea's overwhelming desire for revenge, a well-contrived Conservative–Unionist plot, or the defendant's simple lack of an adequate 'corruption' fund dictated otherwise.

Only one biographer of either Parnell or Katharine offers a reasonable explanation for the 'Steele allegation' and actually suggests that Katharine was 'legally, well informed'[71] in making the allegation. Jane Jordan advances an interesting and plausible case[72] that the reason for the charge of adultery between O'Shea and Anna Steele was because of one of the many legal disadvantages under which women laboured in the late 19th century. Under English law at the time, while a man could divorce his wife on the grounds of adultery, a woman had to prove 'aggravated' adultery or cruelty against her husband. Establishing an O'Shea–Steele affair ('incestuous adultery') would have been sufficient to have secured an end to Katharine's marriage. However, Jordan also points out that Katharine hoped to secure a divorce on the basis of having been deserted by O'Shea. If she was confident of proving her status as a deserted wife it is still possible that the charge against Anna Steele emanated from mere vindictiveness rather than strategic motives. Either way it was ill-judged. The *Times* was able to describe the allegation as a 'shocking charge', and the presiding divorce court judge, Justice Butt,[73] made it clear to the jury that the charge ('simply shocking to my mind'[74]) was an aggravating factor which actually enhanced O'Shea's case.

O'Shea's initial relationship to his own petition was almost as problematic as Parnell's position in the face of Katharine's response. In seeking a legal representative his first recourse was to the familiar. He sought the assistance of Joseph Soames, solicitor for the *Times* at the Special Commission. Fortunately Soames (having at first accepted the Captain's instructions) pointed out to O'Shea the impropriety of taking his case while he was still briefing the Attorney General and his team at a Commission of Inquiry where the former MP had been a star witness against the Irish leader. Unfortunately Soames made a potentially disastrous alternative suggestion when he directed O'Shea instead towards a young, untried solicitor with a mere ten months experience. The difficulty lay not just with the callowness of his proposed replacement, but the parentage. The substitute advocate was the son of Mr Justice Day, who was still sitting in judgement on charges of criminality against Parnell. It was not until the intervention of his lead barrister, Sir Edward Clarke, the Solicitor General, that O'Shea was passed on to the uncircumscribed and interestingly named Muskett, of the London law firm Wontners.[75]

O'Shea had more luck in his (or his legal team's) choice of private detective. Exactly what former Metropolitan Police Inspector James Thomson did for O'Shea's cause is a subject for surmise, but his client was perfectly satisfied with his services. Thomson had retired from the Met in 1887 and had been subsequently employed (along with his wife Martha) by Sir Robert Anderson in covert activities. Both he and his spouse had, for example, been sent on a mission to Boulogne in the summer of 1887 to watch and record the movements of Clan na Gael activist, General Francis Millen, the supposed instigator of the bogus Fenian Jubilee bombing plot. Later Thomson had been employed by the *Times* to try and persuade Millen (who was actually a Foreign Office informer) to testify before the Commission. O'Shea was so enthusiastic about Thomson that he wanted Chamberlain to meet and brief him, describing him as, 'the cleverest man they had at Scotland Yard. I believe if the *Times* had left everything to him we should have seen General Millen and Mr Sheridan both in the witness box ... It was he who frustrated the design for dynamite explosions intended for the Jubilee procession.'[76] If the link to Thomson adds to the circumstantial evidence of a *Times*–Tory–Chamberlain plot, it must be said that Chamberlain's diplomatic refusal to meet him weakens the case.[77] If Thomson was responsible for assembling some of the most damaging evidence in the Captain's action, then it is clear why O'Shea was so wholehearted in praise of his work.

The multi-faceted and ever-changing 'strategy' of the defendants, which in reality did not go much further than the bribery option, finally came down to a stark choice, defend or concede. According to Katharine it was

Parnell who made the decision not to offer any defence. What was to happen to his political reputation and what his political future might be seems to have been of secondary importance to him. In opting not to answer O'Shea's charges, Parnell also knew he was gaining Katharine while 'losing' his two children. The law was clear. A divorced mother was obliged to give up her children to her 'wronged' husband. O'Shea told the divorce court that all five surviving children were his (to have said otherwise would have fatally damaged his case). It is known that Parnell consulted counsel (Inderwick, who ended up assisting Clarke in the divorce on the O'Shea side) some weeks before the trial and inquired about European countries to which he might take Katharine, Clare and Katie without fear of legal consequences.[78] It is significant that Frank Lockwood QC who held a watching brief for Katharine (Parnell was unrepresented) only intervened when it came to the issue of custody. A request to take the matter up in Chambers was denied by Justice Butt and O'Shea was given custody of all five.[79] His own counsel, Sir Edward Clarke, later wrote that the two youngest girls were 'unquestionably his [Parnell's] daughters.'[80] He does not say when or how he came by this information. Although O'Shea never actually seized himself of Clare and Katie they were used as assets. Henry Harrison records that O'Shea, after Parnell's death, used the custody threat as leverage to extract more money from Katharine.

*

Parnell's tactics in refusing to contest (Katharine devotes most of the few pages of her memoir dealing with the divorce to his determination to abort any defence case) may have been based on procrastination. A 'no contest' guaranteed a decree nisi, but the divorce would not be final until the decree absolute, issued after six months. Were any allegations of collusion to be made by the defence during that period, the court could re-examine and reconsider its original decree and refuse to issue a decree absolute. Therefore (assuming he wanted Katharine divorced) it was essential for Parnell not to attempt to justify his behaviour by revealing the truth about the triangular relationship for at least six months. He may have been hinting at this in the Irish Parliamentary Party meeting held in Committee Room 15 of the House of Commons on 25 November 1890, in which he was re-elected chairman of the party. According to T.P. O'Connor he assured his colleagues that:

> ... in a very short period of time, when I am free to do so, I
> will be able to put a complexion on this case very different to
> that which it now bears, and I will then be able to hold my

head as high, aye, and higher, than ever before in the face of
the world. ... I will ask my colleagues to remember that only
one side of the story has been given to the public. I am
accused of breaking up a happy home and of shattering a
scene of domestic bliss and felicity. If this case had been gone
into and a calculation had been made, it would have been
proved that in the twenty-three years of Mr O'Shea's married
life, he spent only four hundred days in his own home. This
was the happy home which I am alleged to have destroyed. I
am also accused of betraying a friend. Mr O'Shea was never
my friend. Since I first met him in Ennis, in 1880, he was
always my enemy – my bitter relentless enemy.[81]

That there can be few certainties as to the true nature of the conduct of
the defence case is illustrated by two extant and somewhat contradictory
accounts of Parnell's relationship with Katharine's counsel, Frank
Lockwood. Both are from former Parnellite lieutenants. The first source
is the wholly partial and relatively unreliable Tim Healy. He quotes an
alleged conversation he had with Lockwood who claimed that it was
Katharine who insisted that Parnell should not testify, a demand with
which he concurred. 'A consultation was held at Lockwood's chambers,'
according to Healy, 'where Parnell came with Mrs O'Shea and announced
that he would not be represented to defend. A violent scene ensued.
Lockwood threatened to throw him out of the window, for he knew that
"collusion" could easily be established and the suit defeated ...'[82] Healy
contended that it was Katharine who dictated the policy of non-engage-
ment because of *her* desire for a divorce. This theory had the double
benefit from his point of view of further demonising 'Kitty O'Shea', while
making Parnell appear weak and subjugated.

The more reliable William O'Brien maintained, in a 1913 article in the
Cork Free Press, in which he also reproduced his former leader's January
1890 letter, that Parnell was eager to testify. 'Parnell afterwards told me
at Boulogne', wrote a much-mellowed O'Brien, 'that the whole complexion of the case would have been changed if he had given evidence as to his
relations with Captain O'Shea; that he had pressed upon Sir Frank
Lockwood (Mrs O'Shea's counsel) in the strongest manner that he should
be examined, and that upon one occasion he and Sir Frank Lockwood
had almost come to blows upon the point. Parnell yielded, with a self-
abnegation to which justice will perhaps be done hereafter.' O'Brien added
that he had once met Lockwood on a cross-Channel journey many years
later and the former Solicitor General had told him, 'I am afraid Parnell

was badly treated. I have some remorse myself.'[83] O'Brien does not specify as to the exact nature of Parnell's ill treatment, but his invocation of the conversation presupposes that Lockwood verified his thesis.

THE DIVORCE COURT[84]

By the time the case of *O'Shea v O'Shea and Parnell (Steele intervening)* was ready to begin on the morning of Saturday 15 November, the court was predictably packed. The cases to be made by the Captain and his wife were first outlined:

> The respondent denied that she had been guilty of adultery, as did also the co-respondent; and the respondent alleged that the petitioner had been guilty of connivance in the adultery,[85] or conduct which had been conducive to the adultery; that he had wilfully separated himself from the respondent; that he had himself been guilty of adultery; that he had unreasonably delayed instituting the suit; and that he had been guilty of cruelty towards the respondent. The petitioner denied the truth of these allegations ...

It is ironic that the reading of the particulars was mostly taken up with the case to be made by Katharine and Parnell because, of course, no attempt was made to justify that case. Within minutes of the commencement of proceedings Frank Lockwood had risen and told Justice Butt that 'I do not intend to cross examine any witnesses, to call any witnesses, nor to take any part in these proceedings.'

Without a defence case, the 'wronged' husband, predictably, had a field day. Because allegations had been made against his good faith, and indeed against his fidelity, two days were spent proving beyond all reasonable doubt what a good and caring spouse Captain William Henry O'Shea had been and what a heinous home-wrecker was one Charles Stewart Parnell. In the absence of any challenge or cross-examination the proceedings of the previous eight years were passed through an O'Shea prism. Letters sent to Katharine by her husband as tacit warnings to keep the relationship covert were interpreted as a thoroughly deceived husband seeking reassurance. There was no defence counsel to ask why, for example, if Eltham was O'Shea's domicile, he needed to write to his wife so often. The many aliases used by Parnell and the frequent changes of address of the couple were portrayed as an attempt to deceive the worthy and put upon Captain, rather than as efforts to comply with his own and Parnell's aversion to publicising the relationship. It was, to use a graphic American expression, a 'turkey shoot'.

In his opening address, Sir Edward Clarke outlined O'Shea's case against his wife and Parnell. He vigorously defended the honour of his client and picked apart the reputation of Parnell, alleging, for example that '... on one occasion he escaped by the balcony in order to avoid Captain O'Shea finding him in the house, and he then came round to the front door a short time afterwards and presented himself as if he had just come to make a call.' This provoked the gallery to its first bout of humiliating laughter. The Tory Solicitor General followed up that scenario with a well-rehearsed and much appreciated witticism at the expense of the entire Irish nationalist movement. In recounting the arrival of the horses, President and Dictator, at Eltham in 1885 he added, 'They were followed in the early part of 1886 by another horse called Home Rule. (Laughter). This horse was described in one of the proofs before him as an old crock, and only fit to go in the shafts. (Laughter) What had become of that horse he did not know. (Laughter.)' Clarke trawled through the *Pall Mall Gazette*, the *Sussex Daily News* and the overwrought letters of criticism and complaint from the petitioner from 1886 and beyond.

When O'Shea took the stand, he allowed himself a few unchallenged lies as well as a number of statements in the immediate neighbourhood of perjury: '... in the early part of 1883', he asserted, 'my daughter Clare was born.' She was, of course, Parnell's daughter and it is morally certain that O'Shea was well aware of that. 'It was not within my knowledge that he was visiting my wife there', was his comment about domestic arrangements at Wonersh Lodge post 1883. 'It was never within my knowledge that he slept in the house or visited there during my absence', was a statement related to Brighton in 1883. 'She said that she knew that Mr Parnell was secretly married', was offered as a pretext in the event of any questions in the minds of jurors as to why he consistently accepted his wife's assurances that nothing untoward was going on. His startling observation that 'I was never away from my wife for a week, not only without her consent, but without her absolute approval', was not, technically, perjury, as his wife was only too delighted to give her tacit consent to his permanent absence.

More embarrassing than the evidence of the Captain himself, was that of former caretaker Caroline Pethers. She had cooked for Katharine during the brief sojourn in 8 Medina Terrace in Brighton. She testified that within days of the O'Shea's arrival 'a gentleman appeared'. He was named as Mr Charles Stewart, but she knew him to be Parnell. 'He sometimes called when Captain O'Shea was at home. He was nearly always there when he was away.' She described how Parnell and Katharine would drive out a lot at night but not during the day, and that 'they were nearly always locked in a room together'. But her most damaging testimony was the evidence that fuelled many a music-hall sketch in London that Christmas. Pethers described how, on more than one occasion, O'Shea had rung the front doorbell when she knew Parnell to be upstairs in the drawing-room. O'Shea had been admitted by her husband and had gone straight upstairs. A few minutes later Parnell had rung at the front door. When asked could Parnell have descended via the staircase, she replied, 'No. There was a balcony outside the drawing-room. There were two rope fire escapes from the window. This happened three or four times.'

It was this vision of the arrogant and dignified Parnell abjectly dangling from a rope in his attempt to avoid detection by O'Shea that became the central iconoclastic image of the O'Shea divorce. The testimony of Pethers subjected Parnell to utter ridicule at the hands of journalists, commentators and music-hall hacks. Once again a competent defence barrister might have asked why, if he was living with his wife in 8 Medina Terrace, O'Shea needed to ring the front doorbell to gain entry. He might also have inquired why Parnell would have needed to be introduced as Mr Stewart if he openly visited O'Shea there under his own name. He might have asked whether Caroline Pethers had ever seen Parnell make the undignified exit she implied (but never stated overtly) in her evidence. Furthermore he might have inquired why she believed Parnell would have bothered presenting himself at the front door, not once but four times, having made his hasty exit from upstairs. The evidence of Pethers possibly offers us an insight into the reasoning behind O'Shea's untrammelled enthusiasm for the methods of his private detective James Thomson.

At the end of the second day, when the petitioner rested his case – an unanswered diatribe which had done unimaginable damage to the reputation of Parnell – two jury members demonstrated what might have been, had the action been defended. Clearly dissatisfied with O'Shea's testimony, they asked that he be recalled and questioned more minutely about Katharine O'Shea's counter-charges. In the absence of an adversarial barrister, Lockwood keeping steadfastly to his seat, Clarke himself went through the motion, in desultory fashion, of cross-examining his own client before indicating that he had no further questions. At that point the two jurors intervened with queries of their own and one of them managed to fluster the petitioner. The interchange concluded as follows:

Juror: Your suspicions were first aroused in 1886?
O'Shea: Yes.
Juror: How do you account for your conduct in, after having challenged Mr Parnell to a duel, inviting him again to dinner?
O'Shea: I did not. The dinner you refer to was before that.
Juror: From your evidence you had him to dinner?
O'Shea: Certainly I did so, because it appeared to me at the time that there was no foundation to my suspicions.[86]

If a mere juror could, simply by paying close attention to the evidence, have forced O'Shea to retract an assertion of fact, what could an experienced QC have done to put serious doubts in the minds of the members of a jury who, in the end, took about 15 minutes to find for the plaintiff?

THE THERMIDOREAN REACTION

The *Times* was suitably exultant:

There is nothing whatever in the evidence to justify the impeachment of Captain O'Shea's good faith. His fault was the generous one of trusting too easily the word of a treacherous friend and of declining to believe in vague rumours affecting the false wife who knew how to keep up to the last the pretence of affection and fidelity. If Captain O'Shea had been a consenting party to the intrigue, according to the baseless and insulting theory which the respondent put forward, but shrank from all attempts to prove, what was the need of Mr Parnell's aliases, disguises and deceiving letters?[87]

The *Times* was not the only English newspaper to roast Parnell over a slow spit. The chorus of disapproval amongst the Tory press was universal.[88] The reaction of Liberal newspapers like the *Star* or the *Manchester Guardian* was more muted and non-committal.

Not unexpectedly *United Ireland* initially took a benevolent view. With O'Brien effectively 'on the run' in the USA, it was his deputy Matthias Bodkin who wrote the leader. 'Of his private life the Irish people have no mission to judge. That they leave to his conscience and his God, who weighs the temptation with the offence. His public career commands their unbounded admiration. It is his public services they will retain, and will repay with loyal support.'[89] It was a viewpoint echoed by the *Freeman's Journal*: 'Our business with Mr Parnell is political. The business of Ireland with him is political. He has ably, faithfully successfully served his country ... Is the most important decade in the latter-day progress of Irishmen to Home Rule to be blotted out, and, as if it had never been, at the hand of an O'Shea? That is what the Unionist and Pigottist press say should happen. That is what Ireland will declare, with no uncertainty, must not happen.'[90] As John Morley had suggested, Ireland was not going to 'throw him over'. The impetus for that, if required, would have to come from elsewhere.

The initial Irish reaction, dictated as it was by a profound sense of shock and disbelief, was not as significant politically as the English response. Gladstone, that pragmatic dweller in the mansion of *Realpolitik* rather than the outhouse of high moral principle (although he frequently gave vent to the latter), waited while others tested the water before committing himself to a formal reaction to the verdict. He would refrain from condemnation in the interests of the Liberal party if there were any way in which Humpty Dumpty could be put back together again. Privately, however, he confided to the Liberal peer, Lord Rendel, that 'Parnell was now impossible! The party would not stand it! Overwhelming evidence had already reached him! Parnell must go!' Rendel himself was more cautious: '... I shrank from giving him a personal opinion. Nor did I even dare to say that, whatever the evidence he had, I hoped he would keep a more open mind until he had seen his leading colleagues.'[91]

One of the most important of those colleagues, John Morley, was hardly less sanguine than Gladstone himself. On the concluding day of the divorce trial he wrote to Harcourt, 'We are in about as bad a fix as Ministers were in the explosion of Pigott. Only the effects of the blow will be more lasting, as Pigott had at least the good sense to take himself off from the sublunary stage. I am most sorry of all for Mr G. The consequences of the dirty malodorous storm will hardly clear away in his time.'[92] As it happened there was a convenient opportunity to test the wind direction, since the fallout from the verdict almost exactly coincided with the National Liberal Federation meeting in Sheffield. Gladstone delegated Harcourt to attend to the grass roots and his report was the second well-struck nail in the coffin of Parnell's political career. 'I have to report to you', he wrote to Gladstone on 22 November, 'that the opinion was *absolutely unanimous and extremely strong* that if Parnell is allowed to remain as the leader of the Irish Party all further co-operation between them and the English Liberals must be at an end. You know that the Nonconformists are the backbone of our party, and their judgement on this matter is unhesitating and decisive.'[93]

The 'unhesitating' nonconformist conscience to which Harcourt referred was exemplified by *Pall Mall Gazette* editor, W.T. Stead. He used the columns of his newspaper to berate Parnell, as he had done Dilke in not dissimilar circumstances. In a contemporary pamphlet, *The Discrowned King of Ireland*, while accepting that Parnell's offence was not nearly as rank as that of Dilke, who had seduced an impressionable young woman, Stead fulminated, 'Nor is it only Christian folk who resent the combination of treachery and deceit by which an adulterer breaks up the home of his friend. It is blankly incredible to the ordinary family man, that any person who stands officially branded by a judge and jury with having accepted his friend's hospitality in order to debauch that friend's wife, can even for a moment venture to take a leading part in political life in civilized society.'[94]

In the aftermath of the free flotation of the nonconformist conscience, the alternatives available to the Liberal and Nationalist leadership were hardly enticing. In the words of Mid-Cork Parnellite MP, D.D. Sheehan, '... the choice thrust upon the Irish people and their representatives was as to whether they should remain faithful to the alliance with the Liberal Party, to which the Irish nation unquestionably stood pledged, or to the leader who had won so much for them and who might win yet more if he had a united Ireland behind him, unseduced and unterrified by the clamour of English Puritan moralists.'[95]

The process by which nationalist Ireland dethroned its 'King' over a period of nine months of bitter in-fighting was tragic, has been told many times and is overwhelmingly a narrative associated with Parnell rather than O'Shea. In the immediate aftermath of the divorce, on 25 November, the party re-elected Parnell as sessional chairman without having been informed by deputy leader Justin McCarthy of a letter sent by Gladstone, which advised the Irish members that to do so, and to continue under the guidance of Parnell, would render his own leadership of the Liberal party 'a nullity'. When this letter was published in the wake of the retention of Parnell's stewardship, the Irish party consensus, which had already been hesitantly moving in the direction of a permanent or temporary departure of their leader, swung against him. By the following day a new meeting had been convened in order, ominously, 'to give Mr Parnell the opportunity of reconsidering his position'. The *Times* wrote that 'His whole conduct in view of the O'Shea divorce suit bespeaks utter indifference to his English allies as well as to their convenience.' Michael Davitt, who had reason to consider that he had been lied to, opposed the continuation of Parnell as Irish party leader. Parnell's response to the Gladstone letter (it had been written to Morley) was to frame a manifesto to the Irish people that poured cold water on the outcome of his Hawarden negotiations with the GOM and asked whether the Irish people proposed to allow their independence of action to be subverted by the Liberal alliance. It burnt virtually every bridge he had built with Gladstone over the previous five years and made the choice of his subordinates starker still.

On 1 December 1890, in Committee Room 15 of the House of Commons, the Irish party tore itself apart in an angry and vicious colloquium where acrimony was a clear winner over collegiality. In the absence of leadership figures like Dillon and O'Brien (both were in the USA and could not return to England because of outstanding warrants against them), Parnell sought to bully and procrastinate, Justin McCarthy sought to mollify, while Tim Healy sought revenge. As the meeting wearily ploughed its way towards an increasingly inevitable conclusion, the Irish Roman Catholic hierarchy, not to be outdone in moral indignation by mere English nonconformists, belatedly issued a statement insisting that Parnell's position was untenable. After six days of discordant and vituperative debate, 'with an almost somnambulistic air of unreality',[96] 45 members of the Irish party, led by Justin McCarthy, abandoned the meeting leaving a Parnellite rump of 28 behind them. Their leisurely departure, shaking hands with Parnellite loyalists as they left, belied the bitterness of the months that lay ahead for the once undisputed leader of Irish nationalism.

William Henry O'Shea can only have observed the rending with a sense of smug fulfillment. Not only had Goliath been brought to earth with his slingshot, but the giant's minions, many of whom had plagued and ridiculed O'Shea as much as he had sneered at them, were in acute political trauma. But feelings of profound contentment were insufficient reward in themselves. Bolstering the suspicion of political collusion, he pressed his claims for a return to the House of Commons. A week after the verdict, he had already communicated with Chamberlain about the possibility of a safe seat and had clearly been encouraged in his desire. 'You are quite right,' he wrote to his, no doubt delighted, mentor, 'A borough would suit me much better than a county. You and I know that Whips (and for the matter of that, the Masters) have a trick of furnishing ... coloured statistics ...' He was referring to Mid-Armagh and the provision by Parnell of dubious ethnic statistics suggesting a possible Liberal Catholic victory where none was on the cards. Buoyed up by a sense of political rehabilitation, he advised Chamberlain, 'If you want me back in the House this is the moment to strike and exact a promise.'[97]

Either Chamberlain was not sufficiently enthusiastic about having O'Shea back in the House, or he was unable to extract the requisite 'promise', but the Captain remained un-anointed and never returned to what he saw as his rightful berth in the Mother of Parliaments.

O'Shea was also quietly busy on his own behalf on the public relations front. In the event that a complete absence of a defence case justifying the allegations of connivance in his own cuckolding was not adequate to stay the doubts of influential observers, O'Shea 'recruited' the Solicitor General himself. An item appeared in the *Times* on 1 December, reporting that a message had been sent by Sir Edward Clarke to Gerard O'Shea. According to the newspaper the message read: 'In the enormous mass of correspondence and documents examined by counsel in the case, your father's life for many years has been laid bare to us. Few men would have emerged with such honour from so searching an ordeal.'[98] Clarke had indeed sent a letter (or had been prevailed upon to do so) to O'Shea's son. But it was devoid of the unctuous phraseology published by the *Times* and no doubt inspired by the Captain. O'Shea gambled that the report would be just sufficiently within the bounds of accuracy not to provoke any amendment or retraction from his former counsel. He lost. On 2 December the *Times* carried Clarke's correction. What he had actually written to Gerard O'Shea was to the effect that he ' ... had carefully examined the correspondence, and that there was not a sentence or word in any of the letters which gave the slightest support to the charge of connivance ...'[99] It was another example of O'Shea's ability to bend the truth out of shape to such an extent as to antagonise even his own allies.

Meanwhile the newly divided Irish party had brought its cudgels home. *United Ireland*, under the temporary editorship of Bodkin, had turned against Parnell. In the wake of the Greek tragedy in Committee Room 15, Bodkin had written: 'Let partisans attempt to disguise it as they may, "Ireland or Parnell" is now the issue on which Irishmen are to decide ... for Ireland's sake, Mr Parnell must go ... no man's personality can be permitted to obstruct the path of Ireland's liberty.'[100] In response to this journalistic *coup d'état*, Parnell organised one of his own, 'retaking' the office of the newspaper by force and ejecting those antipathetic to his cause. On 13 December *United Ireland* and *Suppressed United Ireland*[101] hit the streets of Dublin.

Something very different and more portentous was going on in the streets of Kilkenny. A by-election there in December was the first passage of arms between the two parliamentary factions. The nationalist already chosen, John Pope Hennessy,[102] had become the first anti-Parnellite candidate in the internecine conflict. Parnell put forward in opposition a supporter named Vincent Scully. Tim Healy (who less than a year later would be horsewhipped by one of Parnell's nephews for his vituperative utterances[103]) was at his malicious best in this and the two campaigns that closely followed. He excoriated his former leader from political platforms, combining the rhetorical powers of the advocate with the insidious sniping of the corner-boy. The thin-skinned O'Shea allowed himself to be provoked by scathing references to himself in one Kilkenny stump speech on 14 December.

Claiming that in 1885 Parnell had 'sold' the Liverpool Exchange Division seat to O'Shea he asked, 'What was the price he got for it? (Loud laughter.) In the presence of honest women he would not mention it. Captain O'Shea was defeated and then what did Mr Parnell do? Having failed to prostitute an English seat by securing it for Captain O'Shea, he went off to Galway and, though it was a bond of the Irish Party that every man should sign a pledge to sit, act and vote with the Irish Party, he put in Captain O'Shea as the price of his wife's shame.'[104] Instead of leaving well enough alone, O'Shea reacted as if he still had a reputation to maintain in Ireland. He dashed off a letter to the *Times* claiming that Healy's assertions were 'absolutely false' adding that 'I cannot produce documents or enter into particulars without the consent of others. I am taking steps to obtain it.'[105]

Having entered his protest, and thus having alerted more people to the gibe than would ever have been privy to Healy's invective had he kept his own counsel, he proceeded to try and gather a case together. He told Chamberlain that he intended to write to Lord Stalbridge (the former Lord Richard Grosvenor) to verify his personal fantasy that he was a vaunted and sought-after Liberal standard bearer in Liverpool, whose candidacy had not been dependent on the representations of Parnell.[106] He even contemplated a libel action, but was advised that he had no viable legal redress against Healy. Chamberlain was asked to pitch in to this self-vindicatory *meitheal* with a letter (for publication) confirming O'Shea's contentions, which could be published in refutation of Healy's 'abuse'. He duly obliged. 'According to my recollection,' he wrote, 'Parnell neglected at first to give you any assistance, and did not, in fact would not do so, until he had seen letters from myself and another person pointing out that your services in the past as intermediary between himself and the Liberal Party had been of real advantage to both, and that such services would continue to be equally necessary if it was desired to maintain any kind of friendly relations between the Irish nationalists and the Liberal Party.'[107] This was triumphantly reproduced, along with Chamberlain's mischievous January 1886 letter, advising him to seek a return to parliament via an Irish by-election, and a confirmatory letter from Stalbridge, in the *Times* on 29 December 1890. By then the caravans had moved on. On 22 December Hennessy had defeated Parnell's candidate by a 2 to 1 margin. The King would clearly have a hard struggle to regain his throne. The Captain was abjectly grateful to his Prince. 'Your friendship is worth having;' he wrote to Chamberlain, 'you know how to stand up for a friend.'[108]

A week later two former friends, both adversaries of O'Shea's, met in Boulogne in an attempt to bring a rapid end to the fratricidal conflict that was set to worsen in early 1891 with two further by-elections. But Parnell and William O'Brien (with the later addition of Dillon) were unable to orchestrate the sonata that would allow the former to withdraw from public life with his dignity intact. It may well have been that such a concession was never even a possibility as far as the proud and arrogant Parnell was concerned. He determined to fight on in the increasingly forlorn hope of re-establishing his undisputed hegemony over Irish nationalism. Two further by-election defeats, as well as personal and political humiliation and premature death were to be his lot. Not even his marriage to Katharine O'Shea within days of the decree absolute brought any succour for his cause. If anything, it served to exacerbate the anger and hostility that seemed to follow him wherever he spoke. In a desperate search for new allies he courted some of the same 'hillside men' who had once come to the aid of his nemesis. He had even, belatedly, begun to recognise and address some of the causes of Unionist antagonism to Home Rule. It was all to no avail. A flawed but monumental political career was destroyed by a near perfect political storm.

Meanwhile the man who had been the proximate cause of Parnell's angst was only required to deal with the occasional storm in a teacup. Not even six years in the proving ground of the House of Commons had thickened O'Shea's skin. No slight went unchallenged. Few critical commentaries remained unanswered. Fair comment (albeit much of it vitriolic in the style of Healy) was treated as defamatory. A confessional letter to Chamberlain in February 1891 enclosed an offensive paragraph from *Truth*, accompanied by the observation that 'So far I have taken no notice in this country of Mr Labouchere's mendacities.' The statement must be read in a legalistic sense only. O'Shea had refrained from issuing a writ, but he took notice of every line written about him. The previous year, in the immediate aftermath of the verdict, Labouchere had questioned the court's finding on the accusation of connivance, pointing out that O'Shea had adopted an oddly disengaged approach to his wife's domestic arrangements. 'Mr Parnell was habitually residing in the house in which she and her children were living ...', the newspaper pointed out and wondered why it was that O'Shea was 'perpetually writing to his wife',[109] rather than going to see for himself what was happening.

The Captain was not simply concerned about comments in British newspapers. He was just as exercised about what was being written in the USA where a 'sanguinary campaign' (his own description) was being carried out against him. With that highly developed grasp of public relations that had characterised his career and had long been an inadequate substitute for genuine political skills, O'Shea had sought out the American journalist William Henry Hurlbert, former editor of the *New York World* and a correspondent for the *New York Herald*. Hurlbert (who had tried to persuade P.J. Sheridan to testify for the *Times* at the Special Commission[110]) had sought to establish in a book called *Ireland Under Coercion* (London, 1888) that Parnell and the National League were at the root of Irish violence. So he was an ideal foil for O'Shea's personal propaganda.

O'Shea wanted Hurlbert to establish that 'the lady to whom I was married was *not originally the mistress of a governor of the Bank of England and that I did not marry her for the infamous fortune which I was said in hundreds of American papers to have received in considera-tion !!!*'[111] Aware that his ally was in danger of fighting wars on too many fronts, Chamberlain counselled restraint. O'Shea agreed to 'pay attention only to any really important slander',[112] but his sense of perspective inspired little confidence that he was capable any longer of distinguishing between what was 'important' and what could and should be safely ignored. His spat with the Bishop of Galway was a case in point. The Bishop, Dr MacCormack, had joined the shrill clerical chorus intoning phillipics against Parnell. O'Shea had been caught in the crescendo with a reference in a letter from the Bishop similar to that made by Healy in Kilkenny. MacCormack had written on 14 February, 'In 1886, after having failed to foist Captain O'Shea upon a neighbouring county, the then leader had the effrontery of prostituting the Galway City constituency as a hush gift to O'Shea.'[113]

It was a red rag to the bull in the former Hussar. His first recourse was a letter, on 21 February, to the Archbishop of Tuam, Dr McEvilly, for whom MacCormack was a suffragan bishop. He explained that he was, '... anxious if possible, to avoid taking any action against a Bishop. But it is quite clear that the greatness and sanctity of Dr MacCormack's position render a libel promulgated by him all the more outrageous and damaging, and his lordship must retract or defend his statement.'[114] Having issued his threat to take legal action against MacCormack, he then, at tedious length and with pedantic excess, offered his usual simultaneously self-exculpatory and self-aggrandising narrative of the Galway by-election. The O'Shea frills, omissions, exaggerations and evasions had been honed to perfection. When no reply was forthcoming from Tuam and no apology or defence issued from Galway, he took his case to the Primate in Armagh in a further letter on 10 March, and enclosed his lengthy Galwegian *apologia*.

O'Shea was still particularly sensitive when it came to the clergy, seeing them, not unreasonably, as the true arbiters of Irish public opinion. He told Chamberlain, 'If one were to let this pass unnoticed, the lie in question would soon take a permanent place in the manifestoes of Holy Gentlemen who, like the rest of the Gladstonians, hate me much more than Parnell because it was I who upset the thimblerig at which they were winning, they little cared how.'[115]

O'Shea did not finally receive a withdrawal of the remarks by MacCormack until 30 May. When it came it was grudging, argumentative and private. O'Shea responded six weeks later, having first transmitted MacCormack's partial retraction to Rome for appraisal. It is evident from the context of this particular self-justification (larded with enclosures and political endorsements) that MacCormack had sought to validate some of his original comments. At great length and in familiar style O'Shea wove his narrative web and sought to pummel the prelate into submission with yet more tendentious and wearisome detail. The Captain was clearly a man with much time on his hands and one thing on his mind, the preservation of his 'reputation'. Interestingly he concluded his dreary diatribe by addressing the issue that had long since left his reputation in tatters. 'It is clear to any unprejudiced observer', he bludgeoned the Bishop, 'that if Mr Parnell could in the Divorce Court have shown the slightest ground for the plea of connivance in any shape or way, he would have proved it. He would then have won his case, and if he had won it by any means whatsoever, he would without the shadow of a doubt have been left in undisputed possession of his leadership ...'[116] It is a curious glimpse of O'Shea the counter-factualist as well as a familiar example of O'Shea the fantasist. There were few significant 'unprejudiced observers' of the divorce court proceedings, and even those with a bias against Parnell would hardly have accepted that there were no grounds for a plea of connivance. One wonders whether behind all the bluster and special pleading O'Shea was ever aware that his 'reputation' had been saved from evisceration by the desire of his wife to be finally rid of him and the yearning of Parnell to be married to Katharine. And this at any cost.

Throughout the momentous year of 1891, as Parnell fought and lost further by-elections in Carlow (occasioned by the death of the great old warrior the O'Gorman Mahon) and North Sligo, withstood verbal barracking and physical violence[117] and was forced to endure attacks on Katharine from Healy and others, O'Shea behaved like the little Dutch boy with his finger in the dyke. The difference was that, instead of plugging a single flow, contrary to Chamberlain's advice, he attempted to staunch every haphazard leak that presented itself to his attention. In September he denied a *Freeman's Journal* report that he was about to remarry, asking the newspaper to 'allow me just sufficient space to say that I am a Catholic'.[118] The *Freeman* might well have retaliated by pointing out that his Catholicism had not been allowed to stand in the way of his divorce. It chose not to do so. With far greater justification he responded to a letter from the MP Donal Sullivan to the *National Press*, which quoted Parnell's denial to the party faithful in Committee Room 15 that O'Shea had ever been his friend or that he had ever partaken of his hospitality and promising that, in time, he would vindicate himself. In this instance O'Shea might have been expected to enter the fray with guns blazing, quoting chapter and verse in contradiction of Parnell's claims. Instead he sent a terse reply observing merely that 'Mr Parnell seems to have held a very high opinion of the credulity of his audience.'[119]

The last recorded occasion on which the two men were in physical proximity came less than three months before Parnell's death on 6 October 1891, in Brighton (where O'Shea had by then also taken up residence with Gerard and Carmen). The two men were present in the London Court of Bankruptcy on 29 July for the hearing of an application by Parnell to have set aside a statutory notice of O'Shea's, seeking the payment of £778 in divorce court costs. The sum had been fixed by the Taxing Master and, according to O'Shea, was 'insufficient to cover counsel's fees'.[120] The case was heard in Chambers so there was no way in which the two adversaries could avoid each other. The *Times* reported that 'it is understood the application rested on two grounds'. Parnell claimed that for the greater part of the previous six months he had not lived within the jurisdiction of the court, as his residence was in Avondale. He also made a counter-claim against O'Shea for £3,600, this being money that he claimed had been advanced to the Captain between September 1889 and November 1890. No attempt was made to substantiate the mysterious and fascinating counter-claim and the Judge ruled that, as Parnell had rooms reserved for him in a house in Brighton, he had an English residence, and, consequently, was subject to the jurisdiction of the court. It was the final petty triumph of O'Shea over his enemy.

As Parnell limped and staggered into a hallowed place in the Irish Pantheon, his health failing, his political nous a useless appendage in the face of clerical,[121] pietistic and pragmatic opposition, his most bitter enemy of all lurked in the shadows, emerging from time to time only to defend himself against renewed attack. Like the catalyst in a chemical experiment O'Shea had produced a reaction without actually sharing in its consequences. While Parnell struggled in vain to redefine himself, as well as to redirect Irish nationalism out of what he claimed, rather self-servingly, was the cul-de-sac of the Liberal alliance, O'Shea had the simpler and safer task of attempting to assert some control over his own narrative. As time went on, it was his increasing irrelevance and the indifference of past and potential enemies that allowed him to do this without undue effort. In time the attacks on him became formulaic, desultory and almost apathetic, and he faded into an oblivion of his own.

CHAPTER 14

Finis

Should a gallant captain
Seek to gain our hall,
Fire escapes are handy
To save an ugly fall.

from 'Brighton Over All', Tim Healy after
Edward Harrington

WHERE THERE'S A WILL ...

If the attendance at a funeral indicates some measure of a person's contribution to society, then those of the members of the Parnell–O'Shea triangle could not have provided a starker contrast. When William Henry O'Shea died in 1905 he was interred in a cemetery in Hove in the presence of his son and son-in-law. Katharine O'Shea's obsequies in Littlehampton in February 1921 were attended by four people, the diligent Gerard O'Shea and his wife, her devoted daughter Norah, and the man who had married Parnell's daughter Clare, Dr Bertram Maunsell. In contrast to the anonymity of the burials of the Captain and the Queen, the King was laid to rest with all the trappings of a state funeral in a nation denied statehood.

Perhaps one of the best and most generous things Katharine O'Shea ever did for a country she never visited and might justifiably have blamed for the death of her husband was to accept that he should be buried in Ireland. His Dublin funeral was attended by tens of thousands of mourners.[1] Four cars behind the coffin, immediately after close family, was a carriage containing legendary Fenians John O'Leary and James Stephens, and the less well-known but not insignificant Patrick Neville Fitzgerald, making a final shadowy appearance in this narrative. As is often the case with a tragic and premature demise, if there was any danger that Parnell's achievements in life might fail to immortalise him, his death brought apotheosis.

The myth-making began almost immediately. Parnell's credo was bent into the sort of shape that would allow for his legitimisation in post 1916 Ireland. A marriage of convenience brokered when he was *in extremis* was represented as a return to the recalcitrant and militant convictions of his political youth. To merit inclusion in the pantheon of post-Independence Ireland he had to be distinguished from one of the men who remained loyal to him to the last, John Redmond. Just as Parnell had culpably misinterpreted the true nature of Grattan's Parliament in favour of conferring iconic status on an Ascendancy assembly of strictly limited powers, so was Parnell himself portrayed as a champion of separatism. That he was actually an aristocratic advocate of a rather limited form of legislative independence was conveniently ignored as the Parnellite ploughshare was beaten into a misshapen Fenian sword.

Parnell died as he had lived, close to the edge of bankruptcy. In an attempt to provide for Katharine he had, before they married, written a will in which she and his two children were bequeathed the Parnell family estate of Avondale. Ironically it was his marriage, also designed to regularise her status and secure her future, which invalidated that bequest. Neither Parnell nor Katharine was aware that their nuptials rendered his will null and void and that it would have to be re-made. This was never done and as a consequence his brother John Howard Parnell inherited Avondale. Henry Harrison made one vain attempt to prick the new landlord's conscience but, despite meeting and sympathising with his sister-in-law after his brother's death, John Howard's empathy did not extend as far as honouring his brother's testamentary intentions. It might well have proved more of a burden than a boon for Katharine anyway. It was heavily mortgaged; John Howard Parnell was unable to make a success of it and the estate was sold in 1900.[2]

The last will and testament that was of still greater consequence to Katharine was that of Aunt Ben and, by March 1892, three years after her death, it had progressed no further than the probate court. The brothers Wood were challenging the will on the basis of the alleged 'undue influence' exercised by Katharine on her aunt and the further claim that Mrs Wood was 'not of testamentary capacity',[3] legalese for mentally incompetent to make a will. Their sisters, as well as William, Gerard and Carmen O'Shea, were listed as interveners. Norah O'Shea had declined to join in an action against her mother and the parentage of Clare and Katie was tacitly acknowledged by their absence from the case. The interests of the Wood family and those of the O'Sheas did not exactly coincide. Katharine was the plaintiff, seeking to have the April 1888 will entered into probate. Her siblings were opposing this application and proposed that elements of Aunt Ben's 1847 will should supercede.

O'Shea's intervention was ostensibly on behalf of his two children. However, this can be seen as a convenient fiction to cover his desire for an outcome that placed the legacy within the confines of his marriage settlement. The 1888 will left Aunt Ben's money to her niece in such a manner as to preclude any benefit to O'Shea. In reality, though perhaps not technically, his children's interests were just as well served by the terms of the 1888 will. His own were not. It was to rectify this situation that he intervened. He could not have done so on his own account, consequently, he claimed to be taking action to protect the interests of his children. Although the estate was not 'entailed' (in other words, the entire sum came directly to Katharine, rather than as a life interest to be passed on to her children) it amounted to almost £150,000[4] and was producing an annual income of more than £4,000. Once Katharine treated the legacy as a capital sum and lived off the interest alone, her children's inheritance was secure.

O'Shea's involvement in the case should have been minimally significant. Once Gerard and Carmen's interest in proceedings had been noted, it would have been up to the judge to protect their rights. However, he admitted to Chamberlain in a typically lengthy and self-exculpatory memorandum about the conduct of the case that his letters to Katharine might prove prejudicial. In these, as he declared, 'I certainly pressed my former wife to keep her aunt up to her promises ...' Consequently the correspondence had been cited by the defendants as a clear example of the undue influence over Aunt Ben about which they were complaining. These letters had been lodged with the court during the divorce proceedings and their contents were known to the Woods because of Anna Steele's involvement in that case. Some members of both legal teams had also been briefed in *O'Shea* v *O'Shea and Parnell*. O'Shea confessed to Chamberlain that he had been 'hard up in 1882 owing to the non payment of rent, and other misfortunes ...', adding that 'I was in want of money, owing to political expenses, and , if you will, extravagant personal outlay ...'[5]

The *O'Shea* v *Wood* probate case had become *Parnell (formerly O'Shea)* v *Wood* by the time it was entered on the list for a full hearing before the probate court on 24 March 1892. The mouth-watering prospect of seeing the notorious 'Kitty' O'Shea give evidence in a family row ensured that the courtroom was packed. As her voluntary amanuensis wrote many years later, 'Rumour attributed to her a temperament that would show sport – an indisposition to receive blows without returning them with full measure of interest – and a wallet charged with notes of past negotiations with prominent folk.'⁶ But the curious public and the eager reporters were to be denied their circus. As time ticked on the Judge's Chambers were the scene of last-minute negotiations. According to Henry Harrison, who was not himself directly involved in the settlement, it was the advice of Sir Charles Russell⁷ to his client that had prompted an agreement. As Katharine's solicitor Hawksley told Harrison, 'Russell insists upon a settlement. He says he can't trust the jury – can't be sure of it – and that she might lose everything. The jury might be carried by an outcry that the Mrs O'Shea who had deceived her husband so long was certainly also deceiving her aunt for years – that such a woman would be capable of exercising undue influence ...'⁸

Some time prior to the court appearance O'Shea had engaged in 'undue influence' on his own behalf at the expense of his former wife. According to Henry Harrison the Brighton household was favoured with a visit from Anna Steele. It was the first occasion on which the sisters had spoken since the divorce 15 months before. This fixes the date of the meeting as sometime in February of 1892. Harrison initially assumed Anna Steele to be offering her belated condolences but as it turned out the visit had nothing whatever to do with consoling her sister. She had orders from the Captain. Shortly after the meeting began Norah O'Shea approached Harrison with a letter. It was from O'Shea to his former wife and read: 'Dear Katie, I think that you are worrying yourself unnecessarily about the custody of Clare and Katie because, having regard to the reasonable attitude of your Counsel on the application before the Master on Wednesday, I do not propose to take them away from you.'

It was, on the face of if, a generous and conciliatory letter. But Norah seemed perturbed by it and told Harrison, 'Father wants Mother to agree to something in the Courts to-morrow.' Harrison then noticed that the letter was postdated by two days. He also realised the wording was ambiguous as to time. The reference to 'Wednesday', rather than 'tomorrow' or 'yesterday', meant that the letter could 'relate forward or backward in time, as occasion might require ... The double-jointed phrasing of his letter showed the post-dating to be no accident.'⁹ Harrison concluded that O'Shea 'was making a bargain, and did not wish it subsequently to appear that he had made a bargain.' Rather like a blackmailer who extracts payment for compromising photographs and then refuses to hand them over to his victim, O'Shea was simultaneously playing and keeping his trump card, the custody of Clare and Katie. He had used ingenious phraseology in the letter in order to be able to deny that he had struck a bargain with Katharine over their future. This meant that he would be able to put her under duress again, whenever he chose to do so, by issuing threats to assert his custody rights. Had he dated the letter correctly, he could have left himself open to a legal interpretation that he had 'received consideration and that there has been a contract which can be enforced'.[10] In order to thwart the Captain's machinations Harrison added, in red pen, an addendum to the letter clarifying the date on which it had been written and received. He then had his signature witnessed twice.

The following day matters relating to the O'Shea marriage settlement were being heard in Chambers. Harrison, writing almost four decades after the events in question, is unclear as to the exact nature of these proceedings. They may relate to an application by Katharine to the Court of Chancery for £5,000 from her marriage settlement with O'Shea in order to cover costs of the probate action. As she could claim to be protecting the interests of her children, she could justify such an application. O'Shea was seeking up to £1,500 from the settlement on his own account. He claimed this was to cover his own legal costs[11].

However the proceeding in question may also have referred to a 'rectification of settlement' application on the part of O'Shea. As the Captain was, legally, the innocent party in the divorce and had been given custody of the five children, he was entitled to revisit the divorce settlement to extract additional funds from Katharine should any accrue to her. While the March 1888 will, which was in dispute in the probate court, specifically excluded Aunt Ben's legacy from Katharine's marriage settlement, the divorce action superceded. It allowed O'Shea to seek some of his former wife's 'after acquired' property.[12] As we shall see by the time of the probate action he had forced Katharine to concede a half interest in whatever sum would accrue to her from the Probate Court.[13]

Given that his application for the £1,500 was opposed (to Chamberlain he claimed this was done by her solicitors, but it may also have been by one his children's trustees, Courage of brewery fame[14]) it is more likely that the letter was designed to pressurise her into making a major concession on the issue of the inclusion of her share of the Wood legacy in her marriage settlement. Had she refused to comply, O'Shea might well have returned to the divorce court and forced her to do so anyway, but he had a weapon in his possession that rendered such a move unnecessary. He had legal custody of Parnell's two children. Since the divorce he had made no move to exercise his prerogative but he could do so at any time of his choosing.

The inclusion of whatever legacy accrued from the *Parnell* v *Wood* probate case in the O'Shea marriage settlement meant that O'Shea, while still an intervener, was no longer acting in a fashion antagonistic to his wife's case.[15] Working exclusively in his own interests he attempted to bolster her cause. In a belated attempt to prove Aunt Ben's competence to compose and sign the March 1888 will, he employed an emissary (possibly the admirable James Thomson) to extract affidavits from George Meredith and the Rector of Eltham, among others, that his superannuated financial milch cow had been of sound mind.[16]

His disappointment at the court settlement arrived at on 24 March was profound and bitter. The sum at issue was reduced from £144,500 to £130,000 to cover the legal costs of both sides. This was the Captain's first bone of contention. Webster, Clarke, Russell et al 'have been paid fees of an amount unheard of in such cases within this generation ...'[17] he protested to Chamberlain. What rankled even more was that, despite his understanding that the case would be contested, the settlement left him with 50 per cent of 50 per cent. The agreement worked out in the Chambers of Judge Jeune of the probate court divided £130,000 on a 50:50 basis between Katharine and her Wood siblings. After that, as the *Times* reported, '... the life interest in Mrs Parnell's share will be equally divided between her and Captain O'Shea.'[18] After £15,000 of that capital sum was shared between the two parties to cover large debts and current expenditures, they divided the life interest in £50,000. Invested in Consols at 2.75 per cent, it would produce an annual income stream of just under £700 each.

O'Shea, who the previous year had been writing to Chamberlain in glowing terms about his relations with the Wood family, was infuriated by Katharine's failure to oppose them in the probate court. Three days after the settlement he ascribed this apparent loss of nerve to 'follies actuated by spite against myself'. This, he claimed, had caused his wife to throw away '£75,000 of her children's fortune.'[19] Less than a week after the case his ire had been deflected onto the broad backs of Sir Charles Russell and Gladstone. On the spurious basis that Gladstone's physician, Sir Andrew Clarke, was due to be called as a witness to the sanity of Aunt Ben, he concluded that the future Lord Chief Justice had 'sacrificed his client's interests in order to save Mr Gladstone, whose name and political dodges might have been mentioned in certain examinations or cross-examinations.'[20]

O'Shea's annoyance was probably accentuated by the disappointment that his wife's dealings with the former Prime Minister (which remained out of the public domain until her memoir in 1914) were not going to be explored in open court.

O'Shea's exasperation was no doubt aggravated by the unexpected loss of his trump card. Henry Harrison claims credit for having persuaded Katharine's lawyer, Bourchier Hawksley, to press for a transfer of custody of Clare and Katie. In so doing he made good use of the postdated letter of February 1892, now covered in Harrison's red ink. In the knowledge that he had overplayed his hand and that he could be called upon to explain what he had intended when he wrote the letter, O'Shea did not object when an application was made for custody of the two youngest children to be vested in his wife. He exacted a small measure of revenge within the week.

A few days after the *Parnell* v *Wood* settlement, back in Judge Jeune's Chamber, the portions of the five O'Shea children were allocated. Of the residual sum of £50,000 Gerard O'Shea stood to inherit 40 per cent. Carmen and Norah would be entitled to 22.5 per cent each. In a further manifest acknowledgement of their paternity, the portion allocated to Clare and Katie was a mere 7.5 per cent each. O'Shea had maintained all along that he had been looking after the interests of *his* children. In effecting such a settlement he proved that, quite literally, to be the case.

In order to deflect certain 'nasty hints' as to his conduct in regard to Clare and Katie, O'Shea told Chamberlain that 'I have allowed Mrs Parnell to retain custody of the two youngest children ...' He claimed that this altruistic gesture derived from his having been furnished with medical certificates from a doctor who had examined his wife and declared, '... that if I took them from their mother, he would not answer for the consequences to her.' Having consulted his sisters, 'I agreed to leave these children with their mother.'[21] O'Shea's lengthy (ten closely typed pages) rationalisation may have been prompted by the renewed hope of making a return to the House of Commons which, as we have seen, he had discussed with Chamberlain in the wake of the divorce. On 23 May the *Times* carried a one-line report to the effect that 'It is reported that Captain O'Shea contemplates re-entering political life.'[22] We must presume that the item came from the Captain himself. Such speculative information usually did. Just as in the first flush of excitement after the slaying of Parnell, nothing came of the report.

O'Shea's next imposition on public consciousness was not destined to be on the hustings but in the bankruptcy court. His drawn-out, and ultimately unsuccessful, attempt to avoid a declaration of insolvency began in November 1892, but was largely acted out over the following two years. He had managed to rack up hefty debts of £17,661, of which £12,610 was unsecured. His assets amounted to £4,023. He testified that his income up to 1892 had been around £3,000 a year, but it was now about £700. He told the court that for more than four years past he had been involved in constant litigation, '... and in connexion therewith he has incurred very heavy law costs and expenses. His insolvency is attributable to these costs and expenses, to loss of income, to liabilities incurred on bills accepted by him for the accommodation of others, and to his inability to realise debts due to him.'[23] As was typical with O'Shea, he was blaming others for his misfortunes. His own poor business decisions, litigious nature and excessive lifestyle went unmentioned. He claimed that he had tried to discharge his liabilities in November 1892 by applying to the Probate Division for permission to give up his life interests under his marriage settlement and to receive in lieu the sum of about £6,300. However, there was opposition by the trustees and the order was not finally made until March 1893. The trustees then commenced court proceedings so the money had not been paid over.

Later that week O'Shea's case came before the Official Receiver who heard that a 'scheme of arrangement' was being worked out with creditors to stave off the stigma of bankruptcy.[24] This would involve an immediate payment by the Captain of seven shillings and six pence in the pound. It was apparent during his next court appearance the following month that his financial woes were affecting O'Shea's health. The *Times* reported that '... the debtor, who appeared to be in a delicate state of health, was allowed to be seated during his examination'[25] The previous October the newspaper had reported that the Captain was seriously ill. Bulletins had appeared for four days until his health began to improve.[26] Two years before he had had a bout of scarlet fever.[27] The strain was beginning to show in a man whose lifestyle had never been notably healthy and whose letters frequently included complaints of various ailments, gout in particular. O'Shea testified that, unfortunately, it was '... impossible for him to give any details as to his household and personal expenditure as he had never kept any accounts. He had never been bankrupt before; but he believed that about a quarter of a century ago some arrangement was made with his creditors, but he had no definite recollection on the subject.' It was another example of the Captain's economy with the truth. He had been declared bankrupt in 1869 (see Chapter 1). He explained to the Official Receiver that he had 'made himself responsible for a large amount on behalf of Mr Beerbohm, and he claimed to be a creditor on his estate for £10,000'. The mysterious Beerbohm, a name not mentioned in any of

O'Shea's extant correspondence, had promised him shares in the Hudson Tunnel Company, but the Captain had never received them. As a result of his generosity to Beerbohm '... During the latter part of 1892 several creditors came down upon him, and executions were levied on his property, and his furniture was seized and sold by the sheriff.'

O'Shea's tale of generosity and woe failed to soften the hearts of his creditors. The scheme of arrangement had to be rejected by the bankruptcy court because some of the creditors objected. They had decided, on the basis of what was on offer, what was promised in the future, and what they knew of O'Shea, that their interests would be better served in forcing him into bankruptcy and dividing his assets. Gerard O'Shea had loyally stepped in to help his father, offering security for the proposed payment of seven shillings and sixpence in the pound. But doubts were also expressed about this security. It was agreed that 'the guarantee was not worth anything in its present form' and the application for the arrangement was dismissed.[28] For the second time in his life the Captain had been declared bankrupt. There was no great outburst of Irish *schadenfreude* at the news. The lack of delighted reaction from nationalist Ireland indicated what an irrelevant and marginalised figure he had become.

His son, meanwhile, was proving to be something of a chip off the old block. In 1896 Gerard had married his cousin, Christabel Barrett-Lennard. Joyce Marlow suggests that the marriage may have taken place because his bride was pregnant at the time. The following year he was in the headlines on his own account after a late night fracas in the Raleigh Club in Regent Street. He had been involved in a billiard game with 'a well-known wealthy Scotch laird' called Mackie, a fellow Club member. Mackie had triumphed, in front of a sizeable audience, and after the game the members adjourned to the supper room. There the Scottish laird had 'made some observation respecting Mr O'Shea's mother', prompting O'Shea Jr to throw the contents of his glass over Mackie. The aggrieved Scotsman had immediately threatened to shoot O'Shea. Members had intervened and persuaded Mackie to extend his hand, which O'Shea refused to shake. Instead he had punched his adversary who had hit his head off a fender as he fell. Mackie had remained unconscious for some time. He was gingerly moved to a bed in the club. Two doctors arrived quickly, followed by two brain specialists. There were fears that bones from Mackie's skull had splintered and were pressing on his brain. Fortunately for Gerard O'Shea the Scotsman regained consciousness after a time. O'Shea the Younger sent in his resignation to the Raleigh Club but, according to newspaper reports, members were sympathetic and his resignation was unlikely to be accepted. According to the agency report, 'It is stated that immediately after the fracas Mr. O'Shea laid the facts before his father and other relatives, including his uncle, General Sir Evelyn Wood, all of whom expressed their entire approval of his conduct.'[29]

In 1911, six years after the death of his father, Gerard O'Shea would follow his footsteps into the bankruptcy court. He was far less penitent and clearly under considerably less strain than the Captain had been in 1894. At around the time of the settlement of the probate case he had been allowed to realise a portion of his inheritance and, when examined, he candidly admitted that 'He got rid of his fortune in five or six years, and had a good time while it lasted. He had since earned his living by betting.'[30] He seems to have been refreshingly devoid of at least some of his father's sense of victimhood. When asked about his earnings from gambling, he estimated his average annual income at between five and six hundred pounds.

*

After his second brush with bankruptcy little is heard of or from William O'Shea for a number of years. All pretensions towards a return to public life were at an end and, with an income just in excess of his son's annual gambling receipts, O'Shea was preoccupied with a task he had never found easy, making money on his own account. The last documentary evidence we have of him in that invaluable treasure trove of material that is the Joseph Chamberlain papers is an 1898 letter to his former mentor looking for assistance. By then Chamberlain had been rescued from the political wilderness by the fall of the Liberal government in 1895 and the coming to power of a coalition Unionist Ministry. Proud imperialist that he was, Chamberlain held the position of Colonial Secretary in this new Salisbury administration. O'Shea's latest venture was based in Africa and Chamberlain's return to power offered him an opportunity to exploit one of his few remaining influential contacts. The project he advanced was a scheme involving the development of a railway across part of southern Africa.

The intention was to seek a grant of land from the Colonial Office on the west coast of what is now South Africa at a place called Kosi Bay and run a railway from there to connect with the Transvaal frontier. In February 1898 he wrote to Chamberlain enclosing 'a précis of the business on which I am anxious to see you.' He told his old friend that 'I have devoted much time and labour to bring it into its present shape and I am sure that its conclusion would prove of enormous advantage to England.' A civil service briefing note that accompanied the letter suggested that O'Shea was no William Martin Murphy. He was not going to forge a second career in the African railway business. Three reasons were given by the anonymous civil servant for discouraging O'Shea. These included 'gigantic natural obstacles to the construction of a harbour at Kosi Bay.' As was so often the case with his entrepreneurial projects, the Captain had not done his homework. A curt note dated six days after the receipt of the original letter indicated that 'Mr C has replied'.[31] As far as is known this was the last communication between two men whose correspondence over a period of 16 years offers an often fascinating insight into some curious corners of the history of Ireland in late Victorian times, as well as an insight into some curious corners of the minds of two supreme egotists. The judgment of Chamberlain's hagiographer on the Captain's inglorious declining years is harsh and uncompromising, but his assessment has more than a scintilla of truth. 'Lingering unnoticed, doubtless with a deep sense of the monstrous injustice of life,' J.L. Garvin observed, before he clinically administered the *coup de grâce*, '... After 1891, Parnell's grave was preferable to O'Shea's existence.'[32]

After the divorce, and the death of Parnell in 1891, O'Shea had not offered any further threat to the *Zeitgeist*. This was acknowledged by the newspaper for which he had done some service in 1888. When he died on 22 April 1905 (of chronic interstitial nephritis, leading to cardiac failure) the *Times* wrote that he had 'disappeared almost as completely from political life as his name has disappeared for many years past from public knowledge.'[33] The only political comment the newspaper of record allowed itself in an extraordinarily abbreviated obituary was that the Captain's 'political views were too Whiggish in tendency to suit the character of a thorough Irish Home Ruler at war with the coercive policy of Mr Forster and Mr Gladstone.' It was scant reward for the enthusiastic assistance rendered to the *Times* at the Special Commission. His death went largely unremarked. He was a ghost who had long since lost the power to haunt with any conviction. More Canterville than Baskerville.

One of the few contemporary comments made on his passing was a positive observation from a somewhat surprising source. In his gossipy weekly, *Mostly About People*, one of O'Shea's former adversaries T.P. O'Connor erred on the side of charity in his assessment. 'Whatever his faults, Captain O'Shea was always personally a very agreeable man. Indeed, in the centre of the cyclone which he caused, his own very interesting personality has too often been entirely ignored. As a matter of fact, he was a man of very considerable abilities.'[34] Either the journalist and MP had mellowed considerably, or this was a classic example of *de mortuis nil nisi bonum*. The avuncular TP may have been advertising the very Irish trait of speaking well in death of someone for whom you had no time whatever in life. According to St John Ervine (who dedicates his book on Parnell to Joseph Chamberlain's biographer, J.L. Garvin, so *caveat emptor*), O'Shea 'had great talent, but he seems not to have had character. In suitable circumstances, he might have followed a career of considerable worth, but the circumstances were not created for him.'[35] O'Shea had never been particularly adept in creating positive circumstances for himself. It was ironic that eight years after his death it was another of his most bitter enemies, William O'Brien, who should be instrumental in restoring his name to the public domain.

On 6 September 1913 the *Cork Free Press* published an article by O'Brien that harked back to the divorce scandal. O'Brien had come across three letters written to him by Parnell and they were reproduced in the newspaper.[36] The contents of one of the letters has already been quoted (see p. 344). Written in 1890 it had been intended to reassure O'Brien that there would be no adverse consequences from the divorce proceedings. In his commentary on the letter O'Brien, with the rancour of the party split long past, defended his former leader's reputation. He asserted that if the truth had been allowed to come out 'The Irish leader would have been shown to be rather a victim than a destroyer of a happy home and the divorce would never have taken place. Parnell yielded, with a self-abnegation to which justice will perhaps be done hereafter.'[37] This was, of course, a very different account to that later put forward by Katharine, who would insist the following year that it had been Parnell himself who had wanted the divorce so much that he had refused to press the defendant's claim of collusion.

Gerard O'Shea, who would become a champion of his father's reputation almost as fierce as the Captain himself had been in life, responded in the *Times* to the renewed imputation that his father had colluded in the affair. Describing O'Brien's article as containing 'scandalous insinuations' and adding imperiously that 'I have never heard of Mr William O'Brien', he continued that he believed O'Brien's article to be 'a slander upon my late father' and that he had consulted his mother who had agreed that it was 'an insult to myself, your father's memory, and, above all, to my late husband, Mr Parnell.' Katharine announced that, as soon as possible, she intended to publish Parnell's letters, which she had intended to release after her death. Gerard retained the last word for himself, claiming triumphantly that 'I may say that the letters to which my mother refers constitute an absolute refutation of the allegations ...'[38]

The aggrieved son and the malleable mother were as good as their word. The volume was produced 'with unwashed hands', emerging within a year of the offending article. Serialised with much panoply in the *Daily Sketch* (which, not unnaturally, chose the most salacious extracts), *Charles Stewart Parnell: His Love Story and Political Life* was the publishing sensation of 1914. Largely adverse or, at best, lukewarm British press reaction failed to staunch the flow of the two-volume memoir from British bookshops. Not even the minor matter of the onset of the Great War three months after its publication inhibited its sales. The reaction in Ireland was largely one of embarrassed silence. Most of the mainstream daily newspapers ignored it completely. Only William Martin Murphy's *Irish Independent* reviewed the publication using words like 'shocking ... revolting ... disedifying'[39] to describe its reaction. A highly successful boycott of the book was organised by the ultra-conservative Roman Catholic Vigilance Committee, which would continue to adjudicate on matters of morality for many years to come. So rigorous was this campaign that the Committee even boycotted English newspapers that carried reviews of the book.[40] Many curious Irish readers who did obtain a copy were dismayed at the sheer banality of the relationship between Parnell and Katharine O'Shea once the veneer of intrigue, romance and mystery was removed and the very mundanity of the affair revealed to a disappointed world. Anyone who had bought into the myth of an almost omnipotent Parnell felt cheated by the domesticity of a relationship whose implications and tragic consequences had far exceeded its actual scope.

As we have repeatedly observed, the book (part memoir of Katharine's early life, and part narrative of her unorthodox decade-long 'marriage' to Parnell) was partly intended[41] to counter O'Brien's renewed allegations of collusion on the part of the Captain. This object was largely achieved by sleight of hand. Letters were reproduced from the latter part of the relationship that conveyed the impression of a determined effort at concealment from a suspicious husband. Read in a different context, they can equally stand as a concerted attempt to put the Fourth Estate off the scent. Otherwise the memoir did the Captain few favours. Gerard O'Shea may have been involved in the compilation of the book, but he was not able to censor a largely unflattering portrait of his late father.

However, even in this respect there is some ambiguity. Gerard O'Shea made at least one crucial intervention on behalf of the Captain. Katharine's publication of O'Shea's letters, a move undoubtedly forced on her by her son, created the inescapable impression that they were still on terms of affection up to 1886. The conspiratorial and affectionate tone of his writing sits awkwardly with her allusions to her aversion for her husband. The sense that is often conveyed, far from mutual antipathy, is of a tolerant and reciprocated sisterly affection for an impossible but not irredeemable younger brother. She is 'exasperatedly affectionate'[42] towards her husband until things start to go badly awry in 1886.

It was Henry Harrison's contention that an ailing, vulnerable Katharine O'Shea, verging on dementia, had succumbed to the bullying of her son in the compilation of the book. But, as Roy Foster has demonstrated, the elderly lady who spoke at a press conference on 18 May 1914 to publicise the book was self-possessed, articulate and 'very far from entering a lunatic asylum'.[43] She fielded questions with aplomb. 'All interviewers described her charm, humour and intellectual alertness.' She even finished with an apposite observation about her pugilistic son and his thoughts on William O'Brien. 'He considers two volumes less convincing than one fist.'

Gerard O'Shea was obliged to make one further intervention on behalf of his father. In 1936 he objected to a London West End production of the Elsie T. Schauffer play, *Parnell*, on the basis that the drama, too, suggested that O'Shea had connived in the relationship. In addition, as Joyce Marlow avers in her biography of Katharine, he also replicated his father's snobbery by pointing out a number of technical deficiencies in the writing. 'Captain W.H. O'Shea would have asked his maid to "bring" and not "fetch" the whisky. He had not the misfortune to be educated in the USA, but at Oscott and Trinity College, Dublin. He did not call himself O'Shay, neither did he pronounce the words "sea" and "tea", "say" and "tay".'[44] Gerard managed to delay the production for a short period of time. But when he disappeared to Hollywood to become a technical adviser on the filmed version of the drama, starring Clark Gable and Myrna Loy, the Lord Chamberlain granted *Parnell* a license. His father would most likely have applauded his pragmatism.

While Gerard O'Shea may have maintained contact with his mother, it was left to his sister Norah to look after her in her latter years. She died on 5 February 1921 in a small house in Littlehampton, after suffering from a heart complaint for most of the last years of her life. Her younger daughter, Carmen, herself divorced in 1914, died later that the same year. The faithful Norah O'Shea followed in 1923 and was buried with her mother. The combative Gerard O'Shea survived until 1943.[45]

UN MARI COMPLAISANT?

Henry Harrison takes up many pages of his part-memoir, part-polemic, *Parnell Vindicated: The Lifting of the Veil*, attempting to refute the impression conveyed in Katharine's biography of Parnell; namely that she and her lover conducted a covert affair and struggled, often without success, to conceal this from her husband. In effect, at least according to the voice in *Charles Stewart Parnell: His Love Story and Political Life*, they resorted to lies, pretence, disguise, concealment, misdirection and bogus assurances in order to dupe the suspicious but gullible William Henry O'Shea. In his own 'lifting of the veil', which took place 40 years after Parnell had promised his party that he would do so himself, Harrison argues that the details of the relationship to which Katharine made him privy in 1891–92 were very different from those she published, under duress, in 1914.

To the young Harrison she had claimed that 'she was a free woman and wholly independent of Captain O'Shea'[46] when she met Parnell in 1880. Given that it had been six years since the birth of Carmen, that O'Shea had recently been absent in Spain for 18 months and that he did not contribute to the upkeep of the household, it was a plausible assertion and it is not hard to see how Parnell or Harrison would have taken her at her word. Harrison describes the arrangement between husband and wife as 'an informal separation'.[47] He also declared that 'Sex love between them was long since dead'.[48] From their many conversations on the subject in Brighton, Harrison concluded that in the wake of the 'duel' episode in 1881, '... I am satisfied that Captain O'Shea consciously and deliberately shut his eyes to what was going on.'[49] However, 'appearances' would be kept up. O'Shea was 'not to be driven to an embarrassing choice between forfeiting the benefits which that tacit agreement promised him and being held up to public contempt as one who was clearly conniving at his wife's unfaithfulness.'[50] So Harrison is an 'early adopter', dating the complicity from 1881.

In those Brighton revelations of 1891, when it came to the question of O'Shea's certain and unambiguous knowledge of the affair Katharine was somewhat evasive. She understood that *he* understood the 'arrangement', but they never discussed the matter. When Harrison raised the issue, her response was, '"Did Captain O'Shea know? Of course he knew. I do not mean that I or anybody else told him in so many words ... There was no bargain; there were no discussions; people do not talk of such things. But he knew and he actually encouraged me in it at times.'"[51]

Although she claims never to have raised the issue with her husband out of delicacy, she related a risible anecdote to Harrison that does little to add to the credibility of her assertions. The three principals were involved, she told him, in a late and lengthy conversation one night in Eltham. (No date is offered for the alleged incident.) She had gone to bed first, to be followed by O'Shea who entered her bedroom in order to continue the debate they had been having downstairs. The door had accidentally closed and she told the youthful Parnellite how his party leader had entered the bedroom 'head held high and his eyes snapping'.[52] Parnell had then grabbed her, thrown her over his shoulder and, with no delicacy or ambivalence whatever, carried her across the landing to his room. If such an unlikely incident ever took place there would have been no ambiguity whatever as to the state of O'Shea's knowledge of the true relationship between his wife and Parnell.

In seeking to refute the implication of *Charles Stewart Parnell: His Love Story and Political Life*, that O'Shea was never a *mari complaisant*, Harrison might simply have cited the 'further and better particulars' of the defendants in the divorce case and left it at that. These were outlined a few weeks before the case came to trial, would have been assented to by Katharine, but were never advanced any further in court. The picture drawn in the particulars, in plain, unvarnished and only quasi-legal language, was a stark contradiction of the thesis of her book. The defence case was that:

> The Petitioner constantly connived at and was accessory to the said alleged adultery from the autumn of 1880 to the spring of 1886, by inducing, directing and requiring the Respondent to form the acquaintance of the Co-Respondent and to see him alone in the interest and for the advantage of the Petitioner, by directing the Respondent to invite the Co-Respondent to her house in the absence of the Petitioner in his interest and for his advantage, both before and after he had accused her of adultery with the Co-Respondent, by his knowledge that the Co-Respondent was constantly at the house of the Respondent in the Petitioner's absence and by leaving the Petitioner alone at Wonersh Lodge with the Respondent on most of those occasions when the Petitioner left to go to London or elsewhere.[53]

O'Shea was effectively being accused of trading his wife for 'immoral purposes', pimping her, as well as 'covenanted blindness', to use Harrison's own telling phrase. It is not possible to reconcile such charges with the scenario outlined in Katharine's memoir. Either she lied in furnishing her particulars to the divorce court in 1890, and her husband was neither a pimp nor a conniver, or she lied in her 1914 book and he was both. The overwhelming feeling among historians who have studied the available documentation in detail is that her divorce court submission is the more accurate version of events. Jules Abels, author of a 1966 biography, *The Parnell Tragedy*, is one of the few dissenters. Abels claims that Harrison chose to believe her version of events in 1891–92, '... despite the fact that at the time she was infuriated about Captain O'Shea's part in bringing Parnell to his early death, was also embroiled in litigation with him over her inheritance and was spewing out her hatred Medea-like.'[54] Later Abels advances an unlikely Platonic theory when he suggests that 'It is indisputable that O'Shea knew that Parnell was with his wife when he was not there, but knowledge of illicit love is another matter.'[55] This conveniently ignores the fact that O'Shea went ahead with the divorce without ever having found his wife and Parnell 'in flagrante'. O'Shea could have secured the kind of 'evidence' provided by his son's visit, and which ultimately led to his divorce petition, at any point from the autumn of 1880 onwards. In fact he had himself done so in 1881, had a letter from his son recording the presence of Parnell in the O'Shea 'family home' in 1887, and had done nothing at all until it was financially expedient to do so after the death of Aunt Ben in 1889. So even in 1889 he still had no certain knowledge of 'illicit love'.

O'Shea admitted to one of the inquisitive jurors in the divorce trial that he had not lived with his wife since 1886. This confession, allied to the tempo of hysterically critical correspondence between the Captain and his wife (the hysteria being all on his side) from the middle of 1886 onwards,[56] virtually eliminates all possibility that he was unaware that his wife and Parnell were living together in an adulterous relationship from that date onwards. That he chose to do nothing about this until 1889 is easily explained by the unconscionable longevity of the doughty Aunt Ben. That he chose not to wait until a likely resolution of the probate suit in Katharine's favour (and initially intervened against her interests) is explicable, in that he must have been aware that the delay which had already occurred before his dilatory intervention had jeopardised his chances of a divorce.

So when and how did O'Shea arrive at the conclusion that his wife was having an affair with Charles Stewart Parnell? Unfortunately, in the absence of any definitive documentary evidence, we will never know and it would be dishonest to suggest otherwise. However, despite the fact that we will never catch O'Shea in flagrante, we can proceed on the same basis as he did himself; the basis of moral certainty.

As we have established, he was aware in 1881 that his wife and Parnell were having an affair. His offer of a duel may have been the genuine anger of an outraged husband, or part of a foolish attempt to either intimidate or blackmail the Irish party leader. More likely it was the outrage of a manipulator, hoist with his own petard. While O'Shea was happy to set his wife on to lure Parnell into a liaison, a permanent lasting relationship between the two had not formed any part of his purpose. Whatever the reason, there can be no doubt that O'Shea was 'morally certain' in July 1881 that sexual relations had taken place between Parnell and his wife. He may well have then relapsed into a state of naive and optimistic denial

or collusive 'ignorance' of the affair. It is highly likely that a sporadic continuation of sexual relations with his wife (permitted by her in order to
justify at least one, and possibly two, pregnancies) encouraged him in the
belief that a merely temporary liaison with Parnell (in which he had
actually been complicit) had ended and that the *status quo ante Carolum*
(in other words, a state of quasi-separation between himself and his wife)
had been restored. There is very little doubt that he believed himself to be
the father of Claude Sophie, despite Katharine's attempts to deny this possibility to Henry Harrison in 1891.[57] As far as he was aware, with Parnell
incarcerated in Dublin it would have been impossible for his wife to have
conducted such an affair between October 1881 and May 1882. He was
ignorant of the efficacy of the underground Kilmainham Post Office.

As has already been suggested, the correspondence from the Captain
to his wife (as inserted in the Parnell memoir) points to an enduring
intimacy on his side at least. Many or all of her replies to these letters
were extant at the time of the divorce (upwards of 400 letters between
husband and wife were lodged in the divorce court by O'Shea), but they
were never published and do not survive. As a result we do not know
what was the tenor of her responses to her husband. Were they equally
intimate and conspiratorial in tone? Were they distant and neutral? Were
they curt and discouraging? O'Shea, in his correspondence with
Chamberlain, displayed an innate capacity to ignore brief and businesslike
replies and to be expansive and friendly in response. So we cannot assume
that his continuation of the 'Dick' and 'Boysie' endearments were an echo
of intimacies from his wife. But they are not 'show' letters; their frequency
alone belies this possibility. Neither do they read like the letters of a man
who might suspect that his wife is continuing an affair with his titular
party leader. They are a continuing puzzle and a riposte to those who
believe that O'Shea was a conniving husband from the inception of the
affair. If that was the case, then his wife was a co-conspirator in a
contrived seduction in which her husband believed her to be practising
sexual deception on a trusting Parnell. An unlikely scenario.

The absence of any published correspondence between October 1882
and October 1884 has suggested an estrangement of sorts to some
observers. But the renewal of the correspondence in 1884, on the same
terms of intimacy as existed two years before, also points to the possibility that his letters from this period were excluded by Katharine because
they contained allusions to the 'elephants in the room' of the Parnell
memoir, Clare and Katie. The many scathing references in that correspondence to Parnell himself also suggest that either O'Shea was
deliberately using Katharine as a conduit to convey his dissatisfaction with

the Irish leader, or that he did not believe her to be on intimate terms with Parnell and felt it was safe to unburden himself.

Elsewhere in this volume (see chapter 8) we have speculated that neither a wilfully blind nor cleverly duped O'Shea could have remained in either calculated or genuine ignorance of his wife's affair beyond his discovery that Katharine was pregnant with Katie in early 1884, due to his certain knowledge that he could not possibly be the father. However, either: a) O'Shea was genuinely unconcerned at this 'discovery', in which case we must assume that there had been a compact of some sort between the three all along; b) O'Shea was in no position to express outrage because he *then* chose to become complicit in a conspiracy of silence to his own advantage; or c) he decided to 'forgive' his wife and attempt to win back her affections. Even after Katie's birth (in November 1884) the amiable tone of mutuality in the published letters to Katharine does not change until sometime after December 1885 (the last of the Dick–Boysie salutations). The succession of aggrieved letters from mid-1886 onwards, though expressed in the irate tones of a wronged husband, can be assumed to be either for 'show' or to be genuine complaints about the increasingly indiscreet nature of the affair – or both? A truly suspicious or aggrieved husband would have made a greater personal effort to ascertain the truth of the situation, rather than contrive to prove his non-compliance in any affair by constantly seeking assurances in writing.

There is, of course, an alternative explanation. It is the 'Two Lovers' theory that some biographers, of Parnell in particular, have found unpalatable. As we have already suggested there is internal evidence in the Parnell memoir – if one chooses to recognise or seek it out – that Katharine could have been leading a double life until 1886, from which point the Captain acknowledged that he no longer lived with her.[58] The absences from the domestic scene of both Parnell and O'Shea were frequent and lengthy in duration. Admittedly, on the basis of much of his correspondence with Katharine, Parnell does not appear to be collaborating in the role of 'the other man'; a supplicant paramour accepting of an opportunistic relationship with the object of his affections. But the prevailing assumption that the lover was (for the first half of the affair) not being duped in precisely the same manner as the husband, is based both on Parnell's efficacious qualities and the outmoded notion that Victorian women were as committed to monogamy as their husbands were attracted to adultery. Katharine was a resourceful woman who would do whatever was required for the comfort and well-being of herself and her children – and for as long as was convenient and necessary. The very presence of those three curious children could be advanced as a deterrent for such behaviour on the part of their mother, but the silence of the children in the context of the affair with Parnell has always been a puzzle anyway. It is, therefore, a zero sum argument.

Henry Harrison performs prodigies of mental gymnastics in order to avoid the conclusion that Katharine was physically intimate with both men. He gets something of a 'fool's pardon' because Katharine was not always scrupulously honest with him. In the winter of 1890–91 she told him that O'Shea had no grounds for thinking Claude Sophie was his child.[59] This is in stark contrast to her contention in the Parnell memoir. She was probably telling Harrison what he wanted to hear. She urgently required his zealous efficiency and would have astutely read him as being youthfully priggish and judgmental. Harrison was unready for an admission that it had been necessary for her to continue or resume sexual relations with her husband.

Harrison quotes Sir Edward Clarke as an unimpeachable source on the paternity of Clare and Katie, and insists that 'Captain O'Shea himself was the ultimate originator of the statement'[60] – in other words that Clarke had been given the information by O'Shea himself. Leaving aside the fact that this would not have been the sort of detail that a barrister would have wished to hear from his client if he were to disprove a charge of condonation, Harrison then goes on to use adverse logic in dealing with another of Clarke's assertions. This was that O'Shea 'mistakenly supposed himself to be the father'[61] of Claude Sophie. Rather than suggest that Clarke would have come by this information from the same source (O'Shea) and invite the logical assumption that, consequently, O'Shea must have had (to use Harrison's own phrase) 'sexual access' to his wife, Harrison theorises that 'it was from Mrs Parnell's own book, published in 1914, and not from Captain O'Shea's lips '...that Clarke became acquainted with this fact. Like a self-serving gourmand he manages to have his cake and eat it.

Katharine herself avoids all questions as to O'Shea's awareness of the paternity of Clare and Katie by simply writing them out of the domestic history of the triangle. As we have noted elsewhere, although it is evident that Clare was the child of Parnell, O'Shea may have been gulled into believing that he could have been the father. Such was not the case where Katie was concerned. In the instance of Claude Sophie, while Katharine obviously acknowledges her existence, she simply ignores the issue of why her husband would have been so solicitous for a child (and for her wellbeing) that he knew to be that of another man. Ironically but understandably, although the thrust of *Charles Stewart Parnell: His Love Story and Political Life* is to vindicate the Captain's divorce court testimony that he was an unknowing and unwilling cuckold, she fails, in seeking to promote that cause, to advance the salient information that his ignorance that he was being cuckolded might have been based on the sporadic continuance of their sexual relationship. Evidently her otherwise oppressive son did not require that of her. In much the same way O'Shea, had the divorce been contested, would have failed to advance the paternity of Clare and Katie as proof of adultery because it was, simultaneously, proof of connivance.

Theories about the true nature of this notorious ménage have been based on an understandable hostility to O'Shea. His status in Irish history is on a par with that of the Informer, though he really has more in common with the Place-seeker. He cannot compete with the iconic, albeit flawed, Uncrowned King, therefore observers want to believe that, in addition to being a snake in the Irish Eden, he is a lamentable cuckold and a figure of fun. But neither his connivance in the affair nor his status as a gullible 'cuckold' (whichever happens to be one's favoured theory) is challenged by the notion that he continued to have a fitful relationship, sexual and otherwise, with his wife. Only the dating of the connivance would be at issue. The problem is in accepting that Parnell could have been a cuckold himself.[62]

However, it is still the eminently contradictable and refutable contention of this volume that matters between O'Shea, his wife, and Parnell, came to a head in the summer of 1884. It will be recalled that the Captain wrote an angry letter ('You have behaved badly to me') to the Irish leader, threatening to resign and take his family abroad. There is circumstantial evidence that O'Shea agreed to recognize the de facto Wonersh Lodge relationship in return for guarantees of his continuation in parliament. He was, at the time, under serious threat in his Clare constituency. It is difficult to account for Parnell's exertions on his behalf otherwise. Katharine certainly felt confident enough and secure from detection in early 1885 to build a workshop and a study for Parnell and to stable his horses in Eltham. It was not until 1886 (and the intrusion of the *Pall Mall Gazette*) that the three had to come to terms with the fact that there were other parties who were pruriently interested in their domestic arrangements and that they had teams of eager reporters at their disposal to press home that curiosity. It is relatively easy to dismiss O'Shea's irate 1886–87 letters as warnings to exercise greater discretion or compositions designed for future legal consumption.

It should also be recognised that this theory is not incompatible with the 'Two Lovers' scenario. Just like the 'self-serving gourmand' noted above, we can have our cake and eat it. The only proviso being that the undesired lover was jettisoned after 1884.

THE BOUNDER, THE AUTARCH AND THE CIPHER

The three figures at the centre of the Eltham Triangle, none of whom it should be said are particularly likeable, have all been treated very differently by history. But history, justifiably, smiled on Parnell. Streets, statues, scholarly biographies and veneration have been his lot. He has managed in death to achieve the feat for which he was celebrated in life: being all things to all men. Although he was not hanged, drawn, quartered, shot, assassinated or transported (the fate of many Irish nationalist heroes) his premature death, attributable to his rebellion against English orthodoxy and preceded by his apparent neo-Fenianism means he can safely be conferred the status of nationalist martyr. His rampant parliamentarianism and wholehearted rejection of political violence simultaneously permits of his entry into the Pantheon of Constitutional Nationalism. In one version of heaven it is possible to envisage him sitting alongside Tone and Pearse. In a parallel afterlife he caucuses with O'Connell, Griffith and Collins. If 'success has many fathers' and 'failure is an orphan' he is that paradigmatic Irish success story, a noble failure.

F.S.L. Lyons, in summing up the subject of his monumental biography, talks of 'that career of brilliant light and deepest shade, that enigma which baffled contemporaries and has baffled posterity ever since'.[63] To James Joyce in *Portrait of the Artist as a Young Man* he was the lost leader brought down by cant, hypocrisy and the priesthood. To James Mullin, a 'reformed' Fenian and activist in the Irish National League of Great Britain and someone who had once admired him from afar, the reality of the man was that of a '... high-handed autocrat who secretly despised the homage of his followers, and considered that they only honoured themselves by worshipping his Mightiness.'[64] The more neutral British Liberal peer, Lord Ribblesdale, would have disagreed wholeheartedly. They ended up in a train compartment together on a journey from Euston to Holyhead in the summer of 1887. Ribblesdale '... found him the pleasantest and easiest of travelling companions, and we conversed, apparently without any effort on his side.'[65]

Joseph Chamberlain, a worthy antagonist and former ally who might be expected to disparage his rival's capabilities, told R. Barry O'Brien that Parnell was '... A great man. Unscrupulous, if I may say so ... I mean that he was unscrupulous like every great man. I have often thought Parnell was like Napoleon. He allowed nothing to stand in his way. He stopped at nothing to gain his end. If a man opposed him, he flung him aside and dashed on. He did not care. He did not harbour any enmity. He was too great a man for that.'[66]

Finis

Unfortunately all politicians are also human beings. Parnell's success was based on his frequent ability to be somewhat less than human. He was an appraiser, a scientist with an alchemical bent. His strength lay in the equal disdain with which he treated his manipulative English opponents and his all too malleable Irish colleagues. Labouchere once recounted a conversation he had with Healy during which the acerbic Corkman observed that 'Parnell in his heart cared little for the Irish'.[67] That, of course, was one of the very sources of his power. He cared little for anyone. Just as he did with his scientific experiments, he assayed in politics, weighing things up without emotion, calculating, and then presenting his results. His colleagues, many from the clubbable and clannish Fourth Estate, operated on a much less rigorous basis.

Lyons identifies four Parnells: the country gentleman with an innate sense of the divine right of kingship; the political genius who could bend people to his will; the engaging companion – a charming individual in private belying his rigid public demeanour; and finally a darker Parnell, '... driven by demonic pride and self-will to prodigies of concentrated energy'.[68] It was this aspect of his character, his passionate nature, that both made and unmade him. A little less arrogance and a more empathetic nature might have saved his political career. But without that same arrogance he might never have had a career worth saving.

Unlike O'Shea, a man of meaner spirit, Parnell did not cast about for scapegoats when his own incendiary behaviour razed his political career to the ground. He may have been surprised to have had to face the consequences of his actions, but he was prepared to face them nonetheless. He knowingly and willingly courted disaster in his decade-long relationship with another man's wife. He constructed the gibbet on which lesser men could execute him and then defied them to do so. Eventually they plucked up the courage and hanged him.

If Parnell is a triumph of the new accommodating pluralism, then Katharine O'Shea represents the victory of progressive revisionism. She has moved from obloquy to respectability and metamorphosed from the 'proved British prostitute' of Tim Healy's invective to the forensically reassessed and diligently restored subject of four biographies. She is a woman for the sensibilities of the 21st rather than the 19th century. Arguably there has been some over-balancing of the account. She is presented by her biographers as a strong, resourceful, tenacious woman. She was all of those things, in addition to often being guilty of fickleness, obstinacy, vanity and hubris. Those traits, too, are highlighted by her biographers. What she was not, although she might have believed the contrary, was some sort of political high priestess. She was a conduit, and

381

an efficient and useful one at that, but she was a cipher. 'Katie was like a magic bucket in a fairy story', according to Joyce Marlow, 'When filled she was capable of acting of her own volition, not always in the way her master might have chosen if left to himself, but once the spell was broken she had no reserves with which to fill the bucket.'[69] Parnell spoke through her, and therein lay her claim to attention as far as British high politics was concerned. Like her husband she was an Intermediary. The difference between them was that in his status as messenger O'Shea always seemed to think he could improve the message.

It is interesting that she chose not to publish her own letters in her memoir. This could well have been, bearing in mind some of Parnell's reassuring and pacifying responses, because they would have revealed her as a needy, high-maintenance partner, who did not share or totally understand her husband's devotion to the 'cause'. She was certainly no Kathleen Clarke[70] although she did profess support in her book for the great cause for which Parnell struggled. Her surviving correspondence is that with Gladstone, and for much of that she was merely Parnell's stenographer. Her own voice only comes across where she is seeking favours for her husband or herself. Her background and upbringing, as well as her widely acknowledged association with the most powerful and influential Irish politician of a generation, gave her a sense of entitlement that had her seek out the Prime Minister's doctor to run errands and request the Prime Minister himself to scold the physician when he was dilatory. Throughout their life together she probably shielded Parnell from many of the demands and much of the petulance of her husband. She claims that her sole objective in the divorce was to protect Parnell's political career (which, of course, gave her a vicarious access to an exciting and exhilarating world). But arguably the best way to have protected Parnell would have been to go into the witness box and tell the truth about her appalling treatment at the hands of her neglectful and exploitative husband.

Despite his personal loyalty to her, Henry Harrison is critical of Katharine's handling of the divorce. In observing her dealings with the likes of George Lewis, he noted that 'She was, of course, of the "masterful" type of charming lady whose relationships with their expert advisers of all sorts are often marked by conflict rather than co-operation until sheer incompatibility sunders them.'[71] He also, while acknowledging her intelligence and self-confidence, describes her as 'high-tempered and ... prone to let temperament supplant reason in the determination of both opinion and action.'[72] Notwithstanding these reservations Katharine emerges as the most likeable and human of the three points of the infamous triangle. She has also, in the century or so since she became one of the derided femmes fatales of Irish history, emerged from the outer gloom into which the likes of Healy consigned her. She is, thanks to the work of Joyce Marlow, Mary Rose Callaghan, Jane Jordan and Elisabeth Kehoe (not to mention a more sympathetic treatment in biographies of Parnell), no longer the demonised 'Kitty' O'Shea of nationalist Irish mythology.

While Katharine is a completely rehabilitated figure, her former husband is thoroughly redacted, in both senses of the word. William Henry O'Shea has been 'driven back' and 'reacted against' as well as being 'abridged and edited'.[73] Of course, rarely, if ever, did he assist his own cause. His almost total lack of nobility, when compared with his aristocratic adversary, ensures that he emerges from the 1880s as an undignified figure. 'For Samson to pull down the pillars is intelligible. For Figaro to do it beats the Bible.'[74] Parnell has many of the attributes of a Samson. O'Shea has too many of the traits of a Figaro for comfort. And there are those who would consider such a comparison as being odious where the Beaumarchais character is concerned.

That the 'gallant Captain' was more ebullient, approachable and affable is of no consequence, because he was also more affordable. His price was always too low while Parnell had no price. The Captain's cleverness provides an abject contrast with Parnell's genius. He was Horatio or Donalbain at best, never aiming above their station while not quite sharing their worthier qualities. Parnell was the Negotiator and the Plenipotentiary. O'Shea was merely an Intermediary.

If we are to separate politics and character and deal with O'Shea on a purely political level, the role he chose for himself, according to Robert Kee, was '... that of an agent for the Government between traditional moderate nationalist Ireland and the emergent radical nationalism represented by Parnell.'[75] In the end, though he did succeed in this agency work for a considerable time, he was, ultimately, to become a battered victim of the percussion between the forces of polite moderation and 'slightly constitutional' parliamentary nationalist extremism. For a while he was tolerated as a tame Whig and kept around the house for convenience. But once Parnell became a zealous convert to party discipline (to which he hadn't been quite so attached under the leadership of Butt), O'Shea became, at best, supernumerary; at worst, an irritating embarrassment.

In one of his notes at the end of his only play, *Exiles*,[76] James Joyce breezily dismisses the significance of the relationship between Parnell and Katharine, '... first because Parnell was tongue-tied, and secondly because she was an Englishwoman', before adding with a wealth of potential meaning that 'The character of O'Shea is more typical of Ireland.'[77] Given that the statement probably comes from the disillusioned exile in Joyce, he presumably intends us to infer that the figure of O'Shea is that of the Collaborator. He is self-loathing, obsequious, colonised, neutered Ireland. A true cuckold like the country from which he came. Perhaps that is why it is so difficult to even entertain the notion that the Englishwoman was deceiving both men simultaneously. It is galling to have to accept that neither the acquiescent nor the recalcitrant element within the Irish character and Irish politics was capable of overcoming English perfidy. Or perhaps Joyce intended to suggest that when an Irishman looked in the mirror he expected to see Parnell reflected back. Instead he got O'Shea.

When it came to radical republicanism, Parnell made a more credible extremist than O'Shea. At no point did the deposed Irish leader endorse the Fenian credo and in his final tragic campaign he embraced it only gingerly as a means of political resurrection rather than as a viable alternative to the 'failed' Liberal alliance. O'Shea, too, sought salvation through fraternal dealings with the Brotherhood, but though his involvement (affiliated he was not) was of more significance than would have been known to contemporaries other than the likes of Davitt, it was always a mismatch. It is impossible to see Griffith or Pearse, even if the divorce action had never occurred, annexing O'Shea and placing him in a line of succession from Tone through Young Ireland. And O'Shea himself would have bridled at the prospect.

Parnell rarely, if ever, made representations. He preferred to secure what Britain saw as concessions and he viewed as rights, by dint of political *force majeure*. O'Shea, in contrast, became a slave to representations, bombarding the overseers with requests on his own behalf and on behalf of the other plantation workers. A slave rebellion might only come along once in a generation, but if it did Parnell would have been at its head, not O'Shea. Most of those 'enslaved' had so little to lose they preferred Parnell's defiance to O'Shea's accommodation. That dynamic would alter but the change came 40 years too late for the Captain. Petit bourgeois dominance of the Irish polity would have to wait until the 1920s.

William Henry O'Shea could be unprincipled, narcissistic, self-serving and surprisingly pusillanimous at times. He was also clever, accommodating, flexible and surprisingly hard-working as well. He was not enigmatic and was never in much danger of baffling posterity. Nonetheless he deserves a little more from history than to register in the Irish imagination or collective unconscious as a mere Cuckold in the Gap, a sycophantic tool of British policy who stepped forward with his slingshot to strike a blow for the establishment. Despite his shortcomings, which are legion and legendary, he is something more than the stereotypical bass-baritone in a comic opera. Both the Captain and the King can lay claim to being valedictorians. They are, in a very real as well as symbolic sense, the last of their kind. If O'Shea is Iago rather than Falstaff, a malevolently tragic individual rather than a merely malicious and darkly comic 'trickster' figure then his tragedy is that while he may be the Last of the Irish Whigs, in that same collective unconscious Parnell has long since become the Last of the High Kings.

ENDNOTES

INTRODUCTION

[1] Though the highly distinguished academic, Dr Diarmuid Ferriter, now presents a regular RTÉ Radio 1 programme entitled, *What If*, so the hypothetical has at last acquired some respectability.

[2] O'Shea lost by 55 votes, while Stephens, the Liberal candidate he supplanted, was still on the ballot paper and got 36 votes. Had these votes gone to O'Shea, only ten voters would have needed to switch candidates.

[3] With Parnell (various sources, 1881), James J. O'Kelly (O'Shea, MS 5752, National Library of Ireland, 8 June 1886), Henry Harrison (*Parnell Vindicated: The Lifting of the Veil*, London, 1931) He may also have come close to attracting a challenge from his constituency colleague and veteran duellist, the MP who styled himself the O'Gorman Mahon (O'Gorman/Mahon papers, University of Chicago).

[4] T.P. O'Connor, *Memoirs of an Old Parliamentarian* (London, 1929), vol 1, p. 47.

[5] R. Barry O'Brien, *The Life of Parnell* (London, 1910), p. 382.

[6] Dr Kenny, MP, quoted in F.S.L. Lyons, *Charles Stewart Parnell* (Dublin, 2005), p. 482.

[7] Wilfred Scawen Blunt, *The Land War in Ireland* (London, 1912), p. 143.

[8] *Nation*, 9 February 1884.

[9] O'Shea to Gladstone, May 3 1882 (O'Shea, MS 5752, NLI).

[10] Katharine O'Shea, *Charles Stewart Parnell, His Love Story & Political Life*, (New York, 1914) vol 2, p. 231.

[11] McNally was a barrister who also operated as a Castle spy in the 1790s and, while defending Robert Emmet in 1803, was passing on details of the defence case to his paymasters.

[12] Beach, alias Le Caron, infiltrated the American Fenian movement after the Civil War and operated successfully as a trusted Fenian until he blew his own cover when he testified at the Parnell Commission in 1889.

[13] The amiable Irish MP is the hero of the novels *Phineas Finn* (1867) and *Phineas Redux* (1873). Trollope, ironically, was a good friend of O'Shea's father-in-law, Sir John Page Wood.

[14] In the sense of the word coined by Norman Mailer, i.e. an amalgam of fact and fiction.

Endnotes

[15] W.B. Yeats, *Collected Poems* (London, 1950), p. 356.

[16] Parnell went to schools in Somerset and the Oxfordshire Cotswolds; O'Shea's education took place in Warwickshire.

[17] Parnell initially campaigned in Wicklow for his brother, John Howard, in 1874. O'Shea was inveigled into running in Clare by its former MP, the O'Gorman Mahon, in 1880, though he doesn't appear to have taken much persuading.

[18] Who but the most arrogant of politicians would send his mistress to negotiate on his behalf with the serving Prime Minister?

[19] Andrew Kettle, *Material for Victory: The Memoirs of Andrew J. Kettle* (Dublin, 1958), p. 58.

[20] As had Parnell, famously, when he interrupted a speech by Sir Michael Hicks Beach in 1876 after the latter referred to 'the Manchester murderers'.

[21] Margaret O'Callaghan, *British High Politics and a Nationalist Ireland: Criminality, Land and the Law under Forster and Balfour* (Cork, 1994), p. 121.

[22] O'Shea to Chamberlain, March 9 1887 (*Chamberlain Papers*, University of Birmingham, JC 8/8/1/86).

[23] O'Shea to Chamberlain, April 14 1888 (*Chamberlain Papers,* UB, JC 8/8/1/91).

[24] Robert Kee, *The Laurel and the Ivy* (London, 1993), p. 361.

[25] C.D.H. Howard, 'Documents Relating to the Irish Central Board Scheme', in *Irish Historical Studies*, vol 8, no 31 (Sept 1953).

[26] Paul Bew, *Charles Stewart Parnell* (Dublin, 1980), p. 33.

[27] With reference to the militia force founded in 1778–79, which became the engine of the briefly successful drive towards legislative independence called 'Grattan's Parliament', after the leading patriot, Henry Grattan.

[28] One other party member, Richard Power, had a career that described a similar arc.

CHAPTER 1

[1] O'Shea to Chamberlain, 15 April 1882 (O'Shea, MS 5752, National Library of Ireland). Interestingly the phrase is only used in O'Shea's draft – it is missing from the version finally despatched to Chamberlain.

[2] Parl Debs (series 3) vol 269, col 673 (15 May 1882). All citations from Hansard are given as Parliamentary Debates (Parl Deb) pre-1909.

[3] T.M. Healy, *Letters and Leaders of My Day*, 2 vols (New York, 1929), vol 1, p. 154.

[4] O'Shea family information (O'Shea, MS 18315; ref Parnell genealogy, NLI).

[5] Katharine O'Shea, *Charles Stewart Parnell: His Love Story and Political Life*, 2 vols (New York, 1914), vol 2, p. 24.

[6] O'Shea, Parnell, vol 1, p. 25.

[7] Joyce Marlow, *The Uncrowned Queen of Ireland* (London, 1975), p. 16.

[8] http://www.oscott.net/index.htm. Sadly, you will search this website in vain for any reference to the school's distinguished alumnus, Captain William Henry O'Shea.

[9] Marlow, *Uncrowned Queen*, p. 17. Joyce Marlow's research has shown that, academically, he was in the top five in his class.

[10] Both men were actually born in 1840.

[11] Blunt, *Land War in Ireland*, p. 29.

[12] I am indebted to Professor Donal McCartney for pointing this out to me.

[13] Donal McCartney, *UCD, A National Idea: The History of University College Dublin* (Dublin, 1999), p. 6. Ever the UCD champion, Prof McCartney has observed, tongue-in-cheek, that 'I was tempted to keep it quiet and let Trinity take all the blame for the rascal! But historical truth and honesty prevailed!'

[14] O'Shea, Parnell, vol 1, p. 15.

[15] Basic biographical information from O'Shea, Parnell; and Frank Callanan's *Oxford Dictionary of National Biography* entry for Katharine O'Shea: http://www.oxforddnb.com/.

[16]He was, according to Katie, an excellent if rather reckless horseman.

[17]Jane Jordan, *Kitty O'Shea, An Irish Affair* (Gloucestershire, 2005), p. 3. Jordan's account of the extended Wood family is comprehensive and highly entertaining.

[18]O'Shea, Parnell, vol 1, p. 7.

[19]The campaign colour of the Liberal party.

[20]Farwell Byron, *Eminent Victorian Soldiers* (Ontario, 1985), pp 239–266.

[21]O'Shea, Parnell, vol 1, p. 17.

[22]Farwell, *Eminent Victorian Soldiers*, p. 240.

[23]Marlow, *Uncrowned Queen*, p. 11.

[24]A suspicion that will not be dispelled by the title of one of her novels, *Lesbia* (1867).

[25]O'Shea, Parnell, vol 1, p. 43.

[26]O'Shea, Parnell, vol 1, p. 28.

[27]O'Shea, Parnell, vol 1, p. 21.

[28]O'Shea, Parnell, vol 1, p. 48.

[29] Power Collection – Tasham, Curling and Walls – Costs relating to Miss Katherine (sic) Wood's marriage settlement

[30]Healy, *Letters and Leaders*, vol no 1, p. 154.

[31]O'Shea, *Parnell*, vol 1, p. 50.

[32]Blunt, *Land War*, p. 454.

[33]O'Shea, *Parnell*, vol 1, p. 66.

[34]Marlow, *Uncrowned Queen*, p. 32.

[35] Power Collection – High Court of Justice – Probate Divorce and Admiralty Division – Affidavit – No. 3419 – O'Shea v O'Shea and Parnell.

[36]O'Shea, *Parnell*, vol 1, p. 95.

[37]O'Shea, *Parnell*, vol 1, p. 95.

[38]O'Connor, *Memoirs*, p. 87.

[39]Healy, *Letters and Leaders*, vol no 1, p. 154.

[40]In the same paragraph he, inaccurately, describes O'Shea as Evelyn Wood's 'subaltern' and claims that Katie had a fortune of £30,000.

[41]He was not entirely without business nous, however, but when experiencing good fortune tended to negate this by cultivating an extravagant lifestyle.

[42]Today it is the clubhouse of Blackheath Golf Club.

[43]She spoke fluent French and was a scholar of Greek and Latin.

[44]Information on Anna Maria Wood is taken from Marlow, *Uncrowned Queen*, pp 37–9.

[45]Bew, *Parnell*, p. 4.

[46]Bew, *Parnell*, p. 5.

[47]Who eventually moved to England, was an evicting absentee landlord and became a lifelong Tory.

[48]John Howard Parnell, *Charles Stewart Parnell* (New York, 1914), p. 26.

[49]Alan O'Day, *Charles Stewart Parnell* (Dublin, 1998), p. 13. Being sent to a girls' school was not unusual for small children at that time.

[50]Parnell, *Charles Stewart Parnell*, p. 49.

[51]Parnell, *Charles Stewart Parnell*, p. 53.

[52]Emily Monroe Dickinson, *A Patriot's Mistake: Reminiscences of the Parnell Family* (Dublin, 1905). Her credibility may, however, be somewhat tainted as she goes on to suggest that her brother was responsible for the suicide of a Cambridge girl called Daisy, who killed herself as a consequence of unrequited love for the young Irish student!

[53]Parnell, *Charles Stewart Parnell*, p. 78. According to the author she repented at leisure. John Howard Parnell met her in 1880, the year of Parnell's momentous tour of the USA. She was prosperously married in Newport but she admitted to him her regret that she had not accepted his brother's proposal.

[54]Lyons, Parnell, p. 43.

[55]R.F. Foster, *Charles Stewart Parnell: The Man and his Family* (Sussex, 1979), p. 132.

[56]David Thornley, *Isaac Butt and Home Rule* (London, 1964), p. 210.

[57] R.F. Foster, *Paddy and Mr Punch* (London, 1995), p. 52.
[58] O'Day, *Parnell*, p. 15.
[59] Paul Bew, *Oxford Dictionary of National Biography*, OUP online: http://www.oxforddnb.com/view/article/21384.

CHAPTER 2

[1] Lyons, *Parnell*, p. 59.
[2] Denis Gwynn, *The O'Gorman Mahon: Duellist, Adventurer and Politician* (London, 1934), p. 157.
[3] Gwynn, *O'Gorman Mahon*, p. 159.
[4] Gwynn, *O'Gorman Mahon*, p. 224.
[5] O'Brien became notorious in the 1880s as 'Peter the Packer' for his expertise in selecting juries, even in unsettled counties like Clare, which would convict in cases of agrarian crime. He was rewarded with the position of Lord Chief Justice of Ireland in 1888 and became a peer in 1900.
[6] His name sometimes appears as Finegan, but Finigan is the spelling used in the local newspapers.
[7] Michael Davitt, *The Fall of Feudalism in Ireland* (London, 1904), p. 111.
[8] Davitt, *Fall of Feudalism*, p. 110.
[9] Davitt commented that 'His reputed ignorance ... was only one of the many legends which newspaper gossip has woven round a name and personality of fascinating contemporary interest.'
[10] Davitt, *Fall of Feudalism*, p. 115.
[11] The tautology has been much commented upon.
[12] O'Brien, *Parnell*, p. 134; and Davitt, *Fall of Feudalism*, pp 125–6. O'Brien refers to the telegram as having been sent directly to Parnell. Davitt gives 7 November as its date of despatch.
[13] J.L. Garvin, *Life of Joseph Chamberlain* (London, 1932), pp 317–18.
[14] Later to be Secretary of the Land League.
[15] Davitt, *Fall of Feudalism*, p. 149.
[16] *Freeman's Journal*, 9 June 1879.
[17] Leader of the 1381 Peasants' Revolt in England.
[18] R.V., Comerford, *The Politics of Distress*, vol 6 in W.E. Vaughan (ed), *A New History of Ireland*, (Oxford, 1996), p. 43.
[19] Robert Kee, *Laurel and Ivy* (London, 1993), p. 15.
[20] In this he was to be largely frustrated by Patrick Egan, former Fenian and Treasurer of the Land League.
[21] T.W. Moody, F.X. Martin and F.J. Byrne, *A Chronology of Irish History*, vol 8 in *A New History of Ireland*, (Oxford, 1982), p. 352.
[22] O'Brien, *Parnell*, p. 160.
[23] Kee, *Laurel and Ivy*, p. 219.
[24] Healy, *Letters and Leaders*, vol 1, p. 83.
[25] O'Brien, *Parnell*, p. 165–6.
[26] *Independent and Munster Advertiser*, 18 March 1882.
[27] Bernard Becker, *Disturbed Ireland* (London, 1881), p. 60.
[28] *Clare Freeman*, 13 March 1880.
[29] Pigott to O'Gorman Mahon, 9 March 1880. O'Gorman Mahon Papers (OGM Papers, University of Chicago, Box 4, Folder 22).
[30] The O'Gorman Mahon to Stephen McMahon, 11 March 1880 (OGM Papers, UC, Box 4, Folder 22).
[31] Shaw to Mahon, 12 March 1880 (OGM Papers, UC, Box 4, Folder 22).
[32] *Clare Freeman*, 13 March 1880.

[33] A former Young Irelander and MP for Meath.

[34] O'Shea to Conyngham, 13 March 1880 (OGM Papers, UC, Box 4, Folder 22).

[35] Kenny to Mahon, 19 March 1880 (OGM Papers, UC, Box 4, Folder 22).

[36] Captain Mahon to Mahon, 19 March 1880 (OGM Papers, UC, Box 4, Folder 22).

[37] *Clare Journal*, 11 March 1880.

[38] *Clare Journal*, 18 March 1880.

[39] *Clare Freeman*, 10 March 1880.

[40] *Clare Freeman*, 13 March 1880.

[41] *Clare Freeman*, 27 March 1880.

[42] The *Clare Independent* writing about the meeting said that the slob workers were 'employed by the English capitalist Mr Drinkwater who had been disappointed in his hopes of being chosen to represent either borough or county.'

[43] *Clare Freeman*, 31 March 1880.

[44] *Clare Independent*, 10 April 1880.

[45] O'Shea, Parnell, vol 1, p. 124. She found out when they entertained the O'Gorman Mahon to a fish dinner at Greenwich and her husband admitted that the campaign had cost them £2,000 and that his running mate was penniless: 'this announced by him [Mahon] with the grand air of a conqueror.'

[46] Gwynn, *O'Gorman Mahon*, p. 243.

[47] Gwynn, *O'Gorman Mahon*, pp 245–6.

[48] Conor Cruise O'Brien, *Parnell and his Party* (Oxford, 1964), p. 42.

[49] O'Shea to Mahon, 28 March 1880 (OGM Papers, UC, Box 4, Folder 22).

[50] *Clare Independent*, 10 April 1880. The account of the meeting is taken from the coverage by the *Independent*, the main Home Rule newspaper to have covered proceedings.

[51] Despite the fact that Ennis was, technically, in a different constituency, much Clare county business was conducted there.

[52] He would have required excellent eyesight, as the hills of his native county were the Dublin mountains.

[53] Marie-Louise Legg, *Newspapers and Nationalism: The Irish Provincial Press 1850–1892* (Dublin, 1999), p. 142.

[54] *Clare Independent*, 8 May 1880.

[55] *Clare Independent*, 10 April 1880.

[56] *Clare Freeman*, 3 April 1880.

[57] O'Shea, *Parnell*, vol 1, p. 134.

[58] *Clare Freeman*, 14 April 1880.

[59] O'Shea to Mahon, 25 April 1880 (OGM Papers, UC, Box 4, Folder 23).

[60] O'Shea, *Parnell*, vol 1, p. 123.

[61] *Clare Freeman*, 14 April 1880.

[62] O'Shea to Mahon, 25 April 1880 (OGM Papers, UC, Box 4, Folder 23).

[63] *Clare Independent*, 10 April 1880.

[64] *Clare Journal*, 8 April 1880.

[65] The '40-shilling-freehold' vote that existed in Britain had been abolished in Ireland, making the electoral base even smaller. In Irish boroughs a £4 valuation threshold existed which was not the case in the UK. Conor Cruise O'Brien has pointed out (*Parnell and His Party*) that Leeds, a city the same size as Dublin, returned four times as many MPs.

[66] O'Brien, *Parnell and His Party*, p. 41.

[67] An agreement to allow individual Fenians to support, pro tem, a constitutional strategy was rescinded before the election.

[68] O'Shea to the O'Gorman Mahon, 25 April 1880 (OGM Papers, UC, Box 4, Folder 23).

[69] *Clare Independent*, 24 April 1880.

[70] *Clare Independent*, 17 April 1880.

[71] Thomas Studdert to the O'Gorman Mahon, 13 May 1880 (OGM Papers, UC, Box 4, Folder 23).

[72] *Clare Journal*, 8 April 1880.

CHAPTER 3

1 Comerford, *Politics of Distress*, p. 39.

2 Conor Cruise O'Brien has pointed out that the average age of the Parnellites and of the Liberal Home Rulers was 45. However if the O'Gorman Mahon is removed from the equation the average for the 'advanced' party entitles them to the appellation 'young'.

3 Bew, *Parnell*, p. 37. Paul Bew illustrates the often Janus-like quality of Parnell's stances. He had initially agreed to give the O'Conor Don a free run but, prompted by local sentiment, O'Kelly decided to oppose him. When O'Kelly won, Parnell claimed a major victory and the O'Conor Don was denigrated as a 'West Briton'.

4 O'Shea to the O'Gorman Mahon, 25 April 1880 (OGM Papers, University of Chicago, Box 4, Folder 23).

5 This is based on the *Times* report of 18 May 1880, which names the following members as having attended: Shaw, Parnell, O'Kelly, Commins, Gill, Leahy, A. O'Connor, McCoan, Sullivan, Blake, O'Shea, Nolan, Sexton, McCarthy, O'Shaughnessy, Byrne, Meldon, Marum, Dawson, Brooks, T.P. O'Connor, Gray, McFarlane, Daly, O'Gorman Mahon, Biggar, Lalor, McKenna, Finigan, Leamy, O'Brien, Synan, Power, Smithwick, Callan, Smyth, Gabbett, Foley, Fay, Corbet, Martin, Colthurst, Errington and Barry.

6 *Times,* 18 May 1880.

7 Major Nolan, Shaw and Parnell did not vote.

8 O'Connor, *Memoirs*, p. 47.

9 Marlow, *Uncrowned Queen*, p. 58.

10 O'Shea, *Parnell*, vol 1, p. 134.

11 O'Brien, *Parnell*, p. 193.

12 Parl Debs (series 3) vol 252, cols 46–48 (29 Jun 1880).

13 *Irish Times*, 30 June 1880.

14 *Clare Freeman*, 3 July 1880.

15 *Clare Independent*, 5 June 1880.

16 *Annual Register, 1880* (London, 1881), p 57.

17 Parl Debs (series 3) vol 254, cols 312–13 (12 Jul 1880).

18 Lyons, *Parnell*, p. 127.

19 This was the *Juno*, raided by Fenians in August. Forty cases of firearms were stolen. Attempts by the local Land League in Cork to condemn the raid were countermanded from Headquarters in Dublin.

20 *Annual Register, 1880*, p. 102.

21 O'Brien, *Parnell*, p. 193.

22 'Ribbonmen' were members of agrarian secret societies.

23 *Times*, 24 September 1880.

24 In later years it would become a byword for inefficiency and would be made famous, or notorious, by the Percy French satirical ballad 'Are You Right There Michael'.

25 *Clare Journal*, 9 September 1880; and *Irish Times*, 11 September 1880. The source may well have been the same.

26 *Clare Independent*, 11 September 1880.

27 *Irish Times*, 11 September 1880.

28 *Clare Independent*, 11 September 1880.

29 Interestingly, and perhaps significantly, it was sent from Eltham. In Katharine O'Shea's version of their marriage the two had long since been separated and O'Shea only visited Eltham, on sufferance and by invitation, to convey his children to Sunday Mass and return to his London home the same day. 13 September 1880 was a Monday.

30 More than likely to have been Reverend Matthew Kenny.

31 O'Shea to Gladstone, 13 September 1880 (Gladstone Papers, Add MSS 56446, British Library).

32 For example, *Clare Independent*, 27 November 1880.

33 Aside from his occasional sorties into the government divisional lobbies his attendance

record for votes left a lot to be desired. On 18 September the *Clare Independent* pointed out that in the first session of the new parliament Finigan had votes in 109 divisions, the O'Gorman Mahon in 91 and O'Shea in 71.

34 *Freeman's Journal*, 20 September 1880.
35 *Clare Independent*, 25 September 1880.
36 O'Shea, *Parnell*, vol 1, p. 135.
37 O'Shea, *Parnell*, Vol 1, p. 135
38 O'Shea, *Parnell*, vol 1, pp 139–40.
39 O'Shea, *Parnell*, vol 1, p. 125.
40 O'Shea, *Parnell*, vol 1, p. 142.
41 Stridently expressed by Henry Harrison in *Parnell Vindicated*.
42 They were, in fact, of similar age: the 'age-gap factor' has not been advanced by any bona fide biographers but has, nonetheless, crept into the public domain.
43 These were not necessarily secretive simply in order to deceive her husband alone: had the censorious Aunt Ben stumbled upon the truth, the consequences would have been just as bad as discovery by the husband.
44 Marlow, *Uncrowned Queen*, p. 63.
45 *Clare Independent*, 2 October 1880.
46 Parnell to Katharine O'Shea, 4 November 1880 (O'Shea, Parnell, p. 75).
47 Frank Harris, *My Life and Loves* (New York, 1979), p. 412.
48 Kee, *Laurel and Ivy*, pp 292–3.
49 Including Dillon, Biggar, Sexton, T.D. Sullivan, Egan, Brennan, and full-time activists such as Michael Boyton, Matthew Harris, P.W. Nally and P.J. Sheridan.
50 Parnell to Katharine O'Shea, 4 December 1880 (O'Shea, Parnell, vol 1, p. 82).
51 Parnell to Katharine O'Shea, 12 December 1880 (O'Shea, Parnell, vol 1, p. 83).
52 *Freeman's Journal*, 28 December 1880.

CHAPTER 4

1 In June 1882 (admittedly in the wake of the Phoenix Park murders) Joseph Chamberlain had felt obliged to write to Gladstone to explain himself, following newspaper reports that he had been seen talking to Parnell in the lobby of the House of Commons.
2 Along with Joseph Chamberlain, Dilke was the leading Radical in the House of Commons and well disposed towards Irish issues in the early 1880s.
3 O'Brien, *Parnell*, p. 177.
4 In the many of his speeches he was careful not to overlook the issue of Home Rule and to relate it to the movement for agrarian reform; for example in Cork on 3 October and Galway on 24 October 1880.
5 As did Michael Davitt, though he probably had more to fear from his erstwhile Fenian associates.
6 T.W. Moody and R. Hawkins, *Florence Arnold-Forster's Irish Journal* (Oxford, 1988), p. 489.
7 Albeit from a low figure of 8 to 17.
8 Lyons, *Parnell*, p. 139.
9 Bernard Becker, *Disturbed Ireland* (London, 1881), p. 153.
10 O'Brien, *Parnell*, p. 202.
11 Kee, *Laurel and Ivy*, p. 314.
12 Parl Debs (series 3) vol 257, col 392–94 (10 Jan 1881).
13 Herbert Gladstone, *After Thirty Years* (London, 1928), p. 187.
14 O'Shea to Mahon, 16 March 1881 (OGM Papers, Box 5, Folder 1).
15 *Freeman's Journal*, 25 January 1881.
16 On 30 January in Carlow, for example, he had attacked the 'Chief Slanderer of Ireland Mr Outrage Forster'.

[17] Kee, *Laurel and Ivy*, pp 335–39.
[18] Healy, *Letters and Leaders*, vol 1, p. 110.
[19] Davitt, *Fall of Feudalism*, p. 306.
[20] T.P. O'Connor, *Charles Stewart Parnell: A Memory* (London, 1891), p. 133.
[21] Lyons, *Parnell*, p. 145.
[22] O'Shea, *Parnell*, vol 1, p. 165.
[23] Parl Debs (series 3) vol 259, col 499 (7 Mar 1881).
[24] Lyons, *Parnell*, p. 153.
[25] Kee, *Laurel and Ivy*, p. 353.
[26] Kee, *Laurel and Ivy*, p. 354.
[27] The *Irish Times* reported on 6 May 1881 that 'The military members, Captain O'Shea and Major Nolan, as well as Mr Richard Power, declined to vote on the motion which was thus carried by 17 votes to 12.'
[28] O'Shea to Gladstone, 10 June 1881 (Gladstone Papers, Add MSS 56446, British Library).
[29] O'Shea to Gladstone, 13 June 1881 (Gladstone Papers, Add MSS 44269I, BL).
[30] J.L. Hammond, *Gladstone*, (London, 1938), p. 222.
[31] Gladstone to O'Shea, 14 June 1881 (O'Shea, MS 5752, National Library of Ireland).
[32] Parl Debs (series 3) vol 262, col 1322–24 (19 Jul 1881).
[33] Lyons, *Parnell*, p. 153.
[34] O'Shea, *Parnell*, vol 1, p. 175.
[35] In his book *Long Shadows* (London, 1966), Shane Leslie alleges that O'Shea himself had experience as a 'friend'. 'Not one of the Lives of Lord Randolph Churchill', he wrote, 'records the fantastic fact that he once sent Captain O'Shea to Devonshire House with a challenge to Lord Hartington.'
[36] James Kelly, *That Damn'd Thing Called Honour: Duelling in Ireland 1570-1861* (Cork, 1995), p. 271.
[37] O'Shea, *Parnell*, vol 1, p. 177.
[38] O'Shea, *Parnell*, vol 1, p. 178.
[39] *Times*, 17 November 1890.
[40] O'Shea, *Parnell*, vol 1, p. 159.
[41] Harrison, *Parnell Vindicated*, p. 124
[42] Report of divorce proceedings, *Times*, 17 November 1890.
[43] Harrison, *Parnell Vindicated*, pp 126–7.
[44] Her conversation with Harrison would have taken place in 1891. The memoir was produced 23 years later.
[45] Harrison, *Parnell Vindicated*, p. 223.
[46] F.S.L. Lyons, *The Fall of Parnell, 1890–91* (London, 1960), p. 44.
[47] Now the Bank of Ireland.
[48] Lyons, *Parnell*, p. 162.
[49] So called because of his obsession with coercion, a far cry from his relief work during the Famine.
[50] O'Brien was far from being a creature of Parnell and had a distinct streak of independence. Parnell used the paper in questionable ways, however, occasionally inserting misleading references to journeys he was about to undertake as a cover for lengthy visits to Eltham or Brighton.
[51] O'Brien, *Parnell*, p. 237.
[52] O'Brien, *Parnell*, pp 237–8.
[53] O'Brien, *Parnell*, pp 238–40.
[54] A euphemism for agrarian unrest.
[55] O'Shea, *Parnell*, vol 1, pp 190–1.
[56] O'Shea, *Parnell*, vol 1, pp 187–8.
[57] O'Shea, *Parnell*, vol 1, p. 193.

CHAPTER 5

1 O'Brien, *Parnell*, p. 246.
2 O'Brien, *Parnell and Party*, pp 73–4.
3 O'Brien, *Parnell*, p. 249.
4 William O'Brien ascribed his antipathy to the colour to Parnell's fear of arsenic poisoning.
5 O'Connor, *Parnell: A Memory* (London, 1891), p. 127.
6 O'Shea, *Parnell*, vol 1, p. 225.
7 O'Shea, *Parnell*, vol 1, pp 220–1.
8 O'Shea, *Parnell*, vol 1, p. 225.
9 Healy, *Letters and Leaders*, vol 1, p. 158.
10 *Clare Independent*, 3 December 1881.
11 Parl Debs (series 3) vol 267, col 958 (15 Mar 1882).
12 A taxable valuation of land assigned between 1848–64. It was a government assessment of the rate at which property could be rented and tended, as time went on, to fall well behind the actual rent charged.
13 *Clare Independent*, 25 March 1882.
14 O'Brien, *Parnell*, pp 253–4.
15 Parl Debs (series 3) vol 267, col 1426 (21 Mar 1882).
16 Moody & Hawkins, *Arnold-Forster Journal*, p. 465. Her diary for 30 April 1882, a day on which Lloyd has been invited to lunch, reads, 'I cannot help having a strong feeling for Mr Clifford Lloyd; for I believe that his friendship and loyalty to the Chief Secretary are very sincere ...'
17 *United Ireland*, 7 January 1882.
18 Yet again, the book is uncontaminated by letters from Katharine to O'Shea.
19 O'Shea, *Parnell*, vol 1, p. 210.
20 *Times*, 14 December 1881.
21 O'Shea, *Parnell*, vol 1, p. 230
22 O'Shea, *Parnell*, vol 1, p. 228.
23 Lyons, *Fall of Parnell*, p. 44.
24 Lyons, *Fall of Parnell*, p. 174.
25 According to Katharine the child was named after Parnell's sister and a friend of hers, Claude, Lord Truro (O'Shea, Parnell, vol 1, p. 230).
26 O'Shea, *Parnell*, vol 1, p. 241.
27 Jordan, *Kitty O'Shea*, p. 55.
28 O'Shea, *Parnell*, vol 1, p. 237.
29 O'Shea, *Parnell*, vol 1, p. 240.
30 O'Shea to Chamberlain, 25 April 1882 (Chamberlain Papers, University of Birmingham, JC 8/8/1/1).
31 O'Shea, *Parnell*, vol 1, p. 248.
32 *Annual Register, 1882* (London, 1883), pp 45–6.
33 Parnell to the O'Gorman Mahon, 22 November 1881, 30 November 1881 and 1 December 1881. In the first instance, Parnell says of Dillon, 'I feel convinced he cannot live very long here.'(OGM Papers, University of Chicago, Box 5, Folder 7)
34 Gwynn, *O'Gorman Mahon*, p. 261; and Healy, Letters and Leaders, vol 1, p. 129.
35 Gladstone, *Thirty Years*, pp 273–4.
36 O'Shea to Gladstone, 8 April 1882. Gladstone Papers, Add MSS 62114, British Library.
37 Gladstone to O'Shea, 12 April 1882 (O'Shea, MS 5752, National Library of Ireland).
38 The 'important Irishman' being touted by the self-important O'Shea, was, of course, Parnell.
39 In a draft lodged in the Chamberlain collection the word 'state' is substituted for 'public'.
40 O'Shea to Gladstone, 13 April 1882 (Add MSS 44269, BL).
41 Gladstone to O'Shea, 15 April 1882 (Add MSS 44269, BL).
42 Dudley Bahlman, *The Diary of Sir Edward Hamilton* (London, 1972), p. 253.

Endnotes

[43] Forster to Gladstone, 18 April 1882. Gladstone Papers, Add MSS 44160, BL.

[44] Peter T. Marsh, *Joseph Chamberlain: Entrepreneur in Politics* (New Haven, 1994), p. 153.

[45] Roy Jenkins, *Sir Charles Dilke: A Victorian Tragedy* (London, 1965), p.134.

[46] C.H.D Howard, *Joseph Chamberlain: A Political Memoir:1882–92*, (ed),Connecticut, 1975), pp 18–19.

[47] The reference to Parnell was added between the NLI draft and dispatching the letter to Chamberlain.

[48] O'Shea to Chamberlain, 15 April 1882 (O'Shea, MS 5752, NLI).

[49] Chamberlain to O'Shea, 17 April 1882 (O'Shea, MS 5752, NLI). There is a slightly shorter version of same in Add MSS 62114,BL.

[50] O'Shea to Gladstone, 18 April 1882 (Add MSS 44269, BL); and O'Shea to Chamberlain, 18 April 1882 (O'Shea, MS 5752, NLI).

[51] Forster to Gladstone, 18 April 1882 (Gladstone Papers, Add MSS 44160, BL).

[52] Parnell to Katharine O'Shea, 12 November 1881 (O'Shea, Parnell, vol 1, p. 205); also Moody & Hawkins, Arnold-Forster Journal, p. 455, diary entry for 21 April 1882.

[53] Dilke Papers, Add MSS 43936, British Library, f. 88.

[54] O'Shea, *Parnell*, vol 1, p. 232.

[55] O'Shea, *Parnell*, vol 1, p. 233.

[56] Chamberlain, *Memoir*, p. 39.

[57] It was the bill Parnell had truncated in Kilmainham until he realised that, as a result, it numbered 13 clauses, upon which he rapidly restored the excised clause.

[58] O'Brien, *Parnell*, p. 263.

[59] 'What the Cabinet really decided on the 22nd April was to let out Parnell and his friends and to drop arbitrary arrest, although they did decide to have a new coercion bill on minor fronts; to which coercion bill Parnell himself was favourable'(Dilke Papers, Add MSS 43936, BL, ff. 88–9). Also O'Shea to Chamberlain (Chamberlain, *Memoir*, pp 39–40):'If the country should not settle down as clearly and quickly as Mr Parnell is confident would be the case, I have reason to believe that he would *ipso facto* be brought to see the necessity of not offering an embittered opposition to the passage of temporary provisions aimed at individuals and localities tainted with crime.'

[60] O'Shea to Parnell, 24 April 1882 (O'Shea, MS 5752, NLI).

[61] McCarthy: his home at the time was in Jermyn Street.

[62] Parnell to Katharine O'Shea, 25 April 1882 (O'Shea, Parnell, vol 1, p. 238).

[63] Parl Debs (series 3) vol 268, col 1507–8 (26 Apr 1882).

[64] O'Shea to Parnell, 26 April 1882 (O'Shea, MS 5752, NLI).

[65] Forster to Gladstone, 29 April 1882 (Gladstone Papers, Add MSS 44160, BL).

[66] Of course the deal did no such thing.

[67] Hammond, *Gladstone*, p. 275.

[68] The original version, in the Gladstone papers.

[69] Parnell to O'Shea, 28 April 1882 (O'Shea, MS 5752, NLI). This is a copy in O'Shea's handwriting. Interestingly there is another copy in his papers with no reference to co-operation with the Liberal party. This is the version of the letter read by Parnell in the House of Commons on 15 May 1882

[70] O'Shea, Parnell, vol 1, p. 240.

[71] Bew, Parnell, p. 58.

[72] Given that the McCarthy letter was in play at this time, he might also have had some forlorn hope that what O'Shea had extracted from him would be irrelevant.

[73] Enoch Powell, 'Kilmainham: The Treaty That Never Was', in the *Historical Journal*, vol 21, no 4, December 1978, p 956.

[74] Chamberlain, *Memoir*, pp 48–9.

[75] Hammond, *Gladstone*, p. 275.

[76] Despite this wanton display of independence on O'Shea's part, years later Chamberlain insisted to R. Barry O'Brien that his emissary had simply done as he was told: '... he took

no initiative. He simply took what I said to Parnell, and brought back what Parnell said to me' (O'Brien, *Parnell*, p. 388).

[77] Moody & Hawkins, *Arnold-Forster Journal*, p. 465.

[78] Ironically, as noted elsewhere, Forster's Sunday lunch guest later that day – and a much more welcome visitor, we must assume – was Clifford Lloyd, the most capable and enthusiastic executor of Forster's policy.

[79] All quotes from Forster to Gladstone, 30 April 1882 (Gladstone Papers, Add MSS 44160, BL).

[80] Moody & Hawkins, *Arnold-Forster Journal*, p. 466.

[81] Gladstone to Forster, 30 April 1882 (Gladstone Papers, Add MSS 44160, BL).

[82] Moody and Hawkins, *Arnold-Forster Journal*, p. 469.

[83] *Clare Independent*, 6 May 1882.

[84] Justin McCarthy, *Story of an Irishman* (London, 1904), p. 241 & p. 245.

[85] Bahlman, *Hamilton*, pp 262–3.

CHAPTER 6

[1] O'Shea to Chamberlain, 2 May 1882 (Chamberlain Papers, University of Birmingham, JC 8/8/1/2).

[2] Chamberlain to O'Shea, 2 May 1882 (O'Shea, MS 5752, National Library of Ireland).

[3] O'Shea to Chamberlain, 3 May 1882 (Chamberlain Papers, UB, JC 8/8/1/3).

[4] In those days ministerial appointees were forced to face their constituents before the appointment was confirmed.

[5] Dilke Papers, Add MSS 43936, British Library, f. 91.

[6] O'Shea to Gladstone, 3 May 1882 (O'Shea, MS 5752, NLI; and Gladstone Papers, Add MSS 44269, BL). There are slight but insignificant textual differences between the two.

[7] Bahlman, *Hamilton*, p. 263

[8] Moody & Hawkins, *Arnold-Forster Journal*, p. 473.

[9] An accusation also made against the Tory Prime Minister, Lord Salisbury (Robert Cecil), in the appointment of his nephew, Arthur Balfour, to the same position some years later. Salisbury's inclination to promote family members was immortalised in the phrase 'Bob's your uncle.'

[10] Healy, *Letters and Leaders*, vol 1, p. 156.

[11] Lucy Masterman (ed), *Mary Gladstone: Her Diaries and Letters* (New York, 1930), p. 248.

[12] Moody & Hawkins, *Arnold-Forster Journal*, p. 472.

[13] Moody & Hawkins, *Arnold-Forster Journal*, p. 477.

[14] O'Brien, *Parnell*, p. 559.

[15] O'Shea, *Parnell*, p. 194.

[16] Masterman, *Mary Gladstone: Diaries*, p. 248.

[17] Bahlman, *Hamilton*, p. 264.

[18] *Irish Times*, 6 May 1882.

[19] The background to the murders is best explored in Tom Corfe's *The Phoenix Park Murders: Conflict, Compromise and Tragedy in Ireland, 1879-1882* (London, 1968), while the story of the Invincibles and their individual fates is well told in Senan Molony's *The Phoenix Park Murders: Conspiracy, Betrayal and Retribution* (Cork, 2006).

[20] Other Irish party members, like Tim Healy for example, described the Treaty as a 'surrender' (Healy, *Letters and Leaders*, vol 1, p. 155). In very changed circumstances in 1888 O'Shea himself would use the same word when he described standing over Parnell in Kilmainham 'as he signed his surrender' (the *Times*, 2 August 1888).

[21] Davitt, *Fall of Feudalism*, pp 356–7.

[22] O'Shea, *Parnell*, vol 1, p. 247–8.

[23] Davitt, *Fall of Feudalism*, p. 358.

Endnotes

24 In a letter to Gladstone on 7 May 1882, O'Shea couldn't resist some literary criticism, describing Davitt's language as 'somewhat high-flown' (Gladstone, Add MSS 44269, BL).

25 There are a number of different versions of the sequence of events; this is McCarthy's in Justin McCarthy and Mrs Campbell Praed, *Our Book of Memories* (London, 1912).

26 McCarthy & Campbell Praed, *Memories*, p. 97.

27 Chamberlain, J., *A Political Memoir*, Howard, C.H.D. (ed), (Conneticut, 1975), p. 62

28 O'Shea to Gladstone, 7 May 1882 (Add MSS 44269, BL).

29 Gladstone to O'Shea, 7 May 1882 (Add MSS 44269, BL).

30 Dilke, Add MSS 43936, BL, f. 101–102.

31 McCarthy & Campbell Praed, *Memories*, p 98.

32 Special Commission, Proceedings (1890), vol 1, pp 354 & 381.

33 A.G. Gardiner, *The Life of Sir William Harcourt*, 2 volumes (London, 1923), vol 1, p. 438.

34 Annual Register: 1882, p. 63.

35 Moody & Hawkins, *Arnold-Forster Journal*, p. 485.

36 Davitt, *Fall of Feudalism*, p. 360.

37 John Morley, *Life of Gladstone*, 2 volumes (London, 1908), vol 2, p.230.

38 O'Shea, *Parnell*, vol 1, p. 250.

39 *United Ireland*, 13 May 1882.

40 It was somewhat unusual for Dilke to oppose Chamberlain's will – he once said that their relations were so close 'that I should resign with him if he were to resign because he thought Forster did not have his hair cut sufficiently often.' (Jenkins, *Sir Charles Dilke*, p. 134.)

41 Despite his radical credentials Trevelyan had been elected in 1865 when his second cousin had bought an estate in order to command the votes of the tenants. It was sold after Trevelyan's election (*Dictionary of National Biography* (Oxford, 2004)).

42 *United Ireland*, 17 June 1882.

43 Moody & Hawkins, *Arnold-Forster Journal*, p. 498.

44 Quotes from the first phase of the debate are from Parl Debs (series 3) vol 269, col 672–5 (15 May 1882).

45 Healy, *Letters and Leaders*, vol 1, p. 161.

46 Healy wrote that, 'Hansard [published version, *Parliamentary Debates*, pre-1909] omits this, but records a challenge to O'Shea to "read the whole letter," which Forster then handed him.'

47 *Times*, 16 May 1882.

48 *Irish Times*, 16 May 1882.

49 *Irish Times*, 16 May 1882.

50 Healy, *Letters and Leaders*, vol 1, p. 162.

51 *Times*, 16 May 1882.

52 Quotes from the continued Irish debate are from Parl Debs (series 3) vol 269, col 782–801 (15 May 1882).

53 According to Florence Arnold-Forster this day became known in family circles as 'O'Shea Sunday'.

54 *Times*, 19 May 1882.

55 Davitt, *Fall of Feudalism*, p. 351.

56 Quotes from Parl Debs (series 3) vol 269, col 828–95 (16 May 1882).

57 Moody & Hawkins, *Arnold-Forster Diary*, p. 499.

58 For the rather plodding joke to work, the Clare MP's preferred pronunciation of his name (O'Shee) must be borne in mind.

59 *Punch,* 27 May 1882.

60 Dilke, Add MSS 43936, BL, ff. 111–12.

61 Lyons, *Parnell*, p. 219.

62 Chamberlain's residence in Moor Green in Birmingham.

63 O'Shea to Chamberlain, 23 June 1882 (Chamberlain Papers, UB, JC 8/8/1/7).

64 O'Shea to Gladstone, 9 June 1882 (Gladstone Papers, Add MSS 44269, BL).

65 Arguably his services should not have been required by Chamberlain, who had contact with Parnell through Labouchere.

[66] No date indicated on the invitation, but the dinner was on 13 June 1882 (Gladstone Papers, Add MSS 44787, BL).

[67] Bahlman, *Hamilton*, p. 290.

[68] This is Herbert Gladstone's figure. She herself in her memoir referred to them as having met 'frequently'. Gladstone's son sought to contradict this assertion after the book was published in 1914.

[69] O'Shea, *Parnell*, vol 2, p. 195.

[70] Undated, O'Shea, MS 5752, pp 23–5, NLI.

[71] O'Shea to Chamberlain, 30 March 1892 (Chamberlain Papers, UB, JC 8/8/1/166).

[72] Bahlman, *Hamilton*, pp 327–8.

[73] Gladstone memo to cabinet, 3 November 1882 (Gladstone Papers, Add MSS 44766, BL).

[74] Bahlman, *Hamilton*, p. 357.

[75] Hamilton to Spencer, 24 September 1882 – Gordon, Peter (ed.), *The Red Earl: The Papers of the Fifth Earl Spencer 1835–1910* (2 vols) – vol. 1, p.223

[76] O'Shea, *Parnell*, vol 2, p. 198.

[77] Hammond, *Gladstone*, p. 307.

[78] O'Shea, *Parnell*, vol 2, p. 198.

[79] O'Shea to Chamberlain, 30 March 1892 (Chamberlain Papers, UB, JC 8/8/1/166).

[80] Harrison, *Parnell Vindicated*, p. 192.

CHAPTER 7

[1] In the parliamentary sessions of 1880–3 O'Shea spoke 115 times to Mahon's 9. During the same period the likes of Frank Hugh O'Donnell made 863 interventions and Parnell 1,087. Bear in mind that Parnell was in Kilmainham for almost seven months during that period.

[2] O'Shea kept the local papers well informed of his movements and there is coverage of visits in, for example, October 1882, late June 1883, October 1883, early January 1884, etc.

[3] In 1883, for example, he voted 97 times out of a total of 314 divisions. Parnell voted in 126, the same number as T.P. O'Connor. Frank Hugh O'Donnell was present for 68 divisions and Justin McCarthy for 154. The most prodigious nationalist was Biggar, who voted in all but 27 divisions that year (*United Ireland*, 8 September 1883).

[4] 'It seems probable that even the most moderate Home Rulers, were denied all but morsels of patronage until mid-1882.'Alan O'Day, *The English Face of Irish Nationalism* (Dublin, 1977), p. 72.

[5] These included the Whiggish *Clare Journal*, the nationalistic *Clare Independent* (later the *Independent and Munster Advertiser*) the *Clare Freeman*, *Clare Examiner*, *Clare Advertiser* (based in Kilrush) and the *Kilrush Herald*. The *Examiner* at 1d, the *Independent*, *Freeman* and *Herald* at 2d were the cheapest. The others varied between three and four pence. The Clare *Saturday Record* came on the scene in 1885 when O'Shea had departed it (Legg, *Newspapers and Nationalism*).

[6] *Freeman*, 12 August 1882.

[7] *Independent and Munster Advertiser*, 3 March 1883.

[8] Parl Debs (series 3) vol 274, col 1922 (23 Nov 1882).

[9] Parl Debs (series 3) vol 276, col 1142 (28 Feb 1883).

[10] O'Shea to Gladstone, 6 March 1884 (O'Shea, MS 5752, National Library of Ireland).

[11] Hamilton to O'Shea, 7 March 1884 (O'Shea, MS 5752, NLI).

[12] Equivalent to a county council today.

[13] Chief Secretary's Office Registered Papers (CSORP), National Archive of Ireland, 1880/31241.

[14] Possibly because he knew no better, but more likely to avoid confusing the honourable members, he called them 'little native canoes'.

[15] Debate on Sea Fisheries (Ireland) Bill, Parl Debs (series 3) vol 280, col 1062 (20 Jun 1882).

[16] Considine died in April 1884.

Endnotes

[17] B. Becker, *Disturbed Ireland* (London, 1881), p. 60.

[18] Grosvenor to O'Shea, 13 December 1884 (O'Shea, MS 5752, NLI.)

[19] O'Shea to Grosvenor, 19 December 1884 (O'Shea, MS 5752, NLI.)

[20] Parl Debs (series 3) vol 287, col 930 (27 Apr 1884).

[21] CSORP, 20176/1880, NAI.

[22] Trevelyan to Spencer: 'I have much to say when we meet on the manner of dealing with Irish members, on which I think you can do a great deal by the method of handling patronage.' (O'Day, *Face of Irish Nationalism*, p. 73.)

[23] Grosvenor to O'Shea, 13 December 1884 (O'Shea, MS 5752, NLI.)

[24] He singles out Mahon, O'Shea, Synan, Callan, Marum, Blake, Gray, A.M. Sullivan, O'Shaughnessy and Arthur O'Connor as most frequent recipients. Only O'Connor could be described as a militant supporter of Parnell.

[25] O'Day, *Face of Irish Nationalism*, p. 73.

[26] O'Day, *Face of Irish Nationalism*, p. 75–6.

[27] Ah, the sublime innocence ...

[28] Unless otherwise indicated accounts of the murder of John Doloughty and the trial of Francis Hynes come from the *Clare Freeman*, *Clare Journal* and, most particularly, the *Independent and Munster Advertiser*.

[29] The village became part of Mayo in the Local Government (Ireland) Reform Act of 1898.

[30] In the House of Commons Biggar claimed that ... 'Mr McTiernan and the family of the prisoner had a quarrel about shooting at game and that made him prejudiced against the prisoner.' (*Freeman's Journal*, 18 August 1882) This was denied by McTiernan (*Freeman's Journal*, 19 August 1882).

[31] He would later become Hynes's solicitor.

[32] *Freeman's Journal*, 14 August 1882.

[33] *Freeman's Journal*, 12 August 1882.

[34] According to the *Freeman's Journal* it amounted to eight pints of ale or stout, one bottle of sherry, three bottles of claret, six glasses of gin, one half glass of brandy, a bottle of champagne (divided between two!) and thirty-five and a half glasses of whiskey. Of that total, the six attendants had drunk a glass of whiskey and a pint of stout each. Four members of the jury were teetotallers, so the rest was consumed by eight men (*FJ*, 24 August 1882).

[35] Callan, with typical bombast and hyperbole, had claimed that 'there were 46 Catholics objected to and not a single Protestant.'(*Freeman's Journal*, 16 August 1882.)

[36] Parl Debs (series 3) vol 278, col 1837–42 (15 Aug 1882).

[37] *Independent and Munster Advertiser*, 19 August 1882.

[38] Hammond, *Gladstone*, p. 324.

[39] Members of the jury had publicly denied O'Brien's allegations.

[40] *Independent and Munster Advertiser*, 26 August 1882.

[41] *Freeman's Journal*, 30 August 1882.

[42] *Clare Freeman*, 2 September 1882.

[43] *Freeman's Journal*, 2 September 1882.

[44] *United Ireland*, 2 September 1882.

[45] *Freeman's Journal*, 5 September, 1882

[46] O'Shea, *Parnell*, vol 2, p. 196.

[47] She refers to him as Francis Hymer, which is either an uncorrected typographical error or a misreading of her husband's handwriting.

[48] O'Shea, *Parnell*, vol 2, p. 196.

[49] Katharine O'Shea to Gladstone, 12 September 1882 (O'Shea, Add MS 44269, British Library).

[50] O'Shea, *Parnell*, vol 2, p. 11.

[51] *Freeman's Journal*, 12 September 1882.

[52] *United Ireland*, 16 September 1882.

[53] *United Ireland*, 30 September 1882.

[54] *Independent and Munster Advertiser*, 17 November 1882.

THE CAPTAIN AND THE KING

[55] On 15 August when the matter first came before the House of Commons, he was one of a handful of Irish MPs in attendance. He chose to remain silent while Callan and O'Donnell intervened. Later he would allow Thomas Sexton to make most of the running on the issue in Parliament.

[56] The *Times*, 5 February 1884.

[57] The *Irish Times*, 26 March 1883.

[58] O'Shea to Chamberlain, 1 August 1883 (O'Shea, MS 5752, NLI): 'One can understand Lord Spencer's snapping his fingers at the Boys, but snapping them just as gaily at those who are supposed to save him from the Boys is very funny.'

[59] William O'Brien, *Evening Memories* (Dublin and London, 1920), p. 103.

[60] O'Shea to Grosvenor, December 19 1884 (O'Shea, MS 5752, NLI).

[61] O'Shea to Mahon, 16 March 1881 (OGM Papers, University of Chicago, Box 5, Folder 1).

[62] *United Ireland*, 9 February 1884.

[63] He became Registrar of Petty Sessions Clerks at £700 a year, a reward from a Liberal government aware that he had no chance of re-election in Limerick.

[64] As in 'nominal Home Rulers'; Gladstone was actually the first to use the phrase.

[65] Figures from *United Ireland*, 1 September 1883.

[66] So fleeting was his moment in the limelight we are not even favoured with his first name.

[67] Coverage of the meeting and editorial comment from the *Independent and Munster Advertiser*, 25 August 1883.

[68] The murder of Carey had, in fact, been based on what was an unfortunate coincidence for him. He had been recognised on board ship by a militant nationalist named O'Donnell.

[69] The *Independent and Munster Advertiser*, 8 September 1883.

[70] The *Independent and Munster Advertiser*, 13 October. The letter had been written by Parnell on 2 October and forwarded by O'Shea to T.S. Cleary on 10 October. It had first appeared in the *Freeman's Journal* on that date.

[71] The *Independent and Munster Advertiser*, 27 October 1883.

[72] *United Ireland*, 3 November 1883.

[73] O'Shea to Escott, 18 August 1883. Escott Papers, Add Mss 58789, ff 38–40, BL.

[74] The *Times*, 31 October 1883.

CHAPTER 8

[1] Spencer to O'Shea, 22 June 1882 (O'Shea, MS 5752, National Library of Ireland).

[2] Lloyd to Burke, 24 February 1882 (CSORP, 1882/19433, National Archives of Ireland).

[3] Forster to Burke, 27 February 1882 (CSORP, 1882/19433, NAI).

[4] O'Shea to Forster, 22 March 1882 (CSORP, 1882/20799, NAI).

[5] O'Shea to Forster, 1 April 1882 (CSORP, 1882/20799, NAI).

[6] Response on behalf of W.E. Forster to O'Shea, 3 April 1882 (CSORP, 1882/20799, NAI).

[7] Parl Debs (series 3) vol 264, col 116 (29 Jul 1881).

[8] *Freeman's Journal*, 23 August 1881.

[9] 25 February 1881 (CSORP, 1882/32122, NAI).

[10] CSORP, 1881/27001, NAI. O'Shea's letter was written on 9 August.

[11] Warrant, 25 February (CSORP, 1882/20193, NAI).

[12] This is a standard comment included in Recommendation for Arrest forms.

[13] *Clare Advertiser*, 17 June 1882.

[14] Details from *Clare Freeman*, 21 April 1883 and the *Nation*, 21 April 1883.

[15] *United Ireland*, 28 April 1883.

[16] Parl Debs (series 3) vol 283, col 301–3 (13 Aug 1883).

[17] *Independent and Munster Advertiser*, 28 April 1883.

[18] John O'Connor Power had a similar voting record and was accused by *United Ireland* of 'treason'. O'Shea remained largely untouched by the newspaper. Of course this could reflect

the fact that O'Shea had never adhered to the cause of Irish nationalism in the manner that O'Connor Power once had.

[19] She died on 8 December 1884.

[20] O'Shea to Chamberlain, undated but early December 1884 (Chamberlain Papers, University of Birmingham, JC 8/8/1/33): 'As far as my mite of a vote goes you shall have it for I shall return on Tuesday and be in the House that evening, and either go back to Paris on Wednesday morning or evening, according as the division may be taken. Only one thing shall prevent this – my sister's death or the actual imminence of it.'

[21] Absent for three votes on 8 June 1882 (*United Ireland*, 10 June 1882) and another on 28 June (Parl Debs (series 3) vol 271, (28 Jun 1882)).

[22] *United Ireland*, 14 April 1883: a vote on the sixpence telegram. *United Ireland*, 12 May: seating of Bradlaugh.

[23] *United Ireland*, 21 April 1883: Criminal Code Bill, second reading.

[24] Parl Debs (series 3) vol 297, (5 May 1885). Registration Bill: 'ayes' (Government) 240; 'nays' 237.

[25]

Year	O'Shea	Mahon	O'Donnell	Parnell
1880	7	1	96	221
1881	41	7	296	508
1882	67	1	471	358*
1883	32	1	243	200**
1884	30	2	116	135
1885	14	4	40	130
1886	0	0***	0***	45
Total	191	16	1262	1597

*	Jailed 13 October to 31 December.
**	Jailed 1 January to 4 May.
***	No longer in parliament.

[26] Ireland, 93; Spain, 10; Military/Constabulary, 36; House, 12; other, 40.

[27] Parl Debs (series 3) vol 270, col 1407(16 June 1882).

[28] Unfortunately when she and her husband got there it was over. Though she became a great champion of the defeated Zulu leader Cetewayo.

[29] Christy Campbell, *Fenian Fire: The British Government Plot to Assassinate Queen Victoria* (London, 2003), p. 8.

[30] A story in circulation at the time suggests that the reason for Lady Florence's animosity towards the League was that she had once written an admiring letter to Parnell to which, typically, he had not replied or made any acknowledgement. Her opposition therefore, according to the Irish nationalist press, derived from pique.

[31] Parl Debs (series 3) vol 277, col 939 (20 Mar 1883).

[32] *Irish Times*, 26 March 1883.

[33] Parl Debs (series 3) vol 277, col 993 (29 Mar 1883).

[34] *Punch*, 7 April 1883.

[35] *Irish Times*, 13 August 1883.

[36] O'Brien, *Parnell*, p. 296.

[37] Parl Debs (series 3) vol 276, col 722–5 (23 Feb 1883).

[38] *Times*, 8 March 1883.

[39] *Clare Journal*, 17 July 1882.

[40] Molloy to Mahon, 7 August 1882 (OGM Papers, University of Chicago, Box 5, Folder 12).

[41] *Times*, 22 March 1884.

[42] Parnell himself contributed £2000, which he was in a better position to afford in 1884

than he had been for some time as he had netted more than £37,000 the previous December in the Parnell Tribute. This was a national collection prompted by rumours that Parnell's debts were forcing him to sell Avondale. The final sum collected quadrupled after the Vatican came out against the Tribute.
[43] As Michael Davitt pointed out, this was a figure of 20 times the annual rent. The proper gearing should have been closer to 7:1. Someone had seen them coming.
[44] The *Nation*, 7 June 1884.
[45] Lyons, *Parnell*, p. 267.
[46] O'Shea, *Parnell*, vol 2, p. 69.
[47] Katharine told Henry Harrison that she had details of 17 affairs conducted by her husband.
[48] All O'Connor references from O'Connor, *Memoirs*, pp 207–9.
[49] Clare, the name of his constituency, does come across as one designed to convince O'Shea, or a wider public, of the Captain's paternity.
[50] Healy, *Letters and Leaders*, vol 1, pp 190–1.
[51] On 5, 14, 15, 20, 22 and 25 June. On the middle four dates the Monaghan election campaign was being fought.
[52] O'Shea, *Parnell*, vol 2, p. 65.
[53] O'Shea, *Parnell*, vol 2, p. 66.
[54] O'Connor, *Memoirs*, p. 227.
[55] O'Shea, *Parnell*, vol 2, p. 66
[56] There is no local newspaper record of a visit to his constituency in January but he was certainly in Dublin for the Irish party meeting on 4 February 1884.
[57] *Independent and Munster Advertiser*, 14 June 1884.
[58] *Times*, 17 November 1890. This and the other correspondence that follows was entered into evidence at the divorce and recorded in the *Times*.
[59] *Times*, 17 November 1890.
[60] *Times*, 17 November 1890.
[61] Katharine O'Shea to William O'Shea, 9 April 1887 (O'Shea, MS 35982).
[62] O'Shea note, undated (O'Shea, MS 5752, NLI).
[63] *Times*, 17 November 1890.
[64] O'Shea, Parnell, vol 2, p. 75.

CHAPTER 9

[1] The precise figures are 225,999 and 737,965.
[2] The exception was North East Ulster where eighteen or so seats were virtually certain to go to a Liberal or Conservative candidate.
[3] *United Ireland*, 9 May 1885.
[4] Soon to be dusted off and given a Home Rule connotation.
[5] O'Shea to Chamberlain, 27 November 1884 (Chamberlain Papers, University of Birmingham, JC 8/8/1/26).
[6] Peter Marsh, *Joseph Chamberlain: Entrepreneur in Politics* (New Haven, 1994), p. 193.
[7] Howard, 'Documents: Irish "Central Board" Scheme', p. 241.
[8] Parnell to O'Shea, 5 January 1885 (Chamberlain Papers, UB, JC 8/8/2G/4).
[9] Memo signed by O'Shea and entitled 'Parnell's plan for local government in Ireland, 14 January 1885' (Chamberlain Papers, UB, JC 8/8/1/36).
[10] Although in correspondence with John Morley he drew attention to the measure, saying that 'In one respect it goes much farther than I should have thought possible in the direction of a conservative policy since it proposes a separate representation of landowners both on county boards and on the central board in proportion to their rateable contributions.' He expressed no opposition to the notion. It is hard to imagine Chamberlain willingly accepting a similar measure were it to apply to English local government.

Endnotes

11 O'Shea to Parnell, 6 January 1885 (Chamberlain Papers, UB, JC 8/8/2G/5).

12 O'Shea, *Parnell*, vol 2, p. 202.

13 Parnell to O'Shea, 13 January 1885 (Chamberlain Papers, UB, JC 8/8/2G/6).

14 Garvin, *Joseph Chamberlain*, vol 1, p. 584.

15 Chamberlain to Morley, 21 January 1885 (Howard, 'Documents: Irish Central Board Scheme', p. 249.

16 Henry Harrison, *Parnell, Joseph Chamberlain and Mr Garvin* (London, 1938), pp 97–8.Harrison does, however, point out that 'though it must be admitted, in view of his record, that the latter was quite capable of uttering, or swearing to, any falsehood which seemed convenient to him.'

17 Chamberlain to Miss Endicott, 8 August 1888 (cited in Garvin, Joseph Chamberlain, vol 2, p. 391).

18 O'Shea to Parnell, 19 January 1885 (Chamberlain Papers, UB, JC 8/8/2G/7). A draft version also exists (with slight variations) in O'Shea, MS 5752, National Library of Ireland.

19 Chamberlain to O'Shea, 21 January 1885 (Chamberlain Papers, UB, JC 8/8/1/37).

20 O'Brien, *Evening Memories*, p. 2.

21 Howard, 'Documents: Irish Central Board Scheme', pp 249–51.

22 By June of that year he appears to have lowered his sights somewhat, writing to Chamberlain, 'With reference to recent conversations can you find out for me whether there is a legal impediment to the Under Secretary to the Lord Lieutenant having a seat in the House of Commons?' (17 June 1885, O'Shea, MS 5752, NLI).

23 O'Shea, *Parnell*, vol 2, p. 205.

24 Chamberlain, 11 April; minute on Spencer memo of 25 March 1885 (Howard, 'Documents: Irish Central Board Scheme', pp 252–3).

25 Spencer to Chamberlain, 26 April 1885 (Howard, 'Documents: Irish Central Board Scheme', pp 257–8).

26 Trevelyan minute, 30 April 1885 (Howard, 'Documents: Irish Central Board Scheme', p. 261).

27 Lyons, *Fall of Parnell*, p. 277.

28 O'Shea diary, 1 May 1885 (Chamberlain Papers, UB, JC 8/8/1/40).

29 Note the use of the loaded term 'self-government', of which Chamberlain would not have approved. Could it have been for Parnell's benefit?

30 O'Shea, *Parnell*, vol 2, p. 209.

31 O'Shea diary, 8 May 1885; and Chamberlain Papers, UB, JC 8/8/1/40.

32 Trevelyan to Chamberlain, 6 May 1885 (Howard, 'Documents: Irish Central Board Scheme', p. 263).

33 O'Shea, *Parnell*, vol 2, p. 210.

34 The specific sequence of events, according to Roy Jenkins (Sir Charles Dilke, 1965) was that Dilke resigned when Gladstone announced an extension of land purchase instead of local government reform. Chamberlain was then forced to do likewise although he had privately indicated his support for the measure.

35 Jenkins, *Sir Charles Dilke*, p. 212.

36 *United Ireland*, 27 June 1885.

37 Chamberlain to O'Shea, 8 July 1885 (Chamberlain Papers, UB, JC 8/8/1/49).

38 O'Shea to Chamberlain, 13 July 1885 (Chamberlain Papers, UB, JC 8/8/1/50).

39 O'Shea to Chamberlain, 28 June 1885 (Chamberlain Papers, UB, JC 8/8/1/47).

40 O'Shea to Chamberlain, 13 July 1885 (Chamberlain Papers, UB, JC 8/8/1/50).

41 O'Shea to Chamberlain, 29 June 1885 (Chamberlain Papers, UB, JC 8/8/1/48).

42 O'Shea, *Parnell*, vol 2, pp 212–3.

43 O'Shea to Chamberlain, 29 June 1885 (Chamberlain Papers, UB, JC 8/8/1/48).

44 O'Shea, *Parnell*, vol 2, p. 212

45 The frequent references in his correspondence to the Parnell Tribute are just short of obsessional.

46 *United Ireland*, 12 January 1884.

[47] Speaking in the Liverpool Exchange election in November 1885, he said, 'Captain O'Shea has a clear record on the question of coercion ... he gave hundreds of most valuable votes against coercion, and that in no case was he found in the lobby in favour of coercion.'(*United Ireland*, 28 November 1885.)

[48] *Nation*, 12 January, 1884.

[49] One local newspaper had even announced his death.

[50] In *Parnell and his Island*, George Moore wrote of a character, 'James, on his release from prison, was of course elected Member of Parliament, a few questions were asked as to what he would live on, and the usual answer was given – journalism.' (Dublin, 2004, p. 53.)

[51] *Independent and Munster Advertiser*, 9 February 1884.

[52] *Independent and Munster Advertiser*, 9 February 1884.

[53] *Times*, 11 February 1884.

[54] *United Ireland*, 16 February 1884.

[55] *Independent and Munster Advertiser*, 23 February 1884. Unfortunately no copies of the Kilrush *Herald* survive so all editorial opinions are taken from reprinted pieces in the *Independent*.

[56] 'Hibernicus', *Independent and Munster Advertiser*, 15 March 1884, and J.M. Nagle, *Independent and Munster Advertiser*, 31 October 1884, are two shining examples.

[57] *Independent and Munster Advertiser*, 29 March 1884.

[58] *Independent and Munster Advertiser* 5 April 1884.

[59] *Independent and Munster Advertiser*, 12 April 1884.

[60] *Independent and Munster Advertiser*, 26 June 1884.

[61] He indicated in an undated letter to Parnell in October or November 1885 that he had decided upon 'choosing the Western division'(O'Shea, MS 5752, NLI).

[62] *United Ireland*, 19 April 1884.

[63] *Independent and Munster Advertiser*, 14 June 1884.

[64] The aforementioned John Blake would do so even earlier. The Waterford MP resigned his seat in July 1884, in a very dignified manner, because he said his constituents were out of sympathy with him.

[65] Information from Owen McGee, *The IRB: The Irish Republican Brotherhood from the Land League to Sinn Fein* (Dublin, 2005), pp 78–9, pp 142–3 and pp 154–5.

[66] McGee, IRB, p. 155.

[67] Edited by John A. Carroll it largely consisted of reprinted English newspaper copy and devoted relatively little space to the coverage of Irish National League activities.

[68] *Clare Advertiser*, 14 March 1885.

[69] M. McNamara, a Crusheen conspiracy 'suspect'; John O'Callaghan, who spent time in Limerick prison when Parnell was enjoying the dank pleasures of Kilmainham; John Malone, an associate of P.N. Fitzgerald; John O'Connor of Feakle, an associate of one of the leading IRB men in Clare; Bryan Clune; and James Whelan of Balinahinch, another former prison inmate.

[70] *Independent and Munster Advertiser*, 25 October 1885.

[71] O'Shea, *Parnell*, vol 2, p. 200.

[72] O'Shea to Dilke, 26 October 1884 (Campbell-Bannerman Papers, British Library, Add MSS 41228).

[73] 29 October 1884 (Campbell-Bannerman Papers, BL, Add MSS 41228).

[74] O'Shea, *Parnell*, vol 2, p. 215. John Malone is represented in the text as 'I. Malone', but anyone who can fashion 'Hymer' from 'Hynes' can mistake a capital 'I' for a 'J'.

[75] *Times*, 13 May 1885 and O'Shea, Parnell, vol 2, p. 205.

[76] O'Shea, *Parnell*, vol 2, p. 206.

[77] O'Shea to Chamberlain, 7 January 1885 (Chamberlain Papers, UB, JC 8/8/1/34).

[78] Chamberlain to O'Shea, 23 August 1885, incorrectly dated 3 August (Chamberlain Papers, UB, JC 8/8/1/51).

[79] *Times*, 17 August 1885.

[80] O'Shea to Chamberlain, 22 August 1885 (Chamberlain Papers, UB, JC 8/8/1/54).

[81] Davitt Papers, Trinity College Dublin, MS 9365. Davitt noted in the margins of what looks like an interview done at the time of the Special Commission (1888–89), 'Mulqueeny in service police for ten years.'

[82] Campbell, *Fenian Fire*, p. 188.

[83] O'Connor, *Memoirs*, p. 152.

[84] O'Shea to Chamberlain, 30 August 1885 (Chamberlain Papers, UB, JC 8/8/1/55).

[85] O'Shea, *Parnell*, vol 2, p. 96 and p. 102.

[86] *Clare Advertiser*, 21 March 1885.

[87] *Clare Advertiser*, 9 May 1885.

[88] *Independent and Munster Advertiser*, 16 May 1885,

[89] *Clare Advertiser*, 16 May 1885.

[90] *Clare Advertiser*, 19 June 1885.

[91] *Independent and Munster Advertiser*, 20 June 1885.

[92] One Kilrush supporter, Stephen McMahon, certainly received five pounds from O'Shea. It was claimed this was to assist him to emigrate, but he was still resident in the county and speaking up for O'Shea in late 1885 (*Independent and Munster Advertiser*, 31 October 1885).

[93] O'Shea to Chamberlain, 3 September 1885 (Chamberlain Papers, UB, JC 8/8/1/56).

[94] O'Shea to Chamberlain, 5 September 1885 (Chamberlain Papers, UB, JC 8/8/1/58).

[95] And on O'Shea's role in stymieing an attempt by the Gladstone administration to prevent the appointment of the nationalistic Archbishop Walsh to succeed to the Dublin see after the death of Archbishop McCabe in March 1885. This was designed to reel in the Clare clergy.

[96] Chamberlain to Mulqueeny, 6 October 1885 (O'Shea, MS 5752, NLI, copy of letter written in O'Shea's handwriting).

[97] Finucane to Mahon, 27 October 1885 (OGM Papers, University of Chicago, Box 6, Folder 3).

[98] McGee, *IRB*, p. 142.

[99] O'Shea, *Parnell*, vol 2, p. 215.

[100] O'Shea, *Parnell*, vol 2, p. 86.

[101] J.R. Cox, the Secretary to the Lord Mayor of Dublin and whose family was from Clare, stood for the eastern division, and Jeremiah Jordan, a Fermanagh National League activist unknown in the constituency, stood for West Clare.

[102] *Independent and Munster Advertiser*, 10 October 1885.

[103] *Freeman's Journal*, 9 November 1885.

[104] Which had been solicited of Edmund Dwyer Gray by O'Shea when he submitted the farewell address. The editorial comment closely follows an *apologia* outlined for the Editor by the Captain.

[105] *Freeman's Journal*, 9 November 1885

[106] Moody, 'Parnell and the Galway Election', p. 330.

CHAPTER 10

[1] Punch had first created the character, with its familiar simian characteristics, after the Phoenix Park murders (*Punch*, 20 May 1882).

[2] Frank Callanan, *T.M. Healy* (Cork, 1996), p. 148.

[3] Former Director of Criminal Investigation at Scotland Yard, godson of Cardinal Manning, and putative Tory candidate. His detectives had been energetically following Parnell for years so the irony that he wished to broker a secret meeting cannot have been lost on the Irish leader.

[4] In her memoir Katharine O'Shea sowed the seeds of historiographical confusion by mixing up her copy of the document (sent by her to Gladstone) and passed to Chamberlain by O'Shea in January 1885, which detailed Parnell's plans for a Central Board, with a second document, sent in October 1885, entitled 'A Proposed Constitution for Ireland'. While Chamberlain's biographer J.L. Garvin operated on the assumption that it was the latter

document that Gladstone sought from Spencer and Grosvenor in July 1885, it is clear from J.L. Hammond and F.S.L. Lyons that it was the modest Central Board document that Gladstone had in mind. He was yet to receive the more ambitious constitutional framework.

5 Hammond, *Gladstone*, p. 420.

6 Lyons, *Parnell*, p. 297.

7 O'Brien, *Parnell*, p. 362

8 *Independent and Munster Advertiser*, 29 August 1885.

9 *Times*, 25 August 1885.

10 The estates, respectively, of Gladstone and Salisbury.

11 Hammond, *Gladstone*, p. 422.

12 Hammond, *Gladstone*, p. 424.

13 Algar Labouchere Thorold, *The Life of Henry Labouchere* (London, 1913), p. 239.

14 On 2 November 1885 O'Shea wrote to Chamberlain from Dublin telling him that '... Parnell told me twice "confidentially" ten days ago that the Irish vote might still be cast for the Liberals ...' (Add MSS 62114, British Library).

15 O'Shea, *Parnell*, vol 2, p. 84.

16 Also known as the 'unauthorised programme'. Chamberlain's condemnation of 'the eternal laws of supply and demand ... the necessity of freedom of contract ... the sanctity of every private right of property' as examples of 'the convenient cant of selfish wealth' (Garvin, Joseph Chamberlain, vol 2, p. 62) was not calculated to endear him to the representatives of a nation of would-be peasant proprietors.

17 O'Shea, *Parnell*, vol 2, p. 84.

18 O'Shea, *Parnell*, vol 2, p. 86.

19 O'Shea to Gladstone, 23 October 1885 (Add MSS 44269, BL).

20 Katharine O'Shea to Grosvenor, 23 October 1885 (Gladstone Papers, Add MSS 44316, BL).

21 In a letter to Edmund Dwyer Gray (5 November 1885) O'Shea pointed out that in an electorate of around 8,000 there were 2,847 Catholics (T. W. Moody, 'Parnell and the Galway Election of 1886', in Irish Historical Studies, vol 9, no 35 (March 1955).

22 O'Shea to Chamberlain, 28 October 1885 (Chamberlain Papers, University of Birmingham, JC 8/8/1/62).

23 O'Shea to Grosvenor, undated (Gladstone Papers, Add MSS 44316, BL). His withdrawal was on the basis that 'I have had careful examinations of Mid Armagh made, and finding that Mr Parnell has exaggerated the number of his adherents and that it is impossible to rely upon the casting of a compensating number of Presbyterian votes for a Catholic, I have only to thank you for having taken trouble in the matter ...'

24 O'Shea, *Parnell*, vol 2, p. 89.

25 O'Shea, *Parnell*, vol 2, p. 25.

26 Although, by the time Grosvenor wrote the letter, O'Shea had also spoken to Dickson in Belfast and the Roman Catholic Archbishop McGettigan in Armagh. In a letter to Gladstone Grosvenor blames a Dickson press leak for causing the difficulty, but that was written four days *after* O'Shea was 'outed' by Hamilton.

27 O'Shea to Chamberlain, undated, but late October 1885 (Chamberlain Papers, UB, JC 8/8/1/61). There is an almost identical phrase in O'Shea's letter to Katharine on 25 October 1885 (O'Shea, Parnell, vol 2, p. 89).

28 Which, strictly speaking, is not a constituency. Technically MPs cannot resign. Instead they seek an office of profit under the Crown called Crown Steward and Bailiff of the Three Hundreds of Chiltern and this disqualifies them from continuing as a Member of Parliament. They only relinquish the office when another MP is appointed. At the time of writing the current holder of the office is one Tony Blair!

29 O'Shea to Parnell, undated draft, but probably from 7 November 1885 (O'Shea, MS 5752, National Library of Ireland). This draft (because it is undated) is actually the first note/letter in the file of the O'Shea papers. It is therefore out of sequence, but a letter from O'Shea to Katharine on 8 November 1885 (O'Shea, Parnell, vol 2, p. 92) talks of him having sent just such a letter 'last night'.

Endnotes

[30] The motion (brought by the Conservative leader in the House, Sir Stafford Northcote) was defeated by 311 to 262. The Parnellites voted en masse with the Tories, while the 'nominals' sided with the government (*Times*, 21 February).

[31] *United Ireland*, 23 February 1884.

[32] O'Connor, *Memoirs*, vol 1, p. 323. In her recently published biography of Katharine O'Shea (*Ireland's Misfortune: the Turbulent Life of Kitty O'Shea*, London, 2008, p. 511, fn 46), Elisabeth Kehoe suggests that this might be the division in question. But as O'Shea was not present to vote, it is difficult to support this contention – although she is absolutely correct in her assertion that every Irish vote was important for the Parnellites on that occasion if the attempted political coup were to succeed.

[33] *Times*, 17 March 1884. It is, of course, possible that the *Times* is mistaken in its identification of those who voted 'Aye' and 'Nay' in the division.

[34] O'Shea to Chamberlain, 2 November 1885 (Gladstone Papers, Add MSS 62114, BL).

[35] O'Shea to Parnell, draft/copy, 2 November 1885 (O'Shea, MS 5752, NLI). O'Shea used exactly the same phraseology in a letter of 5 November to Edmund Dwyer Gray (Moody, 'Parnell and the Galway Election', p. 330).

[36] O'Shea, *Parnell*, p. 90, Vol 2; O'Shea to Katharine O'Shea, 2 November 1886.

[37] Chamberlain to O'Shea, 4 November 1885 (O'Shea, MS 5752, NLI).

[38] Labouchere's informant was probably Tim Healy, with whom he was conducting a 'backstairs' negotiation at the time (Callanan, *Healy*, pp 125–150).

[39] Labouchere to Chamberlain, undated (Chamberlain Papers, UB, JC 5/50/32). Also cited in Howard, 'Documents: Irish Central Board Scheme', pp 329–30, fn.

[40] O'Shea to Chamberlain, 8 November 1885 (Chamberlain Papers, UB, JC 8/8/1/64).

[41] Lyons, *Parnell*, p. 326.

[42] Jules Abels, *The Parnell Tragedy* (London, 1966), p. 227.

[43] O'Shea, *Parnell*, vol 2, p. 85.

[44] O'Shea, *Parnell*, vol 2, p. 87.

[45] *Irish Times*, 4 December 1885.

[46] 15 January 1886 (O'Shea, *Parnell*, vol 2, p. 215).

[47] O'Shea, *Parnell*, vol 2, p. 94.

[48] He had never actually issued an address to the Mid Armagh electorate as a Liberal candidate.

[49] Grosvenor to O'Shea, 20 November 1885 (O'Shea, MS 5752, NLI).

[50] Quoted in Lyons, *Parnell*, p. 327. An account of the incident was relayed to Gladstone in November 1890 by E.R. Russell of the Liverpool *Daily Post*.

[51] Typical of the Jesuitical Gladstone that he could correctly deny all personal knowledge of an affair, despite repeatedly being informed of the rumours (by Lord Granville, his secretary Leveson Gower, and almost certainly by Harcourt) on the basis that no one, other than those involved, could be morally certain that any other than a purely platonic relationship existed between Parnell and Katharine O'Shea. (discussed in Herbert Gladstone, *Thirty Years After*, pp 303-305 'He did not listen to gossip and scandal')

[52] Healy, *Letters and Leaders*, vol 1, p. 215. Since the information comes from Healy, who presumably got it from Labouchere , readers can decide for themselves whether or not it is accurate.

[53] A handful of 'deserving' Liberals like Labouchere and Cowen were being supported, but O'Shea clearly did not fall into that category.

[54] Chamberlain to O'Shea, 17 November 1885 (O'Shea, MS 5752, NLI).

[55] Chamberlain to O'Shea, 20 November 1885 (O'Shea, MS 5752, NLI).

[56] O'Shea to Chamberlain, 21 November 1885 (O'Shea, MS 5752, NLI).

[57] Chamberlain to O'Shea, 22 November 1885 (O'Shea, MS 5752, NLI).

[58] *United Ireland*, 28 November 1885.

[59] From a press clipping in O'Shea, MS 5752, NLI.

[60] *Irish Times*, 28 November 1885.

[61] O'Connor, *Parnell: A Memory*, p. 162.

[62] *Times*, 26 November 1885.
[63] Sixteen of those were in Ulster, where the Tories found themselves in a 17 to 16 minority; the other two were in Dublin University.
[64] O'Shea, *Parnell*, vol 2, p 28.
[65] Chamberlain to O'Shea, 9 December 1885 (O'Shea, MS 5752, NLI).
[66] Almost certainly George Mulqueeny.
[67] O'Shea, *Parnell*, vol 2, p. 214.
[68] O'Shea, *Parnell*, vol 2, p. 215.
[69] Sub-Inspector Hubert Crane, 11 April 1881 (CSORP 1882/32122, National Archives of Ireland). The file is about an inch thick and contains ample evidence that Clune was well known to the authorities.
[70] 14 February 1880 (CSORP 1882/32122, NAI).
[71] In one instance against a local school, whose teacher had issued a summons against a fee-defaulter. Subsequently they were suspected of involvement in the beating of two farmers who continued to allow the boycotted schoolteacher to graze his goats on their farm. This sort of behaviour reinforces Margaret O'Callaghan's description of boycotting as 'the private sanctions of an impenetrable community ... it essentially sprang from age-old regulatory rituals.' (O'Callaghan, *British Politics and Nationalist Ireland*, p. 111).
[72] Slattery was one of the 'suspects' visited by O'Shea in Limerick Prison in August 1881.
[73] 21 April 1882 (CSORP 1882/32122, NAI).
[74] Letter from Naas prison Governor, 29 July 1882 (CSORP 1882/32682, NAI).
[75] *Times*, 26 December 1885: 'What the Parnellites Would Accept'.
[76] O'Shea, *Parnell*, vol 2, p. 104.
[77] Chamberlain to O'Shea, 22 January 1886 (O'Shea, *Parnell*, p. 234).
[78] 26 December 1885 (Thorold, *Henry Labouchere*, p. 278).
[79] 1 January 1886 (Thorold, *Henry Labouchere*, p. 278).
[80] Which began life as a Trinity College, Dublin, doctoral thesis supervised by T.W. Moody.
[81] O'Brien, *Parnell and his Party*, p. 176.
[82] Moody, 'Parnell and the Galway Election', p. 333.
[83] Moody, 'Parnell and the Galway Election', p. 335.
[84] O'Shea, *Parnell*, vol 2, p. 105.
[85] O'Shea, *Parnell*, vol 2, p. 106.
[86] O'Shea, *Parnell*, vol 2, p. 107.
[87] O'Connor, *Memoirs*, vol 2, p. 94.
[88] O'Connor wanted to run a friend of his, Thomas Quinn. The local favourite was a Galway National League stalwart, Michael Lynch.
[89] O'Connor, *Memoirs*, vol 1, p. 44.
[90] O'Connor, *Memoirs*, vol 2, p. 94.
[91] O'Brien, *Parnell*, p. 380.
[92] Healy, *Letters and Leaders*, vol 1, pp 239–40.
[93] William O'Brien, *Recollections* (London, 1905), p. 184.
[94] O'Connor, *Memoirs*, vol 2, p. 95.
[95] O'Brien, *Evening Memories*, p. 102.
[96] O'Brien also played a key part in neutralising a highly agitated John Dillon, who agreed not to enter the lists against O'Shea when he was offered similar advice. (Lyons, *Parnell*, p. 334).
[97] O'Brien, *Parnell*, p. 381.
[98] O'Connor, *Memoirs*, vol 2, p. 103.
[99] Moody, 'Parnell and the Galway Election', pp 324–5.
[100] Moody, 'Parnell and the Galway Election', pp 325–6.
[101] Healy, *Letters and Leaders*, vol 1, p. 242.
[102] Healy, *Letters and Leaders*, vol 1, p. 242.
[103] Healy, *Letters and Leaders*, vol 1, p. 242.
[104] Healy, *Letters and Leaders*, vol 1, p. 243.
[105] O'Shea, Parnell, vol 2, p. 230. O'Shea's account was in a response to the allegation made

in 1891 by Dr McCormack, then Bishop of Galway, that Parnell had foisted him on the constituency as 'a hush gift to O'Shea'.

[106] Healy, *Letters and Leaders*, vol 1, p. 241.

[107] Moody, 'Parnell and the Galway Election', p. 326.

[108] Moody, 'Parnell and the Galway Election', p. 326.

[109] Healy, *Letters and Leaders*, vol 1, p. 243.

[110] O'Connor, *Parnell: A Memory*, p. 166.

[111] O'Connor, *Memoirs*, p. 97.

[112] Labouchere to Chamberlain, 19 December 1885 (Thorold, Henry Labouchere, p. 251)

[113] O'Connor, *Parnell: A Memory*, p. 171.

[114] O'Connor, *Memoirs*, vol 2, p. 100.

[115] The phrase echoed one which had appeared in the Freeman earlier, either stolen or inspired by Parnell.

[116] O'Brien, *Parnell*, p. 383.

[117] O'Connor, *Memoirs*, vol 2, p. 100.

[118] O'Connor, *Memoirs*, vol 2, p. 100.

[119] O'Connor, *Memoirs*, vol 2, p. 103.

[120] Moody, 'Parnell and the Galway Election', p. 327

[121] Moody, 'Parnell and the Galway Election', p. 321.

[122] Martin Mansergh, who has seen many chiefs at close quarters, has said of Parnell 'he was not overly concerned with consistency, and was quite happy with the notion that judgements be revised in the light of circumstances and experience.' Though he probably did not have such an egregious example of inconsistency in mind as this. ('Parnell and the Leadership of Nationalist Ireland', in McCartney, Donal (ed), *Parnell: The Politics of Power* (Dublin, 1991).

[123] *United Ireland*, 13 February 1886.

[124] *Nation*, 11 February 1886.

[125] 11 February 1886 (quoted in Lyons, *Parnell*, p. 342).

[126] *Times*, 10 February 1886.

[127] *Irish Times*, 13 February 1886.

[128] O'Connor, *Memoirs*, vol 2, p. 107.

[129] 'Ulster will fight and Ulster will be right', from a coquette who had flirted with the Parnellites.

[130] O'Shea to Churchill, 15 February 1886 (O'Shea, MS 5752, NLI).

[131] R. F. Foster, *Lord Randolph Churchill: A Political Life* (Oxford, 1981), p. 255.

[132] *Times*, 17 February 1886.

[133] Lyons, *Parnell*, p. 349.

[134] Healy, *Letters and Leaders*, vol 1, p. 247.

[135] Lyons, *Parnell*, p. 341.

[136] Margaret Leamy, *Parnell's Faithful Few* (New York, 1936), p. 23. Also related by O'Brien, *Evening Memories*, p. 105.

CHAPTER 11

[1] George D. Boyce, *19th Century Ireland, the Search for Stability* (Gill and Macmillan, Dublin, 1990), p. 174.

[2] Chamberlain to O'Shea and O'Shea to Chamberlain, both on 19 March 1886 (O'Shea, MS 5752, National Library of Ireland).

[3] 'I was surprised afterwards that Mrs O'Shea should have expressed herself annoyed at this note having been sent,' he records in his papers (O'Shea, MS5752, NLI).

[4] O'Shea memo, 25 March 1886 (O'Shea, MS 5752, NLI).

[5] Chamberlain was described in some quarters as not being opposed to the principle of Home Rule, but to the specific terms of Gladstone's Bill: in particular to the exclusion of Irish

members from the English Parliament. In 1898 he told Barry O'Brien that he had 'wanted to kill the Bill' and had used opposition to this clause as a pretext. He also admitted to opposing the accompanying Land Purchase Bill, whose thrust he agreed with, for the same reason. 'I was never near being converted to an Irish Parliament,' he told O'Brien (O'Brien, *Parnell*, p. 393).

6 Chamberlain, *Memoir*, p. 199.

7 Labouchere to Chamberlain, 7 April 1886 (cited in Thorold, *Henry Labouchere*, p. 290).

8 Chamberlain to Labouchere, 8 April 1886 (cited in Thorold, *Henry Labouchere*, p. 290).

9 O'Shea, *Parnell*, vol 2, p. 36.

10 Gladstone, *Thirty Years*, p. 298.

11 Gladstone was 76 at the time.

12 Masterman (ed), *Mary Gladstone: Diaries*, p. 385.

13 The same judge who, in November 1890, would also preside over *O'Shea* v *O'Shea and Parnell*.

14 Marsh, *Chamberlain*, p. 226.

15 Dilke did not recover politically from the divorce proceedings and made an unwise attempt to re-open the case and lost his Chelsea seat in the 1886 election. He did not return to the House of Commons until 1892.

16 Chamberlain to O'Shea, 20 April 1886 (O'Shea, MS 5752, NLI).

17 *Times*, 17 May 1886.

18 *Times*, 17 May 1886.

19 O'Shea to Chamberlain, 4 May 1886 (Chamberlain Papers, University of Birmingham, JC 8/8/1/70).

20 *United Ireland*, 22 May 1886.

21 *United Ireland*, 22 May 1886.

22 *United Ireland*, 22 May 1886.

23 *Times*, 17 May 1886.

24 *Times*, 18 May 1886.

25 O'Shea to Chamberlain, 16 May 1886 (Chamberlain Papers, UB, JC 8/8/1/71).

26 A crestfallen O'Shea refers to him in a note in his collected papers as the 'vexacious [sic] Chief Justice O'Brien' (O'Shea, MS 5752 p. 304, NLI)

27 O'Brien to O'Shea, 18 May 1886 (O'Shea, MS 5752, NLI).

28 *Times*, 19 May 1886.

29 The meeting took place in Committee Room 15, which would be the venue for the Irish party split in November 1890. Bright later expressed annoyance that the contents of the letter had been made public by Chamberlain.

30 Morley, *Gladstone*, vol 2, p. 432.

31 O'Shea to Chamberlain, 1 June 1886 (Chamberlain Papers, UB, JC 8/8/1/73).

32 O'Shea to Chamberlain, 2 June 1886 (Chamberlain Papers, UB, JC 8/8/1/74).

33 Morley, *Gladstone*, vol 2, p. 433.

34 Some historians and contemporary newspapers recorded the count as 341:311, but this figure does not include the two tellers in each lobby.

35 Garvin, *Joseph Chamberlain*, vol 2, p. 382.

36 Kee, *Laurel and Ivy*, p. 519.

37 The theory really emanates from an argument made by Henry Harrison in *Parnell Vindicated*.

38 Harrison, *Parnell Vindicated*, p. 281.

39 *Times*, 9 June 1886.

40 *United Ireland*, 12 June, 1886

41 O'Kelly to O'Shea, 8 June 1886 (O'Shea, MS 5752, NLI).

42 O'Shea to O'Kelly, 12 August 1886 (O'Shea, MS 5752, NLI).

43 Balfour took over as Chief Secretary from Sir Michael Hicks Beach in March 1887 and remained in office until Parnell's death coincided with that of W.H. Smith, whom Balfour then replaced in Cabinet.

Endnotes

44 Lucy, *Sixty Years in the Wilderness* (London, 1912), p. 260.

45 Chamberlain to O'Shea, 16 July 1886 (O'Shea, MS 5752, NLI).

46 On 29 December 1886 Chamberlain wrote to O'Shea about the possibility of a *rapprochement*, but concluded his letter by observing that 'I am as far as ever from seeing my way to anything in the nature of an Irish Parliament with an Irish executive' (O'Shea, MS 5752, NLI).

47 Chamberlain to O'Shea, 1 September 1886 (Chamberlain Papers, UB, JC 8/8/1/76).

48 Foster, *Randolph Churchill*, p. 281.

49 O'Shea to Chamberlain, 13 December, 1886 (Chamberlain Papers, UB, JC 8/8/1/78). O'Shea has just returned from a trip to Ireland and tells Chamberlain: 'I should like to tell you what I have seen and heard.'

50 McGee, *IRB*, p. 111.

51 O'Shea to W.R. Nally, 4 February 1887, MS 22826, NLI.

52 McGee, *IRB*, p. 215.

53 O'Shea to Chamberlain, 3 September 1886 (Chamberlain Papers, UB, JC 8/8/1/77).

54 On 8 May 1888 he made a speech in opposition to the Plan at the Liberal Eighty Club.

55 Alfred Robbins, *Parnell: the Last Five Years* (London, 1926), p. 197–8.

56 Chamberlain to Harcourt, 25 January 1887 (cited in Gardiner, *Sir William Harcourt*, vol 2, p. 30).

57 Harcourt to Chamberlain, 25 February 1887 (cited in Gardiner, *Sir William Harcourt*, vol 2, p. 34).

58 Garvin, *Joseph Chamberlain*, vol 2, p. 383.

59 O'Shea to Chamberlain, 25 February 1887(Chamberlain Papers, UB, JC 8/8/1/83). The letter in question is 17 pages long and most of the quotes that follow, except where otherwise indicated, are taken from it.

60 O'Shea to Chamberlain, 14 April 1888 (Chamberlain Papers, UB, JC 8/8/1/91).

61 O'Shea to Chamberlain, 14 April 1888 (Chamberlain Papers, UB, JC 8/8/1/91).

62 Donal McCartney (ed), *Parnell: The Politics of Power* (Dublin, 1991), p. 17.

63 Katharine O'Shea to Gladstone, 16 April 1886 (Gladstone Papers, Add MSS 56446, British Library).

64 O'Shea, *Parnell*, vol 2, p. 37.

65 William O'Shea to Katharine O'Shea, 23 April 1886 (O'Shea MS 3882–3; ref Tuohy papers, NLI).This much of the letter derives from a fragment which has found its way into the papers of the *Freeman* London correspondent, J.M. Tuohy. There is a longer shorthand version, which Jane Jordan has had 'translated', revealing that the quote refers to a meeting with Gladstone, though that can be reasonably inferred from the context.

66 William O'Shea to Katharine O'Shea, 23 April 1886 (O'Shea, MS 3882–3). Tuohy Papers, NLI – also quoted in the *Times*, 17 November 1890.

67 *Pall Mall Gazette*, 24 May 1886.

68 O'Connor, *Memoirs*, vol 1, p. 302–3.

69 Stead often predicted for himself a death by drowning or lynching. He was proved correct on 15 April 1912, when he died on board the *Titanic* on his way to lecture in New York.

70 This may refer to a meeting that took place between the two men in December 1886. O'Connor does not date his own meeting with Stead.

71 O'Connor, *Memoirs*, vol 2, p. 304.

72 O'Shea to Chamberlain, 13 October 1889 (Chamberlain Papers, UB, JC 8/8/1/1/28).

73 *Times*, 17 November 1890. Much of the correspondence that follows was read out in court on the first day of the divorce proceedings.

74 *Times*, 17 November 1890.

75 *Pall Mall Gazette*, 31 May 1886.

76 He added another layer to his defence in the divorce court, when he claimed that his wife had told him Parnell was secretly married. He also told the court that in 1886 Parnell had spent many Sundays at Eltham, but that the two men had journeyed down and back together. There was no one in court representing Parnell to challenge this assertion.

[77] Clement Preston was a particular favourite, though he also went by the more obvious Mr Stewart. On a couple of occasions the name of Parnell's secretary, Henry Campbell, was used.

[78] He said much more besides but that will be dealt with separately.

[79] Special Commission proceedings, vol 1, p. 367.

[80] Harrison, *Parnell Vindicated*, p. 123.

[81] *Times*, 17 November 1890.

[82] Not unexpectedly this was one letter from wife to husband that was *not* read out at the divorce trial.

[83] Her sister Anna Steele, and her brother Charles Page Wood.

[84] Katharine O'Shea to William O'Shea, 25 August, 1886 (Tuohy Papers, MS 3882-3, NLI).

[85] *Times*, 17 November 1890.

[86] Jordan, *Kitty O'Shea*, p. 147.

[87] *Times*, 17 November 1890.

[88] *Pall Mall Gazette*, 18 December 1886.

[89] O'Shea, *Parnell*, p. 219.

[90] W. T. Stead, an article called 'The Discrowned King of Ireland', in *Review of Reviews*, London, 1890, p. 12.

[91] *Times*, 17 November 1890.

[92] Dilke Papers, Add MSS 43937, BL.

[93] Gerard O'Shea to William O'Shea, 13 April 1887 (MS 35982; ref probate case, NLI).

[94] It might well be argued that this was the blazing row referred to (above) by Katharine, in conversation with Henry Harrison, where she told him directly about her infidelity. However it appears from the context and the internal evidence that O'Shea took the lead in this particular argument. His constant demand throughout the latter half of 1886 and early 1887 was that his wife cease to have any *further* communication with Parnell. Up to the middle of 1886 his avowed object had been to ascertain whether any infidelity had occurred. His letters to Katharine in 1887 would appear to suggest that he was satisfied that it had.

[95] Katharine O'Shea to William O'Shea, 17 April 1887 (MS 35982, NLI).

[96] William O'Shea to Katharine O'Shea, 17 April 1887 (MS 35982, NLI).

[97] *Times*, 17 November 1890.

[98] Pym to O'Shea, 25 April 1887. 'I trust that by this time your eldest boy has returned home as otherwise I foresee his position with Mrs Wood may be very seriously compromised'(MS 35982, NLI).

[99] Pym to O'Shea, 22 April 1887 (MS 35982, NLI).

[100] O'Shea to Pym, 22 April 1887 (MS 35982, NLI).

[101] O'Shea to Parnell, 29 April 1887 (MS 35982, NLI).

[102] Despite assertions to the contrary, including those of Parnell himself, the Pigott forgery is an excellent representation of Parnell's signature. This writer made a comparison between the *Times* facsimile and a Parnell letter that came up for sale in Dublin in 2006 and was unable to find any substantial difference.

[103] Garvin, *Joseph Chamberlain*, vol 2, p. 384.

[104] *Times*, 17 November 1890.

[105] O'Shea to Chamberlain, 13 October 1890 (Chamberlain Papers, UB, JC 8/8/1/128).

CHAPTER 12

[1] Patrick J. Walsh, *William J. Walsh: Archbishop of Dublin* (Dublin & Cork, 1928), p. 393.

[2] *Times*, 7 March 1887.

[3] O'Callaghan, *British Politics and Nationalist Ireland*, p. 114.

[4] Always depicted by *Punch* as a lady with a clock for a face.

[5] *Punch*, 19 March 1887.

[6] The former Chief Secretary had died on 5 April 1886.

Endnotes

[7] L. P. Curtis, *Coercion and Conciliation in Ireland: A Study in Conservative Unionism* (Princeton & Oxford, 1963).

[8] According to Davitt's diligent researches, 'Among the large subscribers to ILPU just prior to purchase of [the] letters were Devonshire & Westminster, Lord Stalbridge, W.H. Smith, Sir Rich[ard] Webster, Mr Balfour, Chamberlain and other prominent Unionists.' (Davitt Papers, MS 9551, 'Notes by an Amateur Detective', Trinity College Dublin.)

[9] The *Times*, *The History of the Times*, 3 vols, (London, 1947), vol 3, p. 44.

[10] The trawl would become even more intense the following year, as the Special Commission of inquiry loomed. A number of examples of Parnell's handwriting were sought and successfully secured: for example, from a Dublin solicitor, Paul Asken, who had had business dealings with Parnell over Avondale. Soames to Asken, 9 & 12 October 1988 and 16 February 1889 (MS 17815,National Library of Ireland).

[11] *Times, History*, vol 3, p. 48.

[12] A series of articles on Irish–American connections was written, anonymously, by Sir Robert Anderson, assistant commissioner for CID. Anderson was also instrumental in one of the great sensations of the Commission, the evidence of 'Henri le Caron' (Thomas Billis Beach), the British agent who had worked at the top echelons of the American Fenian organisation for twenty years.

[13] *Times*, 17 November 1890.

[14] Garvin, *Joseph Chamberlain*, vol 2, p.384.

[15] Davitt, *Fall of Feudalism*, p. 534.

[16] It begins on p. 129 of vol 2 of her memoir (O'Shea, *Parnell*).

[17] Robbins, Sir Alfred, *Parnell: The Last Five Years* (London, 1926), p. 43.

[18] O'Shea, *Parnell*, vol 2, p. 120.

[19] Robbins, *Parnell*, p. 45.

[20] Healy, *Letters and Leaders*, vol 1, p. 271.

[21] Robbins, *Parnell*, p. 49.

[22] Garvin, *Joseph Chamberlain*, vol 2, p. 384.

[23] Frank Hugh O'Donnell, *A History of the Irish Parliamentary Party*, 2 vols (Washington, 1970), vol 2, pp 227–234.

[24] Garvin, *Joseph Chamberlain*, vol 2, p. 384.

[25] O'Donnell claims this was on the advice of Sir Charles Russell, who would later lead Parnell's defence before the Special Commission. Russell's role has never been fully explained. He appears to have played a part in the mishandling of the case. Adding further confusion to an anarchic mix was the fact that at around that time Russell was being paid a retainer by the *Times*.

[26] *Times, History*, vol 3, p. 60.

[27] *Times*, 6 July 1888.

[28] Healy, *Letters and Leaders*, vol 1, p. 279.

[29] An agent.

[30] O'Donnell, *Irish Parliamentary Party*, vol 2, p. 238.

[31] O'Donnell, *Irish Parliamentary Party*, vol 2, p. 239.

[32] Davitt, *Fall of Feudalism*, p. 536.

[33] She did not die until 1957.

[34] Garvin, Joseph Chamberlain, vol 2, p. 386. O'Donnell makes the same point in his book when he cites a memo from his lawyer, R.A. Biale, after a meeting with the Irish leader. It reads, 'Parnell prefers not to be called by O'Donnell as it will expose him to cross-examination' (O'Donnell, *Irish Parliamentary Party*, vol 2, p. 241).

[35] Chamberlain to Endicott, 7 July 1888 (cited in Garvin, *Joseph Chamberlain*, vol 2, p. 386).

[36] Chamberlain to Endicott, 10 July 1888 (cited in Garvin, *Joseph Chamberlain*, vol 2, p. 386).

[37] Henry Harrison, *Parnell, Joseph Chamberlain and the Times* (Belfast & Dublin,1953), p. 18.

[38] Sir Edward Clarke, *The Story of My Life* (London, 1918), pp 274–5.

[39] Lyons, *Parnell*, p. 407.

[40] Edward Byrne (ed Frank Callanan), *Parnell: A Memoir* (Dublin, 1991), p. 30.

[41] Lyons, *Parnell*, p. 408.

[42] Garvin, *Joseph Chamberlain*, vol 2, p. 388.

[43] *Times*, 31 July 1888 For some reason the speech was not recorded in Hansard (Parliamentary Debates).

[44] Garvin, *Joseph Chamberlain*, vol 2, p. 389.

[45] Garvin, *Joseph Chamberlain*, vol 2, p. 391.

[46] Henry Harrison, *Parnell, Joseph Chamberlain and Mr Garvin* (London, 1938), p. 165.

[47] *Times*, 2 August 1888.

[48] *Times*, 6 August 1888.

[49] *Times*, 7 August 1888.

[50] Chamberlain memo, 1 August 1888 (Chamberlain Papers, University of Birmingham, JC 8/8/1/92).

[51] Chamberlain to Mary Endicott, 6 August 1888 (cited in Garvin, *Joseph Chamberlain*, vol 2, p. 391).

[52] O'Shea to Chamberlain, 7 August 1888 (Chamberlain Papers, UB, JC 8/8/1/95).

[53] A draft of this letter, dated 9 August, exists in O'Shea's own papers in the National Library in Dublin. In this version he writes, 'Looking at the ridiculous letter and the absurd way it distorts all we said, I wonder how many years younger I can have been three years and a half ago!' The Captain was a callow youth of 45 when he wrote 'the inconvenient letter'. This particular piece of self-exculpation did not make it into the despatched letter.

[54] O'Shea to Chamberlain, 10 August 1888 (Chamberlain Papers, UB, JC 8/8/1/96). There is also a differently worded draft letter, dated 9 August, in the O'Shea papers (O'Shea, MS 5752, NLI). Annexed to it is O'Shea's copy of the 'inconvenient letter' to Parnell of 19 January 1885.

[55] Chamberlain to Mary Endicott, 8 August 1888 (cited in Garvin, Joseph Chamberlain, vol 2, p. 392).

[56] Chamberlain to Mary Endicott, 9 August 1888 (cited in Garvin, Joseph Chamberlain, vol 2, p. 392).

[57] *Times*, 13 August 1888.

[58] Garvin, *Joseph Chamberlain*, vol 2, p. 392.

[59] O'Shea to Chamberlain, 24 August 1888 (Chamberlain Papers, UB, JC 8/8/1/103)

[60] A number of others, including Davitt who was not then an MP, had also been 'indicted'.

[61] This took the form, for example, of the provision of mountains of documentation by the Dublin Castle administration and the RIC to assist in standing up the *Times* allegations. Much of the fruit of this labour is still to be seen in seven large cartons of documents in the National Archive.

[62] Lyons, *Parnell*, p. 421.

[63] John McDonald, *Daily News*, Diary of the Parnell Commission (London, 1890), p. 6.

[64] The Commission began its proceedings on 17 September 1888 and concluded on 22 November 1889. During that time it sat on 129 days.

[65] Whatever the reason for his sudden appearance, it had nothing to do with his business in Spain. His correspondence with Chamberlain shows that he was travelling over and back to Madrid on a regular basis and, with sufficient notice, could have testified to the Commission with no great inconvenience to himself.

[66] Robbins, *Parnell*, p. 65.

[67] The *Times* account of the Commission appears in volume 3 of its history (*History of the Times*), published in 1947. After disputing its account, Harrison was given access to the relevant papers and pointed out a number of errors which were corrected in volume 4.

[68] Harrison, *Parnell, Chamberlain and the Times*, p. 16. The *Times* accepted Harrison's version of the O'Shea/Chamberlain/Houston/Buckle nexus in the corrigenda to volume 4 of its history (pp 41–2).

[69] O'Shea to Chamberlain, 23 August 1888 (Chamberlain Papers, UB, JC 8/8/1/102).

[70] O'Shea to Chamberlain, undated but probably late August 1888 (Chamberlain Papers, UB, JC 8/8/1/106).

Endnotes

71 O'Shea to Chamberlain, 17 October 1888 (Chamberlain Papers, UB, JC 8/8/1/108).

72 Chamberlain to Endicott, 22 October 1888 (cited in Garvin, Joseph *Chamberlain*, vol 2, p. 393)

73 O'Shea to Chamberlain, 22 October 1888 (Chamberlain Papers, UB, JC 8/8/1/109).

74 O'Shea to Chamberlain, 22 October 1888 (Chamberlain Papers, UB, JC 8/8/1/110).

75 Chamberlain to O'Shea, 23 October 1888 (O'Shea, MS 5752, NLI).

76 This line was repeated, virtually word for word, at the Commission. Davitt was making copious notes throughout O'Shea's evidence. When, for example, O'Shea told Webster that he had resigned from the House of Commons in 1886, Davitt noted in parentheses 'did not'. (He had, but his resignation was overtaken by the dissolution.) When it came to this particular barb Davitt merely recorded it without comment (Davitt Papers, MS 9549, TCD).

77 O'Shea to Chamberlain, 26 October 1888 (Chamberlain Papers, UB, JC 8/8/1/112).

78 Robbins, *Parnell*, p. 67.

79 *United Ireland*, 3 November 1888.

80 Lyons, *Parnell*, p. 427.

81 Robbins, *Parnell*, p. 67.

82 *Punch*, 10 November 1888.

83 Special Commission, Proceedings (1890), 11 vols, Parliamentary Papers, vol 1, p. 344.

84 Robbins, *Parnell*, p. 68.

85 Special Commission, Proceedings, vol 1, p. 353.

86 Special Commission, Proceedings, vol 1, p. 354.

87 Special Commission, Proceedings, vol 1, p. 379.

88 Robbins, *Parnell*, p. 65.

89 Special Commission, Proceedings, vol. 1, p. 357.

90 Special Commission, Proceedings, vol 1, p. 359.

91 Davitt Papers, MS 9549, TCD.

92 Special Commission, Proceedings, vol 1, p. 360.

93 Special Commission, Proceedings, vol 1, p. 364.

94 Davitt Papers, MS 9551, TCD.

95 Special Commission, Proceedings, vol 1, p. 365.

96 One of the few comments Davitt recorded in his Commission notebook about O'Shea's evidence was at the end of his evidence where he noted, 'Point: O'Shea friend of Fenians, also friend of govt, anxious that Land League shd be broke up' (Davitt Papers, MS 9549, TCD).

97 Special Commission, Proceedings, vol 1, p. 365

98 To the intense annoyance of his new boss, Robert Anderson, who had himself been paid for his own services by the *Times*.

99 Affidavit of 'Thompson', alias W.J. Reynolds (Davitt Papers, MS 9441, TCD).

100 Affidavit of 'Thompson', alias W.J.Reynolds (Davitt Papers, MS 9441, TCD). Reynolds wrote to Davitt on May 6 1889, 'As to *myself*: I was in "the Service" when I signed the Requisition to Captain O'Shea at Lynch's [Cowell's], Wardour Street.'

101 Special Commission, Proceedings, vol 1, p. 366.

102 Special Commission, Proceedings, vol 1, p. 366.

103 Robbins, *Parnell*, p. 71.

104 Campbell, *Fenian Fire*, p. 375.

105 'The Irish public house in Wardour Street, London, which Captain O'Shea visited in 1885', Davitt later wrote, 'was then a rendezvous for spies and casual informers ... It was frequented by Mulqueeny, Pigott ... and others of like character. It was in this place, in that year, that Mulqueeny got up the testimonial for Capt O'Shea, protesting against his exclusion from Irish politics, for presentation to Mr Parnell, which testimonial was taken by Mulqueeny to Paris for the signature of Kasey [sic]' (Davitt, *Fall of Feudalism*, p. 633).

106 *United Ireland*, 3 November 1888.

107 *Punch*, 10 November 1888.

108 Special Commission, Proceedings. vol 1, p. 367.

109 Special Commission, Proceedings, vol 1, p. 367.

[110] O'Shea to Chamberlain, 1 November 1888 (Chamberlain Papers, UB, JC 8/8/1/114).

[111] Chamberlain to O'Shea, 2 November 1888 (Chamberlain Papers, UB, JC 8/8/1/115).

[112] The only immediately negative consequence was a public spat with Harcourt over an implication that he had asked O'Shea to destroy all his Kilmainham documents in advance of a Select Committee investigation in 1883. O'Shea, however, had actually made no such claim.

[113] *United Ireland*, 3 November 1888.

[114] Mary Endicott was his third wife.

[115] O'Shea to Chamberlain, 28 December 1888 (Chamberlain Papers, UB, JC 8/8/1/117).

[116] Egan to Labouchere, 2 December 1888 (cited in Thorold, *Henry Labouchere*, p. 346).

[117] Robbins, *Parnell*, p. 84.

[118] Davitt, *Fall of Feudalism*, p. 581.

[119] The soft-hearted Davitt wrote to Soames (the *Times* solicitor) to see if anything could be done for his orphaned children. Their mother had died a couple of years before. Soames responded with a cheque for £10 (Davitt Papers, MS 9441, TCD).

[120] Masterman (ed), *Mary Gladstone: Diaries*, 23 February 1889, p. 407.

[121] Chamberlain to O'Shea, 14 March 1889 (Chamberlain Papers, UB, JC 8/8/1/123).

[122] MacDonald, *Daily News* Diary, p. 188.

[123] Davitt, *Fall of Feudalism*, p. 633.

[124] *Times*, 14 March 1889.

[125] In a statement for the Irish side, Kilkenny MP Thomas Quinn recalled being shown the letter in a meeting with Soames, the *Times* solicitor, the day after the collapse of *O'Donnell v Walter* and four months before the opening statements in the Special Commission. If Quinn is correct, it suggests a level of collusion between the authorities and the *Times*, prior even to the debate to establish the Commission (Callanan, Healy, p. 190).

[126] O'Shea to Chamberlain, 28 December 1888 (Chamberlain Papers, UB, JC 8/8/1/117).

[127] It will be recalled that O'Shea described Campbell as 'one of the treasurers of the Invincibles' (O'Shea to Chamberlain; Chamberlain Papers, UB, JC 8/8/1/92).

[128] McGee, IRB, p. 126.

[129] *Fenian Fire: The British Government Plot to Assassinate Queen Victoria*, by Christy Campbell, is a noble and largely successful effort to plot (no pun intended) a route through the dense Fenian/British Intelligence undergrowth. Where confusion reigns in the mind of the reader, it is not the fault of the writer, but of the baffling array of plotters and often contradictory conspiracies.

[130] Hayes also worked for the *Times* during the Special Commission (Campbell, Fenian Fire, p. 375).

[131] Davitt Papers, MS 9365, TCD.

[132] Callan's name is crossed out but, unlike most of Davitt's (or his wife's) excisions, a pencil is used so that it is possible to make out Callan's name underneath.

[133] Davitt Papers, MS 9551, TCD.

[134] Davitt Papers, MS 9551, TCD.

[135] Davitt Papers, MS 9551, TCD.

[136] Davitt Papers, MS 9551, TCD.

[137] Davitt Papers, MS 9551, TCD.

[138] Davitt drolly referred to it as 'Unionism and Crime' in a later series of articles in his *Labour World* newspaper.

[139] Sir Rowland Blennerhasset, Kerry 'Nominal' Home Rule MP.

[140] Davitt Papers, MS 9551, TCD.

[141] MacDonald, *Daily News* Diary, p. 162.

[142] Callanan, Healy, p. 204.

[143] Davitt, Fall of Feudalism, p. 542.

[144] This was one of Pigott's two final versions of the truth (something with which he had scant acquaintance), made in repudiation of a confession to Labouchere just before his flight, in which he had admitted forging all the letters. He subsequently told the *Times* that some

of the letters had been forged, but others had been provided for him by Patrick Casey. Joseph Casey had actually accompanied Pigott to the hotel in Paris where he had extracted payment for the first batch of letters, though he claimed ignorance of Pigott's intentions. For some time after the conclusion of direct evidence to the Commission, the *Times* continued its attempt to prove that at least some of Pigott's forgeries were genuine.

145 Houston to O'Shea, 6 March 1889 (Chamberlain Papers, UB, JC 8/8/1/122).

146 St John Ervine, *Parnell* (Boston, 1925), p. 256.

147 Later paid by the *Times* to find witnesses for its case.

148 McGee, IRB, p. 126.

149 Casey was offered a large sum of money to testify for the *Times* (Campbell, *Fenian Fire*, p. 375).

150 Special Commission, Proceedings, vol 1, p. 365.

151 Davitt, *Fall of Feudalism*, p. 436.

152 The pamphlet was called 'Parnellism Unmasked'.

153 Davitt, *Fall of Feudalism*, p. 613.

154 Davitt, *Fall of Feudalism*, p. 617.

155 In a subsequent letter to Chamberlain he displays an astonishing level of knowledge of O'Brien, including his abandonment of a woman in the USA and his elopement with another in Ballinasloe, County Galway (O'Shea to Chamberlain, 4 January 1889; Chamberlain Papers, UB, JC 8/8/1/119).

156 O'Shea to Chamberlain, 28 December 1888 (Chamberlain Papers, UB, JC 8/8/1/117.)

157 Patrick Maume, 'Parnell and the IRB Oath', in *Irish Historical Studies*, vol 29, no 115 (May 1995).

158 Campbell, *Fenian Fire*, p. 318.

159 Special Commission, Proceedings, vol 1, p. 361.

160 Though his correspondence shows that he planned to make a return trip to London barely a month after his evidence to the Commission (O'Shea to Chamberlain, 27 November 1888; Chamberlain Papers, UB, JC 8/8/1/116).

161 O'Shea to Chamberlain, 9 March, 1889 (Chamberlain Papers, UB, JC 8/8/1/121).

162 Special Commission, Proceedings, vol 1, p. 370.

163 Garvin, *Joseph Chamberlain*, vol 2, p. 396.

CHAPTER 13

1 See Mathew Sweet, *Inventing the Victorians* (New York, 2001), pp 7–20 for a brief outline of the career of Blondin.

2 The *Times* had also been somewhat more sceptical about the existence of Blondin until his exploits were verified by credible sources. Arguably they placed more trust in Richard Pigott than they had in the great acrobat.

3 8 April 1887, diary entry of Charles Page Wood, discovered to be used by defence in probate case of 1890 (MS 35982; National Library of Ireland).

4 9 May 1887, Charles Page Wood diary entry (MS 35982, NLI).

5 Report of Sir Andrew Clark, filed 20 April 1888 (copy in Chamberlain Papers, University of Birmingham, JC 8/8/1/161).

6 Power Collection – Affidavit of Anne Courage re Chancery proceedings for lunacy in the matter of Anna Maria Wood – Filed 4 May 1888.

7 The estate consisted of land in Gloucestershire and £145,000 in Consols (O'Shea to Chamberlain, 13 October 1889; Chamberlain Papers, UB, JC 8/8/1/127).

8 O'Shea to Chamberlain, 3 November 1888 (JC 8/8/1/115).

9 Chamberlain to O'Shea, 5 December 1888 (Chamberlain Papers, UB, JC 8/8/1/118).

10 He did so on the basis that under the terms of previous wills and codicils he had stood to benefit.

11 O'Shea to Chamberlain, 13 October 1889 (Chamberlain Papers, UB, JC 8/8/1/127).

[12] Chamberlain to O'Shea, 14 October 1889 (Chamberlain Papers, UB, JC 8/8/1/129).

[13] Which, according to his friend Dilke, had been informed by Harcourt of the affair.

[14] Robbins, *Parnell*, p. 132.

[15] Campbell, *Fenian Fire*, p. 352.

[16] O'Shea to Chamberlain, 15 December 1890 (Chamberlain Papers, UB, JC 8/8/1/152).

[17] O'Shea to Chamberlain, 15 August 1890 (Chamberlain Papers, UB, JC 8/8/1/147).

[18] Soames to Louden, 7 September 1888 (Davitt Papers, MS 9441, Trinity College Dublin). This was written by Soames in Dublin, seeking an interview with Louden to 'obtain information about the Land Question'.

[19] O'Shea to Chamberlain, 15 August 1890 (Chamberlain Papers, UB, JC 8/8/1/147).

[20] Louden to Davitt, 9 November 1885 (Davitt Papers, Trinity College Dublin, MS 9329, p. 85). After the divorce verdict Louden wrote again to Davitt expressing no surprise that the case had not been contested and claiming that this was because Katharine (rather than Parnell) had wanted the divorce. He added that 'It is very likely that O'Shea and his wife had a private understanding and that the Captain will get paid by her as well as by the *Times*' (MS 9329, f. 186).

[21] O'Shea to Chamberlain, 15 August 1890 (Chamberlain Papers, UB, JC 8/8/1/148).

[22] O'Shea to Chamberlain, 23 February 1891 (Chamberlain Papers, UB, JC 8/8/1/162).

[23] O'Shea to Chamberlain, 23 February 1891 (Chamberlain Papers, UB, JC 8/8/1/162).

[24] Chamberlain to O'Shea, 25 February 1891 (Chamberlain Papers, UB, JC 8/8/1/163).

[25] O'Shea to Chamberlain, 26 February 1891 (Chamberlain Papers, UB, JC 8/8/1/164).

[26] Marsh, *Chamberlain*, p. 322–3.

[27] Richard Jay, *Joseph Chamberlain: A Political Study* (Oxford, 1981), p. 166.

[28] Moody, 'Parnell and the Galway Election', p. 329.

[29] Harrison, Parnell, Joseph Chamberlain and the *Times* (Introduction).

[30] O'Shea also wrote to Balfour to let him know of his plans. The Tory Chief Secretary professed himself uninterested, though Gosselin was keeping a watching brief on his behalf.

[31] Chamberlain to O'Shea, 14 October 1889 (Chamberlain Papers, UB, JC 8/8/1/129).

[32] The paragraph was actually for 24 May 1886.

[33] O'Shea, *Parnell*, vol 2, pp 221–2.

[34] O'Shea, *Parnell*, vol 2, pp 225–6.

[35] O'Shea to Chamberlain, 30 December 1889 (Chamberlain Papers, UB, JC 8/8/1/130).

[36] Lyons, Parnell, p. 478.

[37] These are, in many instances, unreliable as to fact. For example he calls O'Shea's son 'Harry' and has Justin McCarthy accompany Tim Healy to Galway in 1886 to campaign against O'Shea.

[38] Clarke, *Life*, p. 283.

[39] Harrison, *Parnell Vindicated*, p. 142.

[40] Clarke, *Life*, p. 282.

[41] *Times*, 30 December 1889.

[42] *Evening News and Post*, quoted in *Freeman's Journal*, 30 December 1889.

[43] *Freeman's Journal*, 30 December 1889.

[44] *Freeman's Journal*, 30 December 1889.

[45] *Freeman's Journal*, 31 December 1889.

[46] *Freeman's Journal*, 4 January 1890.

[47] *Times*, 19 February 1890.

[48] Davitt Papers, 1 January 1890 diary entry (MS 9553, TCD).

[49] *Times*, 9 January 1890.

[50] At around this time O'Shea was repudiated in Clare by his erstwhile supporter Fr Patrick White, who compared him to Pigott and said, 'he was sorry he ever shook Captain O'Shea's hand and he would certainly never do it again' (*Times*, 15 January 1890).

[51] Davitt, *Fall of Feudalism*, p. 637.

[52] *Cork Free Press*, 6 September 1913.

[53] Morley to Harcourt, 3 February 1890 (quoted in Gardiner, *Sir William Harcourt*, vol 2, p. 81).

Endnotes

[54] The handshake had obviously had its effect; Parnell did not demur.

[55] John Morley, *Recollections*, 2 vols (New York, 1917), vol 1, pp 253–4.

[56] Morley, *Gladstone*, vol 2, p. 501.

[57] Gardiner, *Sir William Harcourt*, vol 2, p. 82

[58] Harrison, *Parnell Vindicated*, p. 108.

[59] It should be pointed out that some contemporary commentators like Tim Healy and Margaret Leamy maintain that it was Katharine who insisted on the divorce taking place.

[60] £20,000 and £60,000 were the specific sums mentioned.

[61] Clarke, *Life*, p. 289.

[62] In the Gerard O'Shea-inspired memoir, she makes a diametrically opposed statement when she claims, 'I knew absolutely nothing of his private life, and cared less' (O'Shea, *Parnell*, vol 2, p. 159).

[63] Which, as a matter of interest, Katharine fixes as 12 July 1881 (the adultery with Anna Steele is said to have taken place 'on or about the 13th and 14th of July 1881'). This would appear to confirm July rather than January 1881 as the date of the incident.

[64] Power Collection – High Court of Justice – Probate Divorce and Admiralty Division – Affidavit – No. 3419 – O'Shea v O'Shea and Parnell, sworn 24 July 1890. Katharine would have been two months pregnant with Claude Sophie at the time. The copy of the affidavit in the Power Collection (which was originally purchased by Mahon O'Brien) is in the handwriting of O'Shea himself.

[65] O'Shea to Chamberlain, 15 December 1890 (Chamberlain Papers, UB, JC 8/8/1/152).

[66] Harrison, *Parnell Vindicated*, p. 170.

[67] O'Shea, *Parnell*, vol 2, p. 159.

[68] Clarke, *Life*, p. 286.

[69] Katharine did tell Henry Harrison that 'Anna and he had constantly been hunting in couples for many years' (O'Shea, *Parnell*, vol 2, p. 141). Also, in a letter to Katharine in 1886, which may indicate a voluntary confession on the part of her sister, O'Shea wrote, 'You say that Mrs Steele has described me in terms of the vilest character'; however, more innocent constructions can obviously be put on this statement (23 April 1886; MS 3882, NLI, Tuohy Papers).

[70] O'Shea to Chamberlain, 3 August 1890 (Chamberlain Papers, UB, JC 8/8/1/144).

[71] Jordan, *Kitty O'Shea*, p. 177.

[72] It is a case also made by J.L. Hammond in *Gladstone and the Irish Nation*, (London, 1938), p. 615.

[73] The irony that he bore the name of the late Home Rule leader whose later political career had been blighted by Parnell has not been much commented upon.

[74] *Times*, 18 November 1890.

[75] Clarke, *Life*, pp 284–5.

[76] O'Shea to Chamberlain, 19 March 1890 (Chamberlain Papers, UB, JC 8/8/1/137).

[77] O'Shea to Chamberlain, 20 March 1890 (Chamberlain Papers, UB, JC 8/8/1/139). O'Shea wrote in response to an obvious snub from Highbury, 'I think I understand what you mean about the suggested interview.'

[78] Clarke, *Life*, p. 291.

[79] Only Gerard and Carmen ever lived with him. Norah remained with her mother, as did Clare and Katie.

[80] Clarke, *Life*, p. 291.

[81] O'Connor, *Memoirs*, p. 207.

[82] Healy, *Letters and Leaders*, vol 1, p. 318.

[83] *Cork Free Press*, 6 September 1913.

[84] The accounts are taken from the *Times*, 17 & 18 November 1890,

[85] Which, in essence, seems like a bizarre contradiction. It has been suggested that Parnell looked to the Dilke precedent (refusing to testify) to save his political career. The defence appears to be a strange variation of the first Dilke judgement, i.e. O'Shea had connived at adultery, but adultery had not actually taken place!

[86] *Times*, 19 November 1890.
[87] *Times*, 18 November 1890.
[88] *Vanity Fair* caught the mood in a satiric piece, based on the title of a famous H. Rider Haggard novel: the article entitled, 'The Political Princess – O'Shea who must be obeyed' (22 November 1890).
[89] *United Ireland*, 22 November 1890.
[90] *Freeman's Journal*, 18 November 1890.
[91] Lord Rendel, *The Personal Papers of Lord Rendel* (London, 1931), p. 28.
[92] Gardiner, *Sir William Harcourt*, vol 2, p. 83.
[93] Gardiner, *Sir William Harcourt*, vol 2, p. 83.
[94] Stead, *The Discrowned King*, Review of Reviews (London 1890), p. 8.
[95] Captain D.D. Sheehan, *Ireland Since Parnell* (London, 1921), p. 9.
[96] Frank Callanan, *The Parnell Split* (Cork, 1992), p. 53.
[97] O'Shea to Chamberlain, 28 November 1890 (Chamberlain Papers, UB, JC 8/8/1/150).
[98] *Times*, 1 December 1890.
[99] *Times*, 2 December 1890.
[100] *United Ireland*, 6 December 1890.
[101] One of its first headlines was a predictable 'Parnell's Leadership Means Destruction'.
[102] He was, of all things, a former Irish Tory MP and was said to be Trollope's model for Phineas Finn.
[103] *New York Times*, 4 November 1891.
[104] *Times*, 15 December 1890.
[105] *Times*, 16 December 1890.
[106] O'Shea to Chamberlain, 15 December 1890 (Chamberlain Papers, UB, JC 8/8/1/152).
[107] O'Shea, *Parnell*, vol 2, pp 233–4.
[108] O'Shea to Chamberlain, 22 December 1890 (Chamberlain Papers, UB, JC 8/8/1/157).
[109] *Truth*, 20 November 1890.
[110] Davitt, *Fall of Feudalism*, p. 558.
[111] O'Shea to Chamberlain, 12 February, 1891 (Chamberlain Papers, UB, JC 8/8/1/160).
[112] O'Shea to Chamberlain, 23 February, 1891(Chamberlain Papers, UB, JC 8/8/1/162).
[113] O'Shea, *Parnell*, vol 2, p. 229.
[114] O'Shea, *Parnell*, vol 2, p. 229.
[115] O'Shea to Chamberlain, 23 February 1891 (Chamberlain Papers, UB, JC 8/8/1/162).
[116] O'Shea, *Parnell*, vol 2, p. 236.
[117] On one occasion, during the Kilkenny by-election campaign, he had lime thrown in his eye, forcing him to wear a bandage. His opponents claimed that the substance in question had been flour and that he was malingering in order to excite voter sympathy.
[118] *Freeman's Journal*, 3 September 1891.
[119] *National Press*, 22 November 1891.
[120] O'Shea to Chamberlain, 23 February 1891 (Chamberlain Papers, UB, JC 8/8/1/162).
[121] Archbishop Walsh of Dublin, for example, referred to his 'criminal relations with the wife of Captain O'Shea' (*Times*, 25 May 1891).

CHAPTER 14

[1] It was the only one of the three missed by Gerard O'Shea, who once described Parnell as 'the most unmitigated and contemptible villain unhanged'.
[2] Parnell's mother, the redoubtable Delia, died there in a tragic fire there in 1898
[3] *Times*, 16 April 1891.
[4] The precise figure was £144,500, invested at 2.75 per cent per annum.
[5] O'Shea to Chamberlain, 30 March 1892 (Chamberlain Papers, University of Birmingham, JC 8/8/1/166).
[6] Harrison, *Parnell Vindicated*, p. 200.

[7] As far as the line up of counsel went it looked like a re-run of old battles. Russell represented Katharine Parnell, while Attorney General Sir Richard Webster and Solicitor General Sir Edward Clarke represented members of the Wood family.

[8] Harrison, *Parnell Vindicated*, p. 203.

[9] Harrison, *Parnell Vindicated*, pp 111–12.

[10] Harrison, *Parnell Vindicated*, p. 113.

[11] O'Shea to Chamberlain, 30 March 1892 (Chamberlain Papers, UB, JC 8/8/1/166).

[12] Harrison, *Parnell Vindicated*, p. 115.

[13] He had also succeeded in ending her interest in any property brought by him into the marriage.

[14] This could have been on the basis that any reduction of the capital sum for current spending purposes by either parent conflicted with the children's interests, as it reduced the capital sum they would inherit. As these proceedings took place in camera we are reliant on flimsy evidence in correspondence for clues as to what was happening.

[15] The role of O'Shea in the probate suit has been the subject of some confusion and error over the years. Given the relative lack of available manuscript commentary this is not altogether surprising. In addition, as a number of hearings in this and related cases involving the Captain and his wife were heard in Chambers, away from the prying eyes of reporters, newspaper coverage does not always fill the gap. Henry Harrison, for example, would appear to be incorrect in his assertions that O'Shea was an *opponent* of Katharine in the *Parnell (formerly O'Shea)* v *Wood* probate action. On 13 October 1889 O'Shea wrote to Chamberlain about the case pointing out that 'I am chiefly desirous that my friends should know that *notwithstanding the antagonism of our interests* [my italics] in the lawsuit I am not only on terms of intimacy with Mrs O'Shea's family but that I possess their affection, esteem and sympathy in a very marked degree' (Chamberlain Papers, JC 8/8/1/127). By intervening in the challenge to the March 1888 will of Mrs Benjamin Wood, O'Shea placed himself in a separate category. He was avowedly representing the interests of his children – they just happened to coincide with his own. This meant that he had to oppose the Wood family espousal of the 1847 will, which left Aunt Ben's money in equal shares to all of Sir John Page Wood's surviving children. Were this will to be entered into probate it would severely diminish any potential share for O'Shea's own children. However, he could also oppose the 1888 will, which happened to be inimical to his interests as it had been carefully placed outside of his own marriage settlement. This he could do on the basis that the entire fortune had been left to Katharine and might be dissipated by her over the remainder of her life. The enactment of the 1887 will would have protected the interests of his children, as it was not excluded from his marriage settlement. This meant that he and his wife would only have had a life interest in the money and property included in the settlement. The interests of their children were protected by trustees charged with ensuring the capital remained intact.

The effect of his divorce suit, however, was: a) to jeopardise Katharine's chances of success in the case; and b) to offer him the opportunity of capitalising on any such success by dint of his right to claim part of her 'after acquired property', as the innocent party in the divorce charged with the upbringing of five children. Once the divorce went through and in the wake of his 'rectification of settlement' proceedings (where he forced/persuaded his wife to include the legacy in the marriage settlement and give him a life interest in half of it) it was clearly no longer against his or his children's interests that the March 1888 will should be confirmed. Hence, far from being in an antagonistic position towards Katharine on 24 March 1892 in the probate court, as Harrison attests, O'Shea was actually making common cause with his former wife. (My thanks to Frank Callanan for his assistance with the question of the probate case.)

[16] O'Shea to Chamberlain, 30 March 1892 (Chamberlain Papers, UB, JC 8/8/1/166).

[17] O'Shea to Chamberlain, 30 March 1892 (Chamberlain Papers, UB, JC 8/8/1/166).

[18] *Times*, 25 March 1892.

[19] O'Shea to Chamberlain, 27 March 1892 (Chamberlain Papers, UB, JC 8/8/1/165).

[20] O'Shea to Chamberlain, 27 March 1892 (Chamberlain Papers, UB, JC 8/8/1/165).

21 O'Shea to Chamberlain, 30 March 1892 (Chamberlain Papers, UB, JC 8/8/1/166).

22 *Times*, 23 May 1892.

23 *Times* 24 February 1894.

24 *Times*, 28 February 1894.

25 *Times*, 17 March 1894.

26 *Times*, 19 October 1893.

27 *Times*, 30 July 1892.

28 *Times*, 16 & 23 June 1894.

29 *Irish Times*, 10 April 1897.

30 *Times*, 4 November 1911.

31 O'Shea to Chamberlain, 12 February 1898 (Chamberlain Papers, UB, JC 8/8/1/167).

32 Garvin, *Joseph Chamberlain*, vol 2, p. 406.

33 *Times*, 24 April 1905.

34 T.P. O'Connor, *Mostly About People*, cited in Kehoe, Ireland's Misfortune, p. 429.

35 Ervine, *Parnell*, p. 260.

36 Even during this period Parnell's signature is disturbingly similar to the Pigott forgery!

37 *Cork Free Press*, 6 September 1913.

38 *Times*, 10 September 1913.

39 *Irish Independent*, 19 May 1914.

40 Foster, *Paddy and Mr Punch*, p. 127.

41 It was also intended to make money for the perennially hard-up Katharine, who had been cheated by more than one solicitor and business adviser, and perhaps for her alleged literary collaborator, Gerard O'Shea.

42 Foster, *Paddy and Mr Punch*, p. 132.

43 Foster, *Paddy and Mr Punch*, p. 128.

44 Marlow, *Uncrowned Queen*, p. 301.

45 Clare died in childbirth in 1909; her son, Assheton Maunsell, Parnell's sole grandchild, died in India in 1934 of enteric fever. Katie was the last blood relative of Parnell's to die, but she first succumbed to the mental illness that had afflicted many members of the extended family over the years. She died in 1947.

46 Harrison, *Parnell Vindicated*, p. 169.

47 Harrison, *Parnell Vindicated*, p. 121.

48 Harrison, *Parnell Vindicated*, p. 122.

49 Harrison, *Parnell Vindicated*, p. 170.

50 Harrison, *Parnell Vindicated*, p. 171.

51 Harrison, *Parnell Vindicated*, p. 123.

52 Harrison, *Parnell Vindicated*, p. 126.

53 Harrison, *Parnell Vindicated*, pp 147–8

54 Abels, *Parnell Tragedy*, p. 149.

55 Abels, *Parnell Tragedy*, p. 179.

56 This correspondence was discovered to the divorce legal teams and most likely prompted Coward's misgivings. The letters established O'Shea's overwhelming suspicions from the mid 1880s, but failed to establish any resolute attempt to either confirm or assuage his doubts.

57 He wrote, 'There was no suggestion that Captain O'Shea had thought that child to be his own – nor that there could have been the faintest shadow of a justification for such a suggestion'. (Harrison, *Parnell Vindicated*, p. 168). This is palpable nonsense designed by Harrison to preclude the possibility that Katharine was sexually involved with both men at different times in 1881–82.

58 Insofar as his father's letters establish this, their publication can be seen as a form of revenge on his mother by Gerard O'Shea.

59 Harrison, *Parnell Vindicated*, p. 168.

60 Harrison, *Parnell Vindicated*, p. 144.

61 Clarke, *Life*, p. 286.

Endnotes

[62] His period of incarceration in Kilmainham can be discounted, as he seems to have been aware that O'Shea had resumed sexual relations with Katharine.

[63] Lyons, *Parnell*, p. 635.

[64] James Mullin, *Story of a Toiler's Life* (Dublin, 2000), p. 187.

[65] Lord Ribblesdale, *Impressions and Memories* (London, 1907), p. 190.

[66] O'Brien, *Parnell*, p. 386.

[67] Thorold, *Henry Labouchere*, p. 230.

[68] Lyons, *Parnell*, p. 640.

[69] Marlow, *Uncrowned Queen*, p. 297.

[70] Loyal and politically committed wife of executed 1916 leader, Thomas Clarke.

[71] Harrison, *Parnell Vindicated*, p. 140.

[72] Harrison, *Parnell Vindicated*, p. 146.

[73] Oxford English Dictionary definitions.

[74] Garvin, *Joseph Chamberlain*, p. 404.

[75] Kee, *Laurel and Ivy*, p. 359.

[76] The reference was first noted by Joyce Marlow.

[77] James Joyce, *Poems and Exiles*, J.C.C. Mays (ed) (London, 1992), p. 354.

BIBLIOGRAPHY

Manuscript Sources

NATIONAL LIBRARY OF IRELAND
MS 3882–3; ref Tuohy papers
MS 5752; ref O'Shea Papers
MS 17815; ref Times Commission
MS18315; ref Parnell genealogy
MS 21679; ref divorce
MS 22826; O'Shea letter to W.R. Nally
MS 35982; ref probate case

NATIONAL ARCHIVES OF IRELAND
Chief Secretary's Office Registered Papers
CSORP, 1880/20176
CSORP, 1880/31241
CSORP, 1882/19433
CSORP, 1882/20193
CSORP, 1882/20799
CSORP, 1882/24351
CSORP, 1882/32122
CSORP, 1882/32682

TRINITY COLLEGE, DUBLIN
Davitt Papers
MS 9329
MS 9365
MS 9366
MS 9368
MS 9386
MS 9441
MS 9442
MS 9549
MS 9550
MS 9551; 'Notes by an Amateur Detective'
MS 9553

KILMAINHAM GAOL MUSEUM
Parnell Papers
09 MS 1E 13
20 LR 1E 14
08 LR 1E 15

BRITISH LIBRARY
Campbell-Bannerman Papers
Add MSS 41228

Dilke Papers
Add MSS 43913
Add MSS 43936
Add MSS 43927

Escott Papers
Add MSS 58789

Gladstone Papers
Add MSS 44160
Add. MSS 44256
Add MSS 44269
Add MSS 44315–16
Add MSS 44766
Add MSS 44787
Add MSS 56446
Add MSS 61737
Add MSS 62114

UNIVERSITY OF BIRMINGHAM

Joseph Chamberlain Papers
JC 8/8/1/1–176
JC 8/8/2A
JC 8/8/2B
JC 8/8/2C
JC 8/8/2D
JC 8/8/2E
JC 8/8/2F
JC 8/8/2G

UNIVERSITY OF CHICAGO

O'Gorman Mahon Papers
Box 4, Folder 20–6
Box 5, Folder 1–21
Box 6, Folder 3–22
Box 8, Folder 1–4

POWER COLLECTION (PRIVATE)

(Material acquired by Mahon O'Brien and passed on to Patrick Power)
Tasham Curling and Walls, Solicitors – Costs relating to Miss Katherine
(*sic*) Wood's marriage settlement
Affidavits of Robert and Anne Courage and Sir Henry Evelyn Wood re
Chancery proceedings for lunacy in the matter of Anna Maria Wood
High Court of Justice – Probate Divorce and Admiralty Division –
Affidavit – No.3419 – O'Shea v O'Shea and Parnell
Church, Rendell, Todd & Co correspondence re Parnell V Wood Probate
action

Printed Sources

SPECIAL COMMISSION, PROCEEDINGS (1890), PARLIAMENTARY PAPERS

Vol 1
Vol 5
Vol 6

NEWSPAPERS AND PERIODICALS

Clare Advertiser
Kilrush Herald and Kilkee Gazette

Bibliography

Clare Freeman
Clare Independent
Clare Journal
Cork Free Press
Freeman's Journal
Illustrated London News
Independent and Munster Advertiser
Irish Independent
Irish Times
Nation, The
Pall Mall Gazette
Punch
Times, The
United Ireland

MEMOIRS AND DIARIES

Bahlman, Dudley, *The Diary of Sir Edward Hamilton* (London, 1972).

Becker, Bernard, *Disturbed Ireland* (London, 1881).

Blunt, Wilfrid Scawen, *The Land War in Ireland* (London, 1912).

Byrne, Edward (Callanan, F., ed), *Parnell: A Memoir* (Dublin, 1991).

Chamberlain, Joseph – *A Political Memoir*, Howard, C.H.D. (ed), (Connecticut, 1975).

Clarke, Sir Edward, *The Story of My Life* (London, 1918).

Davitt, Michael, *The Fall of Feudalism in Ireland* (London, 1904).

Dickinson, Emily Monroe, *A Patriot's Mistake: Reminiscences of the Parnell Family* (Dublin, 1905).

Fennell, Thomas, *The Royal Irish Constabulary: A History and Personal Memoir* (Dublin, 2003).

Gladstone, Herbert, *After Thirty Years* (London, 1928).

Gordon, Peter (ed.), *The Red Earl: The Papers of the Fifth Earl Spencer 1835–1910*, 2 volumes (Northampton, 1981 & 1986)

Harris, Frank, *My Life and Loves* (New York, 1979).

Healy, T.M., *Letters and Leaders of My Day* (New York, 1929), 2 volumes, vol 1.

Kettle, Andrew, *Material for Victory: The Memoirs of Andrew J. Kettle* (Dublin, 1958).

Leamy, Margaret, *Parnell's Faithful Few* (New York, 1936).

Le Caron, Henry, *Twenty Five Years in the Secret Service* (London, 1892).

Leslie, Shane, *Long Shadows* (London, 1966).

Lucy, Sir Henry, *Sixty Years in the Wilderness* (London, 1912).

Lucy, Sir Henry *A Diary of Two Parliaments* (London, 1886).

Masterman, Lucy, *Mary Gladstone: Her Diaries and Letters* (New York, 1930).

McCarthy, Justin and Mrs Campbell Praed, *Our Book of Memories* (London, 1912).

McDonald, John, *Daily News, Diary of the Parnell Commission* (London, 1890).

Morley, John, *Recollections*, 2 vols, (New York, 1917), vol 1.

Mullin, James, *Story of a Toiler's Life* (Dublin, 2000).

O'Brien, William, *Recollections* (London, 1905).

O'Brien, William, *Evening Memories* (Dublin and London, 1920).

O'Connor, T.P., *Memoirs of an Old Parliamentarian*, 2 vols, vols 1 & 2, (London, 1929).

O'Shea, Katharine, *Charles Stewart Parnell, His Love Story and Political Life*, 2 volumes, (New York, 1914).

Parnell, John Howard, *Charles Stewart Parnell* (New York, 1914).

Rendel, Lord, *The Personal Papers of Lord Rendel* (London, 1931).

Ribblesdale, Lord, *Impressions and Memories* (London, 1907).

Robbins, Alfred, *Parnell: the Last Five Years* (London, 1926).

Sheehan, Captain D.D., *Ireland Since Parnell* (Dublin, 1921).

SECONDARY SOURCES

Abels, Jules, *The Parnell Tragedy* (London, 1966).

Balfour, Michael, *Britain and Joseph Chamberlain* (London, 1985).

Bew, Paul, *Charles Stewart Parnell* (Dublin, 1980).

Boyce, D. George, *19ᵗʰ Century Ireland*, (Dublin, 1990).

Brady, Margery, *The Love Story of Parnell and Katharine O'Shea* (Cork, 1991).

Bussy, Frederick Moir, *Irish Conspiracies* (London, 1910).

Callaghan, Mary Rose, *'Kitty O'Shea': The Story of Katharine Parnell* (London, 1989).

Callanan, Frank, *T.M. Healy* (Cork, 1996).

Callanan, Frank, *The Parnell Split* (Cork, 1992).

Campbell, Christy, *Fenian Fire: The British Government Plot to Assassinate Queen Victoria* (London, 2003).

Cole, J.A., *Prince of Spies: Henri Le Caron* (London, 1984).

Comerford, R.V., *The Politics of Distress*, vol 6 in *A New History of Ireland*, Vaughan, W.E. (ed), 10 vols, (Oxford, 1996).

Cooke, A.B., & Vincent, John, *The Governing Passion: Cabinet Government and Party Politics in Britain 1885-86* (Brighton, 1974).

Corfe, Tom, *The Phoenix Park Murders* (London, 1968).

Curtis, L.P., *Coercion and Conciliation in Ireland: A Study in Conservative Unionism* (Princeton and Oxford, 1963).

Donovan, Dick, *The Crime of the Century* (London, 1904).

English, Richard, *Irish Freedom* (London, 2006).

Ervine, St John, *Parnell* (London, 1928).

Farwell, Byron, *Eminent Victorian Soldiers* (Ontario, 1985).

Foster, R.F., *Charles Stewart Parnell : The Man and his Family* (Sussex, 1979).

Foster, R.F., *Paddy and Mr Punch* (London, 1995).

Foster, R.F., *Lord Randolph Churchill: A Political Life* (Oxford, 1981).

Gardiner, A.G., *The Life of Sir William Harcourt*, 2 vols, (London, 1923), vol 2.

Garvin, J.L., *Life of Joseph Chamberlain*, 3 vols (London, 1933), vols 1 & 2.

Gwynn, Denis, *The O'Gorman Mahon: Duellist, Adventurer and Politician* (London, 1934).

Hamer, D.A., *John Morley: Liberal Intellectual in Politics* (Oxford, 1968).

Hammond, J.L., *Gladstone and the Irish Nation* (London, 1938).

Harrison, Henry, *Parnell Vindicated: The Lifting of the Veil* (London, 1931).

Harrison, Henry, *Parnell, Joseph Chamberlain and the* Times (Belfast & Dublin, 1953).

Harrison, Henry, *Parnell, Joseph Chamberlain and Mr Garvin* (London, 1938).

Haslip, Joan, *Parnell* (London, 1936).

Hurst, Michael, *Joseph Chamberlain and the Liberal Reunion* (Toronto, 1967).

Jackson, Alvin, *Home Rule: An Irish History 1800–2000* (London, 2003).

Jay, Richard, *Joseph Chamberlain: A Political Study* (Oxford, 1981).

Jenkins, Roy, *Sir Charles Dilke: A Victorian Tragedy* (London, 1965).

Jeyes, S.H., *The Life of Sir Howard Vincent* (London, 1912).

Jordan, Jane, *Kitty O'Shea, An Irish Affair* (Gloucestershire, 2005).

Kee, Robert, *The Laurel and the Ivy* (London, 1993).

Kehoe, Elisabeth, *Ireland's Misfortune: The Turbulent Life of Kitty O'Shea* (London, 2008).

Kelly, James, *That Damn'd Thing Called Honour: Duelling in Ireland 1570–1861* (Cork, 1995).

Larkin, Emmet, *The Roman Catholic Church and the Plan of Campaign* (Cork, 1978).

Legg, Marie-Louise, *Newspapers and Nationalism: The Irish Provincial Press 1850–1892* (Dublin, 1999).

Leonard, Hugh, *Parnell and the Englishwoman* (London, 1991). (Fiction)

Lyons, F.S.L., *Charles Stewart Parnell* (Dublin, 2005).

*This paperback reprint of the original was the copy used throughout.

Lyons, F.S.L., *The Fall of Parnell, 1890-91* (Canada, 1960).

McCarthy, Justin, *Story of an Irishman* (London, 1904).

McCartney, Donal, *UCD, a National Idea: The History of University College, Dublin* (Dublin, 1999).

McCartney, Donal, (ed), *Parnell: The Politics of Power* (Dublin, 1991).

McGee, Owen, *The IRB: The Irish Republican Brotherhood from the Land League to Sinn Fein* (Dublin, 2005).

Mallet, Sir Charles, *Herbert Gladstone: A Memoir* (London, 1932).

Marlow, Joyce, *The Uncrowned Queen of Ireland* (London, 1975).

Marsh, Peter. T., *Joseph Chamberlain: Entrepreneur in Politics* (New Haven, 1994).

Molony, Senan, *The Phoenix Park Murders* (Cork, 2006).

Moody, T.W., & Hawkins, Richard, *Florence Arnold-Foster's Irish Journal* (Oxford, 1988).

Moody, T.W., Martin, F.X., & Byrne, F.J., *A Chronology of Irish History*, vol 8 in *A New History of Ireland*, Vaughan, W.E. (ed), 10 vols (Oxford, 1982).

Moore, George, *Parnell and His Island* (Dublin, 2004).

Morley, John, *Life of Gladstone*, 6 vols (London, 1908).

Nicholls, David, *The Lost Prime Minister: A Life of Sir Charles Dilke* (London, 1995).

O'Brien, Conor Cruise, *Parnell and his Party* (Oxford, 1964).

O'Brien, R.Barry, *The Life of Parnell* (London, 1910).

O'Brien, William., *The Parnell of Real Life* (London, 1926).

O'Callaghan, Margaret, *British High Politics and a Nationalist Ireland: Criminality Land and the Law under Forster and Balfour* (Cork, 1994).

O'Connor, T.P., *Charles Stewart Parnell: A Memory* (London, 1891).

O'Connor, T.P., *The Parnell Movement* (London, 1886).

O'Day, Alan, *The English Face of Irish Nationalism* (Dublin, 1977).

O'Day, Alan, *Parnell and the First Home Rule Episode, 1884–87* (Dublin, 1986).

O'Day, Alan, *Charles Stewart Parnell* (Dublin, 1998).

O'Donnell, Frank Hugh, *A History of the Irish Parliamentary Party*, 2 vols (New York, 1970).

Powell, Enoch, *Joseph Chamberlain* (London, 1977).

Reid, T.Wemyss, *The Life of the Right Honourable William Edward Forster* (London, 1888).

Sweet, Matthew, *Inventing the Victorians* (New York, 2001).

Thornley, David, *Isaac Butt and Home Rule* (London, 1964).

Thorold, Algar Labouchere, *The Life of Henry Labouchere* (London, 1913).

Times, *History of the Times: 1884–1912*, 4 vols (London, 1947).

Trollope, Anthony, *Phineas Finn* (Oxford, 1973).

Trollope, Anthony, *Phineas Redux* (Oxford, 1973).

Trollope, Anthony, *The Land Leaguers* (London, 1993).

Vaughan, W.E. (ed), *A New History of Ireland,* 10 vols (Oxford, 1996), vol 6 & 8.

Waldron, Jarlath, *Maamtrasna: The Murders and the Mystery* (Dublin, 1992).

Walsh, Patrick J., *William J. Walsh: Archbishop of Dublin* (Dublin & Cork, 1928).

Yeats, W.B., *Collected Poems* (London, 1950).

ARTICLES

Howard, C.H.D., 'Joseph Chamberlain, Parnell and the Irish "Central Board" Scheme, 1884–5', in *Irish Historical Studies,* vol 8, no 31 (Sept 1953).

Maume, Patrick, 'Parnell and the IRB Oath', in *Irish Historical Studies,* vol 29, no 115 (May 1995).

Moody, T.W., 'Parnell and the Galway Election of 1886', in *Irish Historical Studies,* vol 9, no 35 (March, 1955).

Powell, Enoch, 'Kilmainham: The Treaty That Never Was', in *Historical Journal,* vol 21, no 4 (Dec 1978).

REFERENCE WORKS

Annual Register, 1880–1891 (London, 1881–1892).

Dictionary of National Biography, (Oxford, 2004).

WEBSITES

http://www.oxforddnb.com/

http://www.oscott.net/index.htm

INDEX

Index

Index